CHARLESWORTH AND CAIN
Company Law

ELEVENTH EDITION

By

T. E. CAIN, M.A. (Oxon.),

of the Inner Temple, Barrister-at-Law,
Head of the School of Law at the
Queensland Institute of Technology,
Sometime Member of the Board of Management
of The College of Law

SCOTTISH EDITOR

ENID A. MARSHALL, M.A., LL.B., PH.D.,

Solicitor, Senior Lecturer in Business Law at the University of Stirling,
formerly Lecturer in Law at Dundee College of Technology

CHAPTER 29, TAXATION,
By
L. P. K. BRINDLEY, B.A. (Oxon.), Solicitor,

A Member of the Board of Management
of The College of Law

LONDON
STEVENS & SONS
1977

First Edition	.	.	.	(1932)	By His Honour Judge Charlesworth
Second Edition	.	.	.	(1938)	,, ,, ,, ,,
Third Edition	.	.	.	(1940)	,, ,, ,, ,,
Fourth Edition	.	.	.	(1946)	,, ,, ,, ,,
Second Impression		.	.	(1947)	
Third Impression		.	.	(1948)	
Fifth Edition	.	.	.	(1949)	,, ,, ,, ,,
Second Impression revised		.		(1950)	
Sixth Edition	.	.	.	(1954)	,, ,, ,, ,,
Second Impression revised				(1956)	
Seventh Edition	.	.	.	(1960)	By T. E. Cain
Second Impression		.	.	(1962)	
Eighth Edition	.	.	.	(1965)	,, ,, ,,
Ninth Edition	.	.	.	(1968)	,, ,, ,,
Tenth Edition	.	.	.	(1972)	,, ,, ,,
Eleventh Edition	.	.	.	(1977)	,, ,, ,,

ISBN Hardback   0 420 45330 X
Paperback   0 420 45040 8

Published by Stevens & Sons
of 11 New Fetter Lane, London
Printed in Great Britain by
Richard Clay (The Chaucer Press), Ltd.,
Bungay, Suffolk

PREFACE

This edition had a longer period of gestation and a more difficult birth than its predecessors. For one thing, immediately after the copy had been handed over, I became aware that the Companies Act 1976, the Stock Exchange (Completion of Bargains) Act 1976 and the Insolvency Act 1976 had been passed and that the Report of the Committee of Inquiry on Industrial Democracy had been presented to Parliament, so that a considerable number of amendments had to be made to the copy. The amendments resulting from the Companies Act, which is the most important of the Acts and which affected the Chapters on Accounts and Auditors in particular, have been made to the text and, although it proved to be impossible to deal with the amendments required as a result of the other two Acts and the Report of the Committee of Inquiry in the same way, these are dealt with in the Notes which follow this Preface, as are one or two cases decided since the copy was handed over. It should be noted that sections 1 to 37 inclusive of the Companies Act will be in force by October 1, 1977.

I regret that this edition is some 130 pages longer than the last. There are several reasons for that. One reason is the inclusion of the new material on the Companies Act 1976. Another is that I thought it necessary to include a fair amount of new material on proposals for the reform of Company Law, including those in the Conservative Government White Paper on Company Law Reform, the Labour Party Green Paper on the Reform of Company Law and various Companies Bills, in particular the Companies Bill 1973. A third reason is that I have expanded and, I hope, improved the treatment of a number of topics including the following:— Memorandum of Association (the European Communities Act 1972, section 9, which was dealt with in a Note following the Preface to the Tenth Edition, has been included in the text and a specimen memorandum of association has been included at the end of Chapter 3); Articles of Association (the account of alteration of articles has been improved); Directors (the treatment of directors' powers and of the duties of directors has been expanded); Enforcement of Directors' and Controlling Members' Duties (the account of the rule in *Foss* v.

Harbottle has been expanded and the case of *Re Westbourne Galleries* is dealt with in the text in connection with winding-up by the court on the "just and equitable" ground); Protection of Outsiders (the treatment of the rule in *Royal British Bank* v. *Turquand* has been expanded). Fourthly, there is more Scottish material, *e.g.*, on the Companies (Floating Charges and Receivers) (Scotland) Act 1972, and I have included many more references to Scots authorities. I hope that readers will find the increase in length to be worthwhile.

It will be seen that in one or two instances I have changed the order of treatment of the subject. For example, General Meetings are now dealt with before Directors because I have found it better to teach them in that order.

I was most fortunate in that once again Dr. Enid Marshall agreed to be the Scottish editor and Peter Brindley agreed to be the Taxation editor, and I am much indebted to them. Dr. Marshall supplied a great deal of excellent Scottish material, of which I have included as much as I could, and Peter Brindley provided a completely new chapter on Taxation which I think readers will find very helpful.

I should also like to thank Mrs D. Russell, Mrs N. Weir and Miss P. Starkey, who assisted in a number of ways in producing the copy and checking the proofs.

Having regard to the Notes which follow this Preface I think that it can be said that the law stated in this edition is that based upon the materials available to me in Brisbane in April 1977.

Brisbane,
June 1977

T. E. C.

NOTES ON RECENT DEVELOPMENTS

The Stock Exchange (Completion of Bargains) Act 1976

This Act affects the text in the ways indicated below:—

Immediately before the shoulder heading "Bills of exchange" on page 129, the following new paragraph should be inserted:—

"Section 2(1) of the Stock Exchange (Completion of Bargains) Act 1976 provides that a company may have an official seal for use for sealing securities issued by the company and for sealing documents creating or evidencing securities issued by the company. This official seal must be a facsimile of the common seal of the company with the addition on its face of the word 'Securities'."

After "section 436" on page 196 the following should be inserted:—

"of the Companies Act 1948. The power conferred on a company by section 436 of the 1948 Act to keep a register or other record by recording the matters in question otherwise than by making entries in bound books includes power to keep the register or other record by recording the matters otherwise than in a legible form so long as the recording is capable of being reproduced in a legible form: Stock Exchange (Completion of Bargains) Act 1976, s.3. In other words, a company may now use a computer to keep certain records."

What is said of clause 81 of the Companies Bill 1973 on page 196 may now be disregarded.

In the sixth line of page 246, after the word "company", the following should be inserted:—

"or under the official seal kept by the company by virtue of section 2 of the Stock Exchange (Completion of Bargains) Act 1976 *ante*."

The following new paragraph should be inserted after line 12 on page 246:—

"If shares, debentures or debenture stock are or is allotted to a stock exchange nominee (that is, a person designated as such by the Secretary of State), or a transfer of shares, debentures or debenture stock to a stock exchange nominee is lodged with the company, the company is exempt from the obligation to prepare certificates imposed by section 80 of the Companies Act 1948 *ante:* Stock Exchange (Completion of Bargains) Act 1976, ss. 1, 7."

After the word "seal" in line 14 of page 246, the following should be inserted:—

"or the seal kept by the company by virtue of section 2 of the Stock Exchange (Completion of Bargains) Act 1976,"

After line 4 on page 258, the following new paragraph should be inserted:—

"If shares, debentures or debenture stock are or is allotted to a stock exchange nominee (that is, a person designated as such by the Secretary of State), or a transfer of shares, debentures or debenture stock to a stock exchange nominee is lodged with the company, the company is exempt from the obligation to prepare certificates imposed by section 80 of the Companies Act 1948 *ante:* Stock Exchange (Completion of Bargains) Act 1976, ss. 1. 7."

After the paragraph beginning "(5)" on page 259, the following new paragraph should be inserted:—

"If shares, debentures or debenture stock are or is allotted to a stock exchange nominee (that is, a person designated as such by the Secretary of State), or a transfer of shares, debentures or debenture stock to a stock exchange nominee is lodged with the company, the company is exempt from the obligation to prepare certificates imposed by section 80 of the Companies Act 1948 *ante:* Stock Exchange (Completion of Bargains) Act 1976, ss. 1, 7."

What is said about clause 81 of the Companies Bill 1973 on page 305 may now be disregarded. In its place, the following new sentence should be added: "Section 3 of the Stock Exchange (Completion of Bargains) Act 1976, *ante*, now enables the company to use a computer to keep the minutes."

At the end of the paragraph beginning "By section 436" and ending "falsification" on page 332, the following new sentence should be added: "The company may now use a computer to keep the minutes: Stock Exchange (Completion of Bargains) Act 1976, s. 3, *ante*."

After the fifth paragraph under the centre heading "Issue of Debentures" on page 487, the following new paragraph should be inserted:—

"If shares, debentures or debenture stock are or is allotted to a stock exchange nominee (that is, a person designated as such by the Secretary of State), or a transfer of shares, debentures or debenture stock to a stock exchange nominee is lodged with the company, the company is exempt from the obligation to prepare certificates imposed by section 80 of the Companies Act 1948 *ante:* Stock Exchange (Completion of Bargains) Act 1976, ss. 1, 7."

After the second paragraph under the shoulder heading "Transfer of registered debentures" on page 493, the following new paragraph should be inserted:—

"If shares, debentures or debenture stock are or is allotted to a stock exchange nominee (that is, a person designated as such by the Secretary of State), or a transfer of shares, debentures or debenture stock to a stock exchange nominee is lodged with the company, the company is exempt from the obligation to prepare certificates imposed by section 80 of the Companies Act 1948 *ante:* Stock Exchange (Completion of Bargains) Act 1976, ss. 1, 7."

What is said about clause 81 of the Companies Bill 1973 on page 495 may now be disregarded.

Immediately before the centre heading "BEARER DEBENTURES" on page 495, the following new paragraph should be inserted:—

"Section 3 of the Stock Exchange (Completion of Bargains) Act 1976 now declares that the power conferred on a company by section 436 of the Companies Act 1948 to keep a register or other record by recording the matters in question otherwise than by making entries in bound books includes power to keep the register or other record by recording the matters otherwise than in a legible form so long as the recording is capable of being reproduced in a legible form. In other words, the company may use a computer to keep the register of debenture holders."

The Insolvency Act 1976, section 9

Immediately before the shoulder heading "Register of disqualification orders" on page 316 of the text, the following should be inserted:—

"(5) A person cannot, without leave of the court, be a director of, or be concerned in the management of, a company if, on an application by one of the persons mentioned below, it appeared to the court that—

    (a) he was or had been a director of a company which had at any time gone into liquidation (while he was a director or subsequently) and he was insolvent at that time;

    (b) he was or had been a director of another company which had gone into liquidation within five years of the date on which the first company went into liquidation;

    (c) his conduct as a director of any of those companies made him unfit to be concerned in the management of a company,

and the court ordered that he must not, without its leave, be a director of or in any way be concerned or take part in the management of the company for such period beginning with the date of the order and not exceeding five years as was specified: Insolvency Act 1976, s. 9.

"If a company is being wound up by the court, an application must be made by the Official Receiver or, in Scotland, the Secretary of State, and the power to make a disqualifying order is exerciseable by the court by which the company is being wound up. In any other case, an application must be made by the Secretary of State and the power to make an order is exerciseable by the High Court or, in Scotland, the Court of Session.

"The word 'director' in section 9 includes any person in accordance with whose directions or instructions the directors of the company have been accustomed to act and, for the purposes of the section, a company goes into liquidation, if it is wound up by the court, on the date of the winding-up order and, in any other case, on the date of the passing of the resolution for voluntary winding-up.

"Contravention of an order made under section 9 is an offence punishable, on conviction on indictment, by imprisonment for up to two years or a fine or both or, on summary conviction, by imprisonment for up to six months or a fine of up to £400 or both.

"Section 9 gives effect to a recommendation contained in paragraph 80 of the Jenkins Report."

In the ninth line on page 328, after the reference to section 28 of the 1976 Act, the following should be inserted: "or under section 9 of the Insolvency Act 1976".

The Report of the Committee of Inquiry on Industrial Democracy ((1976) Cmnd. 6706)

Had it been available in time, the Report of this Committee, of which Lord Bullock was the Chairman, would have been dealt with immediately before the shoulder heading "Measures of the European Community" on page 21 of the text. The Report affects pages 14, 17, 350 and 366.

The majority of the members of the Bullock Committee were opposed to the introduction into the U.K. of a statutory two-tier board system and recommended the introduction of a modified unitary board in the case of large companies, *i.e.*, the ultimate holding company of a group which *in toto* employs 2,000 or more people in the U.K. or any individual company which employs 2,000 or more people in the U.K., whether or not it is part of a group. Before a company is required to accept employee representatives on its board, a secret ballot of its employees should be held and the majority required should be a simple majority representing at least one-third of the eligible employees. Where the conditions for employee representation are met, the company's board should be reconstituted so as to be composed of three elements—an equal number of employee and shareholder representatives plus a third group of co-opted directors. The additional directors should be co-opted with the agreement of a majority of each of the employee representatives and the shareholder representatives, be an uneven number greater than one and form less than one-third of the total board (the formula would be $2x + y$, x representing the number of employee representatives and also the number of shareholder representatives and y representing the number of co-opted directors, so there would be minority but equal representation of shareholders and employees). The co-opted directors should be composed of various elements, *e.g.*, senior or middle managers in the company or people from outside the company who are at present non-executive directors. Lastly, directors should continue to be required to act in the best interests of the company but in doing so they should take into account the interests of its employees as well as its shareholders.

Clemens v. Clemens Bros. Ltd. (1976) 2 All E.R. 268

This case concerns controlling members' duties, as to which see pages 372 to 375 of the text.

The case makes it clear that a majority shareholder is not entitled as of right to exercise his majority vote in whatever way he pleases and that such right is subject to equitable considerations which may make it unjust to exercise it in a particular way.

The defendant, who held 55 per cent. of the issued shares of a family company and was one of five directors of it, would have liked the other directors to have shares in the company and a trust set up for long-service employees. The plaintiff, who was the defendant's niece, held 40 per cent. of the shares and was not a director. Resolutions were framed so as to increase the capital and put complete control of the company in the hands of the defendant and her fellow directors, to deprive the plaintiff of her existing rights as a shareholder with more than 25 per cent. of the votes and to ensure that despite her right to pre-emption if the defendant wished to transfer her shares, the plaintiff would never get control of the company. It was held that these considerations were sufficient in equity to prevent the defendant using her votes as she had and the resolutions in general meeting were set aside.

Pedley v. Inland Waterways Association Ltd. [1977] 1 All E.R. 209

This case concerns section 142 of the 1948 Act, as to which see page 295 of the text.

It was held that section 142 does not compel the inclusion of a resolution in the agenda of a general meeting and the phrase in section 142 beginning "and the company shall give its members notice" is merely part of the machinery designed to ensure that members generally, as well as the director or auditor concerned, have at least twenty-one days' notice of any resolution of which such notice is required. Therefore, unless a single member is able to rely on section 140 (page 294 of the text) or a provision of the articles of the company, he has no right to compel the inclusion of such a resolution in the agenda.

Companies (Winding up) (Amendment) Rules 1977 (S.I. 1977/365. April 1, 1977)

The Companies Liquidation Account, referred to on page 598 of the text, has been replaced by the Insolvency Services Account.

CONTENTS

TABLE OF CASES

Table of Cases

TABLE OF STATUTES

TABLE OF STATUTORY INSTRUMENTS

TABLES OF RULES OF THE SUPREME COURT

CHAPTER 1

NATURE OF REGISTERED COMPANIES[1]

THIS book is mostly concerned with registered companies, whether public or private, limited by shares. The term "registered company" means a company incorporated or formed by registration under the Companies Acts, the latest Acts being the Companies Acts 1948 to 1976. The 1948 Act was amended by the 1967 and 1976 Acts in a number of respects but the 1948 Act is the principal Act and in this book, unless it is otherwise stated or the context otherwise requires, references to sections and Schedules are to those of the Companies Act 1948 and references to the "Act" are to the Companies Act 1948.

The Companies Act 1948[1a] provides that for the purpose of the registration of companies under the Act there shall be offices (Companies Registration Offices in England and Scotland) at such places as the Board of Trade (now the Department of Trade) think fit, and that the Board may appoint such registrars, assistant registrars, clerks and servants as they think necessary for the registration of companies and may make regulations with respect to their duties.

Section 1 (1) enables two or more persons associated for any lawful purpose to form an incorporated private company (or seven or more persons to form an incorporated public company), with or without limited liability, by complying with the requirements of the Act in respect of registration. As is explained later in this chapter, the requirements are that certain documents be delivered to the appropriate Registrar of Companies and certain fees and stamp duties paid. Under section 12, for example, a memorandum of association and, usually, articles of association must be delivered to the Registrar, who must retain and register them.

The General Annual Report, Companies in 1974, prepared by the Department of Trade under section 451, states:[2]

"The Companies Acts provide a basic legal framework for the regulation of companies in Great Britain. They make provision for the legal incorporation of enterprises and lay down rules for their constitution, management and dissolution. Although the Acts leave the internal management of companies largely in the hands of the directors, subject to removal by the shareholders, they also confer

[1] See diagram on p. 671.   [1a] s. 424.   [2] See p. 1.

1

certain powers and responsibilities on the Department. The Registrars of Companies in London and Edinburgh administer a number of sections of the Companies Acts. They issue certificates of incorporation and change of name, in connection with which they also control the use of sensitive names. They are responsible for the registration and safe custody of documents required by statute to be filed with them and for pursuing companies which fail to comply with such requirements. They issue certificates of registration for some such documents, mainly those concerned with mortgages or charges. They provide facilities for the examination of filed documents by members of the public and on payment issue copies of or extracts from such documents or certificates relating to a company's corporate existence. In appropriate circumstances they dissolve companies by striking them off the register."

The rest of this chapter attempts first of all to give a simple answer to the question "what is a registered company?" and then to trace briefly the history of the registered company. After that there is a note on various proposals, some recent, some not so recent, for the reform of the law relating to registered companies. Finally, the following topics are dealt with: The procedure to obtain the registration of a company. The effect of the registration of a company— this is that the company is a corporation with a legal existence separate from that of its members, who usually have the privilege of limited personal liability. The management of registered companies. A registered company's securities—these are the shares and debentures which it issues. Registered companies and partnerships contrasted—a partnership is not a corporation and the partners do not have limited liability.

WHAT IS A REGISTERED COMPANY?

A registered company, *i.e.* a company incorporated by registration under the Companies Acts, is regarded by the law as a person, just as a human being, Mr. Smith or Mr. Jones, is a person. This artificial or juristic person can own land and other property, enter into contracts, sue and be sued, have a bank account in its own name, owe money to others and be a creditor of other people and other companies, and employ people to work for it. The company's money and property belong to the company and not to the members or shareholders, although the members or shareholders may be said to own the company. Similarly, the company's debts are the debts of the company and the shareholders cannot be compelled to pay them, although if, for example, the company is being wound up and its assets do not realise a sum sufficient to pay its debts, a shareholder whose liability is limited by shares is liable to contribute to the assets up to the amount, if any, unpaid on his shares. A company, of course, can only act through human agents, and those who manage its business are called directors. But the directors are only agents of the company, with the powers of management given by the company's articles of association and usually with power to delegate any of their powers to a managing director. And the company is liable for torts [2a] and crimes committed by its servants and agents within the scope of their employment or authority. This conception of a company as a corporation, *i.e.* a person separate and distinct from the other persons who are its members and directors, is the fundamental principle of company law.

A company must have members, otherwise it would never exist at all, and in the case of a company with a share capital these members are called shareholders (or, if the shares have been converted into stock, stockholders). The shareholder's position with regard to the company itself and to his fellow shareholders is regulated by the Companies Acts and by the memorandum and the articles of association, and also by the principle that controlling shareholders, *i.e.* those with sufficient votes to pass a resolution in general meeting, must act bona fide for the benefit of the shareholders as a general body. The memorandum and articles vary considerably among different companies, but in every case the shareholder's position is that of the owner of one or more shares in the company, which shares usually carry a right of voting at general meetings, and, if profits are made, he may receive dividends on his shares. His shares are something which he has bought—perhaps from the company, or perhaps from somebody else—and something which he can sell or give away, either in his lifetime or by his will. The general rule is that he cannot get his money back from the company, so long as the company is in existence, because his position is not that of a person who has lent money to the company or has deposited his money as with a bank or a building society—it is that of the owner of property, namely, his shares, which can only be turned into money if a buyer can be found to pay for them. Shares may be fully paid or partly paid. When the shares are only partly paid the shareholder can be compelled to pay them up fully if called upon by the company or, if the company is being wound up and its debts exceed its assets, by the liquidator. In any event it is the policy of the Companies Acts to see that the issued share capital is maintained intact, except for losses in the way of

[2a] (Or, in Scots Law) delicts.

business, so that it may be available to satisfy the company's debts. Accordingly, while the company is a going concern the rule is that no part of the paid-up capital may be returned to the shareholders without the consent of the court.

A company may be formed to acquire and carry on an existing business, which may or may not belong to the promoters, or to start some new business. However, a company is commonly formed as a private company to acquire the promoters' business. In this case a price is put on the business and paid by the issue to the promoters of shares credited as fully or partly paid in the company. Most of the price will be left owing to the promoters so that if the company is later wound up they will rank for repayment of it as unsecured creditors otherwise if they take the whole price in the form of shares credited as fully paid they will rank for repayment of capital after the unsecured creditors. If a company is formed to acquire a business which does not belong to the promoters they may provide the necessary funds for the company by taking shares in the company for cash.

A company can also raise money by borrowing.[3] Persons who lend money to a company may be issued with debentures to show that they have lent money and are entitled to interest on their loans. Unlike shareholders, they are not members of the company and they have no right to vote at general meetings.

Shares in and debentures of public companies are extensively bought as an investment by people who want to derive an income from their capital but who are unable, for reasons of business, age, health or lack of opportunity, to take any part in the management of the company. To protect investors from dishonest or incompetent people who form companies in which the investors are likely to lose their money, disclosure of such things as the company's past financial record and the benefits of being a director, is required in the prospectus on the strength of which the public is invited to subscribe for shares or debentures of the company. Provision is also made for a company's accounts and the balance sheet and profit and loss account to be audited every year by auditors appointed by the shareholders and for the balance sheet and the profit and loss account and certain other documents to be circulated to every shareholder and debenture holder. A copy of the balance sheet and the other documents must also be lodged with the Registrar of Companies.

---

[3] Money borrowed by a company is sometimes called "loan capital." It should not be confused with "share capital": Chap. 11.

The directors of a company, who are usually appointed by the members at their annual general meeting, have wide powers to manage the company's business conferred upon them by the articles. The members cannot control the exercise of these powers, although they can, *e.g.*, alter the articles. The directors owe certain duties of good faith and care to the company.

A registered company is capable of perpetual succession but it may become insolvent or it may decide to retire from business. In such a case it is wound up, *i.e.* it is put, or it goes, into liquidation, and a person, called a liquidator, is appointed to wind up its affairs. He sells the company's property and pays as much of its debts as he can do out of the proceeds of sale. If there is a surplus, he distributes it among the shareholders. When the liquidation is completed the company is dissolved and ceases to exist.

The History of the Registered Company

The modern commercial company, incorporated by registration under the Companies Acts, is the result of the fusion of two different legal principles. A registered company, like a statutory company or a chartered company, is a "corporation,"[4] *i.e.* in the eyes of the law it is a person, capable of perpetual succession and quite distinct from the natural persons who are its members at any given moment.[5] However, the expression "company" is not confined to a corporation but includes a partnership, which is not a corporation but, at least in the case of an English partnership,[6] is merely the aggregate of the individual partners, and the present-day registered company represents the fusion of the principle of incorporation with that of partnership.

At common law the Crown has always had the right of granting charters of incorporation.[7] Non-trading companies, such as the Law Society and the Institute of Chartered Accountants, are the kind of company now incorporated by charter but trading companies have in the past been formed in this way. The right was first used for creating commercial corporations at the end of the sixteenth and the beginning of the seventeenth centuries, when such companies

---

[4] Companies Act 1948, s. 13 (2), *post* p. 27.

[5] *Salomon* v. *Salomon & Co. Ltd.* [1897] A.C. 22, *post* p. 28.

[6] A Scottish partnership, although not a corporation, is a legal person distinct from the partners of whom it is composed: Partnership Act 1890, s. 4 (2).

[7] A chartered company is sometimes referred to as "a common law corporation."

as the Levant Company, the East India Company, the Hudson's Bay Company, and the notorious South Sea Company (afterwards incorporated by special Act of Parliament), were incorporated. As these corporations were legal entities quite distinct from their members, it followed that at common law the members were not liable for the debts of the corporation, and, indeed, the Crown had no power to incorporate persons so as to make them liable for the debts of the corporation.[8] In a partnership, on the other hand, the partners were always liable for all the debts of the firm and their liability was unlimited.

In England trading companies were originally regulated companies, that is, companies in which each member traded with his own stock subject to the rules of the company, but towards the end of the seventeenth century the joint-stock company emerged,[9] and this is the form of company in common use today. In a joint-stock company, the company trades as a single person with a stock which is jointly contributed by its members. Such companies could only be formed by special Act of Parliament or by charter but, as the advantages of the joint-stock form of trading became better known, these methods proved too expensive and dilatory to meet the growing commercial needs of the nation. Accordingly there grew up a new type of company based upon contract. This contract took the form of an elaborate deed of settlement containing provisions regulating the relations of the members among themselves and providing for the transfer of shares. A body formed in this way was only a partnership in the eye of the law and the liability of the members was unlimited. This type of unincorporated company fell into disfavour with the legislature, largely owing to the activities of fraudulent promoters and unscrupulous share dealers, and in 1720 the Bubble Act was passed to deal with it. Unfortunately, that Act had the effect of suppressing unincorporated companies without satisfying the want which had given rise to their existence, so that "joint-stock enterprise had to wait till the middle of the nineteenth century before corporateness 'for any lawful purpose' could be obtained by the simple process of registration, and personal liability be limited by one magic word."[10]

The origins of company law in Scotland were distinct from those

[8] *Per* Lindley L.J. in *Elve* v. *Boyton* [1891] 1 Ch. 501 at p. 507 (C.A.).
[9] Holdsworth, *History of English Law*, Vol. 8, pp. 206–222.
[10] Carr, *Select Charters of Trading Companies*, Selden Society, Vol. 28, p. xx.

in England, although regulated companies and joint-stock companies did exist from at least the latter years of the seventeenth century. The common law of Scotland sanctioned the formation of companies with transferable shares and under the management of directors, and recognised such companies as having a personality separate from that of their members.[11] In Scotland common law companies constituted under contracts of co-partnery corresponded to the English deed of settlement companies. The Bubble Act extended to Scotland but, because of the common law companies, probably had no legal effect there.[12]

In 1825, by the Bubble Companies, etc., Act, the Bubble Act was repealed and the Crown was empowered in grants of future charters to provide that the members of the corporation should be personally liable for the debts of the corporation to such extent as the Crown should think proper. This was the beginning of "limited liability." By the Chartered Companies Act 1837 the Crown was empowered to grant letters patent, *i.e.* to grant the advantages of incorporation *without* granting a charter, to a body of persons associated together for trading purposes. The persons in question had to register a deed of partnership dividing the capital into shares and providing for transfers, and satisfy the other requirements of the Act; limited liability was then granted to them. The association to which the letters patent were granted did not become a body corporate and the grant of limited liability was an advantage to which they would otherwise not have been entitled.

By the Joint Stock Companies Registration, etc., Act 1844 provision was made in England for the incorporation of companies by registration without the necessity of obtaining a Royal Charter or a special Act of Parliament. The peculiarity of this statute was, however, that, instead of allowing the usual common law consequences of incorporation to follow, it proceeded on the lines of the Chartered Companies Act 1837 and merely gave a corporate existence to a body which it still evidently regarded as a partnership, because it imposed much the same liability on the members for the debts of the company as they would have had for the debts of a partnership. This

---

[11] The decision in *Stevenson & Co.* v. *Macnair and ors* (1757) M. 14, 560 and 14, 667, 5 Brown's Supp. 340 suggests that Scottish courts might even, under continental influence, have developed a principle of limited liability in relation to these companies.

[12] An Act of 1825 (6 Geo. 4 c. 131) mentioned with approval the practice which had prevailed in Scotland of forming joint-stock companies with transferable shares.

Act also made it compulsory to register as companies all partnerships with more than 25[13] members. Liability limited by shares, *i.e.* where a member's liability is limited to the amount, if any, unpaid on his shares, was introduced in the case of registered companies by the Limited Liability Act 1855, and the Joint Stock Companies Act 1856 substituted two documents, the memorandum of association and articles of association, for the deed of settlement.

In Scotland the registered company was not introduced until the Act of 1856: neither the 1844 Act nor the 1855 Act applied to Scotland.

The Companies Act 1862 repealed and consolidated the previous Acts. It also established liability limited by guarantee and, in general, prohibited any alteration in the objects clause[14] of the memorandum of association. This prohibition remained until the Companies (Memorandum of Association) Act 1890 enabled the objects to be altered for some purposes with the leave of the court after a special resolution[15] had been passed by the members in general meeting. The Companies Act 1867 contained a power to reduce share capital. The Directors Liability Act 1890 introduced the principle of the liability of the directors to pay compensation to persons who have been induced to take shares on the strength of false statements in a prospectus. The Companies Act 1900 contained the first provisions relating to the contents of prospectuses, the compulsory audit of the company's accounts and the registration of charges with the Registrar.

The Companies Act 1907 made provision for the private (as opposed to the public) company, *i.e.* a company which is prohibited from inviting the public to subscribe for its shares or debentures,[16] and relieved it from the necessity of making its balance sheet public (the public company had to lodge its balance sheet with the Registrar of Companies). The Companies (Consolidation) Act 1908 consolidated the 1862 Act with the various Acts amending it, and this was followed by the Companies Act 1929. The Companies Act 1948, which came into operation on July 1, 1948,[17] introduced the exempt private company, *i.e.* the "family" private company (as opposed to a

---

[13] The maximum number of members for a partnership is now 20, except in the case of certain professional firms: Companies Acts 1948, s. 434; 1967, s. 120, *post* pp. 39, 40.

[14] Dealt with *post* p. 75.

[15] *Post* p. 50.

[16] *Post* p. 35.

[17] s. 462.

private company which was, *e.g.*, a subsidiary of a public company) and called an exempt private company because it was the only kind of private company which was exempt from the necessity of making its balance sheet and profit and loss account public.

The 1948 Act also made far-reaching changes in the law relating to company accounts. As the Cohen Report[18] (on which the 1948 Act was based) said, "The history of company legislation shows the increasing importance attached to publicity in connection with accounts. The Act of 1862 contained no compulsory provisions with regard to audit or accounts, though Table A[19] to that Act did include certain clauses dealing with both matters. In 1879 provision was made for the audit of the accounts of banking companies, but it was not until 1900 that any such provision was made generally applicable. It was only on July 1, 1908, when the Companies Act 1907 came into force, that provision was made for including a statement in the form of a balance sheet in the annual return to the Registrar of Companies, and that provision exempted private companies from this requirement." The Companies Act 1929 required a balance sheet and a profit and loss account to be laid before the company every year, while the present Acts set out in great detail the contents of these accounts, with stringent provisions for their audit. The 1948 Act also for the first time required the auditor of a public or a private company to have a professional qualification.[20]

The present Acts are the Companies Act 1948, the Companies Act 1967 and the Companies Act 1976. The 1948 Act, Parts I and III of the 1967 Act, the Companies (Floating Charges and Receivers) (Scotland) Act 1972, section 9 of the European Communities Act 1972, sections 1 to 4 of the Stock Exchange (Completion of Bargains) Act 1976, section 9 of the Insolvency Act 1976 and the Companies Act 1976 are cited as the Companies Acts 1948 to 1976.[21] In Part I of the 1967 Act, the 1948 Act is referred to as "the principal Act."[22]

A number of the recommendations contained in the Jenkins Report[23] were given effect in the 1967 Act which amended the 1948 Act in a number of respects and came into operation on various dates

---

[18] (1945) Cmd. 6659, para. 96.

[19] A model set of articles of association.

[20] For a fuller treatment of the history of company law, see Gower, *Modern Company Law* (3rd ed., 1969), Chaps. 2 and 3.

[21] 1967 Act, s. 130; 1972 Act, s. 30.

[22] 1967 Act, s. 1.

[23] (1962) Cmnd. 1749.

between July 27, 1967, and July 27, 1968.[24] The status of exempt private company was abolished[25]—the definition of such a company in the 1948 Act was devised to save the small family business from disclosing its affairs to the public but many exempt private companies were not small in membership or in capital or in the extent of their undertakings. There were important new provisions in connection with a company's accounts. For example, a subsidiary company's accounts must disclose the name of its ultimate holding company,[26] accounts must give particulars of the directors' emoluments[27] and of the salaries of employees earning more than £10,000 a year[28] and the turnover for the year must be stated.[29] Other important new provisions were: (1) The provisions in connection with the director's report. For example, the principal activities of the company and its subsidiaries during the year must be stated.[30] The idea is to ensure that shareholders are kept more fully informed of the company's activities. (2) The provisions penalising the dealing by directors, their spouses or children, in certain options to buy or sell shares or debentures of the company or associated companies quoted on a stock exchange, and for securing the disclosure of certain material facts concerning directors.[31] (3) The provisions for securing the disclosure of a person's beneficial ownership of ten per cent. or more of the shares in the company carrying unrestricted voting rights.[32] (It will be seen that the Companies Act 1976 reduced to five per cent. the percentage of shares which, if owned, will require disclosure.) Part III of the 1967 Act gives the Department of Trade wide powers to compel companies to produce books and papers for inspection.[33]

The Companies Acts 1976 enacted the Companies (No. 2) Bill 1976 which itself reproduced a number of the clauses and schedules of the Companies Bill 1973. Sections 24 to 27 and section 30 of the 1976 Act enacted other clauses of the 1973 Bill. The 1976 Act amends the law relating to the filing of company accounts and the keeping of accounting records. It provides for the disqualification of persons taking part in the management of companies if they have been persistently in default in complying with the requirements to deliver documents to the Registrar. The Act also makes new provision with

---

[24] 1967 Act, s. 57.
[25] *Ibid.*, s. 2.
[26] *Ibid.*, s. 5.
[27] *Ibid.*, s. 6.
[28] *Ibid.*, s. 8.
[29] *Ibid.*, s. 9.
[30] *Ibid.*, s. 16.
[31] *Ibid.*, ss. 25–32.
[32] *Ibid.*, ss. 33 and 34.
[33] *Post* p. 406 *et seq.*

respect to the qualifications, appointment, resignation and powers of auditors. It also requires a statement of the first directors and secretary and of the intended situation of the registered office to be delivered to the Registrar on an application for registration of a company, and provides for the regulation of the names of oversea companies.

Companies incorporated by registration under earlier Companies Acts are, of course, just as much subject to the provisions of the Companies Acts 1948, 1967 and 1976 as companies registered under the 1948 Act or the 1948 to 1976 Acts.[34]

Section 9 of the European Communities Act 1972 more or less gave effect to a recommendation of the Jenkins Committee[35] and brought U.K. Company Law into line with that of the EEC when, among other things, it modified the *ultra vires* doctrine.

The Companies (Floating Charges and Receivers) (Scotland) Act 1972 modified the law of Scotland in relation to floating charges and made provision for the appointment of receivers.

The Companies Bill 1973 attempted to give effect to other recommendations of the Jenkins Committee but, as is explained later in this chapter, that Bill lapsed on the dissolution of Parliament in February 1974 and the recommendations still have not been given effect to. It will be found that some of them are referred to at the appropriate places in the text.

Part II of the Industry Act 1975 gives the Secretary of State power to prohibit transfers of control of important manufacturing undertakings to non-residents, and under Part IV manufacturing undertakings can be required to provide information about specified activities to the appropriate minister and, unless, *e.g.*, he decides that it would be contrary to the national interest or to statute, to trade unions recognised by the undertaking. No attempt has been made to codify company law, *i.e.* to reduce to a code all the statute law and common law on the topic. Unlike Acts such as the Partnership Act 1890 the various Companies Acts generally have simply consolidated provisions previously in several other Acts. Consequently a significant part of company law is comprised of decided cases. Further, although the present legislation is mostly applicable to both England and Scotland, the common law of the two countries is not the same.

[34] 1948 Act, s. 377; 1967 Act, s. 53.
[35] Para. 42.

PROPOSALS FOR REFORM OF THE LAW RELATING
TO REGISTERED COMPANIES

Remaining recommendations of Jenkins Committee 1962

Although a number of recommendations contained in the Report of the Jenkins Committee[36] were implemented in the Companies Act 1967,[37] section 9 of the European Communities Act 1972[38] and the Companies Act 1976,[38a] the remaining recommendations have not yet been adopted, although the Companies Bill 1973 attempted to give effect to many of them. Some of them are referred to at the appropriate places in the text.

Conservative Government White Paper on Company Law Reform 1973

In a White Paper on Company Law Reform,[39] presented to Parliament in July, 1973, the then Conservative Government announced its intention to introduce a new Companies Bill. The Government's principle reasons for this were:

(1) Many of the recommendations of the Jenkins Committee that were not included in the Companies Act 1967 were still valid and important.

(2) There was a need for fuller disclosure of information by companies both as a spur to efficiency and as a safeguard against malpractice.

(3) The arrangements for uncovering and dealing with commercial crime and malpractices had proved inadequate.

(4) The existing classification of companies needed to be adapted to present day requirements.

(5) There was a need to consider how far it is desirable and practicable to take further account by statutory means of issues of social responsibility towards employees of a company and the community at large.

Part One of the White Paper set out the major matters to be dealt with in the Bill. These matters, which are dealt with at the appropriate places in the text, were: Disclosure, Insider Dealings, Nominee Shareholdings, Private Interests of Directors, Filing of Company

---

[36] (1962) Cmnd. 1749.   [37] *Ante* p. 9.
[38] *Ante* p. 10.   [38a] *Ante* p. 11.   [39] Cmnd. 5391.

Accounts, The Structure of Incorporation, Disqualification of Directors, Protection of Minorities, Powers to Appoint Inspectors, Financial Assistance by a Company for Purchase of its Own Shares, Limited Voting Rights and No-Par-Value Shares.

The second half of the White Paper discussed briefly some of the major issues on which there would eventually need to be decisions and, probably, legislation. If debate matured a subject to the stage at which broadly acceptable provisions could be included in the forthcoming Companies Bill, the Government would have sought appropriate legislation; but they expected that many of these matters would qualify for inclusion in subsequent legislation.

What follows is a summary of the discussion in Part Two of the White Paper.

The European Economic Community

The Government considered that it would probably be some years before some of the matters discussed in the first part of the White Paper could be effectively harmonised in the member States of the European Economic Community, so that it was appropriate that the U.K. should take independent action where an immediate need could be shown. Some of the matters referred to in the latter part of the Paper needed to be debated both in the U.K. and the Community generally before a basis for common European action could evolve.

Again, some aspects of the existing harmonisation programme had caused real concern in the British commercial and legal community. The Government had therefore suggested a different approach to harmonisation. It should be directed towards identifying those elements of a common company law which each member State would regard as essential to any system of which it formed a part, and towards securing the harmonisation of those elements which could contribute to an early and practical degree of unification of the market.

The public responsibility of the company

The White Paper stated that the directors of a company owe a fiduciary duty to do their best for those whose financial resources they are using but the board has to reconcile several different interests, of which profit is the main but cannot be the only one.

As for an individual, the responsibilities of a company are of two kinds—one specific and one general. The law sets limits to the pursuit of profit—be they limits on acts affecting the public generally, such as fraudulent dealing, exploiting monopolies or polluting the atmosphere, or domestic matters such as the amount of redundancy payment and the keeping of books of account. The other kind of responsibility, a more general and moral kind, is difficult to specify and define in terms that can assist the board in any particular situation or that can be translated into law.

A code of conduct might be appropriate for these wider responsibilities but to be effective a code needs some external sanction. It had been suggested that companies should consider adding to their memoranda a clause empowering the directors to take wider considerations into account when exercising their judgment as directors, and that a code would set such judgments in a general frame of reference. That would protect the directors against any claim by shareholders seeking compensation for loss caused by directors' actions not taken directly and clearly in the shareholders' interest. However, it must be considered whether that would give the necessary positive guidance. Further, some independent source of judgment may be necessary and it was not easy to see what it might be.

A useful step forward would be to impose a duty on directors to report to shareholders on specific parts of the company's response to the social environment. It will be seen later[40] that the Government intended to use for this purpose the powers which they sought to require additional disclosure in directors' reports.

The company and its employees

The Government believed that it was in the interests of all concerned, including those who provided the capital, that the employees should have an appropriate opportunity of influencing decisions which could closely affect their own interest, and a Green Paper on employee participation was to have been published.

The company's responsibility to its shareholders

The "two tier board" is represented by some as a device for bridging the gap that can exist in the larger company between the

[40] *Post* p. 419.

shareholders and the executives. However, the ability of such a board to operate in this way may in part depend on the structure of the ownership of the company. It can be argued that the two tier board is more suited to a situation where the main source of finance is an institution, as is often the case in some other European countries, and less suited to one where the company is largely equity-financed by a considerable number of shareholders, as is usually the case in the U.K. In the latter case, the supervisory, non-executive, board might act not as a bridge but as an additional insulator. On the other hand, it may be that the authority of a large body of shareholders would be more effective if focused by the existence of a supervisory board with powers of ultimate control over the management.

In many companies the non-executive director can play a powerful and useful role, partly by his concern for the interests of the shareholders and partly by obliging executive members to look beyond their immediate concerns to the longer future and to the wider stage. In addition, he may have a particularly active role in matters of management and of succession to the board. There is an argument for saying that every company over a certain size would benefit from the presence on the board of non-executive directors.

Institutional shareholders

An increasingly important part of the shareholding population is now represented by institutional investors such as investment trusts or unit trusts, insurance companies and pension funds. These institutional investors should be better informed than the individual but, because of the size of their investments compared to the size of the market, they do not have the same opportunity of selling out when dissatisfied. Nevertheless, they do not always accept the implications, in terms of the responsibility which they have to their own investors and creditors, for the profitable conduct of the companies in which they are the investors. There is room, for instance, for increasing use of the appointment of suitable non-executive directors.

Some institutions feel that they are investors, and have no special expertise in the management of the companies in which they have invested. However, they have greater resources than the small individual investor to assess the performance of such companies and greater power to press their criticism of inadequate management and, where it might help, to secure the election of non-executive directors.

Conservative Government Companies Bill 1973

As promised in the White Paper *ante*,[41] the Conservative Government introduced a Companies Bill which was first read in the House of Commons on December 18, 1973. Many of the provisions of the Bill are referred to in the text but the Bill was lost when Parliament was dissolved on February 7, 1974, and the Labour Government decided not to re-introduce the Bill but to launch a major review of company law covering employee participation and the supervision of the securities market as well as the more traditional aspects of company law.

Some of the provisions of the 1973 Bill were reproduced in the Labour Government's Companies (No. 2) Bill 1976, which was enacted by the Companies Act 1976, *ante*.[41a]

Labour Party Green Paper on the Reform of Company Law 1974

The Conservative Government's Companies Bill 1973 was said to be inadequate in the Labour Party Green Paper on Company Law Reform called "The Community and the Company." This Green Paper was drafted in December, 1973, and published in May, 1974. It criticised the 1973 Bill on the ground that such Bill did not provide for either the public interest or the employees' interest (the law being based on the rights of shareholders and creditors). The Bill was also criticised in that it relied on self-regulation of city affairs, *e.g.* by the Stock Exchange and the Take-over Panel, and did not provide for the establishment of a Companies Commission.

The proposals in the Green Paper were said to point the way for a Socialist Companies Act to obtain control in the public interest over the private sector by—

(1) establishing a new structure for the relationship of the company and its workers;
(2) regulating companies and financial institutions by a Companies Commission;
(3) widening the scope of disclosure in the public interest and in the interests of employees.

In some ways the provisions of the Australian Corporations and Securities Industry Bill 1974 (Cth) resembled the proposals in the

Green Paper but there was a number of differences. The Green Paper proposed that the duties of directors should be defined so that they should, in deciding what is in the interests of the company,[42] take account of the interests of both employees and shareholders, and perhaps of other interests as well, *e.g.* the national interest.

According to the Green Paper, the interests of employees should be recognised, and there should be increased participation by employees in the decision-making in the company. It was not suggested that employees of a company should be made "members" of it in law, with limited rights, *e.g.* to certain information, although there might be areas of power which shareholders control as "members" in which the employees, through their elected union representatives, should share, *e.g.* the appointment of the liquidator in a shareholders' voluntary winding up.

One of the most interesting proposals was that there should be a two-tier management structure in Britain—a supervisory board and a management board. The management board, which would be responsible for day-to-day "managerial functions," would be appointed by and supervised by the supervisory board. The supervisory board would be composed of shareholders' and workers' representatives and there would be provisions dealing with the situation where there is deadlock in a vote. The supervisory board would have effective control over certain matters of long term policy, including the fundamental nature of the company's operations and association with other companies or enterprises. It would be under a duty to present reports to both the shareholders and the employees constituencies. The directors would be under a duty to act in the interests of the enterprise while at the same time taking special account of their constituency.

The Green Paper was very critical of the present system of self-regulation. It stated that the control and regulation of company affairs is confused and fragmented, and relies too much upon self-regulation, which has failed to work, and that the Department of Trade (of which the Registrar of Companies is an official) is passive and inadequately staffed. To a considerable extent the present system is ineffective in protecting the public interest, the interests of employees and, in some cases, those of shareholders.

The securities market for quoted companies is the responsibility of the Stock Exchange, which formulates its own rules. Its committee membership is made up of stockbrokers and jobbers and therefore

[42] See p. 350.

there is a strong fear that it operates more in its members' interests than those of the investor. Again, it tends to be more concerned with the interests of the large institutional investors than those of small investors. Further, it is unable to police the securities markets effectively, particularly in respect of insider trading.[43]

At present, the monitoring of take-overs is mainly the responsibility of the Panel on Takeovers and Mergers, which is composed of representatives of city interests.[44] It has several basic weaknesses, *e.g.* it operates on a voluntary basis and relies to a large degree on the moral sanctions that it can apply to merchant banks, stock brokers, individuals and companies.

The case for a Companies Commission, a new public supervisory body, which would take over the Companies and Insurance Divisions of the Department of Trade, was therefore overwhelming, the Green Paper stated. Day-to-day control of the Stock Exchange would remain with the Stock Exchange Council, which would decide the Stock Exchange rules in consultation with the Commission, the latter having the final say. The Commission would be in partnership with the appropriate professional bodies in drawing up accounting standards. The Takeover Panel would work to a legally and effectively enforceable code drawn up by the Commission in consultation with the Panel. To make the Commission's work effective, the necessary sanctions must be available.

With regard to warehousing,[45] the Green Paper stated that the threshold for disclosure of a stake in a company could be lowered below five per cent. As to nominee holdings, the Green Paper stated that the principle of full disclosure of the beneficial ownership of shares to the public as a whole must be reasserted. And as to non-voting shares, the Green Paper recommended that the issue of new non-voting shares should be prohibited and existing non-voting shares should be enfranchised over a period of, say, five years.

Finally, in connection with insider trading, the Green Paper agreed with the object of the legislation and with the categories of person included in the definition of "insider" stated in the Conservative Party White Paper,[46] although there was concern that trustees of company pension schemes were not included in the definition where appropriate. However, the Green Paper preferred that the problem

[43] See *post.*
[44] See pp. 641, 648.
[45] *Post* p. 205.
[46] *Ante* p. 12.

should be tackled by saying that a criminal offence is committed by any person who:

(1) possesses inside information of a price-sensitive nature;
(2) knows, or could be reasonably expected to know, that it is inside information;
(3) uses it for the purpose of dealing to make a profit or avoid a loss.

Such a basic provision could be reinforced by restricting the rights of certain defined persons likely to become regularly in possession of inside information, such as directors, in relation to their dealing in the shares concerned and by making it an offence for them to communicate price-sensitive information to third persons with the intent that those persons might engage in dealings or in circumstances where there are grounds for supposing that they might. It seems that the maximum punishment for insider trading is to be seven years imprisonment. As to a civil remedy, ideally the aggrieved party should have the right to reverse the transaction of which he complains and it might be appropriate in certain circumstances for the insider to have to account to the company for his profit. Any change in the law on insider trading should be accompanied by changes in Stock Exchange practice that would enable both principals to any transaction to be identified more readily.

Other proposals in the Green Paper are mentioned at the appropriate places in the text.

Companies Bills 1974 and 1976 and Companies (Audit Committees) Bill 1977

The Companies Bill 1974, a Private Members' Bill, required boards of certain companies to include non-executive directors. However, this Bill was lost when Parliament was dissolved on September 20, 1974. The Companies Bill 1976, which was also a Private Members' Bill, incorporated the provisions of the 1974 Bill.

Companies (Audit Committees) Bill 1977

The Companies (Audit Committees) Bill 1977 provides that the board of a company to which clause 1 applies shall include at least three non-executive directors. Clause 1 applies to a company that is registered in Great Britain, its shares are listed on a recognised stock exchange and at any time within the five years immediately preceding its last annual general meeting it had more than 1,500 employees or £5 million total net assets. It seems that there are about 1,000 such companies. The expression "non-executive director" is defined as a director who is not an employee of, and does not hold any other office or place of profit under, the company or any subsidiary or associated company (clause 8).

The above-mentioned part of the Bill closely follows the lines of the 1974 and 1976 Companies Bills. However, the 1977 Bill goes on to provide that a company to which clause 2 applies must appoint a committee of the board to be known as the audit committee, such committee must include at least three non-executive directors, at least half of the members of the committee must be non-executive directors, one of the non-executive directors must be chairman of the committee and the company secretary must act as secretary of the committee. Clause 2 applies to a company registered in Great Britain whose shares are listed on a recognised stock exchange if at any time within the five years immediately preceding its last annual general meeting it had more than 2,000 employees or more than £10 million total net assets. It seems that there are about 700 such companies.

Clause 3 requires the directors of a company to which clause 2 applies, when required by the audit committee but at least once in each accounting reference period, to secure and collate such data about the company's affairs and transactions and those of its subsidiaries, and to prepare such estimates of the future course of the business, as the audit committee think are required to allow a reasonable assessment to be made of the company's future profitability and of its ability to pay its debts as they fall due. The data and estimates must be provided as soon as reasonably practicable to all the directors, the secretary and the auditors.

Clause 4 specifies the duties of the audit committee. For example, the chairman must convene committee meetings at least twice between any two annual general meetings of the company. The auditors are entitled to receive notices of and to attend every meeting and be heard thereat. The audit committee must undertake reviews of all financial statements prepared by the directors before they are issued to members or published and must consider any matter which the auditors require to be brought to the attention of the board.

At the first suitable opportunity the board must consider matters examined by the audit committee and the opinions of the committee on them (clause 5).

The audit directors must make a statement in each accounting reference period (the "audit directors' statement"). This must say whether they think that the clause 3 data and estimates were properly prepared and their reports to the board duly considered. A copy must be attached to the balance sheet and read before the company in general meeting. Each audit director must sign or resign from the committee. (Clause 6.)

According to the explanatory memorandum, the practice of setting up audit committees is well established in Canada and the United States.

Measures of the European Community

There is a number of measures of the European Community aimed at the harmonisation of the company laws of the Member States. The First Directive of the EEC Council of Ministers was given effect to in the U.K. by the European Communities Act 1972, s. 9, which among other things, modified the *ultra vires* doctrine and is dealt with in a number of places in the text. Other proposals designed to eliminate the major differences between the various company laws are:

Draft Second Directive, submitted by the Commission to the Council on March 5, 1970, concerning company capital. Draft Third Directive, on mergers (June 16, 1970). Draft Fourth Directive, on annual accounts (November 10, 1971). Draft Fifth Directive, on the structure and administration of public companies (October 9, 1972). Draft directive on prospectuses (September 26, 1972).

Draft convention on international mergers.

Convention for the mutual recognition of companies, firms and legal persons (February 29, 1968).

Draft regulation on European groupings (July 18, 1973).

Draft regulation containing the statute for the European company.

Draft Directive on mutual recognition of accountancy qualifications.

Most of the above proposals will be found set out, together with an introductory explanation, in European Company Law Texts by Professor Clive M. Schmitthoff.

PROCEDURE TO OBTAIN REGISTRATION OF A COMPANY

To obtain the registration of a company certain documents must be delivered to the appropriate Registrar of Companies and certain fees and stamp duties must be paid. If the registered office is to be situate in England or in Wales,[47] the appropriate registrar is the Registrar of Companies for England,[48] and his address is now Companies Registration Office, Crown Way, Maindy, Cardiff CF4 3UZ.[49] If the registered office is to be situate in Scotland[47] the appropriate registrar is the Registrar of Companies for Scotland[48] and his address is Companies Registration Office, Exchequer Chambers, 102 George Street, Edinburgh, EH2 3DJ.

Documents which must be delivered to the Registrar

The following documents must be delivered to the Registrar of Companies:

(1) A memorandum of association[50] stating, *inter alia*, the objects of the company and if, as is common, the company is a limited company with a share capital, the amount of share capital with which the company proposes to be registered and its division into shares of a fixed amount,[51] *e.g.* £10,000 divided into 10,000 shares of a nominal amount of £1 each.

The memorandum must be stamped with the standard companies registration fee of £50.[52]

(2) Usually, printed articles of association[53] providing for such matters as the transfer of shares in the company, the holding of general meetings, *i.e.* meetings of the members or shareholders, the directors' powers of management and the extent to which they can delegate their powers to a managing director, and dividends.

(3) If the memorandum states that the registered office is to be

---

[47] See *post* p. 71.
[48] s. 12 of the 1948 Act as amended by Sched. 2 to the 1976 Act.
[49] The main part of the Companies Registration Office is now in Cardiff. There are microfilm reading room facilities in London at Companies House, 55–71 City Road, London, EC1Y 1BB.
[50] s. 12. The memorandum is dealt with in Chap. 3.
[51] s. 2.
[52] *Post* p. 25.
[53] ss. 6, 9, 12. Articles are dealt with in Chap. 4.

situated in Wales and the memorandum and articles are in Welsh, a certified translation in English.[54]

(4) A statement in the prescribed form of the names of the intended first director or directors, and first secretary or joint secretaries, and the particulars specified in section 200 (2) and (3) respectively.[55] Such statement must be signed by or on behalf of the subscribers of the memorandum and must contain a consent to act signed by each of the persons named in it. Where the memorandum is delivered for registration by an agent for the subscribers, such statement must specify that fact and the name and address of that person.[56] The statement must also specify the intended situation of the company's registered office.[57]

(5) A statutory declaration, by a solicitor engaged in the formation of the company or by a person named as director or secretary of the company in the statement delivered under (4) *ante*, of compliance with the requirements of the Acts in respect of registration.[58]

(6) A statement of capital (Form PUC1), unless the company is to have no share capital.

Form PUC1 will bear Inland Revenue capital duty[59] if the subscription shares are being paid for by the subscribers on incorporation.

For the purpose of ensuring that documents delivered to the Registrar are of standard size, durable and easily legible, the Secretary of State may prescribe such requirements as he considers appropriate. If a document delivered to the Registrar does not, in his opinion, comply with such requirements, he may serve a notice on the person or persons by whom the document was required to be delivered whereupon, for the purposes of any enactment which enables a penalty to be imposed in respect of an omission to deliver a document to the Registrar, the duty to deliver is not discharged but the person subject to the duty has fourteen days after the date of service of the notice in which to discharge it.[60]

---

[54] 1976 Act, s. 30 (6).
[55] *Post* pp. 318, 370.
[56] 1976 Act, s. 21.
[57] *Ibid.*, s. 23 (2).
[58] s. 15 (2) of the 1948 Act as amended by Sched. 2 of the 1976 Act.
[59] p. 25.
[60] 1976 Act, s. 35.

The Registrar may, if he thinks fit, accept, under any provision of the Companies Acts requiring a document to be delivered to him, any material other than a document which contains the information in question and is of a kind approved by him. Thus the Registrar has power to accept information on microfilm.[61]

The duty of the Registrar on receiving the above-mentioned documents is to examine them to see whether the statutory requirements have been complied with, but in exercising his duty he has no power to hold a judicial inquiry on evidence.[62] Among the statutory requirements to be observed are:

(1) That the memorandum is signed by at least seven persons, or at least two if the company is to be a private company, and, if the memorandum is accompanied by articles, that the articles are signed by the same persons.[63]

(2) That the company is being formed for a lawful purpose.[64]

If the company is being formed for a purpose prohibited by law, *e.g.* to act as auditor of companies,[65] or for the sale of tickets in a lottery illegal in the United Kingdom, such as the Irish Sweep,[66] the Registrar will decline to register it.

(3) That the other requirements of the Act, *e.g.* as to the contents of the memorandum and articles, are complied with.[67]

(4) That the proposed name is not one which, in the opinion of the Department of Trade, is undesirable.[68]

(5) That the memorandum and articles are in the statutory form.[69]

Any person may inspect the documents or other material kept by the Registrar relative to individual companies on payment of a fee not exceeding five pence per inspection, and may require a sealed copy or extract of them on payment of not more than two and a half pence for each folio of 72 words.[70]

---

[61] *Ibid.*, s. 36.
[62] *R.* v. *Registrar of Companies, ex. p. Bowen* [1914] 3 K.B. 1161.
[63] ss. 1 (1), 3, 6, 9, *post* pp. 61, 105.
[64] s. 1 (1).
[65] s. 161, *post* pp. 454, 455.
[66] *R.* v. *Registrar of Companies, ex p. More* [1931] 2 K.B. 197 (C.A.).
[67] ss. 1 (1), 2, 3, 6, 9, *post* pp. 60, 61, 104, 105.
[68] s. 17, *post* p. 63.
[69] s. 11, *post* p. 61.
[70] 1948 Act, ss. 424 (5), 426; 1976 Act, ss. 36 (3), 38 (3).

Fees and stamp duties

Registration fees

Section 37 of the Companies Act 1976 empowers the Secretary of State, by regulations made by statutory instrument, to require payment to the Registrar of such fees as may be specified in the regulations in respect of the performance by the Registrar of such functions under the Companies Acts as may be specified, including the receipt by him of any notice or other document which the Acts require to be given or delivered to him.

The fee for registration of a company is now a fixed fee of £50[71] irrespective of the amount of nominal capital or, in the case of a company without share capital, the number of members.

Stamp duties

(1) On the formation of a company with limited liability capital duty at the rate of £1 per £100 or part thereof is charged on the greater of the nominal value of the shares issued or allotted on incorporation and the actual value of assets of any kind contributed less any liabilities which have been assumed or discharged by the company in consideration of the contribution.[72]

The duty is impressed on return of allotments Form PUC2 if the allotment is for cash or Form PUC3 if the allotment is for a consideration other than cash.

(2) Conveyance or transfer duty on the transfer of property attaches, *e.g.* when a company is formed to acquire an existing business.[73] An *agreement* in writing for the sale of property (even to a company which is made up of vendors of the property) is, under section 59 of the Stamp Act 1891, as amended, liable to such duty on the consideration for the property, except in so far as that property consists of land, goods and merchandise, ships, stocks, shares or marketable securities. (When any land is *conveyed*, duty will be payable.) This duty

---

[71] Companies (Fees) Regulations 1975 (S.I. 1975/596). But there is power to make new regulations under the Companies Act 1976, s. 37.

[72] Finance Act 1973, ss. 47–49 and Sched. 19. This is to comply with EEC Directive 69/335.

[73] *Post* p. 118.

is now £2 per £100 except that there are reduced rates where the consideration does not exceed £30,000 and the instrument is certified.[74]

It is no longer necessary to stamp the memorandum and articles with a deed stamp.[75]

CERTIFICATE OF INCORPORATION

On the registration of a company the Registrar gives a certificate, authenticated by a seal prepared under section 424 (5) of the 1948 Act, that the company is incorporated and, in the case of a limited company, that it is limited: section 13 (1) of the 1948 Act; s. 38 (2) of the 1976 Act. The certificate of incorporation, which may be described as the company's birth certificate, is in the following form:

CERTIFICATE OF INCORPORATION
I HEREBY CERTIFY that   , Limited, is this day Incorporated under the Companies Act 1948, and that the Company is Limited.
Given under my hand at London this   day of

(seal)

Section 9 (3) of the European Communities Act 1972 requires the Registrar to publish in the *Gazette* notice of the issue of a certificate of incorporation.

Section 15 (1) of the Companies Act 1948 provides that the certificate is conclusive evidence that all the requirements of the Acts in respect of registration and of matters precedent and incidental thereto have been complied with, and that the association is a company authorised to be registered and duly registered.

It is thought that the subsection means that it cannot be argued that a company is not validly incorporated, *e.g.* because the memorandum of association was not subscribed by two persons in the case of a private company or seven in the case of a public company,[76] except where a statutory provision as to substance invalidates the registration.[77] In *Cotman* v. *Brougham*[78] Lord Wrenbury criticised[79] "the pernicious practice of registering memoranda of association

---

[4] Finance Act 1974, s. 49 and Sched. 11.
[75] Finance Act 1970, Sched. 7, para. 1.
[76] *Ante* p. 24.
[77] *Per* Megarry J. in *Gaiman* v. *National Association for Mental Health* [1971] Ch. 317, at p. 329.
[78] [1918] A.C. 514.
[79] At p. 523.

which, under the clause relating to objects,[80] contain paragraph after paragraph not specifying or delimiting the proposed trade or purpose, but confusing power with purpose and indicating every class of act which the corporation is to have power to do." He went on to say: "Such a memorandum is not, I think, a compliance with the Act" but that if the Registrar registers the memorandum the court "must assume that all requirements in respect of matters precedent and incidental to registration have been complied with and confine [itself] to the construction of the document." The certificate of incorporation has been held to be conclusive as to the date of incorporation.[81]

The reason for section 15 (1) is that once a company is registered and has begun business and entered into contracts it would be disastrous if any person could allege that the company was not duly registered.[82]

The certificate will not be conclusive if a trade union should be registered as a company[83]—the registration of a trade union under the Companies Acts is void by statute.[84] Again, the certificate is not conclusive as to the legality of a company's objects—proceedings may be brought to have the registration cancelled where objects are illegal.[85]

EFFECT OF REGISTRATION OF A COMPANY

From the date of incorporation mentioned in the certificate of incorporation, the subscribers of the memorandum, together with such other persons as may from time to time become members of the company, form a body corporate by the name contained in the memorandum, capable forthwith of exercising all the functions of an incorporated company, and having perpetual succession and a common seal, but with such liability on the part of the members to contribute to the assets of the company as is mentioned in the Act: section 13 (2).

[80] *Post* p. 75.
[81] *Jubilee Cotton Mills Ltd.* v. *Lewis* [1924] A.C. 958, where it was also held that "From the date of incorporation" in s. [13 (2)] included any portion of the day on which the company was incorporated.
[82] *Per* Lord Cairns in *Peel's Case* (1867) L.R. 2 Ch.App. 674, at p. 682.
[83] *British Association of Glass Bottle Manufacturers Ltd.* v. *Nettlefold* (1911) 27 T.L.R. 527.
[84] Trade Union Act 1871, s. 5; Companies Act 1948, s. 459 (9).
[85] *Per* Lord Parker of Waddington in *Bowman* v. *Secular Society Ltd.* [1917] A.C. 406, at p. 439.

The registered company is a body corporate, *i.e.* a legal person separate and distinct from its members.

S. had for many years carried on business as a boot manufacturer. His business was solvent when it was converted into a company, *i.e.* a company limited by shares was formed, the subscribers to the memorandum of which were S. and his wife, daughter and four sons (for one share each), and the business was sold to the company at a price of £39,000. The terms of sale were approved by all the shareholders. 20,000 fully paid shares of £1 each were allotted to S. so that S.'s wife and children held one share each and S. held 20,001 shares. S. left the rest of the price on loan to the company and for this sum of £10,000 he was given debentures secured by a charge on the company's assets. It seems that the directors were S. and his sons and that S. was appointed managing director. After a depression the company went into liquidation. The assets were sufficient to satisfy the debentures, but the unsecured creditors, with debts amounting to £7,000, received nothing. *Held,* that the proceedings were not contrary to the true intent and meaning of the Companies Act; that the company was duly registered and was not a mere "alias" or agent of or trustee for the vendor; that he was not liable to indemnify the company against creditors' claims; that there was no fraud upon creditors (or shareholders); that the company (or the liquidator) was not entitled to rescission of the contract of purchase: *Salomon* v. *Salomon & Co. Ltd.* [1897] A.C. 22.[86]

"The company is at law a different person altogether from the subscribers to the memorandum; and, though it may be that after incorporation the business is precisely the same as it was before, and the same persons are managers, and the same hands receive the profits, the company is not in law the agent of the subscribers or trustee for them. Nor are the subscribers as members liable, in any shape or form, except to the extent and in the manner provided by the Act": *per* Lord Macnaghten at p. 51.

One effect is that the property of the company belongs to the company itself and not to the individual members, so that even the largest shareholder has no insurable interest in the property of the company.[87] The managing director, even if he owns all the shares except one, cannot lawfully pay cheques to the company into his own banking account or draw cheques for his own purposes upon the company's banking account.[88] It also means that the company's debts are the obligations of the company alone and normally cannot be enforced against the members, however many shares they may own.[89]

---

[86] Although *Salomon's* case is now generally accepted in Scots law, the Scottish courts were, about the same time and independently of that authority, giving effect to the same principle, *e.g. Henderson* v. *Stubbs' Ltd.* (1894) 22 R. 51, *Grierson, Oldham & Co. Ltd.* v. *Forbes, Maxwell & Co. Ltd.* (1895) 22 R. 812 and *John Wilson & Son Ltd.* v. *Inland Revenue* (1895) 23 R. 18.

[87] *Macaura* v. *Northern Assurance Co. Ltd.* [1925] A.C. 619.

[88] *A. L. Underwood, Ltd.* v. *Bank of Liverpool & Martins Ltd.* [1924] 1 K.B. 775 (C.A.); *cf. Thompson* v. *J. Barke and Company (Caterers) Ltd.,* 1975 S.L.T. 67 (O.H.) (Company's cheques used to repay loan made to director held *ultra vires*).

[89] *Post* p. 30. Two related companies are separate entities: *Taylor, Petitioner,* 1976 S.L.T. ((Sh. Ch. 82).

This principle of the independent corporate existence of a registered company is of the greatest importance in company law. As we shall see, it is this which mainly distinguishes a registered company from a partnership, which is the relation which subsists between persons carrying on a business in common with a view of profit. A partnership is not a corporation but, at least in the case of an English partnership,[90] is only the aggregate of the partners, *i.e.* a partnership has no legal existence but is merely the association of two or more persons carrying on business together. The property of the firm belongs to the partners and the firm's debts are the debts of the partners, *i.e.* the partners are personally liable for the firm's debts, whereas in a registered company the assets and liabilities are those of the company and not of the members.

A registered company is capable forthwith of exercising all the functions of an incorporated company, *e.g.* it can hold land and other property, and it can sue and be sued. If the company is a public company it cannot commence business until the requirements of section 109 have been complied with.[91]

A registered company has perpetual succession unless it is wound up and dissolved.

The liability of a member of a company limited by shares to contribute to the company's assets (for the purpose of enabling its debts to be paid) is limited to the amount, if any, unpaid on his shares.[92] Thus if he has taken one thousand shares of £1 each in the company and the shares are fully paid up he is normally under no further liability to contribute to the assets. In the case of a partnership every partner is jointly liable with the other partners for all the firm's debts.[93]

The veil of incorporation

It was established in *Salomon* v. *Salomon & Co. Ltd.*, *ante*, that a registered company is a legal person separate from its members. This principle may be referred to as "the veil of incorporation."

---

[90] A Scottish partnership or firm has a separate legal existence and is not merely the association of two or more persons. The property of the firm belongs to the firm, and the firm's debts are primarily those of the firm, although each partner may ultimately be made personally liable for the firm's debts.

[91] *Post* p. 182.

[92] s. 1 (2).

[93] Further differences between registered companies and partnerships are dealt with later in this chapter.

In general, the law will not go behind the separate personality of the company to the members, so that, *e.g.* in *Macaura* v. *Northern Assurance Co. Ltd.*, *ante*, it was held that the largest shareholder had no insurable interest in the property of the company. However, there are exceptions to the principle in *Salomon's* case where the veil is lifted and "the law disregards the corporate entity and pays regard instead to the economic realities behind the legal facade. . . . In these exceptional cases the law either goes behind the corporate personality to the individual members, or ignores the separate personality of each company in favour of the economic entity constituted by a group of associated concerns." [94]

Instances of the veil being lifted may be classified as "under express statutory provision" and "under judicial interpretation," [94] or as "statutory," "trading with the enemy" and "common law." [95]

One example of a case where "the veil is lifted" is where a company carries on business for more than six months with less than the statutory minimum of members (seven for a public, two for a private company), in which event every person who is a member during the time that business is so carried on after the end of the six-month period and who knows that business is being so carried on, is severally liable for all the company's debts contracted during such time and may be severally sued therefor (s. 31, intended to ensure that the number of members does not fall below the statutory minimum). This is exceptional because the general rule is that the company's debts cannot be enforced against the members.

Another example occurs in section 154 [96] where the way in which a company's shares are held is relevant in determining whether it is a subsidiary of another company. Thus if more than half of the ordinary shares of a company are held by another company the first will normally be a subsidiary of the second.

Again, where an officer of a company signs, on behalf of the company, a bill of exchange, promissory note, cheque or order for money or goods in which the company's name is not mentioned, the officer is personally liable to the holder of the bill of exchange, etc., for the amount thereof unless it is paid by the company (s. 108 (4)). [97]

At common law, a company registered in England is an alien enemy if its agents or the persons in *de facto* control of its affairs

[94] Gower, *Modern Company Law*, 3rd ed., p. 189.
[95] Ruthven, *Lifting the Veil of Incorporation in Scotland*, 1969 Juridical Review, p. 1.
[96] *Post* p. 57.
[97] *Post* p. 67.

are alien enemies, and in determining whether alien enemies have such control, the number of alien enemy shareholders and the value of their holdings are material.[98]

A fifth example is that in cases such as *Re Express Engineering Works Ltd.*[99] and the other cases dealt with on pages 289, 290, the decision of all the shareholders was held to be the decision of the company, *e.g.* something less formal than a resolution, even a special resolution, duly passed at a general meeting was regarded as the act of the company.

It was held in *Re Bugle Press Ltd.*[1] that if A Ltd. makes an offer for the shares in B Ltd. and in substance A Ltd. is the same as the majority shareholding in B Ltd., A Ltd. will not be able to invoke section 209[2] and compel the minority shareholders in B Ltd. to sell their shares to A Ltd. In these circumstances the law goes behind the corporate personality of A Ltd. to the individual members. The court will not allow the section to be invoked for an improper purpose.

Lord Denning M.R. was prepared to lift the veil in *Wallersteiner* v. *Moir*[3]—he said that in that case the plaintiff was also in breach of section 190 (which in general prohibits a company making a loan to a director) because the company of which he was a director made a loan to another company which was his puppet, so that the loan should be treated as made to him.

The case of *Gilford Motor Co. Ltd.* v. *Horne*[4] shows that the courts will not allow a company to be used as a device to mask the carrying on of a business by a former employee of another person and to enable the former employee to break a valid covenant in restraint of trade contained in the contract under which he was formerly employed. In that case the employee covenanted that after the termination of the employment he would not solicit his employer's customers. Soon after the termination of his employment he formed a company of which the two directors and shareholders were his wife and one other person and which sent out circulars to customers of his former employer. An injunction was granted against the ex-employee and the company. The *Gilford* case was followed in

---

[98] *Daimler Co. Ltd.* v. *Continental Tyre etc. Ltd.* [1916] 2 A.C. 307.
[99] [1920] 1 Ch. 466 (C.A.), *post* p. 289.
[1] [1961] Ch. 270 (C.A.), *post* p. 644.
[2] *Post* p. 642.
[3] [1974] 1 W.L.R. 991 (C.A.).
[4] [1933] Ch. 935 (C.A.).

Jones v. *Lipman*[5] where, having agreed to sell land to the plaintiff, the defendant sold and transferred the land to a company controlled by him. It was held that the company was the creature of the defendant, a mask to avoid recognition by the eye of equity, and therefore specific performance could not be resisted by the defendant. Specific performance was also granted against the company.

Although in *Salomon's* case, *ante*, it was held that the company was not a mere agent for Salomon, in *Smith, Stone & Knight Ltd.* v. *Birmingham Corporation*[6] a subsidiary company which was carrying on the parent company's business was held to be the agent of the parent shareholder. Conversely, in *Wm. Cory & Son Ltd.* v. *Dorman Long & Co. Ltd.*[7] the parent company was held to be the agent of the subsidiary.

In *Smith, Stone & Knight Ltd* v. *Birmingham Corporation* [1939] 4 All E.R. 116, having acquired a partnership business a company registered a new company in which it held all the shares except five which its directors held in trust for it and the directors of which were directors of the parent company. The business was apparently carried on by the subsidiary (its name was on the premises and the notepaper) but the parent had complete control of it (there was no agreement between the companies, the business was not assigned to the subsidiary and, although a manager was appointed by the parent, the books and accounts were kept by the parent). It was held that the six tests for determining whether a subsidiary is carrying on a business as the parent's business or as its own were all satisfied. (1) The profits were treated as those of the parent, (2) which appointed the persons who conducted the business, and (3) was the head and brain of the trading venture, and (4) governed the adventure in that it decided what should be done and what capital should be employed, and (5) made the profits by its skill and direction, and (6) was in effectual and constant control. Therefore the business belonged to the parent, which was the real occupier of the premises. Consequently, the parent was entitled to claim compensation for removal and disturbance when the premises were compulsorily acquired.

The veil is lifted whenever the Act recognises the relationship of holding company and subsidiary.[8] An example is that, except in certain specified cases, group accounts must be laid before the holding company in general meeting (s. 150).[9] The power of an inspector of a company, under sections 166 and 172,[10] to investigate a related company, is also an example of the veil being lifted.

[5] [1962] 1 W.L.R. 832.
[6] [1939] 4 All E.R. 116.
[7] [1936] 2 All E.R. 386 (C.A.).
[7a] *Cf. D. H. N. Food Distributors Ltd.* v. *Tower Hamlets London Borough Council* [1976] 1 W.L.R. 852 (C.A.). *Cf. Woolfson* v. *Strathclyde Regional Council* 1977 S.L.T. 60.
[8] *Post* p. 57.
[9] *Post* p. 434.
[10] *Post* pp. 399, 403.

Other instances of the lifting of the veil of incorporation will be found in the field of taxation, *e.g.* the residence of a company, which is relevant in the ascertainment of the company's liability to U.K. corporation tax,[11] is determined by the location of the central management and control of the company. Another instance occurs when a close company makes inadequate distributions "relevant income" is apportioned among the shareholders under the Finance Act 1972, s. 94 and Sched. 16.[12]

If, in the event of fraudulent trading, an order is made under section 332[13] that parties thereto be personally responsible without limitation of liability for the company's debts, this is better regarded simply as a case where the privilege of limited liability is lost than one where the veil is lifted—creditors of the company have no direct right against those against whom an order is made.[14]

MANAGEMENT OF REGISTERED COMPANIES

We have seen that registered companies, although legal persons, are artificial persons and must act by human agents, the directors and other officers empowered, by the articles to act on the company's behalf. In the case of a private company the shareholders and directors are usually the same persons but that is not so in the case of a public company, where the directors may have few shares in the company,[15] so that management is divorced from ownership of the company. This is important because, as is explained later,[16] under an article like Table A, article 80, *infra*, the company in general meeting, *i.e.* the members or shareholders in general meeting, cannot control the exercise of the directors' powers.

Directors' powers are contained in the articles, *e.g.* Table A, article 80, states that the business of the company shall be managed by the directors who may exercise all the powers of the company except those which are, by the Act or the articles, required to be exercised by the company in general meeting. Thus when section

---

[11] *Post* p. 658. See also *Inland Revenue* v. *Lithgows Ltd.*, 1960 S.C. 405—two companies controlled by two different trusts were held not to be controlled by the same person, although one individual, the first-named trustee in each trust, was entitled to cast the trustees' votes in each company.
[12] *Post* p. 666.
[13] *Post* p. 574.
[14] Palmer's *Company Law*, 21st ed., p. 133.
[15] *Post* p. 316.
[16] *Post* p. 333.

10[17] provides that a company may alter its articles by special resolution the alteration is required to be effected by the company in general meeting and cannot be effected by the directors.

Directors cannot delegate their powers except so far as the articles allow but, *e.g.*, Table A, article 107, empowers the directors to appoint a managing director and article 109 empowers them to delegate any of their powers to him.

It should also be remembered that the directors must exercise their powers for the purposes for which they were granted and *bona fide* for the benefit of the company as a whole, *i.e.* the members as a body.[18]

A REGISTERED COMPANY'S SECURITIES

Two ways in which a registered company with a share capital may raise money to carry on its business are (1) by issuing shares, (2) by borrowing, *e.g.*, on debentures or debenture stock.[19]

Shares

Preference shares and ordinary shares

A registered company's shares may be divided into different classes with different rights, *e.g.* preference shares[20] and ordinary shares. Preference shares give the holders priority in the payment of a dividend at a fixed rate, *e.g.* if a company with ordinary shares and ten per cent. preference shares distributes profits, the preference shareholders are entitled to a dividend of ten per cent. before the ordinary shareholders receive anything. Another difference between ordinary shares and preference shares is that the former usually confer a right of voting at general meetings whereas the latter often deny a right to vote except in certain events.[21]

Shares and stock

Paid-up shares may be converted into stock under section 61,[22] although there is no advantage in adopting such a course today. The

[17] *Post* p. 109.
[18] *Post* p. 350.
[19] A company may borrow without issuing debentures or creating debenture stock.
[20] *Post* p. 212.
[21] *Post* p. 216.   [22] *Post* p. 230.

procedure laid down in the section must be followed. It will be seen that the section provides that in the case of a limited company with a share capital, where there is authority in the articles, paid-up shares may be converted into stock by the company in general meeting, *i.e.* by an ordinary resolution which usually requires a bare majority of the votes of the members entitled to vote at a general meeting of which due notice has been given.[23] For example, a company which has 10,000 paid-up £1 shares may convert them into ten thousand pounds worth of stock. If shares are converted into stock the value of the holder's stake in the company remains the same although it is expressed in different terms, *e.g.* a person who formerly held 100 shares of a nominal amount of £1 each (*market* value £1·50 each) will now hold a nominal amount of one hundred pounds worth of stock (market value £150) and, in the case of ordinary stock, he will normally have a full right of voting at general meetings. Further, if profits are made, he may receive dividends. In the Acts "share" usually includes stock: 1948 Act, s. 455; 1967 Act, s. 56.

Certificates and warrants

A shareholder is usually issued with a *share certificate*[24] in which case, subject to any restrictions contained in the articles, he may transfer the shares, *e.g.*, by executing an instrument of transfer which is registered by the company.[25] Similarly, a stockholder is usually issued with a *stock certificate*, in which case the stock can be transferred in the same way.

Occasionally, a shareholder may be issued with a *share warrant*,[26] in which case the shares may be transferred by simple delivery of the warrant to the transferee. Similarly, a stockholder may be issued with a *stock warrant*, in which case the stock is transferable by delivery of the warrant to the transferee.

Debentures

Debentures and debenture stock

A company limited by shares usually has power to borrow money and to give security for the loan.[27] Lenders may be issued with

---

[23] *Post* p. 305.
[25] *Post* p. 254.
[27] *Post* p. 86.

[24] *Post* p. 245.
[26] *Post* p. 281.

debentures to show that they have lent money to the company, in which event each debenture evidences a distinct debt, *e.g.* for £100. The debentures may give the debenture holders a mortgage[28] or charge on the company's property to secure the loan, in which case, if the company should fail to repay the loan, the debenture holders will have the usual remedies of a mortgagee[28] against the property. There may be a trust deed—as will be seen, there are advantages in having a trust deed.[29]

Debenture stock[30] is borrowed money consolidated into one mass for the sake of convenience. This is done by a trust deed which acknowledges one debt of the amount advanced by the lenders and owing from the company to the trustees. The deed may give the trustees a charge on the company's property as security. Each lender will be given a simple debenture stock certificate evidencing his share of the debt. In the Acts, "debenture" includes debenture stock: 1948 Act, s. 455; 1967 Act, s. 56.

Thus a person who lends £100 to a company may be a debenture holder with a debenture for £100 or a debenture stockholder with a debenture stock certificate for one hundred pounds worth of debenture stock. In either event, unlike a shareholder, he is not a member of the company and has no right to attend and vote at general meetings of the company. He is a creditor of the company and is entitled to interest at the specified rate on his loan.

Registered debentures and bearer debentures

A debenture is usually a registered debenture,[31] in which case the debt may be transferred by an instrument of transfer which is registered by the company. If a debenture is a bearer debenture[32] the debt may be transferred by delivery of the debenture to the transferee.

Debenture stock certificates and debenture stock warrants

If, as is usual, a debenture stock certificate is issued to a debenture stockholder, the debenture stock may be transferred by an instrument of transfer which is registered by the company. If he is issued with a

[28] In Scots law the terms "security" and "security-holder" should be substituted for "mortgage" and "mortgagee" respectively.
[29] *Post* p. 489.   [30] *Post* p. 486.
[31] *Post* p. 491.   [32] *Post* p. 495.

debenture stock warrant the debenture stock may be transferred by delivery of the warrant.

REGISTERED COMPANIES AND PARTNERSHIPS CONTRASTED

Advantages of a registered company

A registered company has many advantages over a partnership, which is defined in the Partnership Act 1890[33] as the relationship which subsists between persons carrying on a business in common with a view of profit, and which is not, *e.g.*, the relation between members of a company registered under the Companies Acts or incorporated by or in pursuance of any other Act of Parliament or Royal Charter. A registered company has the same advantages over an individual trader. These advantages include the following:

(1) A registered company is a corporation,[34] *i.e.* a separate legal person distinct from the members, whereas an English partnership is merely the aggregate of the partners (although a Scottish partnership has one of the attributes of a corporation in that it is "a legal person distinct from the partners of whom it is composed").[35] Consequently:

(*a*) The debts and contracts of a registered company are those of the company and not those of the members, whereas in the case of an English firm every partner is jointly liable with the other partners for all the firm's debts and obligations incurred while he is a partner.[36] (In Scotland the firm's debts are those of the firm but, if the firm fails to pay, each individual partner may be made liable. Further, there is several as well as joint liability. Again, the firm's contracts are those of the firm but the individual partners may be made liable for them.)

(*b*) Unless it is wound up a registered company has perpetual succession,[37] so that it is not affected by the death, bankruptcy, mental disorder or retirement of any of its members. For example, when a shareholder dies or retires the company is not dissolved and no drain is made on its resources or, usually, on the resources of its other members.

[33] s. 1.
[34] s. 13 (2); *Salomon* v. *Salomon & Co. Ltd.* [1897] A.C. 22, *ante* p. 28.
[35] Partnership Act 1890, s. 4 (2).
[36] *Ibid.*, s. 9.   [37] s. 13 (2).

In the case of a partnership, on the other hand, on the death or bankruptcy of a partner, subject to any agreement between the partners the partnership is dissolved as regards all the partners.[38] In practice the share of a partner who dies or retires has to be found out of the business or provided by the other partners, and this may cause serious financial embarrassment to the firm.

(*c*) The property of a registered company belongs to and is vested in the company, so that there is no change in the ownership of, or in the formal title to, the property on a change in the ownership of shares in the company. In an English partnership, the property belongs to the partners and is vested in them. In the case of land, it is vested in the partners or, where they exceed four in number, in up to four of them in trust for all.[39] Consequently there are changes in the ownership of, and in the formal title to, the firm's property from time to time on the death or retirement of a partner or trustee. (In a Scottish partnership, while the partnership property belongs to the firm as a separate *persona*, the formal title to that property may be, and in the case of heritable property must be, in the names of the partners or of other persons in trust for the firm.)

(*d*) A registered company can contract with its members and can sue and be sued on such contracts. In England a partner cannot contract with the firm. (In Scotland, by virtue of the firm's separate personality, a partner can contract with the firm and can sue and be sued on such contracts.)

(*e*) Each partner is normally an agent for the firm for the purpose of the business of the partnership[40] and, subject to any agreement to the contrary between the parties, may take part in the management of the partnership business.[41] The members of a registered company as such are not its agents and have no power to manage its affairs—the directors are limited agents, *i.e.* they have the powers given to them by the articles.[42]

---

[38] Partnership Act 1890, s. 33 (1). As to dissolution by the court in the event of the mental disorder of a partner, see 1890 Act, s. 35, and Mental Health Act 1959, s. 103 (the latter not applicable to Scotland). As to dissolution by notice by a retiring partner, see 1890 Act, s. 32.

[39] See Law of Property Act 1925, s. 34; Trustee Act 1925, s. 34.

[40] Partnership Act 1890, s. 5.

[41] *Ibid.*, s. 24 (5).   [42] *Ante* p. 33.

(*f*) Subject to any restrictions in the articles, which there must be in the articles of a private company,[43] shares in a registered company can be transferred or mortgaged[44] without the consent of the other shareholders. Subject to any agreement to the contrary, a person cannot be introduced as a partner without the consent of all the existing partners[45] and if in England a partner charges his share of the partnership property for his separate debt the other partners normally have the option to dissolve the partnership.[46]

(2) The liability of a member of a registered company to contribute to its assets may be, and usually is, limited, *e.g.* limited, in the case of a company limited by shares, to the amount unpaid on his shares[47] (although the person controlling a private company may have to give a personal guarantee of the company's bank overdraft) but the members of a partnership are jointly (and in Scotland severally also) liable for all the debts of the firm.[48] This advantage can be secured in a partnership by a person's being a limited partner in a limited partnership formed under the Limited Partnerships Act 1907, but few such partnerships have been formed, owing to the superior advantages of the limited company.

(3) The number of members of a private company must not exceed 50[43] and there is no limit to the number of members of a public company, but, except in the case of, *e.g.*, certain partnerships of practising professional men such as solicitors, accountants within section 161 (1) (*a*) or (*b*),[49] stockbrokers who are members of a recognised stock exchange,[50] certain patent agents, surveyors, auctioneers and estate agents, building designers, actuaries and consulting engineers, a partnership with more than 20 members for the purpose of carrying on any business which has for its object the acquisition of gain is prohibited.[51] A partnership of not more than

---

[43] s. 28.
[44] In Scots law "transferred in security."
[45] Partnership Act 1890, s. 24 (7).
[46] *Ibid.*, s. 33 (2) (not applicable to Scotland: see s. 23 (5)).
[47] s. 1.
[48] Partnership Act 1890, s. 9, *ante.*
[49] *Post* p. 454.
[50] *i.e.* recognised for the purposes of the Prevention of Fraud (Investments) Act 1958.
[51] Companies Act 1948, s. 434; Companies Act 1967, s. 120; Partnerships (Unrestricted Size) Regulations: No. 1: S.I. 1968 No. 1222; No. 2: S.I. 1970 No. 835; No. 3: S.I. 1970 No. 992; No. 4: S.I. 1970 No. 1319.

20 members authorised by the Department of Trade in the case of a partnership formed for the purpose of carrying on banking is allowed.[52] As the Jenkins Report[53] said, the purpose of the prohibition is to protect the public from the hazards of dealing with large and fluctuating partnerships. The original restriction to 20 members[54] caused difficulty for large professional firms which cannot by law or professional practice be incorporated, and since the partners in such firms belong to professional organisations which exercise effective control over their members it was not necessary for the protection of the public to maintain the restrictions in their case. One result of the limit on the number of partners is that it is generally impossible for a partnership to raise large sums of capital.

(4) A registered company has greater facilities for borrowing than a partnership, *e.g.* the company may borrow on debentures.[55]

(5) Floating charges can be created by a registered company but not by a partnership.[56]

Advantages of a partnership

A partnership or an individual trader has certain advantages over a registered company (although these are normally outweighed by the advantages of the latter over the former):

(1) There are fewer formalities to be observed, and therefore there is less publicity and less expense involved in forming a partnership, *e.g.* there is no need to be registered, or to file a memorandum and articles, with the Registrar, and therefore there are no registration fees and stamp duty and legal costs are less. A partnership agreement may be oral or even inferred from conduct.

(2) There are fewer formalities and therefore less publicity and less expense in running a partnership, *e.g.* returns do not have to be delivered to a Registrar.

---

[52] 1948 Act, s. 429; 1967 Act, s. 119.
[53] In s. 434.
[54] Paras. 76, 77.
[55] *Ante* p. 35.
[56] *Post* p. 500.

(3) A partnership's accounts are never open to public inspection. Except in the case of certain unlimited companies,[57] those of a registered company are, as are the other documents which any registered company must lodge with the Registrar.[58]

(4) The *ultra vires* doctrine,[59] by which a registered company can only do the things authorised by its memorandum, does not apply to a partnership, which can do anything lawful that all the partners agree to do.

(5) A partnership is not subject to the rules in connection with raising and maintenance of share capital, to which a registered company which is not an unlimited company is subject.[60]

(6) A partnership can make any arrangement with creditors that the partners think fit. A registered company can make only those authorised by the Act.[61]

Taxation

In deciding whether to carry on business by means of a registered company or not, an important factor to consider is the effect of taxation. In some cases a registered company will be advantageous, in others it will not. This is explained in Chapter 29.

[57] *Post* p. 46.
[58] s. 426.
[59] *Post* p. 76.
[60] *Post* pp. 227, 232.
[61] ss. 206, 245, 303, 306.

Chapter 2

CLASSIFICATION OF REGISTERED COMPANIES

THIS chapter deals with the two main classifications of registered companies. The first classifies registered companies as being limited by shares, limited by guarantee or unlimited. The second classifies them as being either public companies or private companies. (Any of the companies in the first classification may be either a public company or a private company.) Finally, something is said of holding companies and subsidiary companies.

COMPANIES LIMITED BY SHARES, COMPANIES LIMITED BY GUARANTEE AND UNLIMITED COMPANIES

A registered company may be—

(1) a company limited by shares, in which case the liability of a member to contribute to the company's assets is limited to the amount, if any, unpaid on his shares; or

(2) a company limited by guarantee, in which case the liability of a member is limited to the amount which he has undertaken to contribute *in the event of its being wound up*; or

(3) an unlimited company, in which case the liability of a member is unlimited: section 1 (2).

The vast majority of registered companies are companies limited by shares. Such companies must have a share capital, whereas companies limited by guarantee and unlimited companies may or may not have a share capital. Companies limited by guarantee are often supported by subscriptions or fees paid by the members.

Companies limited by guarantee

A company limited by guarantee is a registered company, public or private, in which the liability of members is limited to such amount as they respectively undertake to contribute to the assets of the company in the event of its being wound up: section 1. The members are not required to contribute whilst the company is a going concern.

The memorandum of a company limited by guarantee, in addition to containing the clauses normally contained in a memorandum,[1] must state that each member undertakes to contribute to the assets of the company in the event of its being wound up while he is a member, or within one year after he ceases to be a member, for payment of its debts contracted before he ceases to be a member, and of the costs of winding up, and for adjustment of the rights of the contributories, such sum as may be required, not exceeding a specified amount: section 2 (3). The sum specified in Table C, *post*, is £10. Whatever the amount of the guarantee specified in the memorandum, it cannot be increased or reduced.

The amounts which the members have agreed to contribute in a winding up cannot be mortgaged or charged by the company whilst it is a going concern.[2] They are not assets of the company whilst it is a going concern.

A company limited by guarantee may be formed either with or without a share capital, but is usually formed without a share capital, in which event money to acquire such things as premises may be raised by loans from the members. The majority of companies limited by guarantee are formed to incorporate professional, trade and research associations, or clubs supported by annual subscriptions. Many take advantage of section 19[3] and obtain Department of Trade licence to omit the word "Limited" from their names.

Every company limited by guarantee, whether it has a share capital or not, is obliged to register articles of association with the memorandum: section 6. If the company has no share capital, the memorandum and articles must be in the form set out in Table C, or as near thereto as circumstances admit: section 11. Table C is a model form of memorandum and articles for such a company and is set out in the First Schedule to the Act. If the company has a share capital, the memorandum and articles must be in the form set out in Table D, or as near thereto as circumstances admit: section 11. Table D, which is a model form of memorandum and articles for such a company and which is set out in the First Schedule, incorporates the whole of Table A, Part I, a model set of articles for a public company limited by shares.

An article of a company limited by guarantee with no share

---

[1] *Post* p. 60.
[2] *Re Irish Club* [1906] W.N. 127.
[3] *Post* p. 66.

capital is not invalid just because it is not contained in Table C. Section 11 is concerned with the form of the articles of such a company and the word "form" here does not embrace contents. Provided that the draftsman of such articles follows the general form of Table C he is free to add, subtract or vary as the needs of the case suggest.[4]

The articles of a company limited by guarantee must state the number of members with which the company proposes to be registered: section 7. This is to give persons dealing with the company some idea of the value of the guarantee.

Table C, article 2, provides: "The number of members with which the company proposes to be registered is 500, but the directors may from time to time register an increase of members."

Notice of any increase beyond the registered number must be given to the Registrar within 15 days: section 7.

Section 37 of the Companies Act 1976 empowers the Secretary of State to prescribe the fees to be paid to the Registrar upon the registration of a company limited by guarantee.

Every provision in the memorandum or articles of a company limited by guarantee and not having a share capital, or in any resolution of the company, purporting to give any person a right to participate in the divisible profits of the company otherwise than as a member is void, and every provision in the memorandum or articles, or in any resolution, purporting to divide the undertaking of the company into shares or interests is treated as a provision for share capital notwithstanding that the nominal amount or number of the shares or interests is not specified: section 21. The object of this section is to prevent the registration of companies with shares of no par value.[5]

Even a public company need not hold the statutory meeting[6] or forward the statutory report if it is limited by guarantee and has no share capital: see section 130.

If a company limited by guarantee has a share capital it must make the annual return required by section 124.[7] If it has no share capital, it must make an annual return stating:

---

[4] *Gaiman* v. *National Association for Mental Health* [1971] Ch. 317.
[5] Companies of the kind involved in *Malleson* v. *General Mineral Patents Syndicate Ltd.* [1894] 3 Ch. 538.
[6] *Post* p. 284.
[7] *Post* p. 208.

(1) The address of the registered office.
(2) If the register of members is not kept at the registered office, the address of the place where it is kept.
(3) If the register of debenture holders is not kept at the registered office, the address of the place where it is kept.
(4) The particulars of the directors and the secretary which are required to be contained in the register of directors and secretaries.[8]

Particulars of the total amount of the company's indebtedness in respect of all mortgages and charges required to be registered with the Registrar[9] must be annexed: section 125.

If the company has no share capital, an extraordinary general meeting of the company can be requisitioned by the members having at least one-tenth of the voting rights: section 132. If the company has a share capital, members holding at least one-tenth of the paid-up capital carrying the right to vote can requisition a meeting.

Since companies limited by guarantee and having a share capital are very rarely registered the Jenkins Report[10] recommended that such companies should not be registered and the Companies Bill 1973[11] attempted to give effect to the recommendation.

Apart from what has been said in this chapter, most of what is said elsewhere in this work applies to companies limited by guarantee as it does to companies limited by shares.

Unlimited companies

A company may be registered as an unlimited company, in which case there is no limit on the members' liability to contribute to the assets: section 1. In the years immediately preceding 1967 comparatively few such companies were formed, although they are the oldest class of registered company, but the exemption given by section 47 of the 1967 Act (as to which see now section 1 of the Companies Act 1976 *post*), made them more popular.

During 1974, 225 unlimited companies with a share capital were registered.

The memorandum and articles of an unlimited company with a share capital must be in the form set out in Table E, or as near

---

[8] *Post* p. 318.
[9] *Post* p. 510.
[10] Para. 78.
[11] Cl. 1 (3).

thereto as circumstances admit: section 11. Table E is a model form of memorandum and articles in the First Schedule to the Act. The company is obliged to register articles with the memorandum: section 6. The articles must state the number of members with which the company proposes to be registered and, if the company is to have a share capital, the amount of the share capital: section 7. There is no requirement that the division of the share capital into shares of a fixed amount be stated. The name will not, of course, include the word "Limited," and there will be no limitation of liability clause in the memorandum.

Section 37 of the Companies Act 1976 empowers the Secretary of State to prescribe the registration fees to be paid to the Registrar. No capital duty is payable.[12]

Even a public company need not hold the statutory meeting or forward the statutory report if it is an unlimited company: see section 130.

If the company has a share capital it must make the annual return required by section 124.[7] In certain cases an unlimited company is exempted from the requirements of section 1 of the Companies Act 1976 (delivery of accounts to Registrar).[13] If the company has no share capital, the provisions of sections 125 and 132, *ante*, apply to it. No return of allotments need be filed by an unlimited company: see section 52.

An unlimited company is exceptional in that its members may be associated on the terms that they may withdraw in the mode pointed out by the memorandum and articles, so as to be free from liability in the event of a winding up,[14] and it seems that such a company may validly provide by its memorandum and articles for a return of capital to its members, *i.e.* without the consent of the court. Similarly an unlimited company may purchase its own shares if its constituent documents authorise it to do so.[15]

Re-registration of unlimited company as limited

Section 44 of the 1967 Act provides that an unlimited company (not registered by virtue of section 43, *post*) may be re-regis-

---

[12] *Ante* p. 25.
[13] *Post* p. 423.
[14] *Re Borough Commercial and Building Socy.* [1893] 2 Ch. 242.
[15] See, *e.g.*, *Nelson Mitchell* v. *City of Glasgow Bank* (1879) 6 R. (H.L.) 66, (1878) 6 R. 420.

tered as limited if a special resolution to that effect and complying
with the requirements set out below is passed, and the application
for re-registration is in the prescribed form, signed by a director or
the secretary and lodged with the Registrar, together with certain
documents, not earlier than the day on which the copy of the resolution filed under section 143 of the 1948 Act is received by him.

The resolution—
    (1) must state the manner in which the liability of members
        is to be limited and the share capital if the company is
        to have one;
    (2) must provide for the appropriate alterations in and addi-
        tions to the memorandum and articles according to
        whether the company is to be limited by shares or by
        guarantee with or without a share capital.

The documents which must also be lodged are printed copies of
the memorandum and articles as altered.

Section 37 of the Companies Act 1976 empowers the Secretary of
State to prescribe re-registration fees. Capital duty is payable on a
Statement of Capital (Form PUC6).[16]

The Registrar must issue an appropriate certificate of incorporation, whereupon the status of the company is changed and the
alterations in and additions to the memorandum and articles take
effect. Such a certificate is conclusive evidence of compliance with
the requirements of the section with respect to re-registration and of
re-registration.

Section 64 of the 1948 Act (power of unlimited company with a
share capital to provide for reserve liability on re-registration as
limited) applies to a re-registration under section 44.

In the winding up of a company re-registered under section 44—
    (1) notwithstanding section 212 (1) (*a*)[17] of the 1948 Act, a
        past member who was a member at the time of re-registra-
        tion is, where the winding up commences within three
        years after the re-registration, liable to contribute to the
        assets of the company in respect of its debts and liabilities
        contracted before re-registration;
    (2) where no persons who were members at the time of re-
        registration are existing members, a person who was then

---

[16] *Ante* p. 25.   [17] *Post* p. 582.

a present or past member is, subject to section 212 (1) (*a*) of the 1948 Act and (1), *ante*, but notwithstanding section 212 (1) (*c*),[18] liable to contribute as above even though the existing members have satisfied the contributions required of them;

(3) notwithstanding section 212 (1) (*d*)[19] and (*e*) of the 1948 Act, there is no limit on the amount which a person who, at the time of re-registration, was a past or present member is liable to contribute as above.

Re-registration of limited company as unlimited

Section 43 of the Companies Act 1967 enables a limited company (not registered in pursuance of section 44, *ante*) to be re-registered as unlimited with the unanimous consent of its members. The application for re-registration must be in the prescribed form, signed by a director or the secretary and lodged with the Registrar together with certain documents.

The application must set out the appropriate alterations in and additions to the memorandum and, if articles have been registered,[20] the articles, according to whether or not the company is to have a share capital. If articles have not been registered the application must have annexed to it, and request the registration of, appropriate printed articles.

The following documents must be lodged with the application—

(1) the prescribed form of assent to the company's being registered as unlimited *subscribed by or on behalf of all the members* (a subscription by the personal representative of a dead member is deemed to be by him and the trustee in bankruptcy of a member is deemed a member to the exclusion of the member himself);

(2) a statutory declaration by the directors that the subscribers to (1) constitute the whole membership and, if any member has not subscribed himself, that they have taken all reasonable steps to satisfy themselves that the person who subscribed on his behalf was lawfully empowered to do so;

[18] *Post* p. 584.
[19] *Post* p. 583.
[20] *Post* p. 104.

(3) a printed copy of the memorandum incorporating the alterations therein;

(4) if articles have been registered, a printed copy thereof incorporating the alterations to them.

Section 37 of the Companies Act 1976 empowers the Secretary of State to prescribe re-registration fees. No capital duty is payable.

The Registrar must issue an appropriate certificate of incorporation, which will be conclusive evidence of proper re-registration.

Quite a number of former limited companies, such as property and finance companies, have taken advantage of section 43 and re-registered as unlimited in order to preserve secrecy about their affairs.

In a winding up a person who, when the application for re-registration was lodged, was a past member and did not thereafter again become a member is not liable to contribute more than he would have been liable to contribute had there been no re-registration: section 43 (6).

PUBLIC AND PRIVATE COMPANIES

A registered company may be a public company or a private company.

By section 28 a private company is a registered company which by its articles of association—

(1) restricts the right to transfer its shares;

(2) limits the number of members to 50, excluding members who are employees of the company and members who were members when they were employees of the company and who have continued to be members after the determination of the employment, two or more persons who hold one or more shares in the company jointly being treated as a single member;

(3) prohibits any invitation to the public to subscribe for any of the company's shares or debentures, *i.e.* prohibits the issue of a prospectus.

Any registered company whose articles do not contain all the above three provisions is a public company.

As regards (1) above, a common restriction in the articles of a private company is that a member wishing to transfer his shares must first offer them to the other shareholders at a fair value.[21] As to (2), the fact that employee and ex-employee members are not counted enables private companies to issue shares to employees by way of profit-sharing schemes and yet not exceed the permitted maximum of fifty members. The prohibition in (3) is of any invitation, oral or written, to the public (as opposed to a member of the public) to subscribe for shares or debentures of the company, *i.e.* to take such shares or debentures from the company and for cash.[22] The result is that a private company must raise its capital privately, *e.g.* from the members, or a bank, or the Industrial and Commercial Finance Corporation set up by the joint-stock banks.

It may be mentioned here that whereas a public company must have at least seven members, a private company need have only two members: sections 1, 31. The Jenkins Committee considered that this difference is pointless, since a public company whose shares are quoted on a stock exchange will have many more than seven members. Accordingly they recommended[23] that the minimum membership for all registered companies should be two.

Again, whereas a public company must have at least two directors, a private company need have only one director: section 176. The Jenkins Committee recommended[23] that every company should have at least two directors. The idea is to meet the problems which arise on the death of a sole director and to check irresponsible incorporations of "one-man" companies.

It is sometimes said that a company cannot be formed as, *e.g.*, a private company limited by guarantee and not having a share capital, because it cannot comply with the requirement of section 28 that the articles restrict the right to transfer its shares. In fact, the Registrar will register such a company provided that the articles contain a restriction on the right to transfer shares.

We shall see that a private company may be converted into a public company by altering its articles by special resolution so that they no longer contain all three section 28 provisions: section 30. A special resolution requires a majority of at least three-fourths of the votes of the members entitled to vote at a general meeting of which usually at least 21 days' notice has been given (s. 141).[24]

[21] *Post* p. 250.
[22] See further *post* p. 131.
[23] Cmnd. 1749, para. 31.
[24] *Post* p. 306.

Conversely, if there are not more than 50 members, a public company can be converted into a private company by altering its articles so that they contain such provisions and by taking any other appropriate steps. If a private company, without altering its articles, fails to comply with any of the section 28 provisions, it remains a private company but may lose certain of the privileges of a private company, *i.e.* the minimum number of members may be raised to seven: section 29.[25]

In 1974, there were 60 conversions from private to public company, and 120 conversions from public to private company.

Disadvantages of a private company

The three restrictions, which by section 28, *ante*, must be included in the articles of a private company, may be regarded as the disadvantages of a private company as compared with a public company.

Advantages of a private company

A private company has a number of advantages, some of them substantial, over a public company. These advantages include the following:

(1) A private company can commence business (and make binding contracts, and exercise its borrowing powers) immediately on incorporation and without first having to comply with section 109.[26] It will be seen that this is a substantial advantage.

(2) A private company need not hold a statutory meeting, or send a statutory report to its members: section 130.[27] This, too, is a substantial advantage.

(3) A private company need have only two members whereas a public company must have at least seven: sections 1, 31.

(4) A private company need have only one director whereas a public company must have at least two (s. 176), although a private company must have a secretary and a sole director cannot be the secretary (s. 177).

---

[25] As amended by the 1967 Act, *post*, p. 54.
[26] *Post* p. 182.
[27] *Post* p. 284.

(5) Although a private company must not issue a prospectus, it need not register a statement in lieu of prospectus complying with the Fifth Schedule (s. 48) and it is not subject to the other restrictions on the allotment of shares or debentures imposed on a public company by sections 47, 50 and 51.[28]

Other differences between a private company and a public company are:

(1) Directors of a private company are not subject to the requirements of section 181.[29]

(2) Unless the articles otherwise provide, a quorum at a meeting of a private company is two members present in person and at a meeting of a public company three such members: section 134.[30]

(3) At a general meeting of a private company a motion for the appointment of two or more directors may be made by a single resolution: section 183 (1).[31]

(4) A proxy can speak at a meeting of a private company: section 136.[32]

The Jenkins Report[33] recommended that there should be no distinction in the Companies Acts in the treatment of public and private companies, *e.g.* as regards the minimum number of members and the minimum number of directors,[34] and that sections 109, 130 and 181 *ante* should be repealed—the requirements of these sections are now obsolete and unnecessary, and are commonly avoided by the device of incorporating companies as private companies and later converting them to public companies under section 28 *ante*. It was also recommended that the statement in lieu of prospectus should no longer be required. The changes involved would not prevent the formation of privately owned companies with restrictions on the transfer of shares.

[28] *Post* p. 177.
[29] *Post* p. 311.
[30] *Post* p. 296.
[31] *Post* p. 312.
[32] *Post* p. 301.
[33] *Paras.* 64–67; 23, 25 and 31; 252 (j).
[34] *Ante* p. 51.

Table A, Part II

Table A, Part II,[35] in Schedule I to the Act contains model articles which may be adopted by a private company limited by shares. The regulations are the same as those for a public company in Part I with a few modifications necessary to comply with section 28 *ante*. The Registrar will not register articles of a private company unless the issue of share warrants is prohibited—presumably because there is no means of restricting the transfer of shares specified in a share warrant. Another modification is, therefore, that Table A, Part II, article 2 (*d*), prohibits the issue of share warrants to bearer.

Table A, Part II, contains no clause providing that a member wishing to transfer his shares shall first offer them to the other members at a fair value.[36] Article 3 does, however, give the directors an absolute discretion, without assigning a reason, to decline to register any transfer of a share.[37]

The quorum for a general meeting is provided by article 4 to be "two members present in person or by proxy."

Article 5 provides that a resolution in writing signed by all the members entitled to receive notice of and to attend and vote at general meetings is as valid as if it had been passed at a general meeting of the company duly convened and held.

Annual certificates

By section 128 a private company must send, with its annual return to the Registrar, a certificate signed both by a director and by the secretary, that the company has not, since the date of the last return, issued any invitation to the public to subscribe for shares or debentures of the company, *and*, if the number of members exceeds 50, a certificate that the excess consists wholly of persons employed or formerly employed by the company, *i.e.* a certificate or certificates that the section 28 restrictions, *ante*, have been complied with.

Conversion of a private company into a public company

If a private company alters its articles so that they no longer include the provisions which under section 28, *ante*, constitute it a

---

[35] *Post* p. 104.   [36] *Post* p. 250.   [37] *Post* p. 251.

private company, it becomes a public company and must within 14 days, under a penalty of a fine of £50 a day on the company and the officers in default, deliver to the Registrar a statement in lieu of prospectus complying with the Third Schedule, unless within such time a prospectus complying with the Fourth Schedule is issued and delivered to the Registrar as required by section 41:[38] s. 30.

If it is desired to form a public company, the company is usually incorporated as a private company and later converted into a public company. The object is to avoid the necessity of having to comply with sections 109 and 130 *ante*.

Loss of privileges of a private company

If a private company, without altering its articles, fails to comply with any of the section 28 provisions in its articles, it remains a private company but loses the privileges conferred on private companies by sections 31,[39] 222 (*d*)[40] and 224 (1) (*a*) (i),[41] *i.e.* as regards each of these sections the legal minimum number of members is raised from two to seven: Companies Act 1948, s. 29; Companies Act 1967, s. 130 and Sched. 8.

The court may, however, on application by the company or any other person interested, grant relief on such terms as the court thinks just, if it is satisfied either (1) that the failure to comply with the section 28 conditions was (a) accidental, or (b) due to inadvertence, or (c) due to some other sufficient cause, or (2) that on other grounds it is just and equitable to grant relief: section 29.

A private company which advertises for deposits is deemed not to be private for the purposes of, *i.e.* it loses the advantages of a private company under, the following provisions of the 1948 Act: sections 31, 222 (*d*) and 224 (1) (*a*) (minimum number of members); section 176 (number of directors).[42]

---

[38] *Post* p. 142.
[39] *Ante* p. 30.
[40] *Post* p. 540.
[41] *Post* p. 548.
[42] Protection of Depositors Act 1963, s. 4; Companies Act 1967, s. 130 and Sched. 8.

1973 Conservative Government White Paper on Company Law Reform

The 1973 Conservative Government White Paper on Company Law Reform[43] stated that the Government proposed to redefine the status of a private company in a way which would give statutory effect to existing practice and which would require that status to be made explicit in the company's title,[44] and also to define explicitly the term "public company." In addition, despite the conclusion of the Jenkins Committee that a statutory minimum paid-up capital would be too easy to evade,[45] a public company was to be required to have a minimum paid-up capital.

The background to the proposals was that the proliferation of very small companies had increased in the past decade and the public interest did not require the same amount of disclosure (involving the same amount of administration by the company and the Department of Trade) from the smaller as from the larger company. There was, therefore, a case for grading the disclosure requirements, and the administrative effort both by companies themselves and by the Government, in relation to the size and status of the individual company.

Further, despite the Jenkins Committee recommendation,[46] that there should be no distinction in the Companies Acts in the treatment of public and private companies, the Government believed that there remained a valid and important difference between, at the one extreme, a company that owed a wide duty to its numerous shareholders, to the investing public as potential shareholders, to creditors and to the public interest at large; and at the other, a company that owed a duty more narrowly to its creditors (who might for the most part be its current trading partners) and to a restricted number of members. This distinction was broadly reflected in the classification of the public and the private company and to some extent in the different degrees of disclosure required of companies of differing size. However, the definition in section 28 only specified three limiting criteria of a private company and a public company was defined only by exclusion. Moreover, the differences between large public and private companies and between small public and private

[43] Cmnd. 5391, para. 32.
[44] As to how this might be done, see p. 63 *post.*
[45] (1962) Cmnd. 1749, para. 27.
[46] *Ante* p. 52.

companies did not reflect the differences in their economic significance or in their responsibilities.

The requirement that a public company should have a minimum paid-up capital had two objectives—first, to correspond to one of the *indicia* of a public company which the European Economic Community were proposing to adopt and, secondly, to ensure, as the EEC were seeking to do, that any company having public status had a reasonable minimum level of resources of 25,000 units of account, *i.e.* approximately £10,000. It would then be possible to define disclosure requirements by reference to either the size or the status of the company.

It might also be desirable to require a minimum paid-up capital for a private company—obviously by comparison low (say £1,000). That would help to ensure some minimum financial substance as a proper qualification for the protection of limited liability and act as a deterrent to frivolous incorporations. Against such a change was the possibility that the elimination of the very small private company would have an adverse effect on the economic life of small traders and small firms with a useful potential for growth.

An additional form of incorporation, which did not give lightly the privilege of limited liability (with its attendant need for a significant degree of disclosure) but which did afford the benefits of incorporation to the small traders to whom they were of value, might be needed, although it might be that the machinery provided by the Partnership Act 1890, or the Limited Partnership Act 1907, or the unlimited company was already sufficient or could be made so. On the one hand, some argued that limited liability was often a myth for the small man. His sources of funds were trade debts and borrowing from a bank or finance house. If the small trader did not have enough tangible assets to reach the fairly low threshold of £1,000, it was probable that his creditors would seek a charge on his personal assets despite his, theoretical, limited liability. On the other hand, the benefits of incorporation might be real—particularly continuity of legal personality.

1973 Conservative Government Companies Bill

The Conservative Government Companies Bill 1973 provided that for the purposes of the Companies Acts a public company was any company which was not a private company and was either limited by shares or limited by guarantee with a share capital (clause 1 (1)).

Conversely, a private company was a company which fell within the definition in section 28 and which was either limited by shares or limited by guarantee with a share capital (clause 1 (2)).

The Bill also provided that certain sections of the 1948 Act concerned with the minimum number of members, namely sections 1 (1), 31, 222 (*d*) and 224 (1) (*a*) (i), were to apply to an unlimited company as they apply to a private company (clause 1 (5)).

1974 Labour Party Green Paper on the Reform of Company Law

The approach to disclosure adopted in the Labour Party Green Paper on the Reform of Company Law[47] was to define the limits of disclosure not by reference to public and private companies but by reference to broad categories of companies, namely:

Group A—which would include all quoted companies and financial institutions, and "multi-national" companies or companies controlled by non-residents with turnover, gross assets or employees in excess of defined levels.

Group B—Unquoted companies with turnover, etc., in excess of defined levels, and other "multi-national" companies or companies controlled by non-residents.

Group C—Other unquoted companies.

HOLDING AND SUBSIDIARY COMPANIES

It is sometimes important to know whether a registered company is a subsidiary or a holding company. One reason is that section 27[48] generally prevents a subsidiary from being a member of its holding company. The meaning of the terms "subsidiary" and "holding company" is given in section 154 and it is convenient to deal with that section here.

The effect of section 154 is that a company (which we shall call "X") is a subsidiary of another company ("Y") and Y is X's holding company if—

[47] "The Community and the Company."   [48] *Post* p. 192.

(1) Y is a member of X and controls the composition of X's board of directors; or
(2) Y holds more than half of X's equity share capital; or
(3) X is a subsidiary of a third company ("Z") which is itself a subsidiary of Y.

As to (1), Y must be a member of X—holding one share will suffice—*and* must control the composition of X's board. Section 154 (2) provides that Y is deemed to control the composition of X's board only if Y, by the exercise of a power exercisable by it without the consent of any other person, can appoint or remove all or the majority of the directors. Further, that Y is deemed to have power to appoint a director of X if—

(*a*) a person cannot be appointed as a director of X unless Y exercises a power exercisable by it without the consent of any other person; or
(*b*) a person's appointment as a director of X follows necessarily from his being a director of Y; or
(*c*) Y itself or another subsidiary of Y is a director of X.

Y might have a power to appoint a director of X, which power it can exercise without the consent of any other person, *e.g.* by virtue of a provision in a contract between X and Y or of the shares in X held by Y.

As regards (2) above, subsection (5) provides that the "equity share capital" of a company means its issued share capital excluding any part which, neither as respects dividends nor as respects capital, carries any right to participate beyond a specified amount in a distribution. As will be seen, this will normally exclude preference shares so that in effect the equity share capital is the company's issued ordinary shares   It should be noted that in practice one company is in control of another if it holds less than half the other's equity share capital, *e.g.* if the first holds 30 per cent. of the second's ordinary shares. The Jenkins Report[49] recommended that section 154 be amended so that the definition of a subsidiary is based solely on membership and control, *i.e.* that (2) above be repealed.

As to (3), X is a subsidiary of Z and Z is a subsidiary of Y because in each case either the second company is a member of the first and controls its board or the second holds more than half of

[49] Para. 156.

the first's equity share capital. The result of (3) is that X is also a subsidiary of Y.

As one would expect, in (1), (2) and (3) any shares held or power exercisable by a nominee for Y, or by, or by a nominee for, another subsidiary of Y, are treated as held or exercisable by Y (s. 154 (3)).

On the other hand, subsection (3) also provides that:—

(i) Any shares held or power exercisable by Y in a fiduciary capacity are treated as not held or exercisable by it. This would be so where Y is a trustee company which holds shares in X on trust for some beneficiary.

(ii) Any shares held or power exercisable by any person by virtue of the provisions of any debentures of X, or of a trust deed for securing any such debentures, are disregarded. This provision might apply where Y is a member of X and has lent money to it and taken a debenture which gives Y power to appoint the majority of X's directors.

(iii) Any shares held or power exercisable by, or by a nominee for, Y or another subsidiary of Y are treated as not held or exercisable by Y if the ordinary business of Y or the other subsidiary includes the lending of money and the shares are held or the power is exercisable by way of security only for the purposes of a transaction entered into in the ordinary course of such business. This would be so where Y is a money-lending company which has lent money to a shareholder in X who, in order to secure the loan, has transferred his shares to Y by way of mortgage.

Lastly, it should be noted that section 154 (5) also provides that in the section the expression "company" includes any body corporate and that section 455 (3) provides that a reference in the Act to a body corporate is to be construed as including a company incorporated outside Great Britain but as not including a Scottish firm.

CHAPTER 3

MEMORANDUM OF ASSOCIATION

EVERY registered company must have a memorandum of association, which is the registered company's charter.[1] This memorandum regulates the company's external affairs, whilst the articles regulate its internal affairs.[1] The purpose of the memorandum is to enable persons who invest in or deal with the company to ascertain what its name is, whether it is an English or a Scottish company, what its objects, and hence its powers, are, whether the liability of its members is limited and what share capital it is authorised to issue. The memorandum may contain other matters apart from those just referred to. It must contain an association clause and it must be properly subscribed. The provisions of the memorandum can be altered in certain specified cases.

Section 2 of the 1948 Act, as amended by section 30 (1) and (3) of the 1976 Act, provides that the memorandum of every company must state:

(1) The name of the company, with "Limited" as the last word of the name of a company limited by shares or by guarantee or, where the memorandum states that the registered office is to be in Wales, with "Cyfyngedig" as the last word of the name.

(2) Whether the registered office of the company is to be situated in England, Wales or Scotland.

(3) The objects of the company.

(4) That the liability of the members is limited, if the company is limited by shares or by guarantee.

(5) In the case of a limited company having a share capital, the amount of share capital with which the company proposes to be registered and the division thereof into shares of a fixed amount.

In the case of a company limited by guarantee the memorandum must also state that each member undertakes to contribute to the

---

[1] See per Ld. Cairns, L.C., in *Ashbury Railway Carriage Co. Ltd.* v. *Riche* (1875) L.R. 7 H.L. 653, at pp. 667, 668.

assets of the company in the event of its being wound up while he is a member, or within one year after he ceases to be a member, such amount as may be required, not exceeding a specified amount.

The memorandum must state the desire of the subscribers to be formed into a company and the agreement of each to take a specified number of shares in the company.

Seven or more persons or, in the case of a private company, two or more persons, must subscribe their names to the memorandum: section 1 (1).

TABLE B

Form of Memorandum of Association of a Company Limited by Shares

1st. The name of the company is "The Eastern Steam Packet Company Limited."

2nd. The registered office of the company will be situate in England.

3rd. The objects for which the company is established are, "the conveyance of passengers and goods in ships or boats between such places as the company may from time to time determine, and the doing all such other things as are incidental or conducive to the attainment of the above object."

4th. The liability of the members is limited.

5th. The share capital of the company is two hundred thousand pounds, divided into one thousand shares of two hundred pounds each.

We, the several persons whose names and addresses are subscribed, are desirous of being formed into a company, in pursuance of this memorandum of association, and we respectively agree to take the number of shares in the capital of the company set opposite our respective names.

Names, addresses, and descriptions of subscribers	Number of shares taken by each subscriber
1. John Jones, of , in the county of , merchant	200
2. John Smith, of , in the county of , merchant	25
3. Thomas Green, of , in the county of , merchant	30
4. John Thompson, of , in the county of , merchant	40
5. Caleb White, of , in the county of , merchant	15
6. Andrew Brown, of , in the county of , merchant	5
7. Caesar White, of , in the county of , merchant	10
Total shares taken	325

Dated the   day of   , 19 .

Witness to the above signatures,

A. B., No. 13, Hute Street, Clerkenwell, London.

No subscriber may take less than one share and each subscriber must write opposite to his name the number of shares he takes: section 2. Each subscriber must sign the memorandum in the presence of at least one witness, who must attest the signature: section 3.

The form of the memorandum of association of a company limited by shares must be in accordance with the form set out in Table B in the First Schedule to the Act, or as near thereto as circumstances admit: section 11.

Where the memorandum states that the registered office is to be in Wales, the memorandum and the articles may be in Welsh but, if they are, they must be accompanied by a certified translation into English (1976 Act, s. 30 (6)).

However, Table B was taken from the Companies Act 1862 and is very out of date so that, as will be seen, in practice considerable modifications are made to the form set out in it. A specimen memorandum of association is set out at the end of this chapter.

The memorandum must be stamped with a standard registration fee of £50.[2] It is no longer necessary to stamp the memorandum as a deed.[3]

THE NAME

The memorandum must state the name of the company: section 2. The general rule is that any name may be selected. However, a company cannot be registered by a name which in the opinion of the Department of Trade is undesirable: section 17. Further, the last word of the name of a limited company must be the word "Limited" (s. 2), unless permission is given to dispense with the word "Limited" under section 19. Where the memorandum of a limited company states that its registered office is to be in Wales, the last word of the name of the company may be "Cyfyngedig" (s. 30 (3) of the 1976 Act). In selecting a name, it is not necessary to use the word "Company," and the modern tendency is to omit it. A short name is an obvious practical convenience.

The word "Limited" is a misnomer. The company's liability for its own debts is not limited, and the members of the company are not liable for the company's debts (except to the limited extent provided by section 31[4]), because the company is a legal entity separate and

---

[2] *Ante* p. 25.
[3] *Ante* p. 26.
[4] *Ante* p. 30.

distinct from its shareholders. The important thing about the name is that it should show to others that the company is a body corporate, and not a mere unincorporated partnership. It is too late now to reserve the word "Company" for the exclusive use of incorporated companies, because that is in common use by persons who are not incorporated, *e.g.* by partnerships. The American term "Incorporated" expresses the true idea, and that or some synonymous word is to be preferred to "Limited."

The use of the word "Limited" or "Cyfyngedig," or any contraction or imitation of it, as the last word of the name under which any person carries on business without being incorporated with limited liability, is prohibited under a penalty of £5 a day: section 439. It has been held that a solicitor who enters an appearance for such a person, and uses the word "Limited" as describing his client, will be personally liable for the costs.[5]

The Companies Bill 1973 provided that the name of a limited company was to indicate whether it was a public company, a private company or a company limited by guarantee—the name of a limited company was to have as its last part the appropriate designation of the status of the company, which was "public limited company" or "p.l.c." in the case of a public company, "limited" or "ltd." in the case of a private company and "company limited by guarantee" or "c.l.g." in the case of a company limited by guarantee which was not a public company or a private company (clause 2). The Bill also enabled the Secretary of State to license a company limited by guarantee formed for charitable or other specified objects to dispense with the appropriate designation of status in its name (clause 3, which would have superseded s. 19 of the 1948 Act). And clause 103 (3) of the Bill provided that the designation of status appropriate to a limited company whose registered office was situated in Wales was to include the Welsh equivalent (specified in Sched. 6 to the Bill) of the designation specified in clause 2.

Undesirable names

No company can be registered by a name which in the opinion of the Department of Trade is undesirable: section 17. The Department's present practice is explained in "Choice and Approval of Company Names Guidance Notes (C186 (Rev. 74))."

The Notes include the following:
By virtue of section 17 of the Companies Act 1948, the Secretary of State for Trade is empowered to refuse registration of a company by a name which in his opinion is undesirable.

The following notes are given for the guidance of the public though it must be understood that they are in no way exhaustive.

---

[5] *Simmons* v. *Liberal Opinion Ltd.* [1911] 1 K.B. 966 (C.A.).

1. A name will be refused if it is too like the name of an existing company or other body corporate.

2. A name will be refused if it is misleading; for example, if the name of a company with small resources suggests that it is trading on a great scale or over a wide field.

3. A name will be refused if it includes the words "Building Society."

4. Names will not ordinarily be allowed which:—

    (i) suggest a connection with the Crown or member of the Royal Family or suggest royal patronage (including names containing words such as "Royal," "King," "Princess," "Crown").

    (ii) suggest a connection with a Government department, statutory undertaking, local authority, or with any commonwealth or foreign government.

5. The word "British" is not allowed in a name unless the undertaking is British controlled and entirely or almost entirely British owned; nor will it be allowed where the name of the company, taken as a whole, would give the unjustified impression that the company was pre-eminent in its particular field of activity. The same considerations apply to use of the expressions "National," "United Kingdom," "Great Britain," "Northern Ireland," "Scotland," "Europe" and (with appropriate modifications) to "English," "Scottish," "Welsh," and derivatives of all these words.

6. Names including the following words will be allowed only where the circumstances justify it: "Bank," "Chamber of Commerce," "Council," "Co-operative," "Corporation," "Institute," "Insurance," "International," "Investment Trust," "Register," "Trust," "Unit Trust."

7. Members of the public are advised that if they wish to form companies whose names include any of the above mentioned words, then incorporation must necessarily take longer than would otherwise be the case.

8. The words mentioned in this Practice Note should be understood to include all cognate expressions (*e.g.* Bank:—Bankers, Banking; Insurance:—Assurance).

Trade Marks

9. The Registrar does not consult the Trade Marks Index when considering applications for a proposed new company name and the acceptance of a particular name is not an indication that no trade mark rights exist in it. Applicants are therefore advised in their own interests to avoid possible expense and inconvenience by investigating the possibility that others may have trade mark rights in the names—or parts of such names—they require before applying to the Registrar. Searches may be made at the Trade Marks Registry, Patent Office, 25 Southampton Buildings, London WC2A 1AY.

The notes are not exhaustive and do not fetter the discretion of the Secretary of State to refuse registration of a company by a name which he considers undesirable. Their general effect is that a name will not be allowed if it is misleading.

In view of section 17 the persons promoting a company should not incur expenses in the advance printing of business stationery or sign-writing in which the proposed name appears. Further, before

the papers are presented for registration, a preliminary inquiry of the
Registrar should be made as to whether the desired name is too
like that of a company on the register—although a name cannot be
reserved and a reply from the Registrar stating that the proposed
name does not appear to be too like that of another company
confers no priority rights therein.

The Jenkins Report[6] recommended:—

(1) The Registrar should be given power to reserve approved
company names for a period of 30 days on payment
of a fee of £5. At present promoters must proceed with
the preparation and submission of documents in uncertainty until the last moment whether the name which
has been provisionally approved by the Registrar will be
finally allowed.

(2) The Board of Trade[7] should be empowered to control the
corporate names of companies, incorporated abroad and
having an established place of business in Great Britain,
which are, in their opinion, undesirable on grounds other
than similarity. Control over the use of undesirable company names has been evaded by incorporating abroad
by an undesirable name and then establishing a place of
business in Great Britain. It would not be either practicable or desirable to institute any general control over the
use in Great Britain of their own names by companies
incorporated abroad.

Section 17 was designed to make passing-off actions against
registered companies unnecessary and it would appear to have been
very successful. Under the general law, the court has jurisdiction to
grant an injunction[8] to restrain a company from using a trade name
colourably resembling that of the plaintiff if the defendant's trade
name, though innocently adopted, is calculated, *i.e.* likely[9], to
deceive, either by diverting customers from the plaintiff to the defendant or by occasioning confusion between the two businesses,
e.g. by suggesting that the defendant's business is in some way connected with that of the plaintiff.

---

[6] Para. 456.
[7] Now the Department of Trade.
[8] The Scottish equivalent is interdict.
[9] *Per* Earl of Halsbury L.C. in *The N. Cheshire and Manchester Brewery Co. Ltd.*
v. *The Manchester Brewery Co. Ltd.* [1899] A.C. 83 at p. 84.

In *Ewing* v. *Buttercup Margarine Co. Ltd.*,[10] the plaintiff, who carried on business under the trade name of the Buttercup Dairy Company, was held entitled to restrain a newly registered company from carrying on business under the name of the Buttercup Margarine Company Ltd. on the ground that the public might reasonably think that the registered company was connected with his business.

However, if the company's business is or will be different from that of the complaining party, confusion is not likely to arise, and an injunction will not be granted.[11]

A company having a word in ordinary use as part of its name cannot prevent another company from using the same word.

So, Aerators Ltd. were unable to prevent the registration of Automatic Aerators Patents, Ltd. because the word "aerator" was a word in common use in the English language and Aerators Ltd. had no monopoly of it: *Aerators Ltd.* v. *Tollitt* [1902] 2 Ch. 319.

Power to dispense with the word "Limited"

Although section 2 provides that the last word of the name of a limited company must be "Limited," if it is proved to the satisfaction of the Department of Trade that an association about to be formed as a limited company is to be formed for promoting commerce, art, science, religion, charity or any other useful object, and intends to apply its profits, if any, or other income in promoting its objects and to prohibit the payment of any dividend to its members, section 19 empowers the Department by licence to direct that the association may be registered as a company with limited liability without the addition of the word "Limited" to its name.

On proving that the above conditions as to objects and dividends are fulfilled an existing registered company may obtain a licence to make by special resolution a change in its name so as to omit "Limited."

A company to which a licence is granted under section 19 is usually a company limited by guarantee.

A licence may be granted on such conditions as the Department of Trade thinks fit, and may be revoked, subject to the company's right to be heard in opposition to the revocation. A number of documents, including a draft of the proposed memorandum and articles, must be submitted in duplicate with the application for a

---

[10] [1917] 2 Ch. 1 (C.A.).
[11] *Dunlop Pneumatic Tyre Co. Ltd.* v. *Dunlop Motor Co. Ltd.*, 1907 S.C. (H.L.) 15, where the respondents carried on a motor-repairing company.

licence. The Department will require the memorandum to contain a provision, known as a *cy-près* provision, to the effect that on dissolution any surplus assets are to be transferred to some other institution with similar objects.

A company which is licensed under section 19 enjoys all the privileges of a limited company and is subject to all the obligations except that it is relieved from the necessity of (1) having "Limited" as part of its name, (2) publishing its name,[12] and (3) sending lists of members to the Registrar[13] (s. 19 (1), (4)), although the European Communities Act, s. 9 (7), requires the fact that it is a limited company to be mentioned in its business letters and order forms.

In the past, associations such as chambers of commerce, schools and colleges, and research associations have applied for a licence under section 19. More recent applications have been from learned societies, professional qualifying bodies and charitable bodies doing social work.

Companies to which licences have been granted include: Trans-Antarctic Association; Great Britain–U.S.S.R. Association; Institute of Packaging; College of General Practitioners; Scottish Council for the Care of Spastics.

12 licences were granted to proposed companies and 13 to existing companies in 1974.

Clause 3 of the Companies Bill, 1973, which was to have superseded section 19, has been noted already.[14]

Publication of name by company

Section 108 provides that every company must:

(1) Paint or affix its name on the outside of every office or place in which its business is carried on, in a conspicuous position, in letters easily legible.

(2) Engrave its name in legible characters on its seal.

(3) Mention its name in legible characters in all business letters of the company and in all notices and other official publications, and in all bills of exchange, promissory notes, endorsements, cheques and orders for money or goods, bills of parcels, invoices, receipts and letters of credit.

[12] Under s. 108, *post.*
[13] Under s. 124, *post* p. 208 *et seq.*
[14] p. 63.

An exception is that by section 19 (4) a company entitled to dispense with the word "Limited" as part of its name[15] is excepted from the provisions of the Act relating to the publishing of its name, although the European Communities Act, s. 9 (7), requires the fact that it is a limited company to be mentioned in legible characters in all its business letters and order forms.

Where the last word of the name of a limited company is "Cyfyngedig," the fact that the company is a limited company must be stated in English and in legible characters—

(a) in all prospectuses, bill-heads, letter paper, notices and other official publications of the company;

(b) in a notice conspicuously displayed in every place in which the company's business is carried on (s. 30 (5) of the 1976 Act).

Fines are imposed on the company and its officers for non-compliance with the above requirements. Further, if an officer of the company or any person on its behalf, *inter alia*, (a) uses or authorises the use of a seal purporting to be a seal of the company whereon its name is not engraved, or (b) signs or authorises to be signed on behalf of the company any bill of exchange, cheque or order for money or goods in which the company's name is not mentioned, he is liable to a fine of £50 and, in addition, he is personally liable to the holder of the bill of exchange, cheque, or order, for its amount, unless it is paid by the company. Such personal liability is a secondary liability, arising only if the company itself fails to pay, *e.g.* because of liquidation.

A bill was drawn on a limited company described on the bill as "The Saltash Watermen's Steam Packet Company, Saltash," and was accepted by the secretary, who wrote across it "Accepted. John Martyr, Secy. to the sd. Coy." *Held*, when the bill was not honoured, the secretary was personally liable, as the company's correct name was not mentioned in the bill: *Penrose* v. *Martyr* (1858) 120 E.R. 595.

"The intention of the enactment plainly was to prevent persons from being deceived into the belief that they had a security with the unlimited liability of common law, when they had but the security of a Company limited": *per* Crompton J. at p. 597.

In *Durham Fancy Goods Ltd.* v. *Michael Jackson (Fancy Goods) Ltd.* [1968] 2 Q.B. 839, where the plaintiff had prepared the form of acceptance which misdescribed the company's name as "M. Jackson (Fancy Goods) Ltd.," the plaintiff was held estopped from enforcing the personal liability under section 108 of the officer who signed the bill.[16]

---

[15] *Ante* p. 67.
[16] Cf. *Scottish and Newcastle Breweries Ltd.* v. *Blair*, 1967 S.L.T. 72 (O.H.), in which the defence of personal bar was unsuccessful.

If the name of the company appears on the face of the bill it need not appear on the acceptance.

A bill was drawn on "J. & T. H. Wallis Ltd.," and accepted "James Wallis, Thomas Wallis, Henry Bowles, Secty." *Held*, (1) the correct name of the company was mentioned in the bill as required by the Companies Act, (2) the abbreviation "Ltd." might be used for the word "Limited," (3) the individuals who had signed the acceptance were not liable on the bill: *Stacey & Co. Ltd.* v. *Wallis* (1912) 28 T.L.R. 209.

Change of name

1. A company may change its name by special resolution with the approval of the Department of Trade signified in writing: section 18 (1). Section 37 of the 1976 Act empowers the Secretary of State to prescribe the fee to be paid to the Registrar for entering the new name on the register.

Where the memorandum of a limited company states that its registered office is to be in Wales, the approval of the Secretary of State is not required for any change of the name of the company which consists only of substituting "Cyfyngedig" for "Limited" or vice versa (1976 Act, s. 30 (4)).

2. If, through inadvertence or otherwise, a company is registered by a name which in the opinion of the Department of Trade is too like that of a previously registered company, it may change its name with the sanction of the Department. (In this case it is arguable that a special resolution is not necessary and that an ordinary resolution will suffice.) Further, the Department of Trade may, within six months after the registration by that name, direct a change of name, whereupon the company should comply within six weeks from the direction or such longer period as the Department may allow. Default in complying with a direction renders the company liable to a fine of £5 a day whilst the default continues: section 18 (2).

If a company proposes to change its name it should, before passing the special resolution, inquire from the Registrar whether the Department of Trade will be prepared to sanction the change of name. If the answer is in the affirmative the resolution should be passed without delay since the Registrar has no power to reserve a name except upon actual registration.

In 1974 the Department approved a change of name under section 18 (1) in 14,491 cases and directed a change under section 18 (2) in 13 cases.

3. If the Department of Trade considers that a name gives so misleading an indication of the nature of the company's activities as to be likely to cause harm to the public, they may direct a change. A direction must normally be complied with within six weeks, and within three weeks the company may apply to the court to set the direction aside. Default in complying with a direction renders the company liable to a fine of £5 a day: 1967 Act, s. 46.

When a company changes its name a new certificate of incorporation is issued by the Registrar (1948 Act, s. 18 (3); 1967 Act, s. 46), and it has been decided that the company retains its old name until the new certificate is issued.[17]

A change of name does not affect any rights or obligations of the company or any legal proceedings by or against the company: 1948 Act, s. 18 (4); 1967 Act, s. 46.

Business name

If a company carries on business in the United Kingdom under a business name which does not consist of its corporate name without any addition the business name must within fourteen days be registered under the Registration of Business Names Act 1916: 1916 Act, s. 1, as amended by the Companies Act 1947, s. 58.[18] The appropriate form, as well as "Notes for Guidance on Registration of Business Names," can be obtained from the Registry of Business Names, Pembroke House, 40–56 City Road, London, EC1Y 2DN or, in Scotland, Exchequer Chambers, 102 George Street, Edinburgh, EH2 3DJ. Section 14 of the 1916 Act, as amended by the Companies Act 1947, s. 116, gives the Registrar of Business Names power to refuse registration of a business name which is in his opinion undesirable (although he makes only limited use of this power). The Registrar's present practice is set out in "Notes for Guidance." Changes in the registered particulars must be notified on the appropriate form.

Section 32 of the Companies Act 1976 now provides that if a corporation incorporated outside Great Britain has a place of business in Great Britain and carries on business in a business name which does not consist of its incorporated name without any addition, the business name must be registered under the Registration of Business Names Act 1916.

---

[17] *Shackleford, Ford & Co. Ltd.* v. *Dangerfield* (1868) L.R. 3 C.P. 407.
[18] A few sections of the Companies Act 1947 are still in force.

If there is default in registration, the persons in default are liable to a fine and, unless the court gives relief, *e.g.* in the case of accidental default, the rights of the defaulter under a contract made by or on behalf of such defaulter in relation to the business in question are unenforceable by the defaulter by action: Registration of Business Names Act 1916, s. 8.

The certificate of registration must be exhibited at the principal place of business. If the company ceases to carry on business in such circumstances as to require registration the Registrar must be notified. Registrations filed by the Registrar are open to public inspection at a fee of 5p per inspection.

The Jenkins Report[19] recommended:

(1) There should be a substantial increase in the fees charged to the public for the use of the register of business names and a small annual registration fee should be imposed. Despite the fact that the obligation to register is widely disregarded, and that the register contains a lot of "dead wood," the register is extensively used by the public. The latter recommendation is designed to encourage those who cease to use a registered business name to report the fact.

(2) The Registration of Business Names Act should empower the court to order that defaults under the Act be made good. Section 428 of the Companies Act, which empowers the court to order a company or its officers to make good defaults in making returns to the Registrar, has proved efficacious in cases where repeated prosecutions have not, although it should be extended to cover both defaults by the company and defaults by its officers in complying with *any* of their statutory duties.

THE REGISTERED OFFICE

A company must at all times have a registered office to which communications and notices may be addressed: 1976 Act, s. 23 (1). The memorandum must state whether the registered office is to be in England, Wales or Scotland: section 2 of the 1948 Act as amended by section 30 (1) of the 1976 Act. The address of the registered office

[19] Paras. 456, 511.

need not be set out in the memorandum, but notice of the address must be given to the Registrar in the statement which, under section 21 of the 1976 Act *ante*,[20] must be delivered for registration with the memorandum.

Subject to the rule that the registered office cannot be changed from England to Scotland, or vice versa, the address can be changed. Notice of a change must be given to the Registrar within 14 days (1976 Act, s. 23 (3)).[21]

The statement as to the registered office in the memorandum fixes the company's nationality and domicile, *e.g.* if the memorandum states that the office is to be in England (so that the company is registered with the Registrar in Cardiff, as opposed to the Registrar in Edinburgh: section 12) the company is an English company with British nationality and an English domicile. A corporation is domiciled where it is incorporated and cannot change this domicile,[22] except by Act of Parliament, and the law of a corporation's domicile governs all questions of its status, *e.g.* is it duly incorporated, what are its powers, has it been dissolved? The nationality of a corporation is seldom relevant in private international law but also depends on the place of incorporation.

The reason for requiring a company to have a registered office is that, since the company has a legal existence but does not have a physical existence, it is necessary to know where the company can be found, where communications and notices may be addressed and where documents can be served on it. A company need not, and very frequently does not, carry on its business at its registered office. There is nothing, for example, to prevent a company with a registered office in England from carrying on its business abroad.

A document can be served on a company by leaving it at or sending it by post to the registered office of the company: section 437 (1). It is not necessary to send it by registered post.[23]

If a company registered in Scotland carries on business in England, the process of any court in England can be served at the principal place of the company's business in England, a copy being posted at the same time to the registered office: section 437 (2), (3).

Section 9 (3) of the European Communities Act 1972, as amended

---

[20] p. 23.
[21] The change, though resolved on by the directors, does not become effective until this notice has been given: *Ross* v. *Invergordon Distilleries Ltd.*, 1961 S.C. 286.
[22] *Gasque* v. *I.R.C.* [1940] 2 K.B. 80.
[23] *T. O. Supplies (London) Ltd.* v. *Jerry Creighton Ltd.* [1952] 1 K.B. 42.

by section 23 (6) of the Companies Act 1976, provides that the Registrar must publish in the *Gazette* notice of the receipt by him of notice of a change in the situation of a company's registered office. And section 9 (4) provides that a company cannot rely against other persons (as regards service of any document on the company) on any change in the situation of the company's registered office if it had not been officially notified (under s. 9 (3)) at the material time and is not shown by the company to have been known at that time to the person concerned, or if the material time is less than 16 days after official notification and it is shown that the person concerned was unavoidably prevented from knowing of the event at that time.

Section 9 (7) of the 1972 Act requires every company to mention its place of registration and registered number, and the address of its registered office, in legible characters on all its business letters and order forms. A company which fails to comply with the subsection, or an officer of a company or other person on its behalf who issues or authorises the issue of a letter or form which does not comply, is liable to a fine of not more than £50. The phrase "order forms" means forms which the company makes available for other persons to order goods or services from the company and includes, *e.g.*, coupons in newspapers which the public fill in asking for goods to be supplied.[24]

Items which must be kept at the registered office

The following must be kept at the registered office of a company:

(1) The register of members and, if the company has one, the index of members, unless the register is made up at another office of the company, when they may be kept at that office, or is made up by an agent, when they may be kept at the agent's office: sections 110, 111.

(2) The minute books of general meetings: section 146.

(3) The register of interests in the prescribed percentage (five per cent. at present) or more of the shares carrying unrestricted voting rights and, if there is one, the index of names, unless the register of directors' interests is not kept at the registered office, when it must be kept where the register

---

[24] Pamphlet "Company law provisions of the European Communities Act," published by the Department of Trade. And see the Departmental Notice published in Law Notes, December 1972, p. 323.

of directors' interests is kept: 1967 Act, ss. 33, 34; 1976 Act, s. 26.

(4) The register of directors and secretaries: section 200.

(5) The register of directors' interests in shares in, or debentures of, the company or associated companies, together with, if the company has one, the index of names in the register, unless the register of members is not kept at its registered office, when they may be kept where the register of members is kept: 1967 Act, ss. 27–29, 31.

(6) A copy of each director's contract of service or a memorandum thereof, unless kept where the register of members is kept or kept at the company's principal place of business: 1967 Act, s. 26.

(7) If the company has one, the register of debenture holders, unless the register is made up at another office, when it may be kept where it is made up, or is made up by an agent, when it may be kept at the agent's office: section 86.

(8) A copy of every instrument creating any charge requiring registration under Part III of the Act or, in Scotland, Part IIIA: ss. 95, 97, 103 (England), 106A, 106C, 106H (Scotland).[25]

(9) The company's register of charges affecting property of the company: sections 104, 106I.[25]

In general these documents must be kept open to inspection by members without fee during business hours, subject to reasonable restrictions leaving not less than two hours a day for inspection. The minute books are open only to the inspection of members. The register of debenture holders is also open to the inspection of debenture holders without fee. Copies of instruments creating a charge and the register of charges are also open to the inspection of creditors without fee (ss. 105, 106J). The register of members (s. 113), the register of directors and secretaries, the register of directors' interests, the register of debenture holders (s. 87), the register of charges, and, subject to exceptions, the register of interests in five per cent. of the shares, are open to the public on payment of 5p. The register of directors' interests must also be produced at the annual general meeting and remain open and accessible during the meeting to any person attending.

[25] See Companies (Floating Charges and Receivers) (Scotland) Act 1972, s. 6 and Sched.

Every limited banking company, or insurance company, or deposit, provident, or benefit society, must put up in a conspicuous place in its registered office a periodical statement in the prescribed form of its assets and liabilities: section 433.

THE OBJECTS

The memorandum must state the objects of the company: section 2. As Lord Parker of Waddington said in *Cotman* v. *Brougham*,[26] the statement of the objects in the memorandum serves a double purpose: (1) It protects the subscribers, who learn from it the purposes to which their money can be applied.[27] (2) It protects persons dealing with the company, who can discover from it,[28] the extent of the company's powers.

At common law, a corporation has the same legal capacity as a human being[29] but, in order to protect the shareholders and those who deal with the company, the courts evolved the *ultra vires* doctrine to the effect that since a registered company is an artificial person incorporated by Parliament for the objects stated in the memorandum, it has power only to carry out such objects together with anything incidental thereto. The doctrine was to some extent modified by the European Communities Act, s. 9, as will be explained later.

In practice it is, therefore, usual to set out at length in the memorandum all the objects which the company might require, and the short form of objects clause, in the model memorandum in Table B in the First Schedule to the Act, is seldom employed. Further, many powers, *e.g.* a power to borrow money for the purposes of the business, most of which would otherwise be implied, are set out expressly.

Lord Parker continued[26]:

"The narrower the objects expressed in the memorandum the less is the subscribers' risk, but the wider such objects the greater is the security of those who transact business with the company. Moreover, experience soon showed

[26] [1918] A.C. 514 at p. 520. See also *per* Lord Wrenbury at pp. 522, 523.
[27] A member can require the company to send him a copy of the memorandum on payment of 5p: s. 24, *post* p. 114.
[28] They can inspect the memorandum and the other documents kept by the Registrar: s. 426, *post* p. 115.
[29] *Case of Sutton's Hospital* (1612) 10 Co.Rep. 23a; Blackstone, Comm. 1, 593; *University of Glasgow* v. *Faculty of Physicians and Surgeons* (1834) 13 S. 9, (1835) 2 S. & M, 275, (1837) 15 S. 736, (1840) 1 Rob. 397.

that persons who transact business with companies do not like having to depend on inference when the validity of a proposed transaction is in question. Even a power to borrow money could not always be safely inferred, much less such a power as that of underwriting shares in another company. Thus arose the practice of specifying powers as objects, a practice rendered possible by the fact that there is no statutory limit on the number of objects which may be specified. But even then, a person proposing to deal with a company could not be absolutely safe, for powers specified as objects might be read as ancillary to and exercisable only for the purpose of attaining what might be held to be the company's main or paramount object, and on this construction no-one could be quite certain whether the court would not hold any proposed transaction to be *ultra vires*. At any rate, all the surrounding circumstances would require investigation. Fresh clauses were framed to meet this difficulty, and the result is the modern memorandum of association, with its multifarious list of objects and powers specified as objects and its clauses designed to prevent any specified object being read as ancillary to some other object."[30]

The shareholders and persons dealing with the company were also protected by the rule that the stated objects could not be altered except by a Special Act of Parliament or a reconstruction. Later, the objects could be altered for certain specified purposes with the consent of the court and now, as we shall see, they can be altered for certain specified purposes and the consent of the court is generally not required.[31]

Ultra vires doctrine

In order to protect the subscribers and persons dealing with the company the courts held that a company incorporated by registration under the Companies Acts is incorporated by Parliament for the objects stated in the memorandum of association so that it has power only to carry out such objects and anything else which is reasonably incidental thereto. If an act is performed or a transaction carried out which, though legal in itself, is not authorised by the objects clause in the memorandum or by statute, it is *ultra vires*, *i.e.* beyond the powers of, the company and void, so that it cannot be ratified even if all the members wish to ratify.

A registered company has power to carry out the objects set out in the memorandum and also everything which is reasonably necessary to enable it to carry out those objects. As Lord Selborne L.C. said in *Att-Gen.* v. *Great Eastern Railway Co.*[32] the doctrine of

---

[30] For comparable Scottish comments see Lord Skerrington in *John Walker & Sons Ltd., Petitioners,* 1914 S.C. 280 at p. 289, and the reporter in *North of Scotland etc. Steam Navigation Co. Ltd., Petitioners,* 1920 S.C. 633 at p. 637.

[31] And a subsidiary company can be incorporated with other objects.

[32] (1880) 5 App.Cas. 473 at p. 478.

ultra vires "ought to be reasonably, and not unreasonably, understood and applied, and . . . whatever may fairly be regarded as incidental to, or consequential upon, those things which the legislature has authorised, ought not (unless expressly prohibited) to be held, by judicial construction, to be *ultra vires*." For example, a company formed "to buy, sell and deal in coal" may, *for the purpose of carrying out the stated objects,* employ labour, open shops, buy and hire lorries, purchase supplies, draw and accept bills of exchange, borrow and give security, have a banking account, employ agents and pay bonuses and pensions to employees.[33]

In ascertaining whether a particular act is *intra* or *ultra vires* regard must be had to the nature of the transaction and not to the means of execution.[34]

A contract *ultra vires* a company is void and incapable of ratification even if every member wishes to ratify it.

A company was incorporated with the following objects: (1) to make, and sell, or lend on hire, railway carriages and wagons; (2) to carry on the business of mechanical engineers and general contractors; (3) to purchase, lease, work, and sell mines, minerals, land and buildings. The directors contracted to purchase a concession for making a railway in Belgium. *Held,* the contract was *ultra vires* the company and void so that not even the subsequent assent of the whole body of shareholders could ratify it: *Ashbury Railway Carriage Co. Ltd.* v. *Riche* (1875) L.R. 7 H.L. 653. Note that if this case were to occur again it would almost certainly be decided differently because of section 9 (1) of the European Communities Act 1972, *post.*

The words "general contractors" referred to the words which went immediately before and indicated such contracts as mechanical engineers make for the purpose of carrying on their business: see *per* Lord Cairns L.C. at pp. 664, 665.

"This contract was entirely . . . beyond the objects in the memorandum of association. If so, it was thereby placed beyond the powers of the company to make the contract. If so . . . it is not a question whether the contract ever was ratified or was not ratified. If it was a contract void at its beginning, it was void because the company could not make the contract. If . . . every shareholder of the company had said, 'That is a contract which we desire to make . . .', the case would not have stood in any different position from that in which it stands now. The shareholders would thereby, by unanimous consent, have been attempting to do the very thing which, by the Act of Parliament, they were prohibited from doing": *per* Lord Cairns L.C. at p. 672.

A Scottish illustration of the operation of the *ultra vires* doctrine is *Life Association of Scotland* v. *Caledonian Heritable Security Co. Ltd. in Liquidation* (1886) 13 R. 750, in which an agreement entered into by a heritable security company with a prior bondholder for the purpose of preventing an immediate sale by the prior bondholder of the security subjects was held to be *ultra vires*

[33] Palmer's *Company Law*, 21st ed., p. 76.
[34] *Thompson* v. *J. Barke and Company (Caterers) Ltd.,* 1975 S.L.T. 67 (O.H.), *ante* p. 28.

since it was neither expressly authorised by the memorandum nor "incidental or conducive to the attainment" of the stated objects.

It will be seen that, as an exception to the rule in *Foss* v. *Harbottle* or in his own right, an individual member can bring proceedings for an injunction to restrain the company from doing an *ultra vires* act or entering into an *ultra vires* transaction.[35] An unsecured creditor of the company cannot sue to restrain it from acting *ultra vires*[36] but a secured creditor, at least one who has a specific (or fixed) charge[37] on its assets, can.[38]

Main object

As stated earlier,[39] it is usual to set out in the objects clause any object that the company might require, and to set out powers, many of which would otherwise be implied. Once this practice developed the rule that the objects must be stated in the memorandum and the *ultra vires* doctrine ceased to achieve their purpose and, in order to counter the practice, the courts evolved the "main objects" rule of construction by which one of the objects may be held to be the main object of the company and the remainder to be merely ancillary to the main object.

The "main objects" rule of construction is that "where a memorandum of association expresses the objects of the company in a series of paragraphs and one paragraph, or the first two or three paragraphs, appear to embody the 'main object' of the company, all the other paragraphs are treated as merely ancillary to this 'main object,' and as limited or controlled thereby:" *per* Salmon J. in *Anglo-Overseas Agencies Ltd.* v. *Green* [1961] 1 Q.B. 1 at p. 8.

However, the "main objects" rule of construction can be excluded by the appropriate provision in the memorandum. In some cases, *e.g. Cotman* v. *Brougham and Anglo-Overseas Agencies Ltd.* v. *Green, infra,* a sub-clause declares, in effect, that each of the objects is to be regarded as a main object.

An objects clause contained 30 sub-clauses enabling the company to carry on almost every kind of business. The first sub-clause authorised the company to acquire, take over, work, and develop any licences, concessions, estates, plantations and properties, and in particular four specified licences to collect rubber, etc. The twelfth authorised the company to buy or otherwise acquire in any way and hold, sell or deal with or in any stocks or in any shares of any company. The objects clause concluded with a declaration that every sub-clause

[35] *Post* p. 376.
[36] *Mills* v. *Northern Rlwy. of Buenos Ayres Co.* (1870) L.R. 5 Ch.App. 621; *Lawrence* v. *West Somerset Mineral Rlwy. Co.* [1918] 2 Ch.D. 654.
[37] *Post* p. 498.
[38] *Per* Eve J. in *Lawrence's* case *ante,* at p. 257.
[39] p. 75.

should be construed as a substantive clause and not limited or restricted by reference to or inference from any other sub-clause or by the name of the company, and that none of the sub-clauses or the objects or powers therein should be deemed subsidiary merely to the objects in the first sub-clause. The company underwrote and had allotted to it shares in an oil company. When the oil company was wound up the rubber company was placed on the list of contributories. *Held*, the underwriting was *intra vires* the rubber company: *Cotman* v. *Brougham* [1918] A.C. 514.[40]

The objects of a company were, *inter alia*, (A) to carry on business as importers and exporters of merchandise, (E) to acquire any concessions and contracts and to carry the same into effect. The objects clause concluded with a declaration that the objects specified in any paragraph should, except where otherwise expressed in such paragraph, be in no wise limited or restricted by reference to or inference from the terms of any other paragraph or the name of the company. *Inter alia* the company claimed damages against an architect and a firm of estate agents for breach of an agreement to assist the company to obtain a building lease of a site in a shopping centre for a large store, shops and business development. The defence was that the acquisition of a building lease and the making of such an agreement was *ultra vires* the company. *Held*, the "main objects" rule was excluded and the acquisition of the building lease and the agreement were *intra vires*: *Anglo-Overseas Agencies Ltd.* v. *Green* [1961] 1 Q.B. 1.

A declaration like that in the above cases is not the only provision which will exclude the "main objects" rule.

In *Bell Houses Ltd.* v. *City Wall Properties Ltd.* [1966] 2 Q.B. 656 (C.A.), after stating the principal business of the company, which was that of developing housing estates, the objects clause provided that the company was formed "to carry on any other . . . business whatsoever which can, in the opinion of the board of directors, be advantageously carried on by the company in connection with or as ancillary to any of the above businesses or the general business of the company."[41] In one isolated transaction the company agreed, in consideration of the promise of payment of a procuration fee, to introduce to another company a financier prepared to provide a large amount of short-term credit for property development. It was held that since the directors were honestly of the opinion that such an activity could be so advantageously carried on it was *intra vires* even though there was no declaration like that in the *Anglo-Overseas* case.[42]

Other objects were "to . . . turn to account . . . any of the property and assets . . . of the company for such consideration as the company may think fit" and "to do all such other things as are incidental or conducive to the above objects. . . ." The Court of Appeal also held that the contract regarding the procuration fee was authorised by the former clause and Salmon L.J. held that it was further authorised by the latter.

[40] Compare the approval by the Scottish court of an "independent objects" clause in *London and Edinburgh Shipping Co. Ltd., Petitioners*, 1909 S.C. 1, and its rejection of such a clause in *Union Bank of Scotland Ltd., Petitioners*, 1918 S.C. 21, and in the *North of Scotland Case, ante* p. 76.

[41] In the Australian High Court case of *H. A. Stephenson & Son Ltd.* v. *Gillanders, Arbuthnot & Co.* (1931) 45 C.L.R. 476, one of the objects for which the company was formed was "to carry on any other businesses . . . as the company may deem expedient." See, further, Cain, First Australian Supplement to the Tenth Edition of Charlesworth & Cain, p. 54.

[42] In the *Bell Houses* case the test of what was *intra vires* was subjective.

It may be mentioned here that when the main object of a company fails for any reason the substratum of the company is said to have gone and it is just and equitable that the company be wound up, and the "main objects" rule cannot be excluded. The reason is, as Lord Parker of Waddington said in *Cotman* v. *Brougham*,[43] that: "The question whether or not a company can be wound up for failure of substratum is a question of equity between a company and its shareholders. The question whether or not a transaction is *ultra vires* is a question of law between the company and a third party."[44]

The objects of the company included the following—(1) to acquire and use a German patent for manufacturing coffee from dates, (2) to acquire and use any other inventions for that or similar purposes, (3) to import and export all descriptions of produce for the purpose of food. The German patent was never granted, but the company acquired a Swedish patent for the same purpose and also made coffee from dates without a patent in Hamburg. The company was solvent, and the majority of the shareholders wished to continue the company. Two shareholders petitioned for a winding-up on the ground that its objects had entirely failed. *Held*, the substratum had failed as it was impossible to carry out the objects for which the company was formed, and it was just and equitable that the company should be wound up, although the petition was presented within a year after incorporation.[45] The real object was not just to make substitute coffee from dates but to work a particular German patent in Germany. Sub-clauses (2) and (3) were ancillary (subordinate) to that: *Re German Date Coffee Co.* (1882) 20 Ch.D. 169 (C.A.).

"Where on the face of the memorandum you see there is a distinct purpose which is the foundation of the company, then, although the memorandum may contain other general words which include the doing of other objects, those general words must be read as being ancillary to that of which the memorandum shews to be the main purpose, and if the main purpose fails and fails altogether, then, . . . the substratum of the association fails": *per* Kay J. at p. 177.

However, the company will not be wound up if the substratum has not gone.

By the memorandum, the objects of K. Co. were to carry on the business of general engineering *and*, *inter alia*, to acquire a specified existing business. Having acquired the existing business K. Co. later sold it. K. Co. intended to continue with the business of general engineering and to buy another existing business. Certain shareholders petitioned for a winding up, alleging that the substratum of K. Co. had gone. *Held*, since the main object was to carry on an engineering business of a general nature, the substratum had *not* gone, and the company was not wound up: *Re Kitson & Co. Ltd.* [1946] 1 All E.R. 435 (C.A.), distinguishing *Re German Date Coffee Co.*, *ante*. [In the latter case the main object was to acquire and work a *particular* patent.]

---

[43] [1918] A.C. 514 at p. 520. See also *per* Dixon J. in *Stephenson's* case, *supra*, at p. 487, and *Re Tivoli Freeholds* [1972] V.R. 445, *post* p. 385.
[44] Scots law does not distinguish between equity and law in this way.
[45] See p. 543 *post*.

Further, a company can only be wound up on the ground that the substratum has gone on a shareholder's petition and no shareholder is *obliged* to petition to have the company wound up if he would prefer it to carry on some other business authorised by its memorandum.

Effect of ultra vires transactions

In *Mahony* v. *East Holyford Mining Co.*[46] Lord Hatherley said that persons dealing with the company, even if they do not have actual notice of the company's powers because they have not inspected the memorandum, have constructive notice of the powers, *i.e.* they are deemed to know them, because the memorandum, like most of the documents registered with the Registrar of Companies, is open to public inspection under section 426 and could have been inspected. Accordingly, if they make a contract which is to their knowledge, actual or constructive, *ultra vires* the company, and the company takes the point, they cannot enforce it, as is shown, *e.g.*, by *Re Jon Beauforte Ltd.*, *infra*, although this is now subject to section 9 (1) of the European Communities Act 1972 *post*. If they have supplied goods or performed services under such a contract they cannot obtain payment, and if they have lent money the general rule is that they cannot recover it.[47]

A company, authorised by its memorandum to carry on business as costumiers and gown makers, started the business of making veneered panels. This was *ultra vires*. Builders were employed to build a factory, suppliers sold veneers, and coke merchants sold coke. Correspondence showed that the coke suppliers had actual notice that the business being carried on and for which the coke was required was that of veneered panel manufacturers, and they had constructive notice of the contents of the memorandum and hence that the transaction was *ultra vires* the company. *Held*, they could not prove for their debts in the company's liquidation, although this was without prejudice to the questions whether they were entitled to trace their money or other property into any particular asset or the proceeds of sale thereof and to participate in the distribution of surplus assets after the claims of creditors entitled to prove and winding-up costs had been provided for: *Re Jon Beauforte (London) Ltd.* [1953] Ch. 131.[48] [Note: If this case were to recur it would almost certainly be decided differently because of the European Communities Act, s. 9 (1).]

[46] (1875) L.R. 7 H.L. 869 at p. 893.
[47] *Sinclair* v. *Brougham* [1914] A.C. 398, *post* p. 484.
[48] In the *Jon Beauforte* case the test of what was *ultra vires* was subjective. See also the New South Wales case of *Hawkesbury Development Co. Ltd.* v. *Landmark Finance Pty. Ltd.* (1970) 92 W.N. (N.S.W.) 199, which is dealt with in the First Australian Supplement to Charlesworth & Cain at p. 59.

A similar case is *Introductions Ltd.* v. *National Provincial Bank Ltd.*[49]

Money or other property which can be traced into any particular asset of the company or the proceeds of sale of that asset can be claimed, because the company is deemed to hold it as a trustee for the person from whom it was obtained, and, if tracing is impossible, he is entitled to share in the distribution of surplus assets after the creditors entitled to prove and winding-up costs have been provided for.[47] Accordingly, where an *ultra vires* issue of shares has been made, and the company is solvent, the subscribers are entitled to recover their money.[50] However, in *Re Jon Beauforte Ltd.* the creditor's right to trace was worthless since, *e.g.*, the coke had been consumed and so had lost its identity.

It seems that the company can protect its property acquired by an *ultra vires* expenditure.[51]

Subject as below, the company cannot recover its money or other property which it has spent or disposed of for an *ultra vires* purpose. But a director, who parts with the company's money or property for an *ultra vires* purpose, will be liable to the company for the loss it has sustained, even if he acted in good faith, because the company itself cannot legally authorise him to do an *ultra vires* act. The company can, however, in such a case, validly resolve not to sue him, and there is nothing *ultra vires* in its so doing. A guarantee by the directors that the company will perform an *ultra vires* contract to procure the repurchase of its own shares is binding on the directors[52] if the promise is to pay whether the company can lawfully be called upon to pay or not.[53]

In the *Bell Houses* case, *ante*, Mocatta J. held at first instance[54] that a defendant sued on a contract by a company could take the point that the contract was *ultra vires* the company, and it was immaterial whether the contract was executory or executed by the company. In the Court of Appeal, Salmon L.J. said[55] that since the contract was *intra vires* the company it was unnecessary to consider

[49] [1970] Ch. 199 (C.A.), *post* p. 86.
[50] *Per* Lord Simonds in *Linz* v. *Electric Wire Co. of Palestine Ltd.* [1948] A.C. 371 (P.C.) at p. 377. If a shareholder has sold his shares he cannot then say they were unlawfully issued. A Scottish case is *Waverley Hydropathic Co. Ltd.* v. *Barrowman* (1895) 23 R. 136 (*ultra vires* issue of preference shares).
[51] *National Telephone Co. Ltd.* v. *The Constables of St. Peter Port* [1900] A.C. 317 (P.C.).
[52] *Garrard* v. *James* [1925] Ch. 616.
[53] *Per* Fisher J. in *Heald* v. *O'Connor* [1971] 1 W.L.R. 497 at p. 506.
[54] [1966] 1 Q.B. 207.
[55] [1966] 2 Q.B. 656 at pp. 693–694.

the question whether, the plaintiff company having fully performed its part and the defendant having obtained all the benefits under the contract, the defendant could take the point that the contract was *ultra vires* the plaintiff company and so avoid payment, although he added that it seemed strange that the defendant could take advantage of a doctrine, manifestly for the protection of the shareholders, in order to deprive the company of money which in justice should be paid to it by him. However, in the *Anglo-Overseas Agencies* case, *ante*,[56] the defence was that the contract was *ultra vires* the plaintiff company. Again, in the *Charterbridge* case, *infra*, a third party, who was a purchaser of land from the company, took the point that the legal charge on the land which the company had given to a bank was *ultra vires* the company.

In *Charterbridge Corpn.* v. *Lloyds Bank Ltd.* [1970] Ch. 62, the plaintiff, who was a purchaser of land from a company, alleged that a legal charge on the land which the company had given to a bank, was created for purposes not for the benefit of the company—that the bank account of another company in the same group was overdrawn, the first company guaranteed the overdraft and then gave the bank the legal charge on its land to secure its indebtedness to the bank including that under the guarantee. The charge was *intra vires*—it was held that where, as was the case on the facts, a company is carrying out the purposes expressed in its memorandum, and does an act within the scope of a power expressed in it, that act is *intra vires* (the objects were, *inter alia*, to acquire lands for investment and to secure or guarantee by mortgages, charges or otherwise the performance and discharge of any contract, obligation or liability of the company or of any other person or corporation with whom or which it has dealings or having a business or undertaking in which the company is concerned or interested whether directly or indirectly); it would be contrary to the whole function of the memorandum if objects unequivocally set out in it should be subject to some implied limitation by reference to the state of mind of the parties; the state of mind of the officers of the company and the bank as to whether the transaction was intended to benefit the company was irrelevant on the issue of *ultra vires*. Further, that if the intention was relevant, the directors as reasonable men might have concluded that the transaction would benefit the company.[57]

European Communities Act 1972

When it became the practice to draft objects clauses widely and to set out powers in the objects clause,[58] the *ultra vires* doctrine ceased to protect shareholders and persons dealing with a company. Further, in the odd case where the objects were not drafted widely the doctrine was a trap for a person dealing with the company.

[56] p. 79.
[57] And see *Reid Murray Holdings Ltd.* (*In Liq.*) v. *David Murray Holdings Pty. Ltd.* (1972) 5 S.A.S.R. 386.   [58] *Ante* p. 75.

Consequently, statutory modification of the doctrine so as to protect such a person was necessary and was recommended in the Jenkins Report.[59] Effect was more or less given to the recommendation when, in order to bring Company Law in the United Kingdom into line with that of the European Economic Community, the doctrine of *ultra vires* was modified by the European Communities Act 1972, s. 9.[60]

Section 9 (1) provides that in favour of a person dealing with a company in good faith, a transaction decided on by the directors shall be deemed one within the capacity of the company to enter into, and the power of the directors to bind the company shall be deemed free of any limitation under the memorandum or articles; and a party to such a transaction shall not be bound to inquire as to the capacity of the company to enter into it or as to any such limitation on the powers of the directors, and shall be presumed to have acted in good faith unless the contrary is proved.[61]

The above provision means that if, *e.g.*, a person enters into a contract with a company which, although lawful, is *ultra vires* the company, and he does not actually know that it is *ultra vires*, provided that it has been decided on by the directors he can assume that it is *intra vires* and he will be able to enforce the contract against the company, *i.e.* the company will be unable to plead *ultra vires*. The provision operates only in favour of a person dealing with a company in good faith. However, a party to a transaction decided on by the directors is not bound to inquire as to the capacity of the company to enter into the transaction (his omission to inquire is not bad faith) and he is presumed to have acted in good faith unless the contrary is proved (the burden of proving the contrary is on the company). If it can be shown by a company that the other party to an *ultra vires* transaction decided on by the directors had *actual* knowledge, *e.g.* of the company's objects, he is not "a person dealing with a company in good faith" and is not protected by the provision unless he honestly and reasonably failed to appreciate that the transaction was *ultra vires* the company. And if the other party to an *ultra vires* contract decided on by the directors refuses to perform his part of the contract, he is not "a person dealing . . . in good faith"

[59] Para. 42.
[60] S. 9 was intended to give effect to the First Directive of the Council of Ministers of the EEC (March 9, 1968, No. 68/151).
[61] Clause 5 of the Companies Bill 1973 purported to restate s. 9 of the 1972 Act in clearer terms.

and is unable to enforce the contract, *i.e.* the company can plead *ultra vires*.

Section 9 (1) applies only to a transaction decided on by the directors. Presumably this includes, *e.g.*, a transaction decided upon by a managing director where the directors have properly delegated the appropriate powers to him. It follows that a person proposing to enter into a transaction with a company should, before entering into the transaction, satisfy himself that it has been decided upon by the directors or the managing director.

If section 9 (1) operates, a transaction *ultra vires* a company is deemed *intra vires* for some purposes.

The provision does not change the position of the company, or that of the directors or managing director, where a transaction decided on by the directors is *ultra vires*—at least in so far as the company cannot enforce an *ultra vires* contract against the other party and the directors are in breach of duty in deciding that such a contract be made and are liable to the company accordingly. And a shareholder, *e.g.*, can still obtain an injunction to restrain the company from acting *ultra vires*.

The effect of section 9 (1) is that if cases like *Ashbury Railway Carriage Co.* v. *Riche* and *Re Jon Beauforte, ante,*[62] and *Introductions Ltd.* v. *National Provincial Bank, post,*[63] were to occur again in England they would almost certainly be decided differently.

Powers

As was stated earlier, in addition to the objects strictly so called, the memorandum usually sets out expressly a number of powers many of which are reasonably incidental to the attainment of the company's objects and would be implied if not set out. The following are some powers frequently given:

(1) Power to acquire similar businesses.
(2) Power to amalgamate or enter into profit-sharing agreements with other companies, and to borrow money jointly with other companies.

A general power to borrow does not authorise a joint borrowing.[64]

[62] pp. 77 and 81.
[63] p. 86.
[64] *Re Johnston Foreign Patents Co. Ltd.* [1904] 2 Ch. 234 (C.A.).

(3) Power to take shares in another company.[65]
(4) Power to borrow money for the purposes of its business.

> This is implied in the case of a company formed for trading purposes[66]—but an express power removes any difficulty if there is a doubt as to whether the company answers that description.

Since a loan must be for some purpose, borrowing money is not an independent activity even if the memorandum expressly provides that the company has, as an independent object, power to borrow money.

The main object of a company was to provide entertainments and services for overseas visitors. The objects clause also expressly empowered the company to borrow or raise money in such manner as the company should think fit and provided that each of the objects was an independent object. A bank, which was given a copy of the memorandum and which knew that the only business being carried on by the company was pig-breeding, lent money to the company and took debentures as security. *Held*, the loan was for a purpose known to be *ultra vires* and the debentures were void: *Introductions Ltd.* v. *National Provincial Bank Ltd.* [1970] Ch. 199 (C.A.). [Note: It is thought that if this case were to recur it would be decided differently because of section 9 of the European Communities Act 1972.]

(5) Power to issue bills of exchange.
(6) Power to sell or otherwise dispose of any part of the property of the company.

> A colliery company with express power to acquire land has been held to have implied power to sell it from time to time in a proper way.[67]

(7) Power to sell the undertaking of the company for shares in another company or other consideration.

> The Jenkins Report[68] recommended that, notwithstanding anything in the memorandum or articles, the directors should not be able, without the specific approval of the company in general meeting, to dispose of substantially the whole of the company's undertaking or assets.

(8) Power to give gratuities and pay pensions to officers and employees of the company and to their wives and other dependants.

---

[65] See *Re Barned's Banking Co.* (1867) L.R. 3 Ch.App. 105, and *Re Lands Allotment Co.* [1894] 1 Ch. 616 (C.A.), *post* pp. 347, 364.
[66] *General Auction Estate etc. Co.* v. *Smith* [1891] 3 Ch. 432, *post* p. 481.
[67] *Re Kingsbury Collieries Ltd. and Moore's Contract* [1907] 2 Ch. 259.
[68] Para. 122.

A company has implied power to make a gift which is: (a) reasonably incidental to the carrying on of the company's business; (b) a bona fide transaction; (c) done for the benefit of and to promote the prosperity of the company.[69]

In *Re Lee, Behrens & Co. Ltd.*[70] Eve J. held that the above three conditions must also be fulfilled in the case of an express power to make gifts but Pennycuick J. disagreed in the *Charterbridge* case, *ante*[71] and it is thought that condition (a) need not be fulfilled in the case of a gift made under an express power.

However, it is thought that conditions (b) and (c) must be fulfilled in the case of an express power as well as in the case of an implied power because they relate to the directors' duty to exercise their powers bona fide (honestly) and for the benefit of the company.[72] If this view is correct, and directors exercise a power to make a gift otherwise than bona fide for the benefit of the company; this is an abuse of power by the directors which can be ratified by the company in general meeting provided, in the case of an implied power, that the gift is reasonably incidental to the carrying on of the company's business. Of course, if a company with an implied power to make gifts makes one which is not so reasonably incidental, it is *ultra vires* and void and section 9 of the European Communities Act, *ante*,[73] may prevent the company from recovering the money from the donee, although it can recover from the directors. If such a gift is only proposed, a shareholder can bring an action to restrain it.

In *Hutton* v. *West Cork Rlwy. Co.* (1883) 23 Ch.D. 654 (C.A.), a company had disposed of the whole of its undertaking, was not a going concern as a trading body and only existed for the purpose of winding up. The company in general meeting resolved to expend part of the purchase money on a gratuitous payment to officials and directors. A holder of debenture stock with a right to vote at general meetings, who stood in the position of a dissentient shareholder, sought an injunction. *Held*, the resolution was invalid as the company was no longer a going concern.

"The law does not say that there are to be no cakes and ale, but there are to be no cakes and ale except such as are required for the benefit of the company." "Charity has no business to sit at boards of directors *qua* charity. There is, however, a kind of charitable dealing which is for the interest of those who practise it, and to that extent and in that garb (I admit not a very philanthropic garb) charity may sit at the board, but for no other purpose": *per* Bowen L.J. at p. 673.

---

[69] *Hutton* v. *West Cork Rlwy. Co.* (1883) 23 Ch.D. 654 (C.A.); *Parke* v. *Daily News Ltd.* [1962] Ch. 927.

[70] [1932] 2 Ch. 46, applied by Plowman J. in *Re W. & M. Roith Ltd.* [1967] 1 W.L.R. 432.   [71] p. 83.

[72] *Post* p. 350.   [73] p. 84.

In *Re Lee, Behrens & Co. Ltd.* [1932] 2 Ch. 46, the objects clause contained an express power to provide for the welfare of employees and ex-employees of the company, and their widows and children and other dependents, by granting money or pensions. Three years before winding up, the board of directors decided that the company should covenant to pay a pension to the widow of a former managing director. The liquidator rejected the widow's claim to the capitalised value of the pension. *Held*, the transaction was not for the benefit of the company or reasonably incidental to its business and was therefore *ultra vires* and void. The desire of the board was to provide for the widow and the question of what benefit would accrue to the company never presented itself.

Lee's case was applied and *Hutton's* case was followed in *Parke* v. *Daily News Ltd.* [1962] Ch. 927, where the company was not transferring the whole of its undertaking and proposed to continue trading. However, the board had agreed to sell the major part of its business (copyright in two newspapers together with plant and premises) and proposed to distribute the purchase price among former employees. A general meeting was called to approve the transaction. The company was not legally bound to pay any compensation to the employees. Nor was the purchaser. A minority shareholder claimed that the proposed payment was *ultra vires*. Plowman J. held that the proposed payment was *ultra vires* and incapable of ratification by the majority of the shareholders. The decision to pay compensation was motivated by a desire to treat the employees generously and was not taken in the interests of the company as it would remain. [Most of the purchase money later reached the ex-employees after a proper reduction of capital by returning to shareholders the capital paid up on their shares and not required by the company.][74]

Clause 7 of the Companies Bill 1973 provided that a company should have statutory power to make provision for employees or ex-employees on the cessation of the whole or part of its business.

Evans v. *Brunner, Mond & Co. Ltd.* [1921] 1 Ch. 359, is a different kind of case from those mentioned above. In that case a donation for scientific education and research by a chemical manufacturing company was held to be *intra vires*. The objects clause included an express power to do "all such business and things as may be incidental or conducive to the attainment of the above objects, or any of them." Such a power, it was decided, only authorises the company to do that which is incidental or conducive to the main object of the company, but the gift in question was so incidental.

Without any express mention in its memorandum a registered company has power to hold land for the purpose of carrying out the objects set out in the memorandum.[75]

The Jenkins Report recommended[76] that the Act should be amended to provide that every company should have certain specified powers except to the extent that they are excluded, expressly or by implication, by its memorandum; such powers being those which

---

[74] The Redundancy Payments Act 1965 requires employers, including companies, to make specified payments to employees who are dismissed by reason of redundancy.

[75] The Mortmain and Charitable Uses Acts of 1888, 1891 and 1892, and the Companies Act 1948, ss. 14 and 408, were repealed by the Charities Act 1960, s. 38 and Sched. 7, Pt. II A. The Mortmain Acts did not apply to Scotland. Nor did the Charities Act except so far as it repealed the Companies Act.

[76] Para. 54.

any company would normally need in order to pursue its objects. This might result in memoranda of association being drafted in less prolix terms by the omission of many common form powers.

Alteration of objects

If a company wishes to do something *ultra vires* it can usually alter its objects so that the transaction will be *intra vires*.

By section 5 a company may, by special resolution, alter the provisions of its memorandum with respect to its objects to enable the company:

(1) To carry on its business more economically or efficiently.

The objects clause was in the short form set out in Table B. An alteration gave the company general powers likely to be useful to it in its business. *Held*, the alteration enabled the company to carry on business more economically and efficiently: *Re New Westminster Brewery Co. Ltd.* [1911] W.N. 247.[77]

(2) To attain its main purpose by new or improved means.

The word "purpose" is more restricted than the term "object" and consequently the alteration must be one to carry out the main purpose of the company rather than one of the objects of the company, although that object may be described in the memorandum as a main object.[78]

The memorandum of a company, promoted to manage licensed premises mainly with a view to minimising evils of the drink traffic, provided that surplus profits, after payment of a dividend of not more than four per cent. per annum, should be applied to "purposes of public utility." The court doubted whether the company could competently alter the memorandum by deleting the provision as to surplus profits under (5) *infra*, but confirmed an amended alteration which increased the maximum dividend to six per cent., as being, in view of the changed financial situation, an improved means of attaining the company's main purpose: *Kirkcaldy Café Co. Ltd., Petitioners*, 1921 S.C. 681.

(3) To enlarge or change the local area of its operations.[79]

An alteration of this nature may necessitate an alteration in the name of the company.

A company, the principal object of which was to acquire land in Egypt, desired to alter its memorandum so as to give power to acquire land in the

---

[77] A comparable Scottish case is *North of Scotland etc. Steam Navigation Co. Ltd., Petitioners*, 1920 S.C. 633. See also *J. & P. Coats Ltd., Petitioners* (1900) 2 F. 829.
[78] *Re Governments Stock Investment Co.* [1891] 1 Ch. 649.
[79] A Scottish case illustrating "enlarge or change the local area of its operations" is *Scottish Veterans' Garden City Association (Incorporated), Petitioners*, 1946 S.C. 416.

Soudan. *Held*, the alteration could be made provided that the company inserted the words "and Soudan" after the word "Delta" in its name: *Re Egyptian Delta Land and Investment Co.* [1907] W.N. 16.[80]

> (4) To carry on some business which under existing circumstances may conveniently or advantageously be combined with the business of the company.[81] In this connection also a change of name may be required.[82]

The additional business to be carried on may be wholly different from the existing business of the company, and yet be capable of being conveniently or advantageously combined with it. Whether one business can be conveniently combined with another is essentially a business question to be determined by the persons engaged in the business of the company, namely the directors and the shareholders.

The company's business consisted of holding large investments in two companies. A special resolution was passed to enable the company to carry on the business of bankers, financiers, underwriters, and dealers in securities, *and to buy, sell and deal in real and personal estate of every description*. It was conceded that the words italicised were too wide. *Held*, subject to the omission of the words italicised the alteration was valid even though the new business bore no relation to the existing business: *Re Parent Tyre Co. Ltd.* [1923] 2 Ch. 222.[83]

A company may even add some business which its original memorandum specifically forbids.

A company which had power to carry on any kind of insurance business except life insurance was allowed to add life insurance to its objects on condition that it included "and Life" in its name: *Mutual Property Insurance Co. Ltd., Petitioners*, 1934 S.C. 61.

The additional business must not, however, be destructive of or inconsistent with the existing business. It must leave the existing business substantially what it was before.

The company's business was to promote, assist and protect cyclists. It was desired to include among the persons to be assisted all tourists, including motorists. *Held*, it was impossible to combine the two businesses, as one of the objects of the company was to protect cyclists against motorists: *Re Cyclists' Touring Club* [1907] 1 Ch. 269.

[80] Ct. *Kirkcaldy Steam Laundry Co. Ltd., Petitioners* (1904) 6 F. 778.
[81] Scottish cases illustrating this purpose are *Hugh Baird & Sons Ltd., Petitioners*, 1932 S.C. 455, *Dundee Aerated Water Mfg. Co. Ltd., Petitioners*, 1932 S.C. 473, and *King Line Petitioners* (1902) 4 F. 504.
[82] *Scottish Accident Insce. Co. Ltd., Petitioners* (1896) 23 R. 586; *Scottish Employers' Liability etc. Assce. Co. Ltd., Petitioners* (1896) 23 R. 1016.
[83] Scottish judges took a less liberal view: see *Western Ranches Ltd.* v. *Nelson's Trustees* (1899) 1 F. 812, and *Edinburgh Southern Cemetery Co. Ltd., Petitioners*, 1923 S.C. 867.

The provision does not "authorise the company to commit suicide . . . in other words, to do something which is inconsistent with the purpose of its incorporation." [84]

(5) To restrict or abandon any of the objects specified in the memorandum.

This provision cannot be used to enable a company to make a fundamental change in its character by the substitution of a new main object.

The original objects of a company were to build and let a public hall with shops and cellars. The building was destroyed by fire. The court refused to confirm an alteration to substitute for the original objects the erection and letting of shops and houses and warehouses: *Strathspey Public Assembly etc. Hall Co. Ltd.* v. *Anderson's Trustees*, 1934 S.C. 385.

An alteration of objects promoting a default beneficiary to the status of a primary object with regard to taking surplus assets on a winding up is not an alteration for purpose (5).

Clause 3 (1) (*t*) of a memorandum provided that surplus assets on a winding up should go to any institution having objects similar to those of the company and in default to any charity. The clause was altered so as to provide that any balance on a winding up should go to one specified charity. *Held*, the alteration was not one to enable the company "to restrict or abandon" any of its objects and was ineffective: *Re Hampstead Garden Suburb Trust Ltd.* [1962] Ch. 806; compare the *Kirkcaldy Café* case, *supra*.

(6) To sell or dispose of the whole or any part of the undertaking of the company.

(7) To amalgamate with any other company or body of persons.

Section 5 is not restricted to alteration of the objects *clause*. [85]

The section goes on to provide that certain dissentients may, however, within 21 days after the passing of the special resolution, apply to the court for an alteration of objects to be cancelled, and then the alteration is of no effect unless it is confirmed by the court. The application for cancellation can be made by the holders of not less than 15 per cent. in nominal value of the company's issued share capital or any class thereof [86] or, if the company is not limited by shares, not less than 15 per cent. of the members or, when

[84] *Per* Lord President Clyde in *Tayside Floorcloth Co. Ltd., Petitioners*, 1923 S.C. 590 at p. 592.

[85] *Incorporated Glasgow Dental Hospital* v. *Lord Advocate*, 1927 S.C. 400; *Scottish Special Housing Association Ltd., Petitioners*, 1947 S.C. 17.

[86] In the *Hampstead* case, *supra*, the petition was by the holders of not less than 15 per cent. in nominal value of the deferred shares.

debentures entitle the holders to object to an alteration of objects, by the holders of not less than 15 per cent. of the company's debentures. An application cannot be made by a person who consented to or voted for the alteration. Debentures entitling the holders to object are those secured by a floating charge[87] which were issued before December 1, 1947. The holders of such debentures must be given the same notice of a special resolution altering the company's objects as the members. In the *Hampstead* case, *ante*, it was held that notice to trustees for the debenture holders is not enough, even if the trust deed makes the trustees general agents for the debenture holders to receive notices.[88]

The section also provides that on an application for cancellation the court may confirm the alteration of objects wholly or in part and on such terms as it thinks fit, and may adjourn the proceedings to enable an arrangement to be made for the purchase, other than by the company, of the interests of dissentient members. Section 455, the interpretation section, provides that in the Act the expression "the court," used in relation to a company, means the court having jurisdiction to wind up the company. In the case of companies registered in England this is the High Court or, where the paid-up share capital does not exceed £10,000, the County Court of the district in which the registered office is situated, provided that it has jurisdiction in bankruptcy.[89]

Section 5 is thus a "minority section," *i.e.* a section designed to prevent the minority of the members of the company being oppressed by the majority.[90] Even though the special resolution altering the objects was passed by the appropriate majority, the alteration requires confirmation by the court if a dissentient minority of members applies to the court.

A company licensed to omit "Limited" from its name must give notice of a resolution altering its objects to the Department of Trade (s. 5 (6)) whereupon the Department may revoke or vary the licence (s. 19 (6)).

When the objects are altered, a printed copy of the special resolution, or a copy in some other form approved by him, must be delivered to the Registrar within 15 days (1948 Act, s. 143; 1967

---

[87] *Post* p. 498.
[88] The lack of notice to the debenture holders was another reason for the court's refusal to confirm the alteration.
[89] S. 218, *post* p. 539; by the Insolvency Act 1976 £12,000 is to be substituted for £10,000.   [90] *Post* p. 383.

Act, s. 51)[91] and, if no application is made for cancellation of the alteration, a printed copy of the memorandum as altered must be delivered to the Registrar between 21 and 36 days after the date of the resolution.[92] If an application for cancellation is made to the court, the company must forthwith give notice thereof to the Registrar and, on the alteration being cancelled or confirmed, an office copy of the court order must be delivered within 15 days. In the case of confirmation, a printed copy of the memorandum as altered must also be delivered: section 5 (7).

The validity of an alteration of objects cannot be questioned on the ground that it was not authorised by section 5 except in proceedings taken (whether under section 5 or otherwise) within 21 days after the date of the resolution: section 5 (9). The result would seem to be that if, within 21 days after an alteration of objects, an application for cancellation is made by a member or members, whether or not holding 15 per cent. of the issued shares, on the ground that the alteration was not for one of the seven purposes specified in section 5, the court must declare the alteration invalid. If no such application is made, an alteration for a purpose outside the seven specified purposes is valid.

The Jenkins Report recommended[93] that section 5 should be amended by doing away with the list of authorised alterations and substituting a general power of alteration. This amendment would make it appropriate to repeal subsection (9). It was also recommended that the dissentient shareholders or debenture holders who may apply to the court to cancel an alteration of objects should be five per cent. instead of 15 per cent. and the time within which they may apply should be 28 days instead of 21 days. Further, that the court should be enabled to authorise the application of the company's capital in the purchase of the interests of dissentients.

Clause 4 of the Companies Bill 1973 attempted to give effect to the above recommendations.

THE LIMITATION OF LIABILITY

Whether the liability of the members is limited by shares or by guarantee it is enough if the memorandum merely states that the liability of the members is limited: section 2.

[91] *Post* p. 308.
[92] Although the original memorandum need not have been printed.   [93] Para. 54.

Even though a company has under section 19[94] obtained the licence of the Department of Trade to dispense with the word "Limited" as part of its name, the memorandum must contain a statement that the liability of the members is limited.

We saw earlier that under section 31[95] members who know that the company is carrying on business with less than the statutory minimum of members may become severally liable for its debts and may be severally sued therefor, *i.e.* not only do they lose the privilege of limited liability but the veil of incorporation is lifted and they can be sued by the creditors of the company.

It may be noted that a limited company may be re-registered as unlimited (1967 Act, s. 43) and an unlimited company may be re-registered as limited (1967 Act, s. 44).[96]

THE SHARE CAPITAL

In the case of a limited company with a share capital, section 2 provides that the memorandum must state the amount of share capital with which the company proposes to be registered and its division into shares of a fixed amount, *e.g.* one hundred thousand pounds divided into one hundred thousand shares of one pound each. This capital, called the "nominal capital" or the "authorised capital," is that which the company is authorised to raise by the issue of shares. The amount of such capital will be determined by business considerations, and there is no fixed legal minimum or maximum. If it is proposed to purchase some property for £30,000, and £10,000 is wanted for working capital, the founders might fix the nominal capital at £60,000. This capital merely represents the aggregate amount of shares which the company is authorised to issue without paying further duty. The actual or issued capital will depend on how many shares are issued. The stated amount of each share is called its nominal amount or par value. Today it is usual to have shares of a nominal amount of £1 or less each because shares of such a nominal amount are more marketable than shares of £200 each like those in Table B.[97]

In 1974, 25,134 of the 39,884 companies with a share capital registered in England and Wales had a nominal share capital of under £100.

The Second Draft Directive submitted by the Commission to the Council of

---

[94] *Ante* p. 66.   [95] *Ante* p. 30.
[96] *Ante* p. 46 *et seq.*   [97] *Ante* p. 61.

Ministers of the EEC[98] provided that the laws of Member States shall require a minimum capital of 25,000 units of account (approximately £10,000) to be subscribed on formation of a public limited company and 4,000 units of account (£2,000) in the case of a U.K. private company in certain circumstances (Art. 6). If the shares are issued against cash they must be paid up to at least 25 per cent. of their nominal value and if allotted against investment not made in cash they must be entirely paid up (Art. 7). A valuation of assets bought in other than cash must be made prior to formation and published (Art. 8).

The shares into which the nominal capital is divided may be divided into classes, *e.g.* preference and ordinary shares, but it is usual to do this in the articles rather than in the memorandum.[99]

The nominal capital may be increased, if the articles authorise it, by an ordinary resolution under section 61.[1] Again, if the articles authorise it, capital can be reduced by a special resolution and the confirmation of the court under section 66.[2] No special provision need be made for these purposes in the memorandum.

A change in the description of a share from, say, 5s. to 25p is not a change in the fixed amount of the share within section 2 (4) and therefore is not an alteration of a condition of the memorandum so that no formalities are required by virtue of the Act.[3]

OTHER CLAUSES

The matters set out *supra must* be stated in the memorandum: section 2. The contents of the memorandum, however, are not restricted to these and may include any other provisions which the framers desire to insert. Sometimes the memorandum contains provisions dealing with the rights attaching to particular classes of shares such as preference shares, *e.g.* dividend and voting rights and the right to participate in the assets in a winding up. When this is so, the articles cannot be referred to for the purpose of ascertaining the rights of the shareholders, unless there is some ambiguity to be explained or some omission to be supplemented.

A company had ordinary and preference shares. The memorandum provided that the holders of the preference shares should have "a preferential right in the distribution of the assets of the company in the event of a winding up or otherwise." The articles provided that on a winding up the surplus assets after repayment of the whole of the paid-up capital should be divided between all the

[98] On March 5, 1970.
[99] See *Andrews* v. *Gas Meter Co.* [1897] 1 Ch. 361 (C.A.), *post* p. 212.
[1] *Post* p. 228.
[2] *Post* p. 235.
[3] *Re Harris & Sheldon Group Ltd.* [1971] 1 W.L.R. 899.

members in proportion to the capital paid up on their shares, both preference and ordinary. *Held*, (1) the rights conferred by the memorandum on the preference shareholders were exhaustive; (2) they were limited to a preference in the distribution of the assets, and gave no right to participate in the surplus assets in a winding up or otherwise; and (3) the articles could not be referred to for the purpose of construing the memorandum: *Re Duncan Gilmour & Co. Ltd.* [1952] 2 All E.R. 871.[4]

However, the rights of the holders of particular classes of shares are now usually contained in the articles.

THE ASSOCIATION CLAUSE AND SUBSCRIPTION

The association clause is the clause by which the subscribers to the memorandum (at least seven for a public company, two for a private company: section 1) declare that they desire to be formed into a company in pursuance of the memorandum and agree to take the number of shares set opposite their respective names. The subscription contains their names, addresses and descriptions and the number of shares which each subscribes for. The subscribers must take at least one share each: section 2. Each subscriber must write opposite his name the number of shares he takes (s. 2) and must sign in the presence of at least one witness (s. 3). The signatures must be attested but one witness may attest all or both the signatures: section 3. The Registrar requires the date of execution to be given.

It is usual for each subscriber to sign the memorandum for one share only. This is because the subscriber may by contract be bound to take up a definite number of shares in the company, and if he has signed the memorandum for that number he might be bound to take twice the number he intended, once under his contract, and again under the memorandum.

The subscribers need not be independent persons. They may be nominees, or one of two subscribers may be a trustee, of the one share for which he subscribes, for the other subscriber to whom all the rest of the shares issued are allotted,[5] *i.e.* a "one-man" company is legal.

A minor[6] may sign the memorandum because, the contract being voidable and not void, any subsequent avoidance by him will not invalidate the registration.[7]

---

[4] *Cf. Liquidator of the Milford Haven Fishing Co. Ltd.* v. *Jones* (1895) 22 R. 577.
[5] See *Salomon* v. *Salomon & Co. Ltd.* [1897] A.C. 22.
[6] *i.e.* a person under the age of 18: see *post* p. 187.
[7] *Re Laxon & Co.* (*No.* 2) [1892] 3 Ch. 555. And see s. 15 (1), *ante* p. 26.

Another, existing, company may sign the memorandum. So can a person who is a partner in a firm, but an English firm cannot.

It is no objection that all the signatories are foreigners resident abroad,[8] or that the signatories include a person resident outside the "Scheduled Territories," *i.e.* the United Kingdom, the Channel Islands, the Isle of Man, the Republic of Ireland and Gibraltar.[9] If a person resident outside the Scheduled Territories, or a nominee for a person so resident, subscribes a memorandum without Treasury permission, he does not become a member of the company on registration of the memorandum, so that section 31, *ante*, might apply. However, the incorporation of the company is not invalidated.[10]

ALTERATION OF THE MEMORANDUM GENERALLY

A company may alter its memorandum of association only in the cases, in the mode and to the extent for which express provision is made in the Act: section 4. It has been seen that the name, objects and share capital clauses may be altered under sections 18, 5 and 61 and 66 respectively, *ante*. In addition. by section 23, subject to the provisions of sections 22 and 210, *infra*, any condition in the memorandum which could have been in the articles (*i.e.*, not such things as the name, the objects or the share capital, which must be in the memorandum) can be altered by special resolution, unless the memorandum itself provides for or prohibits the alteration of the condition, or it relates to class rights, *i.e.* the special rights of any class of members.

The *Hampstead Garden Suburb* case,[11] *ante*,[12] shows that if a company elects to express a given function as an object, *e.g.* the distribution of surplus assets in a winding up, it must be contained in the memorandum by virtue of section 2 and cannot be altered under section 23. The modes in which class rights may be varied are explained later.[13] Since provisions concerning class rights are the only important provisions which may be in either the memorandum or the articles, and they cannot be altered under section 23 if they are

---

[8] *Princess of Reuss* v. *Bos* (1871) L.R. 5 H.L. 176.
[9] Exchange Control (Scheduled Territories) (No. 2) Order 1972 (S.I. 1972/930. June 23, 1972); Exchange Control (Scheduled Territories) (Amendment) (No. 2) Order 1972 (S.I. 1972/2040. December 21, 1972).
[10] Exchange Control Act 1947, s. 8.
[11] *Re Hampstead Garden Suburb Trust Ltd.* [1962] Ch. 806.
[12] p. 91.
[13] *Post* p. 217.

in the memorandum, it follows that the section is unimportant in practice. Further, as was stated earlier, class rights are normally contained in the articles.

Section 23 contains the same provisions as to application to the court for cancellation of an alteration as section 5,[14] except that debenture holders cannot apply and there is no equivalent of section 5 (9).

Section 22 provides that neither the memorandum nor the articles can be altered so as to require a member to take up more shares, or in any way increase his liability to contribute to the share capital or otherwise pay money to the company, unless he consents in writing. Section 22 is, therefore, a "minority section," *i.e.* a section intended to prevent the minority of the members being oppressed by the majority.[15] Under section 210 the court can make an order to relieve an oppressed part of the members and such an order may alter the memorandum or the articles, in which event the company cannot make a further alteration, inconsistent with the order, without the leave of the court (s. 210 (3)).[16]

Any document making or evidencing an alteration in the memorandum or articles, and any copy of the memorandum or articles as altered, must be in the same language as the memorandum and articles originally registered[17] and, if that language is Welsh, must be accompanied by a certified translation into English (1976 Act, s. 30 (7)).

Section 9 (5) of the European Communities Act 1972 provides that where a company is required to send the Registrar any document making or evidencing an alteration in the company's memorandum or articles (other than a special resolution under section 5) the company must send with it a printed copy of the memorandum or articles as altered. As to what is "printed", see the Pamphlet "Notes for the Guidance of Registered Companies" (C. 56a, 6th revise, October 1974).[18]

Section 9 (3) of the 1972 Act requires the Registrar to publish in the *Gazette* notice of the receipt by him of any document making or evidencing an alteration in the memorandum or articles of a company. Section 9 (4) provides that a company cannot rely against

---

[14] *Ante* p. 91.
[15] *Post* p. 383.
[16] *Post* p. 389.
[17] *Ante* p. 23.
[18] *Post* p. 105.

other persons on any alteration to the memorandum or articles if it had not been officially notified (under s. 9 (3)) at the material time and is not shown by the company to have been known at that time to the person concerned, or if the material time is less than 16 days after official notification and it is shown that the person concerned was unavoidably prevented from knowing of the event at that time.

SPECIMEN MEMORANDUM OF ASSOCIATION
The Companies Acts 1948 *to* 1976

———

COMPANY LIMITED BY SHARES

———

10995293/3
MEMORANDUM OF ASSOCIATION
OF
X.Y.Z. EUROPE LIMITED

1. The name of the Company is "X.Y.Z. EUROPE LIMITED."

2. The registered office of the Company will be situate in England.

3. The objects for which the Company is established are—

   (A) To carry on the business of manufacturers and suppliers of and dealers in products or commodities of all kinds comprising or constituting components of or being associated with or for use in or in connection with, and suppliers of services in relation to, vehicles of all descriptions, including motor vehicles, aircraft and ships, engineering of whatsoever nature, electrical and electronic equipment, cables, chemicals, natural and synthetic rubber and foam, general rubber goods, hose, belting, fire protection, flooring, textiles, sports equipment, footwear, paper, plastics and products, commodities and services of whatever nature which can conveniently be manufactured, supplied or dealt in by the Company, and to carry on any other business which can conveniently be carried on in connection with any of the Company's objects.

   (B) To acquire and hold shares, stocks, debentures, debenture stock or other securities or obligations of any other company incorporated in or carrying on business in any part of the world.

   (C) To carry on the business of planters, growers and cultivators of rubber, gutta percha and other produce of the soil, and to treat, process, prepare, render marketable, buy, sell and dispose of any such products either in their raw or manufactured state and any product or by-product derived therefrom.

   (D) To carry on research and development work and experiments.

(E) To procure the Company to be registered or recognised in any country or place outside the United Kingdom.

(F) To amalgamate or enter into partnership or into any arrangement for sharing of profits, union of interests, co-operation, joint adventure reciprocal concession or otherwise with any person, firm or company carrying on or engaged in or about to carry on or engage in any business or transaction which the Company is authorised to carry on or engage in, or any business or transaction capable of being conducted so as directly or indirectly to benefit the Company.

(G) To carry on any other trade or business whatsoever which can, in the opinion of the Directors, be advantageously carried on by the Company in connection with or as auxiliary to the general business of the Company.

(H) To buy, sell, manufacture, repair, alter, improve, manipulate, prepare for market, let on hire, and generally deal in all kinds of plant, machinery, apparatus, tools, utensils, materials, produce, substances, articles and things for the purpose of any of the businesses specified herein, or likely to be required by customers or other persons having, or about to have, dealings with the Company.

(I) To enter into contracts, agreements and arrangements with any other company for the carrying out by such other company on behalf of the Company of any of the objects for which the Company is formed.

(J) To acquire, undertake and carry on the whole or any part of the business, property and liabilities of any person or company carrying on any business which the Company is authorised to carry on or possess, or which may seem to the Company capable of being conveniently carried on or calculated directly or indirectly to enhance the value of or render profitable any of the Company's property or rights, or any property suitable for the purposes of the Company.

(K) To enter into any arrangements with any government or authorities, supreme, municipal, local or otherwise that may seem conducive to the Company's objects or any of them, and to obtain from any such government or authority any rights, privileges and concessions which the Company may think it desirable to obtain, and to carry out, exercise and comply with any such arrangements, rights, privileges and concessions.

(L) To apply for, or join in applying for, purchase or by other means acquire and protect, prolong and renew, whether in the United Kingdom or elsewhere, any patents, patent rights, brêvets d'invention, licences, registered designs, protections and concessions, which may appear likely to be advantageous or useful to the Company, and to use, and turn to account and to manufacture under or grant licences or privileges in respect of the same, and to expend money in experimenting and testing and making researches, and in improving or seeking to improve any patents, inventions or rights which the Company may acquire or propose to acquire.

(M) To subsidise, assist and guarantee the payment of money by or the performance of any contract, engagement or obligation by any persons or companies and to act as agents for the collection, receipt or payment of money and generally to act as agents for and render services to customers and others.

(N) To promote any company for the purpose of acquiring all or any of the property and liabilities of this Company, or for any other purpose which may seem directly or indirectly calculated to benefit this Company.

(o) To pay out of the funds of the Company all expenses which the Company may lawfully pay of or incidental to the formation, registration and advertising of or raising money for the Company, and the issue of its capital, or for contributing to or assisting any company either issuing or purchasing with a view to issue all or any part of the Company's capital in connection with the advertising or offering the same for sale or subscription, including brokerage and commissions for obtaining applications for or taking, placing or underwriting or procuring the underwriting of shares, debentures or debenture stock.

(P) Generally to purchase, take on lease or exchange, hire, or otherwise acquire any real or personal property and any rights or privileges which the Company may think necessary or convenient for the purposes of its business.

(Q) To receive money on deposit upon such terms as the Company may approve.

(R) To invest and deal with the moneys of the Company in such manner as may from time to time be determined.

(s) To lend money with or without security, but not to carry on the business of a registered money lender.

(T) To borrow or raise or secure the payment of money in such manner as the Company shall think fit, and in particular by the issue of debentures or debenture stock, perpetual or otherwise charged upon all or any of the Company's property (both present and future), including its uncalled capital, and to purchase, redeem or pay off any such securities.

(U) To remunerate any company for services rendered or to be rendered in placing or assisting to place or guaranteeing the placing or procuring the underwriting of any of the shares or debentures or other securities of the Company, or of any company in which this Company may be interested or propose to be interested, or in or about the conduct of the business of the Company, whether by cash payment or by the allotment of shares or securities of the Company credited as paid up in full or in part, or otherwise.

(v) To draw, make, accept, endorse, discount, execute and issue promissory notes, bills of lading, warrants, debentures and other negotiable and transferable instruments.

(w) To sell, lease, exchange, let on hire or dispose of any real or personal property or the undertaking of the Company, or any part or parts thereof, for such consideration as the Company may think fit, and in particular for shares, whether fully or partly paid up, debentures or securities of any other company, whether or not having objects altogether or in part similar to those of the Company, and to hold and retain any shares, debentures or securities so acquired, and to improve, manage, develop, sell, exchange, lease, mortgage, dispose of or turn to account or otherwise deal with all or any part of the property or rights of the Company.

(x) To adopt such means of making known the products of the Company as may seem expedient, and in particular by advertising in the Press, by circulars, by purchase and exhibition of works of art or interest, by publication of books and periodicals, and by granting prizes, rewards and donations.

(Y) To support or subscribe to any charitable or public object and any institution, society or club which may be for the benefit of the Company or its Directors, officers or employees, or the directors, officers and employees of its predecessors in business, or of any subsidiary, allied or associated company, or may be connected with any town or place where the Company carries on business; to give pensions, gratuities or charitable aid to any person who may have served the Company or its predecessors in business, or any subsidiary, allied or associated company, or to the wives, children or other relatives or dependants of such persons; to make payments towards insurance and to form and contribute to provident and benefit funds for the benefit of any Directors or officers of or persons employed by the Company, or of or by its predecessors in business, or of or by any subsidiary, allied or associated company, and to subsidise or assist any association of employers or employees, or any trade association.

(z) To obtain any Provisional Order or Act of Parliament for enabling the Company to carry any of its objects into effect or for effecting any modifications of the Company's constitution, or for any other purposes which may seem expedient, and to oppose any proceedings or applications which may seem calculated directly or indirectly to prejudice the Company's interests.

(AA) To establish, grant and take up agencies in any part of the world, and to do all such other things as the Company may deem conducive to the carrying on of the Company's business, either as principals, or agents, and to remunerate any persons in connection with the establishment or granting of such agencies upon such terms and conditions as the Company may think fit.

(BB) To do all or any of the above things in any part of the world, and as principals, agents, contractors, trustees or otherwise, and by or through trustees, agents or otherwise, and either alone or in conjunction with others.

(CC) To distribute any of the property of the Company in specie among the shareholders.

(DD) To do all such other things whatsoever, whether of the like or other sorts, which the Company consider to be in any way incidental to or conducive with any of the above objects, or conducive to the attainment thereof, or otherwise likely in any respect to be advantageous to the Company.

And it is hereby declared that the word "company" in this clause shall be deemed to include any person or partnership or other body of persons whether domiciled in the United Kingdom or elsewhere, and words denoting the singular number only shall include the plural number and vice versa, and so that the objects specified in each paragraph of this clause shall, except where otherwise expressed in such paragraph, be regarded as independent objects and in nowise limited or restricted by reference to or inference from the terms of any other paragraph or the name of the Company.

4. The liability of the members is limited.

5. The share capital of the Company is £100, divided into 100 Ordinary Shares of £1 each.

WE, the several persons whose names and addresses are subscribed, are desirous of being formed into a Company in pursuance of this Memorandum of Association, and we respectively agree to take the number of shares in the capital of the Company set opposite our respective names.

NAMES, ADDRESSES AND DESCRIPTIONS OF SUBSCRIBERS	Number of Shares taken by each Subscriber
A.B.C. 100A Old Jewry, London EC2 Solicitor	One
D.E.F. 100A Old Jewry, London EC2 Solicitor	One

Dated this 17th day of November, 1976
Witness to the above Signatures—

          G.H.I.
          44 Old Jewry,
          London E.C.2
          Solicitor

CHAPTER 4

ARTICLES OF ASSOCIATION

WHEREAS the memorandum is the company's charter, indicating its nationality, the nature of its business and its capital, the articles of association are the regulations for the internal arrangements and the management of the company. The articles deal with the issue of shares, transfer of shares, alteration of share capital, general meetings, voting rights, directors (including their appointment and powers), managing director, secretary, dividends, accounts, audit of accounts, winding up and various other matters which will be referred to later.

Re Duncan Gilmour, *ante*,[1] shows that, as between the memorandum and the articles, the memorandum is the dominant instrument so that in so far as their provisions conflict the memorandum prevails, although, apart from matters which by statute must be in the memorandum, reference may be made to the articles to explain an ambiguity in the memorandum or to supplement it where it is silent.[2]

Now that all the provisions of the memorandum, other than, *e.g.* the registered office clause, can be freely altered, the memorandum could be combined with the articles, and it is questionable whether there is any reason for having a memorandum and also articles rather than one document embodying the contents of both.

Section 6 provides that articles *may*, in the case of a company limited by shares, and *must* in the case of a company limited by guarantee[3] or an unlimited company,[3] be registered with the memorandum.

Articles may adopt all or any of the regulations in Table A: section 8 (1). Table A in Schedule 1 to the Act is a model form of articles for a company limited by shares. It is in two parts—Part I designed for a public company, Part II for a private company.[4] Thus a company may (1) adopt Table A in full, (2) adopt Table A

---

[1] p. 96.
[2] In *Liquidator of The Humboldt Redwood Co. Ltd.* v. *Coats*, 1908 S.C. 751, the memorandum was silent on the point and so the articles governed.
[3] Chap. 2.
[4] See *post*.

subject to modifications, or (3) register its own articles and exclude Table A.

In the case of a company limited by shares, if articles are not registered, or, if articles are registered, in so far as they do not modify or exclude Table A, Table A will automatically be the company's articles: section 8 (2). Thus, if a public company limited by shares does not register articles, Table A, Part I, will apply.

In the case of companies registered between April 1, 1909, and November 1, 1929, Table A in the Companies (Consolidation) Act 1908, applies, and to companies registered after the latter date and before July 1, 1948, Table A in the Companies Act 1929, applies.

A private company should register articles adopting the restrictive and prohibitive provisions of section 28[5] and indicating how the transfer of shares is restricted. In addition, all or any of the regulations in Table A may be adopted. If, as is preferable, the regulations in Part II of Table A are adopted, the subscribers to the memorandum must indicate their wishes by indorsing on the memorandum some words such as: "Private company limited by shares. Table A, Part II, to apply." In so far as the articles registered do not exclude or modify them, the regulations in Table A, Part II, will apply to the company.

Articles must—

(1) be printed (typewriting is not admissible);
(2) be divided into paragraphs numbered consecutively;
(3) be signed by each subscriber to the memorandum of association in the presence of at least one witness, who must attest the signature. Such attestation is sufficient in Scotland as well as in England: sections 6, 9.[6]

Articles must be dated.

If the memorandum states that the registered office is to be situated in Wales, the memorandum and articles to be delivered for registration under section 12 of the 1948 Act may be in Welsh but, if they are, they must be accompanied by a certificate of translation into English: section 30 (6) of the 1976 Act.

The Registrar accepts the following processes as satisfying the printing stipulation:
Letterpress, gravure, lithography.
Stencil duplicating using waxed stencils and black ink, offset lithography, "office" type-set.

[5] *Ante* p. 49.
[6] As amended by Finance Act 1970, Sched. 7, para. 1, *ante* p. 26.

Electrostatic photocopying.
"Photostat" or similar processes properly washed.[7]

The articles (and the memorandum) form a contract between the company and each member and between the members. The articles can be altered by special resolution.

Effect of memorandum and articles

Subject to the provisions of the Act, the memorandum and articles, when registered, bind the company and the members as if they had been signed and sealed by each member, and contained covenants on the part of each member to observe their provisions: section 20. The result is:

(1) The articles (and the memorandum) form a contract binding the members to the company. Presumably the rule in *Foss* v. *Harbottle infra* applies, *i.e.* an action to enforce the contract must be brought in the name of the company, except where a personal right is infringed.

> The articles provided for the reference of differences between the company and any of the members to arbitration. H., a shareholder, brought an action against the company in connection with a dispute as to his expulsion from the company, *i.e.* a dispute between the company and him in his capacity as a member. *Held*, the company was entitled to have the action stayed, as the articles constituted a contract between the company and its members in respect of their ordinary rights as members: *Hickman* v. *Kent or Romney Marsh Sheep-Breeders' Assocn.* [1915] 1 Ch. 881.[8]
>
> ". . . articles regulating the rights and obligations of the members generally as such do create rights and obligations between them and the company respectively": *per* Astbury J. at p. 900.
>
> A dispute as to a director's right to inspect the company's books, and accounts, including minutes of board meetings, *i.e.* a dispute between the company and the director in his capacity as director, is not within the terms of articles like those in *Hickman's* case *supra* even though the director is also a member. The plaintiff sued for, *inter alia*, a declaration in a representative capacity as a shareholder. It was then claimed that a director had received remuneration to which he was not entitled. He asked for a stay but was refused it: *Beattie* v. *E. & F. Beattie Ltd.* [1938] Ch. 708 (C.A.).

(2) Although section 20 does *not* provide that the memorandum and articles shall bind the company and the members as if

---

[7] Notes for the Guidance of Registered Companies (C. 56a, 6th revise, Oct. 1974).
[8] An article prohibiting any member from taking legal proceedings against his company is contrary to public policy and not binding: *St. Johnstone Football Club Ltd.* v. *Scottish Football Assocn. Ltd.*, 1965 S.L.T. 171 (O.H.).

they had been signed and sealed *by the company*, and contained covenants *on the part of the company* to observe their provisions, the articles constitute a contract binding the company to members.

> A company declared a dividend and passed a resolution to pay it by giving to the shareholders debenture bonds bearing interest and redeemable at par, by an annual drawing, over thirty years. The articles empowered the company to declare a dividend "to be paid" to the shareholders. *Held*, the words "to be paid" meant paid in cash, and a shareholder could restrain the company from acting on the resolution on the ground that it contravened the articles: *Wood* v. *Odessa Waterworks Co.* (1889) 42 Ch.D. 636.

(3) Members are only bound by and entitled on the above-mentioned contract *qua* members, *i.e.* in their capacity as members: *Beattie* v. *E. & F. Beattie Ltd., ante*; *Eley* v. *Positive Life Assurance Co. Ltd., post*.

(4) The articles (and the memorandum) constitute a contract between each individual member and every other member but in most cases the court will not enforce the contract as between individual members [9] it is enforceable only through the company or, if the company is being wound up, the liquidator.

> "It is quite true that . . . there is no contract in terms between the individual members of the company; but the articles . . . regulate their rights *inter se*. Such rights can only be enforced by or against a member through the company, or through the liquidator representing the company; but . . . no member has, as between himself and another member, any right beyond that which the contract with the company gives": *per* Lord Herschell in *Welton* v. *Saffery* [1897] A.C. 299 at p. 315.

It seems that it is the rule in *Foss* v. *Harbottle*[10] which prevents an individual member enforcing the contract. However, the rule is irrelevant where the articles give a member a personal right. In such a case the contract is directly enforceable by one member against another *without* the aid of the company.

> Articles of a private company provided that if a member intending to transfer his shares should inform the directors, the *directors* "will take the said shares equally between them at a fair value." *Held*, the articles bound the defendant directors to buy the plaintiff's shares and related to the relationship between the

[9] *Per* Farwell L.J. in *Salmon* v. *Quin and Axtens Ltd.* [1909] 1 Ch. 311 (C.A.) at p. 318.
[10] *Post* p. 376.

plaintiff as a member and the defendants, not as directors, but as members of the company,[11] and it was not necessary for the company to be a party to the action: *Rayfield* v. *Hands* [1960] Ch. 1.

(5) The provisions of the articles and the memorandum do not constitute a contract binding the company or any member to an outsider,[12] *i.e.* a person who is not a member of the company,[13] or to a member in a capacity other than that of member, *e.g.* that of solicitor, promoter or director of the company.[12]

This is on the general principle that a person not a party to a contract has neither rights nor liabilities under it.

> The articles provided that E. should be the solicitor to the company. He was employed as such for a time but subsequently the company ceased to employ him. *Held*, E. was not entitled to damages for breach of contract against the company. The articles did not create a contract between E. and the company: *Eley* v. *Positive Life Assurance Co. Ltd.* (1876) 1 Ex.D. 88 (C.A.).[14]

However, if a director takes office on the footing of an article providing for remuneration for the director, although the article is not in itself a contract between the company and the director, its terms are part of the contract between the company and the director.

An article provided that the remuneration of the directors should be the annual sum of £1,000. The directors were employed and accepted office on the footing of the article. For some time the directors, who were also members, acted as directors but were not paid. The company went into liquidation. *Held*, the article was embodied in the contract between the company and the directors and they were entitled to recover the arrears of remuneration: *Re New British Iron Co.* [1898] 1 Ch. 324.

(6) Because of the words "Subject to the provisions of this Act" in section 20, the contract constituted by the memorandum and articles can be varied to the extent that those documents can be altered in accordance with the provisions of the Act. The extent to which the memorandum may be altered has been dealt with already.[15] It will be seen shortly that, subject to a number of restrictions, the company may alter the articles by special resolution.

---

[11] As is usual, the directors had shares in the company and so were members.
[12] See *per* Astbury J. in *Hickman's* case at p. 900.
[13] A Scots illustration is *National Bank of Scotland Glasgow Nominees Ltd.* v. *Adamson*, 1932 S.L.T. 492 (O.H.).
[14] A comparable Scottish case is *Muirhead* v. *Forth etc. Steamboat Mutual Insce. Assocn.* (1893) 21R. (H.L.); (1893) 20R. 442.
[15] *Ante* p. 97.

Alteration of articles

Subject to the provisions of the Act and to the conditions in its memorandum, a company may by special resolution alter or add to its articles. An alteration or addition so made is as valid and can be altered in the same way as if originally contained in the articles: section 10. Thus a provision in the articles purporting to deprive the company of its power to alter them is void,[16] *e.g.* a provision that no alteration of articles shall be effective without the consent of X. or that on a proposed alteration only the shares of those opposed shall have a vote.[17]

(1) By section 10 the power to alter articles is subject to the provisions of the Act, *e.g.* sections 22 and 210, *ante*,[18] and section 72.[19]

If, as is common, special rights are attached to a class of shares by the articles and the articles contain a "modification of rights clause" such as Table A. article 4[20] (which provides for alteration of the class rights with the consent of a specified proportion or the sanction of a specified resolution of the shareholders of the class), then it seems that the class rights can only be altered with such consent or sanction.[21] Further, by section 72 dissentient holders of not less in the aggregate than 15 per cent. of the issued shares of the class may, within 21 days after the consent was given, apply to the court to have the variation cancelled.[19]

(2) A company's power to alter its articles is subject to the conditions in the memorandum: section 10. Consequently an alteration of articles must not conflict with the memorandum.

(3) Under the general law the power to alter articles must be exercised bona fide for the benefit of the company as a whole.

Articles gave the company a lien on partly paid shares for all debts and liabilities of a member to the company. Z., on his death, owed money to the company (arrears of calls on partly paid shares), and was the only holder of fully paid shares. The articles were altered so as to give the company a lien on fully paid shares.

---

[16] *Malleson* v. *National Insurance Corporation* [1894] 1 Ch. 200.
[17] *Per* Russell L.J. in *Bushell* v. *Faith* [1969] 2 Ch. 438 (C.A.) at p. 448.
[18] p. 98.
[19] *Post* p. 220.   [20] *Post* p. 219.
[21] *Crumpton* v. *Morrine Hall Pty. Ltd.* [1965] N.S.W.R. 240, *post* p. 113; *Re Old Silkstone Collieries Ltd.* [1954] Ch. 169 (C.A.), *post* p. 240; *Re Holders Investment Trust Ltd.* [1971] 1 W.L.R. 583, *post* p. 220; *contra Fischer* v. *Easthaven Ltd.* [1964] N.S.W.R. 261, *post* p. 113.

Held, the alteration was valid and, as from the date of the alteration, gave the company a lien on Z.'s fully paid shares in respect of the debts contracted before the date of the alteration: *Allen* v. *Gold Reefs of West Africa Ltd.* [1900] 1 Ch. 656 (C.A.).[22]

The power conferred on companies to alter articles "must, like all other powers, be exercised subject to those general principles of law and equity which are applicable to all powers conferred on majorities and enabling them to bind minorities. It must be exercised, not only in the manner required by law, but also bona fide for the benefit of the company as a whole, and it must not be exceeded. These conditions are always implied, and are seldom, if ever, expressed": *Per* Lord Lindley M.R. at p. 671. "The fact that Zuccani's executors were the only persons practically affected at the time by the alterations made in the articles excites suspicion as to the bona fides of the company. But, although the executors were the only persons who were actually affected at the time, that was because Zuccani was the only holder of paid-up shares who at the time was in arrear of calls. The altered articles applied to all holders of fully paid shares, and made no distinction between them. The directors cannot be charged with bad faith": *Per* Lord Lindley M.R. at p. 675. "Further, I may say that the alteration of the articles giving the extended lien was, in my opinion, in no true sense retrospective. The lien given was not made to take effect before the date of the alteration. It operated only from and after that date": *Per* Romer L.J. at p. 682.

It is for the shareholders, and not for the court to say whether an alteration of articles is for the benefit of the company, unless no reasonable man could so regard it.

The articles provided that S. and four others should be permanent directors of the company, unless they should become disqualified by any one of six specified events. None of the six events had occurred. S. on 22 occasions within 12 months failed to account for the company's money he had received, and the articles were accordingly altered by adding a seventh event disqualifying a director, namely, a request in writing signed by all the other directors that he should resign. Such a request was made to S., who was also a shareholder. *Held,* the contract, if any, between the plaintiff and the company contained in the original articles was subject to the statutory power of alteration, and the alteration was bona fide for the benefit of the company as a whole and valid: *Shuttleworth* v. *Cox Bros. & Co. (Maidenhead) Ltd.* [1927] 2 K.B. 9 (C.A.).

"Then the first thing to be considered is whether, in formulating the test I have mentioned, Lindley M.R. [in *Allen's* case *supra*] had in mind two separate and distinct matters; first, bona fides, the state of mind of the persons whose act is complained of, and secondly, whether the alteration is for the benefit of the company, apart altogether from the state of mind of those who procured it. In my opinion this view of the test has been negatived by this Court in *Sidebottom's* case.[22a] So the test is whether the alteration of the articles was in the opinion of the shareholders for the benefit of the company. By what criterion is the Court to ascertain the opinion of the shareholders upon this question? The alteration may be so oppressive as to cast suspicion on the honesty of the persons responsible for it, or so extravagant that no reasonable men could really consider it for the benefit of the company": *Per* Bankes L.J. at p. 18. See also *per* Scrutton L.J. at p. 23.

[22] *Cf. Liquidator of W. & A. M'Arthur Ltd.* v. *Gulf Line Ltd.,* 1909 S.C. 732. For comments on *Allen's* case, see *Moir* v. *Thomas Duff & Co. Ltd.* (1900) 2 F. 1265.
[22a] *Post* p. 111

The expression "bona fide for the benefit of the company as a whole" means that the shareholder must proceed upon what, in his honest opinion, is for the benefit of the company as a whole. The phrase "the company as a whole" does not mean the company as a commercial entity, distinct from the corporators; it means the corporators as a general body. It may be asked whether what is proposed is, in the honest opinion of those who voted in its favour, for the benefit of an individual hypothetical member. Looking at the converse, an alteration of articles is liable to be impeached if its effect is to discriminate between the majority shareholders and the minority so as to give the former an advantage of which the latter are deprived. It is not necessary that persons voting for an alteration of articles should dissociate themselves altogether from their own prospects.[23]

The articles of a private company prohibited a transfer of shares to a non-member so long as another member was willing to buy them at a fair value. The holder of the majority of the shares wished to transfer them to a non-member, so the articles were altered so as to permit a transfer to any person with the sanction of an ordinary resolution. *Held*, the alteration was bona fide and valid, although thereby the minority lost their rights of pre-emption: *Greenhalgh* v. *Arderne Cinemas Ltd.* [1951] Ch. 286 (C.A.).[24]

It has been said that the phrase "corporators as a general body" means both present and future members of the company.[25]

If an alteration of articles is bona fide for the benefit of the company, it is immaterial that it prejudices a minority of the members.

A private company, in which the directors held a majority of the shares, altered its articles so as to give the directors power to require any shareholder who competed with the company's business to transfer his shares, at their fair value, to nominees of the directors. S., who had a minority of the shares and was in competition with the company, brought an action for a declaration that the special resolution was invalid. *Held*, (1) as a power to expel a shareholder by buying him out was valid in the case of original articles it could be introduced in altered articles, provided that the alteration was made bona fide for the benefit of the company as a whole; (2) the alteration was so made and was valid: *Sidebottom* v. *Kershaw, Leese & Co. Ltd.* [1920] 1 Ch. 154 (C.A.).[26]

"I think . . . that it is for the benefit of the company that they should not be obliged to have amongst them as members persons who are competing with them in business and who may get knowledge from their membership which would enable them to compete better": *Per* Lord Sterndale M.R. at p. 166.

[23] *Per* Lord Evershed M.R. in *Greenhalgh* v. *Arderne Cinemas* [1951] Ch. 286 (C.A.) at p. 291.
[24] *Cf. Crumpton* v. *Morrine Hall Pty. Ltd.* [1965] N.S.W.R. 240, *post* p. 113.
[25] *Per* Megarry J. in *Gaiman* v. *National Association of Mental Health* [1971] 1 Ch. 317 at p. 330.
[26] See also *Crookston* v. *Lindsay, Crookston & Co. Ltd.*, 1922 S.L.T. 62 (O.H.)

The principles of natural justice are not applicable in this field.[27]

It has been held that the members of a company, acting in accordance with the Act and the constitution of the company, and subject to any necessary consent on the part of the class affected, can alter the relative voting powers attached by the articles to various classes of shares, provided that the special resolution is passed in good faith for the benefit of the company as a whole.

The issued capital of S. Ltd. comprised 400,000 management shares, which under the articles carried 8 votes each, and 3,600,000 ordinary shares. On the acquisition by S. Ltd. of the shares in B. Ltd. in consideration of the issue of 8,400,000 ordinary shares in S. Ltd., the articles were altered so as to double the votes carried by management shares in order to ensure continuity of management. The special resolution was passed by a large majority at an extraordinary general meeting of the company. The holders of management shares, directors of S. Ltd., did not vote in respect of these shares or their ordinary shares. Nor did they vote at a separate class meeting of the ordinary shareholders which sanctioned the special resolution. *Held*, the alteration was valid: *Rights and Issues Investment Trust Ltd.* v. *Stylo Shoes Ltd.* [1965] Ch. 250.[28]

However, it has been said that the benefit of the company as a whole is an impossible test where the question is simply one as to the relative rights of different classes of shareholders. In this event there must be no fraud or oppression of the minority.[29]

The onus of showing that the power to alter articles has not been properly exercised is on the party complaining.[30]

If, in a rare case, an alteration is not for the benefit of the company as a whole, or its effect is to discriminate between the majority of the shareholders and the minority shareholders, so as to give the former an advantage of which the latter are deprived, the court will restrain the company from making it or acting on it.

In the New South Wales case of *Australian Fixed Trusts Pty. Ltd.* v. *Clyde Industries Ltd.* (1959) S.R.(N.S.W.) 33 the A. Co. held, as trustee for the holders of units in a unit trust, about 300,000 of the 2,000,000 ordinary shares issued by the C. Co. C. Co. proposed to alter its articles so as to provide that a member holding ordinary shares as trustee for the holders of units in a unit trust should not vote in respect of the shares without the direction of the majority of the holders of the units. *Held*, the alteration would be invalid. Its effect was to discriminate between the majority of the shareholders and the minority. No reasonable man could decide that it was for the benefit of the company as a whole.

[27] *Per* Megarry J. in *Gaiman's* case, *ante*, at p. 335.
[28] A comparable Scottish case is *Caledonian Insurance Co.* v. *Scottish American Invest. Co. Ltd.*, 1951 S.L.T. 23 (O.H.).
[29] *Peters' American Delicacy Co. Ltd.* v. *Heath* (1939) 61 C.L.R. 457 (High Court of Australia), *per* Latham C.J. at p. 481 and Rich J. at p. 495. *Peters'* case is dealt with in the First Australian Supplement to Charlesworth & Cain, p. 70.
[30] *Per* Latham C.J. in *Peters'* case *supra* at p. 482.

In another New South Wales case, *Crumpton* v. *Morrine Hall Pty. Ltd.* [1965] N.S.W.R. 240, C. owned a group of shares in a home unit company the articles of which provided that holding a specified group of shares entitled the registered holder to the absolute and exclusive use of a specified unit. The articles also provided that the directors could lease the unit to the holder of the appropriate shares for such period as he was the holder at a rent equivalent to the appropriate share of money payable for such things as maintenance and repairs of the property, rates, and cleaning and furnishing of the hall and stairways. C. was granted a monthly tenancy of her unit which tenancy provided that it would not be determined except by the written consent of each shareholder, *i.e.* including C. Under the articles C. had rights of subletting and licensing others to use the premises. Finally, the articles contained a modification of rights clause in the usual form.

A general meeting passed a special resolution purporting to alter the articles so as to provide that, subject to the prior approval of the directors, the holder of any group of shares should have the right to let his unit for not more than 12 months in any period of 36 consecutive months but otherwise he could not lease, license or part with possession or occupation. C. sought and obtained an injunction restraining the company from acting on the resolution and a declaration that it was void.

Jacobs J. *held*:

(1) That the alteration of articles was a fraud or oppression on the minority. He said that the courts in each generation or decade set a line up to which shareholders are allowed to go in affecting the rights of other shareholders by alterations of articles of association, and that the decision turns on a value judgment formed in respect of the conduct of the majority. Jacobs J. also said that where there is an attempt to take particular rights away from the holders of particular shares then, although the act may appear in theory to be a decision or resolution applicable generally to all holders of shares, if it appears that it affects one or a minority in particular then it should appear that full regard has been had to the proprietary rights involved, and that he did not think it is sufficient merely to say that it is considered that the property of the company will benefit as a result of the alteration of the articles (*cf. Greenhalgh* v. *Arderne Cinemas, ante* p. 111).

(2) That the share capital of the company was divided into different classes within the meaning of the modification of rights clause, the alteration was a variation of class rights, the modification of rights clause should have been complied with and had not been complied with. In this respect the earlier case of *Fischer* v. *Easthaven* [1964] N.S.W.R. 261 was not followed.

Jacobs J. did not follow *Fischer* v. *Easthaven* in another respect when he said that he did not think that the duty on the company could be expressed in terms of a contractual duty not to alter the articles. It was a duty which arose by the application of principles of equity developed in the cases dealing with the power of a company to alter its articles and its inability to alter them so as to commit a fraud on a minority.

In the absence of a prohibition in the memorandum the articles can be altered so as to authorise the issue of preference shares taking priority over existing shares, although no power to issue preference shares is conferred by the memorandum or the original articles.[31]

(4) An alteration of articles in breach of a contract to which the company is a party is valid but the other party is entitled to

[31] *Andrews* v. *Gas Meter Co.* [1897] 1 Ch. 361 (C.A.).

damages. If a person enters into an arrangement which can only take effect by the continuance of an existing state of circumstances, he is under an obligation to do nothing to put an end to that state of circumstances.[32]

> S., a director of B. Co., was properly appointed managing director for ten years by a contract outside the articles. The articles provided that the managing director, *subject to his contract with the company*, was subject to the same provisions as to removal as the other directors, and that if he ceased to be a director, he should *ipso facto* cease to be managing director. The articles also provided that the company could remove a director before the expiration of his period of office. Later, F. Co. acquired the shares in B. Co. and the articles were altered so as to empower F. Co. to remove any director of B. Co. Before the expiration of ten years F. Co. removed S. from the board of directors of B. Co. and he thereby ceased to be managing director. *Held*, it was an implied term of the contract that B. Co. would not remove S. as director during the term of ten years and B. Co. was liable to S. for breach of contract: *Southern Foundries (1926) Ltd.* v. *Shirlaw* [1940] A.C. 701.[33]
>
> "A company cannot be precluded from altering its articles thereby giving itself power to act upon the provisions of the altered articles— but so to act may nevertheless be a breach of contract if it is contrary to a stipulation in a contract validly made before the alteration": *per* Lord Porter at p. 740.

Note what was said earlier of section 9 (3), (4) and (5) of the European Communities Act 1972 and an alteration of articles.[34]

Any document making or evidencing an alteration in the company's memorandum or articles and a copy of the memorandum or articles as altered must be in the same language as the memorandum and articles originally registered and, if that language is Welsh, must be accompanied by a certified translation into English: section 30 (7) of the 1976 Act.

Inspection of articles

A company is required to furnish a copy of its memorandum (embodying any alterations) and of its articles to its members on request, on payment of not more than five new pence a copy: sections 24, 25.

---

[32] *Per* Lords Atkin and Porter in the *Southern Foundries* case at pp. 717 and 741 respectively.
[33] See also *Shindler* v. *Northern Raincoat Co. Ltd.* [1960] 1 W.L.R. 1038, *post* p. 345, and *Carrier Australasia Ltd.* v. *Hunt* (1939) 61 C.L.R. 534, First Australian Supplement to Charlesworth & Cain, p. 71, and *post* p. 344.
[34] p. 98.

Any person, whether a member of the company or not, may inspect the memorandum and articles of association of any company at the office of the Registrar of Companies. He may also have a sealed copy or extract of them: section 426 of the 1948 Act; section 38 (3) and Schedules 2 and 3 of the 1976 Act.

Rectification of articles

The court has no jurisdiction to rectify the articles, even if it is proved that they were not in accordance with the intention of the original signatories.[35]

[35] *Scott* v. *Frank F. Scott (London) Ltd.* [1940] Ch. 794 (C.A.).

CHAPTER 5

PROMOTERS

BEFORE a company can be formed there must be some persons who have an intention to form a company, and who take the necessary steps to carry that intention into operation. Such persons are called "promoters." Promoters stand in a fiduciary position towards the company and, as a result, they owe certain duties.

MEANING OF TERM "PROMOTER"

Apart from the definition for the purposes of section 43,[1] the term "promoter" is not defined in the Act. However, a promoter has been described, for example, as "one who undertakes to form a company with reference to a given project and to set it going, and who takes the necessary steps to accomplish that purpose."[2]

A company may have several promoters and, as is shown by cases such as the *Leeds Theatres* case, *post*, one existing company may promote another new company.

Persons who give instructions for the preparation and registration of the memorandum and articles of association are promoters. So, too, are persons who obtain the directors (very often a promoter is himself a prospective director), issue a prospectus, negotiate underwriting contracts or a contract for the purchase of property by the company, or procure capital.

A person may become a promoter after the company is incorporated, *e.g.* by issuing a prospectus, or by procuring capital to enable the company to carry out a preliminary agreement. Whether a person is actually a promoter and, if so, the date when he became one and whether he is still one, are questions of fact.

A person who has taken no active part in the formation of a company and the raising of the necessary share capital but has left it to others to get up the company on the understanding that he will profit from the operation is a promoter.[3]

---

[1] s. 43 (5) (*a*), *post* p. 154.
[2] *Per* Cockburn C.J. in *Twycross* v. *Grant* (1877) 2 C.P.D. 469 (C.A.) at p. 541.
[3] See *per* Lindley J. in *Emma Silver Mining Co. Ltd.* v. *Lewis* (1879) 4 C.P.D. 396 at

Anyone who acts merely as the servant or agent of a promoter is not himself a promoter. A solicitor, therefore, who merely does the legal work necessary to the formation of a company is not a promoter.[4]

At one time the business of a company promoter was almost a separate business in itself but this is not so today. Further, the increasingly strict provisions of successive Companies Acts in relation to the issue and contents of a prospectus have almost eliminated the fraudulent company promoter.

POSITION AND DUTIES OF PROMOTERS

A promoter is not an agent for the company which he is forming because a company cannot have an agent before it comes into existence.[5] Furthermore, he is usually not treated as a trustee for the future company.[6] However, from the moment he acts with the company in mind, a promoter stands in a fiduciary position [7] towards the company and therefore he must not make any secret profit out of the promotion, *e.g.* a profit on a sale of property to the company.

A promoter must disclose a profit which he is making out of the promotion to either—

(1) an *independent* board of directors [8]; or
(2) the existing and intended shareholders, *e.g.* by making disclosure in a prospectus. [9]

"I do not say that an owner of property may not promote and form a joint stock company, and then sell his property to it, but I do say that if he does he is bound to take care that he sells it to the company through the medium of a board of directors who can and do exercise an independent and intelligent judgment on the transaction." [10]

---

p. 408, and *Tracy* v. *Mandalay Pty. Ltd.* (1952–53) 88 C.L.R. 215, First Australian Supplement to Charlesworth & Cain, p. 73.

[4] *Re Great Wheal Polgooth Ltd.* (1883) 53 L.J.Ch. 42.

[5] *Kelner* v. *Baxter* (1866 (L.R. 2 C.P. 174, *post* p. 124; *Tinnevelly Sugar Refining Co. Ltd.* v. *Mirrlees, Watson & Yaryan Co. Ltd.* (1894) 21 R. 1009, *post* p. 124.

[6] *Omnium Electric Palaces Ltd.* v. *Baines* [1914] 1 Ch. 332, *post*; *Edinburgh Northern Tramways Co.* v. *Mann* (1896) 23 R. 1056, *post*.

[7] *Henderson* v. *The Huntington Copper etc. Co. Ltd.* (1877) 5 R. (H.L.) 1; (1877) 4 R. 294, *post*; the fiduciary relationship was regarded as arising from agency rather than from trust in *Edinburgh Northern Tramways Co.* v. *Mann* (1896) 23 R. 1056, *post*.

[8] *Erlanger* v. *New Sombrero Phosphate Co.* (1878) 3 App.Cas. 1218 (P.C.) *post*; *Tracy* v. *Mandalay Pty. Ltd.* (1952–53) 88 C.L.R. 215.

[9] *Lagunas Nitrate Co.* v. *Lagunas Syndicate* [1899] 2 Ch. 392 (C.A.); *Scottish Pacific Coast Mining Co. Ltd.* v. *Falkner, Bell & Co.* (1888) 15 R. 290.

[10] *Per* Lord Cairns L.C. in *Erlanger's* case, above, at p. 1236.

The requirement of an independent board of directors is one which, in most cases, cannot be complied with, as the promoters, or some of them, are usually the first directors of the company. In the formation of a private company, the promoter usually sells his business to a company, of which he is managing director, and in which he is the largest shareholder, but, nevertheless, the transaction cannot be impeached on the ground that there is no independent board of directors.[11]

"After *Salomon*'s *Case* (*1*) I think it is impossible to hold that it is the duty of the promoters of a company to provide it with an independent board of directors; if the real truth is disclosed to those who are induced by the promoters to join the company."[12]

If there is no disclosure to an independent board, there must be *full* disclosure of the profit made by the promoters to the existing and intended shareholders, either in a prospectus or in some other way.

" 'Disclosure' is not the most appropriate word to use when a person who plays many parts announces to himself in one character what he has done and is doing in another."[13]

If a person buys property with the intention of reselling it to a company which he is forming, he is not presumed to acquire that property as trustee for the company and if, as a matter of fact, he intends to acquire it as a promoter, it is quite legal for him to resell to the company at a profit, provided that he discloses the profit.[14] If he intends to acquire as a trustee, he will have to hand over the property to the company at the price paid by him.

Remedies for breach of duty

If a promoter fails to make full disclosure of a profit made by him out of the promotion the following remedies may be open to the company. Since the promoter's duties are owed to the company the rule in *Foss* v. *Harbottle*[15] is relevant to their enforcement.

(1) Where the promoter has, *e.g.*, sold his own property to the company, the company may rescind the contract and recover the purchase-money paid.

---

[11] *Salomon* v. *Salomon & Co. Ltd.* [1897] A.C. 22, *ante* p. 28.
[12] *Per* Lindley M.R. in the *Lagunas* case, above, at p. 426.
[13] *Per* Lord Macnaghten in *Gluckstein* v. *Barnes* [1900] A.C. 240, *post*, at p. 249.
[14] *Omnium Electric Palaces Ltd.* v. *Baines* [1914] 1 Ch. 332 (C.A.).
[15] *Post* p. 376.

> A syndicate, of which E. was the head, purchased an island in the West Indies said to contain valuable mines of phosphates for £55,000. E. formed a company to buy this island, and a contract was made between X., a nominee of the syndicate, and the company for its purchase at £110,000. *Held*, as there had been no disclosure by the promoters of the profit they were making, the company was entitled to rescind the contract and to recover the purchase-money from E. and the other members of the syndicate: *Erlanger* v. *New Sombrero Phosphate Co.* (1878) 3 App.Cas. 1218 (P.C.).

The right of rescission may be lost in a number of ways. For example, it will be lost if the parties cannot be restored to their original positions, as where the property has been worked so that its character has been altered.[16] However, even if restitution is strictly not possible, rescission may be allowed if restitution is substantially possible. The right to rescind will also be lost if third parties have acquired rights for value, by mortgage or otherwise, under the contract.[17]

(2) The company may compel the promoter to account for any profit he has made.

> Intending to buy property and to form a company and resell the property to the company or another purchaser, a syndicate of four persons bought charges on the property at a discount. They afterwards bought the property for £140,000, formed a company of which they were the first directors and resold the property to the company for £180,000. As a result of this, they made a profit of £40,000 on the property and one of £20,000 on the charges which were paid off in full with the £140,000 received for the property. A prospectus was issued, disclosing the profit of £40,000 but not that of £20,000. It appears that recission had become impossible. *Held*, the £20,000 was a secret profit made by the syndicate as promoters of the company and they were bound to pay it to the company: *Gluckstein* v. *Barnes* [1900] A.C. 240.
>
> A prospectus stated that the company had been formed for the purchase of certain mines at the price of £125,000, and named H. as a director; it did not disclose that H. was receiving £10,000 of the price from the vendor of the mines in consideration, as H. alleged, of services rendered by H. to the company. *Held*, in an action by the company against H., that since H. stood in a fiduciary relation to the company from the date when he agreed to become a director, the company was entitled to recover the £10,000 from H., the true price of the mines being only £115,000: *Henderson* v. *The Huntington Copper and Sulphur Co. Ltd.* (1877) 5 R. (H.L.) 1; (1877) 4 R. 294.

(3) The company may sue the promoter for damages for breach of his fiduciary duty.

[16] As in *Lagunas Nitrate Co.* v. *Lagunas Syndicate* [1899] 2 Ch. 392 (C.A.).
[17] As in *Re Leeds and Hanley Theatres of Varieties Ltd.* [1902] 2 Ch. 809, below, where the mortgagee of the property had sold it.

The F. Co. contracted to purchase two music-halls for £24,000 and had the property conveyed to its nominee, R., intending to sell it to the T. Co. when formed. The F. Co. then promoted the T. Co. and agreed to sell the music-halls to it for £75,000 and directed R. to convey them. The board of directors of T. Co. was not an independent board. A prospectus was issued to the public by the T. Co., giving R. as the vendor, and not disclosing the interest of F. Co. or the profit it was making. *Held*, the prospectus should have disclosed that F. Co. was the real vendor and the amount of profit it was making. For breach of their fiduciary duty to those invited to take shares the promoters were liable in damages to the company and the measure of damages was the promoters' profit: *Re Leeds and Hanley Theatres of Varieties Ltd.* [1902] 2 Ch. 809 (C.A.).

Where promoters sell their own property to the company, the company cannot affirm the contract and at the same time ask for an account of profits or for damages as this would be, in effect, asking the court to vary the contract of sale and order the defendants to sell their assets at a lower price.[18]

Apart from the remedies mentioned above, if a promoter fails to disclose a profit made by him out of the promotion other remedies may be available to the company. The company may be able to recover damages for deceit against the promoter[19] or, perhaps, damages for negligent misrepresentation.[20] And note section 333 *post*.[21]

If a promoter, even though he has not sold property to the company, makes a secret profit out of the promotion of the company, he must account for that profit to the company.[22] He is, however, only bound to account for the profit he has made, that is, after deducting all legitimate expenses, *e.g.* surveyors' and solicitors' charges, and printing costs, incurred in the formation of the company.[23]

---

[18] *Re Cape Breton Co.* (1885) 29 Ch.D. 795 (C.A.); *Jacobus Marler Estates Ltd.* v. *Marler* (1913) 85 L.J.P.C. 167n., *per* Lord Parker; *Tracy* v. *Mandalay Pty. Ltd.* (1952–3) 88 C.L.R. 215, *per* the High Court of Australia at p. 239.

[19] *Per* Romer L.J. in the *Leeds* case, *supra*.

[20] Under the principle in *Hedley Byrne Ltd.* v. *Heller & Partners* [1964] A.C. 645, *Mutual Life and Citizens' Assurance Co. Ltd.* v. *Evatt* [1971] A.C. 793 (P.C.) and cases such as *Esso Petroleum Co. Ltd.* v. *Mardon* [1975] 2 W.L.R. 147 or under the Misrepresentation Act 1967, s. 2 (1), *post* p. 147.

[21] p. 394.

[22] *Henderson* v. *The Huntington Copper etc. Co. Ltd.* (1877) 5 R. (H.L.) 1; (1877) 4 R. 294, *ante*; *Mann* v. *Edinburgh Northern Tramways Co.* (1892) 20 R. (H.L.) 7; (1891) 18 R. 1140.

[23] *Lydney and Wigpool Iron Ore Co.* v. *Bird* (1886) 33 Ch.D. 85 (C.A.).

PAYMENT FOR PROMOTION SERVICES

A promoter has no right against the company to payment for his promotion services in the absence of an express contract with the company. In England such a contract will normally have to be under seal since the company cannot make a valid contract before incorporation and when the contract can be made the consideration by the promoter will normally be past. In the absence of such a contract he cannot even recover from the company payments he has made in connection with the formation of the company.

A syndicate promoted a company and paid £416 2s. in respect of registration fees and *ad valorem* stamp duty incidental to the formation of the company. The company shortly afterwards went into liquidation. *Held*, the syndicate were not entitled to prove for the payments they had made: *Clinton's Claim* [1908] 2 Ch. 515 (C.A.).

The rule that consideration must not be past is not part of Scots law, and the promoter of a Scottish company might be entitled to found on a suitably worded provision in the memorandum or articles to the effect of recovering from the company payments made by him in connection with the formation of the company.[24] The success of a promoter's claim against the company seems to depend on his establishing that the relevant provision creates a *jus quaesitum tertio* in his favour. Where such a right is established, a promoter is entitled to remuneration for professional services rendered.[25] If no such right is established, neither promoters nor experts employed by them have a right to remuneration from the new company; such experts have no claim except against the persons who employed them, namely the promoters.[26]

In both countries it is usual for the articles to give the directors power to pay the preliminary expenses out of the company's funds. By article 80 of Table A: "The directors . . . may pay all expenses incurred in promoting and registering the company." Such an article gives the promoters no right to bring an action against the company for the preliminary expenses, as it only confers a discretion on the directors.[27] However, the promoters are usually directors so that in practice the promoters will receive their expenses.

[24] *Scott* v. *Money Order Co. etc. Ltd.* (1870) 42 Sc. Jur. 212.
[25] See, *e.g.*, *Edinburgh Northern Tramways Co.* v. *Mann* (1896) 23 R. 1056.
[26] *Per* Lord M'Laren in *J. M. & J. H. Robertson* v. *Beatson, M'Leod & Co. Ltd.*, 1908 S.C. 921 at p. 928.
[27] *Melhado* v. *Porto Alegre Ry. Co.* (1874) L.R. 9 C.P. 503. The same interpretation might be adopted in Scotland, but see *Scott's* case *ante*.

Any amount or benefit paid or given within the two preceding years, or intended to be paid or given, to a promoter must normally be disclosed in a prospectus.[28]

SUSPENSION OF PROMOTERS

A person who has been convicted on indictment of any offence in connection with the promotion or formation of a company may have an order made against him by the court that he shall not, without leave of the court, be a director or take part in the management of a company for a period of up to five years: section 188.[29]

[28] s. 38 (1) and Sched. 4, *post* p. 136.
[29] *Post* p. 315.

CHAPTER 6

CONTRACTS

THIS chapter deals first, with contracts made on behalf of a company before it is formed, and secondly, with those made after the company has been formed.

CONTRACTS MADE BEFORE INCORPORATION OF COMPANY

Effect on company

If, before the formation of a company, some person purports to make a contract on its behalf, or as trustee for it, *e.g.* a contract for the sale of property to the company, the contract, or "preliminary agreement" as it is sometimes called, is not binding on the company when it is formed, even if the company takes the benefit of the contract. Before incorporation the company lacks capacity to make the contract, and an agent cannot contract on behalf of a principal who is not in existence.

Solicitors, on the instructions of persons who afterwards became directors of the company, prepared the memorandum and articles of association of the company, and paid the registration fees. *Held*, the company was not liable to pay their costs: *Re English and Colonial Produce Co. Ltd.* [1906] 2 Ch. 435 (C.A.). "There is no binding authority for the proposition that a company, because it has taken the benefit of work done under a contract entered into before the formation of the company, can be made liable in equity under that contract": *per* Vaughan Williams L.J. at p. 442.[1]

Conversely, a company cannot, after incorporation, enforce a contract made in its name before incorporation, or sue for damages for breach of such a contract.

N. Co. agreed with a person acting on behalf of a future company, P. Co., that N. Co. would grant a mining lease to P. Co. P. Co. discovered coal whereupon N. Co. refused to grant the lease. *Held*, P. Co. could not compel N. Co. to grant the lease: *Natal Land etc. Co. Ltd.* v. *Pauline Colliery Syndicate Ltd.* [1904] A.C. 120 (P.C.).[2]

---

[1] For Scots law, *cf.* Lord President Dunedin in *Welsh & Forbes* v. *Johnston* (1906) 8 F. 453 at p. 457, and Lord M'Laren in *J. M. & J. H. Robertson* v. *Beatson, M'Leod & Co. Ltd.* 1908 S.C. 921 at p. 928, *ante* p. 121. See also *F. J. Neale (Glasgow) Ltd.* v. *Vickery*, 1971 S.L.T. (Sh. Ct.) 88.

[2] *Molleson and Grigor* v. *Fraser's Trustees* (1881) 8 R. 630, is a Scottish authority.

D., acting on behalf of a future company, T. Co., entered into a contract with M. Co. for the supply by the latter of certain machinery for a refinery. When T. Co. was registered it alleged that the machinery supplied was defective. *Held*, T. Co. could not sue M. Co. for damages: *Tinnevelly Sugar Refining Co. Ltd*. v. *Mirrlees, Watson & Yaryan Co. Ltd*. (1894) 21 R. 1009.

Further, such a contract cannot be ratified by the company after it is incorporated—the company was not a principal with contractual capacity at the time when the contract was made—although, as is explained later, the contract may be novated.[3]

The Gravesend Royal Alexandra Hotel Company Ltd. was being formed to buy an hotel from K. At a time when all concerned knew that the company had not been formed, a written contract was made "on behalf of" the proposed company by A, B and C for the purchase of £900 worth of wine from K. The company was formed, and the wine handed over to it and consumed, but before payment was made the company went into liquidation. *Held*, A, B and C were personally liable on the contract, and no ratification could release them from their liability: *Kelner* v. *Baxter* (1866) L.R. 2 C.P. 174.

Where a contract is signed by one who professes to be signing "as agent," but who has no principal existing at the time, and the contract would be altogether inoperative unless binding on the person who signed it, he is bound thereby; and a stranger cannot by a subsequent ratification relieve him from that responsibility": *per* Erle C.J. at p. 183.

The Jenkins Report recommended[4] that a company should be enabled unilaterally to adopt, *i.e.* to ratify, contracts which purport to be made on its behalf or in its name prior to incorporation; until the company does so adopt such contracts, the persons who purported to act for the company should be entitled to sue and be liable to be sued thereon. This would have reversed part of the decision in the *Kelner* case and the decision in the *Sensolid* case, below.

It appears that unilateral adoption (ratification) of such contracts by the company is prevented by section 9 (2) of the European Communities Act 1972[5] *infra*, although a novation, *post*, is not.

Clause 6 of the Companies Bill 1973 would have permitted a company, after incorporation, to ratify contracts which purport to have been made in its name or on its behalf before incorporation.

Effect on individuals

Under the general law, if an individual contracts as "agent"[6] or trustee for a future company, whether there is a contract between him

[3] *Kelner* v. *Baxter*, below; *Tinnevelly* case, above.
[4] Para. 54.
[5] p. 125.
[6] Strictly, one cannot be agent for a principal not yet in existence.

and the other person involved depends upon what a reasonable man would think the parties intended. If they have expressed themselves in writing the question is one of construction of the written terms for the judge. If orally, the question is one of fact for the jury if there is one.[7]

In *Kelner* v. *Baxter*, above, it was intended that A, B and C should contract personally. In the *Newborne* case,[8] below, the intention was that the future company should contract.

Tinned ham was sold to S. Ltd. The contract was "We have this day sold to you . . . (Signed) Leopold Newborne (London) Ltd." The signature was typed and underneath was written "Leopold Newborne." The market price of ham fell and S. Ltd. refused to take delivery. When an action was brought it was found that Leopold Newborne (London) Ltd. had not been incorporated at the time of the contract and Leopold Newborne tried to enforce the contract in his own name. *Held*, neither Leopold Newborne (London) Ltd. nor Leopold Newborne could enforce the contract. It was not a case of an agent undertaking to do certain things himself as agent for somebody else. It was a contract in which a company purported to sell. Leopold Newborne did not purport to contract as principal or agent—the contract purported to be made by S. Ltd., on whose behalf it was signed by a future director. "This company was not in existence and . . . the signature on that document, and, indeed, the document itself . . . is a complete nullity": *Newborne* v. *Sensolid* (*Great Britain*) *Ltd.* [1954] 1 Q.B. 45. [*Note:* The decision in this case would be different now by virtue of the European Communities Act 1972, s. 9(2), *infra*.]

It has been said that, in a case like *Newborne*,[8] where the individual who contracts for a future company is not personally bound by the contract the other person involved might be able to sue him for damages for breach of implied warranty of authority, *i.e.* that he was a director of an existing company which had power to contract to buy land,[9] in accordance with the principle in *Collen* v. *Wright*.[10]

If, in a case like *Kelner*, *supra*, the individual is personally bound, the contract should contain a provision (a condition subsequent) that his liability shall cease if and when the company is incorporated and enters into a contract with the vendor on the terms of the preliminary agreement, *i.e.* there is a novation, and a provision that he may rescind if the company does not enter into such a contract by a specified date.

Section 9(2) of the European Communities Act 1972 provides

---

[7] *Per* Fullagar J. in *Summergreene* v. *Parker* (1950) 80 C.L.R. 304, at p. 324.
[8] See also the Australian High Court case of *Black* v. *Smallwood* (1965–66) 117 C.L.R. 52, where it was believed that the company had been formed (First Australian Supplement to Charlesworth & Cain, p. 75).
[9] *Per* Windeyer J. in *Black* v. *Smallwood* (1965–66) 117 C.L.R. 52, at p. 64.
[10] (1857) 8 E. & B. 647.

that where a contract purports to be made by a company, or by a
person as agent for a company, at a time when the company has not
been formed, then subject to any agreement to the contrary the
contract shall have effect as one entered into by the person purporting
to act for the company or as agent for it and he shall be personally
liable on it.

This means that in circumstances like those in *Newborne's* case
ante[8] today, unless there is an agreement to the contrary, there will
be a contract between the individual who acts for the company and
the other person involved. Presumably such individual will be entitled to sue on the contract as well as being liable to be sued on it.
The words "subject to any agreement to the contrary" allow for the
case where there is a novation.

New contract after incorporation

Of course, a company may, after incorporation, enter into a new
contract with the other party to the same effect as a contract made
on its behalf before incorporation, in which event there is a novation,
i.e. the old contract is discharged and replaced by the new. Such a
new contract may be inferred from the acts of the parties after
incorporation.

J. had agreed with W., acting on behalf of a company about to be formed,
to sell certain property to the company. After the company's incorporation, the
directors resolved to adopt the agreement, and to accept J.'s offer to take part of
the purchase-money in debentures instead of cash. *Held*, a contract was entered
into by the company with J. to the effect of the previous agreement as subsequently
modified: *Howard* v. *Patent Ivory Mfg. Co.* (1888) 38 Ch.D. 156.[11]

However, such a new contract will not be inferred if the acts of the
company after incorporation are due to the mistaken belief that it is
bound by the contract made before incorporation.

A contract was made between W. and D., who was acting on behalf of an
intended company, for the grant of a lease to the company. The company, on its
formation, entered on the land the subject of the lease and began to erect buildings
on it but did not make any fresh agreement with respect to the lease. *Held*, the
agreement, being made before the formation of the company, was not binding on
the company, and was incapable of ratification, and the acts of the company were
done in the erroneous belief that the agreement was binding on the company and
not evidence of a fresh agreement between W. and the company: *Re Northumber-
land Avenue Hotel Co.* (1886) 33 Ch.D. 16 (C.A.).

[11] *Cf. James Young & Sons Ltd. and Liquidator* v. *James Young & Sons' Trustee* (1902)
10 S.L.T. 85 (O.H.).

In the case of a public company such a new contract will be provisional only until the company is entitled to commence business: section 109 (4).[12]

Modern practice

Agreements to sell property to a company about to be formed are not now, as a rule, made with a person expressed to be acting on behalf of or as trustee for the company, because of the liability incurred by such person, and the absence of liability incurred by the company unless there is a novation. Although the other party will not be bound before the company is formed, the modern practice is for the promoters[13] to have prepared, before the company is incorporated, a draft agreement to which the company is expressed to be a party, and for the agreement to be executed by the other party and on behalf of the company after incorporation, pursuant to a clause in the company's memorandum to that effect. If, as is common, a company is being formed to acquire the promoters' business,[14] it does not matter that the promoters are not bound.

PROVISIONAL CONTRACTS

Any contract made by a public company after it is incorporated but before it is entitled to commence business is provisional only, and not binding on the company until it is entitled to commence business: section 109 (4). If, therefore, goods are supplied to a company which never becomes entitled to commence business, the company is not liable to pay for them.[15] The company is not entitled to enforce such a contract until it is entitled to commence business.

An action for breach of warranty of authority may be maintained against directors who enter on the company's behalf into contracts which are not binding on the company because of its failure to comply with section 109 (4) where the conduct of the directors has been such that a warranty of their authority to make contracts immediately binding on the company may properly be inferred.[16]

[12] *Post.* [13] *Ante* p. 116.
[14] *Ante* p. 4.
[15] *Re "Otto" Electrical Manufacturing Co. (1905) Ltd.* [1906] 2 Ch. 390, and see *Bond Corporation Pty. Ltd.* v. *Perseus Mining N.L.* [1972] W.A.R. 185, F. Ct.
[16] *Brownett* v. *Newton* (1941) 64 C.L.R. 439.

A private company is entitled to commence business on incorporation, a public company only when it has complied with the requirements of section 109.[17] However, this disability is unimportant in practice since most companies are formed as private companies, even if it is intended that they shall eventually be public companies.[18]

FORM OF CONTRACTS

The rules as to the form of a registered company's contracts are the same as those for contracts made between private persons. Thus a contract on behalf of a company is made (by any person acting under the company's authority) in writing if such a contract is required by law to be in writing when made private persons and orally if it may be made orally when made between private persons. If the contract is, according to English law, required to be under seal even if made between private persons, it may be made under the company's common seal. A deed is validly executed according to Scots law if it is sealed with the company's common seal and subscribed by two directors or by a director and the secretary; witnesses are not required: section 32.[19]

The seal

The company's seal is affixed in the manner laid down in the articles.

Table A, article 113. provides: "The directors shall provide for the safe custody of the seal, which shall only be used by the authority of the directors or of a committee of the directors authorised by the directors in that behalf, and every instrument to which the seal shall be affixed shall be signed by a director and shall be countersigned by the secretary or by a second director or by some other person appointed by the directors for the purpose."

A company whose objects comprise the transaction of business in foreign countries may, if authorised by its articles, have for use in any place outside the United Kingdom, an official seal. The official seal must be a facsimile of the company's common seal, with the addition on its face of the name of every place where it is to be used: section 35.

---

[17] *Post* p. 182.   [18] *Ante* p. 54.
[19] The same rules now apply to other corporations: Corporate Bodies' Contracts Act 1960, which does not apply to Scotland.

A document requiring *authentication* by a company may be signed by a director, secretary or other authorised officer of the company, and need not be under its common seal: section 36.

Bills of exchange

Bills of exchange and promissory notes can be drawn, accepted or indorsed on behalf of a company by any person acting under the company's authority: section 33. Officers who sign their own names without making it clear that they are signing on behalf of the company may incur personal liability.[20]

ULTRA VIRES CONTRACTS

These were dealt with in Chapter 3.[21]

[20] *Brebner* v. *Henderson,* 1925 S.C. 643.
[21] *Ante* p. 76.

CHAPTER 7

PROSPECTUSES

THIS chapter begins by dealing with the question: "What is a prospectus?" This is because it is important for several reasons to be able to tell whether a document is a prospectus. If a document is a prospectus, certain sections of the Companies Act 1948 require it to state certain matters and set out certain reports. This is for the benefit of potential investors. Again, if a document is a prospectus, a section of the Act provides that a copy must be delivered to the Registrar of Companies before the prospectus is issued. Further, if a document is a prospectus and it contains a misleading statement, a section provides that the directors or other persons responsible for the statement are prima facie liable to pay compensation to those members of the public who, *e.g.*, subscribe for shares in the company on the faith of the prospectus. The object of all the sections referred to is to control statements in prospectuses. The various sections are dealt with later in the chapter under the headings "Contents of a Prospectus," "Registration of Prospectus" and "Misrepresentation and Omission."

WHAT IS A PROSPECTUS?

When the public is asked to subscribe for shares or debentures in a company, the invitation involves the issue of a document setting out the advantages to accrue from an investment in the company. This document is termed a prospectus. As will be explained later, it may be issued by the company or a promoter (in which case there is a direct invitation to the public), by an issuing house (in which case there is an offer for sale), or by a share broker (in which case there is said to be a placing).[1] If the existing shareholders are given an option to take further shares in the company there is said to be a rights issue.[2] It is only in the case of a *public* company that an invitation can be made to the public to subscribe for shares or debentures—a private company must raise its capital privately.[3]

[1] *Post* p. 146.   [2] *Post* p. 229.   [3] s. 28, *ante* p. 49.

Section 455 provides that in the Act, unless the context otherwise requires, the expression "prospectus" means any prospectus, notice, circular, advertisement or other invitation, offering to the public for subscription or purchase any shares or debentures of a company. It is only if there is a prospectus as so defined that the provisions of the Act dealing with such things as the contents of a prospectus, registration of a copy of a prospectus and compensation for mis-representation in a prospectus come into play.

The words "invitation" and "offering" in section 455 reflect the fact that sometimes a prospectus is only an invitation to treat and sometimes it is an offer. In the case of a direct invitation the prospectus is an invitation to treat after which the public makes offers for such shares or debentures, as the case may be, as are required.[4] In the case of a rights issue the prospectus (the letter to existing shareholders, giving them an option of taking further shares) is an offer.[5]

Whether an invitation or offer is made to the public is a question of fact but section 55 (1) provides that in the Act subject to any provision to the contrary therein, the term "public" is not restricted to the public at large but includes any section of the public, whether selected as members or debenture holders of the company or as clients of the person issuing the prospectus or in any other manner. There is an offer to the members of a company when a rights issue is made. There may be an offer to clients of the person issuing the prospectus when shares or debentures are placed.

Only 3,000 copies of a document which offered shares for subscription and which was headed "for private circulation only" were distributed to the shareholders of a number of gas companies. *Held*, there was an offer of shares to the public, *i.e.* a prospectus: *Re South of England Natural Gas Co. Ltd.* [1911] 1 Ch. 573.

However, by section 55 (2), an offer or invitation is not treated as made to the public if it can be regarded as not calculated to result in the shares or debentures becoming available for subscription or purchase by persons who have not received the offer or invitation (as will usually be the case where a private company invites its existing members to take more shares[6]), or if it is other-

---

[4] See further *post* p. 168.
[5] *Jackson* v. *Turquand* (1869) L.R. 4 H.L. 305.
[6] This is made clear by s. 55 (2) (*a*) and (*b*) which provide that a provision in a company's articles prohibiting invitations to the public to subscribe for shares or debentures shall not be taken as prohibiting the making to members or debenture holders of an invitation which can be so regarded, and the provisions of the Act relating to private companies shall be construed accordingly.

wise the domestic concern of the persons making and receiving it (*e.g.* where a director of a private company invites only a few friends to take shares[7]).

The word "subscription" in section 455 means acquisition for cash from the company, by issue and allotment by the company, of unissued shares or debentures in the company.[8] The word "purchase" means acquisition for cash, by transfer from a person to whom the company has allotted them, of already issued shares or debentures in the company.[9]

The Jenkins Report stated[10] that:

"It is generally accepted that" subscription or purchase "involves the payment of money and accordingly that a document containing an offer of securities for a consideration other than cash (*e.g.* shares) cannot be a prospectus although it may be a circular to which the Prevention of Fraud (Investments) Act applies."

Clause 31 (3) of the Companies Bill 1973 would have given the Secretary of State power to order that such a document be treated as a prospectus.

British and Commonwealth Shipping Co. Ltd., in a circular accompanied by a "Form of Acceptance and Transfer," offered to acquire all the issued shares in Union-Castle Mail Steamship Co. Ltd. and Clan Line Steamers Ltd. in exchange for shares in British and Commonwealth. *Held*, the circular was not a prospectus. It offered shares neither for purchase (because the shares offered were unissued shares in British and Commonwealth), nor for subscription (because the shares offered were not to be taken for cash). Further, the offer was not made to the public (because the offer could be accepted only by Union-Castle and Clan Line shareholders, and such shareholders as accepted were to be issued with *non*-renounceable letters of allotment, so the case fell within section 55 (2)). The consent of the Board of Trade was obtained under section 13 of the Prevention of Fraud (Investments) Act 1939 on the basis that the circular was not a prospectus. Finally, it was not a form of application for shares within section 38(3) *post*: *Governments Stock, etc., Investment Co. Ltd.* v. *Christopher* [1956] 1 W.L.R. 237.

---

[7] *Sherwell* v. *Combined Incandescent Mantles Syndicate* (*Limited*) (1907) 23 T.L.R. 482; *Sleigh* v. *Glasgow and Transvaal Options Ltd.* (1904) 6 F. 420, in which another reason for the document not being a prospectus was that it did not contain an invitation to take shares and an accompanying letter simply advised the friends to take shares.

[8] *Per* Kekewich J. at p. 357 in *Arnison* v. *Smith* (1889) 41 Ch.D. 348 (C.A.).

[9] *Governments Stock* case, *infra*; *Mutual Home Loans Fund of Australia Ltd.* v. *A.-G.* (*N.S.W.*) (1973) 130 C.L.R. 103. The acquisition of shares in a company by application and allotment is not a "purchase" within section 54, *post*: *Re V.G.M. Holdings Ltd.* [1942] Ch. 235 (C.A.).

". . . the difference between the issue of a share to a subscriber and the purchase of a share from an existing shareholder is the difference between the creation and the transfer of a chose in action": *per* Lord Greene M.R. at p. 241. The Scots law equivalent of "chose in action" is "incorporeal moveable."

[10] Para. 236.

Section 455 speaks only of an invitation offering shares or debentures to the public but defines "debenture" as including debenture stock, bonds and any other securities of a company whether or not constituting a charge on the company's assets. It is thought that the word "share" includes an option to take a share.[11]

The word "company" in the Act means a company formed and registered under the Act or an existing company. An existing company is a company formed and registered under one of the earlier Companies Acts. (s. 455.)

The Jenkins Report[12] recommended that the definition of a prospectus should be extended to cover documents offering securities for a consideration other than cash. Further, that the Board of Trade[13] be empowered to regulate advertisements offering securities by wireless, television or cinematograph.

CONTENTS OF A PROSPECTUS

The object of the legislature is to compel the company to provide in a prospectus the necessary information to enable the would-be investor to decide whether or not to subscribe for the company's shares or debentures. The statutory requirements are designed mainly to provide information about:

(1) Who the directors are, and what benefit they will get from their directorships.
(2) What profit is being made by the promoters.
(3) The amount of capital required by the company to be subscribed, the amount actually received or to be received in cash, and the precise nature of the consideration given for the remaining capital.
(4) What the company's financial record has been in the past.
(5) What the company's obligations are under contracts which it has entered into, and for commission and preliminary expenses.
(6) What are the voting and dividend rights of each class of shares.

[11] *Mutual Home Loans* case *ante.*
[12] Para. 252.
[13] Now the Department of Trade.

Fourth Schedule matters and reports

Section 38 (1) provides that, subject to certain exceptions which will be dealt with later,[14] the general rule is that every prospectus issued by or on behalf of a company or promoter must state the matters specified in Part I of the Fourth Schedule and set out the reports specified in Part II of the Fourth Schedule, whether the prospectus is issued on the formation of the company or subsequently. The company cannot contract out of its obligation to comply with these requirements: section 38 (2).

The Fourth Schedule matters are:

(1) The *number of founders or management or deferred*[15] *shares*, if any, and the nature and extent of the interest of the holders in the property and profits of the company.

(2) The number of shares, if any, fixed by the articles as the *qualification*[16] *of a director*, and any provision in the articles as to the *directors' remuneration*.
The amount of the directors' remuneration need not be set out.

(3) The *names, descriptions and addresses of the directors*.

(4) Where *shares* are offered to the public for subscription, particulars of—

(a) the *minimum subscription, i.e.* the minimum amount which, in the opinion of the directors, must be raised by the issue of such shares to provide for—

(i) the purchase price of any property which is to be defrayed wholly or partly out of the proceeds of the issue;

(ii) preliminary expenses payable by the company, and commission payable by it to persons who have agreed to subscribe or procure subscriptions for shares;

(iii) the repayment of any moneys borrowed by the company in respect of items (i) and (ii);

(iv) working capital; and

(b) the amounts to be provided for (i) to (iv) *ante* otherwise than out of the proceeds of the issue, and the sources from which they are to be provided.

It has been suggested[17] that the provisions relating to the minimum subscription are inadequate in that, *e.g.*, they do not apply to a debenture issue, and the matters enumerated for the purpose of determining the minimum subscription do not include such things as the carrying out of a specific purpose or project the cost of which is to be defrayed in whole or part from the proceeds of the issue and the discharge of any liability due or to become due.

(5) The time of the *opening of the subscription lists*.

(6) The *amount payable on application and allotment* on each share, including

---

[14] Under ss. 38 (5), 39, *post* pp. 138, 139.
[15] *Post* p. 225.   [16] *Post* p. 316.
[17] *Fifth Interim Report of the Australian Company Law Advisory Committee* (1970), paras 67–69.

the amount, if any, payable by way of premium,[18] and, in the case of a second or subsequent offer of shares, the amount offered for subscription on each previous allotment within the two preceding years, the amount actually allotted, and the amount paid on the shares so alloted, including the amount, if any, payable by way of premium.[18]

(7) The *number, description and amount of any shares or debentures for which any person has, or is entitled to be given, an option to subscribe,* the period during which it is exercisable, the price to be paid for the shares or debentures, the consideration given or to be given for the option, and the names and addresses of the persons to whom it was given, or, if given to existing shareholders or debenture holders as such, the relevant shares or debentures.

(8) The *number and amount of shares and debentures* which, within the two preceding years, have been *issued or agreed to be issued as fully or partly paid up otherwise than in cash,* the extent to which they are so paid up, and the consideration for their issue.

(9) The *names and addresses of the vendors of any property* purchased or to be purchased by the company which is to be paid for, wholly or partly, out of the proceeds of the issue offered for subscription by the prospectus (other than property purchased or to be purchased in the ordinary course of the company's business), the amount payable in cash, shares or debentures to each vendor, and short particulars of any transaction relating to the property within the previous two years in which any vendor, director or promoter of the company had any interest.

A vendor is defined[19] as a person who has entered into any contract for the sale or purchase, or for any option of purchase, of any property to be acquired by the company in any case where—

(*a*) the purchase-money is not fully paid at the date of the issue of the prospectus;

(*b*) the purchase-money is to be paid or satisfied wholly or partly out of the proceeds of the issue offered for subscription;

(*c*) the contract depends for its validity or fulfilment on the result of such issue.

Examples.—X buys property from Y for £100,000 and contracts to sell it to the company for £130,000. X completes the purchase on April 30, and on May 1 the prospectus is issued. X's name only need be given as vendor. The price he paid to Y must be disclosed.

R buys property from S for £100,000 and contracts to sell it to the company for £130,000. The purchase is not completed when the prospectus is issued. Both R and S must be given as vendors, and the price at which R is buying from S must be disclosed.

(10) The *amount paid* or payable in cash, shares or debentures *for such property,* specifying the amount payable for goodwill.

(11) The amount paid within the two preceding years, or payable, as *commission* for subscribing or procuring subscriptions for shares or debentures of the company, or the rate of commission.

This includes underwriting commission and brokerage, but not sub-underwriting commission.[20]

(12) The amount or estimated amount of the *preliminary expenses,* and of the

---

[18] This paragraph was amended by s. 33 of the Companies Act 1976.
[19] Sched. 4, Pt. III.
[20] *Post* p. 162.

expenses of the issue, and the persons by whom they have been respectively paid or are payable.

These include the legal expenses incidental to the formation of the company, registration fees and stamp duty, the cost of the prospectus and other out-of-pocket expenses incurred by the promoters in forming the company.

(13) The *amount paid* or benefit given within the two preceding years, or intended to be paid or given, *to any promoter*, and the consideration therefor.

(14) The dates of, parties to and general nature of *every material contract*, not being a contract entered into in the ordinary course of the company's business or made more than two years before the date of issue of the prospectus.

It seems that a material contract is a contract which, whether deterrent or not, an intending investor ought to have an opportunity of considering in order to decide whether to apply for shares or not.[21]

Among material contracts are those for the purchase of property or of a business by the company, for the employment of a promoter as manager, and underwriting contracts.

(15) The names and addresses of *the auditors*.

(16) The nature and extent of *the interest of every director* in the promotion of the company or in the property to be acquired by the company; with a statement of all sums paid or to be paid to him by any person, in cash or shares or otherwise, to induce him to become, or to qualify him as, a director, or for services rendered by him in connection with the promotion or formation of the company.

(17) In a prospectus inviting the public to subscribe for shares the *voting rights* and the rights in respect of dividends and capital attached to the different classes of shares into which the share capital is divided.

(18) The *length of time during which the business of the company* or any business which is to be acquired by the company *has been carried on, if* either business has been carried on for *less than three years*.

Paragraphs (2), (3), (12) (so far as it relates to preliminary expenses) and (16) above do not apply in the case of a prospectus issued more than two years after the company is entitled to commence business.[19]

The Fourth Schedule reports are:

(1) A *report by the company's auditors*, dealing with the profits or losses in each of the five financial years immediately preceding the issue of the prospectus (or, if the company has been carrying on business for less than five years, the years for which its accounts have been made up) and giving the rates of dividends paid on each class of shares during the same period. The report must also deal with the assets and liabilities of the company at the last date to which the accounts of the company were made up.

If the company has subsidiaries[22] the report must deal separately with the company's profits or losses, and in addition deal either—

(a) as a whole with the combined profits or losses of its subsidiaries, so far as they concern members of the company; or

(b) individually with the profits or losses of each subsidiary, so far as they concern members of the company;

or, instead of dealing separately with the company's profits or losses, deal as a whole with the profits or losses of the company and, so far as they concern members of the company, with the combined profits or losses of its subsidiaries.

---

[21] *Broome* v. *Speak* [1903] 1 Ch. 586 (C.A.).
[22] *Ante* p. 57.

Again, if the company has subsidiaries, the report, in addition to dealing separately with the company's assets and liabilities, must deal either—

(a) as a whole with the combined assets and liabilities of the subsidiaries, with or without the company's assets and liabilities; or

(b) individually with the assets and liabilities of each subsidiary,

and must indicate as respects the assets and liabilities of the subsidiaries the allowance to be made for persons other than members of the company.

(2) If the proceeds of the issue of shares or debentures are to be applied in *the purchase of a business*, a report by named accountants (qualified for appointment as auditors of a company)[23] upon the profits or losses of the business in each of the five financial years before the issue of the prospectus, and the assets and liabilities of the business at the last date to which the accounts of the business were made up.

(3) If the proceeds of the issue are to be applied in *the acquisition of shares in another company* which will become a subsidiary of the company issuing the prospectus, a report by named accountants (qualified for appointment as auditors of a company)[23] upon the profits or losses of the other company in each of the five financial years before the issue of the prospectus and upon the assets and liabilities of that company at the last date to which the accounts were made up. The report must also deal with the profits or losses and the assets and liabilities of any subsidiaries of that company, and indicate how the profits or losses of that company would have concerned members of the acquiring company, and what allowance would have been made, in relation to assets and liabilities, for holders of other shares, if it had held the shares to be acquired at all material times.

Clause 31(1) of the Companies Bill 1973 would have given the Secretary of State power to specify the matters to be contained in a prospectus and the documents to be endorsed on or attached to the copy delivered to the Registrar under section 41 *post*.

Expert's consent

Section 40 provides that if a prospectus includes a statement by an expert, he must have given (and not, before delivery of a copy of the prospectus to the Registrar for registration,[24] withdrawn) his written consent to the inclusion of the statement and the prospectus must state that he has done so.

Contravention of the section renders the company and every person knowingly a party to the issue of the prospectus liable to a fine of £500.

The section defines the expression "expert" as including an engineer, valuer, accountant *or any other person whose profession gives authority to a statement made by him.*

[23] Sched. 4, Pt. III, and see *post* p. 454.
[24] *Post* p. 142.

Other requirements

Every prospectus issued by or on behalf of a company or in relation to an intended company must—

(1) be dated, and that date must, unless the contrary is proved, be taken as the date of publication of the prospectus (s. 37);
(2) state on the face of it that a copy has been delivered to the Registrar;
(3) specify any documents required to be indorsed on or attached to such copy (s. 41). Such documents include an expert's consent, above, and will be explained later.[24]

> Clause 22 of the Companies Bill 1973 would have prohibited the issue of a prospectus by a company, other than one whose shares were listed on the stock exchange, unless all its shares carried unqualified voting rights.

When prospectus need not contain Fourth Schedule matters and reports

Section 38 (5) of the 1948 Act, as amended by Schedule 2 of the 1976 Act, provides two exceptions to section 38 (1):

(1) Where the prospectus or form of application is issued to existing members or debenture holders of the company, whether or not an applicant will have the right to renounce in favour of other persons. In this case the issue will normally be a rights issue.[25]
(2) Where the prospectus or form of application relates to shares or debentures uniform with shares or debentures previously issued and for the time being listed on a prescribed stock exchange.

The Stock Exchange is prescribed for the purposes of section 38 (5)[26]—all stock exchanges in Great Britain and Northern Ireland and that in Dublin have been amalgamated.

In these two cases, a prospectus issued by or on behalf of the company or a promoter need not contain the Fourth Schedule matters and reports and is called "an abridged prospectus." In the first case the persons to whom the prospectus is issued explain the

[25] *Post* p. 229.
[26] Companies (Stock Exchange) Order 1973 (S.I. No. 482).

exception; in the second, the kind of shares or debentures being issued.

Forms of application for shares or debentures

By section 38 (3), subject to certain exceptions[27] dealt with below, the general rule is that it is unlawful to issue any form of application for shares or debentures unless the form is accompanied by a prospectus containing the Fourth Schedule matters and reports.

When prospectus not required

There are exceptions to section 38 (3). In these cases a form of application for shares or debentures can be issued *without* a prospectus complying with section 38.

Exceptions are where:

(1) The form of application is issued to existing members or debenture holders of the company: section 38 (5), *ante*.

(2) The form relates to shares or debentures uniform with shares or debentures previously issued and for the time being listed on a prescribed stock exchange: section 38 (5), *ante*.

(3) The form is issued in connection with an invitation to a person to agree to underwrite the shares or debentures: section 38 (3).

(4) The form is issued in relation to shares or debentures which are not offered to the public: section 38 (3).

A person who underwrites shares usually agrees, in return for a commission, to take up to a specified number of shares if the public fail to apply for them.[28] Such a person will have or will obtain, before he agrees to underwrite, all the information he needs about the company.

Certificate of exemption

Section 39 of the 1948 Act, as amended by Schedule 2 of the 1976 Act, provides that section 38, above, is excluded where a prescribed stock exchange grants a certificate of exemption from

[27] Under ss. 38 (3), (5), 39.   [28] *Post* p. 164.

compliance with the Fourth Schedule requirements, which it can do if—

(1) a prospectus is to be issued generally, *i.e.* to non-members or non-debenture holders of the company;
(2) compliance with such requirements would be unduly burdensome, because of the size and other circumstances of the issue, and any limitations on the number and class of persons to whom the offer is to be made; and
(3) application is made to such stock exchange for permission for the shares or debentures to be listed.

When the certificate is granted, the prospectus is deemed to comply with the Fourth Schedule requirements *provided* that it contains the particulars and information which the stock exchange requires to be published in connection with the application for permission ((3) *ante*). A prospectus containing such particulars and information is called "an abridged prospectus."

The stock exchange prescribed for the purposes of section 39 is the same as that for section 38 (5), *ante*.[29]

In 1974, 11 certificates were lodged with the Registrars of Companies.

Clause 29 of the Companies Bill 1973 would have extended the power of the Stock Exchange to authorise abridged prospectuses.

Contravention of section 38

If any person contravenes section 38 (3), *i.e.* issues a form of application for shares or debentures without a prospectus complying with the Act, he is liable to a fine of £500 (s. 38 (3)), and if section 38 (1) is contravened, *i.e.* a prospectus which does not comply with the Act is issued by or on behalf of a company or promoter, it seems that the directors and other persons responsible for the prospectus are liable in damages to a person who takes shares or debentures on the faith of the prospectus and suffers damage by reason of the contravention.

A prospectus was issued which did not disclose the amount offered for subscription and actually allotted on a former prospectus. *Held*, this omission did not entitle an applicant for shares to rescind the contract. The remedy of the allottee was in damages against those responsible for the prospectus: *Re South of England Natural Gas Co. Ltd.* [1911] 1 Ch. 573.[30]

[29] p. 138.
[30] Although Lords Sumner and Warrington said in *Nash* v. *Lynde* [1929] A.C. 158,

Unlike certain other sections, section 38 does not expressly provide that the allottee may rescind his contract for non-compliance with the Act but it does contemplate a liability in damages on the part of the directors and other persons responsible for the prospectus, for subsection (4) exonerates them from liability if they can prove certain matters. "In my opinion the allottee is not entitled to rescind his contract because of any breach of the statutory requirements, which extend to such comparatively unimportant matters as the names and addresses of the company's auditors. His remedy is against the directors and other persons responsible for the prospectus": *per* Swinfen Eady J. at p. 577.

However, in the event of contravention of either section 38 (1) or section 38 (3), section 38 (4) provides that a director or other person responsible for the prospectus is not liable if—

(1) as regards any matter not disclosed, he proves that he did not know of it; or

(2) he proves that the contravention arose from an honest mistake of fact on his part; or

(3) the contravention was in respect of matters which in the opinion of the court were immaterial, or was such as ought, in the opinion of the court, reasonably to be excused.

Clause 28 of the Companies Bill 1973 would have made it an offence to issue a prospectus which does not comply with section 38(1) *ante*.

Stock Exchange listing

If a Stock Exchange listing is desired for the shares or debentures offered to the public by a prospectus, the requirements of The Stock Exchange must be complied with[31] and these are more stringent than those of the Act. For example, the auditors' report must deal with the profits or losses in each of the 10 financial years immediately preceding the issue of the prospectus or in each of the years since incorporation if this occurred less than 10 years prior to publication of the prospectus.[32]

The Jenkins Report[33] recommended that the Fourth Schedule be amended so that it requires information on the lines of that required by the London Stock Exchange[34] about such matters as paid-up capital. It should also require turnover to be disclosed.

---

post p. 143, at pp. 169, 175, that the decision in *Re South of England Natural Gas Co. Ltd.* is open to review.

[31] Rules and Regulations of The Stock Exchange, London, Rule 159 (2) and App. 34, Sched. II.

[32] Compare the corresponding requirement of the Act, *ante* p. 136.

[33] Para. 252.

[34] Now The Stock Exchange.

A Stock Exchange listing for the shares of a public company[3] is advantageous because it makes the shares more marketable. Investors know that the stringent requirements of The Stock Exchange are complied with and that the shares can easily be bought or sold on the Exchange.

REGISTRATION OF PROSPECTUS

By section 41 no prospectus may be issued by or on behalf of a company or in relation to an intended company unless, on or before the date of publication, a copy is delivered to the Registrar for registration. And such copy must—

(1) be signed by every person named in it as a director or proposed director, or by his agent authorised in writing;
(2) have indorsed on or attached to it—
   (*a*) any consent to the issue required from an expert;[36]
   (*b*) when the prospectus is issued generally[37]—

   (i) a copy of any material contract;[38]
   (ii) when the persons making any report required to be set out in the prospectus[39] have made any adjustments as respects the figures of any profits or losses or ass s and liabilities, a signed, written statement by them setting out the adjustments and giving the reasons therefor.

The Registrar requires two copies of the prospectus and of all supporting documents to be lodged.

The Registrar cannot register a prospectus unless it is dated and the above conditions are complied with. The issue of a prospectus before the requisite copy has been registered is punishable by a fine of £5 a day.

The result of section 41 is that a director cannot say that the prospectus was issued without his knowledge or that he was ignorant of the contents of the prospectus. A record is also available for the information of anyone interested in the prospectus, because all

[35] The shares of private companies are not dealt in on The Stock Exchange because of the essential restrictions on their transfer, *ante* p. 49.
[36] *Ante* p. 137.
[37] *Ante* p. 140.
[38] *Ante* p. 136.
[39] *Ante* p. 136.

the documents kept by the Registrar may be inspected: section 426 of the 1948 Act as amended by Schedule 3 to the 1976 Act.

TIME OF ISSUE OF PROSPECTUS

For the purposes of sections 38 and 41, above, it is important to know *when* a prospectus can be said to have been issued. For example, a director or other person responsible will not be liable just because a prospectus which should contain the Fourth Schedule matters and reports does not do so, provided that the prospectus has not been issued.

However, the point has not yet been settled. It may be that a prospectus is issued when it is shown to any person as a member of the public and as an invitation to that person to take some of the shares referred to in the prospectus on the terms set out therein. On the other hand it may be that a prospectus is only issued when it is issued to the public, *i.e.* when there is a general distribution.[40] If this latter view is correct, whether there is a general distribution in any case appears to be a question of degree.

A prospectus was sent by N., the managing director of a company, to a co-director. The co-director sent it to a solicitor who sent it to a client. The client sent it to his brother-in-law, L. The object was to induce L. to become a director, which he did. L. also took some shares in the company. *Held*, the prospectus had *not* been issued: *Nash* v. *Lynde* [1929] A.C. 158.

In a recent case, *R.* v. *Delmayne*,[41] it was held that an advertisement inviting the public to deposit money was issued within the meaning of the Protection of Depositors Act 1963, *post*,[42] when it was issued to a member of a deposit and loan society.

CONTROL OF BORROWING

The Borrowing (Control and Guarantees) Act 1946 provides for the regulation of borrowing and raising of money, the issue of securities, and the circulation of offers of securities for subscription, sale or exchange. However, because of a General Consent given by the Treasury, the control of borrowing machinery is in general not in

[40] See Buckley, *Companies Acts*, 13th ed., p. 85, where the latter view is preferred. In *Nash* v. *Lynde* [1929] A.C. 158, Lord Sumner was in favour of the latter view (p. 168), whereas Lord Hailsham L.C. was in favour of the former view (p. 164).
[41] [1970] 2 Q.B. 170 (C.A.).
[42] p. 159.

use now. The upper limit of the general exemption has been raised from £1 million to £3 million.[43]

DIRECT INVITATIONS, OFFERS FOR SALE, PLACINGS

Shares or debentures may be offered to the public by means of—

(1) a prospectus issued by or on behalf of a company or promoter (in which case there is a direct invitation to the public); or
(2) an offer for sale; or
(3) a "placing."

We shall see that placing securities directly with financial institutions is unfair in that it favours the big investor and deprives the small one of the opportunity to acquire securities at bargain prices (although it must be remembered that The Stock Exchange requires a substantial percentage of a placing to be offered to the market). An offer for sale to the public is fairer. On the other hand, placing is simpler, quicker and cheaper than an offer for sale. Underwriting is unnecessary, advertising is reduced to a minimum and a large number of prospectuses need not be printed.

Offer for sale

An offer for sale is the usual way in which shares or debentures are offered to the public. It occurs when an issuing house (either a specialised concern or a department of a merchant bank) subscribes for an issue of shares or debentures and then invites the public to purchase from it at a higher price. To save stamp duty the issuing house will renounce the allotment to it in favour of those members of the public who apply for shares or debentures.

The offer for sale is within the definition of a prospectus[44] but it is not a prospectus issued by or on behalf of a company or promoter, so that, were it not for section 45, sections 38 and 41, which are concerned with the contents and registration of a copy of a prospectus,[45] would not apply to it. Section 45 provides that where a company allots or agrees to allot shares or debentures of the company with a view to their being offered for sale to the public, the document by which the offer is made is deemed to be a prospectus

---

[43] Control of Borrowing (Amendment) Order 1972 (S.I. 1972/1218. Sept. 1, 1972).
[44] See ss. 455 and 55 (1), *ante* p. 131.   [45] *Ante* pp. 134, 142.

issued by the company, and all enactments and rules of law as to contents of prospectuses and to liability in respect of misrepresentation in prospectuses, or otherwise relating to prospectuses, apply as if the offer had been to the public for subscription and as if persons accepting the offer were subscribers for shares or debentures.

Consequently, subject to sections 38 (5) and 39, the offer must comply with sections 38 and 41. Section 45 goes on to provide that, in addition to the section 38 matters, the offer must state—

(1) the net amount of the consideration received or to be received by the company for the shares or debentures to which the offer relates;

(2) the place and time at which the contract for allotment can be inspected.

The copy registered with the Registrar under section 41 must be signed by the persons making the offer—at least half of the partners if the offer is made by a firm, and two of the directors if made by a company: section 45 (4).

It is presumed, unless the contrary is proved, that an allotment of, or an agreement to allot, shares or debentures was made with a view to their offer for sale to the public if (a) the offer was made within six months after allotment or agreement, or (b) the whole consideration was not received by the company before the offer for sale: section 45 (2).

The persons making the offer for sale are prima facie liable to pay compensation under section 43[46] for damage caused by misleading statements in the offer, as persons who have authorised the issue of a prospectus. The directors of the company at the time are under a similar liability. And by virtue of the provisions of section 45 persons accepting the offer may rescind as against the company.

Where it is difficult to fix the issue price of the shares or debentures being offered to the public, because it is uncertain what the public response to the offer will be, *an offer for sale by tender* may be made. In this event, a minimum price is fixed and the issue price is determined by the prices tendered in the applications. Thus, where 250,000 ordinary 25p shares are offered, a minimum price of 80p a share may be fixed. The prices tendered may range from 80p to £2 and the shares may all be sold at 87½p. The object is to

[46] *Post* p. 153.

ensure that the company receives what the shares are worth to the public, and to defeat stags who, by taking shares and then immediately selling them at a higher price, would otherwise receive the difference between the issue price of a share and its worth to the public.

Placings

An issue of shares or debentures may be placed in one of two ways.[47] An issuing house may subscribe for the issue and then invite its clients (*e.g.* insurance companies and pension funds) to purchase from it at a higher price. Although the invitation is a prospectus unless section 55 (2), *ante*, applies,[48] it is not issued by or on behalf of the company and so is not caught by sections 38 and 41.[45] However, it is caught by section 45, *ante*, and by section 43.[46]

Alternatively, an issuing house or stockbrokers or a bank may, without subscribing, act as agents for the company and invite their clients to take from the company. In this case the agents will be paid a commission called "brokerage" for their services. The invitation to the clients is a prospectus unless section 55 (2)[48] applies and, if it is, it is issued on behalf of the company and so caught by sections 38 and 41,[45] and by section 43.[46]

MISREPRESENTATION AND OMISSION

Civil liability

Since a company is liable for the misrepresentations of its directors and other agents acting within the scope of their authority,[49] a person induced to subscribe for shares or debentures in a company by a misrepresentation, *e.g.* in a prospectus, may have a remedy against the company or the individuals responsible, *e.g.* promoters, directors or expert, or both.[50] The remedy may be available under the general law or it may be statutory.

The main remedy against the *company* is rescission[51] of the

---

[47] See Gower, *Modern Company Law*, 3rd ed., p. 286.   [48] p. 131.
[49] See *per* Lord Hatherley in the *Houldsworth* case, *infra*, at p. 7. R. (H.L.) 60, 5 App. Cas. 331.
[50] As in *Frankenburg* v. *Great Horseless Carriage Co.* [1900] 1 Q.B. 504 (C.A.), *post* p. 154.
[51] The representee may elect to repudiate the contract, and legal proceedings are not essential, in the event of misrepresentation. However, if, as is usual, he wishes to recover money or property transferred by him under the contract he may have to initiate proceedings for rescission.

contract of allotment, with or without an action for damages. A shareholder cannot recover damages for fraud against the company without rescission, because that would be inconsistent with the contract between him and the other shareholders.[52] The same is true of a claim to damages, *e.g.* for breach of contract, which a shareholder *qua* shareholder may seek to enforce against the company.[53] Damages in lieu of rescission may be recovered under the Misrepresentation Act 1967, s. 2 (2), which states that where a person has entered into a contract after a misrepresentation made to him *otherwise than fraudulently*, and he would be entitled to rescind, then if rescission is claimed the court may award damages in lieu of rescission, if of opinion that it would be equitable to do so. Damages for *negligent* misrepresentation may be recovered from the company under section 2 (1) of the Misrepresentation Act, which provides that where a person has entered into a contract after a misrepresentation made to him by another party thereto and as a result has suffered loss, then the representor is liable in damages unless he proves that on reasonable grounds he believed up to the time when the contract was made that the representation was true. Whether a shareholder can recover damages under section 2 (1) without rescission is not clear. Section 2 of the Misrepresentation Act does not apply to Scotland.

The main remedies against the *individuals* responsible are compensation for negligent misrepresentation under section 43[54] and damages for fraud.[55]

It may be possible to claim damages for negligent misrepresentation under the principle in *Hedley Byrne & Co. Ltd.* v. *Heller & Partners Ltd.*,[56] which is that a negligent, although honest, misrepresentation, spoken or written, may give rise to an action for damages for financial loss caused thereby. The law implies a duty of care where one party seeks information or advice from another party and trusts the other to exercise due care, it is reasonable for him to do so, the other knows or ought to know that reliance is being

---

[52] *Houldsworth* v. *City of Glasgow Bank* (1880) 7 R. (H.L.) 53; (1880) 5 App.Cas. 317, where it was too late to rescind since the company had gone into liquidation. See also *Western Bank* v. *Addie* (1867) 5 M. (H.L.) 80.

[53] *Re Dividend Fund Incorporated (In Liquidation)* [1974] V.R. 451, where an unlimited company failed to repurchase shares in accordance with the articles and the shareholder had to pay calls in a liquidation.

[54] *Post* p. 153.

[55] *Post* p. 152.

[56] [1964] A.C. 465.

placed on his skill or judgment or ability to make careful inquiry
and he does not expressly disclaim responsibility for his representation. In *Mutual Life and Citizens' Assurance Co. Ltd.* v. *Evatt*[57]
the Privy Council advised that the party from whom information or
advice is sought must carry on the business of giving advice or in
some other way he must have let it be known that he claims to possess
the necessary skill and competence to do so and is prepared to exercise the necessary diligence to give reliable advice. A duty of care
may also arise where the advisor has a financial interest in the transaction.[58]

Rescission of the contract of allotment

In order to obtain rescission of a contract of allotment on the
ground that it was induced by misrepresentation, the allottee must
prove (1) a material false statement of fact, (2) which induced him
to subscribe.

(1) There must be a material false statement of fact.

A prospectus stated: "a large number of gentlemen in the trade and others
have become shareholders." When the register of members was made up there
were 55 shareholders, of whom 10 or 12 were connected with the trade. *Held*,
there was not a sufficiently material misrepresentation to entitle a person who had
taken shares on the faith of the prospectus to have his name deleted from the
register: *City of Edinburgh Brewery Co. Ltd.* v. *Gibson's Trustee* (1869) 7 M. 886.

A statement of fact must be distinguished from a statement of
opinion.[59] A statement that the property of the company is worth
a certain sum of money, or that the profits are expected to reach a
certain figure, is only opinion and gives no right to rescission except
where it can be shown that the maker of the statement did not hold
the opinion. Statements, on the other hand, that "the surplus
assets, as appear by the last balance sheet, amount to upwards of
£10,000,"[60] that £200,000 of share capital has been subscribed,[61]
and that certain persons have agreed to be directors,[62] are all

---

[57] [1971] A.C. 793 (P.C.).
[58] See *Anderson & Sons* v. *Rhodes Ltd.* [1967] 2 All E.R. 850.
[59] *Liverpool Palace of Varieties Ltd.* v. *Miller* (1896) 4 S.L.T. 153 (O.H.).
[60] *Re London and Staffordshire Fire Insurance Co.* (1883) 24 Ch.D. 149.
[61] *Arnison* v. *Smith* (1889) 41 Ch.D. 348 (C.A.), where the share capital had only
     been allotted *as* fully paid up. But see *Akerhielm* v. *De Mare* [1959] A.C. 789
     (P.C.), *post* p. 152.
[62] *Re Scottish Petroleum Co.* (1883) 23 Ch.D. 413 (C.A.); *Blakiston* v. *London and
     Scottish Banking etc. Corpn. Ltd.* (1894) 21 R. 417; contrast *Chambers* v. *Edinburgh
     etc. Aerated Bread Co. Ltd.* (1891) 18 R. 1039.

material statements of fact and, if false, will give rise to a right to rescission.

Where the facts are not equally well known to both sides a statement of opinion by one who should know the facts often implies a statement of fact, *i.e.* that there are reasonable grounds for his opinion, and if it can be proved that he could not as a reasonable man honestly have had the opinion, there is misrepresentation of fact.[63] Again, a statement of intention does not amount to a representation of fact unless it can be proved that the alleged intention never existed.[64]

If a prospectus refers to a report which contains inaccurate statements of fact, the contract can be rescinded if the company has vouched for the accuracy of the report, but otherwise it cannot. Thus, if the company employs an accountant to go through the books and make a report, and then sets out the report in a prospectus, it will not be liable for any inaccuracy in the report.[65] But if the company makes statements of its own, although they are expressed to be based upon a report, it will be liable for an inaccuracy unless in clear and unambiguous terms it has warned intending applicants that it does not vouch for the accuracy of the report, or of any statement based on it.

A company issued a prospectus inviting subscriptions for the purpose of buying a rubber estate in Peru. The prospectus contained extracts from the report of an expert on the spot, which gave the number of matured rubber trees on the estate, and other information. The report was false. *Held*, the accuracy of the report was prima facie the basis of the contract and, therefore, if the company did not intend to contract on that basis, it should have dissociated itself from the report in clear and unambiguous terms, and warned the public that it did not vouch for the accuracy of the report. As there was no such warning the contracts to take shares could be rescinded: *Re Pacaya Rubber and Produce Co. Ltd.* [1914] 1 Ch. 542.[66]

An *innocent* misrepresentation is a sufficient ground for rescission. It is not necessary to prove knowledge of the untruth of the statement.[67]

Non-disclosure of a material fact amounts to misrepresentation if

[63] *Per* Bowen L.J. in *Smith* v. *Land, etc., Corpn.* (1884) 28 Ch.D. 7 (C.A.) at p. 15.
[64] *Edgington* v. *Fitzmaurice* (1885) 29 Ch.D. 459 (C.A.).
[65] *Bentley & Co.* v. *Black* (1893) 9 T.L.R. 580 (C.A.).
[66] An earlier Scottish case which went to the House of Lords is *Mair* v. *Rio Grande Rubber Estates Ltd.*, 1913 S.C. (H.L.) 74.
[67] *Per* Lord Shaw of Dunfermline in *Mair* v. *Rio Grande Rubber Estates Ltd.*, 1913 S.C. (H.L.) 74 at p. 81.

the omission makes what is stated misleading. It has been said[68] that "It is not that the omission of material facts is an independent ground for rescission, but the omission must be of such a nature as to make the statement actually made misleading." In other words, at least in English law, a contract of allotment is not a true contract *uberrimae fidei*,[69] *i.e.* a contract in which all material facts must be disclosed, although, as has been seen, section 38 and the Fourth Schedule usually require a number of particulars to be disclosed in a prospectus.[70]

A prospectus described a piece of land as "eminently suitable" for greyhound racing. The land in question was, however, affected by a town planning resolution, with the result that, unless the local authority's consent was obtained before any buildings were erected, the company would not be entitled to any compensation in the event of the removal of the buildings under the town planning scheme. The local authority refused its consent. *Held*, the omission to disclose the facts set out above rendered the description of the land as "eminently suitable" misleading, and persons who had subscribed for shares on the strength of the prospectus were entitled to rescind their contracts: *Coles* v. *White City (Manchester) Greyhound Assn. Ltd.* (1929) 45 T.L.R. 230 (C.A.).

It will be remembered that the omission on the part of the company to set out in a prospectus the particulars required to be set out by section 38 does not, of itself, entitle a subscriber to rescind.[71]

(2) The allottee must have been induced to subscribe by the false statement.

Whether or not an allottee was induced to subscribe by reason of the misrepresentation is a question of fact depending on the circumstances of each case. It is not sufficient that the prospectus has been widely advertised in the locality if there is proof that the applicant relied, not on the prospectus, but on independent advice.[72] He is entitled to rely upon the prospectus, and is not bound to verify the statements it contains. Where, therefore, a prospectus simply gave the dates of and parties to contracts and stated where they could be inspected, without indicating that they were material

---

[68] *Per* Rigby L.J. in *McKeown* v. *Boudard Peveril Gear Co. Ltd.* (1896) 74 L.T. 712 at p. 713.

[69] And see *per* Lord Watson in *Aaron's Reefs Ltd.* v. *Twiss* [1896] A.C. 273 at p. 287. There is no definitive authority as to the common law of Scotland on the point and, in view of the statutory provisions, it is now unlikely that there will be.

[70] *Ante* p. 98.

[71] *Re South of England Natural Gas Co. Ltd.* [1911] 1 Ch. 573, *ante* p. 140.

[72] *M'Morland's Trustees* v. *Fraser* (1896) 24 R. 65.

contracts, the omission of the applicant to inspect them did not fix him with notice of their contents.[73]

The false statement need not have been the decisive inducing cause of the contract. It is enough that it was one of the contributory causes.[74]

A later purchaser of shares on the Stock Exchange will usually not be able, on the ground of misrepresentation in a prospectus, to rescind the contract under which he purchased the shares from the allottee, or the contract which arose between the company and the purchaser when his name was entered on the register of members.[75] A purchaser from an issuing house where an offer for sale contains a misrepresentation will be able to rescind as against the company— as stated earlier,[76] section 45 provides that the offer for sale is deemed to be a prospectus issued by the company.

Rescission enables the allottee to recover what he paid for the shares or debentures, plus interest.

The right to rescind is lost—

(1) If, after discovering the misrepresentation, the allottee does an act which shows that he elects to retain the shares and so affirms the contract; for example, he attends and votes at general meetings,[77] receives dividends,[78] or attempts to sell the shares.[79]

(2) If he fails to act within a reasonable time of discovering the true facts.

The right to rescind must be exercised promptly if the company is a going concern, and even a delay of a fortnight has been held to be too long in such a case.[80] When a shareholder was put on inquiry in June, but took no steps to make any investigation until November, his delay prevented him from rescinding the contract.[81]

---

[73] *Aaron's Reefs Ltd.* v. *Twiss* [1896] A.C. 273.

[74] *Edgington* v. *Fitzmaurice* (1885) 29 Ch.D. 459 (C.A.).

[75] *Collins* v. *Associated Greyhound Racecourses Ltd.* [1930] 1 Ch. 1 (C.A.), *post* p. 166.

[76] p. 144.

[77] *Sharpley* v. *Louth and East Coast Ry. Co.* (1876) 2 Ch.D. 663 (C.A.).

[78] *Scholey* v. *Central Ry. of Venezuela* (1868) L.R. 9 Eq. 266n.

[79] *Ex p. Briggs* (1866) L.R. 1 Eq. 483.

[80] See *Re Scottish Petroleum Co.* (1883) 23 Ch.D. 413 (C.A.).

[81] *Re Christineville Rubber Estates Ltd.* [1911] W.N. 216; *cf. Caledonian Debenture Co. Ltd.* v. *Bernard* (1898) 5 S.L.T. 392 (O.H.). See also Lord President Inglis in *City of Edinburgh Brewery Co. Ltd.* v. *Gibson's Trustee* (1869) 7 M. 886 at p. 891.

(3) If restitution is impossible,[82] *e.g.* because he sells the shares.

(4) If the company goes into liquidation.[83]

Events leading up to liquidation may have the same effect, *e.g.* where an unlimited banking company stops payment,[84] or calls a meeting to consider winding up.[85]

Damages for fraud

Fraud is difficult to prove. Nevertheless, promoters, directors, experts or the persons making an offer for sale, are liable for fraud if it can be shown that they signed, or authorised the issue of, a prospectus containing a false statement which they did not honestly believe to be true,[86] with the intention that another person should act upon it, and that he acted on it to his detriment. The test is subjective, *i.e.* did they honestly believe the statement to be true according to its meaning as understood *by them*, albeit erroneously, when it was made?[87] If they cannot be proved to have made a false representation knowingly, or without belief in its truth, or recklessly, careless whether it be true or false, they may have to pay compensation under section 43, *post*, the predecessor of which[88] was first enacted as a result of the decision in *Derry* v. *Peek*.[89]

A tramway company by a special Act had power to move trams by animal power and, with the consent of the Board of Trade, by steam power. A prospectus was issued by the directors stating that the company, under its special Act, had the right to use steam power instead of horses. P. subscribed for shares on the strength of this statement. The Board of Trade afterwards refused its consent, and the company was wound up. P. sued the directors for damages for fraud. *Held*, the directors were not liable, the statement as to steam power having been made in the honest belief that it was true: *Derry* v. *Peek* (1889) 14 App.Cas. 337.

In *Akerhielm* v. *De Mare* [1959] A.C. 789 (P.C.), the representation that capital had been "subscribed in Denmark" was inapt to include shares allotted as fully paid to Kenya residents for services rendered in Denmark in connection with the formation of the company. The representor was not liable for fraud

[82] *Western Bank* v. *Addie* (1867) 5 M. (H.L.) 80.
[83] *Oakes* v. *Turquand* (1867) L.R. 2 H.L. 325; *Western Bank* v. *Addie*, above; *Houldsworth* v. *City of Glasgow Bank* (1800) 7 R. (H.L.) 53; (1879) 6 R. 1164.
[84] *Myles* v. *City of Glasgow Bank* (1879) 6 R. 718.
[85] *Alexander Mitchell* v. *City of Glasgow Bank* (1879) 6 R. (H.L.) 60; (1878) 6 R. 439.
[86] Per Lord Herschell in *Derry* v. *Peek* (1889) 14 App.Cas. 337 at p. 374.
[87] *Akerhielm* v. *De Mare* [1959] A.C. 789 (P.C.), *post*.
[88] *Ante* p. 8
[89] The explanation of fraud given in that case was referred to with approval in the Scottish case of *Boyd & Forrest* v. *Glasgow etc. Rlway Co.*, 1912 S.C. (H.L.) 93. See also *Lees* v. *Tod* (1882) 9 R. 807.

because he honestly believed the representation to be true *in the sense in which he understood it.*

A prospectus may be fraudulent, although it is composed of statements which in themselves are perfectly true, if, by reason of omissions, it is calculated as a whole to give a false impression of the position of the company,[90] but mere concealment, even of a material fact, is not at common law a ground for an action for fraudulent misrepresentation against the directors who have issued the prospectus unless the withholding of what is not stated falsifies that which is stated.[91]

If a prospectus issued in order to induce people to subscribe direct from the company contains a false statement, a later purchaser of shares on the Stock Exchange is not one to whom the prospectus was addressed and cannot bring an action for deceit.[92] If, however, a prospectus is issued not only to induce applications for an allotment of shares but also to induce purchases in the open market, its function is not exhausted when the company has gone to allotment and a purchaser on the strength of false statements in such a prospectus can sue those responsible for it for fraud.[93]

The company can be sued for damages for the fraudulent misrepresentation of its directors and agents acting within the scope of their authority.

The measure of damages for fraud is prima facie the difference between the actual value of the shares at the time of allotment and the sum paid for them.[94] The plaintiff recovers for all the actual damage directly flowing from the fraudulent misrepresentation.[95] It is not an action for breach of contract and therefore no damages in respect of prospective gains can be recovered.

Compensation under section 43

Section 43 provides that a promoter, a director at the time or a person authorising the issue of a prospectus is prima facie liable to pay compensation to those who subscribe on the faith of the

---

[90] *Per* James L.J. in *Arkwright* v. *Newbold* (1881) 17 Ch.D. 301 at p. 318.
[91] *Honeyman* v. *Dickson* (1896) 4 S.L.T. 150 (O.H.).
[92] *Peek* v. *Gurney* (1873) L.R. 6 H.L. 377.
[93] *Andrews* v. *Mockford* [1896] 1 Q.B. 372 (C.A.), where the prospectus was later supplemented by false statements in a telegram published in a financial newspaper.
[94] *McConnel* v. *Wright* [1903] 1 Ch. 546 (C.A.); *Davidson* v. *Tulloch* (1860) 3 Macq. 783; 22 D. (H.L.) 7.
[95] *Doyle* v. *Olby* (*Ironmongers*) *Ltd.* [1969] 2 Q.B. 158 (C.A.).

prospectus for the loss they sustain by reason of any untrue statement contained therein.

The expression "promoter" in the section means a promoter who was a party to the preparation of the relevant portion of the prospectus: section 43 (5) (*a*). The company is not liable under section 43. However, the persons making an offer for sale may be liable, as stated earlier.[96] So may those who place shares.[97] Liability under the section arises only if a prospectus is issued.

It has been held that the measure of compensation is the same as the measure of damages for fraud.[98]

Only a person who subscribes for shares or debentures can claim under section 43. Persons accepting an offer for sale to the public are subscribers by section 45, *ante*.[99]

Section 46 provides that a statement in a prospectus is deemed to be untrue if it is misleading. Of course, an omission from a prospectus may make what is stated misleading. To obtain compensation it is not necessary to prove that the directors knew that a statement was untrue. Under section 43 damages may be recovered for negligent misrepresentation.

Although compensation cannot be obtained from the *company*, a claim against the company for rescission of a contract to take shares, together with a return of the money paid, on the ground of misrepresentation in a prospectus may be joined with an action against the directors for compensation.[1]

No *person other than an expert* is liable to pay compensation under section 43 if he can prove—

(1) that he withdrew his consent to act as *director* before the issue of the prospectus and it was issued without his authority or consent; or

(2) that the prospectus was issued without his knowledge or consent, and on becoming aware of its issue he gave reasonable public notice that it was so issued; or

(3) that he became aware of the untrue statement in the prospectus after it had been issued and before any allotment was made, and he thereupon withdrew his consent and gave

---

[96] *Ante* p. 145.
[97] *Ante* p. 146.
[98] *Clark* v. *Urquhart* [1930] A.C. 28; *Davidson* v. *Hamilton* (1904) 12 S.L.T. 353 (O.H.).
[99] p. 144.
[1] *Frankenburg* v. *Great Horseless Carriage Co.* [1900] 1 Q.B. 504 (C.A.).

reasonable public notice of the withdrawal *and* of the reason for it; or

(4) as regards the *untrue statement*—

(*a*) that he had reasonable ground to believe, and did up to the time of allotment believe, that the statement was true;[2] or

(*b*) that the statement was a fair representation of a statement by an expert,[3] or was contained in a correct copy of or extract from a report or valuation of an expert, and he had reasonable ground to believe, and did up to the issue of the prospectus believe, that the expert was competent; further, that the expert had given the consent required by section 40, *ante*, and had not withdrawn such consent before registration of a copy of the prospectus or, to the defendant's[4] knowledge, before allotment; or

(*c*) that the statement was a correct and fair representation of an official statement or of a copy of or extract from an official document: section 43 (2).

An *expert* is liable to pay compensation in respect of his own untrue statement only (s. 43 (1)) and he will escape liability if he can prove—

(1) that, having given his consent to the issue of the prospectus, he withdrew it in writing before delivery of a copy of the prospectus for registration; or

(2) that, after delivery of a copy of the prospectus for registration and before allotment, he, on becoming aware of the untrue statement, withdrew his consent in writing and gave reasonable public notice of the withdrawal and of the reason for it; or

(3) that he was competent to make the statement and had reasonable ground to believe, and did up to allotment believe, that the statement was true: section 43 (3).

[2] See, *e.g.*, *Smith* v. *Moncrieff* (1894) 2 S.L.T. 140 (O.H.); *cf Gray* v. *Central Finance Corporation Ltd.* (1903) 11 S.L.T. 309 (O.H.).

[3] *Ante* p. 137.

[4] The Scots term for "defendant" is "defender." Similarly, the Scots term for "plaintiff" is "pursuer."

Criminal liability

Section 44 provides that where a prospectus is issued and it includes an untrue statement, *i.e.* by section 46 a misleading statement, any person (other than an expert who has merely given his consent to the inclusion of a statement by him in the prospectus) who authorised the issue of the prospectus is liable to a fine of £500 or imprisonment for two years or both unless he proves—

(a) that he had reasonable ground to believe and did, up to the time of issue of the prospectus, believe that the statement was true; or

(b) that the statement was immaterial.

An intent to defraud is not necessary under section 44.

Section 438 and Schedule 15 provide that a person who wilfully makes a false statement, knowing it to be false, in a prospectus or certain other documents, is liable to penalties.

The Larceny Act 1861, s. 84, provided that a director, manager or public officer of a body corporate who made a written statement, which he knew to be false in any material particular, with intent to deceive or defraud any member, shareholder or creditor, or with intent to induce any person to become a shareholder, or to intrust or advance any property to the company, or to enter into any security for its benefit, was liable to seven years' imprisonment.

A statement was false within section 84 if in its context it conveyed a misleading impression although it was literally correct.

Section 84 did not apply to Scotland.

A prospectus contained a statement, which was true, that the company had paid dividends every year between 1921 and 1927. The result was that the prospectus gave the impression that the company had made trading profits during the years in question. However, during each of those years the company had incurred substantial trading losses and was only able to pay the specified dividends by the introduction into the accounts of non-recurring items, earned in the abnormal war period, such as repayments of excess profits duty, adjustment of income tax reserves and the like. No disclosure was made of these trading losses. *Held*, the prospectus was false, because it put before intending investors figures which apparently disclosed the existing position of the company, but in fact hid it, and K., a director who knew that it was false, was guilty of an offence under the Larceny Act, s. 84: *R.* v. *Kyslant* [1932] 1 K.B. 442 (C.C.A.).

Section 84 of the Larceny Act has been repealed and replaced by section 19 of the Theft Act 1968 but the wording of section 19 is different. It provides that an officer of a body corporate or unincorporated association (or a person purporting to act as such) who, with intent to deceive members or creditors about its affairs, publishes or concurs in publishing a written statement or account which to his knowledge is or may be misleading, false or deceptive in a material particular, is liable to seven years' imprisonment. A person who has entered into a security for the benefit of a body corporate is treated as a creditor of it. In particular, the words "or with intent to induce any person to become a shareholder" do not appear in section 19. This provision of the Theft Act does not apply to Scotland.

Fraudulently inducing a person to acquire securities gives rise to liability under the Prevention of Fraud (Investments) Act 1958, s. 13, as amended by the Protection of Depositors Act 1963, s. 21, *post*.[5]

Fraudulently inducing a person to invest money on deposit gives rise to liability under section 1 of the 1963 Act, *post*.[6]

PREVENTION OF FRAUD (INVESTMENTS) ACT 1958

This Act[7] aims at preventing (1) " share-hawking," (2) the private offer of securities in companies which have filed neither a prospectus nor a statement in lieu of prospectus,[8] and (3) fraud in connection with dealings in securities.

The expression "securities" includes shares, stock, debentures, debenture stock, bonds, and rights or interests (whether described as units or otherwise) in any shares, etc: 1958 Act, s. 26.

Dealing in securities is prohibited except in the case of persons licensed for that purpose by the Department of Trade (1958 Act, s. 1), or persons who do not require a licence. No licence is required by—

(a) a member of any recognised stock exchange or recognised association of dealers in securities; or

(b) the Bank of England, any statutory or municipal corporation or any exempted dealer; or

(c) any person acting in the capacity of manager or trustee under a unit trust scheme authorised by the Department of Trade (1958 Act, s. 2).

---

[5] p. 158.
[6] p. 160.
[7] Which repealed and consolidated, *inter alia*, the Prevention of Fraud (Investments) Act 1939 and the Companies Act 1947, s. 117.
[8] *Post* p. 160.

Contravention of section 1 is punishable by up to two years' imprisonment or a £500 fine or both.

Section 14 of the 1958 Act provides that a person, other than those mentioned above, commits an offence (punishable by up to two years' imprisonment or a £500 fine or both) if he distributes or causes to be distributed circulars which, to his knowledge, invite persons to acquire, dispose of, subscribe for or underwrite[9] securities, unless the circular is—

(a) a prospectus complying with the Companies Act 1948; or
(b) in the case of a corporation incorporated in Great Britain which is not a registered company, a document containing the information required by section 417 of the Companies Act.[10]

A circular may be in the form of a newspaper, journal, magazine or other periodical publication.

No offence is committed if circulars are distributed (i) in connection with a bona fide invitation to enter into an underwriting agreement, or (ii) by or on behalf of a corporation to holders of securities, creditors or employees of the corporation or its subsidiary; or (iii) to a person whose business involves the acquisition and disposal, or the holding, of securities.

By section 13 of the 1958 Act, as amended by the Protection of Depositors Act 1963, s. 21, any person who, by any statement, promise or forecast which he knows to be misleading, false or deceptive, or by any dishonest concealment of material facts, or by the reckless making (dishonestly or otherwise) of any statement, promise or forecast which is misleading, false or deceptive, induces or attempts to induce another person to enter into or offer to enter into any agreement for acquiring, disposing of, subscribing for or underwriting securities is liable to seven years' imprisonment.[11]

The Jenkins Report[12] recommended that the provisions of the Prevention of Fraud (Investments) Act 1958 relating to circulars and to unit trusts might be transferred to the Companies Act.

---

[9] *Post* p. 164.
[10] *Post* p. 654.
[11] As regards the insertion of "dishonestly or otherwise," *R.* v. *Russell* [1953] 1 W.L.R. 77 (C.C.A.), and *R.* v. *Grunwald* [1963] 1 Q.B. 935, were adopted contrary to the recommendations of the Jenkins Report, para. 254.
[12] Para. 234.

PROTECTION OF DEPOSITORS ACT 1963[13]

The objects of this Act are, *inter alia*, to penalise fraudulent inducements to invest on deposit and to restrict and regulate the issue of advertisements for deposits.

Section 2 provides that, subject to a number of exceptions, no person shall issue any advertisement inviting the public to deposit money with him.

The exceptions include advertisements with respect to—

(1) investments within Schedule 1 to the Trustee Investments Act 1961; or

(2) deposits with a bank or discount company, or a building society, friendly society or industrial and provident society; or

(3) deposits with a company[14] incorporated in, or having an established place of business in, Great Britain, provided that the advertisement complies with regulations made by the Department of Trade as to its contents and that any accounts required by the 1963 Act have been delivered by the company; or

(4) deposits prescribed by the Department of Trade (*e.g.* deposits from charities, deposits at a low rate of interest, deposits in connection with an employer's savings or profit-sharing scheme, deposits with an insurance company) or deposits permitted by the Department of Trade.

Contravention is punishable by two years' imprisonment or a fine or both.

In the 1963 Act the word "advertisement" includes every form of advertising, whether in a publication or by the display of notices or by means of circulars or other documents or by an exhibition of photographs or cinematograph films, or by way of sound broadcasting or television: section 26.

Again, the word "deposit" means a loan of money at interest, or repayable at a premium, but does not include, *e.g.*, a loan to a

[13] As amended by the Companies Acts 1967 and 1976.
[14] As has been seen, a private company which advertises for deposits loses the status of a private company for the purposes of certain provisions of the Companies Act. *Ante* p. 54.

company or other body corporate involving the issue of debentures or other securities: section 26.

Any person who, by any statement, promise or forecast which he knows to be misleading, false or deceptive, or by any dishonest concealment of material facts, or by the reckless making (dishonestly or otherwise) of any statement, promise or forecast which is misleading, false or deceptive, induces or attempts to induce another person to invest money on deposit with him or any other person, or to enter into or offer to enter into any agreement for that purpose, is liable to seven years' imprisonment or a fine or both: section 1.

STATEMENT IN LIEU OF PROSPECTUS

Section 48 provides that a company, other than a private company, which has a share capital but does not issue a prospectus on its formation, or which has issued such a prospectus but has not proceeded to allot any of the shares offered to the public for subscription, cannot make a *first* allotment of shares or debentures until at least three days after a statement in lieu of prospectus has been delivered to the Registrar. The statement must be in the form set out in the Fifth Schedule, and must contain practically the same information as a prospectus complying with the Fourth Schedule—one difference is that no minimum subscription[15] is set out in a statement in lieu. The statement must be signed by each director. In the event of contravention of the section a fine of £100 is imposed on the company and on every director who knowingly authorises the contravention.

According to the Jenkins Committee[16] the provisions now contained in section 48 were intended to meet a practice whereby large blocks of a company's securities were disposed of by means of placings[17] which resulted in the securities reaching the public from the original allottee without any offer to the public and therefore without any obligation on the company to provide the public with prospectus information. However, the gaps which the provisions were intended to stop have since been largely stopped in other ways. For example, sections 45 (which covers offers for sale) and 55 (which covers placings) now require prospectus information to be given in the kind of case in question. Consequently the Committee

[15] *Ante* p. 134.
[17] *Ante* p. 146.
[16] Cmnd. 1749, para. 247.

recommended[18] that the provisions of the Act relating to statements in lieu of prospectus, including section 30 *ante*,[19] should be repealed. Clause 32 of the Companies Bill 1973 would have repealed sections 30 and 48.

In certain circumstances section 30 requires a statement in lieu complying with the Third Schedule to be registered.

If a statement in lieu of prospectus contains an untrue, *i.e.* a misleading, statement, the directors and others who authorised its delivery are under the same criminal liability as they would be under section 44 if they issued a prospectus containing an untrue statement.[20]

If an allotment is made in contravention of section 48, it is *voidable* at the instance of the applicant within one month after the statutory meeting, or the allotment, as the case might be, even if the company is being wound up: section 49. As will be explained later,[21] the statutory meeting is the first general meeting of a public company. Section 49 thus provides an exception to the general rule that a right to rescind is lost as against a company if the company goes into liquidation.[22]

A director who knowingly contravenes, or authorises the contravention of, the provisions of section 48 is liable to pay *compensation* to any allottee *and* to the company for any loss they have sustained thereby: section 49. Any action for compensation under this section must be brought within two years from the date of the allotment.

If a statement in lieu of prospectus contains false particulars, and an applicant for shares inspects it and relies upon those false statements, he will be entitled to rescind his contract.[23] He may also be able to recover damages for negligence or for fraud.[24] However, he will not be able to obtain compensation under section 43[25] because this section is limited to a prospectus.

---

[18] Para. 252 (j).
[19] p. 54.
[20] *Ante* p. 156; s. 48 provides much the same defences as s. 44.
[21] *Post* p. 284.
[22] *Ante* p. 152.
[23] *Re Blair Open Hearth Furnace Co. Ltd.* [1914] 1 Ch. 390 (C.A.).
[24] *Ante* p. 147.
[25] *Ante* p. 153.

CHAPTER 8

COMMISSIONS AND DISCOUNTS

IN order to procure capital a company frequently desires to pay a commission or discount to a person introducing capital.

Section 53 (1) allows a company to pay a commission to a person in consideration of his subscribing or agreeing to subscribe, absolutely or conditionally, or procuring or agreeing to procure subscriptions, for *shares* in the company if—

(1) the payment is authorised by the articles (authority in the memorandum is insufficient[1]);
(2) the commission does not exceed either (*a*) 10 per cent, of the price at which the shares are issued, or (*b*) the amount or rate authorised by the articles, whichever is the less;
(3) the amount or rate is (*a*) in the case of shares offered to the public for subscription, disclosed in the prospectus; (*b*) in other cases, disclosed in the statement in lieu of prospectus, or in a statement in the prescribed form delivered to the Registrar before payment of the commission;
(4) the number of shares which persons have agreed for a commission to subscribe absolutely is disclosed in the manner set out above.

This subsection applies as well to private as to public companies.[2] It enables a company to pay underwriting commission or brokerage, which commissions are dealt with in detail later.[3]

Section 53 (2) provides that, except as allowed by subsection (1), no company shall apply any of its shares or capital money, either directly or indirectly, in payment of any commission, discount or allowance to any person in consideration of his subscribing or agreeing to subscribe, whether absolutely or conditionally, or procuring or agreeing to procure subscriptions, absolute or conditional, for any *shares* in the company, whether the shares or money be applied by being added to the purchase money of any property

---

[1] *Re Republic of Bolivia Exploration Syndicate Ltd.* [1914] 1 Ch. 139.
[2] *Dominion of Canada General Trading Syndicate* v. *Brigstocke* [1911] 2 K.B. 648.
[3] pp. 164, 166.

acquired by the company or to the contract price of any work to be done for the company, or the money be paid out of the nominal purchase money or contract price, or otherwise.

In the nineteenth century, and especially after the decision in *Ooregum Gold Mining Co. of India Ltd.* v. *Roper*[4] that shares may not be issued at a discount so as to relieve persons taking shares from liability to pay up their nominal amount in full, there was uncertainty as to whether companies could pay underwriting commission. This uncertainty was removed by the Companies Act 1900, the relevant provisions of which are now embodied in the present section 53. Subsection (1) is intended to allow companies to pay underwriting commission when shares are underwritten, subsection (2) to preclude the issue of shares at a discount. The *Ooregum* case, and section 53 (2), lay down a general rule, intended to protect the creditors of the company, that the company's share capital must be raised, as will be explained later.[5]

An agreement to pay commission in contravention of section 53 is invalid.

The company agreed to pay A. a commission of 10 per cent. on any sum accepted by the company on A.'s introduction. No statement in prescribed form, as required by section 53, was registered with the Registrar. A. was the means of introducing £4,600 to the company, and was paid £200 on account. A. sued for £260, the balance of commission. *Held*, A. was not entitled to recover, as the commission was unlawful, but the company could not recover the £200 already paid to A.: *Andreae* v. *Zinc Mines of Great Britain Ltd.* [1918] 2 K.B. 454.

An agreement by a company to apply some of its shares partly for underwriting services and partly for other services is caught by section 53 (2), *ante*, and the whole agreement is invalid.[6]

If shares are allotted at par to persons who are given an option to subscribe for further shares at par within a certain time, an allotment of such further shares at par is not subject to the provisions of section 53, even though the market value of the shares has risen to a premium, because it does not involve the payment of a commission or discount.[7]

Whenever a company has paid any sums by way of commission in respect of shares or debentures, or allowed discount in respect of shares or debentures, the commission or discount must be stated in

---

[4] [1892] A.C. 125, *post* p. 174. The corresponding Scots case is *Klenck* v. *East India Co. etc. Ltd.* (1888) 16 R. 271. [5] *Post* p. 227.
[6] *Banking Service Corporation Ltd.* v. *Toronto Finance Corporation Ltd.* [1928] A.C. 333 (P.C.).
[7] *Hilder* v. *Dexter* [1902] A.C. 474; *cf. Cameron* v. *Glenmorangie Distillery Co. Ltd.* (1896) 23 R. 1092.

every balance sheet until the whole has been written off: Schedule 8, paragraph 3. Further, the commission or discount must be stated in the annual return to the Registrar: Schedule 6, paragraph 3.

A share premium account may be applied by the company in writing off the commission paid on any issue of shares or debentures of the company: section 56.[8]

UNDERWRITING

Before an issue of shares is made to the public, it is usual to insure the success of the issue by having it underwritten. Underwriting means "agreeing to take so many shares, more or less in number, as are specified in the underwriting letter if the public do not subscribe for them."[9] Another definition is, an agreement "to take up by way of subscription in a new company or new issue a certain number of shares if and so far as not applied for by the public."[10] An underwriter does not guarantee that the public will take up the shares; he agrees with the company to subscribe for them himself on the happening of an event, *i.e.* the failure of the public to subscribe them fully. The underwriter may be, for example, a broker, a bank or an issuing house.

The consideration for underwriting usually takes the form of an underwriting commission which the underwriter receives whether or not the public take up all the shares underwritten. The commission may be in the form of shares or it may be a payment out of the money derived from the issue of shares underwritten. Again, it is thought that it may be a payment out of the company's profits, if the company has profits in hand and they have not been capitalised. In any case, section 53 (1) above must be complied with.

An underwriting contract may take the form of an agreement expressed to be made between the underwriter and the company, not necessarily signed by the underwriter,[11] or an offer may be made by letter from the underwriter which requires an acceptance on the part of the company and notice of acceptance given to the underwriter to make it a contract.[12]

[8] *Post* p. 176.
[9] Per Lindley L.J. in *Re Licensed Victuallers' Mutual Trading Association* (1889) 42 Ch.D. 1 (C.A.) at p. 7.
[10] Per Lord Tomlin in *Australian Investment Trust Ltd.* v. *Strand and Pitt Street Properties Ltd.* [1932] A.C. 735 (P.C.) at p. 745.
[11] *Curnor's Trustee* v. *Caledonian Heritable Security Co. Ltd.* (1880) 7 R. 479.
[12] *Re Consort Deep Level Gold Mines Ltd.* [1897] 1 Ch. 575 (C.A.).

In underwriting contracts the underwriter usually irrevocably appoints some person—frequently a director—to apply in his name for the shares he may have to take up. In such a case the authority being, according to English law, coupled with an interest, cannot be revoked by the underwriter.[13]

The underwriting contract being made before the prospectus is issued, it is usual to enter into it on the basis of a draft prospectus, and to provide that the contract is to be binding notwithstanding any variations between the draft and the final prospectus. If, however, there is a material variation between the draft and the final prospectus, the underwriter will not be bound, in spite of such a clause.[14]

Liability on an underwriting contract passes to the executors of the underwriter, if he dies, as the contract is not one involving personal skill on the part of the underwriter.[15]

Sub-underwriting

It is a common practice for underwriters to relieve themselves from some of their risk by entering into sub-underwriting contracts. In such cases a sub-underwriter, in return for a commission, becomes bound to take and pay for his proportion of the shares sub-underwritten which are not allotted to the public, and "the difference between the commission paid by the company to the principal underwriters and the commission paid by them to the sub-underwriters is known as *overriding commission*."[16]

By the nature of a sub-underwriting contract the sub-underwriter authorises the underwriter to apply for shares on his behalf if the public do not apply for them and he cannot revoke the authority so given, whether or not the sub-underwriting letter contains a formal grant of authority to the underwriter. The authority is coupled with an interest.[17]

In a sub-underwriting contract the personality of the sub-under-

---

[13] *Carmichael's Case* [1896] 2 Ch. 643 (C.A.); *cf. Premier Briquette Co. Ltd.* v. *Gray*, 1922 S.C. 329.

[14] *Warner International, etc., Co. Ltd.* v. *Kilburn, Brown & Co.* (1914) 84 L.J.K.B. 365 (C.A.).

[15] *Warner Engineering Co. Ltd.* v. *Brennan* (1913) 30 T.L.R. 191; *Curror's* case *ante.*

[16] Palmer's *Company Law*, 21st ed, p. 196.

[17] *Re Olympic etc. Reinsurance Co. Ltd.* [1920] 2 Ch. 341 (C.A.); *cf. Premier Briquette Co. Ltd.* v. *Gray*, 1922 S.C. 329.

writer is of importance, and therefore an undisclosed principal cannot sue on such a contract made on his behalf by an agent.

X underwrote shares in a company on the basis of a draft prospectus and Y sub-underwrote some of those shares on the same basis. Y was agent for C., but this was not disclosed to X or the company. The public response to the issue was insufficient and shares were allotted to Y, who renounced in favour of C., who was entered on the register. The prospectus contained misrepresentations and, on learning of this, C. applied for his name to be removed from the register and for repayment of his money. *Held*, C. was not entitled to rescission because (1) the contract between Y and the company was of such a class that Y must be treated as a principal and not as agent for C., and (2) the contract between the company and C. through the entry of C.'s name on the register was not entered into on the basis of the prospectus, the function of the prospectus having been fulfilled before that contract was made: *Collins* v. *Associated Greyhound Racecourses Ltd.* [1930] 1 Ch. 1 (C.A.).

Underwriting debentures

The provisions of section 53 do not apply to the underwriting of debentures, as there is nothing to prevent the issue of debentures at a discount.[18] When commission is paid for underwriting debentures, however, the Act requires:

(1) Particulars of the amount or rate paid to be filed with the Registrar within 21 days of the issue of the debentures: sections 95 (9), 106A (8).

(2) The amount or rate to be disclosed in any prospectus issued within two years thereafter or in a statement in lieu of prospectus: Schedules 4 and 5.

BROKERAGE

Brokerage is a payment made to an issuing house or brokers in return for their placing shares or debentures without subscribing.[19] It differs from underwriting commission in that it is a payment made to a person for placing shares or debentures without involving him in any risk of having to take them. Section 53 (3) provides that nothing in the section affects the power of any company to pay such brokerage as was previously lawful. It was previously held in *Metropolitan Coal Consumers' Association* v. *Scrimgeour*[20] that brokerage of a reasonable amount payable in the ordinary course

[18] *Post* p. 175.
[19] *Ante* p. 146.
[20] [1895] 2 Q.B. 604 (C.A.).

of business was legal. In that case the brokerage was $2\frac{1}{2}$ per cent. but a usual brokerage is $\frac{1}{4}$ per cent. Authority to pay brokerage must be contained in the articles, and need not be given in the memorandum.[21] Table A, article 6, authorises the payment of "such brokerage as may be lawful" on any issue of shares.

A payment is brokerage only if it is paid to "stockbrokers, bankers and the like, who exhibit prospectuses and send them to their customers, and by those mediation the customers are induced to subscribe."[22] The person to whom it is paid must be one who, in some way, carries on the business of a broker. A payment, therefore, to a lady of a percentage on the amount of capital which she induced third parties to subscribe for shares in a company—such a transaction being an isolated one, and not in the ordinary course of the lady's business—was held not to be brokerage.[23]

The amount or rate of brokerage paid or payable must be disclosed in any prospectus issued within two years thereafter or in a statement in lieu of prospectus: Schedules 4 and 5.

---

[21] See *per* Lindley L.J. in [1895] 2 Q.B. 604 at p. 607.
[22] *Per* Bailhache J. in *Andreae* v. *Zinc Mines of Great Britain Ltd.* [1918] 2 K.B. 454 at p. 458.
[23] *Andreae* v. *Zinc Mines of Great Britain Ltd., ante* p. 163.

Chapter 9

ALLOTMENT AND
COMMENCEMENT OF BUSINESS

THIS chapter deals with the contract of allotment under which shares are allotted by a company to a person who has applied for them, certain statutory restrictions on allotment by a public company, and the return which the company usually must deliver to the Registrar after it has allotted shares. Further, this is a convenient place in which to deal with the issue of shares at a discount and the issue of shares at a premium, as well as with certain statutory restrictions on the commencement of business by a public company.

AGREEMENT FOR ALLOTMENT

The ordinary law of contract, which usually requires an offer and an acceptance if there is to be an agreement, applies to agreements to take shares in a company. Where a prospectus is issued by the company the prospectus is not an offer—it is merely an invitation to the public to make offers. An offer is made by the applicant in sending a form of application for shares to the company and it is accepted by the allotment of shares to the applicant. Under normal articles the power to allot shares is vested in the board of directors.

The application for shares is accompanied by a declaration that the applicant is not resident outside the Scheduled Territories[1] and is not making the application as a nominee for a person residing outside them. This is to comply with the Exchange Control Act 1947, Part III, which provides that shares (or stock, debentures, debenture stock or unit trust units) cannot be issued (or transferred) to persons resident outside the Scheduled Territories unless Treasury consent is obtained.

An acceptance must be unconditional[2] and correspond with the terms of the offer. If, therefore, the application was for 100 shares and only 25 were allotted, the allotment would be a counter-offer and the applicant could refuse to take any shares. An issue may be over-

[1] *Ante* p. 97.
[2] *Liquidator of the Consolidated Copper Co. etc. Ltd.* v. *Peddie* (1877) 5 R. 393.

subscribed, and the company unable to make an allotment in full to every applicant; in order to obviate this difficulty the form of application invariably runs, "I agree to accept such shares or any smaller number that may be allotted to me."

To constitute a binding contract, an acceptance must be communicated to the offeror.[3] If the parties must have contemplated that the post might be used to communicate acceptance, the posting of a letter of allotment is sufficient communication to the applicant.

G. applied for shares in the H. company. A letter of allotment was posted, but never reached G. *Held*, G. was a shareholder in the company: *Household Fire Insurance Co.* v. *Grant* (1879) 4 Ex.D. 216 (C.A.).[4]

Communication, however, may be made in any way which shows the applicant that the company has accepted his offer,[5] *e.g.* by a letter demanding payment of an instalment on the shares,[6] or by receipt of a notice calling a general meeting and notification given orally by the secretary that shares have been allotted.[7] The applicant must, however, have *agreed* to take shares and not merely have expressed a "willingness" to take them;[8] the sending to a person who has not so agreed of notices of meetings and of letters making calls on the shares does not of itself make the recipient a shareholder.[9]

An offer can be revoked at any time before acceptance is communicated.

H. applied for shares in a company. Shares were allotted to him, and the letter of allotment sent to the *company's* agent to deliver by hand to H. Before the letter was delivered, H. withdrew his application. *Held*, H. was not a shareholder in the company: *Re National Savings Bank Association* (1867) L.R. 4 Eq. 9.

The above rule is now subject to an exception when the application is made in pursuance of a prospectus issued generally, *i.e.* to persons other than members or debenture holders of the company.[10] In such a case the application cannot be revoked until after the expiration of the third day after the time of the opening of the subscription lists: section 50 (5).[11] This is to prevent the incon-

---

[3] See *Entores Ltd.* v. *Miles Far East Corporation* [1955] 2 Q.B. 327 (C.A.).
[4] Doubted in Scotland: *Mason* v. *Benhar Coal Co. Ltd.* (1882) 9 R. 883, *per* Lord Shand at p. 890.
[5] *Chapman* v. *Sulphite Pulp Co. Ltd.* (1892) 19 R. 837.
[6] *Forget* v. *Cement Products Co. of Canada* [1916] W.N. 259 (P.C.).
[7] *Chapman* v. *Sulphite Pulp Co. Ltd.* (1892) 19 R. 837; see also *Curror's Trustee* v. *Caledonian Heritable Security Co. Ltd.* (1880) 7 R. 479 and *Nelson* v. *Fraser* (1906) 14 S.L.T. 513 (O.H.).
[8] *Mason* v. *Benhar Coal Co. Ltd.* (1882) 9 R. 883.
[9] *Goldie* v. *Torrance* (1882) 10 R. 174; and see *Liquidator of the Florida etc. Co. Ltd.* v *Bayley* (1890) 17 R. 525.   [10] *Ante* p. 140.
[11] *Post* p. 180.

venience caused by "stags" revoking their applications before allotment when they think the issue has not been successful.

To be effective, revocation of an offer must be communicated to the offeree. Thus notice of the revocation of an application must reach the company before the letter of allotment is posted.[12] If the revocation is communicated by post it is not effective until the letter is received by the company.

An offer lapses if it is not accepted within the time prescribed or, if none is prescribed, within a reasonable time. Thus an allotment must be made within a reasonable time after the application, otherwise the application will lapse and the applicant will be entitled to refuse to take the shares.

On June 8 M. offered to take shares in the R. company. He heard nothing until November 23, when he received a letter of acceptance. M. refused to take the shares. *Held*, M. was entitled to refuse, as his offer had lapsed: *Ramsgate Victoria Hotel Co. Ltd.* v. *Montefiore* (1866) L.R. 1 Ex. 109.

An offer is also terminated by the failure of a condition subject to which it was made. Thus if an application for shares is conditional, *e.g.* on the applicant having a contract to supply goods to the company,[13] or on all capital being subscribed,[14] and the condition is not fulfilled when shares are allotted to him, the applicant is under no liability to take the shares.

A conditional application must be distinguished from an application for shares coupled with a collateral agreement, *e.g.* where £10 shares are to be paid up to the extent of £1.50 in cash on allotment, that the balance is to be set-off against goods to be supplied to the company by the allottee. In the latter case, when shares are allotted the applicant becomes a shareholder with the right merely of suing the company on the collateral agreement.[15]

A letter of allotment need not now be stamped.[16]

CONSIDERATION FOR ALLOTMENT

The general rule is that an allottee must pay for his shares in full.[17] However, payment in full need not be made on allotment if the

[12] *Byrne* v. *Van Tienhoven* (1880) 5 C.P.D. 344; *Thomson* v. *James* (1855) 18 D. 1.
[13] *Shackleford's Case* (1866) L.R. 1 Ch.App. 567.
[14] *Swedish Match Co. Ltd.* v. *Seivwright* (1889) 16 R. 989.
[15] *Elkington's Case* (1867) L.R. 2 Ch.App. 511; *cf. Liquidator of the Pelican etc. Insurance Co. Ltd.* v. *Bruce* (1904) 11 S.L.T. 658 (O.H.), and see opinions in *National House Investments Co. Ltd.* v. *Watson*, 1908 S.C. 888.
[16] Finance Act 1949, s. 35 and Sched. VIII, Pt. I, para 17.
[17] *Ooregum Gold Mining Co. of India Ltd.* v. *Roper* [1892] A.C. 125, *post* p. 174; *Klenck* v. *East India Co. etc. Ltd.* (1888) 16 R. 271.

company does not require it, *i.e.* if the shares are allotted in consideration of payment of part of the nominal amount and of a promise of payment of the remainder as and when required by the company. If the company does not require payment in full on allotment, the shares are partly paid shares. Until the allottee has paid for his shares in full he has not fulfilled the condition limiting his liability for the company's debts to "the amount, if any, unpaid on the shares."[18]

"The amount subscribed, which is to make the shareholder a partner in the concern, must be paid, and by no expedient nor indirect arrangement can the company evade the obligation of possessing the capital which the Legislature has enjoined shall be the capital upon which it is to trade. . . . It has also provided that the governing body shall be at liberty either to call up the whole of the agreed sum, or portions of the agreed sum, at such times and in such ways as they think proper by their rules to determine."[19]

Payment for shares may be made either in cash or, with the agreement of the company, in kind.

Payment in cash does not necessarily mean that cash must be handed over by the allottee to the company. It is sufficient if he has a valid claim against the company, *e.g.* if the company owes him a sum of money and agrees to allot him shares to the amount of the debt in extinction of it.

S. sold a mine to a company, and also agreed to take shares. The nominal amount of the shares and purchase price of the mine were payable at once. It was agreed between S. and the company that S. should be debited with the amount payable on the shares and credited with the purchase price of the property. This was done, and S. made up the difference in cash. *Held*, S. had made payment in cash: *Spargo's Case* (1873) L.R. 8 Ch.App. 407.

Where a vendor of property agrees with the company to take part of the price in the form of fully paid shares of the company, that is not payment in cash.[20]

If the sum due to the allottee is not due immediately, *e.g.* if he agrees to supply goods to the company the purchase price of which, when due, is to be set-off against calls in respect of what remains to be paid on the shares, the agreement is in general *ultra vires*.[21]

Shares may, with the consent of the company, be paid for other-

---

[18] *Ante* p. 42.
[19] *Per* Earl of Halsbury L.C. in *Randt Gold Mining Co.* v. *New Balkis Eersteling Ltd.* [1903] 1 K.B. 461 (C.A.) at p. 465.
[20] *Liquidators of Coustonholm Paper Mills Co. Ltd.* v. *Law* (1891) 18 R. 1076.
[21] *Pellatt's Case* (1867) L.R. 2 Ch.App. 527; followed in *National House etc. Investment Co. Ltd.* v. *Watson*, 1908 S.C. 888 (fees for professional services to be performed for company to be set-off).

wise than in cash, *e.g.* by the transfer of property to the company or by the rendering of services to the company, but where shares are allotted as fully or partly paid up otherwise than in cash, a contract constituting the title of the allottee to the allotment together with any contract of sale, or for services or other consideration for the allotment, or, if such a contract is not in writing, particulars of the contract, must, with the return as to allotments, be delivered to the Registrar, usually within a month after the allotment: section 52.[22] Default renders the officers of the company liable to penalties but does not make the allotment void.

Article 7 of the Second Draft Directive submitted by the Commission to the Council of the EEC provides that shares issued against cash must be paid up to at least 25 per cent of their nominal value, and article 8 provides that if shares are to be allotted against investment not made in cash, a report on the value of the assets to be brought in other than cash and on the value of the shares to be issued must be made by an independent valuer prior to the formation of the company.

Registration under section 52 does not make a "contract" binding on the company if there is no consideration for it, and past consideration is no consideration.[23]

A private company decided to turn itself into a public company. Before doing so it resolved to allot £6,000 of fully paid shares to the existing directors and shareholders, and a contract was made agreeing to allot the shares in consideration of their past services and expenses in forming the company and establishing the business. The contract was registered and the shares were allotted. The company afterwards went into liquidation. *Held*, the directors and shareholders were liable to pay for the shares, as there was no consideration in money or money's worth for the allotment, past services being no consideration: *Re Eddystone Marine Insurance Co.* [1893] 3 Ch. 9 (C.A.).

An agreement to allot shares in consideration of services to be performed in the future also renders the allottee liable to pay for the shares.[24] "It is not open to a company to agree with the holder or proposed holder of its shares to replace the statutory liability by a special contract sounding in damages only."[25] However, a company may agree to pay a fixed sum immediately for services to be performed in the future, *e.g.* for the erection of a building, and to satisfy that debt by the allotment of shares.[26]

If there is a contract for the acceptance by the company of

---

[22] *Post* p. 181.
[23] The doctrine of consideration is not part of Scots law. *Cf.*, however, *Liquidator of the Pelican etc. Insurance Co. Ltd.* v. *Bruce* (1904) 11 S.L.T. 658 (O.H.).
[24] *National House etc. Investment Co. Ltd.* v. *Watson*, 1908 S.C. 888.
[25] *Per* Parker J. in *Gardner* v. *Iredale* [1912] 1 Ch. 700 at p. 716.
[26] *Gardner* v. *Iredale*, above.

specified property or services of substantial value in payment for shares, the court will not, whilst the contract stands, inquire into the adequacy of the consideration, as it is for the parties to make their own bargain.

The goodwill, stock-in-trade and property of a business was sold to a company for £46,000, of which £20,000 was to be paid in fully paid shares. The stock-in-trade was shown in the company's books at a figure £11,000 less than the sum allocated to it in the agreement. On the company's going into liquidation, a misfeasance summons was taken out to obtain payment for the shares. *Held*, since the agreement could not be impeached, the adequacy of the consideration could not be gone into: *Re Wragg Ltd.* [1897] 1 Ch. 796 (C.A.).

"Where a company, in good faith, issues shares as fully paid-up in consideration of property transferred or services rendered, the Court will not inquire into the value of that which was accepted by the Company as an equivalent of money": *per* Lord Stormonth Darling (Ordinary) in *Brownlie and ors, Petitioners* (1898) 6 S.L.T. 249 (O.H.) at p. 251.

Where the contract is fraudulent or shows on the face of it that the consideration is illusory, the allottee is liable to pay for the shares.

G. agreed to sell a concession to a company which agreed to allot him as fully paid 400 shares forthwith and also one-fifth of any future increase of capital. *Held*, the agreement was good so far as it obliged the company to allot one-fifth of any future increase of capital but void so far as it relieved G. from paying for the shares. It was apparent that the value of the concession bore no relation to the amount of the shares: *Hong Kong and China Gas Co. Ltd.* v. *Glen* [1914] 1 Ch. 527.

"If the agreement were that the property to be purchased should be valued, and that against this property shares should be issued as fully paid to an extent exceeding the amount of the valuation by one-third, the arrangement would . . . be bad as to this excess of one-third. It would to this extent be apparent on the face of the contract that the attempted discharge of a part of the liability was illusory": *per* Sargant J. at p. 539.

When shares are issued in pursuance of a contract registered under section 52, and the allottee also subscribes the memorandum for the same number of shares, care should be taken to see that the agreement makes it clear that the shares for which the memorandum is signed are the same as those referred to in the agreement, otherwise both lots of shares will have to be paid for.[27] To prevent this from happening, it is usual for the allottee under the agreement not to subscribe the memorandum.

[27] *Fothergill's Case* (1873) L.R. 8 Ch.App. 270.

ISSUE OF SHARES AT A DISCOUNT

The general rule is that shares must *not* be issued at a discount, *i.e.* must not be issued as fully paid for a consideration less than the nominal amount. The shareholder must pay the full nominal value of his shares, although not on allotment if the company does not require payment in full on allotment, whether he pays in cash or in kind.

The market value of the £1 ordinary shares of a company was 2s. 6d. The company thereupon issued preference shares of £1 each with 15s. credited as paid, leaving a liability of only 5s. a share. A contract to this effect was registered under what is now s. 52. *Held*, the issue was *ultra vires*, and the allottees were liable to pay for the shares in full: *Ooregum Gold Mining Co. of India Ltd.* v. *Roper* [1892] A.C. 125.[28]

"The dominant and cardinal principle of [the Companies] Acts is that the investor shall purchase immunity from liability beyond a certain limit, on the terms that there shall be and remain a liability up to that limit": *per* Lord Macnaghten at p. 145.

The share capital of a company must be raised. This means that money or assets equal to the paid-up capital must be received by the company or, in other words, that shares can be treated as paid up only to the extent of the amount actually received by the company in cash or in kind. The idea is to protect creditors of the company.[29] Of course, there may be no substantial issue of share capital by a company—there is no rule that there must be a substantial paid-up capital.

A contract to take shares at a discount cannot be enforced against the person who has agreed to take them, but if such a person allows his name to be put on the register, and deals with the shares as a member, he will be liable to pay the full amount in cash.[30]

There is no issue at a discount where shares are issued at par, *e.g.* after the exercise of an option to take them up at par, even though they could otherwise be issued at a premium,[31] or where shares are issued at a lesser premium than that at which they might have been paid.[32]

---

[28] An earlier Scottish case to the same effect is *Klenck* v. *East India Co. etc. Ltd.* (1888) 16 R. 271, where the memorandum contained a power to issue shares at a discount.

[29] See further *post* p. 227.

[30] *Ex p. Sandys* (1889) 42 Ch.D. 98 (C.A.).

[31] *Hilder* v. *Dexter* [1902] A.C. 474, *ante* p. 163.

[32] *Cameron* v. *Glenmorangie Distillery Co. Ltd.* (1896) 23 R. 1092.

There is nothing to prevent debentures being issued at a discount. However, in the case of convertible debentures, if the debentures are issued at a discount, with a right to exchange them for fully paid shares equal in nominal amount to the par value of the debentures, the right is void as being a right to an issue of shares at a discount.[33] The right will be valid if it is to fully paid shares equal in nominal amount to the issue price of the debentures—the shares will then not be issued at a discount.

The general rule is subject to the following exceptions:

(1) Section 57 provides that a company may issue shares at a discount if—

    (*a*) the shares are of a class already issued (not at a discount);

    (*b*) the issue is authorised by a resolution[34] passed in general meeting and specifying the maximum rate of discount;

    (*c*) the company has been entitled to commence business for at least one year;

    (*d*) the sanction of the court is obtained;

    (*e*) the issue is made within one month after the sanction of the court is obtained, unless the court extends the time;

    (*f*) every prospectus relating to the issue contains particulars of the discount allowed, or so much of it as has not been written off. The same particulars must be given in the annual return and the balance sheet: Schedule 6, paragraph 3 (*g*); Schedule 8, paragraph 3 (*e*).

No express power in the articles is required to issue shares at a discount under section 57.

Section 57 was intended to enable a company to dispose of the "fag-end" of a class of shares. For example, if the issued shares of a class are quoted on a stock exchange at less than their nominal value, no one will take the remaining shares of the class unless they are issued at a price corresponding to that at which the issued shares are quoted. However, it appears that, in practice, the section is not much used.

    (2) There is in effect a discount when shares are issued for an overvalued non-monetary consideration, as in *Re Wragg Ltd.*, *ante*.[35]

---

[33] *Mosely* v. *Koffyfontein Mines Ltd.* [1904] 2 Ch. 108 (C.A.).
[34] An *ordinary* resolution will suffice.   [35] p. 173.

(3) Similarly where, under section 53 (1), *ante*,[36] commission is paid to a person who agrees to subscribe, or to procure subscriptions, for shares in a company.

ISSUE OF SHARES AT A PREMIUM

Where a company's issued shares have a market value greater than the amount paid up on them, when further shares are being issued the company may require applicants to agree to pay more than the nominal amount of the new shares, *i.e.* to pay a premium.

A company may, without any special power in its articles, issue its shares at a premium, *i.e.* for a consideration in cash or in kind which exceeds the nominal amount of the shares, although there is no law which obliges a company to issue its shares above par because they are saleable at a premium in the market.[37] However, by section 56, where shares are issued at a premium, whether for cash or otherwise, a sum equal to the aggregate amount or value of the premiums must be transferred to the "share premium account."

As will be seen later, section 56 extends the principle that the share capital of a company must be maintained[38] to a share premium account, because the section goes on to provide that the provisions of the Act relating to reduction of capital apply to this account, *i.e.* it cannot be reduced without leave of the court, except where it is applied in—

(1) paying up unissued shares of the company to be issued to members as fully paid bonus shares;[39] or

(2) writing off (*a*) the preliminary expenses, or (*b*) the expenses of, or the commission paid or discount allowed on, an issue of shares or debentures of the company; or

(3) providing for the premium payable by the company on the redemption of redeemable preference shares or of debentures.[40]

The object of the provisions relating to the share premium account is to prevent dividends being paid out of premiums received

---

[36] p. 162.
[37] *Per* Lord Davey in *Hilder* v. *Dexter* [1902] A.C. 474 at p. 480; *Cameron's* case *ante*.
[38] *Post* p. 232.
[39] Other ways in which bonus shares can be paid for are dealt with *post* p. 480.
[40] *Post* pp. 222, 496.

on an issue of shares.[41] When, therefore, any part of the share premium account is distributed among the shareholders it is to be treated as if the company were reducing its capital by repaying paid-up share capital.[42] Although share premiums are regarded as capital, it is not capital belonging to any individual shareholder. The shareholder paying the premium has no dividend rights in respect of it and has no right to repayment of it in a winding up.

Shares can be issued at a premium not only for cash but also for a consideration other than cash. If, in the latter case, the value of the consideration received exceeds the nominal value of the shares issued, there is an issue at a premium and section 56 applies.

A Co. and B Co. were amalgamated by the formation of C Co. and by A and B shareholders exchanging their shares for new shares in C. C issued 2,000,000 £1 shares to A and B shareholders in exchange for their shares in A and B on a pound for pound basis. However, the assets of A and B had been written down and were in fact worth £7,000,000. *Held*, there was an issue at a premium and the difference between the nominal value of the shares issued by C and the actual value of the assets of A and B acquired (£5,000,000) had to be carried to C's share premium account: *Head* (*Henry*) *& Co. Ltd.* v. *Ropner Holdings Ltd.* [1952] Ch. 124.

The amount of the share premium account must be specified in the balance sheet: Schedule 8, paragraph 2 (*c*).

The issue of shares at a premium accentuates the unreality of the nominal or par value of a share. The capital in the share premium account is an anomalous form of capital because it is capital on which no dividend is paid, which is not attributable to the ownership of any class of shares, which is not part of the company's nominal capital, which the ordinary investor does not realise is part of the company's actual capital, and which is not capital on which stamp duty is paid.

RESTRICTIONS ON ALLOTMENT

Sections 47 to 51 contain restrictions on allotment by *public* companies.

[41] As in *Drown* v. *Gaumont–British Picture Corporation Ltd.* [1937] Ch. 402, where there was a trading loss in one year but a dividend was paid out of the reserve fund, part of which consisted of premiums on issues of shares.
[42] *Re Duff's Settlements* [1951] Ch. 923 (C.A.).

No allotment unless minimum subscription applied for

Section 47 provides that where a prospectus is issued, a *first* allotment of *shares* offered to the public for subscription cannot be made until—

(1) shares payable *in cash* to the amount of the minimum subscription have been *applied for*;

(2) the money payable on application for such shares has been paid to and *received* by the company.

We have already seen[43] that the minimum subscription is the minimum amount which, in the opinion of the directors, must be raised by the issue of shares to provide for such things as the purchase price of any property which is to be defrayed out of the proceeds of the issue.

The object of section 47 is to prevent a company making a first allotment of shares where the public response to the prospectus has been poor. If, *e.g.*, offers have been made for shares payable in cash to the amount of the minimum subscription such offers can be accepted by the company which will then receive the amount of cash required to be raised by the prospectus. The section is satisfied if shares payable in cash to the amount of the minimum subscription are underwritten.[44]

The money payable on application for each share must be at least 5 per cent. of the nominal value of the share. This condition applies to *all* allotments of shares.

If the above conditions are not satisfied within forty days of the first issue of the prospectus, all money received must be forthwith returned to the applicants without interest. If it is not returned within 48 days of the issue of the prospectus, the directors are jointly and severally liable to repay it with interest at five per cent. per annum. A director is not liable, however, if he proves that the default in repayment was not due to any misconduct or negligence on his part.

A sum is, for the purposes of this section, deemed to have been paid to and received by the company if a cheque for the sum has been received in good faith by the company and the directors have no reason to suspect that it will not be paid.

[43] *Ante* p. 134.
[44] *Ante* p. 164.

Any condition requiring an applicant to waive compliance with any of these requirements is void.

No allotment unless statement in lieu of prospectus registered

We saw in Chapter 7[45] that section 48 provides that if no prospectus is issued on the formation of the company, or a prospectus is issued but no allotment of the shares offered to the public is made, a *public* company cannot make a *first* allotment of *shares or debentures* unless at least three days before the allotment a statement in lieu of prospectus in accordance with the Fifth Schedule, signed by each director, has been delivered to the Registrar.

Effect of irregular allotment

We also saw in Chapter 7[45] that when an allotment is made which does not satisfy the provisions of section 47 or section 48, *ante*, section 49 gives the applicant two remedies, one against the company and the other against the directors.

As against the *company*, the allotment is *voidable* by the allottee within one month after the holding of the statutory meeting or, if such meeting is unnecessary or has been held already, within one month after allotment, even if the company is being wound up.

Legal proceedings need not be taken within a month. Notice of avoidance within the month, followed by prompt legal proceedings after the month, is sufficient.[46]

As against the *directors*, the allottee can sue such of them as knowingly contravened or authorised the contravention of the provisions for any loss, damages or costs he may have sustained or incurred thereby. Any such proceedings against directors must be brought within two years after allotment. The company has a similar remedy against the directors for any loss, damages or costs sustained or incurred by it.

Time of allotment

By section 50, when a prospectus is issued generally, that is, to persons who are not existing members or debenture holders of the

[45] p. 160.
[46] *Re National Motor Mail-Coach Co. Ltd.* [1908] 2 Ch. 228.

company,[47] no allotment or sale of the shares or debentures can be made until the third day after that on which the prospectus is first issued or such later time as is specified in the prospectus—such third day or later time being called "the time of the opening of the subscription lists." The *two*-day interval is to give the Press time to comment and to enable possible applicants to obtain expert advice before applying for securities. When the prospectus is first issued as a newspaper advertisement, the day on which the prospectus is first issued is the day on which the advertisement first appears.

Contravention of these provisions does not render the allotment void, but the company and every officer in default, and, in the case of an offer for sale, the persons making the offer who knowingly and wilfully authorise or permit the contravention, are liable to a fine of £500.

An application for shares or debentures in pursuance of a prospectus issued generally is irrevocable until *after* the expiration of the third day after the time of the opening of the subscription lists, or the giving before the expiration of such third day, by some person responsible under section 43 for the prospectus, of a public notice having the effect of limiting his responsibility: section 50 (5). This is an exception to the general rule that an offer can be revoked at any time before it is accepted. The idea is to restrain "stags" who would otherwise revoke their applications if the shares or debentures cannot be quickly resold at a profit. The company has a *three*-day period in which to accept the "stags'" offers and so prevent them from revoking.

Saturdays, Sundays and bank holidays are not counted for the purposes of this section: section 50 (6).

Section 50 does not apply to a prospectus in respect of which a certificate of exemption under section 39[48] has been obtained: section 50 (7).

The Jenkins Report[49] recommended that applications made in pursuance of a prospectus issued generally should be irrevocable until the expiry of seven working days after the date on which the prospectus is first so issued—the present interval is not long enough —and that no allotment of securities offered to the public should be allowed after three months from the first issue of the prospectus, *i.e.* no allotment should be allowed on a stale prospectus.

[47] *Ante* p. 140. [48] *Ante* p. 139.
[49] Para. 252.

Clause 30 of the Companies Bill 1973 would have given effect to such recommendations and would also have repealed section 50(7).

Stock exchange quotation being sought

If a prospectus states that application has been or will be made for permission for the shares or debentures to be listed on any stock exchange, section 51 of the 1948 Act, as amended by Schedule 2 of the 1976 Act, provides that the money received from applicants must be paid into a separate bank account under penalty of a fine of £500 on the company and every officer in default. The permission must be applied for before the third day after the first issue of the prospectus (Saturdays, Sundays and bank holidays not being counted: section 50 (6)) and if this is not done, or if permission is refused before the end of three weeks from the closing of the subscription lists or such longer period not exceeding six weeks as may be notified by the stock exchange, the allotment or sale is *void* and the money must be returned by the company or the persons making the offer. Subscription lists close when the issue of shares or debentures is fully subscribed or it is obvious that the issue is not going to be so subscribed. If the money is not returned within eight days, the directors are jointly and severally liable to repay it with interest at five per cent. per annum, except that a director is not liable if he proves that the default was not due to misconduct or negligence on his part. Failure to apply for or to obtain permission also renders an allotment under an underwriting contract void. When permission is granted, the money can be taken out of the separate bank account and used in the ordinary way.

If, before the money is returned, the debenture holders appoint a receiver of the company's property, it seems that the money in the separate bank account is not part of the company's property and cannot be claimed by the debenture holders but must be returned to the applicants.[50]

RETURN AS TO ALLOTMENTS

Section 52 of the 1948 Act, as amended by Schedule 2 of the 1976 Act, provides that whenever a limited company with a share capital makes

---

[50] *Per* Harman J., *obiter*, in *Re Nanwa Gold Mines Ltd.* [1955] 1 W.L.R. 1080 at p. 1085.

any allotment of its *shares*, it must, within a month, deliver to the Registrar—

(1) A return of the allotments (on Form PUC 2), stating the number and nominal amount of the shares, the names, addresses and descriptions of the allottees and the amount paid or payable on each share, whether on account of the nominal value of the share or by way of premium.

(2) In the case of shares allotted *otherwise than for cash*, a contract constituting the title of the allottee to the allotment, together with any contract of sale or for services or other consideration for the allotment, and a return (on Form PUC 3) stating the number and nominal amount of shares so allotted, the extent to which they are to be treated as paid up, and the consideration for the allotment.

If such a contract is not in writing, the prescribed particulars of the contract must be filed on Form 52 stamped with the same stamp duty as on a contract.

Forms PUC 2 and PUC 3 bear capital duty at the rate of £1 per £100 or part thereof on the greater of (*a*) the total nominal value of the shares allotted or (*b*) the total amount paid, or due and payable, or treated as paid in respect of the shares. Compliance with these requirements is enforced by a penalty of £50 a day on every director, manager, secretary or other officer of the company who is a party to the default. The court has power to grant relief if the omission to deliver any document within the prescribed time is accidental or due to inadvertence or it is just and equitable to grant relief.

Clause 31 (2) of the Companies Bill 1973 would have given the Secretary of State power to specify the form and contents of annual returns.

RESTRICTIONS ON COMMENCEMENT OF BUSINESS

A private company can commence business, exercise any borrowing power [51] which it has and make a binding contract immediately on incorporation.

By section 109 a public company with a share capital must do none of these things until some further requirements have been complied with. These are:

[51] *Post* p. 481.

(1) Where a prospectus has been issued inviting the public to subscribe for *shares*—

(*a*) shares payable in *cash* to the amount of the minimum subscription must have been *allotted*;

(*b*) every director of the company must have paid on his shares payable in cash a proportion equal to the proportion payable on application and allotment on the shares offered for public subscription;

(*c*) no money must be liable to be repaid to applicants for shares or debentures which have been offered for public subscription by reason of failure to apply for or to obtain permission for the shares or debentures to be listed on any stock exchange, *i.e.* under section 51, *ante*.[52]

(*d*) a statutory declaration by the secretary or one of the directors that the above conditions have been complied with, must have been delivered to the Registrar.

(2) Where no prospectus has been issued—

(*a*) a statement in lieu of prospectus must have been delivered to the Registrar;

(*b*) every director must have paid on his shares payable in cash a proportion equal to the proportion payable by the other allottees on application and allotment on the shares payable in cash;

(*c*) a statutory declaration by the secretary or one of the directors that (*b*) above has been complied with must have been delivered to the Registrar.

On delivery of the appropriate document or documents the Registrar issues a certificate (called a *trading certificate*) which is conclusive evidence that the company is entitled to commence business. If business is commenced or a borrowing power is exercised before the section 109 requirements are complied with, every person responsible for the contravention of the Act is liable to a fine of £50 for every day during which the contravention continues.

A simultaneous offer of shares and debentures is not forbidden by the section (subs. (5)).

We saw in Chapter 6[53] that a contract made by a public company after it is incorporated but before it is entitled to commence business

[52] p. 181.
[53] p. 127.

is provisional only, and does not become binding on the company until it is entitled to commence business: section 109 (4).

Since the requirements of section 109 are commonly avoided by the device of incorporating companies as private companies and later converting them into public companies, the Jenkins Report[54] recommended that there should be no distinction in the Act in the treatment of public and private companies and the section should be repealed.

Clause 8 of the Companies Bill 1973 would have repealed section 109 and replaced it by a provision that a company limited by shares should not commence business or exercise any borrowing powers unless the amount paid up on its shares, whether in cash or other consideration, is not less than the statutory minimum and a statutory declaration of compliance, made by all the directors, has been delivered to the Registrar. The clause would also have given the Secretary of State power to specify the statutory minimum and to specify different amounts for public and private companies.

[54] Para. 67.

CHAPTER 10

MEMBERSHIP

THIS chapter is concerned with the members of a company, *i.e.* in the case of a company limited by shares, the shareholders. In addition to the ways in which a person can become a member and the persons who can become members, the following topics are dealt with: the register of members which every company must keep, disclosure of substantial shareholdings, and the annual return which every company with a share capital must make to the Registrar.

WAYS OF BECOMING A MEMBER

The members of a company consist of:

(1) The subscribers of the memorandum.[1] These are deemed to have agreed to become members, and on the registration of the company they must be entered as members in its register of members: section 26.

(2) Directors who have signed and delivered to the Registrar an undertaking to take and pay for their qualification shares.[2] Such directors are in the same position as if they had signed the memorandum for the shares: section 181 (2).

(3) All other persons who have agreed to become members of the company *and* whose names are entered in the register of members: section 26.

In the case of a company limited by shares the shareholders are the members.

Subscribers of the memorandum

A subscriber of the memorandum becomes a member on registration of the company, and an entry in the register of members is not necessary to make him a member of the company. It is the duty of the directors to enter his name at once in the register, but their failure

[1] *Ante* pp. 61, 96.
[2] *Post* p. 316.

to do this will not enable him to escape liability for calls on the shares for which he has signed the memorandum.[3]

The subscribers to the memorandum of a company limited by shares are liable, by virtue of their subscription, to pay up the amount of their share or shares as and when called up. Until the commencement of winding up the times and amounts of payment depend, apart from express agreement between the company and the signatories, on the articles.[4]

A subscriber's obligation to take the shares for which he has subscribed is not satisfied by the (later) allotment of shares credited as fully paid and to which someone else is entitled.

M. signed the memorandum for five shares. The company had agreed to allot paid up shares to C., as the purchase price of property sold to the company, and C. directed the company to allot five of these shares to M. This was done and the company was afterwards wound up. *Held*, M. was liable to pay for the five shares for which he had signed the memorandum: *Migotti's Case* (1867) L.R. 4 Eq. 238.

If, however, the entire share capital has been allotted to others, the subscriber is under no liability to take shares.[5]

A subscriber of the memorandum cannot rescind the contract to take shares on the ground of a misrepresentation made by a promoter, because (*a*) the company could not appoint an agent before it came into existence and it is therefore not liable for the promoter's acts, and (*b*) by signing the memorandum the subscriber became bound, on the registration of the company, not only as between himself and the company, but also as between himself and the other persons who should become members on the footing that the contract existed.[6]

The foregoing applies equally to directors who have signed and delivered to the Registrar an undertaking to take up their qualification shares as, under section 181 (2), they are in the same position as if they were subscribers of the memorandum.

In Scotland, specific implement is available as a remedy to enforce an undertaking to subscribe for shares.[7]

[3] *Evans's Case* (1867) L.R. 2 Ch.App. 427.
[4] *Per* Lindley M.R. in *Alexander* v. *Automatic Telephone Co.* [1900] 2 Ch. 56 (C.A.) at p. 63.
[5] *Mackley's Case* (1875) 1 Ch.D. 247.
[6] *Lord Lurgan's Case* [1902] 1 Ch. 707.
[7] *Beardmore & Co.* v. *Barry*, 1928 S.C. 101; affd 1928 S.C. (H.L.) 47.

Other members

A person, other than those mentioned above, who has agreed to become a member of the company does not actually become one until his name is entered in the register of members. The section "makes the placing of the name of a shareholder on the register a condition precedent to membership." [8]

Such a person may take an allotment of his shares direct from the company,[9] or may purchase shares from an existing member,[10] or he may succeed to shares on the death or bankruptcy of a member.[11]

WHO CAN BE MEMBERS

Minors

In English law a minor, *i.e.* a person under the age of 18,[12] may be a member unless this is forbidden by the articles. However, a minor's contract to take shares is voidable by him before or within a reasonable time after he attains the age of 18. If he avoids he cannot recover the money paid for the shares unless there has been a total failure of the consideration for which the money was paid.

> S., an infant,[13] agreed to take 500 £1 shares from a company, and paid 10s. on each share. She received no dividend on the shares. While still an infant she repudiated the shares, and brought an action (a) for a declaration that she was entitled to avoid the contract, and (b) to recover the money she had paid. *Held*, (a) S. was entitled to rescind and so was not liable for future calls, but (b) there was no total failure of consideration and S. could not recover money already paid because she had got the thing for which the money was paid, a thing of value: *Steinberg* v. *Scala (Leeds) Ltd.* [1923] 2 Ch. 452 (C.A.).

If the company is wound up the minor member loses his right to avoid unless the liquidator agrees.[14]

Scots law divides persons who are under the age of majority[15] into pupils (boys under 14 and girls under 12) and minors (young persons over the age of pupillarity but under the age of majority). A pupil has no capacity to be a member himself but his "tutor"

---

[8] *Per* Fry L.J. in *Nicol's Case* (1885) 29 Ch.D. 421 (C.A.) at p. 447; *per* Lord Deas in *Macdonald* v. *City of Glasgow Bank* (1879) 6 R. 621 at p. 633.
[9] *Ante* p. 168.   [10] *Post* p. 248.
[11] *Post* p. 265.
[12] Family Law Reform Act 1969, s. 1.
[13] The age of majority was formerly 21 and persons under that age were called "infants."
[14] *Symons' Case* (1870) L.R. 5 Ch. 298.
[15] 18 since January 1, 1970: Age of Majority (Scotland) Act 1969.

(father or mother[16] or other guardian) may be a member on the pupil's behalf.[17] A minor may become a member, but only with the consent of his "curator" (father or mother[16] or other guardian) if he has one; a minor who has no curator may become a member on his own initiative. However, whether a minor has a curator or not, his contract to take shares may be "reduced" (set aside) up to the end of the *quadriennium utile* (*i.e.* the four-year period after he attains majority) on proof of "lesion" (*i.e.* considerable loss to the minor's estate, the contract not being a fair and reasonable one at the time when it was entered into).[18] Lesion is more easily proved in the case of a minor who has no curator than in the case of a minor who transacted with his curator's consent.

Personal representatives

Ownership of the shares of a decreased member is transmitted to his executors[19] or administrators. They must produce to the company the grant of probate of the will, or of letters of administration of the estate, or, in Scotland, of confirmation and, notwithstanding anything in the articles, such document must be accepted by the company as sufficient evidence of the grant: section 82. Production to the company does *not*, however, make the representatives members of the company.[20] The deceased member's estate is the member for some purposes, such as an article providing that on an increase of capital the new shares are to be divided among the existing members in proportion to their existing shareholdings.[21] However, the deceased member is not a member within the meaning of a section such as section 31,[22] which is concerned with reduction of the number of members below the legal minimum.

The personal representatives are liable for calls[23] on partly paid shares only to the extent of the deceased's assets in their hands, and if in England the personal representatives make default in

---

[16] Guardianship Act 1973.
[17] See *Inland Revenue* v. *Wilson*, 1928 S.C.(H.L.) 42; 1927 S.C. 733.
[18] *Hill* v. *City of Glasgow Bank* (1879) 7 R. 68.
[19] In Scots law the term "executors" is used whether there is a will or not, and "confirmation" is the equivalent of both probate and letters of administration.
[20] *Macdonald* v. *City of Glasgow Bank* (1879) 6 R. 621.
[21] *Per* Lord Herschell in *James* v. *Buena Ventura Nitrate Grounds Syndicate Ltd.* [1896] 1 Ch. 456 (C.A.) at p. 464.
[22] *Ante* p. 30. See *Re Bowling & Welby's Contract* [1895] 1 Ch. 663 (C.A.).
[23] *Post* p. 270.

paying calls, the company can obtain an order for administration of the estate of the deceased member: section 215.

The personal representatives are entitled to transfer the shares without being registered as members (s. 76),[24] and to receive all dividends, bonuses or other benefits from the shares, but the articles usually prevent them from voting at general meetings.

Table A, art. 32, provides: "A person becoming entitled to a share by reason of the death or bankruptcy of the holder shall be entitled to the same dividends and other advantages to which he would be entitled if he were the registered holder of the share, except that he shall not, before being registered as a member in respect of the share, be entitled in respect of it to exercise any right conferred by membership in relation to meetings of the company."

Personal representatives may, however, be entitled to be given notice of general meetings, even though they have no right to attend and vote at the meetings. Table A, article 134, gives them a right to be given notice of general meetings.

To prevent the disadvantage of personal representatives who are not members, the articles frequently contain provisions to compel the personal representatives to elect either to be registered in respect of the shares or to transfer them.

In Table A, the proviso to article 32 is: "The directors may at any time give notice requiring any such person to elect either to be registered himself or to transfer the share, and if the notice is not complied with within 90 days the directors may thereafter withhold payment of all dividends, bonuses or other moneys payable in respect of the share until the requirements of the notice have been complied with."

Personal representatives are entitled, if they so choose and there is no contrary provision in the articles, to be registered as members.[25] The articles may give the directors, as does Table A, article 30, the same power to decline to register personal representatives as members as the directors would have had in the case of a transfer by the deceased shareholder before his death.[26]

If personal representatives are registered as members, they become personally liable for calls,[24] although they have a right of indemnity against the deceased's estate.[27]

---

[24] See also *Buchan* v. *City of Glasgow Bank* (1879) 6 R. (H.L.) 44; (1879) 6 R. 567.
[25] *Edwards* v. *Ransomes and Rapier Ltd.* [1930] W.N. 180.
[26] See, *e.g., Shepherd's Trustees* v. *Shepherd,* 1959 S.C. (H.L.) 60. See also *post* p. 249.
[27] *Per* Cotton L.J. in *Duff's Executors' Case* (1886) 32 Ch.D. 301 (C.A.) at p. 309.

Trustees in bankruptcy

A bankrupt may be a member of a company, although the beneficial interest in his shares will be vested in his trustee in bankruptcy as from the time when he is adjudged bankrupt.[28] Unless the articles provide to the contrary, a shareholder does not cease to be a member of the company on becoming bankrupt. Accordingly, as long as he is on the register he is entitled to exercise any vote conferred by his shares at the meetings of the company, even though the articles provide—as does article 134 of Table A—that notice of meetings is to be sent to the trustee in bankruptcy and not to the bankrupt.[29] The bankrupt must vote in accordance with the directions of the trustee.

A minority action[30] may be brought by a bankrupt shareholder who is on the register of members.[31]

The position of the trustee in bankruptcy is similar to that of personal representatives of a deceased member.[32]

Other companies

1. A company may, if authorised by its memorandum, take shares in and be a member of another company. It attends meetings of the other by a representative authorised by resolution of its directors: section 139.[33]

2. *A company usually must not purchase its own shares or be a member of itself.* The company's capital must be maintained and a company must not purchase its own shares because this would involve a reduction of capital, which is illegal without the consent of the court.[34] It is different in the case of a forfeiture of shares by the company or a surrender of shares to the company.[35]

A company was authorised by its articles to purchase its own shares. W. sold his shares to the company, and before the price was paid the company went into liquidation. W. claimed to prove in the liquidation for the price of the shares.

[28] Bankruptcy Act 1914, s. 18.
[29] *Morgan* v. *Gray* [1953] Ch. 83.
[30] *Post* p. 378.
[31] *Birch* v. *Sullivan* [1957] 1 W.L.R. 1247.
[32] Bankruptcy Act 1914, s. 48; Table A, arts. 30–32, *ante* p. 189. The 1914 Act does not apply to Scotland. In Scotland the act and warrant of confirmation in favour of the trustee vests the bankrupt's property in the trustee: Bankruptcy (Scotland) Act 1913, s. 97.
[33] *Post* p. 304.   [34] *Post* pp. 234, 235.
[35] *Post* pp. 277, 280.

Held, the claim failed, as the company had no power to purchase its own shares: *Trevor* v. *Whitworth* (1887) 12 App.Cas. 409.[36]

"One of the main objects contemplated by the legislature, in restricting the power of limited companies to reduce the amount of their capital as set forth in the memorandum, is to protect the interests of the outside public who may become their creditors. In my opinion the effect of these statutory restrictions is to prohibit every transaction between a company and a shareholder, by means of which the money already paid to the company in respect of his shares is returned to him, unless the court has sanctioned the transaction. Paid-up capital may be diminished or lost in the course of the company's trading; that is a result which no legislation can prevent; but persons who deal with, and give credit to a limited company, naturally rely upon the fact that the company is trading with a certain amount of capital already paid, as well as upon the responsibility of its members for the capital remaining at call; and they are entitled to assume that no part of the capital which has been paid into the coffers of the company has been subsequently paid out, except in the legitimate course of its business": *per* Lord Watson at p. 423.

There is nothing to prevent a transfer of shares in a company to a trustee for the company itself, as long as the transfer is voluntary and there is no unpaid liability on the shares.

A partnership business was sold to a company for a sum of money, which was satisfied by the issue of fully paid shares in the company. Owing to a mistake, the partners were overpaid. They therefore voluntarily transferred 3,000 shares to the chairman of the board upon trust for the benefit of the company. *Held*, the transfer did not infringe any of the principles laid down in the decided cases (the company had not parted with money, in cash or money's worth; it was not a member of itself; it had not purchased its own shares; there was no reduction of capital) and it was immaterial that the trust involved an obligation on the trustee to vote in respect of the shares as the company might direct: *Kirby* v. *Wilkins* [1929] 2 Ch. 444.[37]

Similarly, a bequest to a company of fully paid shares in the company is valid. The shares will be transferred to nominees, properly qualified under the articles, upon trust for the company.[38]

The Jenkins Report[39] recommended that shares of a company which are held in trust for the company should carry no right to vote. The idea is to prevent the directors using the votes conferred by such shares towards maintaining themselves in control against the wishes of other shareholders.

A company may purchase its own shares under an order made by the court under section 210[40] to relieve an oppressed part of the

[36] A Scottish case to the same effect is *General Property etc. Co. Ltd.* v. *Matheson's Trustees* (1888) 16 R. 282, where the articles bound a member wishing to sell his shares to offer them to the company in the first instance.

[37] *Cf. Gardiners* v. *Victoria Estates Co. Ltd.* (1885) 12 R. 1356.

[38] *Re Castiglione's Will Trusts* [1958] Ch. 549; *cf. Gill* v. *Arizona Copper Co. Ltd.* (1900) 2 F. 843.

[39] Para. 156.   [40] *Post* p. 389.

members, and in such a case the order will provide for the reduction of the company's capital by the nominal value of the shares purchased.

An unlimited company may purchase its own shares.[41]

Clause 11(1) of the Companies Bill 1973 would have put the decision in *Trevor* v. *Whitworth ante* into statutory form by providing that no company limited by shares or limited by guarantee and having a share capital should purchase or subscribe for its own shares.

3. For the same reason that a company cannot be a member of itself, section 27 provides that, *subject to certain exceptions, a subsidiary company*[42] *cannot be a member of its holding company*,[42] and any allotment or transfer of shares in a holding company to its subsidiary is void.[43] This prohibition cannot be evaded by having a nominee for the subsidiary. Exceptions are where the subsidiary is concerned (a) as a personal representative, or (b) as a trustee, unless the holding company or a subsidiary of it is beneficially interested under the trust otherwise than by way of security for the purposes of a transaction entered into in the ordinary course of a business which includes the lending of money.

For example, as regards (a), Y, who holds shares in X Bank Ltd., appoints its subsidiary, X Bank (Executor & Trustee) Ltd., as his executor and on Y's death the subsidiary is registered in respect of the shares.

As to (b), Y transfers his shares to the subsidiary on trust for a beneficiary, Z, who borrows money from X Bank Ltd. and secures repayment by mortgaging his interest in the shares to X Bank Ltd.

4. To prevent rules 2 and 3 *ante* from being evaded by the device of a loan by the company to a person to enable him to subscribe for or purchase the company's shares, section 54 makes it generally *unlawful for a company to give any kind of financial assistance for the purchase of or subscription for its own shares* or, usually, those of its holding company, *by any person*. It is immaterial whether the financial assistance by the company is by means of a loan, a guarantee, the provision of security or otherwise, and whether it is given directly or indirectly. The section was passed because speculators used to find a company with a cash balance or easily realisable assets, buy up the shares in the company for cash and so arrange

---

[41] *Nelson Mitchell* v. *City of Glasgow Bank* (1879) 6 R.(H.L.) 66; (1878) 6 R. 420, *per* Lord President Inglis at p. 429. And see *ante* p. 46.

[42] *Ante* p. 57.

[43] In Scotland this does not prevent a company from arresting its subsidiary's shares to found jurisdiction, at least where the shares are marketable: *Stenhouse London Ltd.* v. *Allwright*, 1972 S.L.T. 255.

matters that the purchase money which they became bound to provide was advanced to them by the company.[44]

Exception to the section is made in the following cases:

(*a*) Where the lending of money is part of the ordinary business of a company, the lending of money by the company in the ordinary course of its business.

For the lending of money to be part of the ordinary business of a company there must be a lending of money in general, in the sense, *e.g.*, that moneylending is part of the ordinary business of a registered moneylender or a bank—it is not enough that a company from time to time lends money to trade suppliers or purchasers. If the lending of money by a company is to be in the ordinary course of its business the advances must be of a scale and for a purpose similar to those regularly made by the company in carrying out its business—loans deliberately made by a company for the direct purpose of financing a purchase of its shares are not made in the ordinary course of business.

L.S. and J.S. were the directors of a private company, I.V.M., which had three shareholders, L.S., J.S. and S.S. I.V.M.'s business was the sale of automatic vending machines. When a machine was sold a merchandising company, a subsidiary of I.V.M., gave the purchaser an undertaking to stock and operate the machine on his behalf and guaranteed him twenty per cent. per annum on what he had paid for the machine. I.V.M. allowed the merchandising company 10 per cent of the price as a contribution to the obligations undertaken. The operating agreement provided for the setting up in the names of independent trustees of a guarantee fund to secure the purchaser's twenty per cent. I.V.M. advanced to the fund the moneys required to make good the guarantee. With a view to resolving taxation problems I.V.M. was turned into a wholly-owned subsidiary of a public company, A.M.H. The shareholders in I.V.M. sold their shares to A.M.H. for £200,000, which sum was lent by I.V.M. to A.M.H. *Held*, the only lending of money by I.V.M. was the inter-company transfers of funds to enable the merchandising companies to fulfil their obligations and support the guarantee fund. Such operations did not render the lending of money part of the ordinary business of I.V.M.: *Steen* v. *Law* [1964] A.C. 287 (P.C.).

(*b*) The provision by a company, *in accordance with a scheme*, of money for the purchase or subscription by trustees of or for fully paid shares in the company or its holding company to be held by or for the benefit of employees of the company, *including a director holding a salaried employment or office in the company.*

[44] *Per* Lord Greene M.R. in *Re V.G.M. Holdings Ltd.* [1942] Ch. 235 (C.A.) at p. 239.

Clause 11(3) of the Companies Bill 1973 would have extended this paragraph to employees of the company's subsidiary and directors holding salaried employment or office in the subsidiary.

(c) The making by a company of loans to persons, *other than directors*, bona fide in the employment of the company with a view to enabling them to purchase or subscribe for fully paid shares in the company or its holding company to be held by themselves beneficially.

Clause 11(3) of the Companies Bill 1973 would have extended this paragraph to persons, other than directors of the company, bona fide in the employment of the company's subsidiary.

The aggregate amount of any outstanding loans made under heads (b) and (c), *ante*, must be shown as a separate item in the balance sheet: Schedule 8, paragraph 8 (1) (c).

The substance of section 54 is frequently embodied in the articles, as in Table A, article 10.

If the section is contravened, the company and every officer in default is liable to a fine of up to £100: section 54 (2).

A loan by a company for the purchase of its own shares which contravenes section 54 is illegal by statute and void.[45] Neither party can sue on the contract and, in general, money or property passed in pursuance of it cannot be recovered—the courts are not to be instruments for aiding illegality. However, as will be seen, this principle does not prevent the company suing the directors as constructive trustees for doing what is illegal—that is to condemn the illegality.

Further, if a company gives a debenture for a sum lent by one person to another to enable the latter to purchase shares in the company, the debenture is illegal and void—the company is giving financial assistance by means of the provision of a security within section 54—and no liability can arise under a personal guarantee given by the purchaser and endorsed on the debenture.[46]

Where a company contravened section 54 by advancing money to enable a director to complete his purchase of shares from another director it was held that the agreement for the sale of the shares was severable from the agreement by the company to lend its money for the carrying out of the sale and was not invalidated.[47]

---

[45] *Selangor United Rubber Estates Ltd.* v. *Cradock* (*No.* 3) [1968] 1 W.L.R. 1555.
[46] *Heald* v. *O'Connor* [1971] 1 W.L.R. 497, not following *Victor Battery Co. Ltd.* v. *Curry's Ltd.* [1946] Ch. 242.
[47] *Spink* (*Bournemouth*) *Ltd.* v. *Spink* [1936] Ch. 544. Compare *Dey's* case *infra.* Compare *Vam Ltd.* v. *McDonald Industries Ltd.* [1970] 3 N.S.W.R. 3.

Directors who cause a company to enter into a transaction which infringes section 54 are guilty of breach of fiduciary duty and are liable to reimburse the company for the loss which it suffers, even though they are ignorant of the law.[48]

The Jenkins Report[49] recommended that section 54 should be strengthened and recast, *e.g.* so as to make it unlawful for a company to give financial assistance for the acquisition of its shares or those of its holding company unless the transaction has been approved by a special resolution of the company and the directors have filed a declaration that, having effected the transaction, the company will be able to pay its debts as they fall due. The first condition will give some protection to minority shareholders, the second is designed to protect creditors.

However, in their White Paper in 1973,[50] the then Conservative Government took the view that section 54 serves a useful purpose and were not convinced that the additional measures suggested by the Jenkins Committee would be effective. They therefore intended to leave the main principle of the section intact. Clause 11 of their Companies Bill 1973, which would have extended the exceptions to the section, has been dealt with already.

Non-residents

A person who lives outside the Scheduled Territories[51] cannot be a member of or shareholder in a company, except with the permission of the Treasury.[52]

Issuing houses and brokers

A person who has only agreed to place[53] shares does not agree to become a member of the company, and should not be put on the

---

[48] *Steen* v. *Law* [1964] A.C. 287 (P.C.). See also *Curtis's Furnishing Stores Ltd.* v. *Freedman* [1966] 1 W.L.R. 1219, *post* p. 348, and *Wallersteiner* v. *Moir* [1974] 1 W.L.R. 991 (C.A.). Other Australian cases on the equivalent of s. 54 are *Dressy Frocks Pty. Ltd* v. *Bock* (1951 51 S.R.(N.S.W.) 390; *E. H. Dey Pty. Ltd.* v. *Dey* [1966] V.L.R. 464; *Mudge* v. *Wolstenholme* [1965] V.R. 707; *Shearer Transport Co. Pty. Ltd.* v. *McGrath* [1956] V.L.R. 316 (money lent by company to director to enable him to purchase shares in the company recoverable in quasi-contract); and *Niemann* v. *Smedley* [1973] V.R. 769, F.Ct. (title of purchaser or allottee of shares not defeated by illegality under Victorian equivalent of s. 54). Some of these cases are explained in the First Australian Supplement to Charlesworth & Cain, pp. 102, 103.
The Fifth Interim Report of the Australian Company Law Advisory Committee, para. 94, criticises cases like *Dressy Frocks* and *Selangor* as conferring an undeserved benefit on the other party to the transaction.
[49] Para. 187.
[50] Cmnd. 5391, paras. 46 and 47.
[51] *Ante* p. 97.
[52] Exchange Control Act 1947, Part III.
[53] *Ante* p. 146.

register of members. His failure to perform his contract may make him liable in damages, but he is not liable for calls.[54] If, however, a person agrees to take shares himself for the purpose of placing them by the execution of transfers, his name is properly put on the register.[55]

REGISTER OF MEMBERS

Section 110 provides that every company must keep a register of its members containing:

(1) The names and addresses of the members, a statement of the shares held by each member, distinguishing each share by its number[56] so long as it has one, and the amount paid or agreed to be considered as paid on the shares of each member. If the company has converted shares into stock, the register must show the amount of stock held by each member.

(2) The date at which each person was entered in the register as a member.

(3) The date at which any person ceased to be a member.

Default renders the company and every officer in default liable to a default fine.

Where, as in section 110, no amount is specified, a default fine is a fine not exceeding £5 for every day during which the default continues: section 440.

The register may be kept by making entries in a bound book or by recording the required information in any other manner, so long as adequate precautions are taken to guard against falsification: section 436.

Clause 81 of the Companies Bill 1973 would have allowed computers to be used for keeping company registers, minute books and accounting records.

A company with more than 50 members must, unless the register of members constitutes an index, keep an index (which may be a card index) of the names of its members, and must alter the index within 14 days after any alteration in the register. The index must be kept at the same place as the register and must contain sufficient

[54] *Gorrissen's Case* (1873) L.R. 8 Ch.App. 507.
[55] *Miln* v. *North British Fresh Fish etc. Co. Ltd.* (1887) 15 R. 21.
[56] *Post* p. 245.

information to enable the account of each member in the register to be readily found: section 111.

The register of members is prima facie evidence of any matters directed by the Act to be inserted in it: section 118.

Clause 80 of the Companies Bill 1973 would have enabled a company to remove an entry from the register of members 30 years after a person ceased to be a member.

Inspection of register

The register is to be kept at the company's registered office, but if the register is made up at another office of the company, it may be kept there, and if it is made up by an agent, it may be kept at his office. If the company is registered in England, the register must not be kept outside England, and if the company is registered in Scotland, the register must not be kept outside Scotland. When the register has not always been kept at the registered office, notice must be given to the Registrar of the place where it is kept: section 110.

The Jenkins Report[57] recommended that these flexible provisions in section 110 should apply to the other statutory books such as the minutes of general meetings, the register of directors, copies of instruments creating charges registrable under section 95 and the company's own register of charges.

During business hours the register and index are to be open to the inspection of any member without charge, and of any other person on payment of 5p, or less if the company so prescribes. Within ten days after being required to do so, the company is bound to furnish, either to a member or to any other person, a copy of any part of the register on payment of 10 p for every 100 words or part thereof: 1948 Act, s. 113; 1967 Act, s. 52 (2). A person inspecting the register has no right to take extracts from or make copies of the register.[58] The right of inspection terminates on the company going into liquidation.[59] Where there is a winding up the court may allow creditors and contributories to inspect under sections 266 and 307.

The company may, on giving notice by advertisement in some newspaper circulating in the district in which its registered office is

[57] Para. 470.
[58] *Re Balaghat Co.* [1901] 2 K.B. 665.
[59] *Re Kent Coalfields Syndicate Ltd.* [1898] 1 Q.B. 754 (C.A.).

situate, close the register for any time or times not exceeding 30 days in each year: section 115. This is to enable the company to prepare a list of members entitled to payment of a dividend.

Importance of register

The importance of the register as a public representation of who the members are and what their liability is has often been emphasised in Scottish cases,[60] and a company has no power to create a right of pledge or lien over the register, since that would deprive the public of their statutory right of access and inspection.[61] The register and not the share certificate is the document of title to shares, the share certificate being merely an acknowledgment on the part of the company that the name of the person mentioned in it is duly recorded in the register.[62]

Power of court to rectify register

Section 116 gives the court a discretion to rectify the register of members in two cases, namely—

(1) if the name of any person is, without sufficient cause, entered in or omitted from the register;
(2) if default is made or unnecessary delay takes place in entering on the register the fact of any person having ceased to be a member.

Application to the court for rectification may be made by the person aggrieved, or any member of the company, or the company. The application is made in a summary way—by originating summons or originating motion in England: R.S.C., O. 102, r. 3, and by petition in Scotland: R.C. 190.

There is no *Foss* v. *Harbottle*[63] complication—even a single member may apply to the court.

The court may order not only rectification of the register but also payment by the company of any damages sustained by any party aggrieved.

---

[60] *e.g. per* Lord Curriehill in *Liquidator of the Garpel etc. Co. Ltd.* v. *Andrew* (1866) 4 M. 617 at p. 623.
[61] *Liquidator of the Garpel etc. Co. Ltd.* v. *Andrew* (1866) 4 M. 617.
[62] *Per* Lord Sands in *Inland Revenue* v. *Wilson*, 1928 S.C.(H.L.) 42; 1927 S.C. 733 at p. 737.
[63] *Post* p. 376.

If an order is made in the case of a company required to send a list of members to the Registrar,[64] notice of the rectification must be given to the Registrar: section 116 (4).

The period of two months specified in section 78 for giving a transferee of shares notice of the company's refusal to register the transfer is the outside limit after which there is normally unnecessary delay.[65]

An order for rectification may be made even if the company is being wound up.

B, a transferee of shares in a company, sent in his transfer for registration but, by mistake, registration of the transfer was omitted. The company then went into liquidation with a view to reconstruction and B, thinking that he was on the register of members, served the liquidator with notice of dissent to the scheme. The liquidator disregarded the notice on the ground that B was not a member. *Held*, there was such "default or unnecessary delay" in registration as entitled B to rectification of the register: *Re Sussex Brick Co.* [1904] 1 Ch. 598 (C.A.).[66]

Section 116 does not exhaust the court's power to order rectification and does not prevent the court from altering the register in cases other than those specified. Accordingly, where shares were registered in the names of two joint holders, and under the articles the first alone could vote and if the first was ill or absent the second could not vote or be appointed a proxy, an order was made to have the holding split into two holdings with the names of the shareholders in different orders.[67]

In difficult cases the court will refuse to proceed under the section and an action must be brought.[68]

Trusts not to be entered on register in England

Section 117 provides that no notice of any trust shall be entered on the register, or be received by the Registrar, in the case of companies registered in England (which, for this purpose, includes Wales).[69] This means that, subject as below, the company is entitled to treat every person on the register of members as the beneficial owner of shares, even if in fact he holds them on trust for another,

---

[64] See *post*.
[65] *Re Swaledale Cleaners Ltd.* [1968] 1 W.L.R. 1710 (C.A.), *post* p. 253.
[66] See also *Stocker* v. *Liqdrs of the Coustonholm Paper Mills Co. Ltd.* (1891) 19 R. 17.
[67] *Burns* v. *Siemens Brothers Dynamo Works Ltd.* [1919] 1 Ch. 225.
[68] *e.g. Simpson's Case* (1869) L.R. 9 Eq. 91; *Blaikie* v. *Coats* (1893) 21 R. 150.
[69] Wales and Berwick Act 1746, s. 3.

i.e. the company need not take notice of equitable interests in shares. If, therefore, the company registers a transfer of the shares held by a person as trustee, it is under no liability to the beneficiaries even if the sale was a breach of trust and in fraud of the beneficiaries.

> X's shares were, on his death, registered in the name of his executors. They subsequently transferred the shares to Y in breach of the terms of X's will, and the transfer was registered by the company. The company had a copy of the will in its possession, and its president was one of X's executors. *Held,* the company did not act wrongfully, as it was only bound to satisfy itself from the will that the executors were executors, and was not concerned with the disposition by X of his property: *Simpson* v. *Molson's Bank* [1895] A.C. 270.

A further result is that the company is not a trustee for persons claiming the shares under equitable titles. For example, if A, the owner of shares, makes an equitable mortgage of his shares by depositing his share certificate and a blank transfer with B as security for a debt and afterwards makes another equitable mortgage of the same shares by depositing another blank transfer of them with C as security for another debt, saying that he has lost his share certificate, C cannot by giving notice to the company affect the company with notice of his interest in the shares or gain any priority over B.[70] As will be seen later,[71] the proper way to protect the interest of a beneficiary in shares is to serve a stop notice. As a rule, if a company receives notice of an equitable claim it should allow the person giving the notice to apply for a restraining order, if he makes a request to that effect, before registering a transfer to his prejudice.[72]

The articles frequently deal with notice of trusts, as so does Table A, article 7:

> "Except as required by law, no person shall be recognised . . . as holding any share upon any trust, and the company shall not be bound by or be compelled in any way to recognise (even when having notice thereof) any equitable . . . interest in any share . . . or any other rights in respect of any share except an absolute right to the entirety thereof in the registered holder."

It is doubtful whether this adds anything to the effect of section 117, although the section deals only with entries on the register while the article is not limited to entries on the register.[73]

A trustee of shares who is entered on the register is entitled to exercise any vote conferred by the shares although he may be

[70] *Société Générale de Paris* v. *Walker* (1885) 11 App.Cas. 20.
[71] *Post* p. 268.
[72] *Per* Lindley L.J. in *Société Générale de Paris* v. *Tramways Union Co.* (1884) 14 Q.B.D. 424 (C.A.) at p. 453.
[73] See *post* p. 276.

bound to vote in accordance with the directions of the beneficiary. The trustee is personally liable to the company for any calls or other obligations attaching to the shares but is entitled to an indemnity from the beneficiary, not only out of the trust property but to the full extent of his indebtedness in respect of the shares.[74] The company cannot put the beneficiary on the list of contributories but it can, through the trustee, enforce the trustee's right to an indemnity.[75]

A purchase of shares in the name of a nominee, even if an infant or a man of straw, is legal. In such a case the company cannot go behind the nominee to the beneficial owner.

M. and G., a firm of stockbrokers, bought shares which were registered in the name of L., their clerk. L. was an infant. On the company's going into liquidation, the liquidator applied that M. and G.'s names might be substituted for that of L. in the register of members and the list of contributories. *Held*, the application failed, as there was no contractual relation between the company and M. and G.: *Re National Bank of Wales Ltd.* [1907] 1 Ch. 582.

If a person applies for shares in a fictitious name, or in the name of a person who has never agreed to accept the shares, rectification of the register can be obtained so as to place the name of the real owner upon the register.[76]

Trusts may be entered on register in Scotland

It has always been competent for companies registered in Scotland to enter notices of trusts on their registers.[77]

Entry of a notice of trust does *not* have the effect of limiting the liability of the trustees to the amount of the trust estate in their hands.

The legal position of trustees is distinct from that of executors.[78]

On the assumption of a new trustee by deed of assumption his name may be entered on the register without any transfer being executed, and the trustee will then be a member and liable as such.[79]

---

[74] *Hardoon* v. *Belilios* [1901] A.C. 118 (P.C.).
[75] *Per* James L.J. in *Re European Society Arbitration Acts* (1878) 8 Ch.D. 679 (C.A.) at p. 708.
[76] *Pugh and Sharman's Case* (1872) L.R. 13 Eq. 566; *Richardson's Case* (1875) L.R. 19 Eq. 588.
[77] As to the purpose of such entry, see *per* Cairns L.C. in *Muir* v. *City of Glasgow Bank* (1879) 6 R. (H.L.) 21 at p. 26.
[78] *Per* Lord Selborne in *Buchan* v. *City of Glasgow Bank* (1879) 6 R. (H.L.) 44 at p. 50.
[79] Trusts (Scotland) Act 1921, s. 21; *Bell* v. *City of Glasgow Bank* (1879) 6 R. (H.L.) 55; (1879) 6 R. 548.

A trustee who duly resigns his office by minute registered in the Books of Council and Session, and intimated to his co-trustees and to the company, is entitled to have his name removed from the register; no deed of transfer is necessary.[80] When one of several trustees dies, shares registered in the names of the trustees vest in the surviving trustees, and the executors of the deceased trustee are not liable as members even though no intimation of the death has been given to the company.[81] The last surviving trustee, however, is in a different position from the other trustees in that his death does not automatically terminate his liability as a member.[82]

The liability of trustees to the company is *in solidum,* not *pro rata, i.e.* the company may hold any one of the several trustees liable for the full amount due on the shares.[83]

Trustees who have been made liable for calls in respect of shares forming part of the trust estate are entitled to full relief from the trust estate without reference to their own payments or ability to pay; the trust estate may be made liable beyond what the trustees can personally pay, and the company may by diligence compel the trustees to make the right of relief available to the company.[84]

The persons for whom shares are held in trust are *not* members of the company, although their names may appear on the register.[85]

Dominion register

If the objects of a company having a share capital comprise the transaction of business in any part of Her Majesty's dominions outside Great Britain, the Channel Islands, the Isle of Man, or in Malaysia[86] or South Africa,[87] the company may keep a branch register (called a "dominion register") of its members resident in that part. Notice of the situation of the office where the dominion register is kept must be given to the Registrar within fourteen days of the opening of the office or of any change in its situation. The same

[80] 1921 Act, s. 19 (1): *Dalgleish* v. *Land Feuing Co. Ltd.* (1885) 13 R. 223.
[81] *Oswald's Trustees* v. *City of Glasgow Bank* (1879) 6 R. 461.
[82] *Low's Executors* v. *City of Glasgow Bank* (1879) 6 R. 830.
[83] *Cuninghame* v. *City of Glasgow Bank* (1879) 6 R. (H.L.) 98; (1879) 6 R. 679.
[84] *Cuningham* v. *Montgomerie* (1879) 6 R. 1333; *cf. Brownlie* v. *Brownlie's Trustees* (1879) 6 R. 1233.
[85] *Gillespie & Paterson* v. *City of Glasgow Bank* (1879) 6 R. (H.L.) 104; (1879) 6 R. 714.
[86] Companies Registers (Malaysia) Order, 1964 (S.I. 1964 No. 911).
[87] South Africa Act 1962, s. 2 and Sched. 2.

notice must be given if the dominion register is discontinued: section 119.

A dominion register is deemed to be part of the company's register of members ("the principal register"), and it must be kept in the same manner. A copy of every entry in the dominion register must be transmitted to the company's registered office as soon as may be after it is made, and the company must enter it in a duplicate dominion register which it must keep at the same place as the principal register. The dominion register can be rectified on application to the court in the dominion in which it is kept: section 120.

DISCLOSURE OF SUBSTANTIAL SHAREHOLDINGS

Sections 33 and 34 of the Companies Act 1967 contain provisions for securing the disclosure of substantial individual interests in share capital carrying unrestricted voting rights.

The Jenkins Report had stated[88] that in the evidence the Committee had received emphasis was placed on the administrative advantages of the nominee system but that many witnesses had said that disclosure of the beneficial ownership of substantial holdings of shares should be required if it was practicable and did not interfere with the normal working of the nominee system. These witnesses believed that directors, other shareholders and employees of a company ought to be able to ascertain the identity of any substantial holder of the company's shares. This is of particular importance where there is reason to suppose someone may be in the process of buying for control. Further, it may be of interest to know whether someone is in a position to veto a special resolution of the company, and who that person is.

It was also stated that the limitation of the requirement to beneficial owners of shares of quoted companies—and mainly equity shares of such companies—would make the number of persons affected by the new provision relatively few, but the companies concerned would be those whose membership was likely to be a matter of interest to investors, potential investors and the public at large. The new provision would not apply to directors, whose holdings of shares were already required by section 195 to be included in the register of directors' shareholdings.

Obligation to notify company of acquisition and disposal of shares in the company

The following persons—

(a) a person who, being uninterested in shares comprised in the relevant share capital of a company to which the section

[88] *Paras* 142, 143.

applies or being interested in shares of a nominal value less than the prescribed percentage (now five per cent.) of the nominal value of such capital, becomes interested in one twentieth or more of such capital;

(b) a person who, being interested in not less than one twentieth of such capital, increases his shareholding or decreases it but remains a five per cent. shareholder;

(c) a person who, being interested in one twentieth or more of such capital, suffers a decrease in the value of his holding so that it is less than one twentieth;

must, subject as below, notify the company in writing of the occurrence of the event (specifying it), the date on which it occurred and the number of shares comprised in the relevant share capital (specifying it) in which he is interested immediately after the occurrence of the event: 1967 Act, s. 33 (1), as amended by the 1976 Act, s. 26.

Section 33 applies to a company where a recognised stock exchange listing has been granted as regards any part of its capital. "Relevant share capital," in relation to such a company, means issued shares carrying rights to vote in all circumstances at general meetings: s. 33 (10) of the 1967 Act as amended by Schedule 2 of the 1976 Act.

If a company becomes one to which section 33 applies or any class of its capital becomes relevant share capital, every person then interested in one twentieth or more of the relevant shares must notify the company of the subsistence of his interests and the number of shares comprised in the relevant share capital (specifying it) in which each interest subsists: subsections (2), (3).

The rules set out in section 28 [89] of the 1967 Act apply for the interpretation of the above provisions of section 33 except that certain extra interests are disregarded, *e.g.* an interest, for the life of himself or another, of a person under a settlement where the property includes shares, the settlement is irrevocable and the settlor has no interest in any income arising under, or property comprised in, the settlement; an interest of a member of The Stock Exchange who is recognised by the Council as carrying on the business of a jobber, who carries on that business in the U.K. and who holds shares for the purposes of that business; and an interest of a person whose ordinary business includes the lending of money who holds the shares

[89] *Post* p. 321.

by way of security only for the purposes of a transaction entered into in the ordinary course of that business: 1967 Act, s. 33 (4), as amended by the 1976 Act, s. 26 (9).

Section 33 (1) must be complied with within five days after the event if the person concerned knows of the occurrence of the event and of the obligation to which it gives rise; otherwise within five days after he becomes aware that the occurrence of the event gives rise to the obligation. Saturdays, Sundays and bank holidays are disregarded. Subsection (2) must be complied with within five days after the day when the obligation arises thereunder, or after the day when the subsistence of the interest comes to the knowledge of the shareholder, as the case may be: section 33 (5), (9), of the 1967 Act as amended by s. 26 (1) of the 1976 Act.

A notice under this section must identify the shareholder concerned and give his address and, if he is a director, be expressed to be given in fulfilment of an obligation imposed by the section: subsection (7).

Failure to comply with section 33 (1) or (2) of the 1967 Act, or making to the company a statement known to be false or recklessly making a false statement, gives rise to liability to two years' imprisonment or a fine or both. Proceedings under the section cannot in England be instituted except by, or with the consent of, the Department of Trade or the Director of Public Prosecutions: subsections (6), (8).

The Conservative Government White Paper on Company Law Reform[90] stated that there is nothing inherently wrong in the practice of holding shares through nominees, and there were many circumstances in which it was both normal and convenient on commercial or personal grounds. Furthermore, there was a large and complex area of common law and the law of trusts which would be involved in any attempt to forbid the practice. However, there was one area of commercial activity where new legislation was required and that was "warehousing."

"Warehousing" was a situation in which a number of parties acted in undisclosed concert, not sufficiently close to bring them within section 33 of the 1967 Act, each acquiring an interest in the equity of the company below the then "threshold" of ten per cent. at which section 33 required notification to the company, thus enabling one or more of them to acquire by stealth a dominant position in that company. This was usually in preparation for a take-over bid which that company was by then unable to resist.

The Government intended to deal with this situation in two ways: first by lowering the threshold percentage to at most five per cent., and second by reducing the time allowed for notification to the minimum consistent with practical operation.

[90] (1973) Cmnd. 5391, paras 21–24.

The White Paper also stated that a company which had any reason to fear that it might be the subject of a bid, or that a "warehousing" situation might be developing, ought to have a right to know the real identity of the owners of its shares.

The Government therefore proposed to give every company the right reasonably (*i.e.* not vexatiously or capriciously) to demand to know the beneficial as opposed to the nominal owners of its shares.

Power of company to require disclosure of beneficial interest in voting shares

Section 27 of the 1976 Act provides that a company to which section 33 of the 1967 Act *ante* applies may by notice in writing require any member of the company within such reasonable time as is specified in the notice—

(a) to indicate in writing the capacity in which he holds any shares comprised in the relevant share capital of the company;

(b) if he holds them otherwise than as beneficial owner, to indicate in writing so far as it lies within his knowledge the persons who have an interest in them and the nature of their interest.

Where a company is informed that any other person has an interest in shares comprised in relevant share capital, the company may require that other person—

(a) to indicate the capacity in which he holds that interest;

(b) if he holds it otherwise than as beneficial owner, to indicate the persons who have an interest in it and the nature of their interest.

A company to which section 33 applies may require any member to indicate whether any voting rights carried by any shares comprised in relevant share capital held by him are subject to an agreement or an arrangement under which another person is entitled to control his exercise of those rights and, if so, to give particulars of the agreement or arrangement and the parties to it. Where a company is informed that any other person is a party to such agreement or arrangement, the company may require that other person to give particulars thereof.

A person is not obliged to comply with a notice under section 27 if he is exempted by the Secretary of State from the operation of the section.

When a company receives information from a person in pursuance of a requirement under this section, it must inscribe against the name of the member in a separate part of the register kept by it under section 34 *post*—

(a) the fact that the requirement was imposed and the date of imposition;

(b) the information received in pursuance of the requirement;

Subject as below, a person who—

(a) fails to comply with a notice under this section; or

(b) in purported compliance with such a notice makes any statement which he knows to be false in a material particular or recklessly makes any statement which is false in a material particular, is guilty of an offence and liable—

   (i) on conviction on indictment, to imprisonment for up to two years or to a fine or to both; or

  (ii) on summary conviction, to imprisonment for up to six months or to a fine of up to £400 or to both.

A person is not guilty of an offence under (a) above if he proves that the information was already in the possession of the company or that the requirement to give it was frivolous or vexatious.

Register of "5 per cent. shareholders"

Section 34 of the 1967 Act is designed to ensure that the information furnished under section 33, *ante*, is recorded and made available.

Every company to which section 33 applies must keep a register and, within three days after information is received, inscribe therein, against the name of the person giving the information, any information received in consequence of that section and the date of inscription. Saturdays, Sundays and bank holidays are disregarded in computing the three-day period. The entries against the several names inscribed must appear in chronological order.

Anything done for the purposes of section 34 does not affect the company with notice of, or put it upon inquiry as to, the rights of any person in relation to any shares: subsection (4).

The register must be kept where the section 29 register of directors' shareholdings is kept—this will be explained later.[91] There are similar provisions as to inspection except so far as it

[91] *Post* p. 324.

contains information with respect to a holding or other company for the time being entitled to the benefit of section 3 (3) or 4 (3)[92] of the 1967 Act: subs. (5). Unless the register itself is in the form of an index the company must keep an index of the names in the register. So far as the register is open to inspection any member of the company or other person may require a copy on payment of 10p per hundred words or fractional part thereof.

Default in complying with the requirements of section 34 renders the company and every officer in default liable to a fine of £500 and to a default fine.[93] The court is empowered to order inspection of the register and delivery of a copy.

Note what was said *ante*[94] about clause 81 of the Companies Bill 1973.

Annual Return

Every company having a share capital must, once in every year, make a return (called the "annual return") to the Registrar of Companies, except that no annual return need be made in the year of the company's incorporation or, if the company is not required by section 131[95] to hold an annual general meeting during the following year, in that year: section 124. The word "year" means calendar year, *i.e.* the period 1st January to 31st December.[96]

The annual return must contain the matters, and be in the form specified in the Sixth Schedule.

The Sixth Schedule matters are:—

(1) The address of the registered office.
(2) (*a*) If the register of members is not kept at the registered office, the address where it is kept.
   (*b*) If the register of debenture holders is not kept at the registered office, the address where it is kept.
(3) A summary of share capital and debentures, distinguishing between shares issued for cash and shares issued as fully or partly paid up otherwise than in cash, specifying—
   (*a*) the amount of the share capital and the number of shares into which it is divided;
   (*b*) the number of shares taken up to the date of the return;
   (*c*) the amount called up on each share, the amount of calls received and the amount of calls unpaid;
   (*d*) the amount of commission paid in respect of shares or debentures;
   (*e*) the discount allowed on any shares issued at a discount, or so much as has not been written off;

---

[92] *Post* pp. 437, 438.
[93] See s. 440 of the 1948 Act, *ante* p. 196.
[94] p. 196.
[95] *Post* p. 286.
[96] *Gibson* v. *Barton* (1875) L.R. 10 Q.B. 329.

  (*f*) the discount allowed in respect of any debentures since the date of the last return;

  (*g*) the number of shares forfeited;

  (*h*) the amount of shares for which share warrants are outstanding, the number of shares comprised in each warrant, and the amount of share warrants issued and surrendered since the last return.

(4) The amount of indebtedness of the company in respect of all mortgages and charges which are required to be registered with the Registrar.

(5) A list of present and past members—

  (*a*) containing the names and addresses of all persons who, on the fourteenth day after the annual general meeting, are members, and of persons who have ceased to be members since the date of the last return or, in the case of the first return, since incorporation;

  (*b*) stating the number of shares held by each member at the date of the return, specifying shares transferred since the date of the last return and the dates of registration of the transfers;

  (*c*) if the members' names are not arranged in alphabetical order, having an index annexed.

    If any shares have been converted into stock, the amount of stock held by each member must be given: section 124 (1), proviso (*b*). A complete return of the members and their holdings need be made only every third year, and in the intervening two years only a list of changes in the membership need be given: section 124 (1), proviso (*c*). As stated earlier,[97] a company to which a licence is granted under section 19 is excepted from the provisions of the Act relating to sending lists of members to the Registrar: section 19 (4).

(6) The same particulars of the directors and secretary at the date of the return as are required to be in the register of directors and secretaries.[98]

    The return made by a company with no share capital need contain only matters (1), (2), (4) and (6) *ante*: section 125.

The annual return must be completed within 42 days after the annual general meeting and a copy signed by a director and the secretary must be sent forthwith to the Registrar: section 126.

If the annual return is not forwarded, the company and every officer in default is liable to a default fine of £5 for every day of the default: sections 126, 440.

In 1974, there were 1,133 convictions for failure to file annual returns or annex documents to annual returns.

A private company must send with the annual return a certificate, signed by a director and the secretary, that the company has not, since the date of the last return or, in the case of the first return, since incorporation, issued any invitation to the public to subscribe for shares or debentures of the company and, where the number of members exceeds 50, a certificate that the excess consists of members who are or were employees of the company: section 128.

[97] p. 67.   [98] See s. 200, *post* p. 318.

CHAPTER 11

SHARE CAPITAL

THE more important topics dealt with in this chapter are preference
shares, the variation of the special rights of a class of shareholders,
the rules that share capital must be raised and, once raised, must be
maintained, and the reduction of share capital.

MEANING OF "CAPITAL"

The word "capital" used in connection with a company has several
different meanings; thus it may mean the nominal or authorised
share capital, the issued share capital, the paid-up share capital or
the reserve share capital of the company.

The *nominal* or *authorised capital* is the amount of share capital
which the company is authorised to issue. As we have seen,[1] in the
case of a limited company the amount of share capital with which it
proposes to be registered, and the division thereof into shares of a
fixed amount, must be set out in the memorandum of association,
but this amount may be increased or reduced as explained later.[2]
The amount of the company's nominal capital depends on its business requirements, actual or potential.

The *issued capital* is that part of the company's nominal capital
which has been issued to the shareholders. The company is not
bound to issue all its capital at once, and frequently when the nominal
capital is increased the extent of the increase is not limited to the
company's requirements at the time but covers its probable requirements in the future. In such a case, further issues of capital are made
as they are needed.

The *paid-up capital* is that part of the issued capital which has
been paid up by the shareholders. The company may, for example,
have a nominal capital of £500,000 divided into 500,000 shares of
a nominal amount of £1 each, of which £400,000 is issued, *i.e.*
400,000 of the shares have been issued, and only £100,000 is paid

[1] *Ante* p. 94.
[2] *Post* pp. 228, 235.

up, *i.e.* the company has so far required only 25p to be paid up on each share. The *uncalled capital* is the remainder of the issued capital and can be called up at any time by the company from the shareholders in accordance with the provisions of the articles. Uncalled capital is rare today. Since the disastrous experiences of many companies in the years between the wars, when shareholders were often unable to pay calls made in respect of their shares, shares have usually been fully paid up within a short time after issue. Further, at least in the case of the ordinary commercial company, partly paid-up shares are not popular with investors. It follows that reserve capital is rare today.

The *reserve capital*, or reserve liability, is that part of the uncalled capital which a limited company has by special resolution determined shall not be called up except in the event and for the purposes of the company being wound up and which cannot otherwise be called up: section 60. This capital is not under the control of the directors and cannot be reconverted into ordinary uncalled capital, or charged by the company, *e.g.* as security for debentures.[3-4] It is available only for the creditors on the winding up of the company, although it will be seen that it can be reduced with the consent of the court under section 66.[5] Reserve capital must be distinguished from capital reserves, a capital redemption reserve fund, revenue reserves, and a reserve or a general reserve, all of which will be dealt with later.[6]

The European Communities Act 1972, s. 9 (7), provides that if, in the case of a company having a share capital, there is on the stationery used for any business letters, or on the order forms of the company, a reference to the amount of the share capital, the reference must be to paid-up share capital.

As was said earlier,[7] clause 8 of the Companies Bill 1973 would have required a company to have a minimum paid up capital. Clause 9 would have required advertisements and circulars issued to the public which state the amount of the authorised or issued capital to also state the amount of the paid up capital.

And clause 33(2) would have empowered the court on the application of the company, the holder of or other person interested in shares of the company or a creditor of the company, to validate, *inter alia*, an invalid issue of shares where validation is just and equitable. This provision should have applied where a company issues shares in excess of its nominal capital.

[3-4] *Re Mayfair Property Co.* [1898] 2 Ch. 28 (C.A.).
[5] *Re Midland Rlwy. Carriage Co.* (1907) 23 T.L.R. 661.
[6] *Post* pp. 223, 478
[7] p. 184.

CLASSES OF SHARE CAPITAL

A company is not bound to issue all its shares with the same rights but may confer different rights on different classes of shares. Such classes may be described as ordinary shares and preference shares but the name by which a class of shares is called gives only an indication of the rights attaching to it in any particular company, and to ascertain the rights reference must be made to the articles or the terms of issue of the shares.

Although the memorandum of association is required to set out the division of the nominal capital into shares of a fixed amount, it is not required to set out, and in practice it will not usually set out, the different classes of shares into which the capital is divided. However, the articles will normally give the company power to issue different classes of shares.

Table A, article 2, provides: "Without prejudice to any special rights previously conferred on the holders of any existing shares or class of shares, any share in the company may be issued with such preferred, deferred or other special rights or such restrictions, whether in regard to dividend, voting, return of capital or otherwise as the company may from time to time by ordinary resolution determine."

If there is no such provision in the articles, in the absence of a prohibition in the memorandum they may be altered by special resolution to give such a power.[8]

Where a company issues shares with rights which are not stated in its memorandum or articles or in any resolution or document to which section 143 applies, or varies the rights attached to shares otherwise than by amendment of its memorandum or articles or by resolution or document to which section 143 applies, clause 23 of the Companies Bill 1973 would have required the company to deliver particulars to the Registrar unless the shares are uniform with shares previously issued.

Preference shares

Preference shares are shares the issue of which was authorised by the memorandum or the articles and which are entitled to some priority over the other shares in the company. They usually carry a right to preference in payment of dividend (if a dividend is declared) at a fixed rate, and a right to preference in the repayment of capital

---

[8] *Andrews* v. *Gas Meter Co.* [1897] 1 Ch. 361 (C.A.), *ante* p. 113; *cf. Liquidator of The Humboldt Redwood Co. Ltd.* v. *Coats*, 1908 S.C. 751, and *Crookston* v. *Lindsay, Crookston & Co. Ltd.* 1922 S.L.T. 62 (O.H.).

in a winding up. There may be several classes of preference shares, first, second and third, ranking one after the other.

The rights attached to preference shares are always a question of construction of the memorandum, the articles or the terms of issue of the shares. However, unless the articles, etc., otherwise provide, the rights which attach to preference shares are as described below. These prima facie rights differ according to whether the company is a going concern or in liquidation.

When the company is a going concern

1. When a right to a preferential dividend is given without more, it is a right to a *cumulative* dividend, *i.e.* if no preference dividend is declared in any year the arrears of dividend are carried forward and must be paid before a dividend is paid on the other shares.[9] If, however, the shares are declared to be non-cumulative preference shares, or the preferential dividend is to be paid out of the yearly profits,[10] or out of the net profits of each year,[11] the dividend will not be cumulative.

2. Preference shares are *non-participating*, *i.e.* they do not confer any right to a participation in the surplus profits of the company, after payment of a specified rate of dividend on the ordinary shares, in the absence of anything to that effect in the articles, etc. Where a special resolution that the holders of preference shares were entitled to a cumulative preference dividend at the rate of 10 per cent. per annum and that such shares should rank, both as regards capital and dividend in priority to the other shares, the holders were only entitled to a 10 per cent. dividend in the distribution of profits— the provision defined the whole terms of the bargain between the shareholders and the company.[12] Sometimes, however, cumulative and participating preference shares are created, conferring a right to participate in surplus profits up to a fixed percentage, *e.g.* a right to a preferential dividend of seven per cent. may be given, together with a further right, after seven per cent. has been paid on the ordinary shares, to participate in the surplus profits equally with the

---

[9] *Webb* v. *Earle* (1875) L.R. 20 Eq. 556; *Ferguson & Forrester Ltd.* v. *Buchanan*, 1920 S.C. 154. Interest is not payable on the arrears: *Partick etc. Gas Co. Ltd.* v. *Taylor* (1888) 15 R. 711.

[10] *Adair* v. *Old Bushmills Distillery* [1908] W.N. 24.

[11] *Staples* v. *Eastman Photographic Materials Co.* [1896] 2 Ch. 303 (C.A.); contrast *Miln* v. *Arizona Copper Co. Ltd.* (1899) 1 F. 935.

[12] *Will* v. *United Lankat Plantations Co. Ltd.* [1914] A.C. 11.

ordinary shares until an additional seven per cent. has been paid, but no more.

3. Unless the articles, etc., otherwise provide, preference shares carry the *same voting rights* at general meetings as the other shares.[13] However if, as is common, the preference shareholders are expressly given a right to vote in certain specified circumstances, *e.g.* when the preference dividend is in arrears or the rights attached to the preference shares are being varied, prima facie they have no right to vote in other circumstances.

The Jenkins Report[14] recommended that holders of voteless preference shares should receive notices of general meetings and a copy of any chairman's statement which is circulated with the accounts. The majority of the Committee thought that the case for abolition of voteless shares had not been made out and rejected the suggestion that holders of voteless shares should be given a statutory right to attend and speak at company meetings.

When the company is being wound up

1. *In the absence of a provision in the articles, etc., arrears of cumulative preference divivend are not payable out of the assets in a liquidation, unless the dividend has been declared.*[15] If, however, as is usual, the articles provide for the payment of arrears, such arrears are payable out of the surplus assets after payment of the company's debts, whether or not any undistributed profits are included in the assets.[16] If the articles provide only for payment of all arrears "due" at the date of winding up, no arrears will be payable unless dividends have been declared, because a dividend is not due until it has been declared.[17]

A provision that preference shares shall be entitled to "a fixed cumulative preferential dividend at the rate of x per cent. per annum . . . and . . . shall rank both as regards dividends and capital in priority to the ordinary shares, but shall not confer the right to any further participation in profits or assets," entitles the preference

---

[13] See s. 134(e), *post* 300.
[14] Para. 140.
[15] *Re Crichton's Oil Co.* [1902] 2 Ch. 86 (C.A.); *Re Catalinas Warehouses & Mole Co. Ltd.* [1947] 1 All E.R. 51; *Robertson-Durham* v. *Inches*, 1917, 1 S.L.T. 267 (O.H.).
[16] *Re Springbok Agricultural Estates Ltd.* [1920] 1 Ch. 563; *Re Wharfedale Brewery Co. Ltd.* [1952] Ch. 913. In other words, the rule (*post* p. 468) that dividends must only be paid out of profits has no application to the surplus assets in a winding up.
[17] *Re Roberts and Cooper Ltd.* [1929] 2 Ch. 383.

shareholders to receive arrears of dividends, although not declared, in priority to the repayment of capital to the ordinary shareholders— the early part of the provision applies to the state of affairs when the company is a going concern and the words "shall rank . . . as regards dividends . . . in priority to the ordinary shares" obviously apply in a winding up.[18] A similar provision omitting the word "preferential" and any reference to further participation in profits or assets confers no right to undeclared arrears of preference dividend in a winding up—it is not necessary to treat the words "shall rank . . . as regards dividends" as conferring priority in respect of arrears of cumulative preference dividend in a winding up, because there is no prior statement that the preference share-holders are to have a preference dividend.[19] A provision including the word "preferential" and merely omitting any reference to further participation in profits or assets also gives a right to arrears of preference dividend in a winding up in priority to the ordinary shares.[20]

2. *Prima facie, preference shares have no priority in the repayment of capital in a winding up.* However, such a right may be, and usually is, given by the articles, and its effect is that after the company's debts and liabilities, and any arrears of preference dividend which are payable, have been paid, the preference shareholders are entitled to repayment of their capital in full before the ordinary shareholders are repaid their capital.[21]

3. Where there are surplus assets available after the discharge of all the company's liabilities and the repayment of the capital to the shareholders, such *surplus assets are divisible rateably among all classes of shareholders in the absence of any provision in the articles etc. to the contrary.*[22] But, if, as is common, the articles set out the rights attached to a class of shares to participate in profits while the company is a going concern or to share in the property of the company in liquidation, prima facie those rights are exhaus-

---

[18] *Re Walter Symons Ltd.* [1934] Ch. 308; *Re F. de Jong & Co. Ltd.* [1946] Ch. 211 (C.A.).

[19] *Re Wood, Skinner & Co. Ltd.* [1944] Ch. 323; *Robertson-Durham* v. *Inches*, 1917, 1 S.L.T. 267 (O.H.). And see *Re William Bedford Ltd.* [1967] V.R. 490.

[20] *Re E. W. Savory Ltd.* [1951] 2 All E.R. 1036; *Re Wharfedale Brewery Co. Ltd., ante.*

[21] The preference shares were by the articles given priority in the return of capital in the cases cited in notes 18, 19, 20, *ante.*

[22] *Monkland Iron etc. Co. Ltd.* v. *Henderson* (1883) 10 R. 494; *Liquidators of William-son-Buchanan Steamers Ltd., Petitioners*, 1936 S.L.T. 106 (O.H.); *Town and Gown Assocn. Ltd. Liquidator, Petitioner*, 1948 S.L.T. (Notes) 71 (O.H.).

tive. Thus, articles giving preference shareholders priority in the repayment of capital in a liquidation but containing no reference to any further rights in the capital do not entitle the preference shareholders to participate in such surplus assets.[23]

The colliery assets of a coal mining company had been transferred to the National Coal Board under the Coal Industry Nationalisation Act 1946 and the company was to go into voluntary liquidation. Meanwhile the company proposed to reduce its capital by returning their capital to the holders of the preference stock. The articles provided that in the event of a winding up the preference stock ranked before the ordinary stock to the extent of repayment of the amounts called up and paid thereon. *Held*, the proposed reduction was not unfair or inequitable. Even without it, the preference shareholders would not be entitled in a winding up to share in the surplus assets or to receive more than a return of their paid up capital. Accordingly, they could not object to being paid, by means of the reduction, the amount which they would receive in the proposed liquidation: *Wilsons and Clyde Coal Co. Ltd.* v. *Scottish Insurance Corpn. Ltd.*, 1949 S.C. (H.L.) 90; [1949] A.C. 462.

If articles expressly give preference shareholders a right to share in surplus assets after the repayment of capital, they are entitled to share in accumulated profits in a liquidation even if the articles give the ordinary shareholders a right to exclusive enjoyment of accumulated profits not required for the preference dividend—the right of the ordinary shareholders depends on the appropriate resolutions being passed before a winding up.[24]

Preference shares contrasted with ordinary shares

Preference shares are more like debentures than like ordinary shares in that, if profits are available and if a dividend is declared on preference shares, it will be at a fixed rate just as debentures carry a fixed rate of interest (whether profits are available or not), whereas the rate of dividend on ordinary shares varies according to the amount of profits available.

Further, in the case of preference shares the right of the holders to vote at general meetings is usually restricted[25] to when their special rights are being varied, or their dividend is in arrear,[26] and

---

[23] *Wilsons and Clyde Coal Co. Ltd.* v. *Scottish Insurance Corpn. Ltd.*, 1949 S.t. (H.L.) 90; 1948 S.C. 360; *Re The Isle of Thanet Electricity Supply Co. Ltd.* [1950] Ch. 161 (C.A.).

[24] *Dimbula Valley (Ceylon) Tea Co. Ltd.* v. *Laurie* [1961] Ch. 353.

[25] The Stock Exchange requires restricted voting shares to be designated as such: Admission of Securities to Listing, p. 164.

[26] *Ante* p. 214.

debentures normally confer no right to vote at general meetings, whereas ordinary shares usually confer a full right of voting.

The above may be said to be, at least in times of inflation when profits are high, the main disadvantages of preference shares. Another disadvantage is that in a prosperous business the preference shareholder is now regarded as a temporary member of the company, whose rights are limited to his preferential dividend and to priority in the return of capital on a winding up, and whose capital is liable to be returned to him whenever the company can raise the necessary money at a lower dividend rate.[27] The advantage of preference shares is that they are a safe investment. In particular, in a winding up, under normal articles the preference capital is repayable after payment of the company's debts and before the ordinary capital is returned.

A disadvantage from the company's point of view is that dividends on shares are not allowed as a deduction for the purposes of calculating the net profits on which corporation tax is paid whereas debenture interest is so allowed.[28]

Variation of class rights

1. Where a company's shares are divided into classes, "class rights" are special rights of a class of shares, *e.g.* a preferential right as to dividend attached to preference shares where a company's shares are divided into preference shares and ordinary shares.

It has been said that the term "class" must be confined to those persons whose rights are not so dissimilar as to make it impossible for them to consult together with a view to their common interest.[29] In the New South Wales case, *Crumpton* v. *Morrine Hall Pty. Ltd., ante,*[30] each shareholder constituted a separate class of shareholders.

Class rights are usually given to preference shareholders and if articles give the *ordinary* shareholders a right to the distributed profits after payment of a dividend on the preference shares, and a

---

[27] *Post* p. 238.
[28] *Post* pp. 660–665.
[29] *Per* Bowen L.J. in *Sovereign Life Assurance Co.* v. *Dodd* [1892] 2 Q.B. 573 (C.A.) at p. 583. (This case concerned the forerunner of s. 206, *post* p. 218. An arrangement was made between a company in course of being wound up and its creditors. Insured persons whose policies had matured formed a distinct class of creditors from those whose policies had not.)
[30] p. 113.

right to surplus assets on a liquidation, these are *not* class rights—
they are no more than would be implied if the articles did not refer
to them.[31] However, it seems that the original 2s. ordinary shares in
Greenhalgh v. *Arderne Cinemas*,[32] *post*, formed a class of shares
within the meaning of an article providing for variation of the rights
attached to a class of shares. Again, in *Lord St. Davids* v. *Union-
Castle Mail Steamship Co. Ltd.*,[33] where under the articles the large
number of preference shares carried a right to vote when the preference dividend was in arrears and, such dividend being in arrears, the
preference shareholders proposed to alter the articles so as to give
themselves a right to vote on all resolutions, it was held that the
proposed resolution would not affect the rights of the small number
of ordinary shares unless the ordinary shareholders approved in
accordance with an article providing for variation of class rights,
i.e. class rights were attached to the ordinary shares.[34]

Class rights may be attached to a class of shares by the memorandum or the articles of the company, or by the terms of issue of the
shares, or by a special resolution of the company in general meeting
as in *Re Old Silkstone Collieries Ltd.*[35] They are usually concerned
with voting, dividend, and the distribution of assets in the event of
the company's being wound up.

2. *If class rights are set out in the memorandum*, or incorporated
therein by reference to the articles,[36] they are unalterable[37] unless,
e.g., the memorandum itself provides a method of alteration, or a
method of alteration is provided by articles expressly referred to in
the memorandum,[38] or the consent of the court is obtained to a
scheme of arrangement under section 206.[39]

An alteration by a method provided by the memorandum will
probably be subject to section 72, *post*.

Under section 206 a company may make a binding compromise

---

[31] *Hodge* v. *James Howell & Co., The Times*, December 13, 1958 (C.A.).
[32] [1946] 1 All E.R. 512 (C.A.).   [33] *The Times*, November 24, 1934.
[34] See, too, *Rights and Issues Investment Trust Ltd.* v. *Stylo Shoes Ltd.* [1965] Ch. 250, *ante* p. 112.
[35] [1954] Ch. 169, *post* p. 240.
[36] *Dimbula Valley (Ceylon) Tea Co. Ltd.* v. *Laurie* [1961] Ch. 353.
[37] *Ashbury* v. *Watson* (1885) 30 Ch.D. 376 (C.A.).
[38] *Re Welsbach Incandescent Gas Light Co. Ltd.* [1904] 1 Ch. 87 (C.A.). It seems that in Scotland, even where the memorandum is silent as to variation of class rights but contemporaneous articles contain provision for variation, the rights conferred by the memorandum can be varied in accordance with that provision: *Oban etc. Distilleries Ltd., Petitioners* (1903) 5 F. 1140, followed in *Marshall, Fleming & Co. Ltd., Petitioners*, 1938 S.C. 873 (O.H.).
[39] *Post* p. 635.

or arrangement with a class of members. Application must be made to the court to order a meeting of the class. Then the compromise or arrangement must be approved at the meeting by a simple majority in number representing three-fourths in value of those voting in person or by proxy. Finally, the court must approve it.

The power to alter the memorandum conferred by section 23[40] does not authorise any variation or abrogation of the special rights of any class of members.

3. *The rights of different classes of shares are usually set out in the articles and it is usual for the articles to provide for the variation of class rights.*

Table A, article 4, provides: "If at any time the share capital is divided into different classes of shares, the rights attached to any class (unless otherwise provided by the terms of issue of the shares of that class) may, whether or not the company is being wound up, be varied with the consent in writing of the holders of three-fourths of the issued shares of that class, or with the sanction of an extraordinary resolution passed at a separate general meeting of the holders of the shares of the class. To every such separate general meeting the provisions of these regulations relating to general meetings shall apply, but so that the necessary quorum shall be two persons at least holding or representing by proxy one-third of the issued shares of the class and that any holder of shares of the class present in person or by proxy may demand a poll."

If articles attach class rights to a class of shares and contain a "modification of rights clause" like Table A, article, 4, above, the class rights may be varied,[41] with the consent of the specified proportion or resolution of the holders of shares of the class, by a valid alteration of the articles by a special resolution of the company in general meeting.[42]

It has been held that in such a case the modification of rights clause must be complied with if the class rights are to be varied.[43] Section 72, below, appears to have been drafted on this basis, and if the rule were otherwise there would be an implied alteration of the articles.

There is no effectual sanction to a modification of class rights unless those holding a sufficient majority of the shares of the class vote in favour of the modification in the bona fide belief that they

[40] *Ante* p. 97.
[41] A variation of the rights of preference shareholders includes a total abolition of such rights for the purposes of an article like Table A, article 4: *Frazer Brothers Ltd., Petitioners*, 1963 S.C. 139.
[42] *Ante* p. 109.
[43] *e.g. Re Old Silkstone Collieries Ltd., ante* p. 218 and *post* p. 240; *Crumpton* v. *Morrine Hall Pty. Ltd.* [1965] N.S.W.R. 240, *ante* p. 113; *contra Fischer* v. *Easthaven Ltd.* [1964], N.S.W.R. 261.

are acting in the interests of the general body of members of the class, *i.e.* at the class meeting the majority shareholders must consider what is best for the shareholders as a class, not what is best in their own interests.[44]

Where there is in the articles (or the memorandum) a power to vary class rights, the exercise of the power is subject to section 72. This section provides that if, in the case of a company with a share capital divided into different classes of shares, provision is made by the articles (or memorandum) for the variation or abrogation of the rights attached to any class of shares, subject to the consent of a specified proportion of the holders of the shares of the class or the sanction of a resolution passed at a separate meeting of the holders of such shares, and in pursuance of such provision the rights attached to any such class of shares are varied, an application can be made to the court to have the variation cancelled, whereupon it has no effect unless and until it is confirmed by the court.

Those who can apply are the holders of not less in the aggregate than 15 per cent. of the issued shares of the class who did not consent to or vote for the variation. The application must be made within 21 days after the giving of the consent or the passing of the resolution. In England it is made by petition by one or more of the dissenting shareholders authorised in writing by the 15 per cent.: R.S.C., O. 102, r. 5. For Scotland, see R.C. 190.

The court may disallow the variation if, after hearing the various parties interested, it is satisfied that the variation would unfairly prejudice the shareholders of the class in question. If the court is not so satisfied it must confirm the variation.

The company must, within 15 days, send a copy of the order made by the court to the Registrar of Companies: section 72 (5).

The object of the section is to protect shareholders from being prejudiced by the voting of other shareholders who hold shares of another class in addition to those of the class affected by the variation.

For example, if a variation reduces the dividend on preference shares from seven per cent. to six per cent. per annum, and 80 per cent. of the preference shareholders are also ordinary shareholders, the requisite consent of the preference shareholders is likely to be obtained, since the variation will leave more profits for a dividend on the ordinary shares. This would be unfair to the 20 per cent. of the preference shareholders who are not ordinary shareholders and they could apply under section 72.

[44] *Re Holders Investment Trust Ltd.* [1971] 1 W.L.R. 583, *post* p. 225.

Class rights are *not* "varied" by the subdivision of other shares, under a power in the articles, which results in the holders of the shares with the class rights being outvoted by the holders of the other shares.

2s. ordinary shares, as regards voting, ranked *pari passu* with the 10s. ordinary shares. Each 10s share was sub-divided into 5 2s. ordinary shares. *Held*, the voting rights of the original 2s. shares had not been varied. The only voting right attached to that class was one vote per share, and that right remained: *Greenhalgh* v. *Arderne Cinemas Ltd.* [1946] 1 All E.R. 512 (C.A.).[45]

Again, class rights are *not* "affected" by the creation or issue of new shares of the class ranking equally with the old.

Capital was being increased by the issue of 660,000 £1 preference shares ranking *pari passu* with the existing 600,000 £1 preference stock, and 2,640,000 ordinary shares of 10s. each ranking *pari passu* with the existing £3,300,000 ordinary stock. The new shares were to be issued to the ordinary stockholders and paid for out of the reserve fund. *Held*, the proposed issue of new capital did not "affect" the rights of the existing preference shareholders. Only the enjoyment of the rights was affected, the rights themselves were not: *White* v. *Bristol Aeroplane Co. Ltd.* [1953] Ch. 65 (C.A.).[46]

Table A, article 5, states that, unless otherwise expressly provided by the terms of issue of a class of shares, the creation or issue of further shares ranking *pari passu* with the shares of the class is *not* a variation of the class rights.

It is thought that a modification of rights clause in the articles cannot be altered by special resolution without the appropriate consent of shareholders of the class—a class right, that special rights of the class of shares will only be varied in accordance with the clause, is attached to the shares in question.

If, in a rare case, class rights are set out in the articles but the articles do not contain a modification of rights clause, the rights can be varied, *e.g.* under section 206 above, but it is doubtful whether they can be varied by an alteration of the articles whether this amounts to a straightforward alteration of the rights or to the insertion of a modification of rights clause in the articles and compliance with this clause as well as an alteration of the articles. It will be remembered that under section 10[47] a company may by special resolution alter or add to its articles, but the alteration must not be a fraud on a minority of the shareholders. Further, section 72 may

[45] And see the *Dimbula* case, *ante* p. 218.
[46] And see *Re John Smith's Tadcaster Brewery Co. Ltd.* [1953] Ch. 308.
[47] *Ante* p. 109.

be thought to assume that class rights can only be varied in accordance with a modification of rights clause in the articles at the time of issue of the shares in question. However, in *Re National Dwellings Society Ltd.*,[48] where a reduction of capital would affect the rights of preference shareholders, the articles were first altered by the insertion of a modification of rights clause and then the approval of the preference shareholders was obtained, whereupon the court confirmed the reduction.

The Jenkins Report[49] made the following recommendations: Where special rights are attached to a class of shares, otherwise than in the memorandum, and there is no provision in the articles for variation of such rights, the articles should be deemed to include a provision on the lines of Table A, article 4, *ante*, amended in a number of respects, *e.g.* to make it clear that special rights can be varied only with the consent of the prescribed majority of shareholders. It should be made clear that the alteration of a provision relating to the variation of class rights is itself to be treated as a variation of those rights. The decision in the Scots case of *Marshall, Fleming & Co. Ltd.*, *ante*, should apply in England. Section 10[50] should be amended to make clear that the power to alter articles by special resolution cannot be used to override the special rights attached to a class of shares. Section 72 should be amended, *e.g.* to permit an application for cancellation of a variation of class rights to be made by the holders of 10 instead of 15 per cent. of the issued shares of the class and within 28 days instead of 21 days.

Clauses 24 and 25 of the Companies Bill 1973 would have given effect to such recommendations and, indeed, would have reduced the minimum holding entitling a person to object to a variation of class rights to five per cent.

Redeemable preference shares

Section 58 provides that a company, if so authorised by its articles, may issue preference shares which are, or at the option of the company are to be liable, to be redeemed. Issued preference shares cannot be converted into redeemable preference shares under section 58, because that would not be an "issue" within the section.[51] Such a conversion can take place only if the steps appropriate

---

[48] (1898) 78 L.T. 144.
[49] Para. 198.
[50] *Ante* p. 109.
[51] *Re St. James' Court Estate Ltd.* [1944] Ch. 6.

to a reduction and simultaneous increase of capital have been taken, *i.e.* a reduction of capital by cancelling the issued preference shares and an increase of capital by creating the redeemable preference shares. The Jenkins Report[52] recommended that the section be extended to permit the conversion of preference shares into redeemable preference shares by special resolution, subject to any appropriate class consents.

Subject to the provisions of the section, the terms on which redeemable preference shares can be redeemed by the company depend on the articles.

Table A, article 3, provides: "Subject to the provisions of section 58 of the Act, any preference shares may, with the sanction of an ordinary resolution, be issued on the terms that they are, or at the option of the company are liable, to be redeemed on such terms and in such manner as the company before the issue of the shares may by special resolution determine."

The section provides that redeemable preference shares can be redeemed only—

(1) if they are fully paid;
(2) out of profits of the company available for dividend or out of the proceeds of a fresh issue of shares made for the purposes of the redemption.

Requirement (1) is intended to maintain the share capital of the company. As regards (2), the new shares may be ordinary shares.

The section also provides that if the company has bound itself to pay a premium on redemption, this can be paid only out of profits or out of the share premium account.

When the shares are redeemed otherwise than out of the proceeds of a fresh issue, a sum equal to the nominal amount of the shares redeemed must be transferred, out of profits which would otherwise have been available for dividend, to a "capital redemption reserve fund" (s. 58 (1)), which will be shown as a reserve in the balance sheet (Schedule 8, paragraph 4, as amended). The provisions of the Act relating to reduction of capital apply to this fund, as if it were paid-up share capital, except where it is applied in paying up shares issued to members as fully paid bonus shares: section 58 (1). (*Cf.* the share premium account.[53])

The object of this part of section 58 is to prevent the balance

[52] Para. 198.
[53] *Ante* p. 176.

sheet showing a paper profit which might be distributed by way of dividend. The profit would otherwise arise through the current assets being reduced by the amount necessary to redeem the redeemable preference shares, and the share capital *and* the revenue reserves being reduced.[54] The effect of this part of the section is to extend to a capital redemption reserve fund the principle that the share capital of a company must be maintained, which will be explained later.[55]

The redemption of preference shares is not to be taken as a reduction of the company's authorised share capital[56]: section 58 (3). The company can issue new shares of any class up to the nominal amount of the shares redeemed or about to be redeemed. If the new shares are issued before the old shares are redeemed, stamp duty is payable as on an increase of capital unless the old shares are redeemed within a month of the issue of the new shares: section 58 (4).

A company which has issued redeemable preference shares must include details of them in every balance sheet: Schedule 8, paragraph 2, as amended.[57] Within a month after redemption, notice of the number of shares redeemed must be given to the Registrar: section 62.

If a company fails to redeem redeemable preference shares on the due date it seems that the shareholders can obtain as injunction to restrain the payment of any dividends to ordinary shareholders until the preference shares have all been redeemed.[58]

Notwithstanding section 58 *ante*, redeemable preference shares can be redeemed by a reduction of capital under section 66 *post*, *i.e.* by a special resolution of the company in general meeting and with the consent of the court.[59] If redeemable preference shares are being so redeemed, and the reduction is not in accordance with the class rights of the preference shareholders, then at a class meeting of the redeemable preference shareholders, held in accordance with a modification of rights clause in the articles, the majority who vote in favour of the modification of their rights must consider what is best for the shareholders as a class, not what is best in their own interests.

---

[54] See the specimen balance sheet, *post* p. 445.   [55] *Post* p. 232.
[56] *Post* p. 244.   [57] *Post* p. 430.
[58] *Per* Megarry J. in *Re Holders Investment Trust Ltd.* [1971] 1 W.L.R. 583, at p. 590.
[59] *Re Birkenshaw Holdings Pty. Ltd.* (1975) 10 S.A.S.R. 577 (reduction of capital by repayment of redeemable preference shares).

A reduction of capital was to be effected by cancelling the five per cent. £1 cumulative redeemable preference shares (redeemable at par on July 31, 1971) and allotting the holders an equivalent amount of six per cent. unsecured loan stock repayable 1985/90. The majority of the preference shareholders, who supported the reduction, were also holders of 52 per cent. of the company's ordinary stock and non-voting ordinary shares. Minority preference shareholders opposed the reducton. The court refused to confirm it. The majority preference shareholders had considered what was best in their own interests, based on their large equity shareholding, without considering what was best for preference shareholders as a class. Further, the reduction was unfair[60]—the advantages of the exchange into unsecured stock did not compensate for the disadvantages: *Re Holders Investment Trust Ltd.* [1971] 1 W.L.R. 582.

Deferred shares

Deferred shares, which are sometimes called founders or management shares, are usually of small nominal amount with a right to take the whole or a proportion of the profits after a fixed dividend has been paid on the ordinary shares. The rights of the holders of deferred shares depend on the articles or the terms of issue.

The number of founders or management or deferred shares, and the nature and extent of the interest of the holders in the property and profits of the company, must be set out in a prospectus: Schedule 4.

Deferred shares are rarely issued now and the modern tendency is to convert existing deferred shares into ordinary shares.

Non-voting ordinary shares

In recent years a few companies have issued non-voting ordinary shares. The purpose of such issues was to enable the companies concerned to raise money and at the same time enable those with the majority of the existing voting shares to retain control. However, with the idea of ensuring that the public is not misled, The Stock Exchange requires non-voting shares to be designated as such.[61]

The Jenkins Report[62] recommended that holders of voteless equity[63] shares should receive notices of general meetings and a copy of any chairman's statement which is circulated with the accounts.

The Conservative Government White Paper on Company Law Reform[64] accepted the case for prohibiting the issue of equity shares with limited or no

[60] See *post* p. 238.
[61] Admission of Securities to Listing, p. 164.
[62] Para. 140.
[63] *Ante* p. 58.
[64] (1973) Cmnd. 5391, para. 48.

voting rights, and clause 21 of the Companies Bill 1973 would have prevented listed companies from issuing equity shares which do not carry an unqualified right to vote at general meetings or, on a poll, a constant number of votes.

No par value shares

The memorandum of a limited company with a share capital must state the amount of share capital with which the company proposes to be registered and its division into shares of a fixed amount (s. 2), and any provision in the memorandum or articles, or in any resolution, of a company limited by guarantee purporting to divide the undertaking into shares or interests is treated as a provision for a share capital, notwithstanding that the nominal amount or number of the shares or interests is not specified thereby (s. 21). The requirement that the nominal share capital must be divided into shares of a fixed amount means that *shares of no par value cannot be issued*.

Such shares would not give rise to the misleading impression which is often created by the nominal or par value of shares. After a company has been in existence for any length of time, the nominal value of the shares rarely bears any relation to the real value, and so gives no assistance to investors or creditors. For example, after some years, a share of a nominal amount of £1 issued at a price of £1 may be worth £2. Further, if dividends are expressed as a percentage of the nominal value of such share, where the real return is, say, six per cent. on the market value of the share, the dividend will be expressed as 12 per cent. of the nominal value, and this may give rise to the mistaken impression that the dividend is excessive.

The Report of the majority of the Gedge Committee[65] recommended that companies should be able to issue ordinary shares of no par value if they wished, and the Jenkins Report[66] recommended[67] the amendment of the Companies Act to allow the issue of preference and ordinary shares of no par value, but, as yet, effect has not been given to these recommendations. Shares of no par value can be issued in a number of countries, including America. The former Conservative Government did not intend to make any changes in relation to shares of no-par-value. Their White Paper[68] stated

[65] (1954) Cmd. 9112.   [66] (1962) Cmnd. 1749.
[67] Para. 34.
[68] (1973) Cmnd. 5391, para. 49.

that the practical need is now not a strong one—no serious inquirer is likely to be misled by nominal value, particularly as public comment nowadays concentrates on the significant ratios such as price/earnings, dividend cover and earnings per share.

RAISING OF SHARE CAPITAL

The issued share capital of a company is the fund to which creditors of the company can look for payment of their debts and so, to protect the creditors, it has been held that the share capital must be raised. This means that shares can be treated as paid up only to the extent of the amount actually received by the company in cash or in kind, and must not be issued at a discount, *i.e.* must not be issued as fully paid for a consideration less than payment or the promise of payment of the nominal amount of each share,[69] although the company may not require payment in full of the nominal amount on allotment. The rule that the share capital must be raised is intended to ensure that money or assets equal in amount or value to the paid-up capital on paper is or are received by the company. Certain sections of the Act, *e.g.* section 53 (2) which generally prohibits the payment of commissions and discounts out of a company's shares or capital money,[70] section 27 which provides that a subsidiary company generally may not be a member of its holding company,[71] and section 54 which in general prohibits a company from providing financial assistance for the purchase of or subscription for its own shares,[72] also have the effect of ensuring that the capital is raised. Of course, the rule is no protection to creditors where a company does not make a substantial issue of share capital.

There are certain exceptions to the rule that the share capital must be raised. These exceptions have been explained already and are, briefly:

(1) Where shares are issued at a discount under section 57.[73]
(2) Where shares are issued for an over-valued non-monetary consideration, as in *Re Wragg Ltd.*[74]

---

[69] *Ooregum Gold Mining Co.* v. *Roper* [1892] A.C. 125, *ante* p. 174.
[70] *Ante* p. 162.   [71] *Ante* p. 192.
[72] *Ante* p. 192.   [73] *Ante* p. 175.
[74] [1897] 1 Ch. 796 (C.A.), *ante* p. 173. *Cf. Waterhouse* v. *Jamieson* (1870) 8 M. (H.L.) 88 and *Penang Foundry Co. Ltd.* v. *Gardiner*, 1913 S.C. 1203 (O.H.).

    (3) Where a company pays a commission under section 53 (1) to a person who agrees to subscribe, or to procure subscriptions, for shares in the company.[75]

The rule does not apply to an unlimited company.[76]

<h2 style="text-align:center">ALTERATION OF SHARE CAPITAL</h2>

    Section 61 provides that a limited company with a share capital, if so authorised by its articles, may alter the conditions of its memorandum by—

    (1) increasing its share capital by new shares; or
    (2) consolidating and dividing all or any of its share capital into shares of larger amount than its existing shares; or
    (3) converting all or any of its paid-up shares into stock, or reconverting stock into paid-up shares of any denomination; or
    (4) subdividing all or any of its shares into shares of smaller amount than is fixed by the memorandum; or
    (5) cancelling shares which have not been taken or agreed to be taken by any person. (This is called "diminution of capital" and it should not be confused with reduction of capital which will be explained later.[77])

    All these powers require for their exercise a resolution of the company in general meeting.

    It was noted in Chapter 3 [78] that a change in the description of a share from, say, 5s to 25p is not an alteration of a condition in the memorandum so that no formalities are required by the Act.

Increase of capital

    Every increase of capital, *i.e.* nominal capital, must be effected by the company in general meeting: section 61. If the articles authorise the increase of capital, whether an ordinary or a special resolution is required depends on the articles.

---

[75] *Ante* p. 162.
[76] See *Nelson Mitchell* v. *City of Glasgow Bank* (1879) 6 R. (H.L.) 66, (1878) 6 R. 420, *ante* p. 46.
[77] *Post* p. 235.
[78] *Ante* p. 95.

Table A, article 44, provides: "The company may from time to time by *ordinary* resolution increase the share capital by such sum, to be divided into shares of such amount, as the resolution shall prescribe."

If the articles do not give authority to increase capital, the articles must be altered by special resolution so that they do give authority but the one special resolution can both authorise and effect an increase.[79]

The notice convening the meeting must specify the amount of the proposed increase.[80] Within 15 days after the passing of the resolution effecting the increase, a notice in the prescribed form of the amount of the increase must be filed with the Registrar (s. 63). A printed copy of the resolution effecting the increase, or a copy in some other form approved by him, must also be filed with the Registrar (1948 Act, s. 63; 1967 Act, s. 51). The processes which the Registrar is prepared to regard as satisfying the printing requirement have been noted already.[80a]

The articles frequently provide that all new shares shall, before issue, be offered to the existing shareholders in proportion to the shares which they already hold, and that if the shareholders decline to accept the shares so offered, the directors may dispose of them in the manner they think most beneficial to the company. The directors can be restrained by injunction from infringing such an article.

The D. Company's articles provided that new shares should first be issued to existing shareholders. The G. Company held so many shares in D. that it could control the voting power and D. thereupon proposed to offer new shares to all shareholders except G. *Held*, D. could be restrained by injunction from doing this: *Gas Meter Co. Ltd.* v. *Diaphragm and General Leather Co. Ltd.* (1925) 41 T.L.R. 342.

When the existing shareholders are given the right to apply for new shares in proportion to the shares which they already hold, the issue is called a "rights issue." The letter to the shareholders, specifying the number of shares for which they are entitled to apply, is usually accompanied by a letter of renunciation, enabling the shareholders to renounce the shares in favour of a named person. Provision is also made for "splitting" when only part of the new issue is renounced or when part is renounced in favour of one person and part in favour of another.

The conditions on which the new shares are held are set out in the terms of issue. The articles usually provide that they shall be

[79] *Campbell's Case* (1873) L.R. 9 Ch.App. 1.
[80] *MacConnell* v. *E. Prill & Co. Ltd.* [1916] 2 Ch. 57.   [80a] p. 105.

subject to the same provisions with reference to the payment of calls, lien, transfer, transmission, forfeiture, and otherwise as the shares in the original share capital.

Consolidation of shares

This takes place when several shares are consolidated into one, *e.g.* when 20 5p shares are consolidated into one £1 share. Consolidation is effected in the same way as an increase of capital (s. 61), *i.e.* if the articles authorise consolidation, the resolution specified in the articles must be passed. If the articles are silent, a special resolution to give authority and to effect the consolidation is necessary. Table A, article 45, requires an ordinary resolution. Notice must be given to the Registrar within a month of the consolidation (s. 62).

Conversion of shares into stock

The difference between stock and shares was described by Lord Hatherley as follows: "Shares in a company, as shares, cannot be bought in small fractions of any amount, fractions of less than a pound,[81] but the consolidated stock of a company can be bought just in the same way as the stock of the public debt can be bought, split up into as many portions as you like, and subdivided into as small fractions as you please." He also referred to stock as "simply a set of shares put together in a bundle."[82]

A company *cannot issue stock directly* but can only convert shares into stock under section 61, although there seems to be no reason for this rule today. The conversion can only be made if the shares are fully paid (s. 61).

A company had fully paid-up ordinary and preference shares. It then (1) converted its ordinary and preference shares into stock; (2) gave the holders of preference stock carrying a lower rate of dividend extra bonus stock to maintain their former dividends; (3) made a direct issue of new fully paid-up ordinary and preference stock for cash, and (4) issued new partly paid-up ordinary and preference stock. Many years after these issues were made, the company went into liquidation and, after the creditors were paid, there was a surplus to distribute among the members. *Held*, (a) that the bonus stock was *ultra vires* and void, and no distribution could be made in respect of it; (b) that the direct issue of new stock was irregular, but having regard to the lapse of time the irregularity had to be treated as waived, and the holders were entitled to rank for distribution

[81] This only refers to the shares of the particular company under discussion. The nominal value of shares may be less than a pound.
[82] In *Morrice* v. *Aylmer* (1875) L.R. 7 H.L. 717 at pp. 724, 725.

in respect of it; (c) that the partly paid-up stock was *ultra vires* and void and in the same position as the bonus stock; and (d) that the owners of the bonus and the partly paid-up stock were not liable for any calls: *Re Home and Foreign Investment, etc., Co. Ltd.* [1912] 1 Ch. 72.

The conversion of shares into stock (or a reconversion of stock into shares) is effected in the same way as an increase of capital (s. 61). Table A, article 40, provides that the conversion of shares into stock and the reconversion of stock into shares shall be effected by ordinary resolution. Notice must be given to the Registrar within a month (s. 62).

Although in theory stock can be transferred in fractional amounts, in practice the articles usually confer on the directors power to fix the minimum amount transferable. Table A, article 41, gives the directors this power, and provides that such minimum is not to exceed the nominal amount of the shares from which the stock arose. Thus, if the shares were £1 shares, the minimum amount of stock transferable must not exceed £1's worth.

The method of transferring stock is laid down in the articles. Table A, article 41, provides that stock may be transferred in the same manner and subject to the same regulations as the shares from which the stock arose might previously to conversion have been transferred. Article 42 provides that stockholders shall, according to the amount of their stock, have the same rights, privileges and advantages as regards dividends, voting at meetings of the company and other matters as if the conversion had not taken place.

When shares are converted into stock the register of members must show the amount of stock held by each member: section 110. Stock certificates similar in form to share certificates must be issued except that stock warrants transferable by delivery may be issued if the articles so provide [83] and Treasury consent is obtained.[84]

When shares have been converted into stock the annual return must state the amount of stock held by each member: section 124.

The advantage of converting shares into stock was that the work caused by the fact that each share had a separate number was obviated. However, this advantage is now minimised by the proviso to section 74, under which shares need not have a distinguishing number.[85]

---

[83] *Pilkington* v. *United Railways of The Havena etc. Warehouses Ltd.* [1930] 2 Ch. 108.
[84] Exchange Control Act 1947, Pt. III. Such stock warrants must be deposited with an authorised depositary. *Post* p. 283.
[85] *Post* p. 245.

The distinctions between shares and stock can be summarised as follows:

(1) Shares are in units, whereas stock is in a lump holding.
(2) Shares can be issued directly; stock cannot be issued directly.
(3) Shares need not be fully paid; stock must be fully paid.
(4) Shares may be numbered; stock is never numbered.
(5) Shares cannot be transferred in fractional amounts; stock can be so transferred (although there may be a minimum fractional amount of stock which can be transferred).

Clause 34 of the Companies Bill 1973 would have prohibited the conversion of shares into stock.

Subdivision of shares

This is the division of shares into shares of smaller amount, *e.g.* the division of one £1 share into 20 5p shares, and it is often resorted to for the purpose of improving the marketability of expensive shares. Subdivision is effected in the same way as an increase of capital: section 61. Table A, article 45, requires an ordinary resolution. If the shares are not fully paid up, the proportion between the amount paid and the amount unpaid on each reduced share must be the same as it was in the case of the share from which the reduced share is derived (s. 61). The subdivision of shares must be registered with the Registrar within a month (s. 62).

Cancellation of unissued shares

A company can cancel shares which have not been taken or agreed to be taken by any person, and *diminish* the amount of its share capital by the amount of the shares so cancelled. This is not to be deemed a reduction of share capital[86] (s. 61 (3)). Cancellation is effected in the same way as an increase of capital: section 61. Table A, article 45, requires an ordinary resolution. Notice of cancellation must be registered with the Registrar within a month (s. 62).

MAINTENANCE OF SHARE CAPITAL

It is a fundamental principle of company law that the share capital must be maintained. It has been said that "the whole of the sub-

[86] *Post* p. 244.

scribed capital of a company with limited liability, unless diminished by expenditure upon the company's objects (or, of course, by means sanctioned by statute) shall remain available for the discharge of its liabilities." [87] The term "subscribed capital" means "issued capital." Capital may be lost as a result of ordinary business risks and, as we shall see, it may be returned to the shareholders with the consent of the court under section 66, but otherwise it must be maintained since it is the fund to which creditors of the company look for payment of their debts. [88] Except under section 66 money or assets representing the paid-up share capital must not be returned to the members, nor must the liability of the members in respect of any share capital not paid up be reduced. Of course, capital may be returned to the members when the company is being wound up, after its debts have been paid, [89] and in certain circumstances interest on shares may be paid out of capital under section 65. [90] Originating in cases such as *Trevor* v. *Whitworth*, [91] the principle is now assisted by a number of sections of the Act, *e.g.* sections 27 and 54.

The principle that the share capital of a company must be maintained boils down to this—paid up share capital must not be returned to the members and their liability in respect of capital not paid up on their shares must not be reduced.

The principle has the following consequences:—

(1) A company generally must not purchase its own shares, or be a member of itself, as was decided in *Trevor* v. *Whitworth*. [92]

(2) A subsidiary company generally must not be a member of its holding company and any allotment or transfer of shares in a holding company to its subsidiary is void: section 27. [92]

(3) It is generally unlawful for a company to give any kind of financial assistance for the purchase of or subscription for its own shares or those of its holding company, by any person: section 54. [93]

---

[87] *Per* Kitto J. in *Davis Investments Pty. Ltd.* v. *Commissioner of Stamp Duties (N.S.W.)* (1957–58) 100 C.L.R. 392, at p. 413. And see *per* Lord Herschell at p. 415, and Lord Watson at p. 423, in *Trevor* v. *Whitworth* (1887) 12 A.C. 409, *ante* p. 191.

[88] See, *e.g.*, *Jenkins* v. *Harbour View Courts Ltd.* [1966] N.Z.L.R. 1 (C.A.), *post* p. 244, and *Australasian Oil Exploration Ltd.* v. *Lachberg* (1958) 101 C.L.R. 119.

[89] *Post* p. 597.

[90] *Post* p. 475.

[91] (1887) 12 App.Cas. 409, *ante* p. 191.

[92] *Ante* p. 192.

[93] *Ante* p. 192.

(4) Dividends must not be paid to the shareholders except out of profits, as was established in cases such as *Flitcroft's Case*.[94]

There are certain exceptions to the principle:—

(1) A company may reduce its share capital with the consent of the court under section 66, *post*.[95]
(2) A company may purchase its own shares under a court order made under section 210 to relieve an oppressed part of the members.[96]
(3) Capital may be returned to the members, after the company's debts have been paid, in a winding up.[89]
(4) Under section 65[90] interest on share capital may be paid out of capital in certain circumstances.

Other exceptions are forfeiture of shares and surrender to avoid a forfeiture, although here the amount paid on the shares remains with the company when the shareholder unable to pay a call is relieved of liability for future calls, and the shares revert to the company, bear no dividend and may be re-issued.[97]

Finally, the principle as to maintenance of share capital has been extended:—

(1) By section 58, to a capital redemption reserve fund set up when redeemable preference shares are redeemed by the company out of profits.[98]
(2) By section 56, to a share premium account.[99]

A company limited by guarantee and not having a share capital is subject to the principle of raising and maintenance of capital as far as the guarantee fund is concerned. The principle as applied to such a company is stricter than as applied to the company limited by shares, since in the latter type of company the principle does not prevent the creation of security over called or uncalled capital.[1]

The principle does not apply to an unlimited company.[2]

---

[94] (1881) 21 Ch.D. 519 (C.A.), *post* p. 476; *Liquidators of City of Glasgow Bank* v. *Mackinnon* (1881) 9 R. 535.
[95] p. 235.   [96] *Post* p. 389.
[97] *Per* Lord Herschell at p. 417, and Lord Watson at p. 424, in *Trevor* v. *Whitworth supra*.
[98] *Ante* p. 223.   [99] *Ante* p. 176.
[1] *Robertson* v. *British Linen Co.* (1890) 18 R. 1125 (O.H.); approved *obiter* in *Lloyds Bank Ltd.* v. *Morrison and Son*, 1927, S.C. 571.
[2] *Nelson Mitchell* v. *City of Glasgow Bank* (1879) 6 R. (H.L.) 66, (1878) 6 R. 420.

REDUCTION OF CAPITAL

The share capital of the company must be subscribed in money or money's worth. This capital may be lost or diminished according to the fluctuations of the business, but otherwise it generally cannot be reduced without the sanction of the court. The object of requiring this sanction is threefold—(1) to protect persons dealing with the company, so that the fund available for satisfying their claims shall not be diminished except by ordinary business risks; (2) to ensure that the reduction is equitable as between the various classes of shareholders in the company; (3) to protect the interests of the public.[3]

The Second Draft Directive submitted by the Commission to the Council of the EEC, articles 27–34, would allow reduction of capital without the sanction of the court, and article 16 provides that in the case of serious loss of the subscribed capital, *i.e.* a loss of not more than half the subscribed capital, a meeting of shareholders must be called for the purpose of taking the necessary measures or considering whether the company should be dissolved.

Reduction procedure

Section 66 provides that, subject to confirmation by the court, a limited company with a share capital may, if authorised by its articles, by *special* resolution, reduce its share capital and, if and so far as is necessary, alter its memorandum by reducing the amount of its share capital and of its shares.

"The court," in relation to a company, means the court with jurisdiction to wind up the company: section 455. The courts with jurisdiction to wind up a company are set out in sections 218 and 220 and will be dealt with later.[4] The application for confirmation is by petition: R.S.C., O. 102, r. 5 (England); R.C., 190 (Scotland).[5]

Power to reduce must be given in the articles; power in the memorandum is not effective.[6] The power must be a specific power to reduce.[7]

---

[3] *Per* Lord Watson in *Trevor* v. *Whitworth* (1887) 12 App.Cas. 409, at p. 423, *ante* p. 191; *per* Lord Macnaghten in *British and American Finance Corporation Ltd.* v. *Couper* [1894] A.C. 399 at p. 411.   [4] *Post* p. 539.
[5] In Scotland the petition is presented to the Inner House of the Court of Session and, as a rule, a remit is made by the court to a "reporter" (a man of business, usually a solicitor of standing) who scrutinises the proposed reduction and draws the attention of the court to any doubtful points: *Scottish Stamping etc. Co. Ltd., Petitioners,* 1928 S.C. 484; *J. Hay x Sons Ltd., Petitioners,* 1928 S.C. 662.
[6] *Re Dexine Rubber Co.* [1903] W.N. 82.
[7] *John Avery & Co. Ltd., Petitioners* (1890) 17 R. 1101.

Table A, article 46, provides: "The company may by special resolution reduce its share capital, any capital redemption reserve fund or any share premium account in any manner and with, and subject to, any incident authorised, and consent required, by law."

If the articles do not authorise the reduction of capital, *two* special resolutions—one to alter the articles so as to give authority and the other to effect the reduction—will be necessary, in addition to the consent of the court.[8]

The court cannot condone a reduction which has been carried out without its prior approval.[9]

Stock[10] may be reduced without being first converted into shares.[11] Reserve liability, *i.e.* capital which can only be called up on a winding up of the company, may also be reduced.[12]

Cases of reduction

The power to reduce capital given by section 66 is general, *i.e.* if the proper procedure is adopted a company can reduce its share capital in any case. However, the section specifies three particular cases of reduction—

(1) the extinction or reduction of the liability on shares in respect of capital not paid up;

(2) with or without the extinction or reduction of liability on shares, the cancellation of paid-up share capital which is lost or unrepresented by available assets;

(3) with or without the extinction or reduction of liability on shares, the payment off of any paid-up share capital which is in excess of the wants of the company.

For example, if a company has more than enough capital, it may reduce the nominal amount of shares by repaying paid-up capital, as where fully paid shares of a nominal amount of £5 each are reduced to £2 fully paid shares and £3 is paid back on each share. This would reduce the company's nominal, issued and paid-up capital and, so far as the nominal capital and the nominal amount of the shares are concerned, alter the memorandum. In one case 10 per cent.

---

[8] *Re Patent Invert Sugar Co.* (1885) 31 Ch.D. 166 (C.A.); *Oregon Mortgage Co. Ltd., Petitioners*, 1910 S.C. 964.

[9] *Alexander Henderson Ltd., Petitioners*, 1967 S.L.T. (Notes) 17.

[10] *Ante* p. 230.

[11] *Re House Property and Investment Co.* [1912] W.N. 110; cf. *Doloi Tea Co. Ltd., Petitioners*, 1961 S.L.T. 168.

[12] *Re Midland Rlway. Carriage Co.* (1907) 23 T.L.R. 661.

of the capital was returned on the footing that the amount returned could be called up again.[13]

A return of capital to shareholders may, in some cases, be taxed as a dividend;[14] however it will normally rank as a disposal or part disposal for the purpose of Capital Gains tax, by the shareholder of his shares.

A return of capital may be at a premium.

A reduction of capital involved repaying the capital paid-up on each of the company's preference shares of 10s. each plus a premium of 5s. per share. The court confirmed the reduction: *Re Saltdean Estate Co. Ltd.* [1968] 1 W.L.R. 1844.

A reduction may involve the company paying off part of its share capital not with money but by transferring to the shareholders shares of another company.[15]

Moneys withdrawn from the capital and set free by the reduction can be employed in the purchase of the company's own shares which it is intended to extinguish.[16]

The reduction procedure cannot be used as a device to raise new capital to replace capital which has disappeared, *e.g.* by the conversion of £1 fully paid shares into £1 shares with only 75p paid, thus imposing an additional liability on shareholders.[17]

Clause 8(8) of the Companies Bill 1973 would have prevented a company limited by shares from reducing its share capital when the nominal value of its paid up capital does not exceed a statutory minimum or so as reduce such nominal value below that minimum.

Questions for the court on reduction

Subject to the discretion conferred on the court by section 66 and the statutory provisions for the protection of creditors, *post*, whether there should be a reduction of capital and, if so, how it should be effected, is a domestic question for the prescribed majority of the shareholders to decide.[18] The court should sanction a reduction unless what is proposed to be done is unfair or inequitable in the interests of (1) the creditors, (2) the shareholders and (3) the public

[13] *Scottish Vulcanite Co. Ltd., Petitioners* (1894) 21 R. 752.
[14] *Post* p. 662.
[15] *Westburn Sugar Refineries Ltd., Petitioners,* 1951 S.C. (H.L.) 57; [1951] A.C. 625.
[16] *Per* Lord Macnaghten in *British and American Finance Corporation* v. *Couper* [1894] A.C. 399 at p. 414.
[17] See s. 22, and also *W. Morrison & Co. Ltd., Petitioners* (1892) 19 R. 1049.
[18] *British and American Finance Corpn.* v. *Couper* [1894] A.C. 399. See Lord President Inglis in *Hoggan* v. *Tharsis Sulphur etc. Co. Ltd.* (1882) 9 R. 1191 at p. 1272.

who may have dealings with the company or may invest in its securities.[19] When creditors are not concerned (because the reduction does not involve the diminution of any liability in respect of unpaid capital or the payment to any shareholder of any paid-up capital) the questions to be considered by the court are:

(1) Ought the court to refuse its sanction to the reduction out of regard to the interests of those members of the public who may be induced to take shares in the company?

(2) Is the reduction fair and equitable as between the different classes of shareholders?[20]

In considering what is fair as between different classes of shareholders, the court proceeds upon the basis that a reduction is a sort of anticipation to a limited extent of what would take place in a winding up, *i.e.* the various classes of shareholders have the rights which they would have in a liquidation. Accordingly, if capital is lost, the loss should, prima facie, fall upon all the shareholders equally if their rights in respect of capital are equal. If, therefore, preference shareholders are only preferential as to dividend and not as to capital, a reduction of capital should be borne rateably by the preference and the ordinary shareholders.[21] On the other hand, if on a winding up the preference shareholders are entitled to preference as to capital, the ordinary shares should bear the loss first.[22]

If, under the memorandum and articles, preference shareholders have no priority as to capital and no voting power but are merely entitled to a fixed cumulative preference dividend on the amount paid up on their shares, a rateable reduction on all the shares, preference and ordinary, cancelling lost paid-up capital, though diminishing the preference dividend, is not an alteration of the rights of the preference shareholders so as to require their sanction under an ordinary modification of rights clause: *Re Mackenzie & Co. Ltd.* [1916] 2 Ch. 450.

When capital is being returned as surplus to the company's requirements, it should normally[23] be returned first to the class of shareholders with priority as to capital in a winding up,[24] at any

---

[19] *Westburn Sugar Refineries Ltd., Petitioners*, 1951 S.C. (H.L.) 57; [1951] A.C. 625.

[20] *Poole* v. *National Bank of China Ltd.* [1907] A.C. 229. See Lord Parker of Waddington in *Caldwell & Co. Ltd.* v. *Caldwell*, 1916 S.C. (H.L.) 120 at p. 121.

[21] *Bannatyne* v. *Direct Spanish Telegraph Co.* (1886) 34 Ch.D. 287 (C.A.).

[22] *Re Floating Dock Co. of St. Thomas Ltd.* [1895] 1 Ch. 691.

[23] But not always: see *William Dixon Ltd., Petitioners*, 1948 S.C. 511.

[24] *Wilsons and Clyde Coal Co. Ltd.* v. *Scottish Insurance Corporation Ltd.*, 1949 S.C. (H.L.) 90; 1948 S.C. 360; *Prudential Assurance Co. Ltd.* v. *Chatterley-Whitfield Collieries Ltd.* [1949] A.C. 512.

rate where preference shares are not entitled to participate in surplus assets.[25]

> A coal company with a capital of £400,000, half of which was in ordinary shares and half in 6 per cent. preference shares, had a surplus of capital as a result of nationalisation. A special resolution was passed reducing the capital by paying off the preference shares. By the articles, the preference shareholders in the event of a winding up had a right to priority of repayment of capital *but no further right to participate in the surplus assets. Held*, the reduction should be confirmed as fair and equitable, the preference shareholders having no right to a continuance of their rate of dividend during the life of the company if the company desired and had the means to pay them off. The preference shareholders were being treated in accordance with their rights and it was immaterial that the elimination of their shares extinguished any hopes which they had of obtaining some additional advantage as a result of regulations to be made under the Coal Industry Nationalisation Act 1946, s. 25: *Prudential Assurance Co. Ltd.* v. *Chatterley-Whitfield Collieries Ltd.* [1949] A.C. 512.

> In *Re Fowlers Vacola Mfg. Co. Ltd.* [1966] V.R. 97, it was held that a reduction of capital by return to shareholders is prima facie unfair if it is made otherwise than according to priorities on winding up. Capital was to be reduced by the return of excess capital to the ordinary shareholders. The articles gave the preference shareholders priority in the return of capital in a winding up. In the circumstances, the reduction was not fair and equitable, and the confirmation of the court was refused.

It is not necessary for the company to show by how much its capital is surplus to its requirements. "Public policy" is not a ground for the court's refusing to confirm a reduction which is otherwise unobjectionable, *e.g.* reduction may be confirmed although the motive for it may have been avoidance of the consequences of possible future nationalisation,[19] or minimisation of tax liability.[26]

A modification of rights clause in the articles has no application to a cancellation of shares on a reduction of capital which is in accord with the rights attached to the shares.[27]

If a modification of rights clause in the articles provides that the special rights of the holders of any class of shares can be modified with the sanction of a specified majority of the shareholders of that class, a reduction modifying such rights which is so sanctioned will be approved unless it is unfair or has been sanctioned by the influence of some improper or extraneous consideration.[28] The burden of proving that the reduction is unfair lies on those

[25] Per Lord Greene M.R. in the *Prudential* case, *supra*, in the Court of Appeal [1948] 2 All E.R. 593, at pp. 596, 600.
[26] *David Bell Ltd., Petitioners*, 1954 S.C. 33.
[27] *Re Saltdean Estate Co. Ltd.* [1968] 1 W.L.R. 1844, *ante* p. 237.
[28] *Re Welsbach Incandescent Gas Light Co. Ltd.* [1904] 1 Ch. 87 (C.A.).

who oppose it.[29] (If the proper sanction is not obtained the burden of proving that the reduction is fair lies on those in favour.)[29]

A company had an authorised capital of £95,000,000 divided into £1 ordinary, £1 preference and 10s. deferred shares. It was proposed to reduce the capital to £89,565,859 by cancelling half the amount of each of the 10s. deferred shares and then converting and consolidating each four deferred shares into one £1 ordinary share. The articles required any alteration of the rights of any class of shareholder to be approved by a meeting of the members of that class. Notices were sent out summoning an extraordinary general meeting of the shareholders, a class meeting of the ordinary shareholders and a class meeting of the deferred shareholders, at the same time and place. The resolutions sanctioning the proposed reduction were passed at each of the meetings. At the deferred shareholders' meeting the ordinary shareholders were present but neither spoke nor voted at the meeting and no objection was made to their presence. *Held*, (1) the objection which might have been taken by the deferred shareholders to the presence of the ordinary shareholders at their meeting had been waived, (2) as the reduction was approved by the deferred shareholders at their meeting they could not complain that it was unfair in the absence of proof that their interests were unfairly overridden by persons with other and conflicting interests (such as persons who held both ordinary and deferred shares), (3) on the evidence, the deferred shareholders were not unfairly treated for the benefit of the ordinary shareholders, and therefore (4) the reduction should be confirmed: *Carruth* v. *I.C.I. Ltd.* [1937] A.C. 707.

However, if a reduction of capital involves a variation of class rights, and a modification of rights clause in the articles is not complied with, the court will refuse to confirm the reduction.

A colliery company was nationalised and its assets vested in the National Coal Board. A reduction of capital, by the repayment of part of the capital paid up on preference shares, expressly reserved any rights which the preference shareholders might have as a result of regulations (for the adjustment of rights as between preference and ordinary shareholders) to be made under the Coal Industry Nationalisation Act 1946, s. 25, until the amount of the compensation payable to the company had been determined. When the directors later formed the opinion that such rights had no monetary value the court refused to confirm a later reduction by the repayment of the rest of the capital paid up on the preference shares. The first reduction attached a special right to the preference shares and the sanction of the preference shareholders, necessary under the modification of rights clause in the articles, had not been obtained to the second reduction, which reduction would have had the effect of extinguishing the special right: *Re Old Silkstone Collieries Ltd.* [1954] Ch. 169 (C.A.).[30]

In one case, where there were special circumstances, a reduction involving a variation of class rights was confirmed although no class meeting of the class of shareholders (the preference shareholders) had been held—no one objected, there was no prospect of liquidation (when the preference shareholders had the right to

---

[29] *Re Holders Investment Trust Ltd.* [1971] 1 W.L.R. 583, *ante* p. 225.
[30] See also *Frazer Brothers Ltd., Petitioners*, 1963 S.C. 139, *ante* p. 219.

participate in surplus assets after repayment of capital), and the preference shareholders received more than they would have received by selling.[31]

When one part of a class of equity shareholders is treated differently from another, the usual practice is to proceed by scheme of arrangement under section 206, under which the interests of the minority are better protected.[32]

In England, where reduction is required on the ground that capital has been lost or is not represented by available assets, evidence of the loss or that the available assets do not represent the capital must be given.[33] A reduction may be confirmed where capital has been lost but it is still represented by available assets.

A company had built up a reserve fund. It had incurred a loss arising from the depreciation in the value of its public-houses below the amount stated in the balance sheet, and it proposed to reduce its capital by apportioning the loss between its capital account and the reserve. *Held*, the loss ought to be rateably apportioned between the capital account and the reserve, and the company was not bound to apply the whole of its reserve to wipe out the loss: *Re Hoare & Co. Ltd.* [1904] 2 Ch. 208 (C.A.).

Creditors' right to object to reduction

If a proposed reduction of share capital involves either (1) diminution of liability in respect of unpaid share capital, or (2) payment to any shareholder of any paid-up capital,[34] and (3) in any other case where the court so directs, creditors who, if the company were being wound up, would be able to prove against it, are entitled to object to the reduction. For this purpose the court must settle a list of creditors, with the nature and amount of their claims, and may publish notices fixing a day by which creditors not entered on the list are to claim to be entered. Such of the creditors as do not consent to the reduction must be paid off, or the company must secure payment of their claims by appropriating such amount as the court directs: section 67. In special circumstances the court may

[31] *Re William Jones & Sons Ltd.* [1969] 1 W.L.R. 146.
[32] *Re Robert Stephen Holdings Ltd.* [1968] 1 W.L.R. 522.
[33] *Per* Lord Parker of Waddington in *Caldwell & Co. Ltd.* v. *Caldwell*, 1916 S.C. (H.L.) 120 at p. 121. Scottish courts dispense with such evidence where there is no reason to suspect the *bona fides* of the parties: *Caldwell's* case.
[34] Replacement of preference shares with loan stock, which has recently become a common practice for the purposes of reducing liability to corporation tax, counts as such payment, although the loan stock does not fall to be repaid by the company until a future date: *Lawrie & Symington Ltd., Petitioners*, 1969 S.L.T. 221.

dispense with these requirements: section 67 (3). The court might dispense with the requirements where the company has sufficient cash, trustee securities and good sundry debtors[35] to more than cover any capital to be returned to shareholders and the company's debts, or if the discharge of the debts is guaranteed to the court's satisfaction, or if a simultaneous increase in capital results in the paid-up capital being the same as it was before the reduction.[36]

Before dispensing with a list of creditors under section 67 (3) the court must be satisfied that no creditor who might be entitled to object to the reduction would be prejudiced by it.

A company had sufficient cash resources to cover paid-up capital being paid to preference shareholders and its liabilities but not rents prospectively payable in respect of long leases during the residues of the terms or ten years, whichever was less, and so a direction extending to the lessors could not be given under section 67 (3): *Re Lucania Temperance Billiard Halls (London) Ltd.* [1966] Ch. 98.[37]

In cases not within (1) and (2) above, the creditors have, prima facie, no right to object to the proposed reduction of capital, because no asset out of which their claims could be satisfied is being given up or returned to the shareholders.

A company had a paid-up share capital of £1,000,000, and had also issued £1,000,000 debentures secured by a trust deed constituting a floating charge. In 1904 losses to the extent of £800,000 were incurred and no dividends had since been paid, any profits being applied in reduction of the deficiency. By 1917 the deficiency had been reduced to £640,000, and the company proposed to reduce its capital to £360,000 by writing off the lost capital. The latest balance sheet showed assets worth £1,500,000. The debenture holders objected. *Held*, as the reduction involved no diminution of unpaid capital or repayment to shareholders of paid-up capital, creditors were not entitled to object unless a strong case was made out, and the debenture holders had not made out any such case: *Re Meux's Brewery Co. Ltd.* [1919] 1 Ch. 28.

The object of reducing capital, where capital has been lost or is not represented by available assets, is to enable the accounts to present a realistic picture of the company's financial position, which may permit the company to pay dividends. To safeguard the creditors in the case of an application by a company to write off capital not lost or unrepresented by available assets, thereby setting free capital which might be distributed among the shareholders, the court is empowered by section 67 to give effect to a creditor's objection "in any other case."

[35] *Anderson, Brown & Co. Ltd., Petitioners,* 1965 S.C. 81.
[36] *New Duff House Sanitarium, Petitioners,* 1931 S.L.T. 337 (O.H.).
[37] *Cf. Palace Billiard Rooms Ltd.* v. *City etc. Trust Corpn.,* 1912 S.C. 5.

Order for reduction. Minute of reduction

Confirmation by the court must precede the actual reduction of capital.[38]

On making an order confirming the reduction, the court may direct:

(1) For special reasons, that the company add the words "and reduced" to its name for a specified time.

(2) That the reasons for reduction and the causes leading to the reduction be published, with a view to giving proper information to the public (s. 68).

These powers are rarely used today and the Jenkins Report recommended their repeal.[39] Clause 10 of the Companies Bill 1973 would have given effect to the recommendation.

Section 69 provides that the order for reduction must be produced to the Registrar, and a copy of the order and a minute approved by the court showing the amount of the share capital, the number of shares into which it is divided, the amount of each share and the amount, if any, deemed to be paid up on each share, must be registered with him. The Registrar then grants a certificate of registration, which is conclusive evidence of the reduction and that all the requirements of the Act with respect to reduction have been complied with—even if it is afterwards discovered that the special resolution for reduction was not properly passed,[40] or that there was no power in the articles to reduce capital.[41] The reduction takes effect as from the date of registration. By section 143,[42] a copy of the special resolution must be forwarded to the Registrar within 15 days.

Reduction without the consent of the court

There is a number of cases in which, despite section 66, capital can be reduced without the consent of the court. Two such cases are:

(1) Where, under power in the articles, shares are forfeited by the company for non-payment of a call or an instalment[43]—and

---

[38] *Alexander Henderson Ltd., Petitioners,* 1967 S.L.T. (Notes) 17.
[39] Paras 159, 187.
[40] *Ladies' Dress Association* v. *Pulbrook* [1900] 2 Q.B. 376 (C.A.).
[41] *Re Walker and Smith Ltd.* [1903] W.N. 82.
[42] *Post* p. 308.   [43] *Post* p. 277.

in this rare case, as was stated earlier,[44] the forfeited shares may be re-issued, in which event there is no permanent reduction.

(2) Where, under power in the articles, shares are surrendered to the company to avoid a forfeiture—in this rare case, too, the shares may be re-issued.[45]

There are, however, cases in which at first sight there appears to be a reduction without consent but there is no reduction for the purposes of the Act, *e.g.*—

(1) where redeemable preference shares are redeemed under section 58[46]—there is no real reduction, whether the shares are redeemed out of profits (because of the provisions with regard to the capital redemption reserve fund) or out of the proceeds of a fresh issue of shares (because the fresh capital will replace the redeemed capital);

(2) where unissued shares are cancelled under section 61[47]—there is no real reduction because the issued capital is not reduced.

An example of an improper reduction of capital is the New Zealand case of *Jenkins* v. *Harbour View Courts Ltd.*[48] where the articles provided that each A class share should confer on the holder a right to occupy a flat in a block owned by the company on the terms of a lease in the schedule. The aggregate annual rentals were not to exceed the sum necessary to provide for rates, insurance and other outgoings as well as management and maintenance of the block. The plaintiff took 3,580 ordinary shares of £1 each and one A class share for which he paid £3,580. Since substantially the block was to be made the subject of leases for 99 years to shareholders for no rent in the form of landlord's reward to the company, this was held to be just as much an illegal return of capital to shareholders as if, from a fund of money, a substantial part was distributed among them. It made no difference that the plaintiff by a different transaction might for the same expenditure have purchased a valid lease of her flat if the agreement between the company and the shareholder had been for the "purchase" and allotment of one share followed by a purchase for £3,580 of the lease.[49]

As to the liability of the officers responsible and of the shareholders concerned in the event of an illegal reduction of capital, see what is said later[50] as to the effect of paying dividends out of capital.

---

[44] p. 234.
[45] *Post* p. 281.
[46] *Ante* p. 222.
[47] *Ante* p. 232.
[48] [1966] N.Z.L.R. 1 (C.A.).
[49] Another example of improper reduction is the Australian case of *Australasian Oil Exploration Ltd.* v. *Lachberg* (1958) 101 C.L.R. 119, which is dealt with in the First Australian Supplement to Charlesworth & Cain, p. 233.
[50] p. 475.

Chapter 12

SHARES

A SHARE has been defined as "the interest of a shareholder in the company measured by a sum of money, for the purpose of liability in the first place, and of interest in the second, but also consisting of a series of mutual covenants entered into by all the shareholders *inter se* in accordance with [the Companies Act 1948, s. 20[1]]. The contract contained in the articles of association is one of the original incidents of the share."[2] The share is measured by a sum of money, namely, the nominal amount of the share, and also by the rights and obligations belonging to it as defined by the Companies Acts and by the memorandum and articles of the company.

Each share in a company must be distinguished by its appropriate number, provided that it need not have a number if all the issued shares, or all the issued shares of a particular class, are fully paid up and rank *pari passu* for all purposes: section 74. Numbers are often dispensed with today under the proviso to section 74.

A share certificate, which specifies the shares held by the member and which is prima facie evidence of his title to the shares (s. 81), is usually issued to a shareholder.

Shares in a company are personal[3] estate, transferable in the manner provided by the articles of the company: section 73.

A shareholder may borrow money on the security of his shares, *i.e.*, in England, he may give the lender a mortgage over the shares to secure the payment of interest and repayment of the principal sum.

SHARE CERTIFICATE

Every company must complete the share certificates and have them ready for delivery within two months[4] after the allotment of any of

---

[1] *Ante* p. 106.
[2] *Per* Farwell J. in *Borland's Trustee* v. *Steel Bros. & Co. Ltd.* [1901] 1 Ch. 279 at p. 288.
[3] The Scottish equivalent of "personal" is "moveable": s. 455.
[4] Fourteen days if the shares are quoted on a stock exchange: Rules of The Stock Exchange, App. 34, Sched. VIII.

its shares or after the date on which a transfer of its shares is lodged for registration, unless the conditions of issue otherwise provide, under a penalty of a default fine of £5 a day: sections 80, 440. The form of the certificate is governed by the articles. Table A, article 8, gives the right to a certificate without payment and provides that it shall be under the seal of the company, and shall specify the shares to which it relates and the amount paid up thereon. If a quotation on the Stock Exchange is desired, the certificate must also have a footnote to the effect that no transfer will be registered without production of the share certificate and, in the case of preference shares, must state the conditions conferred thereon as to capital and dividends.[5]

The certificate is a formal statement by the company under its common seal that the person named therein is the holder of the number of shares in the company specified in the certificate. It is prima facie evidence of the title of that person to the shares: section 81.[6] It is not a document of title (as the register of members is).[7] The object of the certificate is to facilitate dealings with the shares, whether by way of sale or security, and so make them more valuable to their owner. On the other hand, a share certificate is not a negotiable instrument, so that its accidental loss or destruction is not a matter of great moment. The articles usually make provision for the granting of a new certificate in such a case.

Table A, article 9, provides: "If a share certificate be defaced, lost or destroyed, it may be renewed on payment of a fee of 12½p or such less sum and on such terms (if any) as to evidence and indemnity and the payment of out-of-pocket expenses of the company of investigating evidence as the directors think fit."

In England a share certificate is not a deed for the purposes of the Law of Property Act 1925, section 74,[8] *post.*[9]

---

[5] Rules of The Stock Exchange, App. 34, Sched. IV. See *Rainford* v. *James Keith & Blackman Co. Ltd., post* p. 268.
[6] See, *e.g., Woodhouse & Rawson Ltd.* v. *Hosack* (1894) 2 S.L.T. 279 (O.H.).
[7] *Ante* p. 198.
[8] *Per* Clauson J. in *South London Greyhound Racecourses Ltd.* v. *Wake* [1931] 1 Ch. 496 at p. 503.
[9] p. 410.

Estoppel[10] as to statements in a certificate

The issue of a share certificate may give rise to an estoppel against the company. The company cannot deny the truth of the certificate as against a person who has relied on the certificate and in consequence has changed his position.

T., the registered holder of shares, left the share certificate with her broker. T.'s signature was forged to a transfer in favour of S., T. did not reply to notice of the transfer sent to him by the company and a new certificate in the name of S. was issued by the company. A. bought from S. and paid for the shares on delivery of the share certificate and a new share certificate was issued to A. The fraud was subsequently discovered and T.'s name was restored to the register. *Held*, the company was liable to indemnify A. The giving of the certificate to S. amounted to a statement by the company, intended to be acted upon by purchasers of shares in the market, that S. was entitled to the shares, and A. having acted on the statement, the company was estopped from denying it. A. was entitled to recover from the company as damages the value of the shares at the time when the company first refused to recognise him as a shareholder, with interest: *Re Bahia and San Francisco Rlwy. Co.* (1868) L.R. 3 Q.B. 584.

There is no estoppel in favour of a person, such as S. in the above case, who procures the granting of a certificate on a forged transfer[11] or forged power of attorney,[12] even if he has acted in good faith.

The company may be estopped from denying the title to shares of the person to whom it has issued a share certificate.[13]

D. bought 30 shares through a broker, L., who was also secretary of the company, and paid L. She received and returned to L. a transfer of shares executed to L.'s direction by his clerk, P., who was never a man of substance and who did not hold any shares. The transfer, which did not specify the numbers of the shares, was put before the board by L. and passed without production of P.'s certificate being required, and a new certificate prepared by L. was issued to the effect that D. held 30 shares, numbers 115–144 inclusive. The chairman, who did not sign the certificate, did not notice that the shares were part of his holding (numbers 1–333). The board properly relied on the secretary to check transfers and certificates with the register. Two years later the board notified D. that P.'s transfer was invalid and declined to recognise her as a shareholder. L. was bankrupt by then and the company could not prove that he could not have reimbursed D. if, when the certificate was issued, the company had refused to issue it. *Held*, D. was entitled to damages: *Dixon* v. *Kennaway & Co.* [1900] 1 Ch. 833.

The company may be estopped from denying the amount stated to be paid up on shares.

[10] Personal bar is the Scottish equivalent of "estoppel." See per Lord Kyllachy (Ordinary) in *Clavering, Son & Co.* v. *Goodwins, Jardine & Co. Ltd.* (1891) 18 R. 652 at p. 657.
[11] *Sheffield Corporation* v. *Barclay* [1905] A.C. 392, *post*, p. 265.
[12] *Starkey* v. *Bank of England* [1903] A.C. 114.
[13] *Balkis Consolidated Co. Ltd.* v. *Tomkinson* [1893] A.C. 396.

B. lent money to a company on the security of fully paid shares in the company and was handed by the company share certificates for 10,000 shares of £1 each which the certificates stated to be fully paid up. No money had been paid on the shares, which had been issued direct by the company to B., but B. did not know this. On the company's going into liquidation, B. was placed on the list of contributories in respect of these shares. *Held*, the company was estopped by the certificate from denying that the shares were fully paid up and B. was entitled to have his name removed from the list of contributories: *Bloomenthal* v. *Ford* [1897] A.C. 156.[14]

The company may be made liable in damages to the person who has relied on the statement in the share certificate.[15]

If B., in the last case, had known that the shares were not fully paid up, there would have been no estoppel—there is no estoppel in favour of a person who knows the untruth of statements in a share certificate.[16] An original allottee, therefore, will seldom be in a position to benefit from the principle.

The company is not estopped where[13] a certificate is a forgery.

R. lent money to the secretary of a company for his own purposes on the security of a share certificate issued to R. by the secretary and certifying that R. was registered as transferee of the shares. The secretary issued the share certificate without authority, affixed the common seal and forged the signatures of two directors, so that the certificate apparently complied with the articles. R. sued the company for damages for refusal to register him. *Held*, in the absence of evidence that the company had held out the secretary as having authority to do more than the mere ministerial act of delivering share certificates, when duly made, to those entitled to them, the company was not estopped from disputing the claim or responsible for the secretary's act: *Ruben* v. *Great Fingall Consolidated* [1906] A.C. 439.

TRANSFER OF SHARES

There is a distinction between a transfer of shares and a transmission of shares. A transfer is by the act of the member, while a transmission occurs by operation of law on the death or the bankruptcy of a member.[17]

---

[14] *Cf. Waterhouse* v. *Jamieson* (1870) 8 M. (H.L.) 88, in which it was held that statements in the memorandum and articles, which also appeared in share certificates, as to the amount paid up on shares could not be contradicted by the liquidator.

[15] *Clavering, Son & Co.* v. *Goodwins, Jardine & Co. Ltd.* (1891) 18 R. 652.

[16] See *Crickmer's Case* (1875) L.R. 10. Ch.App. 614. In England, if the shares had been transferred to a purchaser without notice that they were not fully paid up he could give a good title to a purchaser from him with or without notice: *Barrow's Case* (1880) 14 Ch.D. 432 (C.A.).

[17] *Post* p. 265.

Restrictions on transfer

Every shareholder has a right to transfer his shares to whom he likes, unless the articles provide to the contrary.[18]

By the Companies Acts "it is provided that the shares in a company under these Acts shall be capable of being transferred in manner provided by the regulations of the company. The regulations of the company may impose fetters upon the right of transfer. In the absence of restrictions in the articles the shareholder has by virtue of the statute the right to transfer his shares without the consent of anybody to any transferee, even though he be a man of straw, provided it is a bona-fide transaction in the sense that it is an out-and-out disposal of the property without retaining any interest in the shares—that the transferor bona fide divests himself of all benefit. . . . In the absence of restrictions it is competent to a transferor, notwithstanding that the company is *in extremis*, to compel registration of a transfer to a transferee notwithstanding that the latter is a person not competent to meet the unpaid liability upon the shares. Even if the transfer be executed for the express purpose of relieving the transferor from liability, the directors cannot upon that ground refuse to register it unless there is in the articles some provision so enabling them": *per* Buckley L.J. in *Lindlar's Case* [1910] 1 Ch. 312 (C.A.) at p. 316.[19]

However, a transfer of shares to a person resident outside the Scheduled Territories, as defined by the Exchange Control Act 1947, is forbidden without the consent of the Treasury,[20] and the directors must decline to register a transfer which is not properly stamped.[21]

An article providing that on the bankruptcy of a member he shall sell his shares to particular persons at a particular price, which is fixed for all persons alike and is not shown to be an unfair price, is valid.[22] So, too, is an article providing that on the death of a member his shares must be offered to "the other members" at par, even though there is only one surviving member.[23]

Table A, article 24, provides: "The directors may decline to register the transfer of a share (not being a fully paid share) to a person of whom they shall not approve, and they may also decline to register the transfer of a share on which the company has a lien."

[18] *Weston's Case* (1868) L.R. 4 Ch.App. 20. It is otherwise, *e.g.*, where the company is being wound up and a transfer is prevented by s. 227, *post* p. 557.
[19] For Scottish authority to the same effect, see, *e.g.*, *per* Lord Kincairney (Ordinary) in *Stewart* v. *James Keiller & Sons Ltd.* (1902) 4 F. 657 at p. 667.
[20] Exchange Control Act 1947, Pt. III, *ante* p. 168.
[21] *Maynard* v. *Consolidated Kent Collieries Corpn.* [1903] 2 K.B. 121; Stamp Act, 1891, s. 17.
[22] *Borland's Trustee* v. *Steel Bros. & Co. Ltd.* [1901] 1 Ch. 279.
[23] *Jarvis Motors (Harrow) Ltd.* v. *Carabott* [1964] 1 W.L.R. 1101, where one of the two members of a company, who each held half of the shares, died, and the executors of the deceased had to offer his shares at par to the surviving member.

In the case of a private company, the articles must restrict the right to transfer its shares: section 28.[24] In the case of a public company, shares must normally be free from restrictions on the right of transfer if a stock exchange quotation is to be obtained.[25]

Any restrictions on the transfer of shares are a derogation from the common law right of free transfer. Any rights conferred by the articles will not be extended to situations not covered by them;[26] the procedure laid down in the articles for the exercise of the rights must be strictly followed;[27] and if the rights are not actively exercised the right of free transfer will revive.[28]

Pre-emption clauses

The articles of a private company usually contain a pre-emption clause, *e.g.* to the effect that no shares shall be transferred to any person not a member of the company so long as a member can be found to purchase them at a fair price to be determined in accordance with the articles.[29] Such a pre-emption clause does not entitle the company to refuse to register a transfer of shares from one member to another member of the company.[30] Where the value of shares for the purpose of such a clause falls to be fixed by the directors, the court will not review the directors' valuation provided that they have acted fairly and honestly.[31]

Sometimes the articles provide that a member desiring to sell any of his shares must inform the directors of the number of shares, the price and the name of the proposed transferee, and the directors must first offer the shares at that price to the other shareholders. In such a case, any member to whom the shares are offered cannot buy part only of the shares, and if none of the members is willing to buy all the shares the proposed transfer can be carried out.[32]

A member whose shares have been offered to other members

---

[24] *Ante* p. 49. The necessary restriction on the transfer of shares in a private company is one reason why such shares are not dealt in on stock exchanges.

[25] Rules of The Stock Exchange, App. 34, Sched. VII. The main advantage of a stock exchange quotation is that it makes the securities more marketable.

[26] *Furness & Co.* v. *Liquidators of "Cynthiana" Steamship Co. Ltd.* (1893) 21 R. 239.

[27] *Neilson* v. *Ayr Race Meetings Syndicate Ltd.*, 1918 1 S.L.T. 63 (O.H.).

[28] *Shepherd's Trustees* v. *Shepherd*, 1950 S.C. (H.L.) 60 (application for registration granted, the two directors having failed to agree to refuse registration).

[29] *Post* p. 467.

[30] *Delavenne* v. *Broadhurst* [1931] 1 Ch. 234.

[31] *Stewart* v. *James Keiller & Sons Ltd.* (1902) 4 F. 657.

[32] *The Ocean Coal Co. Ltd.* v. *The Powell Duffryn Steam Coal Co. Ltd.* [1932] 1 Ch. 654.

under a pre-emption clause has been held entitled to withdraw his offer at any time before its acceptance.[33]

> Articles provided that no transfer of shares should take place so long as any other shareholder was willing to purchase at a price to be ascertained by agreement between the intending transferor and the directors, or, failing agreement, at a price to be fixed by the auditors, and that any shareholder who was "desirous of transferring" his shares should inform the secretary of the number of shares which he desired to transfer. *Held*, shareholders who, on a take-over bid, accepted an outside offer to buy their shares, received the price, gave the purchaser general proxies, and agreed to execute transfers and deliver up the share certificates when called upon to do so, were "desirous of transferring" their shares and had to comply with the pre-emption clause, unless they gave notice that they had changed their minds before the other shareholders exercised their pre-emption rights: *Lyle & Scott Ltd.* v. *Scott's Trustees*, 1959 S.C. (H.L.) 64; [1959] A.C. 763.

If the provision in the articles relating to the offer of the shares to the existing shareholders before a transfer is made is disregarded, the transferee will not be entitled to be entered on the register. In England the same is true in the case of a sale, in disregard of the articles, by a mortgagee under his power of sale.[34] However, a transfer by a shareholder, in breach of the pre-emptive rights given by the articles, to a person who has paid for the shares operates as a transfer of the *beneficial interest* in the shares, so that the transferee takes priority over a judgment creditor who subsequently obtains a charging order[35] on the shares.[36]

Articles may provide that the other members are bound to buy the shares of a member who wishes to transfer them.[37]

Note what is said later as to the duty of care owed by an auditor who values shares in the knowledge that his valuation will determine the price to be paid under a contract.[38]

Directors' power to refuse transfers

In addition to containing a pre-emption clause, the articles of a private company usually contain an article like Table A, Part II,

---

[33] *J. M. Smith Ltd.* v. *Colquhoun's Trustee* (1901) 3 F. 981.
[34] *Hunter* v. *Hunter* [1936] A.C. 222.　　[35] *Post* p. 268.
[36] *Hawks* v. *McArthur* [1951] 1 All E.R. 22.
　　Similarly, in Scotland, in a competition between a transferee and an arrester, the arrester was held not to be entitled to found on an alleged failure on the part of the company to observe the proper procedure relating to pre-emption and registration of transfers, with the result that the court declared that the shares had vested in the transferee: *National Bank of Scotland Glasgow Nominees Ltd.* v. *Adamson*, 1932 S.L.T. 492 (O.H.).
[37] *Rayfield* v. *Hands* [1960] Ch. 1, *ante* p. 108.
[38] *Arenson* v. *Casson Beckman Rutley & Co.* [1975] 3 W.L.R. 815, (H.L.), *post* p. 467.

article 3, providing that the directors may, in their absolute discretion and without assigning any reason therefor, refuse to register any transfer of any share. In such a case, if the directors refuse to register a transfer the court will not interfere unless it can be shown that the directors are exercising their discretion improperly.[39]

When directors have power to decline to register a transfer, whether their power is absolute or limited to certain specified grounds, they need not disclose their reasons for refusing registration and if, having considered the questions, they refuse registration without giving any reasons, their refusal cannot be questioned unless there is evidence (which will be hard to come by) that they have not acted in good faith.[40]

The directors' discretionary power is a fiduciary power and must be exercised in good faith, *i.e.* legitimately for the purpose for which it is conferred. In exercising it the directors must act in good faith in the interest of the company and with due regard to the shareholder's right to transfer his shares, and they must fairly consider the question at a board meeting.[41]

Articles gave the directors "an absolute and uncontrolled discretion" to refuse to register any transfer of shares. The two directors each held 4,001 of the 8,002 ordinary shares. F. died and his son, as his executor, applied for the shares to be registered in his name. S. refused, but offered to register 2,001 shares if 2,000 were sold to him at a fixed price. F.'s son applied for rectification of the register but failed. There was nothing to show that the director's power was not exercised in the company's interest: *Re Smith and Fawcett Ltd.* [1942] Ch. 304 (C.A.).

There is a presumption that the directors have acted *in bona fide* and reasonably.[42]

If the articles empower the directors to decline to register transfers on certain grounds, *e.g.* on the ground that the transferor is indebted to the company, or that the transferee is a person of whom they do not approve, they can be interrogated as to the ground on which they have refused registration, although not as to the reasons for their refusal, unless the articles provide that they shall not be

---

[39] See *Stewart* v. *James Keiller & Sons Ltd.* (1902) 4 F. 657.
[40] *Re Coalport China Co.* [1895] 2 Ch. 404; *Kennedy* v. *North British Wireless Schools Ltd.*, 1916 1 S.L.T. 407; 1915 1 S.L.T. 196 (O.H.).
[41] *Per* Chitty J. in *Re Bell Bros. Ltd.* (1891) 65 L.T. 245 at p. 245; and see *per* Lord Trayner in *Stewart* v. *James Keiller & Sons Ltd.* (1902) 4 F. 657 at p. 678.
[42] *Per* Lord Anderson (Ordinary) in *Kennedy* v. *North British Wireless Schools Ltd.*, 1916 1 S.L.T. 407; 1915 1 S.L.T. 196 (O.H.) at p. 198.

bound to specify the grounds for their refusal, in which case they cannot be interrogated at all.[43]

If the directors give reasons for their refusal, the court can decide whether they are sufficient to justify the refusal.

The articles empowered the directors to refuse to register a transfer if "in their opinion it is contrary to the interests of the company that the proposed transferee should be a member thereof." The directors declined to register transfers of single shares, stating that it was contrary to the interests of the company that shares should be transferred singly or in small amounts to outside persons with no interest in, or knowledge of, shipping. *Held*, this was a bad reason for refusing—refusal should have been on grounds personal to the transferee—and the transfers were directed to be registered: *Re Bede S.S. Co. Ltd.* [1917] 1 Ch. 123 (C.A.).

"A formal active exercise of the right of refusal to register is required before the company is authorised to refuse to register" shares in the names of the transferees. Where directors are equally divided and so come to no decision to decline to register, the transfer must be registered.[44]

Where the articles provided that no share should be transferred to a person not already a member of the company without the consent of the directors and, to prevent a particular transfer from being registered, a director purposely abstained from attending board meetings so that a quorum could not be obtained, it was held that the transferee was entitled to an order directing the company to register the transfer.[45]

In one case the board lost their right to veto a transfer because they were guilty of an unreasonable delay of four months in deciding whether or not to exercise the veto—the period of two months specified in section 78 for giving a transferee notice of the company's refusal to register a transfer is the outside limit after which there is unnecessary delay, unless in an exceptional case it is impossible to constitute a board.[46]

In a rare case, the remedy of the transferee, or of the transferor, on a refusal to register a transfer is to apply to the court to rectify the register of members by substituting his name for that of the transferor under section 116. Unnecessary delay in registering a

---

[43] *Berry and Stewart* v. *Tottenham Hotspur Football Co. Ltd.* [1935] Ch. 718.
[44] *Shepherd's Trustees* v. *Shepherd*, 1950 S.C.(H.L.) 60, *per* Lord Porter at p. 66; *Re Hackney Pavilion Ltd.* [1924] 1 Ch. 276.
[45] *Re Copal Varnish Co. Ltd.* [1917] 2 Ch. 349.
[46] *Re Swaledale Cleaners Ltd.* [1968] 1 W.L.R. 1710 (C.A.).

transfer does not in itself constitute a ground for rectification, and a transferor applying for rectification must be able to show that he has been prejudiced by the delay.[47] A winding-up petition is not the proper remedy for the transferor where registration of a transfer is refused.[48]

The former Conservative Government White Paper[49] proposed to accept the recommendations of the Jenkins Committee[50] that persons such as legal personal representatives or trustees in bankruptcy, to whom shares are transmitted by process of law[51] but who are refused registration by the directors, should have a right to present a petition or seek an injunction under section 210[52] and, unless a prompt explanation is provided as to why they should not be registered, to registration subject to the priority of pre-emptive rights, and the Government proposed to extend such recommendations to cover persons to whom shares are transferred as well as those to whom they are transmitted. Further, the directors should be required, if they refuse to register, to serve upon the applicant within 28 days a written statement setting out the reasons why it is not in the interests of the company that the applicant should be entered upon the register. In default of such service, the directors should be required to register the shares in the applicant's name. If he considers those reasons open to challenge, it will be open to him to apply to the court for rectification of the register under section 116.

The Companies Bill 1973 would have given effect to those proposals. Clause 20(2) provided that where an application is made to a company for a person to be registered as a member in respect of shares which have been transferred or transmitted to him by act of parties or operation of law, the company shall not refuse registration by virtue of any discretion conferred by the articles unless it has served on the applicant, within the period of 28 days beginning with the day on which the application was made, a notice in writing stating the facts which are considered to justify refusal.

Form of transfer

Section 75, which was passed to make sure that there is an instrument which can be stamped with stamp duty, provides that it is unlawful for a company to register a transfer of shares unless a "proper instrument of transfer" has been delivered to the company. Consequently it is illegal to have an article that upon the death of a shareholder his shares shall be deemed to have passed to his widow, without any transfer.[53]

The form of the transfer may be that prescribed by the articles,

---

[47] *Property Investment Co. of Scotland Ltd.* v. *Duncan* (1897) 14 R. 299.
[48] *Charles Forte Investments Ltd.* v. *Amanda* [1964] Ch. 240 (C.A.).
[49] (1973) Cmnd. 5391, paras 38, 39.
[50] (1962) Cmnd. 1749, para. 212.
[51] *Post* p. 265.
[52] *Post* p. 389.
[53] *Re Greene* [1949] Ch. 333.

but a "proper instrument" for the purposes of section 75 does not necessarily mean an instrument complying with the formalities prescribed by the articles—it means an instrument such as will attract stamp duty.[54] The articles may require transfers to be made in writing under seal.

Table A in the Companies Act 1948, as amended by the 1967 Act, contains the following provisions:

Article 22.—"The instrument of transfer of any share shall be executed by or on behalf of the transferor and transferee, and the transferor shall be deemed to remain a holder of the share until the name of the transferee is entered in the register of members in respect thereof."

Article 23.—"Subject to such of the restrictions of these regulations as may be applicable, any member may transfer all or any of his shares by instrument in writing in any usual or common form or any other form which the directors may approve."

Formerly, the common form of transfer of shares had to be executed by the transferee as well as by the transferor and had to be attested.

Now, in the case of a company limited by shares, if shares are fully paid they may be transferred by a simplified form of transfer, namely a stock transfer under hand in the form set out in Schedule 1 to the Stock Transfer Act 1963.[55] Such a transfer need be executed only by the transferor and need not be attested: 1963 Act, section 1.

The 1963 Act applies to, *inter alia*, fully paid up registered securities issued by a company limited by shares, or by a statutory company or a chartered company (but not by a building society or an industrial and provident society), or, subject to exceptions, by the Government or by a local authority, or which are units of a unit trust scheme: section 1. The expression "registered securities" means transferable securities the holders of which are entered in a register, and "securities" includes shares, stock, debentures, debenture stock, loan stock, bonds and units of a unit trust scheme: section 4.

Where a stock transfer has been executed for the purpose of a stock exchange transaction, particulars of the consideration and of the transferee may be either inserted in such transfer or, where there are several transferees, supplied by brokers' transfers, *i.e.*

---

[54] *Re Paradise Motor Co. Ltd.* [1968] 1 W.L.R. 1125 (C.A.).
[55] As amended by the Stock Transfer (Amendment of Forms) Order 1974 (S.I. No. 1214).

separate instruments in the form set out in Schedule 2 to the 1963 Act, identifying the stock transfer and specifying the securities to which each relates. The transferor need not sign a brokers' transfer: section 1.

STOCK TRANSFER FORM		Certificate lodged with the Registrar
Consideration Money £.............		(For completion by the Registrar/Stock Exchange)
Name of Undertaking.		
Description of security.		
Number or amount of Shares, Stock or other security and, in figures column only, number and denomination of units, if any.	Words	Figures
		(units of)
Name(s) of registered holder(s) should be given in full: the address should be given where there is only one holder.	in the name(s) of	
If the transfer is not made by the registered holder(s) insert also the name(s) and capacity (e.g., Executor(s)), of the person(s) making the transfer.		
Delete words in italics except for stock exchange transactions. Bodies corporate should execute under their common seal.	I/We hereby transfer the above security out of the name(s) aforesaid to the person(s) named below *or to the several persons named in Parts 2 of Brokers Transfer Forms relating to the above security:*	Stamp of Selling Broker(s), or, for transactions which are not stock exchange transactions, of Agent(s), if any, acting for the Transferor(s).
Signature(s) of transferor(s) 1................................ 2................................	3................................ 4................................	Date...............
Full name(s), full postal address(es) (including County or, if applicable, Postal District number) of the person(s) to whom the security is transferred. Please state title, if any, or whether Mr., Mrs. or Miss, Please complete in typewriting or in Block Capitals.		

I/We request that such entries be made in the register as are necessary to give effect to this transfer.

Stamp of Buying Broker(s) (if any)	Stamp or name and address of person lodging this form (if other than the Buying Broker(s))

(Endorsement for use only in stock exchange transactions)
The security represented by the transfer overleaf has been sold as follows:—

.... Shares/Stock	.... Shares/Stock
.... Shares/Stock	.... Shares/Stock
.... Shares/Stock	.... Shares/Stock
.... Shares/Stock	.... Shares/Stock
.... Shares/Stock	.... Shares/Stock
.... Shares/Stock	.... Shares/Stock
.... Shares/Stock	.... Shares/Stock

Balance (if any) due to Selling Broker(s)   ....

Amount of Certificate(s)

Brokers Transfer Forms for above amounts certified

Stamp of certifying Stock Exchange   Stamp of Selling Broker(s)

The only stock exchange now recognised for the purposes of the 1963 Act is The Stock Exchange.[56]

Procedure on transfer

If a shareholder has sold all his shares comprised in one share certificate[57] to one person,[58] the transfer is effected as follows:

(1) The transferor sends the transferee a "proper instrument of transfer" required by section 75 and complying with the articles or the Stock Transfer Act 1963, *ante*, and executed by the transferor, together with the share certificate relating to the shares comprised in the transfer.

(2) The transferee then executes the transfer if it is in accordance with the articles, stamps it and forwards it, with the share certificate and the registration fee, to the company for registration.

(3) Within two months[59] after the transfer is lodged the com-

---

[56] 1963 Act, s. 4; Stock Transfer (Recognised Stock Exchanges) Order 1973 (S.I. No. 536).

[57] As to shares comprised in a share warrant, see *post* p. 281.

[58] As to the procedure when, *e.g.*, part only of the holding is being sold, see Certification of Transfers, *post*.

[59] Fourteen days if the shares are quoted on a stock exchange: Rules of The Stock Exchange, App. 34, Sched. VIII, Pt. A.

pany must either issue a new share certificate to the transferee or, where the directors are exercising a power to refuse
registration, send *him* notice of its refusal to register the
transfer: sections 80, 78.

The Jenkins Report[60] recommended that the period be five
weeks and that notice of a refusal be given to the transferor too.
Clause 20(1) of the Companies Bill 1973 would have given effect to
these recommendations and, indeed, would have shortened the period
to 28 days.

The penalty for non-compliance is a default fine of £5 a day on
the company and every officer who knowingly authorises or permits
the default: sections 78, 80, 440.

Table A contains the following provisions as to transfers of
shares:

Article 25.—"The directors may also decline to recognise any
instrument of transfer unless:—

(a) a fee of $12\frac{1}{2}$p or such lesser sum as the directors may from
    time to time require is paid to the company in respect
    thereof;[61]
(b) the instrument of transfer is accompanied by the certificate
    of the shares to which it relates, and such other evidence
    as the directors may reasonably require to show the right
    of the transferor to make the transfer; and
(c) the instrument of transfer is in respect of only one class of
    share."

Article 27.—"The registration of transfers may be suspended at
such times and for such periods as the directors may from time to
time determine, provided always that such registration shall not be
suspended for more than thirty days in any year."

Directors must not register a transfer unless it is correctly
stamped.[62] If the consideration expressed is substantially below
the value of the shares, they should make inquiry as to the true
consideration; even if the stamp duty is in accordance with the
consideration expressed on the transfer, they are entitled to make

---

[60] Para. 483.
[61] No fee is payable for registration of transfers if the shares are quoted on a stock
exchange: Rules of The Stock Exchange, App. 34, Sched. VIII, Pt. A.
[62] Stamp Act 1891, s. 17 (the penalty is a fine of £10).

inquiries as to the true consideration and to decline registration until the correct stamp duty is paid.[63]

The stamp duty on transfers is at the rate of £1 per cent. on the price.[64]

A transfer may also be registered, at the request of the transferor, in the same manner and subject to the same conditions as if registration were applied for by the transferee: section 77.

Certification of transfer

If a holder of shares sells some only of his shares comprised in a share certificate, *e.g.* 250 shares out of 1,000, it will be unsafe for him to deliver his share certificate for 1,000 shares to the purchaser. Similarly if he sells some of the shares to one person and the rest to another. The usual procedure in such cases is, therefore:

(1) The transferor executes the transfer and sends it, with the share certificate, to the company.

(2) The secretary indorses on the transfer the words "certificate lodged" or similar words, and returns the transfer so certificated to the transferor.

(3) The transferor hands over this certificated transfer to the transferee against payment of the price.

(4) The transferee executes the transfer if it is in the form prescribed by the articles, has it stamped, and forwards it to the company for registration.

(5) Within two months[59] the company either issues new share certificates or, where a power to refuse registration is being exercised, informs the *transferee* of its refusal to register him: sections 80, 78, *ante*.

The certification of a transfer is a representation by the company to any person acting on the faith of the certification that there have been produced to the company such documents as show a prima facie title to the shares in the transferor, but it is not a representation that the transferor has any title: section 79 (1). However, if a company *fraudulently or negligently* makes a false certification the company is liable in damages to a person who acts on the faith of it to his detriment: section 79 (2).

[63] *Maynard* v. *Consolidated Kent Collieries* [1903] 2 K.B. 121.
[64] Stamp Act 1891, s. 1, Sched. 1; Finance Act 1963, s. 55, Sched. 2.

Suppose that P transferred all his shares to X and his certificate was lodged by X with the company. Before registration was completed, P executed a transfer of some of the shares to Y, who sold them to B. Y's transfer to B was negligently certificated by the company and, on the strength of this, B paid Y. The company registered X and refused to register B. The company is liable in damages to B.

A certification is deemed to be made by the company if it is made by a person, such as the secretary, authorised to issue certificated transfers on the company's behalf and if it is signed by a person authorised to certificate transfers on the company's behalf: section 79 (3).

When a transfer is certificated the company destroys the original certificate and issues new certificates. But if it *negligently* returns the original certificate with the certificated transfer to the transferor and the transferor then fraudulently deals with the original certificate so as to inflict loss on a third party, *e.g.* the transferor purports to transfer *all* the shares comprised in the original certificate to the third party, the company is not liable to the third party. The reason is that the share certificate is neither a negotiable instrument nor a warranty of title on the part of the company issuing it, and the company owes no duty to the public as to the custody of the certificate. Further, the company is not estopped from denying the validity of the transferor's title to the shares *previously* transferred, because the proximate cause of the third party's loss is the fraud of the transferor and not the negligence of the company.[65]

Rights as between vendor and purchaser

On a sale of shares the ordinary contract between the parties is that the vendor shall give to the purchaser a valid transfer and do all that is required to enable the purchaser to be registered as a member in respect of the shares, the purchaser's duty being to get himself registered.[66] The vendor's duty is not only to give a genuine transfer but also, where the vendor is not the transferor, one which is signed by a transferor willing that the transfer shall be registered.

[65] *Longman* v. *Bath Electric Tramways Ltd.* [1905] 1 Ch. 646. The Scottish equivalent of "estoppel" is personal bar, but, in the absence of Scottish authority on certification, it seems doubtful whether a company would be entitled to deny the validity of a share certificate in the circumstances mentioned: *cf. Clavering, Son & Co.* v. *Goodwins, Jardine & Co. Ltd.* (1891) 18 R. 652.

[66] *Skinner* v. *City of London Marine Insce. Corpn.* (1885) 14 Q.B.D. 882 (C.A.).

Solicitors instructed stockbrokers to sell stock and enclosed the certificate and a blank transfer (*i.e.* a transfer in which the transferee's name had still to be inserted)[67] signed by the stockholder. The stockbrokers sold the stock but the stockholder repudiated the contract and the company, on her instructions, refused to register the transfer. The stockbrokers replaced the stock by a purchase on the Stock Exchange and sued the solicitors for an indemnity. *Held*, (1) the solicitors were principals of the stockbrokers as regards the sale, (2) it was the solicitor's duty to deliver a transfer executed by a transferor willing that it should be registered, and (3) the solicitors were liable: *Hichens, Harrison, Woolston & Co.* v. *Jackson & Sons* [1943] A.C. 266.

If the directors, in pursuance of a power in the articles, decline to register the transfer, the purchaser, unless he bought "with registration guaranteed," will be unable to sue the vendor for damages or rescind and recover the price from the vendor—there is no implied condition subsequent to such effect.[68] In such a case the vendor will be a trustee of the shares for the purchaser.[69] The vendor is, of course, under a duty to the purchaser not to prevent or delay the registration of the transfer.[70]

As from the time of the contract of sale, the equitable or beneficial interest in the shares passes to the purchaser, and the vendor holds the legal title as quasi-trustee for the purchaser.[69] The purchaser does not obtain the legal or complete title until his name is entered on the register of members.[71]

Until the transfer is registered, the vendor will receive any dividends or other benefits declared on the shares and, in the case of partly paid shares, calls may be made on him. As between the vendor and the purchaser the rights and liabilities depend on the terms of the contract. The shares may be bought "cum" or "ex" dividends or rights, or with a specified sum paid. In the absence of any such agreement, the purchaser is entitled to dividends or other benefits declared after the *date of the contract*.[72]

In September, 1935, R. sold shares privately to W. In April, 1936, the company declared a dividend for the year ending December 31, 1935. *Held*, the sale being by private bargain and not governed by Stock Exchange rules,

[67] Such a transfer may be invalid in Scots law: *post* p. 269.
[68] *London Founders Assocn. Ltd.* v. *Clarke* (1888) 20 Q.B.D. 576 (C.A.).
[69] *Stevenson* v. *Wilson*, 1907 S.C. 445; this quasi-trust would not, however, defeat a subsequent arrestment of the shares by a creditor of the transferor: *per* Lord Moncrieff (Ordinary) in *National Bank of Scotland Glasgow Nominees Ltd.* v. *Adamson*, 1932 S.L.T. 492 (O.H.) at p. 495.
[70] *Hooper* v. *Herts* [1906] 1 Ch. 549 (C.A.).
[71] See *per* Lord Gifford in *Morrison* v. *Harrison* (1876) 3 R. 406 at p. 411; see also *Tennant's Trustees* v. *Tennant*, 1946 S.C. 420.
[72] *Black* v. *Homersham* (1878) 4 Ex.D. 24; *Re Kidner* [1929] 2 Ch. 121.

W. was entitled to the whole dividend and it was not apportionable between W. and R.: *Re Wimbush* [1940] Ch. 92.

Subject to contrary agreement, the purchaser must indemnify the vendor against calls made after the date of the contract.

X, owner of shares not fully paid up, sold to Y, giving him a blank transfer. Y, without being entered on the register, sold to Z, giving Z a blank transfer. Z was not entered on the register, and became bankrupt. The company made a call on X. *Held*, Y was bound to indemnify X, although Y had then no beneficial interest. The implied obligation arose out of the contract between them: *Spencer* v. *Ashworth, Partington & Co.* [1925] 1 K.B. 589 (C.A.).

Note: Z would have been liable to indemnify X only during the period of Z's beneficial ownership. The obligation would have arisen from the relationship of trustee and beneficiary between them.

Again, until the transfer is registered, the vendor is entitled to exercise any vote conferred by the shares but he must vote as directed by the purchaser.

An unpaid vendor of shares who remains on the register of members after the contract of sale retains *vis-à-vis* the purchaser the right to vote in respect of those shares unless the contract restricts such right.[73]

Priorities

In England, when the same shares are claimed by two innocent parties the general rules are:

(1) The party who is on the register of members and therefore has the legal title has priority.

(2) If neither party is on the register, the party whose equitable title is first in time has priority.

For example, if X, the registered owner, is trustee of the shares for Y and, in breach of trust, sells the shares to Z, who buys without notice of the trust and becomes registered as owner before the company knows of the trust, Z will have priority over Y. A company, however, is entitled to a reasonable time for the consideration of every transfer before it registers the transfer,[74] and therefore if Y, in the example just given, had given notice of his claim to the company before Z was actually registered as owner, he would

---

[73] *Musselwhite* v. *C. H. Musselwhite & Son Ltd.* [1962] Ch. 964, where a contract for the sale of shares provided that the transfer and share certificate should be held by a third party until the price was paid by instalments over a period of years.

[74] *Re Ottos Kopje Diamond Mines Ltd.* [1893] 1 Ch. 618 (C.A.).

have been entitled to priority over Z, as his equitable title would have been first in time.[75]

C. assigned all his property to P. as trustee for C's creditors. The property included some shares. P. asked for the share certificates but was unable to obtain them from C.; he then gave notice of the assignment to the company. C., after the date of the assignment to P., sold the shares to X, who applied for registration. *Held*, P., having an equitable title which was prior in time, was entitled to registration: *Peat* v. *Clayton* [1906] 1 Ch. 659.

Entry on the register after notice of a prior equitable claim will not give priority.

In 1893 X transferred debentures of a private company to Y on trust for X for life with remainder to X's sons. The transfer was not registered. In 1894 one son sold his share of the debentures to Z. In 1911 X deposited the debentures with the bank as security for the company's overdraft. In 1914 the bank, on learning of the settlement and transfer to Y, took a transfer of the debentures from X, and were registered as owners. *Held*, Z was entitled to priority over the bank: *Coleman* v. *London County and Westminster Bank Ltd.* [1916] 2 Ch. 353.

It has been said [75] that even if a complete legal title has not been obtained, a person who has, as between himself and the company, a present, absolute, unconditional right to registration before the company learns of a better title, has the same priority as if he were actually registered. It is doubtful, however, whether anything short of registration will give priority, except perhaps in very special circumstances. Directors should refuse to register a transfer after receiving notice of an adverse equitable claim to the shares, unless the transfer has already been passed for registration.[76]

Delay in obtaining registration is dangerous to a transferee for two reasons: a later transferee may gain priority by obtaining registration first, or an earlier equity may come to light.

A husband mortgaged shares of which he was trustee for his wife. Before the mortgagee was registered the wife successfully claimed that her equitable title prevailed over that of the mortgagee: *Ireland* v. *Hart* [1902] 1 Ch. 522.

In Scotland, if there are competing claims for membership of a company, the person preferred is the one who first completes his title to the shares by having his name entered on the register; a mere assignation of shares, even though intimated to the company, does not make the assignee a member.[77]

Where a competition arises between a transferee and an arrester,

---

[75] *Per* Romer J. in *Moore* v. *North Western Bank* [1891] 2 Ch. 599 at pp. 602, 603.
[76] *Per* Joyce J. in *Ireland* v. *Hart* [1902] 1 Ch. 522 at p. 529.
[77] *Morrison* v. *Harrison* (1876) 3 R. 406.

the transferee is preferred to the arrester as soon as the transfer has been registered.[78] In a question between a transferee whose transfer has been duly intimated to the company but not registered and a subsequent arrester, the intimation of the transfer has been held to cut out the arrestment.[79]

Directors may delay registration where they suspect that a transfer is affected by fraud or dishonesty[80] but, if they receive intimation of a competing interest in the shares from some party other than the transferee, they are entitled to register the transfer unless the intimation is followed up by a legal measure such as interdict.[81] The company must be made a party to any such interdict process, and interdict has been refused where it was alleged that share transfers, bearing that the beneficial interest remained in the transferors, had been executed by a body of trustees to certain of their own number and another person in order to give the transferors a qualification to act as directors; the possibility that the shares had been transferred in breach of trust was not, the court held, a matter which concerned the company or which made the registration of the transferees invalid.[82]

Forged transfer

A forged transfer of shares is a nullity and cannot affect the title of the shareholder whose signature is forged. If the company, therefore, has registered the forged transfer and removed the true owner of the shares from the register, it can be compelled to replace him.[83] It can then claim an indemnity from the person who sent the forged transfer for registration if it has sustained loss through acting thereon. No estoppel in favour of such a person arises from a share certificate issued to him even though he knows nothing of the forgery—he has not relied on the act of the company in issuing the certificate.

B. sent to the corporation for registration a transfer of stock which stood in the names of T. and H. The transfer was a forgery, T. having forged H.'s signature to the transfer, but B. was ignorant of this. The corporation registered the

---

[78] *National Bank of Scotland Glasgow Nominees Ltd.* v. *Adamson*, 1932 S.L.T. 492 (O.H.).
[79] *Jackson* v. *Elphick* (1902) 10 S.L.T. 146 (O.H.).
[80] *Property Investment Co. of Scotland Ltd.* v. *Duncan* (1897) 14 R. 299.
[81] *Per* Lord M'Laren in *Shaw* v. *Caledonian Rlwy. Co.* (1890) 17 R. 466 at p. 482.
[82] *Elliot* v. *J. W. Mackie & Sons Ltd.*, 1935 S.C. 81.
[83] *Barton* v. *N. Staffordshire Rlwy. Co.* (1888) 38 Ch.D. 458.

transfer. B. transferred the stock to third parties to whom certificates were issued. The corporation was estopped from denying that those registered were the stockholders entitled. H. subsequently discovered the forgery and compelled the corporation to buy him an equivalent amount of stock and to pay him the missing dividends with interest. *Held*, B. was bound to indemnify the corporation upon an implied contract that the transfer was genuine: *Sheffield Corporation* v. *Barclay* [1905] A.C. 392.[84]

In an effort to prevent the registration of a forged transfer, companies usually, on a transfer being lodged for registration, write to the shareholder informing him of the transfer and of their intention to register it unless by return of post they hear that he objects. The neglect of the shareholder to reply to this communication does not estop him from proving that the transfer is a forgery.[85]

By the Forged Transfers Acts 1891 and 1892 companies are empowered to pay compensation for any loss sustained owing to forged transfers, even if they are under no legal obligation to pay it. The Acts provide for the formation of a fund, if the company thinks fit, to meet claims for compensation. Many companies insure against the risk of forged transfers.

TRANSMISSION OF SHARES

Section 75 *ante*[86] provides that it does prejudice any power of a company to register as shareholder any person to whom the right to any shares in the company has been transmitted by operation of law. Transmission of shares occurs on the death or the bankruptcy of a member, or, if the member is a company, on its going into liquidation.

On the death of a sole shareholder the shares vest in his personal representative,[87] *i.e.* his executor or administrator.[88] The company is bound to accept production of the probate of the will or, in the case of an intestacy, letters of administration of the estate, or, in Scotland, the confirmation as executor, as sufficient evidence of the grant: section 82. Table A, article 28, provides that the company may charge a fee for the registration of any such instrument. Subject to any restrictions in the articles, the personal representative may

---

[84] *Cf.* Lord Kyllachy (Ordinary) in *Clavering, Son & Co.* v. *Goodwins, Jardine & Co. Ltd.* (1891) 18 R. 652 at p. 657.

[85] *Re Bahia and San Francisco Rlwy. Co.* (1868) L.R. 3 Q.B. 584, *ante* p. 247. *Barton* v. *L. & N.W. Rlwy Co.* (1890) 24 Q.B.D. 77 (C.A.).

[86] p. 254.

[87] *Re Greene* [1949] Ch. 333.

[88] Executor in Scots law: see p. 188 *ante*.

be registered as a member or transfer the shares without himself becoming a member: section 76.[89]

> Table A, article 30, provides: "Any person becoming entitled to a share in consequence of the death or bankruptcy of a member may, upon such evidence being produced as may from time to time properly be required by the directors and subject as hereinafter provided, elect either to be registered himself as holder of the share or to have some person nominated by him registered as the transferee thereof, but the directors shall, in either case, have the same right to decline or suspend registration as they would have had in the case of a transfer of the share by that member before his death or bankruptcy, as the case may be."

Note what was said earlier[90] as to proposals for changes in the law and Clause 20 (2) of the Companies Bill 1973.

When shares are jointly held, the surviving holder becomes the sole holder. Under Table A, article 29, the estate of the deceased joint holder is not released from any liability in respect of the shares.

On the bankruptcy of a member, his shares vest in his trustee in bankruptcy who may,[91] subject to the articles, either be registered as a member himself or transfer the shares without being registered as a member.[92]

MORTGAGE OF SHARES (ENGLISH LAW)

In England, a shareholder who borrows money on the security of his shares may give the lender either a legal mortgage or an equitable mortgage over the shares.

Legal mortgage

A legal mortgage of shares is effected by transfer of the shares to the lender (the mortgagee) followed by registration of the transfer by the company. There should also be a document setting out the terms of the loan and containing an agreement to retransfer the shares on repayment of the amount borrowed with interest. The document will empower the lender to sell the shares in the event of default by the borrower (the mortgagor).

This form of mortgage gives the lender complete security up to the value of the shares. He will be entitled to dividends and to exercise any voting rights in respect of the shares, unless it is agreed

---

[89] *Ante* p. 189.
[90] p. 254.
[91] Bankruptcy Act 1914, ss. 18(1), 53(1), (2). Bankruptcy (Scotland) Act 1913, s. 70, and Sched. D 97.
[92] *Ante* p. 190.

that the dividends shall be paid to the borrower and that he shall exercise the voting rights as the borrower directs.[93]

However, restrictions on the transfer of shares contained in the articles[94] may prevent this kind of mortgage being made. Further, it might not be advisable where the shares are not fully paid because the lender on the register would be personally liable for calls.

Equitable mortgage

1. An equitable mortgage of shares may be made by depositing the share certificate with the lender as security for a loan. In such a case the lender can enforce his security by applying to the court for a sale of the shares or for an order for transfer and foreclosure.[95]

2. A method more commonly adopted is for the borrower to deposit with the lender the share certificate together with a blank transfer, *i.e.* a transfer signed by the borrower with the transferee's name left blank. In such a case the lender has an *implied* power to sell the shares if default is made by the borrower in making repayment at the agreed time or, if no time for repayment is agreed, within a reasonable time after notice.[96] The implied power of sale includes power to insert the name of the buyer in the blank transfer if, as is usual, the articles provide for transfers to be in writing. The borrower is under an implied obligation not to delay registration of the transfer so filled up.[97]

3. If the articles require transfers to be by deed, the lender cannot fill up a blank transfer unless he is authorised by deed. In such a case an equitable mortgage may be made by deposit of the share certificate plus a transfer by deed to the lender. If the borrower defaults, the lender can lodge the transfer for registration.

No equitable mortgage is in itself absolutely secure because the borrower remains on the register and may sell the shares and procure the registration of the purchaser with priority over the lender, who would have no remedy against the company.

C. deposited his share certificate and a blank transfer with R. as a security for a loan. Upon the certificate was printed: "Without the production of this certificate no transfer of the shares mentioned therein can be registered." C. sold

---

[93] *Siemens Brothers & Co. Ltd.* v. *Burns* [1918] 2 Ch. 324.
[94] *Ante* p. 249.
[95] *Harrold* v. *Plenty* [1901] 2 Ch. 314.
[96] *Hooper* v. *Herts* [1906] 1 Ch. 549.
[97] *Powell* v. *London and Provincial Bank* [1893] 2 Ch. 555 (C.A.).

the shares to Y. and induced the company to register Y. as owner of the shares without the production of the share certificate. R. sued the company for wrongfully registering the shares in Y's name. *Held*, the company was not liable as it owed no duty of care to R., and the statement on the certificate was only a warning to the owner of the shares to take care of the certificate and not a statement of fact giving rise to an estoppel: *Rainford* v. *James Keith & Blackman Co. Ltd.* [1905] 1 Ch. 296.[98]

However, the mortgagor must exercise any voting rights as directed by the mortgagee.[99]

Stop notice

To obtain complete protection, an equitable mortgagee of shares should serve a stop notice. This is done by filing an affidavit setting out the facts, and a notice in the prescribed form, in the Central Office of the Supreme Court or in a District Registry and serving an office copy of the affidavit and a duplicate notice on the company. The effect of the notice is that, whilst it continues in force, if the company receives any request to register a transfer of the shares in question it must give notice in writing to the person who has served the notice. Within eight days, such person must apply for an injunction restraining the transfer or the company will be at liberty to register the transfer.[1]

Charging order

A judgment creditor of the registered owner of shares may obtain an order charging the shares with payment of the judgment debt,[2] after which, until the order is discharged, the company cannot permit a transfer except with the authority of the court. A charging order will not have priority over a mortgage created by deposit of the share certificate and a blank transfer before the date of the charging order, as the judgment creditor can be in no better position than the judgment debtor at the time when the order was made.

---

[98] Reversed on the facts [1905] 2 Ch. 147 (C.A.). On the facts the company was affected with notice of R's charge and he was able to recover the price of the shares which had been paid to the company in repayment of a loan made by the company to C.

[99] *Wise* v. *Landsell* [1921] 1 Ch. 420.

[1] R.S.C., O. 50, rr. 11–15.

[2] R.S.C., O. 50, rr. 2–7.

ASSIGNATION OF SHARES IN SECURITY (SCOTS LAW)

The only effective way of assigning shares in security is by the execution and registration of a transfer in favour of the lender. See the section headed "Legal mortgage," *ante*.[3]

No form of the equitable mortgage recognised by English law gives the lender any real security in competition with the general creditors of the borrower.[4] Accordingly, where a borrower delivers the share certificate to the lender and undertakes to transfer the shares to the lender when requested to do so, a transfer executed within six months before the borrower's notour bankruptcy is reducible as a fraudulent preference under the Bankruptcy Act 1696 (Scots Act 1696, c. 5) as amended by the Companies Act 1947, section 115, and even intimation to the company of the lender's right to the shares will not avail the lender unless his right is completed by his actually becoming a shareholder.[6] Where, however, a completed transfer has been delivered to the lender along with the share certificate so that the lender is in a position to have himself registered as a member without further interposition of the borrower, registration of the transfer on the eve of the borrower's sequestration is not open to challenge as a fraudulent preference provided the delivery of the documents to the lender was made more than six months before the borrower's notour bankruptcy.[7] A blank transfer may be invalid under the Blank Bonds and Trusts Act 1696 (Scots Act 1696 c. 25) which declares null "bonds, assignations, dispositions or other deeds" subscribed blank in the name of the person or persons in whose favour they are conceived.

Stop notices and charging orders are not part of Scots law. When a company called on to register a transfer receives intimation from some person other than the transferee that that other person has an interest in the shares, the company is entitled to proceed to register the transfer unless the intimation is followed up by an application for interdict or other legal measure.[8]

---

[3] p. 266.
[4] *Gourlay* v. *Mackie* (1887) 14 R. 403; *per* Lord Gifford in *Morrison* v. *Harrison* (1876) 3 R. 406 at p. 411; *ct. Guild* v. *Young* (1884) 22 S.L.R. 520 (O.H.).
[5] *Gourlay* v. *Mackie* (1887) 14 R. 403.
[6] *Per* Lord Gifford in *Morrison* v. *Harrison* (1876) 3 R. 406 at p. 411.
[7] *Guild* v. *Young* (1884) 22 S.L.R. 520 (O.H.).
[8] *Per* Lord M'Laren in *Shaw* v. *Caledonian Rlwy. Co.* (1890) 17 R. 466 at p. 482.

Shares are subject to arrestment at the instance of the creditors of the shareholder, whether the arrestment is in execution[9] or merely to found jurisdiction.[10] Where competition arises between a transferee and an arrester the transferee has the preferable right to the shares as soon as his transfer has been lodged, even although it is not registered before the lodging of the arrestment.

In January S. transferred 200 shares to M. and 1,000 shares to F., and the transfers were received by the secretary of the company on 19th January and 2nd February respectively. Because of an arrestment lodged the previous November against S. at the instance of a bank, the transfers were not registered. On 30th March arrestments were executed at the instance of D. against S. *Held*, the transfers to M. and F. were preferable to D.'s arrestments: *Harvey's Yoker Distillery Ltd.* v. *Singleton* (1901) 8 S.L.T. 369 (O.H.).

"An arrestment can only attach property belonging truly and in substance to the common debtor. Now these shares did not belong in substance to Singleton at the time of the arrestment, because he had by that time done all in his power to dispose of them by executing the transfers": *per* Lord Stormonth Darling (Ordinary) at p. 370.

An arrester is not entitled to found on any irregularity in the registration procedure to the effect of defeating the transferee's title.[11] Intimation to the company of a transfer, even without registration, has the effect, in a question between the transferee and a subsequent arrester, of cutting out the arrestment.[12]

CALLS ON SHARES

A call on shares is a demand by the directors that a member pay to the company money which is unpaid on his shares, whether on account of the nominal value of the shares or by way of premium. Since shares are now usually fully paid up, calls are uncommon today.[13] If, when shares are issued, the full amount of each share is not payable at once, the terms of issue will provide that part is payable on application, part on allotment and the remainder by instalments at fixed dates, in which case the instalments are not calls,[14] as the obligation of the shareholder to pay is not dependent on a call from the company. However, in a rare case, the company may not require all the nominal amount of a share, or the full amount of a

---

[9] *Sinclair* v. *Staples* (1860) 22 D. 600.

[10] *American Mortgage Co. of Scotland Ltd.* v. *Sidway*, 1908 S.C. 500.

[11] *National Bank of Scotland Glasgow Nominees Ltd.* v. *Adamson*, 1932 S.L.T. 492 (O.H.); for an arrestment made effective by the granting by the court of a warrant to sell the shares, see *Valentine* v. *Grangemouth Coal Co. Ltd.* (1897) 35 S.L.R. 12 (O.H.).

[12] *Jackson* v. *Elphick* (1902) 10 S.L.T. 146 (O.H.).

[13] *Ante* p. 211.

[14] But articles may provide that they shall be *deemed* to be calls: see Table A, art. 19.

premium on a share, to be paid at or soon after allotment but may leave part to be called up in accordance with the provisions of the articles as and when required by the company or, in the event of a winding up, by the liquidator. If so, a shareholder is bound to pay the whole or part of the balance unpaid on his shares "as and when called on," in accordance with the provisions of the articles. Calls must be made in the manner laid down in the articles.

Table A, article 15, provides: "The directors may from time to time make calls upon the members in respect of any moneys unpaid on their shares (whether on account of the nominal value of the shares or by way of premium) and not by the conditions of allotment thereof made payable at fixed times, provided that no call shall exceed one-fourth of the nominal value of the share or be payable at less than one month from the date fixed for the payment of the last preceding call, and each member shall (subject to receiving at least fourteen day's notice specifying the time or times and place of payment) pay to the company at the time or times and place so specified the amount called on his shares. A call may be revoked or postponed as the directors may determine."

Table A, article 16, provides: "A call shall be deemed to have been made at the time when the resolution of the directors authorising the call was passed. . . ."

Where the articles require the time and place of payment and the amount of the call to be specified, a call is not properly made if the resolution of the directors authorising the call specifies the amount of the call but not the date of payment.[15] A verbal direction to the secretary fixing the date of payment is not enough.[16]

In England a call creates a specialty debt due from the shareholder to the company (s. 20 (2)), and so the period within which an action can be brought for payment of it is 12 years.[17] In Scotland a call remains enforceable until the expiry of 20 years.[18] Table A, article 18, provides for payment of interest at the rate of five per cent. from the date fixed for payment until actual payment.

If authorised by the articles, a company may make arrangements on the issue of shares for a difference between the shareholders in the amounts and times of payment of calls: section 59 (*a*). Table A, article 20, authorises such an arrangement. Such a power does not entitle directors to make calls on all the shareholders except themselves,[19] at any rate without the knowledge and sanction of the other shareholders—the directors' power to make calls must be

[15] *Re Cawley & Co.* (1889) 42 Ch.D. 209 (C.A.).
[16] *Per* James L.J. in *Johnson* v. *Lyttle's Iron Agency* (1877) 5 Ch.D. 687 (C.A.) at p. 694.
[17] Limitation Act 1939, s. 2.
[18] Prescription and Limitation (Scotland) Act 1973, s. 7.
[19] *Alexander* v. *Automatic Telephone Co.* [1900] 2 Ch. 56 (C.A.).

exercised bona fide for the benefit of the company as a whole, and not so as to give themselves an advantage over other shareholders.[20]

Any arrangement made under section 59 (*a*) must be made at the time of the issue of shares. If no such arrangement is made, the rule is that "prima facie it is entirely improper for the directors to make a call on some members of a class of shareholders who stand in the same relation to the company as the other members of the class without making a similar call on all the other members of that class."[21]

Table A, articles 33 to 39, provides for forfeiture for non-payment of a call or an instalment.[22]

In an action to enforce payment of a call it is no defence for the shareholder to say that he has repudiated the contract because of misrepresentations in the prospectus. To succeed he must show that he has taken steps to have his name removed from the register of members.[23]

Calls made by a liquidator in the course of a winding up are in some respects different from calls made by directors during the active existence of the company.[24]

Payment in advance of calls

If authorised by the articles, a company may accept payment from a member of the whole or a part of the amount remaining unpaid on his shares, although no part of this amount has been called up: section 59 (*b*).

Table A, article 21, provides: "The directors may, if they think fit, receive from any member willing to advance the same, all or any part of the moneys uncalled and unpaid upon any shares held by him, and upon all or any of the moneys so advanced may (until the same would, but for such advance, become payable) pay interest at such rate not exceeding (unless the company in general meeting shall otherwise direct) 5 per cent. per annum, as may be agreed upon between the directors and the member paying such sum in advance."

When a payment in advance of calls has been made the consequences are:

[20] *Post* p. 350.
[21] *Per* Sargant J. in *Galloway* v. *Hallé Concerts Society* [1915] 2 Ch. 233 at p. 239.
[22] *Post* p. 277.
[23] *First National Reinsurance Co.* v. *Greenfield* [1921] 2 K.B. 260; *Scottish Amalgamated Silks Ltd.* v. *Macalister*, 1930 S.L.T. 593 (O.H.); see, however, *Liquidators of Mount Morgan (West) Gold Mine Ltd.* v. *M'Mahon* (1891) 18 R. 772.
[24] *Mitchell, Petitioner*, (1863) 1 M. 1116; *Liquidators of Benhar Coal Co. Ltd., Petitioners* (1882) 9 R. 763.

(1) The shareholder's liability to the company is extinguished or reduced, as the case may be.

(2) He becomes a creditor to the extent of the payment in advance, so that interest on it can be paid out of capital,[25] *i.e.* whether profits are made by the company or not.

(3) The company cannot be compelled to repay the payment,[26] except in a winding up, *post*.

(4) The company cannot repay without the consent of the shareholder.[27]

(5) In a winding up he will rank after the other creditors but will be entitled to repayment of the advance with interest in priority to the other shareholders who have not paid in advance.[28]

The power of receiving payment in advance of calls is a fiduciary power and must be exercised by the directors bona fide for the benefit of the company as a whole, and not for the private ends of the directors. Accordingly, where directors, knowing the company to be insolvent, paid the amount remaining unpaid on their shares and on the same day appropriated the money in payment of their fees, it was held that they still remained liable on the shares.[29] However, although directors are trustees of their powers for the shareholders,[30] they are not trustees for the company's creditors, and where, the company being insolvent, they paid in advance the amount of their calls and applied the money in discharging the company's bank overdraft, which they had guaranteed, it was held that their shares were fully paid up.[31]

LIEN ON SHARES (ENGLISH LAW)

The articles may give the company a lien on the shares held by a member for his unpaid call or instalment, or for some other debt due from him to the company. Such a lien is an equitable charge upon the shares, and gives rise to the same rights as if the shares

---

[25] *Lock* v. *Queensland Investment and Land Mortgage Co.* [1896] A.C. 461; *Myles, Petitioner* (1893) 1 S.L.T. 90 (O.H.).

[26] *Per* Lindley and Kay L.JJ. in *Lock* v. *Queensland Investment etc. Co.* [1896] 1 Ch. 397 (C.A.) at pp. 405, 407.

[27] *London and Northern Steamship Co.* v. *Farmer* (1914) 111 L.T. 204.

[28] *Re Exchange Drapery Co.* (1888) 38 Ch.D. 171.

[29] *Sykes' Case* (1872) L.R. 13 Eq. 255.

[30] *Post* p. 347.

[31] *Poole's Case* (1878) 9 Ch.D. 322 (C.A.).

had been expressly charged by the member in favour of the company.[32]

Table A, article 11, provides: "The company shall have a first and paramount lien on every share (not being a fully paid share) for all moneys (whether presently payable or not) called or payable at a fixed time in respect of that share, and the company shall also have a first and paramount lien on all shares (other than fully paid shares) standing registered in the name of a single person for all moneys presently payable by him or his estate to the company; but the directors may at any time declare any share to be wholly or in part exempt from the provisions of this regulation. The company's lien, if any, on a share shall extend to all dividends payable thereon."

The articles may grant a lien on shares which are fully paid but in such a case an official quotation on The Stock Exchange cannot be obtained.[33] If the lien given by the articles extends only to shares not fully paid, the company can alter its articles so as to give a lien on all shares, even if only one member will be affected by the alteration.[34]

Table A, article 24, empowers the directors to decline to register the transfer of a share on which the company has a lien.

A shareholder against whom a lien is to be enforced can compel the company to assign its lien to his nominee who is willing to pay off the amount of the lien.[32]

How a lien is enforced

A lien is enforced, like any other equitable charge, by a sale. If the articles do not give the company power to sell the shares, an application for an order for sale may be necessary. It is probable that the company has the implied power of sale given by the Law of Property Act 1925, section 101, to a mortgagee whose mortgage is made by deed. However, since it is uncertain that the articles, which create the lien, are a deed for the purposes of section 101,[35] to avoid the necessity of an application to the court the articles usually give an express power of sale.

Table A provides: "12. The company may sell, in such manner as the directors think fit, any shares on which the company has a lien, but no sale shall be made unless a sum in respect of which the lien exists is presently payable, nor until the expiration of fourteen days after a notice in writing, stating and

[32] *Everitt* v. *Automatic Weighing Machine Co.* [1892] 3 Ch. 506.
[33] Rules of The Stock Exchange, App. 34, Sched. VII.
[34] *Allen* v. *Gold Reefs of West Africa Ltd.* [1900] 1 Ch. 656 (C.A.), *ante* p. 110.
[35] See s. 20, *ante* p. 106.

demanding payment of such part of the amount in respect of which the lien exists as is presently payable, has been given to the registered holder for the time being of the share, or the person entitled thereto by reason of his death or bankruptcy."

Further, articles usually give the company power to nominate someone to execute the transfer.

Table A provides: "13. To give effect to any such sale the directors may authorise some person to transfer the shares sold to the purchaser thereof. The purchaser shall be registered as the holder of the shares comprised in any such transfer, and he shall not be bound to see to the application of the purchase money, nor shall his title to the shares be affected by any irregularity or invalidity in the proceedings in reference to the sale."

The first part of article 13 is necessitated by section 75, which requires a proper instrument of transfer to be produced before a transfer is registered.

Table A continues: "14. The proceeds of the sale shall be received by the company and applied in payment of such part of the amount in respect of which the lien exists as is presently payable, and the residue, if any, shall (subject to a like lien for sums not presently payable as existed upon the shares before the sale) be paid to the person entitled to the shares at the date of the sale."

A lien cannot be enforced by forfeiture even if power to forfeit is contained in the articles.

The articles of a company provided that the company should have a lien on shares for the debts of the shareholder, and also provided that the lien could be enforced by forfeiture. *Held*, (1) forfeiture for debts generally, as distinct from debts due from the shareholder as a contributory, amounted to an illegal reduction of capital; (2) power to forfeit on failure to redeem after notice amounted to a clog on the shareholder's equity of redemption, and was invalid and *ultra vires*: *Hopkinson* v. *Mortimer, Harley & Co. Ltd.* [1917] 1 Ch. 646.

Priority of lien

When a third party advances money on the security of shares, a question may arise as to whether the third party has priority over the company's lien. In such a case, if the third party gives notice of his security to the company before the company's lien arises, the third party will have priority, but otherwise not.

The articles of a company gave "a first and paramount lien and charge" on shares for debts due from the shareholder. A shareholder created an equitable mortgage of his shares by depositing the share certificate with a bank as security for an overdraft and the bank gave notice of the deposit to the company. The shareholder subsequently became indebted to the company whereupon a lien arose in favour of the company. *Held*, the bank had priority as the company's lien arose after notice of their equitable mortgage. The notice was not notice of a trust contrary to what is now section 117 but notice affecting the company, in its character of trader, with knowledge of the bank's interest: *Bradford Banking Co.* v. *Briggs & Co.* (1886) 12 App. Cas. 29.

It seems that the position is the same even if the articles contain a clause like Table A, article 7,[36] relieving the company of the obligation to take notice of equities in relation to shares.[37]

Similarly, where the shareholder is a trustee, the company's lien will prevail over the claims of the beneficial owners unless the company is given notice, before the lien arises, that the shareholder is a trustee.

Trustees held shares in a company, the articles of which gave the company a lien on shares standing either in a single name or in joint names for any debt due from any of the holders, either separately or jointly with any other person. There was also an article like Table A, article 7.[36] Long after the registration of the shares in the trustees' names, one of the trustees incurred a liability to the company. It was *not* alleged that the company had notice of the trust before the lien arose. *Held*, the company's lien prevailed over the title of the *cestuis que trust*: *New London and Brazilian Bank* v. *Brocklebank* (1882) 21 Ch.D. 302 (C.A.).

The title of the beneficial owners, however, will have priority if the company has notice, before the lien arises, that the shareholder is a trustee of the shares.[38]

The company has no lien on the shares registered in the name of a trustee for debts due to it from the beneficial owner.[39]

If a lien in favour of the company has arisen and the shareholder sells part only of his shares, the purchaser can require the company to discharge the lien primarily out of the shares not sold.[40]

A lien does not cease on the shareholder's death, but may be enforced against his executors.[41]

LIEN ON SHARES (SCOTS LAW)

A company has at common law and independently of any provision in its articles a lien on shares held by a member for debts due by the member to the company.[42] Articles, however, usually make express provision to the same effect. The lien enables the company to refuse to register any transfer of the shares until the transferor's debt to the company has been satisfied.

A company whose articles expressly limit the lien to partly paid

---

[36] *Ante* p. 200.
[37] *Rainford* v. *James Keith & Blackman Co. Ltd.* [1905] 2 Ch. 147 (C.A.), *ante* p. 268.
[38] *Mackereth* v. *Wigan Coal Co. Ltd.* [1916] 2 Ch. 293.
[39] *Re Perkins* (1890) 24 Q.B.D. 613 (C.A.).
[40] *Gray* v. *Stone* (1893) 69 L.T. 282.
[41] *Allen* v. *Gold Reefs of West Africa Ltd.* [1900] 1 Ch. 656 (C.A.), *ante* p. 110.
[42] *Hotchkis* v. *Royal Bank* (1797) 3 Paton 618; (1797) M. 2673; *Bell's Trustee* v. *Coatbridge Tinplate Co. Ltd.* (1886) 14 R. 246.

shares may alter the articles so as to extend the lien to all shares, but if such an alteration is not made until after a transfer of fully paid shares has been presented for registration the transferee's right to be registered is not affected by that alteration.[43]

A lien can be enforced by a sale only if the power of sale has been conferred by the articles, or a warrant is obtained from the court. A lien in respect of debts other than calls or instalments could not be enforced by forfeiture, since that would be an illegal reduction of capital.

Where X, a shareholder, has assigned his shares in security to Y who has completed his title to the shares by being registered as the holder of them, the company is no longer entitled to a lien on the shares in respect of debts due to it by X, since X is not the registered holder.[44]

For the provisions of Table A on lien, see "Lien (English Law)," above.

FORFEITURE OF SHARES

Although a forfeiture of a member's shares by the company is recognised by the Act, the directors may forfeit shares only if expressly authorised to do so by the articles and only for non-payment of a call or an instalment.

Table A provides: "33. If a member fails to pay any call or instalment of a call on the day appointed for payment thereof, the directors may, at any time thereafter during such time as any part of the call or instalment remains unpaid, serve a notice on him requiring payment of so much of the call or instalment as is unpaid, together with any interest which may have accrued.

"34. The notice shall name a further day (not earlier than the expiration of fourteen days from the date of service of the notice) on or before which the payment required by the notice is to be made, and shall state that in the event of non-payment at or before the time appointed the shares in respect of which the call was made will be liable to be forfeited.

"35. If the requirements of any such notice as aforesaid are not complied with, any share in respect of which the notice has been given may at any time thereafter, before the payment required by the notice has been made, be forfeited by a resolution of the directors to that effect."

Article 131 *post*[45] deals with the way in which notice may be given to a member.

---

[43] *Liquidator of W. & A. M'Arthur Ltd.* v. *Gulf Line Ltd.*, 1909 S.C. 732.
[44] *Paul's Trustee* v. *Thomas Justice & Sons Ltd.*, 1912 S.C. 1303.
[45] p. 291.

Forfeiture, being in the nature of a penal proceeding, is valid only if the provisions of the articles, *e.g.* as to notice, are strictly followed. Any irregularity will avoid the forfeiture.[46] To protect purchasers of the forfeited shares against possible irregularities in the forfeiture, the articles usually provide, as does Table A, article 38, that the title of the purchaser shall not be affected by any invalidity in the proceedings in reference to the forfeiture.

The power of the directors to forfeit shares must be exercised in good faith and not for the purpose of relieving shareholders with whom the directors are friendly from their liability.[47]

Forfeiture, when exercised, amounts to a reduction of capital, and it therefore seems certain that the articles cannot authorise forfeiture except on the ground of non-payment of calls or instalments. Table A, article 39, authorises forfeiture for non-payment of any sum which, by the terms of the issue of a share, is payable at a fixed time, including premiums. Forfeiture for non-payment of other debts due to the company is invalid.[48] Similarly, an article which authorises the forfeiture of shares held by a member who sues the company or the directors is invalid.[49]

An invalid forfeiture can be restrained by injunction.[46]

Forfeited shares may be sold or reissued by the company according to the provisions of the articles.

Table A, article 36, provides: "A forfeited share may be sold or otherwise disposed of on such terms and in such manner as the directors think fit, and at any time before a sale or disposition the forfeiture may be cancelled on such terms as the directors think fit."

A forfeiture cannot be cancelled without the consent of the person whose shares have been forfeited.[50]

Forfeited shares can be reissued at less than the amount which has been paid on them.

A company had forfeited a number of shares of £5 5s. each, £2 5s. paid, and proposed to reissue them at the price of 30s. a share. *Held*, the company could do so, as it was not bound to treat the forfeited shares as if nothing had been paid upon them: *Morrison* v. *Trustees, etc., Corpn. Ltd.* (1898) 68 L.J.Ch. 11 (C.A.).

The purchaser of the reissued shares is liable for the payment of all future calls duly made, including one for the amount of the

[46] *Johnson* v. *Lyttle's Iron Agency* (1877) 5 Ch.D. 687 (C.A.).
[47] *Re Esparto Trading Co.* (1879) 12 Ch.D. 191; *Gower's Case* (1868) L.R. 6 Eq. 77.
[48] *Hopkinson* v. *Mortimer, Harley & Co.* [1917] 1 Ch. 646, *ante* p. 275.
[49] *Hope* v. *International Financial Socy.* (1876) 4 Ch.D. 327 (C.A.).
[50] *Larkworthy's Case* [1903] 1 Ch. 711.

call which occasioned the forfeiture.[51] Consequently, there is no issue of shares at a discount, as the company has already received the amount paid up. The purchaser should be credited with any subsequent payments made by the ex-owner.[52]

The effect of the forfeiture on the former owner of the shares is to discharge him from his liability on the shares.[53] "The company on forfeiture gets its shares back, and the shareholder who has had his shares forfeited is wholly discharged from his liability."[54] To prevent this position from arising, the articles usually preserve the liability of the former owner.

Table A, article 37, provides: "A person whose shares have been forfeited shall cease to be a member in respect of the forfeited shares, but shall, notwithstanding, remain liable to pay to the company all moneys which, at the date of forfeiture, were payable by him to the company in respect of the shares, but his liability shall cease if and when the company shall have received payment in full of all such moneys in respect of the shares."

Such an article makes the person whose shares have been forfeited for non-payment of calls liable as a debtor to the company, and not as a contributory,[55] so that where, more than a year after the forfeiture, the company went into liquidation, it was held that the former owner of the shares was still liable.[56]

Even without the last part of Table A, article 37, the company cannot recover more than the difference between the calls due and the amount received on reissue.

B. underwrote two blocks of shares in a company. The issue to the public was a failure and B. was consequently allotted (*inter alia*) 8,200 £1 shares in the company. He was unable to pay the calls on these shares, which were forfeited. They were then reissued so that the company received the balance of the calls in full, but to obtain the new allottees the company had to pay £1,018 by way of commission. B. became bankrupt. The articles provided that the holder of forfeited shares should remain liable for calls notwithstanding the forfeiture and the company attempted to prove for the balance of calls due from B. *Held*, the

---

[51] *New Balkis Eersteling Ltd.* v. *Randt Gold Mining Co.* [1904] A.C. 165, where the purchaser was to hold the shares "discharged from all calls due prior to such purchase."

[52] *Re Randt Gold Mining Co.* [1904] 2 Ch. 468. *Re Bolton*, below, shows that the converse is true.

[53] *Stocken's Case* (1868) L.R. 3 Ch.App. 412; in *Goldsmith* v. *Colonial Finance etc. Corpn. Ltd.* [1909] 8 C.L.R. 241, Griffith C.J., at p. 249, and Barton J., at p. 253, thought that what Lord Cairns L.J. said in *Stocken* was founded on the particular article there in question.

[54] *Per* Luxmoore J. in *Re Bolton* [1930] 2 Ch. 48, *post*, at p. 59.

[55] *Post*, p. 582.

[56] *Ladies' Dress Assocn. Ltd.* v. *Pulbrook* [1900] 2 Q.B. 376 (C.A.); *cf. Ferguson* v. *Central Halls Co. Ltd.* (1881) 8 R. 997, and *Liquidators of Mount Morgan (West) Gold Mine Ltd.* v. *M'Mahon* (1891) 18 R. 772.

company could not receive payment of the calls twice over and could only prove for the actual loss sustained, *viz.* the £1,018 commission: *Re Bolton* [1930] 2 Ch. 48.

A surety for calls is released on forfeiture of the shares without his consent.[57]

SURRENDER OF SHARES

A surrender of his shares by a member to the company is not recognised by the Act, and Table A gives no power to accept a surrender. A company's articles, however, frequently give power to the directors to accept a surrender of shares where they are in a position to forfeit such shares and in any other case where a surrender of shares is allowed by law.

A surrender of shares is lawful where it is accepted to save the company from going through the formalities of forfeiture.[58]

"These [surrenders of shares] have been admitted by the Courts upon the principle, as I understand it, that they have practically the same effect as forfeiture, the main difference being that the one is a proceeding *in invitum*, and the other a proceeding taken with the assent of the shareholder, who is unable to retain and pay future calls on his shares."[59]

Surrender in these circumstances has been described as an "apparent exception" only to the principle of maintenance of capital,[60] since "the extinction of the obligation of a bankrupt shareholder can injure nobody."[61]

It seems that a surrender is also lawful where a surrender of fully paid shares is accepted in exchange for new shares of the same nominal value.

The holders of six per cent. fully paid preference shares surrendered them to the company in exchange for five per cent. fully paid preference shares. The surrendered shares were not cancelled but could be reissued by the company. *Held*, the surrender was valid, as it did not involve any reduction of capital or the purchase by the company of its own shares; and that the new shares issued in exchange were fully paid up: *Rowell* v. *John Rowell & Sons Ltd.* [1912] 2 Ch. 609.[62]

---

[57] *Re Darwen and Pearce* [1927] 1 Ch. 176.
[58] E.g. *General Property Investment Co. Ltd. and Liquidator* v. *Craig* (1890) 18 R. 389.
[59] *Per* Lord Watson in *Trevor* v. *Whitworth* (1887) 12 App.Cas. 409 at p. 429.
[60] *Ante* p. 244.
[61] *Per* Lord M'Laren in *Gill* v. *Arizona Copper Co. Ltd.* (1900) 2 F. 843 at p. 860.
[62] This case followed *Teasdale's Case* (1873) L.R. 9 Ch.App. 54 and *Eichbaum* v. *City of Chicago Grain Elevators Ltd.* [1891] 3 Ch. 459, in spite of the disapproval of the latter case expressed by the Court of Appeal in *Bellerby's* case (referred to in the text).

On the other hand, a surrender of partly paid shares, not liable to forfeiture, is unlawful, as it (*a*) releases the shareholder from further liability in respect of the shares, (*b*) amounts to a purchase by the company of its own shares, and (*c*) is a reduction of capital without the sanction of the court.

A company sustained a loss of £4,000 and the directors agreed to share the loss between themselves. They therefore surrendered shares to the amount of £4,000. The shares were £11 each, £10 paid, and the intention was that the directors should be released from the remaining £1 a share unpaid. The company subsequently became more prosperous and the directors took proceedings to have the surrender declared invalid. *Held*, the surrender was invalid as amounting to a purchase by the company of its own shares: *Bellerby* v. *Rowland & Marwood, Steamship Co. Ltd.* [1902] 2 Ch. 14 (C.A.).

Shares which have been validly surrendered can be reissued in the same way as forfeited shares, if the articles authorise their reissue.

SHARE WARRANT

A share warrant is a document issued by a company under its common seal stating that the bearer of the warrant is entitled to the shares specified therein: section 83.

Before share warrants can be issued the following conditions must be satisfied:

(1) The company must be a public company and limited by shares.
(2) There must be authority in the articles. (Table A does not authorise the issue of share warrants.)
(3) The shares must be fully paid up: section 83.
(4) Treasury consent is necessary.[63]

A share warrant must be stamped with a duty of three per cent., three times the usual rate.[64]

In the case of a private company, an article authorising the issue of share warrants, the shares specified in which could be transferred by delivery of the warrants, would be contrary to the essential restriction on the transfer of shares.

When the issue of share warrants is authorised the articles

---

[63] Exchange Control Act 1947, Pt. III, although, subject to exceptions, a general consent has been given: Bank of England Notice E.C. Securities 10 (3rd Issue).
[64] Stamp Act 1891, s. 1, Sched. 1; Finance Act 1963, s. 59.

usually provide for such matters as the deposit of the share warrant with the company a certain number of days before any right is exercised, and for the giving of notices of meetings by advertisement.

On issuing a share warrant, the company must strike out of its register of members the name of the holder of the shares as if he had ceased to be a member and make the following entries in the register:

(1) The fact of the issue of the warrant.

(2) A statement of the shares included in the warrant, distinguishing each share by its number, so long as the share has a number.

(3) The date of issue of the warrant: section 112 (1).

The bearer of a share warrant may, however, if the articles so provide, be deemed to be a member of the company either to the full extent or for any purposes defined in the articles: section 112 (5).

A share warrant can, subject to the articles, be surrendered for cancellation, whereupon the holder is entitled to be entered in the register of members: section 112 (2).

Stock warrants to bearer can be issued on the same terms as share warrants.[65]

When share warrants are issued, the annual return[66] must show—

(1) the total amount of shares for which share warrants are outstanding at the date of the return;

(2) the total amount of share warrants issued and surrendered respectively since the last return;

(3) the number of shares comprised in each warrant: Schedule 6, Part I, paragraph 3 (*j*).

A share warrant differs from a share certificate[67] in the following respects:

(1) The bearer of a warrant is not entered in a register: section 112.

(2) He is entitled to the shares specified in the warrant: section 83.

(3) The shares are transferable by delivery of the warrant: section 83.

---

[65] *Pilkington* v. *United Railways of Havana* [1930] 2 Ch. 108.
[66] *Ante* p. 208.   [67] *Ante* p. 245.

(4) A warrant is a negotiable instrument and if it is stolen and afterwards gets into the hands of a bona fide purchaser for value without notice of the fraud, he can enforce against the company payment of coupons for dividends due in respect of such share warrant.[68]

(5) Coupons for dividends may be attached to a warrant: section 83.

Dividends are advertised, and then collected upon the handing over of the appropriate coupon. This procedure is necessary because the company does not know to whom to send the dividend.

(6) Holding a share warrant is not enough where the articles require a director to hold a specified share qualification: section 182 (2).[69]

(7) A warrant held in the United Kingdom or held on behalf of a U.K. resident must be deposited with an authorised depositary, such as a member of a stock exchange or a solicitor.[70] The idea is to prevent currency being smuggled out of the country.

Share warrants are not very common. This is because they cannot be issued without Treasury consent and they must be deposited with an authorised depositary, because of the serious consequences of loss or theft, and also because of the heavy stamp duty. Another reason is that the company has to advertise in newspapers to get in touch with the shareholders.

Section 85 makes special provision for certain offences in connection with share warrants in Scotland.

[68] *Webb, Hale & Co.* v. *Alexandria Water Co. Ltd.* (1905) 93 L.T. 339.
[69] *Post* p. 318.
[70] Exchange Control Act 1947, Part III.

CHAPTER 13

GENERAL MEETINGS

THIS chapter is concerned with general meetings, *i.e.* meetings of the members or shareholders of a company and certain other persons (the auditors, the personal representatives of a deceased member and the trustee in bankruptcy of a bankrupt member). The various kinds of general meeting are dealt with first and it will be seen that the Act requires that certain meetings, *e.g.* an annual general meeting and, in the case of some companies, the statutory meeting, are held and allows other meetings, called extraordinary general meetings, to be held, usually when the directors think fit. Then the notice that the members must be given of general meetings is explained. Thirdly, proceedings at general meetings are dealt with—how many members must be present to constitute a meeting and enable it to transact business, who takes the chair, how a vote is taken and so on. Finally, the various kinds of resolution that may be passed at a meeting are explained.

If a company has more than one class of shares, class meetings, *i.e.* meetings of the holders of the shares of a certain class, may be held. Some of the sections referred to below, *e.g.* section 136 with regard to proxies, also apply to meetings of any class of members of a company as they apply to general meetings of the company. Table A, article 4, provides that the provisions of Table A relating to general meetings apply to class meetings except that a quorum shall be two persons at least holding or representing by proxy one-third of the issued shares of the class and that any holder of shares of the class present in person or by proxy may demand a poll.

KINDS OF GENERAL MEETING

Statutory meeting

Section 130 provides that every *public* limited company with a share capital must hold a general meeting of the members of the company, to be called "the statutory meeting," not less than one month and not more than three months from the date at which it is entitled to commence business.[1]

At least 14 days before this meeting is held the directors must send a report, called "the statutory report," to every member. This report must state the following matters:

(1) The number of shares allotted, the extent to which they are paid up, and the consideration for allotment.
(2) The cash received in respect of the shares allotted.
(3) An abstract of the receipts and payments of the company, the balance in hand, and the estimated amount of the preliminary expenses.
(4) The names, addresses and descriptions of the directors, auditors, managers and secretary.
(5) Particulars of any contract the modification of which is to be submitted to the statutory meeting for approval, with particulars of the proposed modification.

The number of shares allotted, the cash received in respect of them, and the receipts and payments on capital account must be certified by the auditors. The report must be certified by two directors.

A copy of the statutory report must be delivered to the Registrar of Companies.

A list of members, showing the number of shares held by them respectively, must be produced at the meeting.

Section 42 provides that the company must not, before the statutory meeting, vary the terms of a contract referred to in the prospectus or statement in lieu of prospectus, except subject to the approval of the statutory meeting.

The object of the statutory report and meeting is to furnish the shareholders with full information as to the results of the formation of the company and an opportunity of discussing those results before the company has embarked on trading to any appreciable extent. Section 130 (7) provides that the members present at the meeting may discuss any matter relating to the formation of the company or arising out of the statutory report, whether previous notice has been given or not, but that no resolution of which notice has not been given in accordance with the articles may be passed.

It will be seen[2] that default in delivering the report to the Registrar

---

[1] *Ante* p. 182.　　　　　　　　　　[2] *Post* p. 540.

or in holding the meeting is a ground on which the company may be wound up by the court. However, since companies are usually formed as private companies, statutory meetings are rarely held[3] and statutory reports rarely sent. Accordingly, the Jenkins Report[4] recommended that section 130 should be repealed and clause 77 (1) of the Companies Bill 1973 would have given effect to that recommendation.

Annual general meeting

By section 131 the general rule is that every company must hold an annual general meeting, specified as such in the notice calling it, every year, with an interval of not more than 15 months between one annual general meeting of the company and the next. The word "year" means calendar year, *i.e.* the period January 1 to December 31.[5] A limited exception is that as long as a company holds its first annual general meeting within 18 months of incorporation it need not hold it in the year of incorporation or, sometimes, in the following year, *e.g.* a company incorporated on October 1, 1977, might hold its first annual general meeting in March 1977.

The directors must call the annual general meeting (see Table A, article 80). The object of section 131 is to ensure that those members who wish to do so can meet together and confront the directors at least once a year. Table A, article 52, provides in effect that the business at an annual general meeting is—

(1) the declaration of a dividend, the consideration of the accounts, balance sheets and the reports of the directors and auditors, the election of directors in place of those retiring, and the appointment of, and the fixing of the remuneration of, the auditors;

(2) special business, *i.e.* any other business.

If default is made in holding an annual general meeting, the Department of Trade may, on the application of any member of the company, call or direct the calling of a meeting and give such ancillary directions as the Department thinks expedient, including a direction that one member present in person or by proxy shall be deemed to constitute the meeting: section 131.

[3] *Ante* p. 54.
[4] Para. 67.
[5] *Gibson* v. *Barton* (1875) L.R. 10 Q.B. 329.

The Jenkins Report[6] recommended that the Board of Trade[7] be empowered to extend the period within which a company is required to hold its annual general meeting. The idea is to assist companies endeavouring to avoid being in default, *e.g.* because no quorum is available.

Extraordinary general meetings

Any general meeting of a company, other than an annual general meeting, is an extraordinary general meeting. Table A, article 48, so provides and article 49 provides that the directors *may*, whenever they think fit, convene an extraordinary general meeting.

Further, by section 132, despite anything in the articles, the directors are *bound* to convene an extraordinary general meeting on the requisition of the holders of not less than one-tenth of the paid-up capital of the company carrying the right of voting at general meetings or, if the company has no share capital, of members representing not less than one-tenth of the total voting rights. The requisition must state the objects of the meeting and be signed by the requisitionists. If the directors do not, within 21 days of the deposit of the requisition at the registered office of the company, proceed to convene the meeting, the requisitionists, or the holders of more than half their voting rights, may convene it themselves so long as it is held within three months after such deposit.[8] The reasonable expenses of the requisitionists in convening the meeting must be repaid by the company, which must retain them out of any remuneration of the directors in default.

The business at an extraordinary general meeting is special business (Table A, article 52).

The Jenkins Report[9] recommended that section 132 be amended to enable the requisitionists to convene a meeting if the directors do not do so for a date not later than 28 days after the notice convening the meeting. At present directors may defeat the purposes of the section by calling an extraordinary requisition meeting for a date, say, six months ahead. Clause 77 (2) of the Companies Bill 1973 would have given effect to the recommendation.

[6] Para. 468.   [7] Department of Trade now.
[8] This right may be abrogated if the requisionists are themselves directors who have, by failing to attend board meetings, been the cause of the directors' default: *Thyne* v. *Lauder*, 1925 S.N. 123 (O.H.).
[9] Para. 468.

By section 135, if for any reason it is impracticable to call a meeting in any manner in which meetings may be called, or to conduct a meeting in the manner prescribed by the articles or the Act, the court may, either of its own motion or on application by any director or any member entitled to vote at the meeting, order a meeting to be called, held and conducted in such manner as the court thinks fit, and may give such ancillary directions as it thinks expedient, including a direction that one member present in person or by proxy shall be deemed to constitute the meeting.

E. Ltd. had three members, A, B and C. A and B were directors and held five per cent. of the shares each. C, who was not a director, held 90 per cent. of the shares. No general meetings were held. The articles provided that a quorum at a meeting should be two members. A and B frustrated C's efforts to call a meeting under section 132 by refusing to attend. C gave special notice of his intention to move ordinary resolutions to remove the directors at the next extraordinary general meeting, and asked the court to call a meeting under section 135 and to direct that one member should be a quorum. C's application was opposed by the directors. *Held*, the application should be granted because (1) otherwise C would be deprived of his right to remove the directors under section 184; (2) the directors were in breach of their statutory duty by not holding an annual general meeting: *Re El Sombrero Ltd.* [1958] Ch. 900.[10]

The Jenkins Report[11] recommended that section 135 should be amended so that personal representatives of deceased members should be treated, for the purposes of the section, as members of the company, *i.e.* able to apply under the section, and as having the same voting rights as the dead members would have had. This would enable the company to appoint directors when all directors and shareholders have died. Clause 76 (1) and (2) of the Companies Bill 1973 would have given effect to the recommendation.

NOTICE OF GENERAL MEETINGS

Length of notice for calling meetings

The effect of section 133 is that notwithstanding a provision in the articles providing for shorter notice:

(1) An annual general meeting must be called by not less than 21 days' written notice.

(2) Any other general meeting of a limited company must be

---

[10] For a Scottish instance, see *Edinburgh Workmen's Houses Improvement Co. Ltd., Petitioners*, 1935 S.C. 56.
[11] Para. 31.

called by not less than 14 days' written notice, unless a special resolution is to be proposed, in which case, by section 141, not less than 21 days' such notice is required.

Table A, article 50, provides that the notice shall be clear notice, *i.e.* exclusive of the day on which it is served or deemed to be served and of the day for which it is given.[12]

A meeting may be called by shorter notice than that specified above or in the articles if that is agreed to by—(1) all the members entitled to attend and vote in the case of an annual general meeting; (2) a majority in number of the members holding not less than 95 per cent. of the shares giving the right to attend and vote or, in the case of a company without a share capital, representing not less than 95 per cent. of the total voting rights, in the case of any other meeting: sections 133 (3); 141 (2). Such agreement is likely to be obtained only in the case of a company with few members.

Clause 86 of the Companies Bill 1973 would have required a minimum notice of at least 7 days' notice of a special resolution for voluntary winding up except where a declaration of solvency has been delivered to the Registrar.

If a resolution is to be passed on short notice, it must be appreciated that the resolution is being so passed.[13]

Sections 133 (3) and 141 (2) are derived from cases like *Re Express Engineering Works Ltd.*[14] and *Re Oxted Motor Co. Ltd.*[15] which established that it is competent to all the shareholders to waive all formalities as regards notice of meetings, etc.

In the *Express Engineering* case five persons formed a private company in which they were the sole shareholders. They sold to the company for £15,000 a property which they had just bought for £7,000. The price was to be paid by the issue of debentures for £15,000 by the company. The transaction was carried out at a "board" meeting of the five individuals who appointed themselves the directors. The articles forbade a director to vote in respect of a contract in which he was interested. It was held that there was no fraud and the company was bound in the matter by the unanimous agreement of the members. Consequently the debentures were valid.

In the *Oxted Motor* case both the members of a company waived the normal length of notice of a meeting at which an extraordinary resolution for voluntary winding up was validly passed.

[12] In Scotland articles may be so worded as not to require *clear* notice, *e.g.* a provision that "days shall be reckoned, excluding the first and including the last of such days," allows the day of the meeting to be counted: *The Aberdeen Comb Works Co. Ltd., Petitioners* (1902) 10 S.L.T. 210.
[13] *Re Pearce Duff & Co. Ltd.* [1960] 1 W.L.R. 1014.
[14] [1920] 1 Ch. 466 (C.A.), followed in the Victorian case of *E. H. Dey Pty. Ltd.* v. *Dey* [1966] V.R. 464.
[15] [1921] 3 K.B. 32.

The *Express Engineering* case and the *Parker & Cooper* case below were applied in *Re Bailey, Hay & Co. Ltd.*[16] where short notice was given of a meeting to pass an extraordinary resolution for voluntary winding up but all five corporators attended and the resolution was passed by the votes of two shareholders, the other shareholders abstaining from voting. The resolution was deemed to have been passed with the unanimous agreement of all the corporators and those who abstained were treated as having acquiesced in the winding-up.

Cases such as *Parker & Cooper Ltd.* v. *Reading*[17] have gone further than the *Express Engineering* and *Oxted Motor* cases. It was decided in *Parker & Cooper* that if all the members assent to a transaction *intra vires* the company, although beyond the powers of the board, the company is bound and it is not necessary that they should hold a meeting in one room or one place to express that assent simultaneously.

In *Parker & Cooper* there was no actual meeting but the members individually and at different times informally ratified a debenture granted by the directors which, although *intra vires* the company, was beyond the powers of the directors because two directors had been invalidly appointed.

Parker & Cooper was applied in *Re Duomatic Ltd.*[18] in which it was held that when it can be shown that all shareholders who have a right to attend and vote at a general meeting of the company assent to some matter which a general meeting of the company could carry into effect, that assent is as binding as a resolution in general meeting

Despite the *Oxted Motor* and *Bailey, Hay* cases, the words "passed . . . at a general meeting" in the definitions of a special resolution and of an extraordinary resolution in section 141[19] might be thought to suggest that such resolutions can only be passed at a meeting. However, section 143 (4) (*c*)[20] appears to contemplate the contrary so long as all the members have agreed to the resolution —it provides for the registration of a copy of a resolution agreed to by all the members of a company which would otherwise not be effective unless passed as a special or as an extraordinary resolution as the case may be. And in the Victorian case of *Re Meyer Douglas Pty. Ltd.*[21] Gowans J. accepted the principle that even a special resolution is merely machinery for securing the assent of members. Further, in the case of a private company, Table A, Part II, article 5,

[16] [1971] 1 W.L.R. 1357.
[17] [1926] Ch. 975, doubted in the Victorian case of *Re Meyer Douglas Pty. Ltd.* [1965] V.R. 638.
[18] [1969] 2 Ch. 365.
[19] *Post* p. 305.
[20] *Post* p. 308.
[21] [1965] V.R. 638.

provides that, subject to the provisions of the Act, a written resolution signed by all the members entitled to attend and vote at general meetings shall be as valid and effective as if passed at a general meeting of the company duly convened and held. The Jenkins Report[22] recommended that the Act should expressly provide that in the case of any company such a resolution shall be equivalent to an ordinary or a special resolution duly passed at a general meeting and clause 77 (5) of the Companies Bill 1973 would have given effect to the recommendation.

Service of notice of meetings

Section 134 of the 1948 Act provides that, unless the articles provide to the contrary, notice of the meeting of a company is to be served on every member of the company as required by Table A. Section 14 of the 1967 Act requires that notice of every general meeting be given to the auditors.

Table A provides in effect:

Article 131.—Notice may be given to any member either personally or by sending it by post to his registered address or, if he has no registered address within the United Kingdom, to the address within the United Kingdom supplied by him to the company for the giving of notice to him.

Where notice is sent by post, service is deemed to be effected by properly addressing, prepaying and posting a letter containing the notice, and to have been effected, in the case of notice of a meeting, at the expiration of 24 hours after posting, and, in other cases, at the time when the letter would be delivered in ordinary course of post.

Article 132.—Notice to joint holders of a share is given to the joint holder first named in the register of members.

Article 133.—On the death or bankruptcy of a member, notice is given to the personal representatives or the trustee in bankruptcy at the address within the United Kingdom supplied for the purpose.

Article 134.—Notice must be given to—

(1) every member except members who (having no registered address within the United Kingdom) have not supplied an address within the United Kingdom for the giving of notices to them;
(2) the personal representative or the trustee in bankruptcy of a member who, but for his death or bankruptcy, would be entitled to notice;
(3) the auditor.

No other person is entitled to notice of a general meeting.

Clause 73(1) of the Companies Bill 1973 provided that notice of every general meeting of a company shall be served on every member of the company and every person on whom the ownership of a share devolves by reason of his being a personal representative or a trustee in bankruptcy of a member.

[22] Para. 468.

If notice of a meeting is not given to every person entitled to notice, any resolution passed at the meeting will be of no effect.

A committee of a club met and passed a resolution expelling Y from the club. X, a member of the committee, was not summoned to the meeting, as she had previously informed the chairman that she would be unable to attend meetings. *Held*, the omission to summon X invalidated the proceedings of the committee: *Young* v. *Ladies' Imperial Club Ltd.* [1920] 2 K.B. 523 (C.A.).

To obviate this result it is usually provided in the articles, as in Table A, article 51, that the accidental omission to give notice to, or the non-receipt of notice by, any person entitled to receive notice shall not invalidate the proceedings at that meeting.

In *Re West Canadian Collieries Ltd.* [1962] Ch. 370, the omission to give notice of a meeting to a few members, because the plates for these members were inadvertently kept out of the machine when the envelopes for the notices were being addressographed, was an accidental omission within an article like Table A, article 51.

However, in *Musselwhite* v. *C. H. Musselwhite & Son Ltd.* [1962] Ch. 964,[23] the omission to give notice of a general meeting to the unpaid vendors of shares who remained on the register of members, because the directors erroneously believed the vendors were no longer members, was due to an error of law and was not an accidental omission within such an article.

If the 1973 Bill had become law, Clause 73(4) would have resulted, there being a section of the Act to the same effect as Table A, article 51.

Nature of notice of meetings

The articles of a company will contain provisions dealing with the nature of the notice to be given of meetings. Table A, article 50, provides that the notice of a meeting shall state the place, date and hour of the meeting and, in the case of special business, the general nature of that business.

Notice of an annual general meeting was in common form and included in the business was "to elect directors." C., the retiring director, offered himself for re-election, but was not elected. A motion was proposed for the election of three new directors to fill up the places of the retiring director and two vacancies, but the chairman refused to accept it. *Held*, the refusal was wrong, as the notice sufficiently specified the general nature of the special business to bring it within the competence of the meeting to elect directors up to the number permitted by the articles: *Choppington Collieries Ltd.* v. *Johnson* [1944] 1 All E.R. 762 (C.A.).

Notice of special business must "state the resolution to be passed in such a way as fairly to state the purpose for which the meeting is convened, so that every shareholder may make up his mind whether he will or will not attend, with knowledge of the result of his act."[24]

[23] *Ante* p. 262.   [24] Stiebel's *Company Law*, 3rd ed., p. 335.

Directors of a holding company had from 1907 to 1914 been receiving remuneration as directors of a subsidiary company without the knowledge of the shareholders of the holding company. Special resolutions, authorising the directors to retain the remuneration and altering the articles to allow the directors to receive remuneration as directors of subsidiary companies, were proposed and an extraordinary general meeting summoned to pass them. The notice did not specify the amount of the remuneration, which was £44,876. The resolution was passed. A shareholder brought an action on behalf of himself and all other shareholders of the company against the company and its directors claiming, *inter alia*, a declaration that the resolution was not binding upon the company. *Held*, the resolution was not binding as the notice was insufficient: *Baillie* v. *Oriental Telephone etc. Co. Ltd.* [1915] 1 Ch. 503 (C.A.).

A notice convening a meeting stated that it was being held for receiving the directors' report, and the election of directors and auditors. The directors' report sent therewith stated that the meeting would be asked to confirm the appointment of R. as director. *Held*, the notice and the report together were sufficient notice of this special business: *Boschoek Proprietary Co. Ltd.* v. *Fuke* [1906] 1 Ch. 148.

The notice of a general meeting at which a special resolution or an extraordinary resolution is to be proposed must specify the intention to propose the resolution as a special resolution or an extraordinary resolution[25] as the case might be: section 141. It appears that the *exact wording* of the resolution to be proposed must be set out in the notice.[26]

Where a meeting has been requisitioned under section 132, *ante*,[27] it may competently deal with business additional to that specified in the requisition, provided adequate notice of the additional business has been duly given.[28]

Every notice calling a meeting of a company with a share capital must contain a statement, given reasonable prominence, that a member entitled to attend and vote may appoint a proxy to attend and vote instead of him, and that the proxy need not be a member of the company: section 136.

Clause 74 of the Companies Bill 1973 would have required notices of resolutions to contain an explanation of their effect and particulars of material interests of any director or member of his family.

[25] Strictly interpreted in *Rennie* v. *Crichton's* (*Strichen*) *Ltd.*, 1927 S.L.T. 459 (O.H.), in which a notice of a resolution for voluntary winding up was held invalid because it did not specify the intention to propose the resolution *as an extraordinary resolution*; for *obiter dicta* to the contrary see *North of Scotland etc. Steam Navigation Co. Ltd., Petitioners*, 1920 S.C. 94.

[26] *MacConnell* v. *E. Prill & Co. Ltd.* [1916] 2 Ch. 57.

[27] p. 287.

[28] *Per* Lord Hill Watson (Ordinary, in *Ball* v. *Metal Industries Ltd.*, 1957 S.C. 315 (O.H.) at p. 316.

Notice of members' resolutions and statements

If some of the members of a company themselves wish to move a resolution at an *annual general meeting*, or to circulate to members a statement relating to any proposed resolution or the business to be dealt with at *any general meeting*, they can do so under section 140. The section provides that on the written requisition of members holding not less than one-twentieth of the voting rights of the members entitled to vote at the relevant meeting, or of one hundred members on whose shares there has been paid up an average sum of not less than £100 a member, the company must—

(1) give notice to every member entitled to receive notice of the annual general meeting of any resolution which may properly be moved and is intended to be moved at that meeting;

(2) circulate to every member entitled to receive notice of any general meeting any statement, of not more than 1,000 words, relating to any proposed resolution or the business to be dealt with at the meeting.

The notice of the resolution must be given, and any statement must be circulated, with the notice of the meeting or, if that is impracticable, as soon as possible afterwards. The company is not bound to circulate a *statement* if, on the application of the company or any aggrieved person, the court is satisfied that the rights given by the section are being abused to secure needless publicity for defamatory matter.

The requisition must be signed by the requisitionists and deposited at the registered office (1) at least six weeks before the meeting when notice of a resolution is required; (2) at least one week before the meeting in any other case. A sum to cover the company's expenses must also be deposited (although at the meeting it may be resolved that the expenses shall be borne by the company, in which case the deposit will be returned).

If the directors call an annual general meeting for a date six weeks or less after deposit of the requisition, the requisition is deemed to have been properly deposited.

Special notice

Section 142 provides that where under the Act special notice is required of a resolution, notice of the intention to move it must be given *to the company* not less than 28 days before the meeting at which it is to be moved, *and* the company must give notice of the resolution *to the members* when it gives them notice of the meeting (or, if that is not practicable, either by advertisement in a newspaper having an appropriate circulation or in any other mode allowed by the articles, not less than 21 days before the meeting). To close a loophole which would otherwise allow directors to avoid the provision by claiming that the notice had not been given in time, the section also provides that if the directors call a meeting for a date 28 days or less after the notice has been given to the company, the notice is deemed to have been properly given. The notice to the company may be left at or sent by post to the registered office: section 437.[29]

Special notice is only required by sections 184 and 185 of the 1948 Act (removal of directors and appointment of a director who has attained the age of 70 respectively) and section 15 of the 1976 Act (appointment and removal of auditors).

PROCEEDINGS AT GENERAL MEETINGS

Quorum

Under Table A, Part I, article 53, no business is to be transacted at a general meeting unless a quorum of members is present when the meeting proceeds to business. In England this article has been held to be satisfied if the quorum is present at the beginning of the meeting,[30] but in Scotland there is authority to the contrary.[31]

The quorum must be an effective quorum, *i.e.* it must consist of members qualified to take part in and decide upon questions before the meeting,[32] and where articles require a quorum of members to be "present" (without any such addition as "personally or by proxy") that word means "present in person."[33]

---

[29] *Ante* p. 72.
[30] *Re Hartley Baird Ltd.* [1955] Ch. 143, distinguished in *Re London Flats Ltd.* [1969] 1 W.L.R. 711.　　[31] *Henderson* v. *Louttit & Co. Ltd.* (1894) 21 R. 674.
[32] *Henderson's* case, above, *per* Lord President Robertson at p. 676.
[33] *M. Harris Ltd., Petitioners*, 1956 S.C. 207, in which a member represented by an attorney was held not be to be "present."

By section 134, unless the articles otherwise provide, a quorum is three members present in person for a public company and two such members for a private company. Table A, Part I, article 53, fixes three members present in person as a quorum in the case of a public company. Although proxies cannot be counted for this purpose, one individual may count as more than one member if he attends the meeting in more than one capacity, *e.g.* as a member holding shares in his own right and as a member entitled to vote in person in respect of a trust holding.[34] Table A, Part II, article 4, fixes two members present in person *or by proxy* in the case of a private company. As to a quorum at a class meeting, see Table A. Part I, article 4, *ante*.[35]

Strictly, since the word "meeting" prima facie means a coming together of more than one person, one person cannot constitute a meeting,[36] even where he attends in more than one capacity or holds proxies for other persons.[37] However, in *East* v. *Bennett Bros. Ltd.*[38] it was held that one member, who held all the shares of a class, constituted a class meeting. Further, under sections 131[39] and 135,[40] the Department of Trade and the court, respectively, may direct that one member shall be deemed to constitute a meeting.

If a quorum is not present within half an hour of the time appointed for the meeting, Table A, article 54, provides that the meeting, if convened upon the requisition of members, shall be dissolved, but in any other case it shall stand adjourned to the same day in the next week at the same time and place, or to such other day and at such other time and place as the directors may determine, and if at the adjourned meeting a quorum is not present within half an hour, the members present shall form a quorum. It is thought that a single member can constitute a quorum at an adjourned meeting.[41]

---

[34] *Neil M'Leod & Sons Ltd., Petitioners*, 1967 S.C. 16.
[35] p. 284.
[36] *Sharp* v. *Dawes* (1876) 2 Q.B.D. 26 (C.A.), applied in *Re London Flats*, above.
[37] *James Prain & Sons Ltd., Petitioners*, 1947 S.C. 325.
[38] [1911] 1 Ch. 163.
[39] *Ante* p. 286.
[40] *Ante* p. 288.
[41] See *Jarvis Motors (Harrow) Ltd.* v. *Carabott* [1964] 1 W.L.R. 1101, *ante* p. 249, where it was held that the Interpretation Act 1889, s. 1 (1), applied to the articles so that words in the plural included words in the singular and "members" included sole surviving member.

Chairman

Section 134 provides that, unless the articles otherwise provide, the members present at a meeting may elect any member as a chairman. However, the articles usually provide who is to be chairman. Table A, article 55, states that the chairman of the board of directors shall preside at every general meeting of the company, or if there is no such chairman, or if he is not present within 15 minutes after the time appointed for the meeting or is unwilling to act, the directors present shall elect one of themselves to be chairman. Article 56 provides that if no director is willing to act as chairman or if no director is present within 15 minutes, the members present may elect one of their number to be chairman of the meeting.

It is the duty of the chairman:

(1) To preserve order.
(2) To see that the proceedings are regularly conducted.
(3) To take care that the sense of the meeting is properly ascertained with regard to any question properly before it.[42]
(4) To decide incidental questions arising for decision during the meeting, *e.g.* whether proxies are valid.[43]

He must allow the minority of the shareholders to have a reasonable time to put forward their arguments, but at the expiration of that time he is entitled, if he thinks fit, to put a motion to the meeting that the discussion be terminated.[44]

The chairman has no casting vote unless expressly given one by the articles.[45] Table A, article 60, gives him a casting vote.

Adjournment

A chairman cannot adjourn a meeting at his own will, except in case of disorder. If, in any other case, he purports to do so, the meeting may elect another chairman and proceed with the business.[42]

The chairman is not bound to adjourn a meeting, even if the majority desire him to do so,[46] unless the articles otherwise provide.

---

[42] *National Dwellings Society* v. *Sykes* [1894] 3 Ch. 159.
[43] *Post* p. 303.
[44] *Wall* v. *London and Northern Assets Corporation* [1898] 2 Ch. 469 (C.A.).
[45] *Nell* v. *Longbottom* [1894] 1 Q.B. 767.
[46] *Salisbury Gold Mining Co. Ltd.* v. *Hathorn* [1897] A.C. 268.

Table A, article 57, provides: "The chairman may, with the consent of any meeting at which a quorum is present (and shall if so directed by the meeting), adjourn the meeting from time to time and from place to place, but no business shall be transacted at any adjourned meeting other than the business left unfinished at the meeting from which the adjournment took place. When a meeting is adjourned for thirty days or more, notice of the adjourned meeting shall be given as in the case of an original meeting. Save as aforesaid it shall not be necessary to give any notice of an adjournment or of the business to be transacted at an adjourned meeting."

Conduct of a meeting

Subject to the provisions of the Companies Acts and the articles, the way in which the business at a meeting is to be conducted is decided by the meeting itself.

"There are many matters relating to the conduct of a meeting which lie entirely in the hands of those persons who are present and constitute the meeting. Thus it rests with the meeting to decide whether notices, resolutions, minutes, accounts, and such like shall be read to the meeting or be taken as read; whether representatives of the Press, or any other persons not qualified to be summoned to the meeting, shall be permitted to be present, or if present shall be permitted to remain; whether and when discussion shall be terminated and a vote taken; whether the meeting shall be adjourned. In all these matters, and they are only instances, the meeting decides, and if necessary a vote must be taken to ascertain the wishes of the majority. If no objection is taken by any constituent of the meeting, the meeting must be taken to be assenting to the course adopted": *per* Lord Russell of Killowen in *Carruth* v. *I.C.I. Ltd.* [1937] A.C. 707,[47] at p. 761.

Voting

1. *A show of hands*

The common law rule is that, unless the articles otherwise provide, a resolution put to a meeting is normally decided in the first instance by a show of hands.[48] Further, on a show of hands each member entitled to vote and present in person has one vote only, *i.e.* proxies[49] are not counted. In practice articles do not provide otherwise, *e.g.* Table A, article 58, below, provides that a vote shall be by a show of hands unless a poll is demanded and article 62 provides that subject to any rights or restrictions attached to any class of shares,[50] every member present in person shall have one vote on a show of hands, *i.e.* proxies cannot vote.

[47] *Ante* p. 240.
[48] *Re Horbury Bridge Coal Co.* (1879) 11 Ch.D. 109 (C.A.).
[49] *Post* p. 301.
[50] *Ante* p. 217.

Table A further provides, in effect:

Article 63.—In the case of joint holders, the vote of the holder whose name appears first in the register of members shall be accepted to the exclusion of the others.

Article 65.—No member shall be entitled to vote at any general meeting unless all calls or other sums presently payable by him in respect of shares in the company have been paid.

Article 66.—Objections to the qualification of a voter can only be raised at the meeting at which the vote is tendered. Objections are to be referred to the chairman and his decision is to be final.

In *Marx* v. *Estates & General Investments Ltd.* [1976] 1 W.L.R. 380, Brightman J. said that there is much to be said for an article like article 66. In that case a proxy form, which was liable to stamp duty because it authorised a proxy to vote at more than one meeting but which was unstamped, was not void but a valid authority capable of being stamped, and since the company had accepted it without objection at the meeting the votes cast by the proxy were valid. Further, by virtue of article 66 the objection taken several days after the meeting was made too late.

A bankrupt shareholder may vote if he is still on the register.[51]

A shareholder, even if he is a director, can vote although he has an interest in the question to be voted on, provided that the majority of the members do not unfairly oppress the minority.[52]

"The shareholder's vote is a right of property, and prima facie may be exercised by a shareholder as he thinks fit in his own interest": *per* Lord Maugham in *Carruth* v. *I.C.I. Ltd.* [1937] A.C. 707, at p. 765.

Table A, article 58, provides that, unless a poll is demanded, a declaration by the chairman that a resolution has on a show of hands been carried, or carried by a particular majority, or lost, and an entry to that effect in the minutes, is conclusive evidence of the fact without proof of the number or proportion of the votes recorded for or against.[53] See also section 141 (3), *post*.[54]

2. *A poll*

Although a show of hands can be taken quickly, it is not an accurate method of ascertaining the wishes of the members of a

---

[51] *Morgan* v. *Gray* [1953] Ch. 83, *ante* p. 190.   [52] *Post* p. 378.
[53] Where a show of hands has been taken and the minutes record the passing of the resolution but omit any mention of the show of hands, further evidence may be required to establish the validity of the procedure: *Fraserburgh Commercial Co. Ltd., Petitioners*, 1946 S.C. 444.
[54] p. 307.

company because the votes of those voting by proxy are not counted. Again, it does not pay due regard to the wishes of a member holding a large number of shares since he has only one vote on a show of hands. Consequently, although the right to demand a poll exists at common law,[55] section 141 (3) and (4) give a statutory right to demand a poll in the case of a special resolution or an extraordinary resolution and articles always make provision for taking a poll. The effect of Table A, article 58, is that a poll may be demanded before, or on the declaration of the result of, a show of hands, *i.e.* it is not necessary to have a show of hands before a poll is taken.[56] A proper demand for a poll does away with the need for, or the result of, a show of hands.

The number of votes which a member has on a poll depends upon the articles. Section 134 (e) states that unless the articles otherwise provide a member shall have one vote in respect of each share or each £10 of stock held by him, and articles 62 and 67 of Table A provide that, subject to any rights or restrictions attached to any class of shares, on a poll every member present in person or by proxy shall have one vote for each share of which he is the holder, *i.e.* proxies can be counted.

A poll is complete when the result is ascertained, not on an earlier day when the votes are cast.[57]

Section 137 provides that, on any question other than the election of the chairman or the adjournment of the meeting, any article is void in so far as it excludes the right to demand a poll or requires more persons to demand a poll than (*a*) five members entitled to vote at the meeting, or (*b*) members representing one-tenth of the voting rights, or (*c*) members holding one-tenth of the paid-up capital conferring a right to vote. Further, a proxy has the same right to demand a poll as the member he represents. If articles could require a considerable number of members to demand a poll the right would be worthless. It is essential that a proxy be able to demand a poll—he has no vote on a show of hands.

Table A, article 58, provides that in addition to the members in (*b*) or (*c*), *ante*, a poll may be demanded by the chairman or by three members present in person or by proxy, and that the demand for a poll may be withdrawn.

[55] *R.* v. *Wimbledon Local Board* (1882) 8 Q.B.D. 459 (C.A.).
[56] *Per* Jenkins L.J. in *Holmes* v. *Keyes* [1959] Ch. 199 (C.A.) at p. 212, although see *per* Lord Blanesburgh in *Carruth's* case, *ante*, at p. 755.
[57] *Holmes* v. *Keyes, post* p. 317.

The poll is taken as laid down in the articles. Table A, article 61, provides that a poll demanded on the election of a chairman or on a question of adjournment shall be taken forthwith. If demanded on any other question, it shall be taken at such time as the chairman directs. Where, under articles similar to Table A, a poll was demanded on a question of adjournment and taken, but the scrutineers informed the chairman that the result could not be announced within the time during which the meeting hall was available, it was held that the meeting subsequently convened to hear the result was a continuation of the original meeting, with the result that no proxies deposited between the date of the original meeting and the date of the continuation meeting were valid, as the articles required proxies to be deposited 48 hours before the meeting.[58]

On a poll, a member entitled to more than one vote need not cast all his votes or cast them all in the same way: section 138. This provision was introduced to meet the difficulties of a large trust corporation which might hold shares in a company on behalf of two or more different trusts, whose respective interests might well require different exercises of its votes.[59]

Proxies

Although there is no common law right to vote by proxy,[60] section 136 gives such a right.

The section contains the following provisions: Any member entitled to attend and vote at a company meeting may appoint another person, whether a member of the company or not, to attend and vote as his proxy, and if the company is a private company, to speak as his proxy—the Jenkins Report[61] recommended that a proxy be allowed to speak at a meeting of any company. Every notice calling a meeting must state this right of a member to appoint a proxy. Unless the articles otherwise provide, a proxy can only vote on a poll, a member of a private company cannot appoint more than one proxy to attend on the same occasion, and a member of a company without a share capital cannot appoint a proxy.

---

[58] *Jackson* v. *Hamlyn* [1953] Ch. 577, applying *Shaw* v. *Tati Concessions Ltd.* [1913] 1 Ch. 292.

[59] *Per* Walton J. in *Northern Counties Securities Ltd.* v. *Jackson & Steeple Ltd.* [1974] 1 W.L.R. 1133, at p. 1147.

[60] *Per* Lord Hanworth M.R. in *Cousins* v. *International Brick Co. Ltd.* [1931] 2 Ch. 90 (C.A.) at p. 100.

[61] Para. 468.

Articles cannot require the instrument appointing a proxy to be deposited with the company more than 48 hours before a meeting or an adjourned meeting. If articles could require the instrument to be deposited a considerable time before a meeting the right to appoint a proxy would be worthless.

Clause 75 of the Companies Bill 1973 (1) would have extended section 136 to a company not having a share capital, (2) would have enabled a proxy to speak at a meeting of any company, (3) would have enabled a member holding non-voting equity shares to appoint a proxy, and (4) would have empowered a member to appoint two proxies to attend on the same occasion to represent respectively such number of his shares as may be specified in their instruments of appointment.

A proxy is appointed by an instrument in writing in accordance with the articles. There are two forms of proxy in use—a general proxy appointing a person to vote as he thinks fit, having regard to what is said at the meeting, and a special proxy appointing a person to vote for or against a particular resolution. A special proxy is often called "a two-way proxy." The Stock Exchange requires two-way proxy forms to be sent to shareholders.[62]

The articles usually provide for the form and proof of proxies.

Table A contains the following provisions:

Article 67.—"On a poll votes may be given either personally or by proxy."

Article 68.—The instrument appointing a proxy must be in writing signed by the appointer; the proxy need not be a member.

Article 69.—The instrument must be deposited at the registered office at least 48 hours before the holding of the meeting or adjourned meeting—24 hours in the case of a poll—otherwise it is invalid.

Article 70.—Prescribes the form of a general proxy.

Article 71.—Prescribes the form of a special proxy.

Article 72.—The instrument appointing a proxy is deemed to confer authority to demand a poll.

Article 73.—A vote by proxy is valid notwithstanding the previous death or insanity[63] of the principal or revocation of the proxy, as long as no intimation in writing of such death, etc., has been received by the company at the registered office before the commencement of the meeting or adjourned meeting.

It has been held that directors acting bona fide in the interests of the company are entitled to send out to the shareholders proxy papers in favour of named directors at the expense of the company.[64] However, section 136 (4) provides that if invitations to appoint as proxy a person or one of a number of persons specified in the invitations are issued at the company's expense to some only of the members entitled to vote at a meeting, every officer of the company who knowingly and wilfully authorises or permits their issue is

---

[62] Admission of Securities to Listing, pp. 164, 171.
[63] The death or mental disorder of the principal revokes a proxy.
[64] *Peel* v. *L. & N.W. Rlwy. Co.* [1907] 1 Ch. 5 (C.A.).

liable to a fine of up to £100, although an officer is not liable by reason only of the issue to a member, at his written request, of a form of appointment naming the proxy or of a list of persons willing to act as proxy, if the form or list is available to every member entitled to vote. If this were not so the directors might send the proxy papers to friendly shareholders only. The Jenkins Report[65] recommended that proxy forms issued by a board of directors should permit the member to instruct his proxy to vote for or against (or to exercise his discretion in respect of) each resolution dealing with special business, and clause 75 (5) of the Companies Bill 1973 would have given effect to that recommendation.

It is the duty of the chairman to decide on the validity of proxies. If the articles provide, as does Table A, article 66, that votes tendered at a meeting and not disallowed shall be deemed to be valid, the court will not review the chairman's decision, even if it is wrong, in the absence of fraud or bad faith on his part.[66] Where articles do not incorporate Table A a mere misprint or some quite palpable mistake on the face of a proxy form does not entitle the company to refuse to accept the proxy.[67]

Where proxy forms were sent out to all the stockholders in a company and the chairman was named as their proxy, it was held that he was bound to demand a poll in order to ascertain the sense of the meeting, and bound to exercise all the proxies in accordance with the instructions which they contained.[68]

A shareholder who has given a proxy is free to attend the meeting and vote in person, in which case the vote tendered by the proxy may properly be rejected.[69] He does not thereby revoke the proxy and the proxy may, *e.g.*, vote on a second resolution on which the shareholder does not vote.[70]

A corporation, whether a company within the meaning of the Act or not, may, if it is a member of another corporation which is

---

[65] Para. 468.

[66] *Wall* v. *Exchange Investment Corporation* [1926] Ch. 143 (C.A.). And see *Marx* v. *Estates and General Investments Ltd.* [1976] 1 W.L.R. 380, *ante* p. 299.

[67] *Oliver* v. *Dalgleish* [1963] 1 W.L.R. 1274, where the proxies referred to the "annual general meeting" instead of to the "extraordinary general meeting" and there was no other meeting which could be confused with that the date of which was stated in the proxies.

[68] *Second Consolidated Trust Ltd.* v. *Ceylon, etc. Rubber Estates Ltd.* [1943] 2 All E.R. 567.

[69] *Cousins* v. *International Brick Co. Ltd.*, *ante*, where the proxy had not been revoked under Table A, art. 73, above.

[70] *Ansett* v. *Butler Air Transport Ltd.* (*No. 2*) (1958) 75 W.N.(N.S.W.) 306.

such a company, by resolution of its directors or other governing body authorise such person as it thinks fit to act as its representative at any meeting of the company or of any class of members of the company. The representative is entitled to exercise on behalf of the corporation the powers which the corporation could exercise if it were an individual shareholder of the company: section 139. Such a representative is *not* a proxy and may vote on a show of hands as well as on a poll, and may address the meeting even if the company is not a private company.

In one case,[71] where no committee of inspection had been appointed and no directions had been received from the body of creditors or the court, the liquidator in a creditors' voluntary winding up was held to be within the phrase "or other governing body" in section 139 *ante*, and entitled to appoint himself as representative of the company at general meetings of subsidiary companies.

Minutes

Every company must keep minutes of all proceedings of general meetings. Such minutes, signed by the chairman of the meeting at which the proceedings were had or of the next succeeding meeting, are evidence of the proceedings: section 145. Unless the articles so provide, they are not conclusive evidence, and so, if a resolution has been passed, but is not entered in the minutes, other evidence to prove it will be admitted.[72] However, when the articles provide that the minutes, signed by the chairman, shall be "conclusive evidence without any further proof of the facts therein stated," as between those bound by the articles, namely the company and the members *qua* members,[73] evidence cannot be called to contradict the minutes unless they have been fraudulently written up.[74]

When minutes have been duly made, there is a presumption that all the proceedings were in order, and all appointments of directors, managers or liquidators are deemed to be valid: section 145.

The books containing minutes of general meetings are to be kept at the registered office and open to the inspection of any member

---

[71] *Hillman* v. *Crystal Bowl Amusements Ltd.* [1973] 1 W.L.R. 162 (C.A.).
[72] *Re Fireproof Doors* [1916] 2 Ch. 142; *cf. Fraserburgh Commercial Co. Ltd., Petitioners*, 1946 S.C. 444.
[73] *Ante* p. 106.
[74] *Kerr* v. *Mottram* [1940] Ch. 657.

without charge for at least two hours a day. A member is entitled to be furnished, within seven days, with a copy on payment of not more than 2½p per 100 words. If inspection is refused or copies are not sent, the court can compel immediate inspection of the books [75] or direct that copies be sent to those requiring them: section 146. The minute books may be bound, or loose-leaf provided that adequate precautions are taken for guarding against falsification: section 436. Clause 81 of the Companies Bill 1973 would have allowed the use of computers for keeping minute books.

RESOLUTIONS

Kinds of resolution

In the absence of a contrary provision in the Act or in the memorandum or the articles the company in general meeting acts by ordinary resolution. Sometimes, however, the Act or the memorandum or articles require a special resolution or, occasionally, an extraordinary resolution. The Jenkins Report [76] recommended that references to extraordinary resolutions be omitted from the Act and special resolutions required in their stead. Clause 77 (4) of the Companies Bill 1973 would have given effect to such recommendation.

An *ordinary resolution*, which is not defined in the Act, is a resolution passed by a simple majority of the votes of the members entitled to vote [77] and voting in person or, where allowed, by proxy, at a meeting of which notice has been duly given. The length of the notice depends upon a number of factors including the kind of meeting at which the resolution is passed. [78]

Section 141 defines an *extraordinary resolution* as a resolution passed by at least a three-fourths' majority of [the votes of] the members entitled to vote [77] and voting, in person or, where allowed, by proxy, at a general meeting of which notice specifying the intention to propose the resolution as an extraordinary resolution has been duly given. Again, the length of the notice depends upon a number of factors including the kind of meeting at which the resolution is passed. [78]

[75] By the member himself or by a named expert on his behalf: *M'Cusker* v. *M'Rae* 1966 S.C. 253.
[76] Para. 468.   [77] *Ante* p. 216.
[78] *Ante* p. 288.

A *special resolution* is defined as a resolution passed by a majority of at least three-fourths of [the votes of] the members entitled to vote[77] and voting, in person or, where allowed, by proxy, at a general meeting of which at least 21 days' notice specifying the intention to propose the resolution as a special resolution has been given: section 141.

The words in brackets must be read into section 141 because voting may be on a show of hands, in which case each member will usually have one vote, or on a poll, in which case each member will usually have one vote for each of his shares.

Table A, article 50, provides that the notice must be *clear* notice, *i.e.* exclusive of the day on which it is served or deemed to be served and of the day for which it is given. In England a provision in the articles that the day of service is to be included in the number of days' notice to be given does not apply to notice of a special resolution, *i.e.* the period of not less than 21 days prescribed by section 141 is a period of not less than 21 clear days, exclusive of the day of service of the notice and of the day on which the meeting is to be held. Articles cannot curtail the length of time which Parliament has said must elapse between the date on which the notice is served and the date on which the meeting is held.[79] In Scotland the requisite notice under section 141 (2) means a notice of not less than 21 days computed by excluding the day on which the notice is received by the shareholder but including the day on which the meeting is to be held.[80] We have seen[81] that less than 21 days' notice of a special resolution may be given if it is so agreed by a majority in number of the members holding not less than 95 per cent. of the shares giving the right to attend and vote at the meeting: section 141 (2).

It was also stated earlier that it appears that the notice of a special resolution or of an extraordinary resolution must set out the exact wording of the resolution,[82] and that there is some uncertainty as to whether special and extraordinary resolutions can only be passed at a meeting.[83]

At a meeting at which a special resolution or an extraordinary

[79] *Re Hector Whaling Ltd.* [1936] Ch. 208, applied in *Thompson* v. *Stimpson* [1961] 1 Q.B. 195.
[80] *Neil M'Leod & Sons Ltd., Petitioners,* 1967 S.C. 16, *per* Lord President Clyde at p. 20.
[81] *Ante* p. 289.
[82] *MacConnell* v. *E. Prill & Co. Ltd.* [1916] 2 Ch. 57, *ante* p. 293.
[83] *Ante* p. 290.

resolution is submitted to be passed, a declaration of the chairman
that the resolution is carried is, unless a poll is demanded, conclusive
evidence of the fact without proof of the number or proportion
of the votes recorded in favour of or against the resolution: section
141 (3). This provision prevents a resolution from being challenged
on the ground, *e.g.*, that certain shareholders were not qualified to
vote.[84] If, however, the declaration of the chairman is fraudulent, or
shows on the face of it that the proper majority has not been obtained,
it is not conclusive.

A special resolution was put to the meeting. The chairman then said: "Those
in favour 6; those against 23; but there are 200 voting by proxy,[85] and I declare
the resolution carried." *Held*, the declaration was not conclusive, and the
resolution was not passed: *Re Caratal (New) Mines Ltd.* [1902] 2 Ch. 498.[86]

Further, the chairman's declaration is not conclusive where the
resolution has not been effectively submitted to the meeting, *e.g.* if
a show of hands has not been taken as required by the articles.[87]

The chairman can put a resolution to the meeting without its
being seconded, unless the articles prohibit it.

Amendments

If a positive amendment, pertinent to the subject-matter of the
proposed resolution, is proposed, it must be voted upon first. If
the chairman refuses to put a proper amendment to the meeting, the
resolution, if passed, is not binding.[88]

An amendment cannot be moved if it goes beyond the notice
convening the meeting. Because notice of special business must
state the resolution to be passed in such a way as fairly to state the
purpose for which the meeting is convened,[89] there is little scope
for amendment where a resolution is special business. Where a
notice of a meeting stated that it was to pass, with such amendments as should be determined, a resolution that three named persons
be appointed directors, an amendment to elect two other directors as
well was held valid.[90] Again, there is little scope for amendment of

[84] *Grahams' Morocco Co. Ltd., Petitioners*, 1932 S.C. 269.
[85] Those "voting" by proxy could not vote on a show of hands.
[86] A corresponding Scottish case is *Cowan* v. *Scottish Publishing Co. Ltd.* (1892) 19 R.
437.
[87] *Citizens Theatre Ltd., Petitioners*, 1946 S.C. 14; *cf. Fraserburgh Commercial Co. Ltd.,
Petitioners*, 1946 S.C. 444.
[88] *Henderson* v. *Bank of Australasia* (1890) 45 Ch.D. 330 (C.A.).
[89] *Ante* p. 292.   [90] *Betts & Co. Ltd.* v. *Macnaghten* [1910] 1 Ch. 430.

special and extraordinary resolutions since it appears that the notice of a special resolution or an extraordinary resolution must set out the exact wording of the resolution.[89] However, where a notice of a meeting stated that it was to pass special resolutions to wind up voluntarily and to appoint X as liquidator, and the second resolution was dropped and a new one to appoint Y as liquidator was passed, it was held that Y's appointment was valid because as soon as the resolution to wind up was passed a liquidator could be appointed, without notice, under the Act.[91]

Registration and copies of certain resolutions

A printed copy of certain resolutions and agreements, or a copy in some other form approved by him, must be forwarded to the Registrar within 15 days after they are passed or made and, where articles have been registered, a copy must be annexed to every copy of the articles issued subsequently: 1948 Act, s. 143; 1967 Act, s. 51.

Section 143 applies to, *inter alia*, special and extraordinary resolutions, resolutions agreed to by all the members which would otherwise not have been effective unless passed as special resolutions or extraordinary resolutions, and resolutions agreed to by all the members of a class of shareholders.

Clause 77 (3) of the Companies Bill 1973 would have extended section 143 to an ordinary resolution limiting or altering the extent to which the company's borrowing powers may be exercised by the directors.

A resolution passed at an adjourned meeting is treated as having been passed on the date on which it was in fact passed, and is not deemed to have been passed on the date of the original meeting: section 144.

It will be remembered that a printed copy of a resolution effecting an increase of capital, or a copy in some other form approved by the Registrar, must also be filed within 15 days: 1948 Act, s. 63; 1967 Act, s. 51.

The various processes which the Registrar is prepared to regard as satisfying the printing stipulation have been dealt with already.[92]

[91] *Re Trench Tubeless Tyre Co.* [1900] 1 Ch. 408 (C.A.).
[92] p. 105.

When various resolutions required

The company in general meeting acts by ordinary resolution unless another kind of resolution is required by the Act or by the memorandum or the articles. Thus an ordinary resolution is enough under section 57 (issue of shares at a discount) or section 14 of the 1976 Act (appointment of auditors).[93] In practice an increase of capital is effected by an ordinary resolution.[94] An ordinary resolution is *expressly* provided for by section 184 of the 1948 Act (removal of a director) and section 14 (6) of the 1976 Act (removal of an auditor).

An extraordinary resolution is required in a few cases, for example by section 278[95] (initiation of a creditors' voluntary winding up, when the company is insolvent), by section 303[96] (to sanction the exercise of certain of the powers of the liquidator in a members' voluntary winding up) and by section 306[97] (arrangement between a company being wound up voluntarily and its creditors).

A special resolution is required for the more important matters, for example by section 18 (1) (change of name), section 5 (alteration of objects), section 10 (alteration of articles), section 66 (reduction of capital), section 278[95] (initiation of a members' voluntary winding up), section 287[98] (authority for the liquidator in a voluntary winding up to sell the company's business to another company for cash or shares in the other company).

The Jenkins Committee did not support the view that the Act should be amended to provide generally for voting on the above mentioned resolutions by postal ballot. They thought that where there is a possibility of there being a difference of opinion between members about such matters there should be a meeting at which the matter in question may be discussed (although they saw no need for a meeting where all the members entitled to vote are unanimous).[99]

[93] *Post* p. 452.
[94] *Ante* p. 228.
[95] *Post* p. 614.
[96] *Post* p. 624.
[97] *Post* p. 628.
[98] *Post* p. 632.
[99] *Para.* 460.

Chapter 14

DIRECTORS

The management of a company is usually entrusted to a small body of persons called "directors," although they are sometimes called "governors," or, in the case of a private company, "governing directors." It will be seen later that the Act requires a public company to have at least two directors and a private company to have at least one. The exact name by which a person occupying the position of director is called is immaterial as, under section 455 (1), in the Act the expression "director" includes any person occupying the position of director by whatever name called. Section 455 (1) also provides that in the Act the expression "officer" in relation to a corporation includes a director or manager.

Among other things, this chapter deals with the appointment, remuneration and vacation of office of directors. It also shows that the directors of a company act as a board, that normal articles (*e.g.* Table A, article 80) give the directors extensive powers to manage the the company's business (and that so long as the directors act within their powers, the company in general meeting cannot overrule then), and that articles usually empower the directors to appoint a managing director and delegate any of their powers to him.

One of the most important topics dealt with in the chapter is the fiduciary duties and duties of care which a director owes to his company.

It should be noted that in a private company the directors are usually substantial shareholders. In a public company, the directors normally have few shares, their fees and other emoluments, rather than their dividends, being their main sources of profit from the company, with the result that management and ownership of the company are divorced.

Number and Appointment of Directors

Every public company registered on or after November 1, 1929, must have at least two directors. Companies registered before that date, and every private company, must have at least one director: section 176. The Jenkins Committee recommended that every company should have at least two directors[1] but that recommendation has not yet been implemented, although clause 41 of the Companies Bill 1973 attempted to give effect to it. Apart from section 176, the number of directors is regulated by the articles.

As to the *first directors*, section 21 (5) of the Companies Act 1976 provides that the persons named in the statement of first directors and secretary, which must be delivered for registration with the memorandum, shall, on the incorporation of the company, be deemed to have been appointed as the first directors and secretary, and any appointment by any articles delivered with the memorandum shall be void unless the person concerned is named as a director or secretary in the statement.

Section 181 (1) of the 1948 Act as amended by Schedule 3 of the 1976 Act provides that a person cannot be named as a director in a prospectus or statement in lieu of prospectus unless, before the issue of the prospectus or the registration of the statement in lieu of prospectus, as the case may be, he has—

(*a*) signed and delivered to the Registrar a consent in writing to act as director; and

(*b*) (i) signed the memorandum for his qualification shares, if any; or

 (ii) taken his qualification shares from the company; or

 (iii) delivered to the Registrar an undertaking in writing to take from the company and pay for his qualification shares; or

 (iv) delivered to the Registrar a statutory declaration that the qualification shares are registered in his name.

These requirements do not apply in the case of, *e.g.*, (*a*) a company which is or was a private company, and (*b*) a public company when the prospectus is issued more than a year from the date on which the company was entitled to commence business[2] (s. 181 (5)).

The Jenkins Report[3] recommended the repeal of section 181.

Clause 57 (3) of the 1973 Bill attempted to effect such repeal.

[1] *Ante* p. 50.
[2] *Ante* p. 182.
[3] Para. 67.

Subsequent directors are appointed in the way laid down in the articles, *e.g.* by the company in annual general meeting.

Table A provides:
"89. At the first annual general meeting of the company all the directors shall retire from office, and at the annual general meeting in every subsequent year one-third of the directors for the time being, or, if their number is not three or a multiple of three, then the number nearest one-third, shall retire from office.

90. The directors to retire in every year shall be those who have been longest in office since their last election, but as between persons who became directors on the same day those to retire shall (unless they otherwise agree among themselves) be determined by lot.

91. A retiring director shall be eligible for re-election."

The articles also usually contain clauses, as does Table A in articles 94 and 95, providing that the company may by ordinary resolution increase or reduce the number of directors, and that casual vacancies, *i.e.* vacancies occurring between two annual general meetings, may be filled by the directors. Article 95 also provides that the directors may appoint additional directors to hold office until the next annual general meeting but so that the total number of directors fixed in accordance with the articles is not exceeded. Where there are articles similar to articles 94 and 95 the power of appointing additional directors has not been delegated to the directors so as to exclude the inherent power of the company in general meeting to appoint directors.[4]

The appointment of directors at a general meeting, except in the case of a private company, must be voted on individually unless a resolution to the contrary has first been agreed to by the meeting without any vote being given against it. A motion for the appointment of two or more persons as directors of a public company by a single resolution is void (although the operation of section 180,[5] by which the acts of the "directors" are valid, is not excluded and no provision in the articles for the automatic reappointment of retiring directors in default of another appointment applies): section 183.

Table A, article 92, provides that the company at the meeting at which a director retires by rotation may elect a director to fill the vacancy and that the retiring director, if offering himself for re-election, is deemed to have been re-elected unless (*a*) another person is elected, (*b*) a resolution not to fill the vacancy is passed, or (*c*) a resolution for his re-election is lost. In the absence of a provision

---

[4] *Worcester Corsetry Ltd.* v. *Witting* [1936] Ch. 640.
[5] *Post* p. 417.

like (*c*), a retiring director will be deemed to be re-elected even though a resolution that he be re-elected is lost.[6] It is also provided, by article 93, that no person, other than the retiring director or a person recommended by the directors, is eligible for election as a director unless notice of intention to propose him, signed by a member entitled to vote, is left at the registered office not less than three nor more than 21 days before the meeting, together with a signed notice of his willingness to act.

The articles may appoint a named person a permanent director of the company, so that no re-election is necessary in his case. This was common in the case of the former exempt private companies.[7] The appointment of such a director, when the only contract he has is that contained in the articles, can be terminated by an alteration of the articles, or by his removal under section 184,[8] or by the company's going into liquidation.

The articles appointed F. governing director of the company for his life, or until he should resign or be removed by a special resolution of the company, at a salary of £300 a year. F. acted for 16 years, when the company went into voluntary liquidation. *Held*, F.'s employment was conditional on the continued existence of the company and ceased automatically when it was wound up, so that F. could not claim damages for breach of contract: *Re T. N. Farrer Ltd.* (1937) Ch. 352.

Power may be given to a particular person or company to nominate one or more directors; this is often done in the case of subsidiary companies.

Assignment of office by directors

If the articles or any agreement contains power for a director to assign his office to another person, an assignment is of no effect unless and until it is approved by a special resolution of the company: section 204.

Alternate directors

Although the Act does not say so, section 204, above, does not prevent the appointment by a director, if authorised by the articles and subject thereto, of an alternate or substitute director to act for him in certain circumstances. Because of the wide definition of the

---

[6] *Grundt* v. *Great Boulder Proprietary Mines Ltd.* [1948] Ch. 145 (C.A.).
[7] *Ante* p. 10. [8] *Post* p. 328.

word "director" in section 455 it seems that an alternate is a director
for the purposes of the Act, so that particulars with respect to him
must be shown in registers such as the register of directors, *post*.[9]

PERSONS WHO CANNOT BE DIRECTORS

Certain persons cannot be appointed or act as directors:

(1) A person who has reached the age of 70 cannot be *appointed*
director *unless* the company is private and not the subsidiary of a
public company, *or* the articles otherwise provide, *or* he is appointed
or approved by a resolution of which special notice, stating his
age, has been given: section 185. The exceptions are such as to make
this section ineffective.

Clause 43 of the 1973 Companies Bill would have repealed those parts of
section 185 whereby the section does not apply to private companies and has
effect subject to a contrary provision in a company's articles.

A person who is *first* appointed a director of a company, other
than a private company which is not the subsidiary of a public
company, after he has reached the age at which the directors retire
under the Act[10] or the articles, must give notice of his age to the
company: section 186.

(2) An undischarged bankrupt must not act as director of, or be
concerned in the management of, a company without the leave of the
court by which he was adjudged bankrupt,[11] under penalty of two
years' imprisonment or a fine of £500 or both: section 187.

In England, on an application for leave to act as director, notice
must be given to the Official Receiver, who can oppose the application if he is of opinion that it is contrary to the public interest.

(3) A person cannot, without leave of the court, be a director
of or be concerned in the management of a company if he has been
convicted of an indictable offence in connection with the promotion,
formation or management of a company, or if in a winding up it has
appeared that he has been guilty of fraudulent trading[12] or that he has
been guilty, while an officer, of fraud or breach of duty in relation to
the company, and the court has ordered that he shall not be a di-

[9] p. 318. And see the Jenkins Report, para. 83.
[10] See s. 185, above.
[11] For Scotland, substitute "sequestration of his estates was awarded" for "he was
adjudged bankrupt."
[12] *Post* p. 574.

rector or be concerned in management for up to five years: section 188.

The period of disqualification must date from conviction, not, *e.g.*, from the convicted person's release from prison.[13]

The Jenkins Report[14] recommended that section 188 be extended to cover, *e.g.*, persons who have been persistently in default in complying with the Act (it will be seen that this recommendation was enacted by section 28 of the Companies Act 1976 *post*), and that disqualification should continue for up to five years after a convicted person's release from prison.

The 1973 White Paper[15] stated that the then Conservative Government intended to give effect to such recommendation except for the proposal that disqualification should be possible when a person has been incompetent (as opposed to guilty of impropriety or recklessness). Consequently, certain clauses of the 1973 Companies Bill would have provided wider grounds of disqualification, *e.g.* reckless conduct, in relation to the management of a company, by an officer of the company.

The Jenkins Report further recommended that corporate bodies and Scottish firms should be prohibited from being directors.

Clause 40 of the 1973 Bill would have given effect to that recommendation and would also have disqualified minors from acting as directors. Clause 45 would have prohibited a person from acting as a director of a company which controls another company in which he has an interest.

(4) A person cannot, without leave of the court with jurisdiction to wind up the company, be a director of or be concerned in the management of a company if he has been persistently in default in relation to any provision of the Companies Acts which requires any document to be delivered, or notice of any matter to be given, to the Registrar and, on the application of the Secretary of State, the High Court (Court of Session in Scotland) has ordered that he shall not be a director or be concerned in the management of the company for up to five years: section 28 of the 1976 Act.

The fact that a person has been persistently in default in relation to any provision of the Companies Acts may be conclusively proved by showing that in the five years ending with the date of the application of the Secretary of State he has been adjudged guilty (whether or not on the same occasion) of three or more defaults. A person is to be treated as being adjudged guilty of a default if—

[13] *R.* v. *Bradley* [1961] 1 W.L.R. 398 (C.C.A.).
[14] Para. 85.
[15] Company Law Reform, (1973) Cmnd. 5391, paras. 36, 37.

(a) he is convicted of any offence by virtue of any contravention of or failure to comply with any provision of the Companies Acts (whether on his own part or on the part of the company); or

(b) an order is made against him under section 428 of the 1948 Act *ante* or section 5 (1) of the 1976 Act *post*.

The Secretary of State must give at least ten days' notice of his intention to apply for an order under section 28 and on the hearing of the application the person concerned may appear and himself give evidence or call witnesses.

If a person contravenes an order under section 28 he is in respect of each offence liable—

(a) on conviction on indictment, to up to two years' imprisonment or to a fine or to both; or

(b) on summary conviction, to imprisonment for up to six months or to a fine of up to £400 or to both.

Register of disqualification orders

Section 29 of the 1976 Act provides that the prescribed officer of any court which makes an order that a person shall not, without the leave of the court, be a director of or be concerned in the management of a company for a specified period, or grants leave in relation to such an order, must furnish the Secretary of State with particulars of the order or the grant of leave whether the order is made under section 188 of the Companies Act 1948 *ante*, section 9 of the Insolvency Act 1976 or section 28 of the Companies Act 1976 *ante*.

The Secretary of State must maintain a register of such orders and grants of leave, which register is open to inspection on payment of such fee as may be specified by the Secretary of State in regulations made by statutory instrument.

SHARE QUALIFICATION OF DIRECTORS

A share qualification is a specified number of shares which a person must hold in the company to qualify him for appointment as a director of it. There is no share qualification unless the articles otherwise provide, as they frequently do. The Rules of The Stock Exchange,

London, do not require a qualification, nor does Table A provide for one.

Article 77 of Table A merely provides: "The shareholding qualification for directors may be fixed by the company in general meeting, and unless and until so fixed no qualification shall be required."

It should be remembered that in the case of a private company a director will in any event usually be a substantial shareholder.

When a qualification is imposed, a director not already qualified must obtain his qualification within two months of his appointment or the shorter time fixed by the articles: section 182. Where he is appointed by a resolution decided on a poll (on which each member usually has one vote for each of his shares) the two months' period, within which his name must be entered in the register of members, runs from midnight on the day on which the votes are counted and the result of the poll ascertained, not from midnight on an earlier date on which the votes are cast.[16]

If a director fails to obtain his qualification within the appropriate period, or if he thereafter ceases to hold it, his office is vacated and he is liable to a fine of £5 a day until he ceases to act as director: section 182.

A provision in the articles that "no person shall be eligible to, or shall continue in, the office of director" unless he holds a specified number of shares does not apply to persons who are expressly and unconditionally named as directors in the articles.[17]

Qualification shares normally[18] need not be obtained from the company; the director may obtain them by transfer from a member,[19] but he should not obtain them by way of gift from a promoter.[20]

Where articles provide that a first director is to "be deemed to have agreed to take" his qualifying shares from the company, a person who has accepted office as one of the first directors and has acted as such is bound to accept an allotment of shares made in accordance with that provision.[21]

Shares held jointly with another person are a sufficient qualification, unless the articles otherwise provide.[22]

---

[16] *Holmes* v. *Keyes* [1959] Ch. 199 (C.A.).
[17] *Liquidator of the Consolidated Copper Co. etc. Ltd.* v. *Peddie* (1877) 5 R. 393.
[18] s. 181 (1) (*b*) (ii), *ante* p. 311, is an exception.
[19] *Brown's Case* (1874) L.R. 9 Ch. 102.
[20] *Eden* v. *Ridsdales Railway Lamp Co. Ltd.* (1899) 23 Q.B.D. 368, *post* p. 357.
[21] *The Kingsburgh Motor Construction Co. Ltd.* v. *Scott* (1902) 10 S.L.T. 424 (O.H.).
[22] *Grundy* v. *Briggs* [1910] 1 Ch. 444.

The holding of a share warrant does not constitute the holding of qualification shares (s. 182 (2)), as the shares can be transferred at any time by delivery of the warrant.

Sometimes the articles provide that the director must hold his qualification shares "in his own right." This does not mean that he must be the beneficial owner of them.[23] It means "holding in his own right as distinguished from holding in the right of somebody else. . . . It means that a person shall hold shares in such a way that the company can safely deal with him in respect of his shares whatever his interest may be in the shares."[24] It is sufficient if the director holds the shares as trustee.[25]

A person described in the register as the liquidator of another company does not hold shares in his own right.[26] Nor does a bankrupt director whose trustee in bankruptcy has given the company notice that he is claiming the shares.[27]

REGISTER OF DIRECTORS AND SECRETARIES

Section 200 of the 1948 Act as amended by section 22 (1) of the 1976 Act provides that a company must keep at its registered office a register of its directors and secretaries. In the case of an individual director the register must contain his name and any former name, address, nationality and business occupation, together with particulars of any other directorships held by him (except directorships of companies of which the company is the wholly owned subsidiary, or which are wholly owned subsidiaries either of the company or of another company of which the company is the wholly owned subsidiary) and the date of his birth (except in the case of a private company which is not a subsidiary of a public company). The register is open to inspection by members without fee and by others on payment of 5p.

Within 14 days of any change in the directors or secretary or in the particulars contained in the register, the company must notify

---

[23] *Howard* v. *Sadler* [1893] 1 Q.B. 1; *The Galloway Saloon Steam Packet Co.* v. *Wallace* (1891) 19 R. 330.

[24] *Per* Lindley L.J. in *Bainbridge* v. *Smith* (1889) 41 Ch.D. 462 (C.A.) at p. 474.

[25] *Pulbrook* v. *Richmond, etc., Mining Co.* (1878) 9 Ch.D. 610, where the director was held entitled to an order restraining his co-directors from excluding him from the board. See further on this point *Hayes* v. *Bristol Plant Hire Ltd.* [1957] 1 W.L.R. 499 and *Elliot* v. *J. W. Mackie & Sons Ltd.*, 1935 S.C. 81.

[26] *Boschoek Proprietary Co. Ltd.* v. *Fuke* [1906] 1 Ch. 148.

[27] *Sutton* v. *English and Colonial Produce Co.* [1902] 2 Ch. 502.

the Registrar of the change and the date when it occurred. A notification of a person having become a director or secretary must contain his signed consent to act as such.

Section 9 (3) of the European Communities Act 1972 as amended by section 22 (3) of the Companies Act 1976 requires the Registrar to publish in the *Gazette* notice of the receipt by him of any notification of a change among the directors of a company. And subsection (4) provides that a company cannot rely against other persons on any change among its directors if it had not been officially notified at the material time and is not shown by the company to have been known at that time to the person concerned, or if the material time is less than 16 days after official notification and it is shown that the person concerned was unavoidably prevented from knowing of the event at that time.

Clause 57 of the Companies Bill 1973 would have imposed on a director or secretary of a company a duty to give written notice to the company of such matters relating to himself as may be necessary for the purposes of section 200.

PARTICULARS OF DIRECTORS IN TRADE CATALOGUES, ETC.

Unless exemption is granted by the Department of Trade, the name and any former name and the nationality, if not British,[28] of each director must be stated in all trade catalogues, trade circulars, showcards and business letters issued by the company if the company was registered after November 23, 1916, and whether it is a public or a private company: section 201.

In 1974 exemption was granted in 1,006 cases.

The Jenkins Report[29] recommended that section 201 be repealed. Particularly in the case of larger companies, where changes in directors may be frequent, the requirements of the section may be unduly onerous.

Clause 56 of the Companies Bill 1973 would have extended the requirements of section 201 in some ways, *e.g.* by requiring, in the case of a subsidiary company, that the name of the company's ultimate holding company also be stated in the section 201 documents.

[28] The Companies (Disclosure of Directors' Nationalities) (Exemption) Order 1974 exempts companies from the obligation to state the nationality of a non-British director where he is a citizen of an EEC Member State.
[29] Para. 456.

DISCLOSURE OF DIRECTORS' SHAREHOLDINGS, ETC.

Obligation of director to notify company of his interests in shares in, or debentures of, it or associated companies

Subject to any exceptions made by the Department of Trade, a person who becomes a director when he is interested in shares in or debentures of the company or its subsidiary, holding company or co-subsidiary, must, within five days[30] (or, if he does not know of the interest, within five days after it comes to his knowledge), give the company written notice of his interests and of the number of shares of each class in, and the amount of debentures of each class of, the company and each of the associated companies: Companies Act 1967, s. 27 (1) (*a*) as amended by Companies Act 1976, s. 24 (1).

A person in accordance with whose directions the directors are accustomed to act is deemed to be a director of the company.

A director must (within five days, if he knows of the event and that its occurrence gives rise to the obligation; otherwise within five days after he becomes aware that the occurrence of the event gives rise to the obligation) give the company written notice if, while he is a director—

(i) an event occurs in consequence of which he becomes or ceases to be interested in shares in or debentures of the company or an associated company; or

(ii) he contracts to sell any such shares or debentures; or

(iii) he assigns a right given to him by the company to subscribe for shares in or debentures of the company; or

(iv) he is granted by an associated company a right to subscribe for shares in or debentures of that other company, or he exercises or assigns such a right;

stating the number or amount, and class, of shares or debentures involved: section 27 (1) (*b*) of the 1967 Act as amended by section 24 (1) of the 1976 Act. Certain other matters such as the price or consideration must be stated too.

The 1973 Conservative Government White Paper[31] stated that the Government intended to require a director who deals in his company's shares to notify the company within the shortest practicable time, and clause 17 of the 1973 Companies Bill would have reduced the statutory period from 14 days to three days.

[30] Excluding Saturdays, Sundays and bank holidays.
[31] Cmnd. 5391, para. 20.

Contravention of section 27 (1), or making to the company a statement known to be false or recklessly making a false statement, gives rise to liability to two years' imprisonment or a fine or both. Proceedings can, in England or Wales, be instituted only by or with the consent of the Department of Trade or the Director of Public Prosecutions.

If it appears that section 27 has been contravened the Department of Trade may order an investigation: section 32.[32]

Rules for giving effect to obligation to disclose

Section 28 of the Companies Act 1967 contains the following rules for giving effect to section 27 (1), *ante*:

(1) An interest in shares or debentures is not excluded by reason of its remoteness or the manner in which it arises or that the exercise of a right conferred by ownership is or may be made subject to restraint.

(2) An interest under a trust whereof the property comprises shares or debentures (other than a discretionary interest) is deemed an interest in the shares or debentures.

(3) A person is deemed interested in shares or debentures if a company is interested in them and—

(*a*) it or its directors are accustomed to act in accordance with his directions; or

(*b*) he is entitled to exercise or control the exercise of one-third or more of its voting power at any general meeting.

(4) A person is deemed interested in shares or debentures if—

(*a*) he contracts for the purchase of them; or

(*b*) he has a right, otherwise than by virtue of having an interest under a trust, to call for delivery of them; or

(*c*) not being a registered holder, he is entitled (otherwise than by virtue of having been appointed a proxy or as representative of a corporation) to exercise any right conferred by the holding thereof.

(5) Each of persons with a joint interest is deemed to have an interest.

---

[32] *Post* p. 406.

(6) It is immaterial that the shares or debentures are unidentifiable.

(7) Interests in reversion or remainder, or (as regards Scotland) in fee, are disregarded so long as a person is entitled to receive, during the lifetime of himself or another, income from trust property comprising shares or debentures.

(8) An interest in England and Wales as bare trustee or as custodian trustee, or in Scotland as simple trustee, is disregarded.

(9) An interest subsisting by virtue of, *inter alia*, an authorised unit trust scheme[33] is disregarded.

(10) An interest of the Church of Scotland General Trustees or of the Church of Scotland Trust is disregarded.

(11) Delivery to a person's order of shares or debentures in fulfilment of a contract to purchase by him or in satisfaction of his right to call for delivery thereof, or failure to deliver to him in accordance with such a contract or right, or the lapse of his right to call for delivery, is deemed an event in consequence of which he ceases to be interested in them.[34]

Extension of obligation to disclose to interests of spouses and children

For the purposes of section 27 of the Companies Act 1967, *ante*, an interest of the spouse of, or of a child under the age of majority of, a director (not being himself or herself a director) in shares or debentures is treated as the director's interest, and a contract, assignment or right of subscription entered into, exercised or made by, or a grant made to, such a spouse or child is treated as that of the director: section 31 (1).

Within five days after the event in question comes to his knowledge, a director must notify the company in writing if, while he or she is a director—

(*a*) the company grants the director's spouse or child a right to subscribe for shares in or debentures of the company; or

(*b*) such spouse or child exercises such a right.

In each case the like information as is required by section 27, *ante*,

---

[33] *Ante* p. 157.
[34] The necessity for s. 28 (11) was questioned in the Second Interim Report of the Australian Company Law Advisory Committee, February 1969, at p. 5. It was also said that if the sub-section is to be included in Australian legislation it should be redrafted to express more clearly what is intended.

must be stated: section 31 (2) of the 1967 Act as amended by section 24 (1) of the 1976 Act. If section 31 (2) appears to have been contravened the Department of Trade may order an investigation: section 32.[35]

In section 31, "son" includes step-son and adopted son, and "daughter" includes step-daughter and adopted daughter.

Register of directors' shareholdings, etc.

The Companies Act 1967, s. 29, contains provisions for securing that information furnished under section 27,[36] and certain other information about directors' interests, is recorded and made available.

Every company must keep a register for the purposes of section 27 and whenever it receives information from a director in consequence of that section, within three days[30] thereafter it must inscribe in the register, against his name, the information and the date of inscription.

When a company grants a director a right to subscribe for shares or debentures it must, within a similar time, inscribe against his name the date of the grant, the period during or time at which it is exercisable, the consideration for the grant, the description of the shares or debentures and the number or amount thereof, and the price to be paid. When such a right is exercised there must be inscribed that fact (identifying the right), the number or amount of shares or debentures involved, the fact that they were registered in his name or the names of the persons in whose names they were registered, together with the number or amount registered in the name of each person.

The entries against the names in the register must appear in chronological order. If a director requires it, the nature and extent of his interest in shares or debentures must also be recorded.

The company is not, by virtue of anything done for the purposes of section 29, affected with notice of, or put upon inquiry as to, the rights of any person in relation to shares or debentures.

Clause 81 of the Companies Bill 1973 would have allowed the use of computers for company registers.

[35] *Post* p. 406.
[36] *Ante* p. 320.

Inspection of register

The register must be kept at the registered office or where the register of members is kept[37] and must be open during business hours for at least two hours each day to the inspection of members without charge and other persons on payment of 5p per inspection. Except where it has always been kept at the registered office the company must notify the Registrar of the place where the register is kept. Any person may require a copy of the register or part thereof on payment of 10p per 100 words or fractional part thereof. Any copy must be sent by the company within ten days after the requirement is received. The register must also be produced at the commencement of the annual general meeting and remain open and accessible during the meeting to any person attending.[38]

Index of names

Unless the register is in the form of an index the company must also keep an index of the names inscribed therein. The index must give a sufficient indication to enable the information against each name to be readily found and must be altered within 14 days after the date on which a name is entered in the register.

Contravention of section 29

There are default fines[39] and other fines for contravention of section 29, and the court is empowered to order inspection of the register and delivery of a copy.

Duty of company to notify stock exchange of acquisition of its securities by director

Section 25 of the 1976 Act provides that when a company whose shares or debentures are listed on a recognised stock exchange is notified of any matter by a director under section 27 or section 31 of the 1967 Act *ante* and that matter relates to shares or debentures listed on a stock exchange. the company must notify that stock exchange of the matter before the end of the following day (Satur-

[37] *Ante* p. 197.   [38] *Ante* p. 286.
[39] *Ante* pp. 196.

days, Sundays and Bank Holidays in any part of Great Britain being disregarded).

If there is default in complying with the section the company and every officer in default is guilty of an offence and liable on summary conviction to a fine not exceeding £500 and further to a default fine, although proceedings in England and Wales cannot be instituted except by, or with the consent of, the Secretary of State or the Director of Public Prosecutions.

INSPECTION OF DIRECTORS' SERVICE CONTRACTS

Section 26 of the Companies Act 1967 provides that, subject as below, every company must keep a copy of each director's contract of service[40] or of any variation thereof, or a memorandum thereof setting out its terms if it is not in writing, at one place. This place may be—

(1) the company's registered office; or
(2) the other place where the register of members is kept; or
(3) its principal place of business in England, if the company is registered in England, or in Scotland if the company is registered in Scotland.

The documents must be kept open to the inspection of members without charge during business hours for at least two hours a day.

Notice of such place and of any changes in it must be given to the Registrar except where the documents have always been kept at the registered office.

Contracts requiring a director to work mainly outside the United Kingdom are excluded, as are those where the unexpired term of the contract is less than 12 months or the contract can be terminated by the company without payment of compensation within 12 months.

There are default fines[39] and other fines for contravention of section 26 and the court is empowered to order an inspection.

Clauses 48 and 49 of the 1973 Companies Bill would have required agreements for the management of the company to which a director is a party or in which he has a close interest, to be notified to the company and filed with the Registrar.

[40] *Post* p. 336.

DEALING BY DIRECTORS IN CERTAIN OPTIONS

The Jenkins Report[41] stated that a director should not deal in options in securities of his company or of the group to which the company belongs—a director who speculates in such a way with special inside information is clearly acting improperly. However, it was said that the prohibition should not extend to options to subscribe for securities given to directors by the company or another member of the group—the terms of such options are a matter for the company.

Accordingly, the Companies Act 1967, ss. 25 and 30, penalise the dealing by directors, their spouses or children, in options to buy or sell quoted shares in, or quoted debentures of, the company or associated companies.

A director who buys a right to call for delivery, or a right to make delivery, or, at his election, a right either to call for or to make delivery, at a specified price and within a specified time of a specified number of relevant shares or a specified amount of relevant debentures, is liable to two years' imprisonment or a fine or both: section 25.

"Relevant shares" and "relevant debentures" mean, respectively, shares in, or debentures of, the company or its subsidiary, holding company or co-subsidiary, as respects which a stock exchange listing has been granted in Great Britain or elsewhere. A person in accordance with whose directions the directors are accustomed to act is deemed a director of the company, (although section 56 (3) provides that a person is not to be deemed one in accordance with whose directions the directors are accustomed to act by reason only that they act on advice given by him in a professional capacity).

Buying a right to subscribe for shares or debentures is not penalised, nor is buying debentures which carry a right to subscribe for or convert into shares.

Section 30 extends section 25 to the spouse of, or child under the age of majority of, a director, not being herself or himself a director of the company, except that it is a defence for such a spouse or child, charged with an offence under section 25, to prove that he had no reason to believe that his spouse or parent was a director of the company in question. "Child" includes step-child and adopted child.

[41] Para. 90.

If it appears that section 25 has been contravened the Department of Trade may order an investigation: section 32.[42]

VACATION OF OFFICE BY DIRECTORS

A director may cease to be such for various reasons, *e.g.* death, dissolution of the company, retirement by rotation under articles like Table A, articles 89–92, *ante*,[43] or retirement under an age limit, disqualification, or removal under section 184.

Clause 43 of the 1973 Companies Bill would have limited the length of time a director appointed by the company in general meeting or by the directors may hold office, without re-election by the company in general meeting, to the end of the third annual general meeting after his appointment in the first case and the end of the next annual general meeting after his appointment in the second case.

Retirement of directors under age limit

A director must retire at the end of the first annual general meeting after he reaches 70 *unless*—

(1) the company is a private company which is not the subsidiary of a public company; or

(2) the articles otherwise provide; or

(3) he was appointed or approved by the company in general meeting by a resolution, *i.e.* an ordinary resolution, of which special notice,[38] stating his age, was given: section 185.

If a director should have to retire under this section he may be reappointed by an ordinary resolution of which special notice,[44] stating his age, has been given. The result is that the section is a weak one and unimportant in practice. In particular, the articles may alter the age limit or provide that directors shall not be obliged to retire on reaching any age. The Jenkins Report[45] recommended that the section be strengthened, simplified and made to apply to all companies.

[42] *Post* p. 406.
[43] p. 312.
[44] *Ante* p. 295.
[45] Para. 85.

Disqualification of directors

The articles usually provide for the vacation of office by directors on the happening of certain events, *e.g.* bankruptcy or resignation.

Table A, article 88, provides: "The office of director shall be vacated if the director—

(a) ceases to be a director by virtue of section 182[46] or 185[47] of the Act; or
(b) becomes bankrupt or makes any arrangement or composition with his creditors generally; or
(c) becomes prohibited from being a director by reason of any order made under section 188[48] of the 1948 Act or section 28 of the 1976 Act; or
(d) becomes of unsound mind; or
(e) resigns his office by notice in writing to the company; or
(f) shall for more than six months have been absent without permission of the directors from meetings of the directors held during that period."

When the articles provide that a director shall vacate his office if he absents himself from board meetings for a certain time, the office will not be vacated if the absence is involuntary, as where the director is ill and unable to travel.[49] On the other hand, if the director is absent because his doctor has advised that his health will be benefited by going abroad, the office will be vacated.[50]

On the happening of any of the events mentioned in the articles, the vacation of office is automatic and the board of directors has no power to waive the offence or condone the act.[51] Similarly, on the resignation of a director the office is automatically vacated, so that the resignation cannot be withdrawn without the consent of the company.[52]

Removal of directors

By section 184 a company may by ordinary resolution[53] remove a director (other than, in the case of a private company, a director holding office for life on July 18, 1945) before the expiration of his period of office, *notwithstanding* anything in the articles or in any agreement between him and the company. Special notice[44] must be given of any

---

[46] *Ante* p. 317.
[47] *Ante.*
[48] *Ante* p. 315.
[49] *Mack's Claim* [1900] W.N. 114.
[50] *McConnell's Claim* [1901] 1 Ch. 728.
[51] *Re The Bodega Co. Ltd.* [1904] 1 Ch. 276.
[52] *Glossop* v. *Glossop* [1907] 2 Ch. 370.
[53] This is the only case where the Act *expressly* provides for an ordinary resolution. But see now 1976 Act s. 14 (6)—a company may by ordinary resolution remove an auditor; *post* p. 455.

resolution to remove a director or to appoint another person in place of a removed director at the meeting at which he is removed. On receipt of notice of an intended resolution to remove a director the company must send a copy to the director concerned, who is entitled to have his representations in writing of a reasonable length sent to the members of the company or read out at the meeting and also to be heard on the resolution at the meeting. The director may be deprived of the former right if the court is satisfied that it is being abused to secure needless publicity for defamatory matter.

It has been held that nothing in the Act prevents the articles giving a director's shares special voting rights, *e.g.* three votes per share on a poll, on a resolution to remove him.[54]

Clause 44 of the Companies Bill 1973 would have prevented the exercise of special voting rights on resolutions to remove directors.

Subsection (6) provides that nothing in section 184 deprives a removed director of any compensation or damages payable to him in respect of the termination of his appointment as director or of any appointment, *e.g.* as managing director, terminating with that as director; and nothing in the section derogates from any power of removal which may exist apart from the section, *e.g.* a power of removal given by the articles of the company. For example, as will be explained later,[55] he will be entitled to damages if he has a contract of service, outside the articles, appointing him managing director for a specified period which has not yet expired, and his removal is inconsistent with such contract. The Companies Act 1967, s. 26, *ante*,[56] enables members to inspect the service contract and ascertain how much it will cost to remove a director.

A director suing for damages must, of course, try to mitigate his loss by obtaining suitable alternative employment. And in calculating the damages, as to £5,000 of the amount claimed, the court will deduct the tax which the removed director would have paid had he not been removed, *i.e.* he will be awarded a net sum. As to the excess over £5,000, the director will have to pay tax to the Revenue.[57] If compensation, *i.e.* liquidated damages or damages for breach of contract where the amount of damages is agreed in the contract, is

[54] *Bushell* v. *Faith* [1970] A.C. 1099.
[55] p. 344.
[56] p. 325.
[57] *Parsons* v. *B.N.M. Laboratories Ltd.* [1964] 1 Q.B. 95 (C.A.); *Bold* v. *Brough, Nicholson & Hall* [1964] 1 W.L.R. 201.

paid, it is chargeable to tax in the recipient's hands in so far as it exceeds £5,000.[58]

A director validly removed from office may, in appropriate circumstances, be entitled to an order under section 210 where the affairs of the company have been conducted oppressively,[59] or an order that the company be wound up by the court on the ground that winding up is just and equitable.[60]

It has been held that the New South Wales section 120, which corresponds to, although it differs in some respects from, section 184 *ante*, empowers a public company to remove not only particular directors but the board of directors as a whole by a single resolution.[61]

PROCEEDINGS OF DIRECTORS

Unless the articles otherwise provide, the directors must act as a board. Table A, article 98, provides that they "may meet together for the despatch of business, adjourn, and otherwise regulate their meetings, as they think fit."

Article 98 further provides that a director may, and the secretary on the requisition of a director must, at any time summon a board meeting.

Every director is entitled to have reasonable notice of a meeting except that article 98, *ante*, provides that notice need not be given to a director who is absent from the United Kingdom. What is reasonable notice depends on the practice of the company, but if a director wishes to complain of the shortness of the notice he should act promptly, otherwise the court will not interfere.[62]

If notice is not properly given, the proceedings at the meeting are void.

Application was invited for 106,000 shares, and the directors resolved not to allot until 14,000 shares were applied for. A subsequent meeting was held at which two directors, a quorum, were present, when a resolution was passed to allot the shares applied for, about 3,000. The meeting was held at a few hours' notice at 2 o'clock. This was much shorter notice than had ever been given before. One director did not receive notice until next day, and another gave notice that he could not attend until 3 o'clock. *Held*, the allotment was void: *Re Homer District Gold Mines* (1888) 39 Ch.D. 546.

[58] Income and Corporation Taxes Act 1970, ss. 187–188
[59] *Post* p. 389.
[60] *Re Westbourne Galleries Ltd.* [1973] A.C. 360, *post* p. 384.
[61] *Taylor* v. *McNamara* [1974] 1 N.S.W. L.R. 164.
[62] See *Browne* v. *La Trinidad* (1887) 37 Ch.D. 1 (C.A.).

A quorum is that number of directors which must be present to make the proceedings of the board valid. The articles usually fix a quorum. Table A, article 99, provides: "The quorum necessary for the transaction of the business of the directors may be fixed by the directors, and unless so fixed shall be two."

If the number of directors sinks below the quorum, the directors cannot act unless the articles provide, as they usually do, that the continuing directors can act.

Table A, article 100, provides that if and so long as the number of directors is reduced below the number constituting a quorum, "the continuing directors or director may act for the purpose of increasing the number of directors to that number, or of summoning a general meeting of the company, but for no other purpose."

In ascertaining whether a quorum is present, those directors who are incompentent to vote on the matter under discussion must not be counted,[63] as is now provided by Table A, article 84, *post*.[64] Directors, however, can attend the meeting even if they are unable to vote.[65] One transaction cannot be split up into two resolutions so as to qualify directors to vote.

Y. and D., two directors of a company, had made advances to the company in consideration of receiving debentures. The company had four directors, three of whom were a quorum. A resolution was passed granting a debenture to Y. Y. did not vote on this resolution. Another resolution was then passed granting a debenture to D., on which D. did not vote. The two debentures ranked equally among themselves. *Held*, the issue of the two debentures formed one transaction in which Y. and D. were equally interested and that the two resolutions were invalid for want of a quorum: *Re North Eastern Insurance Co. Ltd.* [1919] 1 Ch. 198.

If an allotment is invalid owing to some informality in the constitution of the board it will in most cases be binding on the company, either because of the rule in *Royal British Bank* v. *Turquand* or section 180, *post*,[66] or because of subsequent ratification by a properly constituted board.[67]

The articles deal with the election of a chairman. By Table A, article 101, the directors may elect a chairman of their meetings and determine the period for which he is to hold office. Article 98 provides that questions arising at a board meeting shall be decided by a

---

[63] *Re Greymouth Point Elizabeth Ry., etc., Co. Ltd.* [1904] 1 Ch. 32.
[64] p. 357.
[65] *Grimwade* v. *B.P.S. Syndicate Ltd.* (1915) 31 T.L.R. 531.
[66] pp. 410, 417.
[67] *Re Portuguese Consolidated Copper Mines Ltd.* (1890) 45 Ch.D. 16 (C.A.).

majority of votes, and that in case of an equality of votes the chairman shall have a second or casting vote. (The chairman has no casting vote at common law.[68])

Table A, article 106, provides that a resolution in writing, signed by all the directors entitled to receive notice of a meeting of the directors, shall be as valid as if it had been passed at a board meeting duly convened and held. (The position is the same at common law.[69])

Section 145 provides that minutes of proceedings at directors' meetings must be entered in books kept for the purpose, and such minutes signed by the chairman of the meeting at which the proceedings were had, or by the chairman of the next succeeding meeting, are evidence of the proceedings. Where minutes have been duly made there is a presumption that the meeting was duly held and convened, that all proceedings were duly had and that all appointments of directors and managers were valid.

By section 436 the minutes may be kept in a bound book, or in a loose-leaf book provided that adequate precautions are taken for guarding against falsification.

If the minutes are incomplete, a resolution duly passed can be proved by other evidence.[70]

Although section 145 contains no provision for the inspection of the minutes, the Court of Session may, on the petition of a director presented to the *nobile officium*, ordain a company to make them available for inspection by the director and by a named accountant on his behalf.[71]

POWERS OF DIRECTORS

The powers of the directors depend on the articles since, apart from requiring that certain things, *e.g.* alterations to the articles (s. 10) or the capital (ss. 61, 66), shall be done by the members in general meeting, the Act leaves the distribution of powers between the general meeting and the board to the articles, which always give the directors extensive powers.

Table A, article 80, provides: "The business of the company shall be managed by the directors, who may pay all expenses incurred in promoting and registering the company, and may exercise all such powers of the company as are not, by the

---

[68] *Wall* v. *London and Northern Assets Corpn.* [1898] 2 Ch. 469 (C.A.).
[69] *Re Bonelli's Telegraph Co.* (1871) L.R. 12 Eq. 246.
[70] *Re Fireproof Doors Ltd.* [1916] 2 Ch. 142.
[71] *M'Cusker* v. *M'Rae*, 1966 S.C. 253.

Act or by these regulations, required to be exercised by the company in general meeting, subject, nevertheless, to any of these regulations, to the provisions of the Act and to such regulations, being not inconsistent with the aforesaid regulations or provisions, as may be prescribed by the company in general meeting; but no regulation made by the company in general meeting shall invalidate any prior act of the directors which would have been valid if that regulation had not been made."

If they act within the powers given to them by such an article, directors are not bound to obey resolutions passed by the share-holders at a general meeting; such resolutions cannot override a decision of the directors or control the exercise of their powers in the future.[72] The directors' powers can be altered for the future by an alteration of the articles in the proper way,[73] but the articles cannot be altered with retrospective effect. And it may be that the directors can be removed from office in the proper way.[74]

"A company cannot by ordinary resolution dictate to or overrule the directors in respect of matters entrusted to them by the articles. To do that it is necessary to have a special resolution": *per* Plowman J. in *Bamford* v. *Bamford* [1970] Ch. 212 at p. 220.

The articles of a company contained an article like Table A, article 80, except that it was stated to be "subject to such regulations as might be made by the company by extraordinary resolution." The majority of the shareholders arranged a sale of the company's undertaking and requisitioned a meeting at which an ordinary resolution requiring the directors to seal the contract was passed. *Held*, the directors were not bound to obey the resolution: *Automatic Self-Cleansing Filter Syndicate Co. Ltd.* v. *Cuninghame* [1906] 2 Ch. 34 (C.A.).

The articles contained an article like Table A, article 80, and also provided that no resolution of the directors to acquire or dispose of premises was to be valid unless neither A nor B dissented. (A and B were the managing directors.) The directors resolved to acquire premises. B dissented. An ordinary resolution to the same effect as the board resolution was passed at an extraordinary general meeting of the company. *Held*, the ordinary resolution was inconsistent with the articles and the company was restrained from acting on it: *Salmon* v. *Quin & Axtens Ltd.* [1909] 1 Ch. 311 (C.A.); [1909] A.C. 442.

"This Court decided not long since, in [the *Automatic Self-Cleaning* case], that even a resolution of a numerical majority at a general meeting of the company cannot impose its will upon the directors when the articles have confided to them the control of the company's affairs": *per* Farwell L.J. in [1909] 1 Ch. 311 at p. 319, quoting Buckley L.J. in *Gramophone & Typewriter Ltd.* v. *Stanley* [1908] 2 K.B. 89 (C.A.).

In accordance with the principle set out above, a resolution passed by a company in general meeting that the directors should make an

---

[72] *Automatic Self-Cleansing Filter Syndicate Co. Ltd.*, v. *Cuninghame* [1906] 2 Ch. 34 (C.A.); *Salmon* v. *Quin Axtens Ltd.* [1909] 1 Ch. 311 (C.A.); [1909] A.C. 442.
[73] *Ante* p. 109.
[74] *Ante* p. 328.

advance of money to the shareholders pending the declaration of a dividend was held to be inoperative.[75]

If directors are unable to exercise one of their powers because of deadlock on the board or because their number has fallen below the number required for a quorum, the company in general meeting may exercise the power.[76]

The position is similar if a company has no directors.[77] Where a company has no directors and two individuals, acting without the authority of the company, commence an action in the company's name, the company in general meeting or, if the company is being wound up, the liquidator can ratify the proceedings.[78]

If directors exceed or improperly exercise their powers, their action can be ratified by an ordinary resolution of the company in general meeting.[79]

By way of defence to a take-over bid directors allotted 500,000 shares at par for cash to a third company which was the principal distributor of the products of the company to be taken over. The articles provided that the unissued shares were to be at the directors' disposal. Two shareholders brought an action against the three directors, the third company, and the company, claiming a declaration that the allotment was invalid in that the directors had not acted bona fide in the interests of the company. *Held*, assuming that the allotment was *intra vires* the company and the directors but not bona fide in the interests of the company and therefore voidable, it could after full disclosure be ratified by an ordinary resolution at a general meeting: *Bamford* v. *Bamford* [1970] Ch. 212 (C.A.), approving *Hogg* v. *Cramphorn Ltd.*, *post*.[80]

If directors improperly refuse to exercise a power to initiate an action in the company's name, a minority shareholders' action may be brought by way of exception to the rule in *Foss* v. *Harbottle*.[81]

Power to manage the business of the company does not give directors power to fix their own remuneration.[82] The articles, however, may empower them, as does Table A, article 87, to pay a gratuity or pension or allowance on retirement to a director who has

[75] *Scott* v. *Scott* [1943] 1 All E.R. 582.
[76] *Barron* v. *Potter* [1914] 1 Ch. 895, where the articles gave the board of directors power to appoint an additional director and, owing to differences between the directors, no board meeting could be held for the purpose. *Held*, the company retained power to appoint additional directors in general meeting.
[77] *Per* Lord Hailsham of St. Marylebone in *Alexander Ward & Co. Ltd.* v. *Samyang Navigation Co. Ltd.*, 1975 S.L.T. 126 (H.L.) at p. 129.
[78] *Alexander Ward* case, *ante*.
[79] *Grant* v. *United Kingdom Switchback Rlwys. Co.* (1888) 40 Ch.D. 135 (C.A.).
[80] p. 351.
[81] *Cook* v. *Deeks* [1916] 1 A.C. 554, *post* p. 379; *per* Hudson J. in *Kraus* v. *J. G. Lloyd Pty. Ltd.* [1965] V.R. 232, at pp. 236, 237, *post* p. 380.
[82] *Foster* v. *Foster* [1916] 1 Ch. 532.

held a salaried office with the company, or to his widow or dependants.

The Jenkins Report[83] recommended that directors should not have the power to issue any shares without the prior approval of the company in general meeting. The Committee were not prepared to make statutory the requirement of The Stock Exchange, that issues for cash of equity shares or securities convertible into equity shares should in the first instance be offered *pro rata* to the existing equity shareholders unless the company has otherwise resolved. The Report[83] also recommended that directors should not be able to dispose of the whole or substantially the whole of the company's undertaking or assets without the approval of a general meeting.

Clauses 54 and 55 of the Companies Bill 1973 would have given effect to both recommendations.

The directors cannot delegate their powers unless empowered to do so by the articles. It will be seen later[84] that the articles usually provide for delegation to a managing director. They usually also provide for delegation to a committee of directors.

Table A, article 102, provides: "The directors may delegate any of their powers to committees consisting of such member or members of their body as they think fit; any committee so formed shall in the exercise of the powers so delegated conform to any regulations that may be imposed on it by the directors."

REMUNERATION OF DIRECTORS

Directors as such are not servants of the company,[85] but managers or controllers of the company's affairs. Accordingly they have no claim to payment for their services unless, as is usual, there is a provision for payment in the articles.[86]

Table A, article 76, provides: "The remuneration of the directors shall from time to time be determined by the company in general meeting. Such remuneration shall be deemed to accrue from day to day. The directors may also be paid all travelling, hotel and other expenses properly incurred by them in attending and returning from meetings of the directors or any committee of the directors or general meetings of the company or in connection with the business of the company."

[83] Para. 122.
[84] p. 343.
[85] *Post* p. 346.
[86] *Per* McCardie J. in *Moriarty* v. *Regent's Garage Co. Ltd.* [1921] 1 K.B. 423, at p. 446; *cf.* Lord President Inglis in *M'Naughtan Brunton* (1882) 10 R. 111 at p. 113.

It should be remembered that a director may hold some other position with the company, *e.g.* he may also be the managing director, in which case he will be a servant of the company as regards that other position and will receive a salary fixed by his contract of service or employment with the company.[87]

If remuneration is voted to the directors, it constitutes a debt due from the company and is consequently payable not only out of profits but also out of capital.[88] As was shown earlier,[89] a clause in the articles that directors shall receive a certain sum as remuneration, although it cannot be directly enforced against the company, is binding if the directors have accepted office on the footing of the articles.[90]

A director who is entitled to remuneration for his services is not entitled to his travelling and other expenses in attending board and other meetings unless the articles expressly so provide.

The articles, which were not like Table A, article 76, provided that each director should be paid £200 a year by way of remuneration for his services, and that the company should pay all costs and expenses which any officer of the company should incur in the discharge of his duties. Y. was appointed a director, and shortly afterwards the directors passed a resolution that all reasonable travelling expenses should be reimbursed to the directors. *Held*, the resolution was *ultra vires* the directors, and Y. must repay the travelling expenses received. His expenses of attending directors' meetings were covered by his remuneration: *Young* v. *Naval and Military Society* [1905] 1 K.B. 687.[91]

It is unlawful for a company to make tax-free payments to directors. A provision for payment to a director of remuneration tax free has effect as if it were for payment, as a gross sum subject to income tax and surtax, of the net sum for which it actually provides: section 189. For example, a provision for payment of £100 free of tax has effect as if it were for payment of £100 subject to tax.[92]

---

[87] *Anderson* v. *James Sutherland (Peterhead) Ltd.*, 1941 S.C. 203, in which a managing director was held to be a person "employed by the company in any capacity" within an article which enabled the directors to remove such a person from membership when he was dismissed as managing director for misconduct (assaulting a co-director by the firing of a revolver at a directors' meeting).

[88] *Re Lundy Granite Co.* (1872) 26 L.T. 673.

[89] p. 108.

[90] *Re New British Iron Co.* [1898] 1 Ch. 324.

[91] See also *Marmor Ltd.* v. *Alexander*, 1908 S.C. 78 and *Tomlinson* v. *Liquidators of Scottish Amalgamated Silks Ltd.*, 1935 S.C. (H.L.) 1; 1934 S.C. 85.

[92] *Owens* v. *Multilux Ltd.*, 1974 S.L.T. 189 (N.I.R.C.) (provision in contract between company and managing director for a "salary of £2,500 per annum net of deductions" held to give the managing director a legal right to payment of a gross sum of £2,500 per annum subject to income tax).

Unless authorised by the articles, directors cannot vote remuneration to one of themselves or appoint one of their number to a salaried position with the company. It has been said that "Directors have no right to be paid for their services, and cannot pay themselves or each other, or make presents to themselves out of the company's assets, unless authorised so to do by the instrument which regulates the company or by the shareholders at a properly convened meeting." [93]

The article governing directors' remuneration was the same as Table A, article 76.[94] The *directors* passed a resolution appointing K., one of the directors, "overseas director" at a salary of £1,800 a year. In pursuance of this appointment K. was obliged to go, and did go, to Australia. He sued for arrears of salary. *Held*, the appointment was *ultra vires* the board, so that K. could not recover the arrears of salary and was liable to refund salary already received: *Kerr* v. *Marine Products Ltd.* (1928) 44 T.L.R. 292.

However, where directors held a majority of the shares and in virtue thereof secured the passing of a resolution increasing their remuneration, the resolution was held not invalid unless fraud was proved or the resolution was *ultra vires* the company.[95]

A resolution of the directors to forgo fees to which they are entitled is binding on them and on the company if the company is a party to the agreement.[96] Otherwise the directors may rescind the resolution and claim for fees.[97]

On a liquidation, directors are not entitled to preferential payment of fees owing to them, since as directors they are not servants of the company.[98] It is otherwise with regard to salary owing to them where they hold some other position with the company.[99]

When a director ceases to be a director during a year of office, a question arises as to whether he is entitled to have his remuneration apportioned. If, *e.g.*, the articles say that he is to be paid "at the rate of" so much a year, he is entitled to be paid for the period during which he was a director.[1] On the other hand, if he is to be paid £100 a year, or in any way other than at the rate of so much a year, it has

[93] *Per* Lindley L.J. in *Re George Newman & Co.* [1895[1 Ch. 674 (C.A.) at p. 686.
[94] *Ante* p. 335.
[95] *Harris* v. *A. Harris Ltd.*, 1936 S.C. 183.
[96] *West Yorkshire Darracq Agency Ltd.* v. *Coleridge* [1911] 2 K.B. 326.
[97] *Re Consolidated Nickel Mines Ltd.* [1914] 1 Ch. 883.
[98] *Re Newspaper Proprietary Syndicate Ltd.* [1900] 2 Ch. 349.
[99] *Post* p. 594.
[1] *Swabey* v. *Port Darwin Gold Mining Co.* (1889) 1 Meg. 385, although despite the report, the articles did not contain the words "at the rate of," as pointed out in *Inman's* case *post*.

been held that he is entitled to be paid only for each complete year he serves, and not for any broken period.[2]

The Apportionment Act 1870, ss. 2 and 5, provides that all salaries and other periodical payments in the nature of income shall be considered as accruing from day to day and apportionable in respect of time accordingly but, in *Moriarty* v. *Regent's Garage Co. Ltd.*,[3] although a Divisional Court held that, in the absence of agreement to the contrary, that Act applied to directors' remuneration, the decision was reversed in the Court of Appeal on other grounds.[4] Whether or not that Act applies to directors' remuneration is, therefore, an open question. It is submitted that it applies. Further, it will be remembered that Table A, article 76, provides that remuneration shall accrue from day to day, with the result that, in cases to which such an article applies, the remuneration is definitely apportionable.

Clause 51 of the Companies Bill 1973 purported to prohibit the alteration of a company's articles so as to provide for or improve directors' emoluments except by a resolution which does not deal with other matters.

Disclosure of directors' emoluments

Any provision in the articles as to the directors' remuneration must usually be disclosed in a prospectus issued by the company: Schedule 4.[5]

By section 196 the accounts which must be laid before the company in general meeting must show certain particulars of directors' salaries, pensions, etc.

The particulars are:

(1) The aggregate amount of the directors' emoluments.

These include fees and percentages, sums paid as expenses allowances which are charged to income tax,[6] contributions paid in respect of the directors under any pension scheme, and the estimated money value of any other benefits received otherwise than in cash. The accounts must distinguish between emoluments in respect of services as directors and other emoluments such as sums received by the directors as salaried employees of the company.

[2] *Salton* v. *New Beeston Cycle Co.* [1899] 1 Ch. 775; *Inman* v. *Ackroyd & Best Ltd.* [1901] 1 Q.B. 613 (C.A.), (followed in *Liquidator of the Fife Linoleum, etc., Co. Ltd.* v. *Lornie* (1905) 13 S.L.T. 670 (O.H.).
[3] [1921] 1 K.B. 423.
[4] [1921] 2 K.B. 766.
[5] *Ante* p. 134.
[6] See Finance Act 1976, ss. 60–72.

(2) The aggregate amount of directors' or past directors' pensions.

This does not include pensions paid under a pension scheme where the contributions are substantially adequate for the maintenance of the scheme, but does include a pension paid to a director's widow or other dependent.

(3) The aggregate amount of any compensation paid to directors or past directors for loss of office.

This includes sums paid on a director's retirement from office.

These amounts must include all relevant sums received from the company, the company's subsidiaries and any other person. The amount shown under (3), above, must distinguish between sums received from the company, the company's subsidiaries and other persons.

Further, sections 6 and 7 of the Companies Act 1967 provide that, subject as below, the accounts must contain certain additional particulars of directors' emoluments.

The additional particulars are:

(4) With respect to each person who has been chairman of the directors' meetings during the year, his emoluments so far as attributable to his period of office (unless his duties were mainly discharged outside the United Kingdom).

(5) With respect to all the directors (other than any whose duties were mainly discharged abroad), the number whose several emoluments did not exceed £2,500, exceeded £2,500 but not £15,000,[7] and so on in bands of £2,500.

(6) If the emoluments of one or more directors exceed the chairman's or chairmen's emoluments, his emoluments or the greater or, as the case may be, the greatest emoluments.

Emoluments include all such amounts (other than contributions paid in respect of a person under a pension scheme) as are caught by (1) above.

(7) The number of directors who have waived rights to receive emoluments and the aggregate amount of such emoluments.

Sections 6 and 7 do not apply to a company which is neither a holding company nor a subsidiary as respects a financial year in which the aggregate amount of the directors' emoluments does not exceed £15,000.

If accounts do not comply with sections 6 and 7 the auditors must, so far as they reasonably can, include the required particulars in their report.

Each director is under a duty to give notice to the company of such matters relating to himself as may be necessary to enable the above information to be shown in the accounts, under penalty of a fine of £50: 1948 Act, s. 198; 1967 Act, ss. 6, 7.

COMPENSATION TO DIRECTORS FOR LOSS OF OFFICE

It is unlawful for a company to make to a director any payment by way of compensation for loss of office, or as consideration for or in

---

[7] Companies (Accounts) Regulations 1971 (S.I. 1971 No. 2044).

connection with retirement, unless particulars of the proposed payment, including the amount, are disclosed to the members and the proposal is approved by the company: section 191. It was held in *Re Duomatic Ltd.*[8] that disclosure must be made to *all* the members, even those with no right to attend and vote at general meetings, whilst the payment is still a proposed payment, although in *Wallersteiner* v. *Moir*[9] Lord Denning M.R. said that he imagined that payment could be later approved by the company in general meeting.

The section does not apply to a payment to a *managing director as such*.[10] Nor does it apply to a payment to a director who does not retire.

It is unlawful for anyone to make to a director a payment by way of compensation for loss of office, etc., in connection with the transfer of the whole or part of the company's undertaking or property unless particulars are disclosed and approved. If such a payment is not disclosed the director holds it upon trust for the company: section 192.

When, in connection with a transfer of all or any of the shares in the company resulting from (*a*) an offer made to the general body of shareholders, (*b*) an offer made with a view to the company becoming the subsidiary of another, (*c*) an offer made with a view to an individual obtaining control of not less than one-third of the voting power at a general meeting, or (*d*) any other offer conditional on acceptance to a given extent, a payment is to be made to a director as compensation for loss of or retirement from office, he must take reasonable steps to see that particulars of the proposed payment, including the amount, are sent with any notice of the offer for their shares given to the shareholders. If this is not done, or the payment is not, before the transfer of the shares, approved by a meeting of the shareholders summoned for the purpose, the director holds the payment on trust for the persons who have sold their shares as a result of the offer: section 193.

Sections 192 and 193 cannot be avoided, *e.g.* by paying more than the market value for a director's shares, because section 194 provides that, in connection with sections 192 and 193, the price paid to a director for any of his shares in the company in excess of the price which could have been obtained by other shareholders, or the

[8] [1969] 2 Ch. 365.
[9] [1974] 1 W.L.R. 991 (C.A.). at p. 1016.
[10] *Lincoln Mills* v. *Gough* [1964] V.R. 193.

money value of any valuable consideration given to him, is deemed to have been a payment to him of compensation for loss of office. References in sections 191, 192 and 193 to payments of compensation for loss of office exclude bona fide payments of damages for breach of contract or of pensions in respect of past services.

In so far as the compensation for loss of office paid to a director exceeds £5,000, it is liable to tax in his hands.[11]

The Jenkins Report[12] recommended that sections 191, 192 and 193 be extended to payments to former directors, to payments in respect of any other office in connection with the management of the company's affairs (*e.g.* the office of managing director) and to payments in respect of the office of director or any other office in connection with the management of the affairs of a subsidiary of the company. Further, that the approval required by sections 191, 192 and 193 should be by special resolution. Finally, that where the sections require disclosure, any payment of damages for breach of contract or of pensions should also be required to be disclosed.

Clause 50 of the 1973 Companies Bill would have given effect to these recommendations.

LOANS TO DIRECTORS

Section 190 is another section intended to ensure that a director does not abuse his position. The section provides that it is unlawful for a company to make a loan to a director of it or of its holding company, or to guarantee or provide security for a loan made to a director by another person, unless—

(1) the company is a subsidiary company and the director is its holding company; or

(2) the ordinary business of the company includes the lending of money or the giving of guarantees, and the loan or guarantee is made or given in the ordinary course of that business; or

(3) the loan is made to provide funds to enable the director to meet expenditure incurred by him for the purposes of the company, or to enable him to perform his duties properly.

In the last case the company in general meeting must first approve, or a condition must be imposed that if the company does not approve at or before the next annual general meeting the loan must be repaid, or the guarantee or security discharged, within six months after such meeting. If the approval of the company is not given as required by

[11] Income and Corporation Taxes Act 1970, ss. 187–188.　　[12] Para. 99.

such a condition, the directors authorising the loan, guarantee or security are jointly and severally liable to indemnify the company against any loss arising therefrom.

The general prohibition of loans, etc., by companies to their directors is reasonable. The Report of the Cohen Committee,[13] which led to the introduction of section 190, stated that it is "undesirable that directors should borrow from their companies. If the director can offer good security, it is no hardship to him to borrow from other sources. If he cannot offer good security, it is undesirable that he should obtain from the company credit which he would not be able to obtain elsewhere. Several cases have occurred in recent years where directors have borrowed money from their companies on inadequate security and have been unable to repay the loans."

The exceptions to the rule are reasonable, too. As regards the first exception, the holding company may hold all or a majority of the shares in the subsidiary, so that if it borrows from the subsidiary it is in effect borrowing from itself. The other exceptions are obviously necessary.

It should be noted that the prohibition does not apply to a loan to a person who later becomes a director of the company. A question arises as to the meaning of the word "loan"—does it include a sale of goods on credit by a company to a director?[14] As regards the second exception, reference should be made to the case of *Steen* v. *Law* which was dealt with in Chapter 10.[15]

The Jenkins Report[16] recommended that section 190 be extended to prohibit loans by a company to another company in which one or more of the directors of the lending company have a controlling interest. It was thought that the section could be circumvented in such a case but in *Wallersteiner* v. *Moir*[17] Lord Denning M.R. said that if another company to which money is lent is the puppet of a director of the lending company, the loan should be treated as made to him.

Clause 46 of the Companies Bill 1973 would also have prohibited a loan to a member of a director's family or to another company in which a director has a significant interest.

If a loan is made in contravention of section 190 the company will not be entitled to recover the amount from the director—the

[13] (1945) Cmd. 6659, para. 94.
[14] Parsons & Kenneally, *Principles of Company Law in N.S.W.*, Ch. VI, p. 49.
[15] *Ante* p. 193.   [16] Para. 99.
[17] [1974] 1 W.L.R. 991 (C.A.), at p. 1015.

contract is illegal by statute as formed and so neither party can sue on it. This is why the New South Wales equivalent of section 190[18] provides, *inter alia*, that nothing in it shall operate to prevent the company from recovering the amount of any loan given contrary to the provisions of the section. However, in *Wallersteiner* v. *Moir ante*, where the loan was unlawful under section 190, Lord Denning said[19] that the director was guilty of misfeasance and liable to indemnify the company against any loss arising therefrom.

Particulars of loans made to directors or other officers or guaranteed or secured by the company or one of its subsidiaries must be shown in the accounts: section 197. A director is under a general duty to make disclosure for the purposes of section 197: section 198.

MANAGING DIRECTOR

Unless the directors are empowered to appoint a managing director[20] by the memorandum[21] or the articles, as they usually are by the articles, the directors cannot appoint a managing director.[22] When the articles empower the directors to appoint a managing director, the company in general meeting cannot itself make such an appointment without first altering the articles.[23]

Table A, article 107, provides that the directors may appoint *one or more of their body* to the office of managing director for such period and on such terms as they think fit, and, *subject to the terms of any particular agreement*, may revoke such appointment; that a director so appointed shall not, whilst holding that office, retire by rotation,[24] but that the appointment shall be automatically determined if he ceases to be a director.

A managing director has two functions and two capacities, those of director and managing director. As managing director, he is a party to a contract of employment or service with the company.[25]

---

[18] Companies Act, 1961 as amended (N.S.W.), s. 125.   [19] At p. 1015.

[20] For a discussion of the general nature of the post of managing director, see *Anderson* v. *James Sutherland (Peterhead) Ltd.*, 1941 S.C. 203, *ante* p. 336; also *Hindle* v. *John Cotton Ltd.* (1919) 56 S.L.R. 625 (H.L.) (managing director held to be an "employee" within the meaning of the articles) and opinions in *Kerr* v. *Walker*, 1933 S.C. 458.

[21] *Re Scottish Loan & Finance Co. Ltd.* (1944) 44 S.R. (N.S.W.) 461.

[22] *Per* Swinfen Eady J. in *Boschoek Proprietary Co. Ltd.* v. *Fuke* [1906] 1 Ch. 148 at p. 159.   [23] *Thomas Logan Ltd.* v. *Davis* (1911) 104 L.T. 914; 105 L.T. 419.

[24] *Ante* p. 312.

[25] *Per* Lord Normand in *Anderson* v. *James Sutherland (Peterhead) Ltd.*, 1941 S.C. 203, at p. 218; *per* Jenkins L.J. in *Goodwin* v. *Brewster* (1951) 32 T.C. 80, at p. 96.

Subject to the articles, the powers and duties of a managing director depend upon his contract of service with the company.

Table A provides:
"109. The directors may entrust to and confer upon a managing director any of the powers exercisable by them upon such terms and conditions and with such restrictions as they may think fit, and either collaterally with or to the exclusion of their own powers and may from time to time revoke, withdraw, alter or vary all or any of such powers."

C. was appointed a managing director of H. Co. His service agreement provided that he should perform the duties and exercise the powers in relation to the business of H. Co. and the businesses of its existing subsidiary companies which might from time to time be assigned to or vested in him by the directors. Later the directors resolved that C. should confine his attention to a particular subsidiary company. C. sued for damages for breach of contract. C.'s action was dismissed: *Caddies* v. *Harold Holdsworth & Co.* (*Wakefield*) *Ltd.*, 1955 S.C.(H.L.) 27; [1955] 1 All E.R. 725 (H.L.).

As will be seen in Chapter 18, a managing director may have implied power to enter into certain agreements on behalf of the company even though there has been no express delegation of the power to him by the board.[26]

Where a managing director is appointed under an article like Table A, article 107, above, his appointment may be prematurely determined by his removal from his directorship,[27] *e.g.* under section 184,[28] but the company will be liable in damages if this is in breach of his contract of service, as it usually will be. In fact the company will often have to pay a large sum by way of liquidated damages.

S. was appointed managing director of N. Ltd., a subsidiary of L. Co., for ten years. The articles of N. Ltd. included article 68 of Table A in the 1929 Act (which provided that a managing director's appointment should be automatically determined if he ceased to be a director or if the company in general meeting resolved to terminate his appointment). M. Co. bought the shares in L. Co., and, at a general meeting of N. Ltd., resolutions were passed removing S. from office

---

[26] *Allison* v. *Scotia Motor, etc., Co. Ltd.* (1906) 14 S.L.T. 9 (O.H.) (implied power to engage a works manager for a period of five years).

[27] *Southern Foundries* (*1926*) *Ltd.* v. *Shirlaw* [1940] A.C. 701, *ante* p. 114; *Nelson* v. *James Nelson & Sons Ltd.* [1914] 2 K.B. 770 (C.A.); *Carrier Australasia Ltd.* v. *Hunt* (1939) 61 C.L.R. 534. (First Australian Supplement to Charlesworth & Cain, p. 71.) In the *Nelson* case the articles empowered the board to appoint a managing director and to revoke the appointment. The Board appointed the plaintiff managing director, the agreement providing that he was to hold the office so long as, *inter alia*, he efficiently performed the duties. The board revoked his appointment whilst he was still fulfilling the conditions of the agreement and he was held entitled to damages for breach of contract. In the *Carrier Australasia* case the articles empowered the company to remove a director, subject to the provisions of any agreement. The articles were altered so as to delete the words "subject to . . . any agreement" and then the managing director was removed from his directorship. He was held to be entitled to damages.

[28] *Ante* p. 328.

as a director and terminating his service agreement. S. sued for damages for wrongful dismissal. *Held*, S. succeeded. It was an implied term of the service agreement that N. Ltd. would do nothing of its own motion to put an end to the state of circumstances which enabled S. to continue as managing director: *Shindler* v. *Northern Raincoat Co. Ltd.* [1960] 1 W.L.R. 1038, applying *Stirling* v. *Maitland* (1865) 34 L.J. Q.B. 1 and *Southern Foundries (1926) Ltd.* v. *Shirlaw* [1940] A.C. 701.[29]

Per Diplock J., quoting Cockburn C.J. in *Stirling* v. *Maitland ante*: "If a party enters into an arrangement which can only take effect by the continuance of a certain existing set of circumstances, there is an implied engagement on his part that he shall do nothing of his own motion to put an end to that state of circumstances."

R. was appointed managing director at £7 a week, the duration of his appointment not being specified. Article 68 of Table A in the 1929 Act, *ante*, was one of the articles. Later, the directors dismissed R. on a month's notice and their action was confirmed by the company in general meeting. R. sued for damages for wrongful dismissal on the ground that he was not given reasonable notice. *Held*, the claim failed, because R.'s contract incorporated article 68 which empowered the company to dismiss him without notice by a resolution in general meeting. In the absence of any contract independent of article 68 and the directors' resolution appointing him, there was no ground for implying a term as to reasonable notice: *Read* v. *Astoria Garage (Streatham) Ltd.* [1952] Ch. 637 (C.A.).

Where directors have a discretionary power to dismiss a managing director, this power must be exercised in good faith in the interests of the company and not for some ulterior purpose such as appropriation of the managing director's shares.[30]

The articles usually provide for the remuneration of a managing director.

Table A provides: "108. A managing director shall receive such remuneration (whether by way of salary, commission or participation in profits, or partly in one way and partly in another) as the directors may determine."

Table A, article 108, is an independent article providing for the remuneration of a managing director whether appointed by the articles or by the board under Table A, article 107.[31]

In a case[31] where a member was appointed managing director by the articles which also incorporated Table A, article 108, it was said[32] that "The effect of . . . article 108 . . . coupled with the fact that the applicant was a member of the company, . . . is that a contract exists between himself and the company for payment to him of remuneration as managing director, and that remuneration depends on article 108. . . ."

In practice a managing director's remuneration will be specified in his contract of service which the directors will negotiate on behalf of the company.

---

[29] *Ante* p. 114.   [30] *Hindle* v. *John Cotton Ltd.* (1919) 56 S.L.R. 625 (H.L.).
[31] *Re Richmond Gate Property Co. Ltd.* [1965] 1 W.L.R. 335.
[32] *Per* Plowman J. at p. 337.

If, where the appointment of a managing director is in fact void, he performs services which are accepted by the company, he is entitled to reasonable remuneration.

The articles authorised the directors to appoint one of their number managing director. By contract under the company's seal, C. was appointed managing director at a salary. The seal was affixed to the contract by a resolution of the board of directors but none of the directors had acquired his qualification shares. C. himself acted as managing director, but also failed to acquire his qualification shares. *Held*, C.'s contract was void and C. was not properly appointed managing director. His claim for remuneration in contract failed but the alternative claim in quasi-contract succeeded, *i.e.* he was entitled to payment on a *quantum meruit* basis arising from the performance of services and their acceptance by the company: *Craven-Ellis* v. *Canons Ltd.* [1936] 2 K.B. 403 (C.A.).

A managing director has been held not to be a "servant" of the company so as to be entitled to preferential payment of his salary on a winding up,[33] and has been held to be an "officer" of the company for the purpose of the provision, now in section 258, empowering the court to require any officer of the company to deliver property to the liquidator.[34]

Position of Directors

As a company has no physical but only a legal existence, the management of its affairs is entrusted to human instruments called "directors" whose exact position in relation to the company is rather hard to define. Directors as such are not servants of the company, but are rather managers who in some respects may be said to be (1) quasi-trustees, and (2) agents for the company. The result is that they owe fiduciary duties and certain duties of care to the company, *i.e.* the members as a body, as will be explained later.

"The Directors are a body to whom is delegated the duty of managing the general affairs of the Company. A corporate body can only act by agents, and it is of course the duty of those agents so to act as best to promote the interests of the corporation whose affairs they are conducting. Such agents have duties to discharge of a fiduciary nature towards their principal. And it is a rule of universal application, that no one, having such duties to discharge, shall be allowed to enter into engagements in which he has, or can have, a personal interest conflicting, or which possibly may conflict, with the interests of those whom he is bound to protect": *per* Lord Cranworth L.C. in *Aberdeen Rlwy. Co.* v. *Blaikie Bros.* (1854) 1 Macq. 461 at p. 471.

"The directors are the mere trustees or agents of the company—trustees of the company's money and property—agents in the transactions which they enter into

[33] *Re Newspaper Proprietary Syndicate Ltd.* [1900] 2 Ch. 349, *post* p. 594.
[34] *Dunlop* v. *Donald* (1893) 21 R. 125.

on behalf of the company": *per* Lord Selborne L. C. in *Great Eastern Rlwy. Co.* v. *Turner* (1872) L.R. 8 Ch. 149 at p. 152.

"The director's functions are in one view those of an agent, and in another those of a trustee. But the former predominate over the latter": *per* Lord Johnston in *M'Lintock* v. *Campbell*, 1916 S.C. 966 at p. 980.

Not being in a fiduciary position towards the company *qua* shareholder, a director has the same right as any other shareholder to transfer his shares to a man of straw in order to avoid payment of a call,[35] and he may exercise his voting power at general meetings, even although the effect is to increase his own remuneration[36] or to prevent the calling up of a loan made by the company to himself.[37]

Directors as trustees

Directors have been described as trustees (1) of the company's money and property,[38] and (2) of the powers entrusted to them.

They hold the company's property in their hands or under their control on trust for the company. Such property must be applied for the specified purposes of the company and a misapplication of it is a breach of trust.[39] Where a person has improperly profited from his fiduciary position the court has equitable jurisdiction to award interest on the judgment for damages for misfeasance or breach of duty as a director.[40]

In an action to recover moneys of the company misapplied by them, directors can in England rely on the Limitation Act 1939, s. 19, as if they were trustees,[41] *i.e.* the action must be brought within six years except where they have been guilty of fraud, or where the property is still in their possession or has been previously converted to their own use.

Directors are trustees of their powers in that, as will be explained later,[42] they must exercise them for the purposes for which they were conferred and bona fide for the benefit of the company as a whole.

---

[35] *M'Lintock* v. *Campbell*, 1916 S.C. 966.

[36] *Harris* v. *A. Harris Ltd.*, 1936 S.C. 183.

[37] *Baird* v. *J. Baird & Co. (Falkirk) Ltd.*, 1949 S.L.T. 368 (O.H.).

[38] *Per* Lord Selborne L.C. in *Great Eastern Rlwy. Co.* v. *Turner* (1872) L.R. 8 Ch. 149 at p. 152.

[39] *Selangor United Rubber Estates Ltd.* v. *Cradock (No. 3)* [1968] 1 W.L.R. 1555, *post* p. 355.

[40] *Wallersteiner* v. *Moir (No. 2)* [1975] Q.B. 373 (C.A.), where the interest awarded was compound interest at one per cent. per annum above the official bank rate or minimum lending rate in operation at the time.

[41] *Re Lands Allotment Co.* [1894] 1 Ch. 616 (C.A.), *ante* p. 86; *cf. John S. Boyle Ltd.* v. *Boyle's Trustees*, 1949 S.L.T. (Notes) 45 (O.H.). [42] p. 350.

Directors had power to issue the unissued shares of the company. The company was in no need of further capital, but the directors made a fresh issue to themselves and their supporters with the object of maintaining control of the company and resisting the election of three additional directors which would have made the two existing directors a minority on the board: *Held*, the allotment of the shares was invalid and void. Directors are not entitled to use their power of issuing shares merely for the purpose of maintaining their control or the control of themselves and their friends over the affairs of the company, or merely for the purpose of defeating the wishes of the existing majority of shareholders. The power to issue shares is primarily given to directors for the purpose of enabling them to raise capital when required for the company: *Piercy* v. *S. Mills & Co. Ltd.* [1920] 1 Ch. 77.[43]

If a director, who is about to retire and sell his shares in the company, makes a bargain with his intended successor and the purchaser of the shares that, when the latter controls the company, he will procure it to make a present to the former out of its assets, the recipient of the proceeds is as guilty of misfeasance or breach of trust as the directors who have procured it, *i.e.* the principle of the law of trusts, referred to in *Head* v. *Gould*,[44] applies.[45]

Directors really quasi-trustees

Directors are really only quasi-trustees because (1) the company's money and property are not vested in them but in the company, (2) their functions are not the same as those of trustees, (3) their duties of care are not as onerous as those of trustees.[46]

"The distinction between a director and a trustee is an essential distinction founded on the very nature of things. A trustee is a man who is the owner of the property and deals with it as principal, as owner, and as master, subject only to an equitable obligation to account to some persons to whom he stands in the relation of trustee, and who are his *cestuis que trust* . . . The office of director is that of a paid servant of the company:"[47] *per* James L.J. in *Smith* v. *Anderson* (1880) 15 Ch.D. 247 (C.A.) at p. 275.

"It is sometimes said that directors are trustees. If this means no more than that directors in the performance of their duties stand in a fiduciary relationship to the company, the statement is true enough. But if the statement is meant to be an indication by way of analogy of what those duties are, it appears to me to be wholly misleading. I can see but little resemblance between the duties of a director and the duties of a trustee of a will or of a marriage settlement. It is indeed impossible to describe the duty of directors in general terms, whether by way of analogy or otherwise. The position of a director of a company carrying on a small

---

[43] *Cook* v. *Barry, Henry & Cook Ltd.*, 1923 S.L.T. 692 (O.H.).
[44] [1898] 2 Ch. 250.
[45] *Curtis's Furnishing Stores Ltd.* v. *Freedman* [1966] 1 W.L.R. 1219.
[46] Directors' duties of care are explained *post* p. 362.
[47] "Paid manager" would be more accurate.

retail business is very different from that of a director of a railway company. The duties of a bank director may differ widely from those of an insurance director, and the duties of a director of one insurance company may differ from those of another. . . . The larger the business carried on by the company the more numerous, and the more important, the matters that must of necessity be left to the managers, the accountants and the rest of the staff": *per* Romer J. in *Re City Equitable Fire Insce. Co. Ltd.* [1925] Ch. 407 at p. 426.[48]

Directors as agents

Directors are agents by whom a company acts and[49] it is largely because they are agents that they owe fiduciary duties and contain duties of care to the company.

"Directors of a company are fiduciary agents, and a power conferred upon them cannot be exercised in order to obtain some private advantage or for any purpose foreign to the power": *per* Dixon J. in *Mills* v. *Mills* (1938) 60 C.L.R. 150 at p. 186.

Like other agents, directors incur no personal liability on contracts made by them on behalf of the company, within the scope of their authority.[50]

E. contracted to supply goods to a company of which H. was chairman of directors, payment to be made by the issue of £600 of the company's debentures. The contract was made at a board meeting at which H. was chairman. E. constantly pressed for the debentures, but none was issued, and eventually the company was wound up. *Held*, H. was not liable to an action at the suit of E.: *Elkington & Co.* v. *Hürter* [1892] 2 Ch. 452.

If, however, directors exceed the powers given to them by the memorandum and articles they will be liable for breach of warranty of authority.[51] Their actions may be ratified by the company in general meeting if they act within the powers in the memorandum but outside the powers conferred on them by the articles.

Directors may be *specifically appointed* agents for the shareholders to negotiate a sale of the company's shares. If so, the shareholders are liable for their fraud.

R., managing director of N. Ltd., by frauds of which the other directors were ignorant, made N. Ltd. profitable, and negotiated with E. Ltd. for the sale of the shares in N. Ltd. without disclosing that the profits were based on dishonest trading. The negotiations were reported to the shareholders who, in ignorance of R.s' fraud, authorised R. to complete the sale on the basis of his negotiations. The fraud was subsequently discovered and the shareholders were sued for

---

[48] And see *per* Lord Johnson in *M'Lintock* v. *Campbell*, 1916 S.C. 966 at p. 980.
[49] See, *e.g.*, *per* Lord Selborne L.C. in *Great Eastern Rlwy. Co.* v. *Turner* (1872) L.R. 8 Ch. 149 at p. 152.
[50] Directors may be personally liable under s. 108 (4), *ante* p. 67.
[51] *Firbank's Exors.* v. *Humphreys* (1886) 18 Q.B.D. 54 (C.A.), *post* p. 485.

damages. *Held*, they were liable as R. was their agent to negotiate the sale of their shares, and they were liable for his fraud even though it preceded his appointment as agent: *Briess* v. *Woolley* [1954] A.C. 333.

Further, directors may *hold themselves out* to the shareholders as agents for the shareholders, in which case the directors must disclose any profit made by them to the shareholders.

Directors entered into negotiations for the amalgamation of the company with other companies. Before the negotiations were completed they induced a number of shareholders to give them options on their shares at par, representing that this was necessary to effect the amalgamation. The directors then exercised the option and thereby made a handsome profit. *Held*, they had to account for this profit to the shareholders: *Allen* v. *Hyatt* (1914) 30 T.L.R. 444, distinguishing *Percival* v. *Wright*, below.

DUTIES OF DIRECTORS

Under the general law directors (and other agents of the company) owe fiduciary duties [52] and certain duties of care [53] to the company, *i.e.* the members as a body, and, except in a case like *Allen* v. *Hyatt ante*, not to the individual shareholders or to anyone else. [54]

The directors of a company bought shares from X. They did not disclose to him that negotiations were being conducted for the sale of all the company's shares at a higher price than that asked by X. The negotiations proved abortive. X sued to have his sale set aside on the ground that the directors ought to have disclosed the negotiations. *Held*, the sale was binding, as the directors were under no obligation to disclose the negotiations to X: *Percival* v. *Wright* [1902] 2 Ch. 421.

Clause 53 of the Companies Bill 1973 would have empowered directors, in exercising their powers, to have regard to the interests of the company's employees generally as well as the interests of its members.

The fact that the duties of directors are owed to the company and not the individual shareholders means that the enforcement of the duties may, in theory, be a problem where the directors who are in breach of duty control the company, as will be explained later. [55]

Fiduciary duties

The fiduciary duties of directors are—

(1) to exercise their powers for the purposes for which they were conferred and bona fide for the benefit of the company as a whole;

[52] *Per* Lord Cranworth L.C. in *Aberdeen Rlwy. Co.* v. *Blaikie Bros.* (1854) 1 Macq. 461 at p. 471, *ante* p. 346.
[53] *Per* Romer J. in *Re City Equitable Fire Insce. Co. Ltd.* [1925] Ch. 407 at p. 428.
[54] *e.g.*, not to applicants for shares: *Brown* v. *Stewart* (1898) 1 F. 316; *Wilson* v. *Dunlop, Bremner & Co. Ltd.*, 1921, 1 S.L.T. 35 and 354.   [55] p. 376.

(2) not to put themselves in a position in which their duties to the company and their personal interests may conflict.[56]

As to duty (1), directors' discretionary power to refuse to register a transfer of shares is a fiduciary power.[57] The directors' power to issue shares is also a fiduciary power and the exercise of such a power is invalid if it is not exercised for the purpose for which it was granted, which is primarily to raise capital when required by the company. Thus an issue of shares is invalid if the directors are motivated by self-interest, *e.g.* a desire to preserve their control of the company.[58]

Directors, in an endeavour to secure control in order to forestall a take-over bid, issued unissued shares in the company to trustees to be held for the benefit of employees, the shares being paid for by the trustees out of an interest-free loan from the company. *Held*, the issue exceeded the directors' fiduciary power, it being immaterial that it was made in the bona fide belief that it was in the interests of the company. Since the directors did not hold the majority of the shares before the new issue, the issue could be ratified by the company in general meeting, the votes carried by the shares issued to the trustees not being exercised: *Hogg* v. *Cramphorn Ltd.* [1967] Ch. 254.

Where the self-interest of the directors is involved, they are not permitted to assert that their action was bona fide thought to be, or was, in the interest of the company.[59] However, self-interest is only one instance of improper motive—in the recent Privy Council case of *Howard Smith Ltd.* v. *Ampol Petroleum Ltd.*[60] the directors were not motivated by any purpose of personal gain but an allotment was set aside because they issued the shares for the purpose of destroying the existing majority bloc of shares.

On the other hand, it is wrong to say that the only valid purpose for which shares can be issued is to raise capital for the company.

---

[56] *Per* Lord Cranworth L.C. in *Aberdeen Rlwy. Co.* v. *Blaikie Bros.* (1854) 1 Macq. 461 at p. 471 and *per* Viscount Finlay and Lord Shaw in *Hindle* v. *John Cotton Ltd.* (1919) 56 S.L.R. 625 (H.L.) at p. 631.

[57] See *Re Smith and Fawcett Ltd.* [1942] Ch. 304 (C.A.), *ante* p. 252.

[58] *Piercy* v. *S. Mills & Co. Ltd.* [1920] 1 Ch. 77, *ante* p. 348; *Hogg* v. *Cramphorn Ltd.* [1967] Ch. 254; *Bamford* v. *Bamford* [1970] Ch. 212 (C.A.), *ante* p. 334; *Ngurli* v. *McCann* (1954) 90 C.L.R. 425 (First Australian Supplement to the 10th edn. of Charlesworth & Cain, p. 156), where there was no take-over bid, shares were issued to a shareholder to give him control of the company, the interests of the company as a whole were not considered, and an attempted ratification was a fraud on the minority and so ineffective. See *post* p. 353.

[59] *Hogg's* case, *ante*.

[60] [1974] A.C. 821 (P.C.) (First Australian Supplement, *ante*, p. 158). See also *Ashburton Oil N.L.* v. *Alpha Minerals N.L.* (1971) 45 A.L.J.R. 162.

In a High Court of Australia case[61] the company had no immediate need of fresh capital but it was held that the directors' purpose in allotting shares to another company was to ensure the financial stability of the first company and the allotment was valid.

The phrase "bona fide in the interest of the company as a whole," if it does anything more than restate the general principle applicable to fiduciary powers, at best serves, negatively, to invalidate issues where the directors are acting sectionally, or partially, *i.e.* improperly favouring one section of the shareholders against another. It has been said[62] of such cases that: "The question which arises is sometimes not a question of the interest of the company at all, but a question of what is fair between different classes of shareholders. Where such a case arises some other test than that of the 'interest of the company' must be applied." In other words, where the interests of two or more classes of shareholders are fundamentally different and opposed, and it is virtually impossible to determine the interests of the company as a whole,[62a] the directors must act fairly between the different classes.

If directors exercise a power for a proper purpose and in good faith, their judgment is not open to review by the courts.[63] However, although it would be wrong for the courts to question the correctness of the management's decision on a question of management, if bona fide arrived at, when the question is whether directors exercised a power for one purpose or another, the courts are entitled to look at the situation objectively in order to ascertain how substantial an alleged requirement may have been.[64]

Where a director is also a shareholder in the company he may promote his own interests so long as his dominant motive is to benefit the company.[65]

---

[61] *Harlowe's Nominees Pty. Ltd.* v. *Woodside (Lakes Entrance) Oil Co. N.L.* (1969–70) 121 C.L.R. 483 (First Australian Supplement, *ante*, p. 157).

[62] *Per* Latham C.J. in *Mills* v. *Mills* (1938) 60 C.L.R. 150 (First Australian Supplement, *ante*, p. 156).

[62a] *Woods* v. *Cann* (1963) 80 W.N. (N.S.W.) 1583 (First Australian Supplement, *ante*, p. 159) was such a case but the articles had been drafted to meet the impossibility.

[63] See the *Howard Smith* case, *ante*, at p. 9 and *per* Barwick C.J., McTiernan J. and Kitto J. at p. 493 in *Harlowe's* case, quoted in the *Howard Smith* case at p. 10.

[64] *Howard Smith* case, *ante*, at p. 8.

[65] *Mills* v. *Mills* (1938) 60 C.L.R. 150 (First Australian Supplement to Charlesworth & Cain, p. 156), where the directors believed that the bonus issue was in the best interests of the company and it was immaterial that one director derived some benefit from the passing of the board resolution.

A nominee director, *e.g.* a director appointed by a shareholder, owes the same duties to the company as any other director.[66]

Because a director owes a fiduciary duty, where in England a company owes a statute-barred debt, a balance sheet signed by a director (whose signature was necessary to its validity) who is himself interested in the debt, cannot constitute an acknowledgment for the purposes of the Limitation Act 1939, ss. 23 and 24. and the time within which an action may be brought does not run afresh,[67] unless it is sanctioned by every member of the company, in which event it cannot be said that the directors are in breach of their fiduciary duty.[68]

The Jenkins Report merely recommended[69] (1) that the Companies Act should provide that a director must observe the utmost good faith towards the company in any transaction with it or on its behalf and must act honestly in the exercise of his powers and the discharge of the duties of his office, (2) that a director who commits a breach of such statutory duty is liable to the company for any profit made by him and for any damage suffered by the company as a result of the breach and (3) that such statutory duty is in addition to and not in derogation of the general law duties of a director.

Clause 52 of the Companies Bill 1973 would have given effect to such recommendations.[70]

Relief of directors from liability for breach of duty

By a resolution in general meeting

Since directors' fiduciary duties are owed to the members as a body, the majority of the members in general meeting may, after full disclosure of all material circumstances, waive a breach of fiduciary duty by a director[71] and, if he is a member, the director may vote in

---

[66] *Per* Lord Denning in *Meyer* v. *Scottish C.W.S. Ltd.*, 1958 S.C. (H.L.) 40 at pp. 67. [68] [1959] A.C. 324 at pp. 366, 367, *post* p. 392; *per* Ungoed-Thomas J. in *Selangor United Rubber Estates Ltd.* v. *Cradock* (*No. 3*) [1968] 1 W.L.R. 1555, at pp. 1613, 1614. *Cf, e.g., per* Jacobs J. in *Re Broadcasting Station 2 GB Pty. Ltd.* [1964–65] N.S.W.R. 1648 (First Australian Supplement, p. 192) at p. 1663, where he said that so long as the nominee directors believed that the interests of the shareholder who nominated them were identical with those of the company, they could follow the wishes of the shareholder without a close personal analysis of the issues.

[67] *Re Transplanters* (*Holding Company*) *Ltd.* [1958] 1 W.L.R. 822, *post* p. 433.

[68] *Re Gee & Co.* (*Woolwich*) *Ltd.* [1975] Ch.D. 52, applying *Re Duomatic Ltd.* [1969] 2 Ch. 365, *ante* p. 290.

[69] Para. 99 (a) (i), (iii) and (iv).

[70] *Cf.* s. 124 (1), (3) and (4) of the New South Wales Companies Act, 1961 (First Australian Supplement to Charlesworth & Cain, p. 160).

[71] *Bamford* v. *Bamford* [1970] Ch. 212 (C.A.), *ante* p. 334.

favour of waiver, provided that there is no fraud on the minority of the members.

The directors of a company contracted to buy a ship from a vendor who was a director. (This was a breach of duty by him since the articles contained no clause authorising a director to contract with the company. Further, there was at the time no section like the present section 199, *post*.) At a general meeting a resolution affirming the contract was carried, against the wishes of the minority shareholders, by reason of the fact that the vendor held the majority of the shares in the company. *Held*, the resolution was valid. As a shareholder, the vendor was merely using his voting power to his own advantage, and there was no question of a fraud on the minority—there was no unfairness or impropriety: *N.-W. Transportation Co.* v. *Beatty* (1887) 12 App.Cas. 589 (P.C.).

Two directors of a construction company negotiated for a construction contract in the usual way in which the company's business was carried on, and then took the contract in their own names. A meeting of the company was called, and by their votes as holders of three-quarters of the shares a resolution was passed declaring that the company had no interest in the contract. *Held*, the benefit of the contract belonged to the company and the directors must account to the company for it, and the purported ratification was a fraud on the minority and ineffective: *Cook* v. *Deeks* [1916] 1 A.C. 554 (P.C.).

The general meeting may give advance authority for an exercise of power by the directors which would otherwise involve a breach of their fiduciary duty.[72]

Not by a provision in the articles

Under the general law a director can be exempted from liability for breach of duty by a provision in the articles of the company. However, section 205, first introduced in 1929, states that, subject as below, any provision, whether in the articles or in any contract with the company or otherwise, for exempting a director or other officer or the auditor from liability for negligence, default, breach of duty or breach of trust in relation to the company, or indemnifying him against such liability, is void.

The section goes on to provide that the company may, in pursuance of a provision in the articles, etc., indemnify such a person against any liability, *i.e.* against any costs, incurred by him in defending any proceedings, civil or criminal, in which judgment is given in his favour

---

[72] *Winthrop Investments Ltd.* v. *Winns Ltd.* [1975] 2 N.S.W. L.R. 666 (C.A.). But not, according to Samuels J.A., if to do so would be to usurp the directors' powers. The notice convening the meeting must set out clearly the nature of the contemplated breach of the directors' duty, and state that the directors seek to be absolved from such breach and that the meeting will be asked to authorise the breach and waive its consequences.

or in which he is acquitted,[73] or in connection with any application under section 448 in which relief is granted to him by the court. Table A, article 136, contains such a provision.

By the court

Section 448 provides that if, in proceedings for negligence, default, breach of duty or breach of trust against a director or other officer or auditor of a company, it appears that he has acted honestly and reasonably, and that, having regard to all the circumstances, including those connected with his appointment, he ought fairly to be excused, the court may relieve him, wholly or partly, from liability on such terms as it thinks fit.

Relief can be given even when the director has done an act *ultra vires* the company, as where the company's money was applied for a purpose which was *ultra vires*, but which the director, acting on counsel's opinion, thought to be *intra vires*.[74]

A director does not act reasonably unless he does everything which a normal man would do in the conduct of his own affairs.

B. and G., two of the directors of a company, were present at a finance committee in June at which it was resolved to sell £60,000 War Bonds and to reinvest the proceeds at B.'s discretion. In September, G. inquired about the reinvestment of the proceeds and was told that they had been temporarily invested on the Stock Exchange. B. misappropriated the proceeds of sale. *Held*, (1) G. was negligent in allowing the money to remain in B.'s hands longer than was reasonable and in not making inquiries as to its permanent investment, and (2) though G. had acted honestly, he had not acted reasonably and ought not to be granted relief: *Re City of London Insurance Co.* (1925) 41 T.L.R. 521.

In *Selangor United Rubber Estates Ltd.* v. *Cradock* (*No. 3*)[75] directors of a public company who disposed of virtually all its assets without regard for minority shareholders, and without consideration, but blindly at the behest of the majority shareholder who nominated them to the board, did not act reasonably and could not be relieved. In *Re Duomatic Ltd.*[76] a director dealing with payment to another director of compensation for loss of office, who did not seek legal advice but dealt with the matter himself without a proper exploration of what should be done on the company's behalf, did not act reasonably.

In a recent Australian case, *Lawson* v. *Mitchell*,[77] two English cases were not followed[78] and it was held that the Victorian section corresponding to section 448 has no application to criminal proceedings in respect of offences against the

[73] *Cf. Tomlinson* v. *Liquidators of Scottish Amalgamated Silks Ltd.*, 1935 S.C. (H.L.) 1.
[74] *Re Claridge's Patent Asphalte Co.* [1921] 1 Ch. 543.
[75] [1968] 1 W.L.R. 1555.
[76] [1969] 2 Ch. 365.
[77] [1975] V.R. 579, Full Ct.
[78] *Re Barry & Staines Linoleum Ltd.* [1934] Ch. 227; *Re Gilt Edge Safety Glass Ltd.* [1940] Ch. 495.

Companies Act (and that the word "court" in the Victorian section may include other courts besides the Supreme Court or a judge thereof).

Secret benefits of directors

Because a director is in a fiduciary position,[79] he must not make a secret profit by reason of that position. If he does, he must account for it to the company. It is immaterial that the company itself could not have obtained the profit. The company in general meeting may consent to such a profit being made or kept.

A. was a director of B. Co. and, on the company's behalf, contracted for the building of fishing smacks. Unknown to the company, he was paid a commission on the contract by the shipbuilders. A. was also a shareholder in an ice company which, in addition to dividends, paid bonuses to shareholders who were owners of fishing smacks and who employed the ice company in supplying ice to the fishing smacks. A. employed the ice company in respect of B. Co.'s fishing smacks and received the bonus. *Held*, A. must account to B. Co. for both the commission and the bonus, although the bonus could never have been received by B. Co. as it was not a shareholder in the ice company: *Boston Deep Sea Fishing Co.* v. *Ansell* (1888) 39 Ch.D. 339 (C.A.).

R. Ltd. owned one cinema and wanted to buy two others with a view to selling the three together. R. Ltd. formed a subsidiary company to buy the two cinemas, but was unable to provide all the capital required, so all the directors of R. Ltd. except one subscribed for some of the shares in the subsidiary themselves. The cinemas were acquired and the shares in R. Ltd. and the subsidiary sold at a profit. *Held*, the former directors who subscribed for shares in the subsidiary themselves must account to R. Ltd. for the profit they made, because it was only through the knowledge and opportunity they gained as directors of R. Ltd. that they were able to obtain the shares. The one former director who did not himself subscribe but merely found someone else to do so was under no liability nor was a solicitor who was invited to subscribe by the directors: *Regal* (*Hastings*) *Ltd.* v. *Gulliver* [1967] 2 A.C. 134 (Note).[80]

In the *Regal* case the directors could have protected themselves by a resolution (either antecedent or subsequent) of the Regal shareholders in general meeting,[81] and the case was distinguished in *Lindgren* v. *L. & P. Estates Ltd*[82] where the directors were released from liability by the company retaining them on the board, after it had knowledge of the facts (the alleged breach of duty was that the directors had merely "rubber-stamped" the decisions of other persons).

"The rule of equity which insists on those, who by use of a fiduciary position make a profit, being liable to account for that profit, in no way depends on fraud, or absence of bona fides; or upon such questions or considerations as

---

[79] p. 346.

[80] [1967] 2 A.C. 134 (Note), applied in *Phipps* v. *Boardman* [1967] 2 A.C. 46. See also *Industrial Development Consultants Ltd.* v. *Cooley* [1972] 1 W.L.R. 443 and *Furs Ltd.* v. *Tomkies* (1935–36) 54 C.L.R. 583 (First Australian Supplement to Charlesworth & Cain, p. 164).

[81] *Per* Lord Russell of Killowen at p. 150.

[82] [1968] Ch. 572 (C.A.), in which it was also held that prospective directors of a company owe no duty to it and that directors of a parent company owe no duty to, and are not debarred from contracting with, a subsidiary with an independent board.

whether the profit would or should otherwise have gone to the plaintiff [*i.e.* the company], or whether the profiteer was under a duty to obtain the source of the profit for the plaintiff, or whether he took a risk or acted as he did for the benefit of the plaintiff, or whether the plaintiff has in fact been damaged or benefited by his action. The liability arises from the mere fact of a profit having, in the stated circumstances, been made. The profiteer, however honest and well-intentioned, cannot escape the risk of being called upon to account:" *per* Lord Russell of Killowen in the *Regal* case at p. 144.

Another example of the principle that a director must not make a secret profit out of his position is that a director must not, without the consent of the company, accept from a promoter any gift, *e.g.* of shares or money, either while any negotiations between the promoter and the company are still going on or after they have been completed.[83]

The Jenkins Committee recommended[84] (1) that the Companies Act should provide that a director of a company must not make use of any money or other property of the company, or of any information acquired by virtue of his position as a director or officer of the company, to gain directly or indirectly an improper advantage for himself at the expense of the company, (2) that a director who commits a breach of such statutory duty is liable to the company for any profit made by him and for any damage suffered by the company as a result of the breach and (3) that such statutory duty is in addition to the general law duties of a director.

Clause 52 of the Companies Bill 1973 would have given effect to such recommendations.[85]

Contracts of directors with their company

A consequence of the general law duty of a director towards the company, not to allow conflict between duty and interest,[86] is that even if he makes no profit, a director must not be interested in a contract or proposed contract with the company unless the articles permit it, as they usually do, *e.g.* Table A, article 84. If this rule is broken the contract is prima facie voidable by the company.

This is so even if his interest is only that of a shareholder in

---

[83] *Eden* v. *Ridsdales Railway Lamp Co. Ltd.* (1889) 23 Q.B.D. 368 (C.A.); *Archer's Case* [1892] 1 Ch. 322 (C.A.); *Henderson* v. *The Huntingdon Copper, etc., Co. Ltd.* (1877) 5.R. (H.L.) 1.

[84] Para. 99 (a) (ii), (iii) and (iv).

[85] *Cf.* s. 124 (2), (3) and (4) of the New South Wales Companies Act, 1961 (First Australian Supplement, p. 165).

[86] *Ante* p. 351.

another company which contracts with the company of which he is a director.

T. Co. bought some shares in L. Co. from N.B. Co. H. was a shareholder in both T. Co. and N.B.Co. and also a director of T. Co. As such director he voted for the purchase and N.B. Co. had notice of it. H. did not disclose the nature of his interest (his shareholding in N.B. Co.) as required by the articles of T. Co., which also provided that a director was not to vote in respect of any contract in which he was concerned. *Held*, the contract was voidable at the option of T. Co.: *Transvaal Lands Co.* v. *New Belgium* (*Transvaal*) *Land, etc., Co.* [1914] 2 Ch. 488 (C.A.).

"Where a director of a company has an interest as shareholder in another company or is in a fiduciary position towards and owes a duty to another company which is proposing to enter into engagements with the company of which he is a director, he is in our opinion within this rule. He has a personal interest within this rule or owes a duty which conflicts with his duty to the company of which he is a director. It is immaterial whether this conflicting interest belongs to him beneficially or as trustee for others": *per* Swinfen Eady L.J., reading the judgment of the court, at p. 503.

His interest may be that of a partner in a firm which contracts with his company.[87]

It is usual to provide in the articles that a director who is interested in a contract with the company must declare his interest as required by section 199 *post*, that he shall not vote on any such contract, and that if he does vote his vote shall not be counted. The effect of this is to allow the director to contract with the company, on disclosing his interest, and to keep any profit he may make.[88]

Table A, article 84, provides: "(1) A director who is in any way, whether directly or indirectly, interested in a contract or proposed contract with the company shall declare the nature of his interest at a meeting of the directors in accordance with section 199. . . ."

"(2) A director shall not vote in respect of any contract or arrangement in which he is interested, and if he shall do so his vote shall not be counted, nor shall he be counted in the quorum present at the meeting, but neither of these prohibitions shall apply to—

(a) any arrangement for giving any director any security or indemnity in respect of money lent by him to or obligations undertaken by him for the benefit of the company; or

(b) any arrangement for the giving by the company of any security to a third party in respect of a debt or obligation of the company for which the director himself has assumed responsibility in whole or in part under a guarantee or indemnity or by the deposit of a security; or

(c) any contract by a director to subscribe for or underwrite shares or debentures of the company; or

(d) any contract or arrangement with any other company in which he is

---

[87] *Aberdeen Rlwy. Co.* v. *Blaikie Bros.* (1854) 1 Macq. 461.
[88] *Costa Rica Rlwy.* v. *Forwood* [1901] 1 Ch. 746. (C.A.).

interested only as an officer of the company or as a holder of shares or other securities;

and these prohibitions may at any time be suspended or relaxed to any extent, and either generally or in respect of any particular contract, arrangement or transaction, by the company in general meeting."

(3) [A director may hold any other office of profit under the company (other than that of auditor) with the consent of the directors and may contract with the company.]

(4) [A director may be counted in the quorum present at a meeting at which he is appointed to hold any other office of profit under the company.]

"(5) Any director may act by himself or his firm in a professional capacity for the company, and he or his firm shall be entitled to remuneration for professional services as if he were not a director; provided that nothing herein contained shall authorise a director or his firm to act as auditor to the company."

Section 199 (a section first introduced in 1929 and intended to ensure that a director does not abuse his position) provides that a director who is any way interested in a contract or proposed contract with the company must declare the nature of his interest at a board meeting. Where a director is interested in a proposed contract, the declaration must be made at the meeting of the directors at which the question of entering into the contract is first considered. Otherwise, the declaration must be made at the first meeting after the director becomes interested in the contract or proposed contract. However, a general notice by a director that he is a member of a specified company or firm and is to be regarded as interested in all contracts made with that company or firm is a sufficient declaration of interest if it is given at a meeting of the directors or the director takes reasonable steps to secure that it is brought up and read at the next meeting of the directors after it is given. Compliance with this statutory duty is enforced by a fine of £100.[89]

It should be noted that only the nature of the interest need be declared, that the declaration of interest need not be to the company in general meeting (although in certain circumstances section 16 (1) (c) of the 1967 Act, *post*,[90] requires details of a contract with the company in which a director is interested to be given in the directors' report) and that a general declaration of interest is sufficient.

The section also provides that it does not prejudice the operation of any rule of law restricting directors from having an interest in

[89] As to the effect of a breach of the N.S.W. section corresponding to s. 199, see *Castlereagh Motels Ltd.* v. *Davis-Roe* [1966] 2 N.S.W.R. 79 (C.A.), particularly at p. 84.

[90] p. 440.

contracts with the company. This means that the section does not imply in the articles a provision allowing a director to contract with the company.

If the articles do not contain such a provision and a director is interested in a contract with the company, the contract may be affirmed by the company in general meeting and, if the director is a member of the company, he can cast the votes conferred by his shares in favour of the resolution, so long as it is not a fraud on the minority of the shareholders.[91]

If a director does not disclose his interest in a contract with his company in accordance with section 199, the contract is *prima facie* voidable by the company[92] and the director must account to it for any secret profit which he has made out of the contract.[93]

Section 205 *ante*[94] is qualified by section 199, which is a statutory extension of the general law in that, *e.g.*, it imposes a penalty of £100 for a breach of the section.

The Jenkins Report[95] recommended that section 199 be amended so as to require a director to disclose only material interests in contracts, including contracts which do not come before the board.

Clause 47 of the Companies Bill 1973 would have given effect to such recommendation and would have extended it to disclosure of interests of members of a director's family.

Insider trading

"Insider trading" can be defined as "dealing in the securities of a company by a person such as a director, substantial shareholder, employee, or professional adviser, of the company, who is in possession of information which is not generally known but which would be likely, if generally known, to have a material effect on the market price of those securities."

Under the general law, market trading, although clearly wrong, is not prohibited, as is shown by *Percival* v. *Wright ante*.[96]

The Jenkins Report[97] recommended that a director who, in any

---

[91] *N.-W. Transportation Co.* v. *Beatty* (1887) 12 App. Cas. 589 (P.C.), *ante* p. 354.
[92] *Hely-Hutchinson* v. *Brayhead Ltd.* [1968] 1 Q.B. 549 (C.A.), *post* p. 413, where it was too late to avoid because *restitutio* was impossible.
[93] *Per* Lord Cairns L.C. in *Parker* v. *McKenna* (1874) L.R. 10 Ch.App. 96 at p. 118.
[94] p. 354.   [95] Para. 99.
[96] p. 350.
[97] Para. 99 (b). See also para. 89. The recommendation that a director should not deal in options is dealt with *ante*, p. 326.

transaction relating to the securities of his company or of any other company in the same group, makes improper use of a particular piece of confidential information which might be expected materially to affect the value of such securities, should be liable to compensate a person who suffers loss from his action unless that information was known to that person.

The Conservative Government White Paper on Company Law Reform[98] stated that unfair benefits can on occasion be made in share dealings by the improper use of confidential, price-sensitive information that is not generally available to the investing public. Consequently, the Government concluded that in principle insider dealings should be made a criminal offence. The White Paper stated that the object of legislation on insider dealing must be to ensure that anyone who is in possession of information which would be likely, if generally known, to have a material effect on the price of the relevant securities refrains from dealing until the material information has properly been made generally available. It would seem that the Government had in mind legislation very much on the lines of section 75A of the N.S.W. Securities Industry Act, 1970.[99]

The Government's view was that the definition of insider should include directors, employees, major shareholders and professional advisers of a company, together with the near relations of each of these people. The Government also took the view that dealing in a company's securities by anyone who, by reason of his relationship with the company or its officers, has information which he knows to be price-sensitive, should be a criminal offence unless he can show that his primary intention in dealing at that particular time was not to make a profit or avoid a loss.

The Government also concluded that the law should confer a civil remedy on persons who can establish that by reason of the misuse of materially significant information they have suffered an identifiable loss and that the law should preserve the present position whereby an insider may be accountable to the company for his profit.

Clauses 12–16 of the Companies Bill 1973 would have more than given effect to the above-mentioned views.

The Labour Party Green Paper on the Reform of Company Law[1] considered that the definition of insider should also include trustees of company pension schemes.

Sections 27 and 29 of the Companies Act 1967 (Register of directors' shareholdings, etc.)[2] may be of assistance in proving insider trading. So may sections 164–175 of the 1948 Act (Inspection).[3]

---

[98] (1973) Cmnd. 5391, para. 15.
[99] First Australian Supplement to Charlesworth & Cain, p. 166. The N.S.W. 1970 Act has been repealed and extended by the 1975 Act, ss. 112–114 of which are based on clauses 12, 15 and 16 of the U.K. Companies Bill 1973 *post*.
[1] *Ante* p. 18.
[2] *Ante* p. 320.
[3] *Post* p. 396.

Directors competing with company

Under the general law, apart from the case where a director has a service agreement with the company which requires him to serve only the company, there is authority to the effect that he may become a director of a rival company, *i.e.* that in this way he may compete with the first company, provided that he does not disclose to the second company any confidential information obtained by him as a director of the first company, and that what he may do for a rival company he may do for himself[4] or a rival firm. However, it has been said that he must not subordinate the interests of the first company to those of the second and that if he does so it is at the risk of an application under section 210 (Remedy in case of oppression).[5,6]

Duties of care

Directors' duties of care towards the company cannot be said to be unduly burdensome, as will be seen from the three propositions laid down by Romer J. in *Re City Equitable Fire Insurance Co. Ltd.*[7] These were:

(1) A director need not exhibit in the performance of his duties (*i.e.* his functions) a greater degree of skill than may reasonably be expected from a person of his knowledge and experience (*i.e.* the particular director's own knowledge and experience). A director of a life insurance company, for instance, does not guarantee that he has the skill of an actuary or of a physician. It is perhaps only another way of stating the same proposition to say that directors are not liable for mere errors of judgment.

(2) A director is not bound to give continuous attention to the affairs of his company. His duties are of an intermittent nature to be performed at periodical board meetings. He is not, however, bound

[4] *London & Mashonaland Exploration Co.* v. *New Mashonaland Exploration Co.* [1891] W.N. 165; *per* Lord Blanesburgh in *Bell* v. *Lever Bros. Ltd.* [1932] A.C. 161 at p. 195.

[5] *Post* p. 389.

[6] *Per* Lord Denning in *Meyer* v. *Scottish C.W.S. Ltd.*, 1958 S.C. (H.L.) 40 at p. 68; [1959] A.C. 324 at p. 368.

[7] [1925] Ch. 407 at p. 428. The *City Equitable* case was applied in *Huckerby* v. *Elliott* [1970] 1 All E.R. 189. For a similar description of a director's duties, see *per* Lord Justice-Clerk Moncrieff in *Western Bank* v. *Baird's Trustees* (1872) 11 M. 96 at p. 112, and on the extent to which directors are entitled to rely on other officials, see *Western Bank* v. *Addie* (1867) 5 M. (H.L.) 80; (1865) 3 M. 899, and *Lees* v. *Tod* (1882) 9 R. 807.

to attend all such meetings, though he ought to attend whenever, in the circumstances, he is reasonably able to do so.

(3) In respect of all duties that, having regard to the exigencies of business, and the articles of association, may properly be left to some other official, a director is, in the absence of grounds for suspicion, justified in trusting that official to perform such duties honestly.

As to (1) *ante*, a greater degree of skill than that indicated by Romer J. must be shown, *e.g.*, by an executive director, such as a finance or legal director—it is an implied term of his contract of service that he will use reasonable skill in the performance of the duties of his office, *i.e.* the degree of skill which may reasonably be expected of a person in such a position.[8]

Further, the duties of directors vary according to the nature of the company and of its business, *e.g.* the responsibilities of directors of small private companies consisting of only two members differ from the responsibilities of directors of a large public company.[9]

As to (2), greater diligence than that indicated is required of, *e.g.*, an executive director, such as a managing director, whose contract of service requires him to work full time for the company.

The directors of an insurance company left the management of the company's affairs almost entirely to B., the managing director. Owing to B.'s fraud a large amount of the company's assets disappeared. Items appeared in the balance sheet under the headings of "loans at call or at short notice" and "cash at bank or in hand," but the directors never inquired how these items were made up. Had they done so, they would have discovered that the loans were chiefly to B. and to the company's general manager, and that the "cash at bank or in hand" included £73,000 in the hands of a firm of stockbrokers in which B. was a partner. *Held*, the directors were negligent: *Re City Equitable Fire Insce. Co.* [1925] Ch. 407. [In this case the articles protected the directors from liability except in case of wilful neglect or default, and consequently the directors were held not liable. Section 205, *ante*,[10] now makes any such article void.]

What was said earlier[10] as to the relief of directors from liability for breach of duty in connection with their fiduciary duties applies also to their duties of care. As to relief by a resolution of the company in general meeting, it was held in *Pavlides* v. *Jensen*[11] that if the directors by their negligence had sold the company's mine at an undervalue, it was open to the company by a vote of the majority to decide that proceedings should not be taken against them.

[8] *Lister* v. *Romford Ice and Cold Storage Co. Ltd.* [1957] A.C. 555.
[9] *Per* Lord Johnson in *Brenes & Co.* v. *Downie*, 1914 S.C. 97 at p. 104.
[10] p. 353.
[11] [1956] Ch. 565, *post* p. 377.

The Jenkins Committee did not recommend that directors should have a statutory duty of care on the lines of that in section 124 (1) of the New South Wales Companies Act[12] and the Companies Bill 1973 contained no provisions dealing with the matter.

Liability for acts of co-directors

A director is not liable for the acts of his co-directors of which he has no knowledge and in which he has taken no part,[13] as his fellow directors are not his servants or agents to impose liability on him.[14] Moreover, if an *ultra vires* investment is made at a directors' meeting, a director who was not present at the meeting is not liable for the investment merely because he was present at a meeting at which the minutes of the meeting authorising the investment were confirmed.[15]

If a director is fraudulent, his co-directors are not liable for not discovering his fraud in the absence of circumstances to arouse their suspicions.

A bank sustained heavy losses by advances to customers made improperly. The irregular nature of the advances was concealed by means of fraudulent balance sheets, the work of the general manager and the chairman. *Held*, a co-director was not liable for not having discovered the frauds, as he was not, in the absence of circumstances of suspicion, bound to examine entries in the company's books to see that the balance sheets were correct: *Dovey* v. *Cory* [1901] A.C. 477.

Non-attendance at board meetings has been held not to impose liability on a director for the acts of the board.[16]

Where more than one director is alleged to have neglected his duties of care, both or all are jointly and severally liable, with the result that if an action is brought by the company against only one of them he is not entitled to plead that all parties interested have not been called.[17] However, the director sued is entitled to contribution from the other directors.

[12] First Australian Supplement to Charlesworth & Cain, p. 171.
[13] *Perry's Case* (1876) 34 L.T. 716.
[14] *Cullerne* v. *London and Suburban Bldg. Socy.* (1890) 25 Q.B.D. 485 (C.A.).
[15] *Re Lands Allotment Co.* [1894] 1 Ch. 616 (C.A.), *ante* p. 86.
[16] *Re Denham & Co.* (1884) 25 Ch.D. 752.
[17] *Liquidators of Western Bank* v. *Douglas* (1860) 20 D. 447, the reason being that the action is based on delict and not on contract *per* Lord Justice-Clerk Inglis at p. 476.

Contribution between directors

When directors have misapplied the company's funds, as by paying dividends out of capital or advancing money for an unauthorised purpose, a director who has been sued for the misapplication is entitled to contribution from the other directors who were parties to it.[18] If, however, the money misappropriated has been applied for the sole benefit of one of the directors, that director is not entitled to obtain contribution.[19]

DIRECTORS' POWERS AND SHAREHOLDERS' CONTROL

We have seen that in modern public companies the directors have usually but a small shareholding, their salaries and other emoluments, rather than their dividends, being their main sources of profit from the company, with the result that management and ownership of the company have become divorced.[20]

We have also seen that the articles commonly delegate extensive powers to the directors, although there can be no delegation of powers which are required by the Act to be exercised by the company in general meeting, *e.g.* those of altering the articles (s. 10), or the capital (ss. 61, 66).[21] The Jenkins Committee[22] thought that wide delegation is necessary if the directors are to manage the company efficiently and that members are persistently reluctant to concern themselves with management.

The Committee[23] also thought that as a general rule directors exercise their powers in what they conceive to be the best interests of the company. Again, the Act provides shareholders with powerful weapons if they choose to use them. *e.g.* the powers of requisitioning meetings and of requiring the giving of notice of members' resolutions to be proposed at meetings (ss. 132 and 140[24]), and there are various sources of information available to members, *e.g.* the balance sheet and profit and loss account (s. 158[25]), and, even if practical considera-

---

[18] *Ramskill* v. *Edwards* (1886) 31 Ch.D. 100; see also (for England) Law Reform (Married Women and Tortfeasors) Act 1935, s. 6, and (for Scotland) Law Reform (Miscellaneous Provisions) (Scotland) Act 1940, s. 3.

[19] *Walsh* v. *Bardsley* (1931) 47 T.L.R. 564.

[20] *Ante* p. 310.

[21] *Ante* p. 332.

[22] Paras. 104 and 109 of the Report.

[23] Para. 110 of the Report.

[24] *Ante*, pp. 287, 294.

[25] *Post* p. 440.

tions (the large number of shareholders in the company, the lack of interest normally shown by the general body of shareholders, the difficulty of rallying support) make such weapons difficult for the small investor to wield, the institutional investors (such as insurance companies) are not likely to submit to any major abuse of power by the directors.[26] Further, where quoted companies are concerned, the Stock Exchange requirements and the sanction for them in the shape of a suspension of quotation provide some protection.[26]

However, there are rare cases where directors abuse their power[27] and the Committee made certain recommendations[28] designed to protect the vital interests of shareholders without hampering directors in their conduct of the day-to-day business of the company. Sections 16 to 23 of the 1967 Act gave effect to one of these recommendations —that suggesting that the directors' report should contain certain additional information.[29] Other recommendations with regard to disposal of assets and the issue of shares are set out earlier in this chapter.[30]

PROPOSALS FOR REFORM OF THE LAW RELATING TO DIRECTORS

The proposal in the Labour Party Green Paper, that there should be a two-tier management structure—a supervisory board and a management board—was dealt with in Chapter 1,[31] and it is only necessary to add here that the Fifth Draft Directive of the EEC Council of Ministers contains a requirement to the same effect in the case of companies of the public type.

[26] Jenkins Report, para. 106.
[27] *Ibid.* para. 111.
[28] *Ibid.* para. 122.
[29] *Post* p. 440 *et seq.*
[30] *Ante* p. 335.
[31] p. 17.

CHAPTER 15

THE SECRETARY

EVERY company must have a secretary and a sole director cannot also be secretary: section 177. The secretary may be an individual or a Scottish firm or a corporation, but a corporation cannot be the secretary if its sole director is also the sole director of the company: section 178. A company may have joint secretaries: see section 200 (3).

The Act does not require the secretary to have a professional qualification, but he is often, *e.g.*, a Chartered Secretary.

He is usually appointed by the directors, but sometimes he is named in the articles.[1]

Table A, article 110, of the 1948 Act, as amended by Schedule 2 of the 1976 Act, provides: "Subject to section 21 (5) of the Companies Act 1976, the secretary shall be appointed by the directors for such term, at such remuneration and upon such conditions as they may think fit; and any secretary so appointed may be removed by them."

The position of a company's secretary has changed a great deal in the last seventy five years. In 1887 it was said that: "a secretary is a mere servant; his position is that he is to do what he is told, and no person can assume that he has any authority to represent anything at all; nor can anyone assume that statements made by him are necessarily to be accepted as trustworthy without further inquiry."[2] Even in 1902 his duties were described as "of a limited and of a somewhat humble character."[3] Accordingly, it has been held that a company is not liable for the act of its secretary in fraudulently making representations to induce persons to take shares in the company,[4] or in issuing a forged share certificate.[5] The secretary is, however, the proper official to issue share certificates, and so the company

[1] As to which see *Eley* v. *Positive Life Assurance Co. Ltd.* (1876) 1 Ex.D. 88 (C.A.), *ante* p. 108.
[2] *Per* Lord Esher M.R. in *Barnett, Hoares & Co.* v. *South London Tramways Co.* (1887) 18 Q.B.D. 815 (C.A.) at p. 817.
[3] *Per* Lord Macnaghten in *George Whitechurch Ltd.* v. *Cavanagh* [1902] A.C. 117 at p. 124.
[4] *Barnett, Hoares & Co.* v. *South London Tramways Co., ante.*
[5] *Ruben* v. *Great Fingall Consolidated* [1906] A.C. 439, *ante* p. 248.

is estopped or barred from denying the truth of genuine share certificates issued by him without the authority of the company.[6]

It has also been held the the secretary has no independent authority to bind the company by contract.[7]

> L., a director of N. Co., without any authority from the company, made a contract with H. The contract was confirmed by a letter written by the secretary on behalf of the company. *Held*, the secretary, as such, had no power to bind the company, and N. Co. was not liable on the contract: *Houghton & Co.* v. *Nothard, Lowe & Wills Ltd.* [1928] A.C. 1, *post*.[8]

Similarly, it has been held that he cannot borrow money on behalf of the company.

> At the request of the secretary, a director, C., lent £17,353 to the company to discharge debts guaranteed by the company. The loans were confirmed by a meeting of the directors at which C. and one other director were present. The articles provided that two directors were a quorum, but that a director could not vote in respect of a contract in which he was interested. The company went into liquidation. *Held*, C. was not entitled to recover the money advanced. The secretary had no power to borrow on behalf of the company and his request was not made or confirmed at a properly constituted meeting of the directors: *Re Cleadon Trust Ltd.* [1939] Ch. 286 (C.A.).

Also, without the authority of the company, he cannot issue a writ in the company's name[9] or lodge defences in the company's name,[10] and it is not his duty as secretary to instruct the company as to its legal rights.[11]

> The secretary of a company is not "an official who *virtute officii* can manage all its affairs, with or without the help of servants, in the absence of a regular directorate": *per* Lord Parker in *Daimler Co. Ltd.* v. *Continental Tyre Co. Ltd.* [1916] 2 A.C. 307 at p. 337.

Again, the secretary cannot register a transfer until he is authorised to do so by the directors;[12] he cannot, without such authority, strike a name off the register of shareholders;[13] and he cannot summon a general meeting on his own authority.[14]

However, in a recent case[15] it was said[16] that a company secretary

---

[6] *Clavering, Son & Co.* v. *Goodwins, Jardine & Co. Ltd.* (1891) 18 R. 652.

[7] *Williams* v. *The Chester and Holyhead Ry. Co.* (1851) 15 Jur. 828.

[8] p. 415.

[9] *Daimler Co. Ltd.* v. *Continental Tyre, etc., Co. Ltd.* [1916] 2 A.C. 307.

[10] *Edington* v. *Dunbar Steam Laundry Co.* (1903) 11 S.L.T. 117 (O.H.).

[11] *Niven* v. *Collins Patent Lever Gear Co. Ltd.* (1900) 7 S.L.T. 476 (O.H.).

[12] *Chida Mines Ltd.* v. *Anderson* (1905) 22 T.L.R. 27.

[13] *Re Indo-China Steam Navigation Co.* [1917] 2 Ch. 100.

[14] *Re State of Wyoming Syndicate* [1901] 2 Ch. 431.

[15] *Panorama Developments (Guildford) Ltd.* v. *Fidelis Furnishing Fabrics Ltd.* [1971] 2 Q.B. 711 (C.A.).

[16] *Per* Lord Denning M.R. and Salmon L.J. at pp. 716, 717.

is a much more important person now than he was in 1887. He is the chief administrative officer of the company with extensive duties and responsibilities. This appears not only in the modern Companies Acts but in the role which he plays in the day-to-day business of the company. He is no longer a mere clerk. He regularly makes representations on behalf of the company and enters into contracts on its behalf which come within the day-to-day running of its business. So much so that he may be regarded as held out as having authority to do such things on behalf of the company. He is certainly entitled to sign contracts connected with the administrative side of a company's affairs, such as employing staff and ordering cars. All such matters come within the ostensible authority of a company's secretary.

The secretary, purportedly on behalf of the company, fraudulently hired cars, ostensibly for the purpose of meeting customers, and used the cars for his own private purposes. Held, the secretary had ostensible authority to enter into contracts for the hire of cars on behalf of the company and the company was liable to pay the hire charges: *Panorama Developments (Guildford) Ltd.* v. *Fidelis Furnishing Fabrics Ltd.* [1971] 2 Q.B. 711 (C.A.).

The duties of the secretary depend on the size and nature of the company, and on the arrangement made with him. In any case he will be present at all meetings of the company, and of the directors, and will make proper minutes of the proceedings. He will issue, under the direction of the board, all notices to members and others. In practice he will countersign every instrument to which the seal of the company is affixed. He or his department will conduct all correspondence with shareholders in regard to transfers and otherwise, will certify transfers, and will keep the books of the company, or such of them as relate to the internal business of the company, *e.g.* the register of members, the share ledger, the transfer book, the register of charges, etc. He will also make all necessary returns to the Registrar, *e.g.* the annual return, return of allotments, notice of increase of capital, etc.

If a provision requires or authorises a thing to be done by or to a director and the secretary, it is not satisfied by the thing being done by or to the same person acting both as director and as secretary: section 179.

If a person is secretary of two companies, a fact which comes to his knowledge as secretary of one company is not notice to him as secretary of the other company, unless it was his duty to the first company to communicate his knowledge to the second company.

H. was secretary of two companies, A. Co. and B. Co. B. Co. drew a bill on a third company, C. Co., and indorsed it in favour of A. Co. The bill was dishonoured by C. Co. and no notice of dishonour was given to B. Co. It was claimed that as H., in his capacity of secretary, knew of the dishonour, no notice was necessary. *Held*, notice to H., as secretary of A. Co., was not notice to B. Co.: *Re Fenwick, Stobart & Co.* [1902] 1 Ch. 507.

In England a full-time secretary is a "clerk or servant" so as to be entitled to preferential payment of his salary on a winding up, but a part-time secretary is not.[17]

The secretary is an officer of the company: section 455. Accordingly, he is in the same position as a director with regard to loans made to him by the company having to be disclosed in the accounts under section 197.[18] Similarly, a provision in the articles or in any contract for relieving him from liability is void: section 205.[19] Again, the court can relieve him from liability in certain cases: section 448.[20] His present Christian name and surname, any former Christian name and surname and his address must be set out in the register of directors and secretaries: section 200.[21]

A secretary has been held to have no lien over the books of the company coming into his possession in the course of his duties.[22]

The appointment of the secretary may be terminated by giving the agreed notice or, if no notice is agreed, by giving reasonable notice.[23] It may be terminated without any notice if the secretary makes a secret profit.[24]

If the secretary is an employee he is entitled to the minimum period of notice applicable to him under the provisions of the Contracts of Employment Act 1963 (as amended).

The appointment in England of a receiver and manager in a debenture-holders' action,[25] and the making of an order for the com-

---

[17] *Cairney* v. *Back* [1906] 2 K.B. 746, *post* p. 594. Scottish cases in which a secretary was held not to be a "clerk or servant" for this purpose are *Scottish Poultry Journal Co.* (1896) 4 S.L.T. 167 (O.H.), *Clyde Football etc. Co. Ltd.* (1900) 8 S.L.T. 328 (O.H.) and *Laing* v. *Gowans* (1902) 10 S.L.T. 461 (O.H.).

[18] *Ante* p. 343.

[19] *Ante* p. 354.

[20] *Ante* p. 355.

[21] *Ante* p. 318.

[22] *Gladstone* v. *M'Callum* (1896) 23 R. 783 (minute book); *Barnton Hotel Co. Ltd.* v. *Cook* (1899) 1 F. 1190 (register of members and other books and documents at secretary's own premises).

[23] *Creen* v. *Wright* (1876) 1 C.P.D. 591.

[24] *McKay's Case* (1875) 2 Ch.D. 1.

[25] *Reid* v. *Explosives Co.* (1887) 19 Q.B.D. 264 (C.A.), *post* p. 523.

pulsory winding up of the company,[26] both operate as a dismissal of
the secretary. The passing of a resolution for a voluntary winding up
usually has this effect too.[27]

[26] *Chapman's Case* (1866) L.R. 1 Eq. 346, *post* p. 560; *Laing* v. *Gowans* (1902) 10
560 S.L.T. 461 (O.H.), *ante* p. 370.
[27] *Reigate* v. *Union Manufacturing Co.* (*Ramsbottom*) *Ltd.* [1918] 1 K.B. 592 (C.A.);
per Lord Stormonth Darling (Ordinary) in *Day* v. *Tait* (1900) 8 S.L.T. 40 (O.H.) at
p. 41. And see *post* p. 621.

CHAPTER 16

CONTROLLING MEMBERS' DUTIES

IN this chapter the term "controlling members" means those members of a company who between them possess sufficient voting power to pass the appropriate resolution in general meeting, usually an ordinary resolution.

We have seen that directors occupy a fiduciary position and owe fiduciary duties to the company.[1] However, shareholders occupy no fiduciary position and are under no fiduciary duties. A share is property and the right to vote is attached to the share as an incident of property which is to be enjoyed and exercised for the owner's personal advantage,[2] as we saw in *N.-W. Transportation Co.* v. *Beatty*.[3]

Again, a shareholder may bind himself by contract to vote in a particular way, whereas a director may not.

"When a director votes as a director for or against any particular resolution in a directors' meeting he is voting as a person under a fiduciary duty to the company for the proposition that the company should take a certain course of action. When a shareholder is voting for or against a particular resolution he is voting as a person owing no fiduciary duty to the company and who is exercising his own right of property, to vote as he thinks fit. The fact that the result of the voting at the meeting (or at a subsequent poll) will bind the company cannot affect the position that, in voting, he is voting simply in exercise of his own property rights . . . a director is an agent, who casts his vote to decide in what manner his principal shall act through the collective agency of the board of directors; a shareholder who casts his vote in general meeting is not casting it as an agent of the company in any shape or form. His act therefore, in voting as he pleases, cannot in any way be regarded as an act of the company": *per* Walton J. in *Northern Counties Securities Ltd.* v. *Jackson & Steeple Ltd.* [1974] 1 W.L.R. 1133, at p. 1144.

In *Greenwell* v. *Porter*,[4] where executors and trustees of a will who held shares agreed to sell some to G., who stipulated that he should nominate X as a director and that the executors should, when X retired by rotation, vote for his re-election, it was held that the executors were bound by the agreement. It may

---

[1] *Ante* p. 350.
[2] *Per* Latham C.J. and Dixon J. in *Peters' American Delicacy Co. Ltd.* v. *Heath* (1939) 61 C.L.R. 457 at pp. 482, 504, and the High Court of Australia in *Ngurli Ltd.* v. *McCann* (1954) 90 C.L.R. 425 at p. 439.
[3] (1887) 12 App.Cas. 589 (P.C.), *ante* p. 354.
[4] [1902] 1 Ch. 530. See also *Puddephatt* v. *Leith* [1916] 1 Ch. 200.

be mentioned that there was a voting agreement in *Greenhalgh* v. *Mallard*[5] but it was held that the shareholders who agreed to vote in a certain way were under no obligation to retain their shares and there was no continuing obligation running with the shares.

We have seen, too, that the company in general meeting, *i.e.* the members or corporators of the company assembled in general meeting,[6] may waive a breach of fiduciary duty by a director who contracts with the company as in the *N.-W. Transportation* case,[3] or who makes a secret profit out of his position as in *Regal (Hastings) Ltd.* v. *Gulliver*,[7] or who issues shares to preserve his control of the company, at least where voting rights conferred by the new shares are not exercised on the question of ratification, as in *Hogg* v. *Cramphorn Ltd.*[8] and *Bamford* v. *Bamford*,[9] provided always that there is no fraud on the minority of the shareholders.

Again, the company in general meeting may waive a breach of a director's duty of care, as in *Pavlides* v. *Jensen*,[10] where no fraud on the minority was alleged.

The company in general meeting cannot waive a breach of a director's fiduciary duty by approving a misappropriation by him of the company's property which would be a fraud on the minority. That is what the company tried to do in *Cook* v. *Deeks*.[11]

The same is true where there is an attempted confirmation of a share issue made by a director in order to give him control of the company and benefit the majority to the detriment of the minority, *i.e.* the general meeting cannot waive the director's breach of duty.[12]

Members cannot, by resolution in general meeting, expropriate the company's property.

The shareholders in E. Co., which was formed with the object of constructing a submarine telegraph, were H. Co. with 3,000 shares, M. with 2,000 and thirteen other persons with 325 between them. H. Co. was to make and lay cables for E. Co. The directors of E. Co., who were nominees of H. Co., and H. Co., decided not to pursue an action in which E. Co. was claiming a concession to construct the telegraph, procured the passing of a resolution in general meeting to put E. Co. into voluntary winding up and concealed the fact that they had agreed to end the agreement between E. Co. and H. Co. so that H. Co. could

[5] [1943] 2 All E.R. 234 (C.A.).
[6] *Per* Walton J. in *Northern Counties Securities Ltd.* v. *Jackson & Steeple Ltd.* [1974] 1 W.L.R. 1133 at p. 1144.
[7] [1942] 1 All E.R. 378 (H.L.), *ante* p. 356.
[8] [1967] Ch. 254, *ante* p. 351.
[9] [1970] Ch. 212 (C.A.), *ante* p. 334.
[10] [1956] Ch. 565, *post* p. 377.
[11] [1916] 1 A.C. 554, *ante* p. 354.
[12] *Ngurli* v. *McCann* (1954) 90 C.L.R. 425, *ante* p. 351.

sell the cable to a third company. M. brought an action on behalf of himself and
the other shareholders, except those who were defendants, in which he joined
E. Co. as a defendant. He claimed, *inter alia*, a declaration that H. Co. was a
trustee of the resulting profit for M. and the other shareholders in E. Co. *Held*,
M. succeeded. The majority shareholder had obtained certain advantages by
dealing with something which was the property of the whole company: *Menier* v.
Hooper's Telegraph Works (1874) L.R. 9 Ch.App. 350.

As regards the property of other members of the company, we
saw in Chapter 4 that, on the authority of *Sidebottom* v. *Kershaw,
Leese & Co.*,[13] an alteration of the articles by special resolution in
general meeting in order to enable some members to acquire the
shares of other members must be bona fide for the benefit of the
company as a whole.

Further, we saw that cases such as *Greenhalgh* v. *Arderne
Cinemas Ltd.*,[14] *Shuttleworth* v. *Cox Bros. Ltd.*,[15] *Australian Fixed
Trusts Pty. Ltd.* v. *Clyde Industries*[16] and *Peters' American Delicacy
Co. Ltd.* v. *Heath*[17] established the rule that in making any alteration
to the articles the general meeting must act bona fide for the benefit
of the company as a whole. Similarly, a class meeting of preference
shareholders sanctioning a modification of the special rights of the
preference shares must act bona fide for the benefit of the class as a
whole.[18]

It was said in a Scots case[19] that: "Prima facie, the shareholders are the best
judges of their own affairs, and it is only where it appears that some sinister
motive has operated, or that interests other than the interest of the company
have plainly prevailed, that the Court will entertain a complaint. The test
always is—Is the thing complained of a thing done in the interest of the company?—or, to put it perhaps more accurately, Is the action of the majority
irreconcilable with their having proceeded upon any reasonable view of the
company's interest?" In the case in question a resolution of a general meeting
to issue unissued shares to the managing director at a lower premium than would
have been obtained on the market was valid. In another Scots case it was said[20]
that "The question . . . is whether the resolution complained of . . . can be held
to be so oppressive and extravagant that no reasonable man could consider it
to be for the benefit of the Company."

Thus controlling members owe a duty to the company, *i.e.* the
corporators as a body, to act bona fide for the benefit of the company
as a whole and not to commit a fraud on the minority.

---

[13] [1920] 1 Ch. 154 (C.A.), *ante* p. 111.
[14] [1951] Ch. 286 (C.A.), *ante* p. 111.   [15] [1927] 2 K.B. 9 (C.A.).
[16] (1959) S.R. (N.S.W.) 33.   [17] (1939) 61 C.L.R. 457.
[18] *Re Holders Investment Trust Ltd.* [1971] 1 W.L.R. 583, *ante* p. 225.
[19] *Per* Lord Kyllachy (Ordinary) in *Cameron* v. *Glenmorangie Distillery Co. Ltd.*
(1896) 23 R. 1092 at p. 1095.
[20] *Per* Lord Wark (Ordinary) in *Harris* v. *A. Harris Ltd.*, 1936 S.C. 183 at p. 192.

It has been said that a higher standard is required from directors exercising a fiduciary power than from shareholders who do not, in voting at a meeting, exercise any power of a fiduciary nature,[21] and the court is more ready to interfere to prevent an abuse by directors of the powers conferred on them by the articles than to prevent an abuse by the majority of the powers conferred upon a company in general meeting.[22]

[21] *Per* Latham C.J. in *Peters'* case, *ante*, at p. 482.
[22] *Per* the High Court of Australia in *Ngurli* v. *McCann* (1954) 90 C.L.R. 425 at pp. 438, 439.

CHAPTER 17

ENFORCEMENT OF DIRECTORS' AND CONTROLLING MEMBERS' DUTIES

THIS chapter attempts to present in a coherent form a number of matters, some of which have been explained already and others of which have been referred to.

One of the matters which has been referred to on more than one occasion is the rule in *Foss* v. *Harbottle* to the effect that the company is usually the proper plaintiff in an action to enforce the duties of directors and controlling members.

Majority rule and its counter balance, minority protection, are dealt with—under the general law the wishes of the majority of the members normally prevail over those of the minority but the majority must not perpetrate a fraud on the minority.

Finally, statutory protection of the minority against the majority is explained, for example, under sections 222 and 224 of the Companies Act even a single member can have the company wound up by the court if that is just and equitable and under section 210 a single member can obtain other relief from the court where the company's affairs are being conducted in an oppressive way.

THE RULE IN FOSS *v.* HARBOTTLE[1]

The rule is that, as one would expect, the proper plaintiff[2] in an action to redress an alleged wrong to a company on the part of anyone, whether director, member or outsider, or to recover money or damages alleged to be due to it, is prima facie the company and, where the alleged wrong is any irregularity which might be made binding on the company by a simple majority of members, no individual member can bring an action in respect of it.[3]

In other words, the company is normally the proper plaintiff in an

[1] The account which follows is largely based on the judgment of Jenkins L.J. in *Edwards* v. *Halliwell* [1950] 2 All E.R. 1064 (C.A.) at p. 1066 *et seq.*
[2] The Scots term is "pursuer."
[3] See *per* Lord Davey delivering the judgment of the court in *Burland* v. *Earle* [1902] A.C. 82 (P.C.) at pp. 93, 94.

action to enforce a duty owed to the company by directors or controlling members, and where the breach of duty can be condoned by an ordinary resolution of the members in general meeting, no individual member or minority of members may sue. A general meeting may be held so that the members may by ordinary resolution decide whether to sue or not.

It has been said[4] that there are two branches of the rule and these have been described[5] as—

(1) the proper plaintiff principle,
(2) the internal management principle.

Two members took proceedings on behalf of themselves and all other members except those who were defendants against the directors of a company to compel them to make good losses sustained by the company owing to the directors buying their own land for the company's use and paying themselves a price greater than its value. *Held*, as there was nothing to prevent the company from taking the proceedings, if it thought fit to do so, the action failed: *Foss* v. *Harbottle* (1843) 2 Ha. 461; 67 E.R. 189.[6]

A minority shareholder sought to bring an action on behalf of himself and all other shareholders, save three who were directors, against those directors and the company for damages, alleging that the directors had been negligent in selling an asset of the company for less than its market value. Most of the shares in the company were held by another company the directors of which were also directors of the first company. *Held*, since the sale of the mine was *intra vires* the company, and there was no allegation of fraud by the directors or appropriation of assets of the company by the majority shareholders in fraud of the minority, the action was not maintainable. It was open to the company, on the resolution of a majority of the shareholders, to sell the mine at a price decided by the company in that manner, and it was open to the company by a vote of the majority to decide that, if the directors by their negligence had sold the mine at an undervalue, proceedings should not be taken by the company against the directors. *Semble*, it is sometimes admissible to go behind the apparent ownership of shares to discover whether a company is in fact controlled by wrongdoers, *e.g.* where the shares are held by nominees: *Pavlides* v. *Jensen* [1956] Ch. 565.[7]

---

[4] *Per* Jordan C.J. in *Australian Coal etc. Employees' Fedn.* v. *Smith* (1937) 38 S.R. (N.S.W.) 48.

[5] *Per* Street J. in *Hawkesbury Development Co. Ltd.* v. *Landmark Finance Pty. Ltd.* (1970) 92 W.N. (N.S.W.) 199 (First Australian Supplement to Charlesworth & Cain, p. 59).

[6] Applied in the *Hawkesbury* case *ante*.
    In a corresponding Scottish case, *Orr* v. *Glasgow, etc., Rlwy. Co.* (1860) 3 Macqueen 799, "the ground of action . . . was that the directors were also directors of a rival company, and that they had acted in the interests of this latter company to the prejudice of the shareholders of the first. The action was dismissed on the ground that although the transaction complained of was beyond the powers of the directors, it was competent for the shareholders to sanction it, and therefore that a single shareholder, or a minority, had no title to sue": *per* Lord Kinnear (Ordinary) in *Rixon* v. *Edinburgh Northern Tramways Co.* (1889) 16 R. 653 at p. 656.

[7] Scottish illustrations are *Lee* v. *Crawford* (1890) 17 R. 1094 (action against director for payment to the company of funds alleged to have been illegally lent to officials

The rule avoids multiplicity of suits. The reason for the last part of the rule is that litigation at the suit of a minority of the members is futile if the majority do not wish it.

"If the thing complained of is a thing which in substance the majority of the company are entitled to do, or if something has been done irregularly which the majority of the company are entitled to do regularly, or if something has been done illegally which the majority of the company are entitled to do legally, there can be no use in having litigation about it, the ultimate end of which is only that a meeting has to be called, and then ultimately the majority gets its wishes": *per* Mellish L.J. in *MacDougall* v. *Gardiner* (1875) 1 Ch.D. 13 (C.A.) at p. 25.

Under this rule, the court will not interfere with irregularities at meetings at the instance of a shareholder.

The articles empowered the chairman, with the consent of the meeting, to adjourn a meeting, and also provided for taking a poll if demanded by five shareholders. The adjournment was moved, and declared by the chairman to be carried; a poll was then demanded and refused by the chairman. A shareholder suing on behalf of himself and all other shareholders except those who were directors brought an action against the directors and the company for a declaration that the chairman's conduct was illegal and an injunction to restrain the directors from carrying out certain arrangements without the shareholders' approval. *Held*, the action could not be brought by a shareholder; if the chairman was wrong, the company alone could sue: *MacDougall* v. *Gardiner* (1875) 1 Ch.D. 13 (C.A.).

The rule is subject to a number of exceptions, in which cases a minority of shareholders, or even an individual shareholder, may bring a minority shareholders' action, usually under R.S.C., O. 15, r. 12, *i.e.* the minority shareholders sue on behalf of themselves and all other shareholders except those who are defendants, and may join the company as a defendant. The directors are usually defendants. This action is brought instead of an action in the name of the company.

"The form of the action is always 'A.B. (a minority shareholder) on behalf of himself and all other shareholders of the company' against the wrongdoing directors and the company": *per* Lord Denning M.R. in *Wallersteiner* v. *Moir* (*No. 2*) [1975] Q.B. 373 (C.A.) at p. 390.

The exceptions are:—

(1) Where the wrong complained of is a fraud by the majority of

---

of the company), *Cameron* v. *Glenmorangie Distillery Co. Ltd.* (1896) 23 R. 1092 (directors carrying out shareholders' resolution to allot to managing director unissued shares at a premium considered by a shareholder to be inadequate) and *Brown* v. *Stewart* (1898) 1F 316 (claim for damages against directors on ground that they had acted recklessly in commencing business when so few shares had been applied for).

the members on the minority and the wrongdoers are in
control of the company in general meeting, *i.e.* they control
the majority of the shares in the company, and they will not
permit an action to be brought in the name of the company.
If the aggrieved minority could not bring a minority shareholders' action in this case their grievance would never reach
the courts. Where an action is brought under this exception
the wrongdoers are usually both directors and controlling
shareholders.

In *Cook* v. *Deeks*[8] a shareholder brought a minority shareholders' action to
compel the directors to account to the company for the profits made out of the
construction contract which they took in their own names.[9]

(2) Where the act complained of is one which is illegal, or *ultra
vires* the company.[10] Such an act cannot be condoned by the
majority of the members.

(3) Where the matter is one which can be validly done or
sanctioned, not by a simple majority, but only by some
special majority, *e.g.* a special resolution, which has not been
obtained. If an action could not be brought in this case the
company could, in breach of the articles, do *de facto* by
ordinary resolution that which according to its regulations
can only be done by a special resolution.

Thus in *Baillie* v. *Oriental Telephone Co. Ltd.*,[11] a shareholder was able to
bring a minority shareholders' action to restrain the company from acting on a
special resolution of which insufficient notice had been given.[12]

It was assumed, although not decided, in *Heyting* v. *Dupont*[13]
that there may be a further exception to the rule in *Foss* v. *Harbottle*
—namely where justice demands that an action be brought, *e.g.*
where all that is alleged is damage to the company arising from a
director's misfeasance in withholding an asset of the company without fraud or *ultra vires*. The company was to exploit an invention of
the defendant's consisting of a machine for making plastic pipes and
the defendant withheld the company's patent application. However,

---

[8] [1916] 1 A.C. 554, *ante* p. 354.
[9] See also *Menier* v. *Hooper's Telegraph Works* (1874) L.R. 9 Ch.App. 350, *ante* p
374.
[10] *Flitcroft's Case* (1882) 21 Ch.D. 519 (C.A.). And see the *Hawkesbury* case, referred
to in footnote 5.
[11] [1915] 1 Ch. 503 (C.A.), *ante* p. 293.
[12] And see *Dunn* v. *Banknock Coal Co. Ltd.* (1901) 9 S.L.T. 51 (O.H.).
[13] [1964] 1 W.L.R. 843 (C.A.), *per* Russell and Harman L.JJ. at pp. 851, 854.

the company could not have exploited the invention because it was in a state of paralysis owing to discord, so there was no damage to the company and therefore justice did not require that exception be made. Again, there is some authority to the effect that justice may demand that exception be made where the directors are in breach of duty which the company in general meeting could but will not condone and although the directors are not controlling shareholders they prevent the company suing because an article like Table A, article 80, gives them most of the powers of the company.[14]

In *Hawkesbury Development Co. Ltd.* v. *Landmark Finance Pty. Ltd.*,[15] it was held that if there is an exception to the rule where justice so requires—and for the purposes of the case Street J. was prepared to assume that there was—the facts that the plaintiff was a substantial creditor of the company and that the company was in the hands of a receiver and manager were insufficient to bring the case within such an exception. There may be an exception to the rule where a shareholder seeks to restrain the company or its officers from disregarding the terms of the articles. In the *Hawkesbury* case it was alleged that there is such an exception and that in such a suit relief can also be sought for the benefit of the company against a stranger, such stranger being said to be a proper defendant to such a suit. Street J. did not wish to be taken to assent to a general proposition in these terms but in any event the suit in the case was not one to restrain either the company or its officers from disregarding the requirements of the articles. It was also held in the *Hawkesbury* case that there is no exception to the rule where the plaintiff is the sole shareholder in the company.

The minority shareholders' action is sometimes called a derivative action[16] to indicate that the right being enforced is that of the company. The Legal Aid Act 1974 makes no provision for legal aid in a minority shareholders' action but it is open to the court in such an action to order the company to indemnify the plaintiff against the costs of the action. The minority shareholder should apply for the sanction of the court soon after issuing his writ. It would be unlawful as being contrary to public policy for a solicitor to accept a

---

[14] See *per* Hudson J. in *Kraus* v. *J. G. Lloyd Pty. Ltd.* [1965] V.R. 232 at pp. 236, 237.
[15] (1970) 92 W.N. (N.S.W.) 199 (First Australian Supplement to Charlesworth & Cain, p. 59).
[16] In Gower, *Modern Company Law*, 3rd ed., p. 587; *per* Lord Denning M.R. at p. 390 and Scarman L.J. at p. 406 in *Wallersteiner* v. *Moir* [1975] Q.B. 373 (C.A.). Scarman L.J. said that the American description of a minority shareholders' action, brought to obtain redress for the company, as a stockholders' derivative action, is apt.

retainer from the plaintiff(s) to conduct the action on a contingency fee basis (*i.e.* he is paid the fee if he wins but not if he loses).[17]

In *Hogg* v. *Cramphorn*[18] the plaintiff was held to be justified in suing in a representative capacity in respect of the alleged wrongful disposition of the company's money by the directors which could be condoned by a resolution in general meeting, so that the action should have been dismissed unless it was not a *derivative* representative action but an *individual rights* representative action.

A member of a company may enjoy a right alone or in common with other members of the company and the rule in *Foss* v. *Harbottle* has no application where individual members sue, not in right of the company, but in their own right to protect their *individual* rights as members[19]—in such a case a member can bring an action in his own name and may sue on behalf of himself and other members, and the breach of duty owed to an individual shareholder cannot be ratified by a majority of shareholders. Thus in *Pender* v. *Lushington*,[20] *ante*, a shareholder was able to enforce the article giving him a right to vote at meetings and compel the directors to record his vote.[22]

Circumstances in which an individual member can sue in his own name are:—

(1) Where the company is acting illegally or *ultra vires*.[23]
(2) Where a special majority is required and has not been obtained.[24]
(3) Where the company is acting contrary to its articles.

It follows that because the wrong complained of may be an invasion of the rights of individual members as well as a breach of duty to the company and because an individual member can usually sue in his own name where his individual rights are being invaded, the rule in *Foss* v. *Harbottle* is not as important as it might be thought to be.

---

[17] *Wallersteiner* case *ante*.   [18] [1967] Ch. 254, *ante* p. 351.

[19] *Per* Sir Geo. Jessel M.R. in *Pender* v. *Lushington* (1877) 6 Ch.D. 70 at pp. 80, 81.

[20] (1877) 6 Ch.D. 70.

[22] See also *Ngurli* v. *McCann* (1954) 90 C.L.R. 425, *ante* p. 373, as explained in *Provident International Corpn.* v. *International Leasing Corpn. Ltd.* (1969) 89 W.N. (Pt. 1) (N.S.W.) 370.

[23] *Per* Lord Campbell L.C. in *Simpson* v. *Westminster Palace Hotel* (1860) VIII H.L.C. 712, 11 E.R. 608 at p. 610; *Russell* v. *Wakefield Waterworks Co.* (1875) L.R. 20 Eq. 474 at p. 481; *per* Street J. in the *Hawkesbury* case, *ante*, at pp. 212, 213.

[24] *Edwards* v. *Halliwell ante*.

The rule does not apply where a shareholder relies on a statutory right, *e.g.* a right to have the register of members rectified under section 116.

MAJORITY RULE AND MINORITY PROTECTION

Majority rule

The members of a company can express their wishes at general meetings by voting for or against the resolutions proposed. However, the will of the majority of the members usually prevails and if the appropriate majority is obtained a resolution binds all the members, including those who voted against it. Sometimes the majority is a simple majority and sometimes it is a three-quarters majority—for example, an ordinary resolution is a resolution passed by a simple majority of the votes of the members entitled to vote and voting; a special resolution is a resolution passed by a three-fourths majority of the votes of such members.[25] This can be said to be the first example of what is called "majority rule."

Further, it should be remembered that, subject to a few restrictions, the articles of a company, which constitute a contract binding the company and the members, can be altered by special resolution.[26]

Another example of majority rule is the rule in *Foss* v. *Harbottle*, by which, subject to certain exceptions, if a wrong to a company is alleged, or if there is an alleged irregularity in its internal management which is capable of confirmation by a simple majority of the members, the court will not interfere at the suit of a minority of the members.[27]

Minority protection

Both under the general law and under the Companies Acts there is some protection of the minority of the members against the acts of the majority. "A proper balance of the rights of the majority and minority shareholders is essential for the smooth functioning of the company. Since the passing of the Joint Stock Companies Act 1856, most Acts have extended the protection of the minority. The Act of 1948, and the relevant case law, attempt to maintain that balance by

[25] *Ante* p. 305.
[26] *Ante* p. 109.
[27] *Ante* p. 376.

admitting, on principle, the rule of the majority but limiting it, at the same time, by a number of well-defined minority rights."[28]

Examples of minority protection are:

(1) Under the general law, the doctrine that the majority of the members must not commit a fraud on the minority but must act bona fide for the benefit of the company as a whole.[29] Thus, in *Cook* v. *Deeks*[30] an individual shareholder was able, despite *Foss* v. *Harbottle*, to bring an action to recover the company's property from those who had taken it and who, by their voting power, prevented the company itself from suing. Again, an alteration of articles must not be in fraud of the minority.[31]

(2) The other exceptions to the rule in *Foss* v. *Harbottle*,[32] in which cases an individual member may bring a minority share-holders' action.

(3) The various sections of the Act intended to protect a minority of members. Under some minority sections even a single shareholder can defy the majority. Thus under sections 222 and 224[33] a member can petition the court to wind up the company on the ground that it is just and equitable that the company be wound up. And under section 210[34] a member can petition the court for relief other than a winding-up order where the company's affairs are being conducted in a manner oppressive to some of the members, including himself. Other minority sections enable a number of shareholders to defy the majority. For example, under section 5, dissentient holders of 15 per cent. of the issued shares can apply to the court for cancellation of an alteration of objects.[35] Again, under section 72, where class rights are varied in pursuance of a clause in the articles, dissentient holders of 15 per cent. of the issued shares of the class can apply for cancellation of the variation.[36] Finally, under sections 164 and 172,[37] 200 members or the holders of one-tenth of the issued shares can apply to the Department of Trade for an investigation of the company's affairs or of the ownership of the company.

Some of these minority sections will now be examined in detail.

[28] Palmer's *Company Law*, 21st ed., p. 498.
[29] *Ante* p. 374.
[30] *Ante* pp. 354, 379.
[31] *Ante* p. 109.
[32] *Ante* p. 379.
[33] *Post* p. 384.
[34] *Post* p. 389.
[35] *Ante* p. 91.
[36] *Ante* p. 220.
[37] *Post* pp. 397, 403.

STATUTORY PROTECTION OF MINORITY SHAREHOLDERS

Winding up by the court on the "just and equitable" ground

Under sections 222 and 224 a contributory may petition that a company be wound up by the court and where the court is of opinion that it is just and equitable that the company should be wound up, the court may order winding up.

A member of a company is a contributory by sections 212 and 213, and it has been held that a holder of fully paid-up shares is a contributory.[38] Thus in appropriate circumstances even a single member can petition for a winding up. We shall see[39] that section 224 generally prevents a contributory from petitioning unless he has held his shares for at least six months.

In petitioning for a winding up on the just and equitable ground a member is not confined to such circumstances as affect him as a shareholder, *i.e.* he is not confined to cases where his position as a shareholder has been worsened by the action of which he complains; he is entitled to rely on any circumstances of justice or equity which affect him in his relations with the company or with the other shareholders,[40] although it is otherwise under section 210 *post.*

The court will not, as a rule, order a winding up on a contributory's petition unless, *e.g.*, he alleges and proves, at least to the extent of a prima facie case, that there will be assets for distribution among the shareholders.[41] The reason is that unless there are such assets the contributory has no interest in a winding up. And a contributory's petition which is opposed by the majority of the contributories will usually not be granted except where the conduct of the majority is something of which the minority have a right to complain,[42] or the main object of the company has failed.[43] The petitioner need not establish that the other members have not acted bona fide in the interests of the company.[40]

---

[38] *Re National Savings Bank Assocn.* (1866) L.R. 1 Ch.App. 547; *Walker and ors, Petitioners* (1894) 2 S.L.T. 230 and 397 (O.H.).

[39] *Post* p. 548.   [40] *Re Westbourne Galleries Ltd.* [1973] A.C. 360.

[41] *Re Rica Gold Washing Co.* (1879) 11 Ch.D. 36 (C.A.), distinguished in *Re W. R. Willcocks & Co. Ltd.* [1974] Ch.D. 163; *per* Lord Trayner in *Black* v. *United Collieries Ltd.* (1904) 7 F. 18. And see *post* p. 549.

[42] *Re Middlesbrough Assembly Rooms Co.* (1880) 14 Ch.D. 104 (C.A.), *post* p. 542; *Re Tivoli Freeholds Ltd.* [1972] V.R. 445 (First Australian Supplement to Charlesworth & Cain, pp. 55, 56).

[43] *Re German Date Coffee Co.* (1882) 20 Ch.D. 169, *ante* p. 80; *Pirie* v. *Stewart* (1904) 6 F. 847; *ct Cox* v. *"Gosford" Ship Co. Ltd.* (1894) 21 R. 334 and *Galbraith* v. *Merito Shipping Co. Ltd.*, 1947 S.C. 446.

Even where the minority is entitled to complain of the conduct of the majority a contributories' petition is uncommon. For one thing, winding up is a drastic remedy. For another, an alternative remedy may be available under section 210, *post*, now.

An order for winding up will be made, *e.g.* in the following circumstances, some of which do not involve oppression of the minority:—

(1) Where the main object of the company has failed[43]—we saw in Chapter 3 that a clause excluding the "main objects" rule is irrelevant in this event—or the company is engaging in acts which are entirely outside what can fairly be regarded as having been within the general intention or common understanding of the members when they became members.[44] Oppression within the meaning of section 210 need not be shown.[44]

A company was formed to acquire the English portion of the aircraft business of M. Blériot, a well-known airman. M. Blériot refused to carry out the contract. *Held*, the company should be wound up because its substratum had gone: *Re Blériot Aircraft Co.* (1916) 32 T.L.R. 253.

A company formed to purchase, charter and work ships and to carry on the business of shipowners lost its only vessel. Its remaining asset was a balance of £363 in the bank. A majority in number and value of shareholders petitioned for compulsory winding up, but a minority of shareholders desired to carry on the business as charterers. *Held*, it was just and equitable that the company should be wound up: *Pirie* v. *Stewart* (1904) 6 F. 847.

(2) If the company is a "bubble," *i.e.* there is no bona fide intent on the part of the directors to carry on business in a proper manner.[45]

The court will not order a solvent company to be wound up merely because it is making a loss or is deeply indebted if the majority of the shareholders are against a winding up,[46] or if no meeting of shareholders has been held to consider winding up.[47]

(3) Where the company was formed to carry out a fraud, or to carry on an illegal business.

[44] *Re Tivoli Freeholds ante.*
[45] *Re London and County Coal Co.* (1866) L.R. 3 Eq. 355.
[46] *Re Suburban Hotel Co.* (1867) L.R. 2 Ch.App. 737 (company making a loss), *Black* v. *United Collieries Ltd.* (1904) 7 F. 18 (company deeply indebted). See also *Galbraith* v. *Merito Shipping Co. Ltd.*, 1947 S.C. 446, *per* Lord Mackay at p. 458.
[47] *Cox* v. *"Gosford" Ship Co. Ltd.* (1894) 21 R. 334; *Scobie* v. *Atlas Steel Works Ltd.* (1906) 8 F. 1052.

T. E. B. and his sons were relatives of, and had been employed by, persons who carried on the business of piano manufacturers under the name of J.B. & Sons. They left J. B. & Sons and formed a company called T. E. B. & Sons Ltd. for carrying on a similar business. A prospectus was issued which stated that the price paid for the business was £76,650, when it was really only £1,000 in cash together with £5,000 in shares in the company. Money was subscribed by the public and most of this money found its way into the hands of the persons who were the real, though not the ostensible, promoters. J. B. & Sons obtained an injunction restraining the company from using the name B., and it was found that the company was formed to filch as much trade as possible from J. B. & Sons. Numerous actions were brought against the company for fraud in the prospectus. *Held*, the company should be wound up: *Re Thomas Edward Brinsmead & Sons* [1897] 1 Ch. 45; 406 (C.A.).

Fraudulent misrepresentation in the prospectus[48] or fraud in the course of business with the outside world[49] are not, by themselves, grounds for winding the company up, as the majority of the share-holders may waive the fraud, or there may be a change of management; but fraud in the real, though not the ostensible, object of the company will be such a ground.

A company formed to carry on an illegal business, *e.g.* one which infringes the Betting, Gaming and Lotteries Act, will be wound up.[50]

(4) Where the mutual rights of the members are not exhaustively defined in the articles, *e.g.* where they entered into membership on the basis of a personal relationship involving mutual confidence or an understanding as to the extent to which each is to participate in the management of the company's business, and the right to transfer shares in the company is restricted, and the confidence is not maintained or the petitioner is excluded from the management. Section 210 oppression need not be shown.

From about 1945 E. and N. were partners in a carpet dealing business with an equal share in the management and profits. In 1958 they formed a private company to take the business over. E. and N. were the first directors and each held 500 £1 shares. The articles provided that shares could not be transferred without the directors' consent. Later, N's son, G., was appointed a director and E. and N. each transferred 100 shares to him. The company made good profits which were all distributed by way of directors' remuneration, *i.e.* no dividends were paid. After a disagreement between E. and N., with whom G. sided, N. and G. at a general meeting removed E. as a director by ordinary resolution under section 184, and thereafter excluded him from the conduct of the company's business. E. petitioned for an order under section 210 that N. and G. buy his

[48] *Re Haven Gold Mining Co.* (1882) 20 Ch.D. 151 (C.A.).
[49] *Re Medical Battery Co.* [1894] 1 Ch. 444.
[50] *Re International Securities Corpn. (Ltd.)* (1908) 24 T.L.R. 837; 25 T.L.R. 31 (C.A.).

shares and, in the alternative, for an order under section 222(f) that the company be wound up on the ground that it was just and equitable. *Held*, (at first instance) there was no such course of oppressive conduct as to justify an order under section 210, but (by the House of Lords) it was just and equitable that the company be wound up. After a long association in partnership, during which he had had an equal share in the management and profits, E. had joined in the formation of the company; the inference was indisputable that he and N. had done so on the basis that the character of the association would, as a matter of personal faith, remain the same; and E. had established that N. and G. were not entitled, in justice and equity, to make use of their legal powers of expulsion. Furthermore E. was unable to dispose of his interest in the company without the consent of N. and G.: *Re Westbourne Galleries Ltd.* [1973] A.C. 360.

Per Lord Wilberforce at pp. 374, 375: "there has been a tendency to create categories or headings under which cases must be brought if the [just and equitable] clause is to apply. This is wrong. Illustrations may arise but general words should remain general and not be reduced to the sum of particular instances."

And at p. 379: "The words [just and equitable] are a recognition of the fact that a limited company is more than a mere legal entity, with a personality in law of its own: that there is room in company law for recognition of the fact that behind it, or amongst it, there are individuals, with rights, expectations and obligations inter se which are not necessarily submerged in the company structure. That structure is defined by the Companies Act and by the articles of association by which shareholders agree to be bound. In most companies and in most contexts, this definition is sufficient and exhaustive, equally so whether the company is large or small. The 'just and equitable' provision does not . . . entitle one party to disregard the obligation he assumes by entering a company, nor the court to dispense him from it. It does, as equity always does, enable the court to subject the exercise of legal rights to equitable considerations; considerations, that is, of a personal character arising between one individual and another, which may make it unjust, or inequitable, to insist on legal rights, or to exercise them in a particular way.

It would be impossible, and wholly undesirable, to define the circumstances in which these considerations may arise. Certainly the fact that the company is a small one, or a private company, is not enough. There are very many of these where the association is a purely commercial one, of which it can safely be said that the basis of association is adequately and exhaustively laid down in the articles. The superimposition of equitable considerations requires something more [than the fact that the company is a small one, or a private company], which typically may include one, or probably more, of the following elements: (i) an association formed or continued on the basis of a personal relationship, involving mutual confidence—this element will often be found where a pre-existing partnership has been converted into a limited company; (ii) an agreement, or understanding, that all, or some (for there may be 'sleeping members'), of the shareholders shall participate in the conduct of the business; (iii) restriction on the transfer of the members' interest in the company—so that if confidence is lost, or one member removed from management, he cannot take out his stake and go elsewhere."

Per Lord Cross of Chelsea at p. 383: ". . . it is not a condition precedent to the making of an order under [s. 222(f)] that the conduct of those who oppose it should have been 'unjust or inequitable'."

And at p. 387: "A petitioner who relies on the 'just and equitable' clause must come to court with clean hands, and if the breakdown in confidence between him and the other parties to the dispute appears to have been due to his misconduct he cannot insist on the company being wound up if they wish it to continue."

Re Westbourne Galleries was applied in *Re A. & B. C. Chewing Gum Ltd.* [1975] 1 W.L.R. 579, where the petitioners held one-third of the company's shares on the basis that they should have equal control with the two individual respondents, who were brothers and directors of the company and owned the other two-thirds of the shares. To achieve equality of control, the articles were altered so as to provide, *inter alia*, that the petitioners could appoint and remove a director representing them, and that decisions at board meetings should be unanimous. The petitioners, the respondents and the company also signed and sealed a shareholders' agreement setting out the way in which the day to day business was to be conducted. The respondents refused to recognise the petitioner's removal of their director and the appointment of another in his place. This was not a case of one side making use of its legal rights to the prejudice of another—the petitioners were excluded from their legal and contractual rights. Their right to management participation was repudiated.

Weinberg and Rothman were the sole shareholders in and directors of a company, with equal rights of management and voting power. After a time they became bitterly hostile to one another and disagreed about the appointment of important servants of the company. All communications between them were made through the secretary. The company made large profits in spite of the disagreement. *Held*, mutual confidence had been lost between W. and R. and the company should be wound up: *Re Yenidje Tobacco Co. Ltd.* [1916] 2 Ch. 426 (C.A.).

A family company was formed to carry on a testator's business and to divide the profits among his family entitled under his will to share them. The managing director, who had a preponderating voting power, omitted to hold general meetings, submit accounts or recommend dividends, and laid himself open to the suspicion that his object in so doing was to acquire the minority's shares at an undervalue. *Held*, the company should be wound up. Confidence in the management was, justifiably, at an end: *Loch* v. *John Blackwood Ltd.* [1924] A.C. 783 (P.C.).[51]

Whether it is just and equitable to wind up a company depends on facts which exist at the time of the hearing and a petitioner is confined to heads of complaint set out in his petition.[52]

A shareholder is not entitled to a winding-up order on the "just and equitable" ground if his object is not a company purpose but the securing for himself of an advantage in a question between himself and other shareholders.[53]

If, in the case of a contributories' petition, the court is of opinion that it is just and equitable that the company should be wound up and some other remedy, *e.g.* an injunction, or the removal from office of a director guilty of mismanagement, or an order under section 210, *post*, is available to the petitioners, the court *must* make

---

[51] And see *Re Wondoflex Textiles Pty. Ltd.* [1951] V.L.R. 458. Scottish cases are *Symington* v. *Symington's Quarries Ltd.* (1905) 8 F. 121, *Thomson* v. *Drysdale*, 1925 S.C. 311, *Baird* v. *Lees*, 1924 S.C. 83 and *Lewis* v. *Haas*, 1971 S.L.T. 57 (O.H.).

[52] *Re Fildes Bros. Ltd.* [1970] 1 All E.R. 923.

[53] *Anglo-American Brush etc. Corpn. Ltd.* v. *Scottish Brush Co. Ltd.* (1882) 9 R. 972.

a winding-up order unless it is of the opinion that the petitioners are acting unreasonably in not pursuing the other remedy: section 225 (2). The Jenkins Report[54] recommended that this provision be amended so as to remove the limitations on the court's discretion.

Alternative remedy to winding up in cases of oppression

Section 210 provides that any member[55] who complains that the affairs of the company are being conducted in a manner oppressive to some part of the members, including himself, may petition the court for an order under the section.

Even a single member has a statutory individual right to petition under the section and the rule in *Foss* v. *Harbottle ante* is irrelevant.[55a] The term "member" in section 210 includes the personal representative of a deceased member even if the personal representative is not entered in the register of members.[56]

The section is available in respect of oppression within a company limited by guarantee as well as within one limited by shares.[57]

The petitioner must prove that, on a consideration of the whole course of events in the period complained of, some part of the members suffered, in a pecuniary sense, as members, as a result of a visible departure from the standards of fair dealing,[58] or of conduct which is "burdensome, harsh and wrongful"[59] or which suggests a lack of probity.[60]

A continuing process of oppression is required[61]—an isolated incident is not sufficient ground for an order under section 210, which requires a course of oppressive conduct continued up to the date of the petition,[62] although under the general law an injunction may be obtained where there is an isolated act of oppression.[63] And

---

[54] *Para.* 503(i).
[55] A creditor cannot petition under s. 210. *Cf.* s. 224 *ante.*
[55a] *Per* Joske J. in *Re Associated Tool Industries Ltd.* [1964] A.L.R. 73 at p. 83.
[56] *Re Jermyn Street Turkish Baths Ltd.* [1970] 1 W.L.R. 1194, although in the Court of Appeal ([1971] 1 W.L.R. 1042) the personal representative was treated as a duly registered member. According to *Re Meyer Douglas Pty. Ltd.* [1965] V.R. 638 "member" in s. 210 does not include such a personal representative but "contributory" in s. 224 *ante* does.
[57] *Re Ingleburn Horse and Pony Club Ltd.* [1973] 1 N.S.W.L.R. 641.
[58] *Elder* v. *Elder & Watson Ltd.*, 1952 S.C. 49, *post.*
[59] *Meyer* v. *Scottish C.W.S. Ltd.*, 1958 S.C. (H.L.) 40; [1959] A.C. 324, *post.*
[60] *Re Broadcasting Station 2 GB Pty. Ltd.* [1964–65] N.S.W.R. 1648. (First Australian Supplement to Charlesworth & Cain p. 192; Second Australian Supplement, p. 23).
[61] *Re H. R. Harmer Ltd.* [1959] 1 W.L.R. 62 (C.A.), *post.*
[62] *Re Jermyn Street Turkish Baths Ltd.* [1971] 1 W.L.R. 1042 (C.A.).
[63] *Per* Jacobs J. in *Re Broadcasting Station 2 GB, ante,* at p. 1662.

the court cannot anticipate oppression—there is no oppression until the majority shareholder actually prefers his own interests to those of the company. Oppression at the time when the petition is presented must be established.[64]

The oppression must be suffered by the petitioners in their character as members and not, *e.g.*, in their character of director or secretary or manager.[65]

In a family company, the petitioning shareholders had been removed from office as directors and from employment as secretary and factory manager but there was no allegation that the business was mismanaged or that registration had been refused of any transfers of their shares by the petitioners. *Held*, no case for relief had been stated. There was no oppression of the petitioners as members, and it was not just and equitable that the company should be wound up: *Elder* v. *Elder & Watson Ltd.*, 1952 S.C. 49.

Oppression is not limited to that designed to obtain pecuniary advantage as opposed to that which is due to an overwhelming desire for power.[61] However, it is not enough to prove that a person is unwise, inefficient and careless in the performance of his duties as managing director.[64] The oppression need not be by a controlling majority. Oppression by anyone in fact taking part in the affairs of the company is enough.[66]

A remedy sought under section 210 is not barred by the fact that the majority shareholder's own shares have depreciated in value *pro rata* with those of the minority.

"It is maintained that the section has no operation where Samson destroys himself as well as the Philistines in a single catastrophe, the point being that in this case the society hold 4,000 of the shares the value of which they are said to have deliberately depressed. I have come to think that this is to give too narrow a meaning to this remedial provision": *per* Lord President Cooper in *Meyer* v. *Scottish C.W.S. Ltd.*, 1954 S.C. 381 at p. 392.

The Department of Trade may petition where, as a result of an investigation of the company's affairs, there appears to have been oppression of members.[67]

A section 210 petition must set out in clear terms the general nature of the relief sought.[68]

If the real object of a petition alleging oppression is to obtain

---

[64] *Re Five Minute Car Wash Service Ltd.* [1966] 1 W.L.R. 745.
[65] A member petitioning under s. 224 *ante* is not confined to such circumstances as affect him as a shareholder.
[66] *Per* Jenkins L.J. in *Re H. R. Harmer Ltd.* [1959] 1 W.L.R. 62 (C.A.) at p. 75; *Re Associated Tool Industries Ltd.* [1964] A.L.R. 73.
[67] *post* p. 401.
[68] *Re Antigen Laboratories Ltd.* [1951] 1 All E.R. 110.

repayment of a loan owed by the company to the petitioner, the presentation of the petition to achieve the collateral purpose is an abuse of the process of the court and the petition will be dismissed.[69]

The section also provides that if the court is of opinion—

(1) that the company's affairs are being conducted as alleged;

(2) that it is just and equitable that the company should be wound up by the court[70]; but

(3) that to wind up the company would unfairly prejudice the oppressed part of the members;[71]

then, instead of making a winding up order, the court may, with a view to bringing to an end the matters complained of, make such order as it thinks fit, whether for regulating the future conduct of the company's affairs, or for the purchase of any member's shares by other members or by the company or otherwise. In the case of purchase by the company the order will provide for the reduction of the company's capital.[72]

An 88 years old controlling shareholder and his wife had the majority of the shares carrying a right to vote but the minority of the different class of shares carrying a right to share in the distributed profits of a private company. The majority of the latter class of shares were held by his sons, whose shares he had given to them. The controlling shareholder, who had founded the company and transferred his business to it, continued to regard the business as his own and ignored the wishes of the other shareholders and of his co-directors, including the petitioners, his sons. Viscount Simonds' definition of "oppressive" as meaning "burdensome, harsh and wrongful" in *Meyer's* case[73] was adopted, and an order was made under section 210 that the controlling shareholder was not to interfere in the company's affairs except in accordance with board decisions: *Re H. R. Harmer Ltd.* [1959] 1 W.L.R. 62 (C.A.).

A holding company, engaged in the same class of business as its subsidiary which had an independent minority of members, ruined the subsidiary in the interests of the holding company and its controllers by cutting off supplies. Three of the subsidiary's directors were nominated by, and were also directors of, the holding company. These nominee directors actively supported the policy of the holding company. The minority shareholders of the subsidiary petitioned for an order that the holding company should purchase their £1 shares. At one time the shares had been worth £6 but by the time of the action they were practically worthless. *Held*, the conduct of the holding company through the nominee directors was conduct of the affairs of the subsidiary and was oppressive to the minority. The order made under section 210 was that the holding company buy

---

[69] *Re Bellador Silk Ltd.* [1965] 1 All E.R. 667.
[70] *Ante* p. 384.
[71] *e.g.* because the petitioners will recover only the break up value of their shares: see *per* Lord Denning M.R. in *Meyer* v. *Scottish C.W.S. Ltd.* [1959] A.C. 324 at p. 368.
[72] *Cf.* s. 5, *ante* p. 92.
[73] At 1958 S.C. (H.L.) p. 47. [1959] A.C. at p. 342.

the minority's shares at a fair price, namely £3 15s. per share: *Meyer* v. *Scottish C.W.S. Ltd.*, 1958 S.C.(H.L.) 40; [1959] A.C. 324.[74]

"Whenever a subsidiary is formed . . . with an independent minority of shareholders, the parent company must, if it is engaged in the same class of business, accept . . . an obligation so to conduct what are in a sense its own affairs as to deal fairly with its subsidiary:" *per* Viscount Simonds at p. 48 and Lord Keith at p. 63.[75]

Where other members are ordered to buy the petitioner's shares the court has no power under the section to charge payment for the shares on the shares in the company already held by the respondents.[66]

If an order under section 210 alters the company's memorandum or articles then, subject to the order, the company cannot, without leave of the court, make any further alteration inconsistent with the order.

An office copy of a section 210 order, or of an order giving leave to alter the memorandum or articles, must be delivered to the Registrar within 14 days after it is made.[76]

However, condition (2) *ante* is the weakness of section 210. If, *e.g.*, it is not just and equitable that a company should be wound up since the assets will be swallowed up by claims of creditors leaving nothing for the contributories, no order can be made under the section.[69] On the other hand the section does not apply in every case where winding up is just and equitable but only to cases of that character which have in them the requisite element of oppression.[61]

The Cohen Committee intended[77] the section to be useful, *e.g.*, where on the death of a shareholder, the directors, under powers in the articles, refuse to register transfers by the personal representatives and so are able to buy the deceased's shares at their own price, or where directors absorb an undue proportion of the profits of a company in remuneration for their services so that little or nothing is left for distribution among the shareholders by way of dividend, as may happen where two persons are the working directors and shareholders of a company and one dies, leaving his shares to his widow who takes no active part in the business. If a director draws remuneration to which he is not legally entitled this might found

---

[74] The nominee directors were in breach of their duties to the subsidiary. See also *Re Broadcasting Station 2 GB Pty. Ltd.*, *ante*, and *Re Bright Pine Mills Pty. Ltd.* [1969] V.R. 1002 (F.Ct.) (First Australian Supplement, p. 193).

[75] And *vice versa*: *per* Joske J. in *Re Associated Tool Industries Ltd.* [1964] A.L.R. 73 at p. 82.

[76] And in England see the Companies (Winding-up) Rules 1949, r. 42.

[77] Cmd. 6659, paras. 58–60. See also the Jenkins Report (Cmnd. 1749), para. 205.

misfeasance proceedings or proceedings for some other kind of relief but it does not of itself amount to oppression. The fact that he is a majority shareholder makes no difference unless he uses his voting power to procure or retain the remuneration, or to stifle proceedings by the company or other shareholders in relation to it.[78]

The kinds of order which the court may make under the section mean that it is more effective than section 224 *ante* (under which only an order for winding up can be made) or the general law (under which, in the event of, *e.g.*, a breach or threatened breach of duty by directors or by controlling shareholders, the principal remedies are a declaration and an injunction, generally available to the company.[79]

The Jenkins Committee thought that an action under section 210 might also be appropriate where shares are issued to directors and others on advantageous terms or non-cumulative preference dividends are passed on shares held by the minority.

Apart from any restrictions on transfer,[80] the market for the purchase of a minority shareholding in a private company is a very restricted one and, if the majority shareholders are unwilling to buy, the minority shares may be unsaleable at anything like their true value. The only available remedy would seem to be in the nature of prevention rather than cure, namely, to take the greatest care in the drafting of the articles, so as to provide for the disposal of the shares on the death or retirement of the shareholders, and to have not less than one-quarter of the voting power so that the articles cannot be altered without the minority shareholders' consent. The extension of section 222[81] as recommended by the Jenkins Committee would assist in this connection.

The Jenkins Report[82] recommended that section 210 should no longer make the establishment of a case for winding up under the just and equitable rule an essential condition of intervention by the court—one reason why the section has not afforded effective protection to minorities is that such a case at the instance of a contributory is difficult to establish, as is noted above. It was further recommended that the section should be amended so as to—

---

[78] *Re Jermyn Street Turkish Baths Ltd.* [1971] 1 W.L.R. 1042 (C.A.), where the resolution of the board fixing the remuneration of the directors was *ultra vires* the directors since the articles required directors' remuneration to be fixed by the company in general meeting.
[79] Para. 205.
[80] See, *e.g.*, *Re Westbourne Galleries Ltd.* [1973] A.C. 360, *ante* p. 387.
[81] *Post* p. 432.
[82] Para. 212. And see paras. 199–211.

(1) make clear that it covers isolated acts as well as a course of conduct and that it extends to cases where the affairs of the company are being conducted in a manner unfairly prejudicial to the interests of some part of the members and not merely in an "oppressive" manner;

(2) enable the court to restrain the commission or continuance of any act which would support a petition under the section;

(3) enable the court to authorise the bringing of proceedings in the name of the company against a third party where a wrong is done to the company and the control vested in the majority is wrongfully used to prevent an action, so that the minority is indirectly wronged;

(4) make clear that personal representatives to whom shares are transmitted by operation of law, but who are not registered as members, are entitled to present a petition or seek an injunction under the section and so as to entitle personal representatives to require the directors to furnish a written statement of their reasons if they refuse them registration.

The former Conservative Government proposed to accept the recommendations of the Jenkins Committee as to amendment of section 210 but with some modification in detail.[83] In particular, they proposed to extend the recommendations as to personal representatives and others to whom shares are transmitted by process of law to cover persons to whom shares are transferred. Clause 70 of the 1973 Companies Bill would have given effect to these proposals.

Misfeasance proceedings in a winding up

Section 333 provides that if in a winding up it appears that any promoter, past or present director, manager or liquidator, or any officer of the company, has misapplied or retained or become liable or accountable for any money or property of the company, or been guilty of any misfeasance or breach of trust in relation to the company, the court may, on the application of the Official Receiver, the liquidator or any creditor or contributory,[84] examine the conduct of such promoter, director, manager, liquidator or officer, and order him to repay or restore with interest, or to contribute to the assets of the company such sum as the court thinks just. Although "misfeasance" is not a Scots law term, the section does apply to Scotland.

The section is procedural only. It gives a summary remedy, not

[83] White Paper on Company Law Reform, (1973) Cmnd. 5391, para. 39.
[84] *Ante* p. 384.

a new cause of action.[85] It has been said that it "does not create any new liability, any new right, but only provides a summary mode of enforcing rights which must otherwise have been enforced by the ordinary procedure of the Courts." Also, that the applicant "must shew something which would have been the ground of an action by the company if it had not been wound up." Further, that the word "misfeasance" in the section means "misfeasance in the nature of a breach of trust, that is to say, it refers to something which the officer . . . has done wrongly by misapplying or retaining in his own hands any moneys of the company, or by which the company's property has been wasted, or the company's credit improperly pledged. It must be some act resulting in some actual loss to the company." [86]

It follows that section 333 is not available in all cases in which the company has a right of action against an officer of the company. It is not available where a company has a right of action against an officer for common law negligence[87]—in this case an ordinary action must be brought.

A misfeasance summons[88] was taken out by the liquidator against the secretary of a company for sums overdrawn by him on account of his salary on the instructions of the managing director. *Held*, as this was a claim for repayment of an ordinary debt due from the secretary without any wrongful conduct on his part, no order on the summons ought to be made: *Re Etic Ltd.* [1928] Ch. 861.

Section 333 "is limited to cases where there has been something in the nature of a breach of duty by an officer of the company as such which has caused pecuniary loss to the company. Breach of duty of course would include a misfeasance or a breach of trust in the stricter sense, and the section will apply to a true case of misapplication of money or property of the company, or a case where there has been retention of money or property which the officer was bound to have paid or returned to the company": *per* Maugham J. at p. 875.

In England a receiver and manager appointed by a debenture holder has been held not to be a person whose conduct can be examined under the section.[87] He is not an "officer" of the company within section 455 because any work of management he might do is not done by virtue of any office which he holds in the company; nor

---

[85] *Coventry and Dixon's Case* (1880) 14 Ch.D. 660 (C.A.). See Lord President Inglis in *Liquidators of City of Glasgow Bank* v. *Mackinnon* (1881) 9 R. 535, at p. 564, and Lord Guest (Ordinary) in *Lord Advocate* v. *Liquidators of Purvis Industries Ltd.*, 1958 S.C. 338 (O.H.), at p. 342.

[86] *Per* James L.J. in *Coventry and Dixon's Case* at p. 670.

[87] *Re B. Johnson & Co. (Builders) Ltd.* [1955] Ch. 634 (C.A.); *per* Mason J. (Barwick C.J. concurring) in *Walker* v. *Wimborne* (1976) 50 A.L.J.R. 446.

[88] In Scotland the application to the court would take the form of a note in the petition process (compulsory winding up) or of a petition (voluntary winding up): R.C. 215.

is he a "manager" of the company because he is managing, not on behalf of the company, but on behalf of the debenture holders.

The Jenkins Report[89] recommended that section 333 be amended to deal with actionable negligence by directors and others, and to bring within its scope a receiver of any property of the company.

Instances of misfeasance are the improper receipt by a director of his qualification shares from a promoter,[90] the certifying by an auditor of erroneous accounts whereby dividends were paid out of capital,[91] the receipt by the secretary of a secret profit from a person who sold a mine to the company,[92] the acts of a director in procuring the company to buy shares in another company from himself at an over-value, and making an unsecured loan to enable him and his co-directors to pay calls[93] and failure by a liquidator to make proper provision for the equal ranking and payment of all preferential claims.[94]

No set-off is allowed to a claim for misfeasance.[95]

The court has a discretion as to the amount to be ordered to be paid on an application under section 333.

A liquidator negligently admitted a proof, which he should have disallowed, and as a result the company paid £38,000 to a creditor. An attempt to recover this failed, as there was no mistake of fact on the liquidator's part. *Held*, the liquidator was liable for misfeasance, but the court, in the exercise of its discretion, ordered him to pay only such a sum as would enable the creditors to be paid in full with interest at 5 per cent.: *Re Home and Colonial Insce. Co. Ltd.* [1930] 1 Ch. 102.

Further, the court's power under the section is not merely to specify a sum by way of compensation but to apportion it between co-defendants in such way and with such priority of liability as the court thinks fit.[96]

Inspection

Statutory provision is made for a number of forms of inspection. These comprise investigation of a company's affairs, investigation of

[89] Para. 503.
[90] Which occurred in *Eden* v. *Ridsdales Railway Lamp Co. Ltd.* (1889) 23 Q.B.D. 368 (C.A.).
[91] See *Re Kingston Cotton Mill Co.* (*No. 2*) [1896] 2 Ch. 279 (C.A.), *post* p. 465.
[92] *McKay's Case* (1875) 2 Ch.D. 1 (C.A.).
[93] *Re V.G.M. Holdings Ltd.* [1942] Ch. 235 (C.A.).
[94] *Lord Advocate* v. *Liquidators of Purvis Industries Ltd.* 1958 S.C. 338 (O.H.), *post* p. 594.   [95] *Ex p. Pelly* (1882) 21 Ch.D. 492 (C.A.).
[96] *Re Morecambe Bowling Ltd.* [1969] 1 W.L.R. 133.

the ownership of a company, investigation of share dealings, and inspection of companies' books and papers.

Investigation of a company's affairs[97]

Appointment of inspectors

1. In the case of a company with a share capital, *on the application of not less than 200 members or of members holding not less than one-tenth of the shares issued,* the Department of Trade *may* appoint one or more competent inspectors to investigate the affairs of the company and to report on them. The application must be supported by evidence showing that the applicants have good reason for requiring the investigation. Security, not exceeding £100, for the costs of the inquiry, may be required by the Department of Trade: section 164.

An inspector is usually a Queen's Counsel, a Chartered Accountant or an official of the Department of Trade.

2. The Department *must* appoint an inspector or inspectors *if* (i) *the company by special resolution, or* (ii) *the court by order,*[98] *declares that an investigation ought to be made:* section 165 (*a*).

In certain circumstances the transactions of a receiver and manager of the property of a company appointed by a debenture holder are affairs of the company within section 165 (*a*).[99]

The Jenkins Report[1] recommended that section 164 be repealed and section 165 (*a*) extended, *e.g.* so as to require the appointment of an inspector when over two hundred members or holders of one-quarter or more of the issued shares of any class request it, unless sufficient facts are known to the applicants to enable them to assert their rights on their own behalf.

The former Conservative Government did not propose to amend section 165 or to repeal section 164 as suggested by the Jenkins Committee.[2]
It considered that the recommendations of the Jenkins Committee raise

---

[97] *e.g.* the investigation, by Mr. E. Milner Holland Q.C., of the affairs of the Savoy Hotel Limited, *post* p. 405.
[98] The procedure in England is to apply to the Companies Court by originating motion under R.S.C., O. 102, r. 4. For Scotland, see R.C. 190.
[99] *R.* v. *B.o.T., ex p. St. Martins Preserving Co. Ltd.* [1965] 1 Q.B. 603, where, since the company by special resolution had declared that such transactions ought to be investigated, the Board of Trade (now the Department of Trade) had to appoint an inspector.
[1] Para. 218.
[2] White Paper on Company Law Reform, (1973) Cmnd. 5391, paras. 42–44.

conflicting considerations. The Conservative Government philosophy was that on the one hand, it is essential that the appointment of an inspector by the Secretary of State should not be seen as a convenient substitute for appeal to the court, which is normally the proper course for an aggrieved individual. On the other hand, shareholders may be unable to establish the facts on which an action might be based, and there may then be a public interest in an official investigation to establish the facts. The Government ought not to try to cushion investors from the results of their own decisions, or to seek to intervene in the internal management of companies, by the appointment of inspectors; however, the power to appoint must extend to all cases where there is reason to believe that there has been fraud, misfeasance or impropriety in the conduct of a company's affairs. In each case, the Secretary of State has to judge where the public interest lies, and must be scrupulous to see that his powers are not used to support the pursuit of a wholly private interest.

Thus there is still a place for a power (as opposed to an obligation) to appoint inspectors when a body of shareholders seek an investigation. The cost of an investigation can be very considerable. Under section 165 there is no power, nor should there be, to require the applicants to contribute to the cost; but under section 164 it is reasonable to have the power to require the applicants to contribute. It should not be mandatory for an appointment to be made and an investigation carried out at the public expense or that of the company on the application of a minority of shareholders.

The Conservative Government also considered that the upper limit of £100 which the applicants under section 164 may be required to give as security for their contribution to the costs of the investigation should be removed, and applicants should in appropriate cases be required to give security reasonably related to the probable cost.

Clause 71 (1) of the Companies Bill 1973 would have substituted "such amount as appears to the Secretary of State to be reasonable in the circumstances" for "£100" in section 164 and clause 71 (3) would have substituted "unfairly prejudicial to the interests" for "oppressive" in 3 (i) *post*.

3. The Department *may, on their own initiative*, appoint inspectors if it appears—

> (i) that a company's business is being or has been[3] conducted for a fraudulent or unlawful purpose or in a manner oppressive to part of its members or that it was formed for a fraudulent or unlawful purpose; or
>
> (ii) that the promoters or the persons managing its affairs have been guilty of misconduct towards the company or its members; or
>
> (iii) that the members have not been given reasonable information as to the company's affairs: section 165 (*b*).

The Department's power under 3, *ante*, is exercisable even if the company is being voluntarily wound up.[3]

In 1974 there were 438 applications to the Department under sections 164, 165 and 172 of the 1948 Act, and section 109 of the 1967 Act, *post*. 158 applica-

---

[3] Companies Act 1967, s. 38.

tions were approved, 130 being under section 109 of the 1967 Act and 25 under section 165 of the 1948 Act.

Powers of inspectors

1. An inspector may, if he thinks it necessary, investigate any other body corporate which is or has been a related company, *i.e.* the company's subsidiary[4] or holding company[4] or a subsidiary of its holding company or a holding company of its subsidiary: section 166.

2. He may call for the production of documents by past or present officers and agents (including bankers, solicitors and auditors) of the company or related company, whose duty it is to produce to the inspector all books and documents of or relating to the company or related company which are in their custody or power, to attend before the inspector when required[5] and to give the inspector all reasonable assistance: section 167. If an officer or agent refuses to perform his duties under section 167, the court may punish him as if he were in contempt of court.

Clause 71 (4) of the Companies Bill 1973 would have inserted a new sub-section (1A) into section 167 extending the section to persons other than officers and agents which persons the inspectors consider are or may be in possession of property of the company, or indebted to it, or able to give information concerning it.

A solicitor need not disclose a privileged communication made to him, except as regards the name and address of his client, and a banker need not disclose the affairs of his customers other than the company: section 175.

3. The inspector may examine on oath past or present officers and agents[6] of the company or related company in relation to its business.

If the inspector thinks it necessary that some other person be examined, the court may order that such person be examined on oath before it: section 167.

An answer given by a person to a question put under powers given by section 167 of the 1948 Act (or section 32 of the 1967 Act or rules made under section 365 (1) of the 1948 Act) may be used

---

[4] *Ante* p. 57.
[5] Companies Act 1967, s. 39.
[6] In the *St. Martins* case, *ante*, Winn J. thought that the receiver and manager was an agent of the company within s. 167.

in evidence against him (and a statement of the company's affairs, which by section 235 of the 1948 Act must be submitted to the Official Receiver in an English winding up, may be used in evidence against any person making or concurring in it): 1967 Act, section 50.

The only answers admissible in evidence under section 50 are those given on oath in the course of an examination by inspectors under section 167 (2) and, while it is not improper to question a person informally, his unsworn answers are inadmissible.[7]

4. The inspector may at any time during his investigation, without making an interim report, inform the Department of Trade of matters tending to show that an offence has been committed: 1967 Act, section 41.

It has been held that the inspectors' function is investigatory and not judicial but they must, in view of the consequences which may follow from their report, act fairly and, before they condemn or criticise a man, give him a fair opportunity to answer what is alleged against him.[8] It is sufficient for the inspectors to put to witnesses what has been said against them by other persons or in documents to enable them to deal with those criticisms in the course of the inquiry; it is not necessary for the inspectors to put their tentative conclusions to the witnesses in order to give them an opportunity to refute them.[9]

It has been said[10] that the considerations which are to be borne in mind in respect of an inquiry under the Companies Act are:

(a) It is a very special kind of inquiry. It is not a trial. There is no accused, no prosecutor, no charge. It is simply an investigation.

(b) There is no one to present a case to the inspector. There is no "counsel for the Commission." The inspector has to do it all himself.

(c) The investigation is in private. This is necessary because witnesses may say something defamatory of someone else, and it

---

[7] *Karak Rubber Co.* v. *Burden* [1971] 1 W.L.R. 1748.

[8] *Re Pergamon Press Ltd.* [1971] Ch. 388 (C.A.), where the persons who were required to give evidence were not entitled to see the transcripts of evidence of witnesses. In *Testro Bros. Pty. Ltd.* v. *Tait* (1963) 109 C.L.R. 353, the majority of the High Court of Australia held that the inspector need not, before making a report on the company's affairs, give the company an opportunity of answering or explaining matters which, if unanswered or unexplained, might give rise to adverse findings or comment in the report.

[9] *Maxwell* v. *Department of Trade and Industry* [1974] 1 Q.B. 523 (C.A.).

[10] *Per* Lord Denning M.R. in *Maxwell's* case, *ante*, at p. 533.

would be quite wrong for it to be published without the party
affected being able to challenge it.

(*d*) The inspectors have to make their report. They should state
their findings on the evidence and their opinions on the
matters referred to them. They should make it with courage
and frankness, keeping nothing back. Before they condemn
or criticise a man they must act fairly by him.

Inspectors' report

The inspectors may make interim reports, and on the conclusion
of the investigation they must make a final report to the Department
of Trade.

The Department of Trade must send a copy of a report to the
company's registered office, and if the Department think fit, they
must furnish a copy on request and on payment of the prescribed fee
to any member of the company or a related company dealt with in
the report or to any creditor whose interests appear to be affected.
Where the inspectors were appointed under section 164, a copy must,
on request, be furnished to the applicants for the investigation, and
where the appointment was under section 165 in pursuance of a
court order, a copy must be furnished to the court: section 168.

Clause 71 (6) of the 1973 Bill would have enabled any person whose conduct
is referred to in the report or whose financial interests appear to be affected by
it, to request a copy.

Proceedings on inspectors' report

Section 35 of the 1967 Act, as amended by Schedule 3 of the 1976
Act, provides that if it appears to the Department of Trade from the
inspectors' report, or from any information or document obtained
under Part III of the 1967 Act,[11] that it is expedient in the public
interest that the company be wound up, the Department may present
a petition that it be wound up by the court if the court thinks it just
and equitable that the company be wound up[12]: subsection (1). No
evidence of fraud or misfeasance is necessary.

The affidavit verifying the petition should describe the position of
the relevant officer in the Department, depose that he is entrusted

[11] *Post* p. 406.
[12] *Ante* p. 384.

with the section 35 power and explain that it appears to him to be expedient in the public interest that the company should be wound up.[13]

If it appears that the company's business is being conducted in a manner oppressive to any part of its members, the Department may present a petition for an order under section 210[14] of the 1948 Act: subsection (2).

If from the report, etc., it appears that civil proceedings ought in the public interest to be brought by any company, section 37 of the 1967 Act empowers the Department to bring such proceedings in the name and on behalf of the company. The Department must indemnify the company against costs or expenses incurred by it in connection with any such proceedings. If civil proceedings are properly brought under this section and there is no evidence to show that the company will be able to pay the defendant's costs if the defence is successful, the defendant is fully protected by the indemnity provision in the section and security cannot be ordered under section 447 of the 1948 Act.[15]

Expenses of investigation

The expenses of an investigation of a company's affairs are defrayed in the first instance by the Department of Trade but the following persons are liable to repay the Department:—

(1) Any person convicted on a prosecution instituted as a result of the investigation, or ordered to pay the costs of proceedings brought by virtue of section 37 of the 1967 Act, *ante*, may in the same proceedings be ordered to repay.

(2) Any company in whose name proceedings are brought is liable to repay to the extent of money or property recovered by it as a result of the proceedings.

(3) A company dealt with by the inspectors' report, where the inspectors were appointed otherwise than of the Department's own motion, is liable except so far as the Department otherwise direct.

(4) The applicants for the investigation, where the inspector was appointed under section 164 of the 1948 Act, *ante*, are liable

---

[13] *Re Golden Chemical Products Ltd.* [1976] Ch.D 300.
[14] *Ante* p. 389.
[15] *Selangor United Rubber Estates Ltd.* v. *Cradock* [1967] 1 W.L.R. 1168.

to such extent as the Department may direct: 1948 Act, section 170; 1967 Act, sections 36, 40.

In Australia, the Company Law Advisory Committee[16] has expressed the view that it is wrong that the expenses of the investigation of a company's affairs should be paid otherwise than out of public money and that the Government should accept the responsibility for seeing that justice is done, both criminal and civil.

Extension of Department of Trade's powers of investigation

Sections 165 to 171 and 175 of the 1948 Act now apply to all companies incorporated outside Great Britain which are carrying on business in Great Britain or have at any time carried on business therein, subject to any adaptations the Department of Trade may specify by statutory instrument: 1967 Act, section 42.

Investigation of the ownership of a company[17]

Appointment of inspectors

1. *Where they consider that there is good reason to do so*, the Department of Trade *may* appoint one or more inspectors to investigate and report on the membership of a company, for the purpose of determining the persons who are, or have been, financially interested in the success or failure of the company, or able to control or materially influence its policy: section 172 (1).

2. Unless the application is vexatious, the Department *must* appoint an inspector, *on the application*, with regard to particular shares or debentures, *of those members who can apply under section 164*[18] for an investigation of the company's affairs: section 172 (3).

Powers of inspectors. Inspectors' report

An inspector appointed under section 172, above, has the same powers as an inspector appointed to investigate the affairs of a company has under sections 166 and 167; section 168 applies to the report of inspectors appointed under section 172.[19]

---

[16] Third Interim Report 1969, paras. 26, 33.
[17] *e.g.* the investigation, by Mr. J. B. Lindon Q.C., of the membership of the Savoy Hotel Limited, *post* p. 405.
[18] *Ante* p. 397.   [19] *Ante* p. 399 *et seq.*

In addition, the sections apply in relation to all persons whom the inspector reasonably believes to be or to have been financially interested in the success or failure of the company or related company, or able to control or materially influence its policy. However, the Department of Trade are not bound to furnish the company or any person with a copy or a complete copy of the report if they believe that there is good reason for not divulging the whole or part of it: section 172 (5).

Expenses of investigation

The expenses of an investigation under section 172 are defrayed by the Department of Trade out of moneys provided by Parliament: section 172 (6).

Power to require information as to persons interested in shares, etc.

Where it appears that there is good reason to investigate the ownership of any shares or debentures of a company, and that it is unnecessary to appoint an inspector for the purpose, the Department of Trade may require any person whom they reasonably believe to be, or to have been, interested in such shares or debentures, or to act, or to have acted, as the solicitor or agent of someone interested therein, to give information as to the present and past interests in the shares or debentures and the names and addresses of the persons interested therein and of any persons who act or have acted for them in relation to the shares or debentures.

A person is deemed to have an interest in a share or debenture if he has a right to acquire or dispose of it or any interest therein, or to vote in respect thereof, or if his consent is necessary for the exercise of any right of other persons interested therein, or if such other persons can be required or are accustomed to exercise their rights in accordance with his instructions.

Failure to give information required under this section, or making a statement known to be false in a material particular, or recklessly making a statement false in a material particular, is punishable by six months' imprisonment or a £500 fine or both: section 173.

Power to impose restrictions on shares, etc.

If the Department of Trade find unwillingness on the part of the persons concerned to disclose the relevant facts about any shares or debentures, they may, subject to an appeal to the court, direct that the shares or debentures shall be subject to restrictions. The restrictions prevent transfers, the exercise of voting rights, the issue of further shares or debentures in right of the shares or debentures or to the holder thereof and, except in a liquidation, payment of any sums due from the company on the shares or debentures, whether in respect of capital or otherwise, *e.g.* payment of a dividend. Contravention of such restrictions renders the person or company concerned liable to penalties, although a prosecution in England can be instituted only by or with the consent of the Department of Trade: section 174.

The Savoy Hotel investigations

In 1953 there was heavy buying of Savoy Hotel stock on the Stock Exchange. The real buyers were unknown since the buying was through nominees. The object of the buyers was to obtain control of the Savoy Hotel Limited and develop its assets. 224 members of the company applied to the Board of Trade under sections 172 and 173 and Mr. J. B. Lindon Q.C. was appointed to investigate the ownership of the company. From the inspector's interim report,[20] it appears that Land Securities Investment Trust Limited, of which Mr. Harold Samuel was chairman and principal shareholder, had bought Savoy stock carrying 20 per cent. of the votes on a poll at a general meeting of Savoy Hotel Limited, and Princes Investments Limited, controlled by Mr. Charles Clore, had bought stock carrying 9 per cent. of the votes.

The Berkeley Hotel Company Limited was a subsidiary of the Savoy Company, with substantially the same directors, and it would have been possible to make a large immediate profit by turning the Berkeley Hotel into offices. To put the Berkeley Hotel out of the reach of anyone who might obtain control of the Savoy Company, the Savoy directors formed Worcester Buildings Company Limited and sold the Berkeley Hotel to the Worcester Company at a price satisfied by the issue to the Berkeley Company of fully paid preference shares in the Worcester Company. The Worcester Company gave the Berkeley Company a lease of the hotel for 50 years at a rent. The hotel could not be used otherwise than as a hotel without the consent of the Worcester Company. However, the Worcester Company was controlled by a number of ordinary shares of small nominal amount which were issued for cash to the trustees of the Savoy Company's benevolent fund. The cash was provided from the fund, which had been transferred to the trustees. The Board of Trade, under section 165 (*b*), appointed Mr. E. Milner Holland Q.C. to investigate the affairs of the Savoy Company.

[20] Dated November 28, 1953, and published by H.M.S.O.

His report[21] stated that, on the analogy of *Piercy* v. *Mills & Co.*,[22] the transaction was an invalid use of the powers of management of the Savoy directors, even though they thought they were acting for the benefit of the companies and their shareholders, and even though they had legal advice that they could act as they did. The purpose of the transaction was to deny to the majority holding voting control of the Savoy Company the power, by the exercise of that control, to cause the Berkeley Hotel to be used otherwise than as a hotel.

Investigation of share dealings

The 1967 Act, section 32, provides that if it appears to the Department of Trade that section 25[23] or 27[24] or 31 (2)[25] of the 1967 Act (these sections being concerned with penalisation of dealing in options by, and notification of interests of, directors or their spouses or children) may have been contravened, they may appoint one or more competent inspectors to investigate and report to them.

Section 167[26] of the 1948 Act, which imposes on officers and agents the duty to assist inspectors, applies with one or two modifications. Thus section 32 applies, *e.g.*, to members of a recognised stock exchange or of an association of dealers in securities who are individuals and to officers (past and present) of members who are companies.

Section 175[27] of the 1948 Act (savings for solicitors and bankers) applies.

The expenses of an investigation under section 32 are defrayed by the Department of Trade.

Clause 15 (5) of the Companies Bill 1973 would have extended section 32 to contraventions of the proposed provision prohibiting insider trading.[28]

Inspection of companies' books and papers

This is dealt with in Part III (sections 109 to 118) of the 1967 Act as follows—

Power of Department of Trade to require production of documents

Section 109 of the 1967 Act provides that the Department of Trade may, if they think there is good reason to do so, require certain

---

[21] Dated June 14, 1954, and published by H.M.S.O.
[22] [1920] 1 Ch. 77, *ante* p. 348.
[23] *Ante* p. 326.
[24] *Ante* p. 320.
[25] *Ante* p. 323.
[26] *Ante* p. 399.
[27] *Ante* p. 399.
[28] *Ante* p. 361.

companies, including a company formed and registered under the 1948 Act and a company incorporated outside Great Britain which is carrying on or has carried on business in Great Britain, to produce such books or papers (including accounts, deeds, writings and documents: section 117) as may be specified.

This section gives effect to a recommendation of the Jenkins Committee and is intended to make it easier for the Department of Trade to decide when an inspection of a company's affairs is justified.[29] The Department will be less likely to be inhibited from appointing inspectors by fear of causing unnecessary damage to a company. Further, the Department can now test the complainants' Statement of Facts without necessarily revealing to the directors the case against them and without the delays sometimes involved in awaiting the directors' reply.[30]

Without prejudice to any lien he may have, production of documents may be required from any person who appears to be in possession of them. Copies or extracts may be taken, and explanations may be required from such person or from present or past officers or employees of the company. If the documents are not produced, the person required to produce may be required to state, to the best of his knowledge and belief, where they are: section 109.

Nothing in Part III compels a solicitor to produce a document containing a privileged communication made by or to him: section 116.

Non-compliance with a requirement to produce documents or provide an explanation or make a statement renders the company or person concerned liable to three months' imprisonment or a £200 fine or both. Where a person is charged with failing to produce books it is a defence for him to prove that they were not in his possession or under his control and that it was not reasonably practicable for him to produce them: section 109.

If a person provides or makes an explanation or statement which he knows to be false, or recklessly provides or makes a false explanation or statement, he is liable to two years' imprisonment or a fine or both: section 114.

---

[29] *Ante* p. 397.
[30] Cmnd. 1749, paras. 215, 218.

Entry and search of premises

If a justice of the peace, or in Scotland the sheriff or a magistrate, is satisfied, on information on oath laid by an officer of the Department of Trade, that there are reasonable grounds for suspecting that there are on any premises any books or papers of which production has been required under section 109, *ante*, and which have not been produced, he may issue a warrant authorising any constable to enter and search the premises and take possession of any books or papers appearing to be such.

Any documents of which possession is taken may be retained for three months or, if within that period there are commenced certain criminal proceedings mentioned in section 111 *post* (being proceedings to which the documents are relevant), until the conclusion of the proceedings.

Penalties are imposed for obstructing the exercise of a right of entry or search, or of a right to take possession of documents: 1967 Act, s. 110.

Provision for security of information

No information or document obtained under section 109 or 110, *ante*, may, without the previous written consent of the company, be published or disclosed, except to a competent authority (normally the Department of Trade, an officer of the Department, an inspector appointed under the 1948 Act by the Department, the Treasury or an officer thereof), unless the publication or disclosure is required, *e.g.*—

(1) with a view to the institution of, or for the purposes of, any criminal proceedings pursuant to certain Acts, including the Companies Act 1948, the Insurance Companies Act 1974, the Protection of Depositors Act 1963, and the Companies Act 1967, or any criminal proceedings for an offence entailing misconduct in connection with the management of the company or misapplication or wrongful retainer of its property; or

(2) for the purpose of complying with any requirement, or exercising any power, imposed or conferred, by the 1948 Act with respect to inspectors' reports; or

(3) in connection with proceedings by the Department with respect to the company under section 37 of the 1967 Act; or

(4) in connection with proceedings by the Department for the winding up of the company.

Publication or disclosure of any information or document in contravention of the section is punishable by up to two years' imprisonment or a fine or both: 1967 Act, s. 111.

Clause 109 (2) of the Companies Bill 1973 would have extended (1) *ante* to include criminal proceedings, whether in the U.K. or in any other country, in respect of any offence of dishonesty wherever committed.

Penalisation of destruction, etc., of company documents

Section 113 of the 1967 Act provides that an officer of a company mentioned in section 109, *ante*, who destroys, mutilates or falsifies, or is privy to the destruction, etc., of a document affecting or relating to the property or affairs of the company is guilty of an offence unless he proves that he did not intend to conceal the state of affairs of the company or to defeat the law. Similarly if he fraudulently parts with, alters or makes an omission in, any such document. The penalty is up to two years' imprisonment or a fine or both.

Section 329 of the 1948 Act contains a similar provision with regard to an officer or contributory of a company being wound up.

CHAPTER 18

PROTECTION OF OUTSIDERS

THIS chapter is concerned with a number of rules, some of which are general law rules and others of which are statutory, for the protection of persons other than members, *i.e.* non-members who deal with the company and who are sometimes referred to as "outsiders."

If a person, *e.g.* a director, purports to act for a company without actual authority, the other person with whom he deals (the outsider) will be able to hold the company bound by the act if the rule in *Royal British Bank* v. *Turquand post* applies.

Where there is a defect in the appointment of a director who acts for the company, the outsider may be able to rely on section 180 (which provides that the acts of a director or manager are valid despite any defect in his appointment or qualification) and an article like Table A, article 105, *post*.[1]

The outsider may sometimes be able to rely on an article like Table A, article 79 (directors' borrowing power), *post*.[2]

In England he may be able to rely on the Law of Property Act 1925, section 74, where he is a purchaser and there is a defect in the sealing of a deed. Section 74 provides that in favour of a purchaser —by section 205, one who acquires an interest in property in good faith and for valuable consideration—a deed is deemed to have been duly executed by a corporation if it purports to have been sealed in the presence of and attested by a director and the secretary. For Scottish deeds, see Chapter 6.[3]

Again, the outsider may be able to rely on section 145 (minutes of meetings) *ante*,[4] as regards the onus of proof.

If, *e.g.*, a director acts for a company without authority and the outsider has no actual or constructive knowledge of the lack of authority, the director is liable to the outsider in damages for breach of express or implied warranty of authority.[5]

[1] p. 417.
[2] p. 482.
[3] *Ante* p. 128.
[4] p. 332.
[5] *Hely-Hutchinson* v. *Brayhead Ltd.* [1968] 1 Q.B. 549 (C.A.); *Firbank's Exors.* v. *Humphreys* (1886) 18 Q.B.D. 54 (C.A.), *post* p. 485.

The rule in Royal British Bank v. Turquand

The so-called[6] rule in *Royal British Bank* v. *Turquand*[7] may protect a person dealing with a company (an "outsider") where there is some irregularity in its internal management, *e.g.* where the board of directors contract with him on behalf of the company without authority. (A person dealing with a company in good faith in a case like that given in such example is now protected by the European Communities Act 1972, s. 9 (1), *ante*.)[8]

A person dealing with a company, even if he does not have actual notice, has constructive notice of the contents of its public documents, such as the memorandum and articles, special resolutions, register of charges[9] and, presumably, list of directors, because they are open to public inspection at the Companies Registration Office,[10] but, where the persons entitled to manage its affairs do so in a manner apparently consistent with such documents, then, subject as below, he is not affected by an internal irregularity, *e.g.* the lack of an ordinary resolution required by the articles as authority for the directors to enter into the transaction. The maxim *omnia praesumuntur rite esse acta* (all things are presumed to have been done rightly) applies.

The reason is that since documents such as the memorandum and articles are registered, and accessible to all who care to consult them, persons dealing in good faith with the company are bound to see that externally everything is in order, but they are not concerned with the indoor management because they cannot check that the rules of internal management have been complied with. Thus the doctrine of constructive notice of the contents of such documents is qualified by the rule in *Turquand's* case.

A company issued a bond under its common seal, signed by two directors. The registered deed of settlement (the equivalent of the modern memorandum and articles) provided that the directors might borrow on bond such sums as they should be authorised by an ordinary resolution of the company. No such resolution was passed. *Held*, the bond was binding on the company, as the lenders were entitled to assume that a resolution authorising the borrowing had been passed: *Royal British Bank* v. *Turquand* (1856) 6 El. & Bl. 327; 119 E.R. 886.[11]

[6] *Per* Lord Simonds in *Morris* v. *Kanssen* [1946] A.C. 459 at p. 474.
[7] (1856) 6 El. & Bl. 327; 119 E.R. 886.
[8] p. 84.
[9] See *per* Eve J. in *Wilson* v. *Kelland* [1910] 2 Ch. 306 at p. 313, *post* p. 502.
[10] Under s. 426, *ante* p. 81.
[11] Applied in *Albert Gardens* (*Manly*) *Pty. Ltd.* v. *Mercantile Credits Ltd.* (1973) 131 C.L.R. 60 (Second Australian Supplement to Charlesworth & Cain, p. 24). For a

The maxim is also illustrated by the doctrine of ostensible or apparent authority in the law of agency.[12]

A company is bound by the acts of its agent within his actual authority, express or implied. As to express actual authority, an individual director may be specifically authorised by the board of directors to make a particular contract on behalf of the company.[13] As to implied actual authority, a director may, under a power in the articles, be appointed to an office, *e.g.* that of managing director, which carries with it authority to make a contract on behalf of the company.[14] However, the question of implication does not stop there and authority may be implied from the conduct of the parties and the circumstances of the case.[15] A person with actual authority to obtain quotations of prices has no implied actual authority to communicate acceptance of such quotes where no decision to purchase has been made by his principal—at most such a person may have an ostensible authority.[16]

A company is also bound by the acts of its agent within his apparent authority where he lacks actual authority (although actual authority and apparent authority are not mutually exclusive and generally co-exist).[17] Thus an outsider may be protected where an individual director acts on behalf of the company without actual authority but with apparent authority, which apparent authority may arise from a representation that he has authority made by the board of directors or such a representation contained in the company's public documents.

If a person acts on behalf of a company without actual authority the company, *i.e.* usually the board of directors, may ratify the contract, in which case the company will be bound by it.

---

full exposition of the rule in a Scottish case see the opinions of Lord President Inglis and Lord Shand in *Heiton* v. *Waverley Hydropathic Co. Ltd.* (1877) 4 R. 830.

[12] *Per* Lord Simonds in *Morris* v. *Kanssen* [1943] A.C. 459 at p. 475.

[13] Or a board of directors may pass a resolution authorising two of their number to sign cheques: *per* Lord Denning M.R. in *Hely-Hutchinson* v. *Brayhead Ltd.* [1968] 1 Q.B. 549 (C.A.) at p. 583.

[14] *Per* Willmer L.J. in *Freeman & Lockyer* v. *Buckhurst Park Properties (Mangal) Ltd.* [1964] 2 Q.B. 480 (C.A.) at pp. 488, 489. Diplock L.J. agreed. And see *Paterson's Trustees* v. *Caledonian Heritable Security Co. Ltd. etc.* (1885) 13 R. 369 (manager borrowed money for purposes of company, and used money to purchase heritable property the title to which was taken in his own name).

[15] As in *Hely-Hutchinson's* case, *ante.*

[16] *Crabtree-Vickers Pty. Ltd.* v. *Australian Direct Mail Advertising etc. Co. Pty. Ltd.* (1976) 50 A.L.J.R. 203, following the *Freeman & Lockyer* case and *Turquand's* case

[17] *Panorama Developments (Guildford) Ltd.* v. *Fidelis Furnishing Fabrics Ltd.* [1971] 2 Q.B. 711 (C.A.), *ante* p. 369, where the secretary had apparent authority to hire cars on behalf of the company.

Further, if in such a case the company does not ratify, then, subject as below, the company will still be bound if the other party can prove—

(1) that he was induced to make the contract by the agent being held out as occupying a certain position in the company;

(2) that the representation, which is usually by conduct, was made by the persons with actual authority to manage the company, generally or in respect of the matters to which the contract relates, who are usually the board of directors;[18] and

(3) that the contract was one which a person in the position which the agent was held out as occupying would usually have actual authority to make.

Condition (2) *ante* is due to the fact that the principal, the company, is not a natural person. It follows from the condition that the outsider cannot as a rule[19] rely on the agent's own representation that he has authority.[20]

R., the chairman of the directors of the defendant company, B. Ltd., acted as its *de facto* managing director. The board knew of and acquiesced in that and the articles of B. Ltd. empowered the board to appoint a managing director. H. was the chairman and managing director of a public company, P. Ltd., which needed financial assistance. B. Ltd. was prepared to help and accordingly in January, 1965, B. Ltd. bought shares in P. Ltd. from H. for £100,000 and proposed to inject £150,000 into P. Ltd. H. became a director of B. Ltd. but never saw its memorandum and articles and did not attend board meetings until May 19, 1965. After that meeting R. and H. agreed that H. would put more money into P. Ltd. if B. Ltd. would secure his position. R., on behalf of B. Ltd., signed letters to H. in which B. Ltd. purported to indemnify H. against loss on his guarantee of a bank loan of £50,000 to P. Ltd. and to guarantee a loan by H. to P. Ltd. H. then advanced £45,000 to P. Ltd. When P. Ltd. went into liquidation H. had to honour his guarantee and he claimed the £50,000 and the £45,000 from B. Ltd. B. Ltd. denied liability and said that R. had no authority to sign the letters (and that the contracts were unenforceable for non-disclosure of H.'s interest in accordance with s. 199). *Held*, that on the facts R. had actual authority implied from the conduct of the parties and the circumstances of the case to enter into the contracts with H. (and that it was too late to avoid them for non-disclosure of H.'s interest as required by the articles): *Hely-Hutchinson* v. *Brayhead Ltd.* [1968] 1 Q.B. 549 (C.A.),[21] applying the *Freeman & Lockyer* case below.

[18] But occasionally the shareholders: *Mahony* v. *East Holyford Mining Co.* (1875) L.R. 7 H.L. 869, *post*.

[19] See the *Crabtree-Vickers* case *ante*.

[20] *Per* Diplock L.J. in the *Freeman & Lockyer* case, *ante*, at p. 505, and Lord Pearson in the *Hely-Hutchinson* case, *ante*, at p. 593.

[21] And see *ante* p. 360. A corresponding Scots case is *Allison* v. *Scotia Motor, etc., Co. Ltd.* (1906) 14 S.L.T. 9 (O.H.), where a *de facto* managing director engaged a works manager of the company for a period of five years.

The articles of a company formed to purchase and resell an estate empowered the directors to appoint one of their body managing director. K., a director, was never appointed managing director but, to the knowledge of the board, he acted as such. On behalf of the company he instructed architects to do certain work in connection with the estate. *Held*, the company was bound by the contract and liable for the architects' fees. K. had apparent authority because he had been held out by the board as managing director and, therefore, as having authority to do what a managing director would usually be authorised to do on behalf of the company, and his act was within the usual authority of a managing director. Accordingly, the plaintiffs could assume that he had been properly appointed: *Freeman & Lockyer* v. *Buckhurst Park Properties (Mangal) Ltd.* [1964] 2 Q.B. 480 (C.A.).[22]

"It must be shown:

(1) that a representation that the agent had authority to enter on behalf of the company into a contract of the kind sought to be enforced was made to the contractor;

(2) that such representation was made by a person or persons who had 'actual' authority to manage the business of the company either generally or in respect of those matters to which the contract relates;

(3) that he (the contractor) was induced by such representation to enter into the contract, that is, that he in fact relied upon it; and

(4) that under its memorandum or articles of association the company was not deprived of the capacity either to enter into a contract of the kind sought to be enforced or to delegate authority to enter into a contract of that kind to the agent:" *per* Diplock L.J. at pp. 505, 506.

The persons who signed the articles of a company, and who under the articles were entitled to appoint directors, treated some of themselves as directors although there was no proper appointment. The articles provided that cheques should be signed as directed by the board. The person acting as secretary informed the company's bank that the "board" had resolved that cheques should be signed by two of three named directors and countersigned by the secretary. The bank acted on the communication and honoured cheques so signed. *Held*, the bank was entitled to honour the cheques and was not liable to refund the money paid. The rule in *Turquand's* case applied and there was an article like Table A, article 105: *Mahony* v. *East Holyford Mining Co.* (1875) L.R. 7 H.L. 869.

Where the outsider relies on a representation by the board of directors it is not necessary that he should actually have inspected the company's public documents but where he is seeking to rely on a representation in the public documents it is essential that he inspected them. A party seeking to set up an estoppel (or, in Scots law, a personal bar) must show that he relied on the representation which he alleges, be it a representation in words or a representation by conduct.

A director purported to make, on behalf of the company, an agreement whereby an outsider was to sell on commission goods imported by the company

---

[22] Applying *Biggerstaff* v. *Rowatt's Wharf Ltd.* [1896] 2 Ch. 93 (C.A.) and *British Thomson-Houston Co.* v. *Federated European Bank Ltd.* [1932] 2 K.B. 176 (C.A.). See also *Clay Hill Brick Co. Ltd.* v. *Rawlings* [1938] 4 All E.R. 100.

and to retain the proceeds as security for a debt due from another company. The outsider had not inspected the company's public documents and did not know of the power of delegation contained in the articles. Further, the agreement was so unusual as to put the outsider upon inquiry to ascertain whether the director had authority in fact. *Held*, the company was not bound: *Houghton & Co.* v. *Nothard, Lowe and Wills Ltd.* [1927] 1 K.B. 246 (C.A.); affirmed on other grounds [1928] A.C. 1.

R. Co., by their principal director, A., purported to enter into an oral contract with B., who was a director of and purported to act for P. Co. but had no actual authority. The alleged contract was that the two companies should finance the sale of a telephone directory holder produced by a third company. R. Co. claimed repayment of money paid by them to B. as agent for P. Co. in pursuance of the contract. R. Co. alleged that P. Co. were estopped from denying B.'s authority because the P. Co'.s articles provided that the directors could delegate their powers to a committee of one or more directors. However, A. had not inspected the articles until after the action began (and even if A had inspected the articles a single director would not normally have authority to act for the company). *Held*, because A had not inspected the articles when the contract was made, they could not be relied on as conferring ostensible or apparent authority on B, and the action failed: *Rama Corporation Ltd.* v. *Proved Tin, etc., Ltd.* [1952] 2 Q.B. 147.

Further, even in the case of a representation by the board of directors, the company is not bound where the public documents show that the contract is *ultra vires* the company—the outsider will have constructive notice of the fact—although, by the European Communities Act 1972, s. 9 (1), *ante*,[23] in favour of a person dealing with a company in good faith, the company is bound even if the public documents show that a contract is *ultra vires* the company, provided that the transaction is decided upon by the directors or the managing director where the directors have properly delegated the appropriate powers to him. Similarly, the company is not bound where the public documents show that authority to make the contract cannot be delegated to the particular agent.

The rule in *Turquand's* case does not apply, *i.e.* the company is not bound and the outsider is not protected, in the following cases:—

(1) Where the outsider knows of the irregularity or lack of actual authority.

Under the articles the directors had power to borrow up to £1,000 on behalf of the company without the consent of a general meeting and to borrow further money with such consent. The directors themselves lent £3,500 to the company without such consent, and took debentures. *Held*, the company was liable, and the debentures were valid, only to the extent of £1,000: *Howard* v. *Patent Ivory Manufacturing Co.* (1888) 38 Ch.D. 156.

[23] p. 84.

(2) Where the outsider purported to act as a director in the transaction, *i.e.* to act for and on behalf of the company in the transaction. On the other hand, if a director, acting in his private capacity, contracts with his company, acting by another director, the former director is not automatically to be treated as having constructive knowledge of any defect in the latter's authority, so as to exclude the rule.[24]

C., whose appointment as director had ceased, and S., who had never been appointed a director, purported to hold a board meeting and appoint M. a director. Then all three purported to allot shares to M. *Held*, the invalid appointment of M. and allotment to him were not validated by what are now section 180 and Table A, article 105, *post*, because there was no appointment of C. and S. as directors after C.'s appointment had expired. Further, the rule in *Royal British Bank* v. *Turquand* did not apply to the allotment since M. purported to act as a director in the transaction: *Morris* v. *Kanssen* [1946] A.C. 459.

(3) Where there are suspicious circumstances putting the outsider on inquiry.

The sole director of and main shareholder in a company paid cheques, drawn in favour of the company, into his own account. *Held*, the bank was put upon inquiry and not entitled to rely on his ostensible authority, and could not rely on the rule: *A. L. Underwood Ltd.* v. *Bank of Liverpool & Martins* [1924] 1 K.B. 775 (C.A.).

The articles of a company carrying on business as forwarding agents empowered the directors to determine who should have authority to draw bills of exchange on the company's behalf. C., the company's Manchester manager, drew bills on the company's behalf in favour of K., who took them, believing C. to be authorised to draw them. C. had no such authority, and it was unusual for a branch manager to have such authority. *Held*, the company was not liable to the holders on the bills because (1) K. did not know of the power of delegation in the articles and therefore could not rely on its supposed exercise; (2) the bills were forgeries; (3) even if K. had known of the power of delegation, he was not entitled to assume that a branch manager had ostensible authority to draw bills on behalf of his company: *Kreditbank Cassel G.m.b.H.* v. *Schenkers Ltd.* [1927] 1 K.B. 826 (C.A.).

(4) Where a document is forged so as to purport to be the company's document, unless, perhaps, it is held out as genuine by an officer of the company acting within the scope of his authority.[25]

Prior to the European Communities Act 1972, s. 9 (1) *ante*, there was another exception to the rule in *Turquand's* case where, *e.g.*, a special resolution of the company in general meeting, required by the

---

[24] *Hely-Hutchinson* v. *Brayhead Ltd.* [1968] 1 Q.B. 549 (Roskill J.).
[25] *Ruben* v. *Great Fingall Consolidated* [1906] A.C. 439, *ante* p. 248, particularly *per* Lord Loreburn L.C. at p. 443.

articles as authority for the transaction, had not been passed—the public documents of the company at the Companies Registration Office would not include a copy of the resolution[26] and the outsider would have constructive notice of the irregularity.[27] In favour of a person dealing with the company in good faith, at least in the case of a transaction decided on by the directors, the powers of the directors to bind the company are deemed free of any limitation under the memorandum or the articles today.

Validity of acts of directors

Where there is a defect in the appointment of a director who has acted for the company, the outsider may be protected by section 180 and an article like Table A, article 105. The section provides that the acts of a director or manager are valid notwithstanding any defect that may afterwards be discovered in his appointment or qualification. Table A, article 105, provides that all acts done by any meeting of the directors or of a committee of directors or by any person acting as a director shall, notwithstanding that it be afterwards discovered that there was some defect in the appointment of any such director or person acting as aforesaid, or that they or any of them were disqualified, be as valid as if every such person had been duly appointed and was qualified to be a director.[28]

The effect of these provisions is to validate the acts of a director who has not been validly appointed because there was some slip or irregularity in his appointment. Thus, an outsider dealing with the company, *or a member*, is entitled to assume that a person who appears to be a duly appointed and qualified director is so in fact.

The articles included an article like Table A, article 105. T., N. and S., *de facto* directors, made a call, payment of which was resisted by some shareholders on the ground that T., N. and S. were not *de jure* directors. For example, unknown to his co-directors, N. had vacated office by parting with his qualification shares, although he later acquired a share qualification and continued to act as a director. *Held*, the article operated not only as between the company and outsiders but also as between the company and its members, and covered the irregularities alleged, so that the call was valid: *Dawson* v. *African Consolidated Land etc. Co.* [1898] 1 Ch. 6 (C.A.).

---

[26] *Ante* p. 308.
[27] *Irvine* v. *Union Bank of Australia* (1877) 2 App.Cas. 366 (P.C.), *post* p. 485.
[28] The N.S.W. section corresponding to s. 180 and the rule in *Turquand's* case applied in *Albert Gardens (Manly) Pty. Ltd.* v. *Mercantile Credits Ltd.* (1973) 131 C.L.R. 60 (Second Australian Supplement, p. 24).

It is immaterial that it is clear from the company's public documents that a director is not duly qualified to act.[29]

The provisions do not validate acts where there has been no appointment at all.[30]

Nor do they validate acts which could not have been done even by a properly qualified director. Thus, in *Craven-Ellis* v. *Canons Ltd.*,[31] what is now section 180 did not empower improperly qualified directors to do what properly qualified directors could not do, namely, appoint an improperly qualified director as managing director.

[29] *Per* Farwell J. in *British Asbestos Co. Ltd.* v. *Boyd* [1903] 2 Ch. 439 at p. 444. In this case a director vacated office on becoming secretary.

[30] *Morris* v. *Kanssen* [1946] A.C. 459, *ante* p. 416, appled in *Grant* v. *John Grant & Sons Pty. Ltd.* (1950) 82 C.L.R. 1.

[31] [1936] 2 K.B. 403 (C.A.), *ante* p. 346.

CHAPTER 19

ACCOUNTS

AT one time, the keeping of accounts by a company was considered merely as the domestic concern of the company and its shareholders, but the tendency of modern legislation has been to secure more and more publicity of the financial affairs of companies. Publication of accounts is now insisted upon primarily to provide shareholders with all necessary information of the financial position of the company in a form that they can understand, and secondarily to put such information, which is, at any rate in large companies, a matter of public importance, at the disposal of creditors of the company, employees and the public at large.

This chapter deals first with the accounting records which must be kept by a company and, secondly, with the profit and loss account and balance sheet which must be laid before the company in general meeting. Then there is a note on the documents, such as the auditors' report and the directors' report, which must be attached to the balance sheet. There is a note on the persons entitled to a copy of the balance sheet and the attached documents, and an account of the directors' report (an account of the auditors' report will be found in the next chapter). A specimen set of reports and accounts is included and, finally, there is a brief note on the disclosure of information that certain companies may be required to make under Part IV of the Industry Act 1975.

The 1973 Conservative Government White Paper on Company Law Reform stated[1] that openness in company affairs was the first principle in securing responsible behaviour. The Government already had substantial powers to require further disclosure in company accounts, and they intended to seek a similar power in respect of directors' reports and then to use these two powers in concert to require companies to report a much wider range of matters.

For public and large private companies these powers would be used to give shareholders and the public the chance to judge companies' behaviour by social as well as financial criteria. Existing law required disclosure in the accounts of the rates at which directors and senior employees were paid. The directors' report might be required to disclose the performance of the company in regard to the safety and health of its employees, the number of consumer complaints and how they were dealt with and the conduct of industrial relations. The report would be

[1] (1973) Cmnd. 5391, paras. 10–12.

required to include particulars of the directors' contracts of service, of their other interests, of any dealings they had in the company's shares, and of transactions by the company and other companies in which they had any significant interest. Most of this information was already required to be shown in a publicly available record but it was desirable that it should be given in the directors' report rather than merely available to those who could go to examine the record. It might also be desirable for the directors to disclose more fully details of significant material acquisitions, realisations and contracts since the previous year.

For smaller private companies the same levels of disclosure were not appropriate because there was no element of investment by the general public and the public interest was not involved to the same extent. For such companies also the burden of disclosure was greater and the commercial dangers might be greater.

The above approach was criticised in the 1974 Labour Party Green Paper.[2]

The 1973 White Paper went on to say that the principle of openness needed to be applied to international enterprises as well as to national ones. In reviewing the general disclosure requirements in the U.K., the Government would pay particular attention to the public interest about the activities of these enterprises, bearing in mind the contribution that they made to the national economy. The Government would also take account of disclosure requirements in the EEC and elsewhere. U.K. disclosure requirements were already more extensive than those of most other advanced countries. The Government's aim was to secure improvements in both the quality and the comparability of information available in all members of the EEC and of the OECD about the activities of international enterprises.[3]

It should be noted that the Fourth Draft Directive submitted by the Commission to the Council of the EEC is concerned with the annual accounts of limited liability companies.

ACCOUNTING RECORDS

Section 12 of the Companies Act 1976 requires every company to cause accounting records to be kept: subsection (1).

Such accounting records must be sufficient to show and explain the company's transactions, and must be such as to—

(a) disclose with reasonable accuracy, at any time, the financial position of the company;

(b) enable the directors to ensure that any balance sheet or profit and loss account prepared by them under section 1 of the 1976 Act complies with the requirements of section 149 of the 1948 Act, *post*: subsections (2), (3).

In particular, the accounting records must contain—

(a) entries from day to day of all sums of money received and expended by the company and the matters in respect of which the receipt or expenditure takes place;

(b) a record of the assets and liabilities of the company;

[2] p. 27.
[3] Para. 14.

(c) where the company's business involves dealing in goods, the following statements—

    (i) statements of stock held by the company at the end of each financial year of the company;

    (ii) all statements of stocktakings from which (i) above have been or are to be prepared;

    (iii) except in the case of goods sold by way of ordinary retail trade, statements of all goods sold and purchased showing the goods and the buyers and sellers in sufficient detail to enable them to be identified: subsections (4), (5).

The accounting records must be kept at the company's registered office or at such other place as the directors think fit, and must at all times be open to inspection by the company's officers: subsection (6). Although there is no express statutory provision authorising the court to compel inspection (contrast section 146 *ante*), the Court of Session may, on the petition of a director presented to the *nobile officium*, ordain a company to make the accounting records available for inspection by the director and by a named accountant on his behalf.[4] If the accounting records are kept outside Great Britain, such accounts and returns must be kept in Britain as will disclose the financial position of the business at intervals not exceeding six months and will enable the directors to ensure that any balance sheet or profit and loss account prepared by them complies with section 149 of the 1948 Act: section 12 (7), (8), of the 1976 Act.

The accounting records normally must be preserved—

(a) by a private company, for three years;

(b) by a public company, for six years;

in either case, from the date on which they are made: subsection (9).

If a company fails to comply with subsections (1) to (7) of section 12, every officer in default is guilty of an offence unless he shows that he acted honestly and that in the circumstances in which the business was carried on the default was excusable. If any officer of the company fails to take all reasonable steps to secure compliance by the company with subsection (9) or has intentionally caused any default by the company thereunder, he is guilty of an offence. Any person guilty of an offence under section 12 is liable—

[4] *M'Cusker* v. *M'Rae*, 1966 S.C. 253.

(a) on conviction on indictment, to imprisonment for up to two years or a fine or both;

(b) on summary conviction, to imprisonment for up to six months or a fine of up to £400 or both: subsections (10), (11).

A shareholder has no right to inspect the books of account of the company unless one is given to him by the articles.

Table A, article 125, provides: The directors shall from time to time determine whether and to what extent and at what times and places and under what conditions or regulations the accounts and books of the company or any of them shall be open to the inspection of members not being directors, and no member (not being a director) shall have any right of inspecting any account or book or document of the company except as conferred by statute or authorised by the directors or by the company in general meeting.

The Jenkins Report[5] recommended that, if necessary, section 147 of the 1948 Act (now superseded by section 12 of the 1976 Act) be amended to permit companies to use modern accounting machinery to keep their accounts, and clause 81 of the Companies Bill 1973 would have given effect to this recommendation.

DUTY TO PREPARE, LAY AND DELIVER ACCOUNTS BY REFERENCE TO ACCOUNTING REFERENCE PERIODS

Section 1 of the Companies Act 1976 provides that the directors of every company must in respect of each accounting reference period of the company prepare a profit and loss account (or, in the case of a company not trading for profit,[6] an income and expenditure account). The period in respect of which any such account is made up is a financial year of the company (whether it is a year or not) and, in respect of the first accounting period of the company, must begin with the first day of that accounting reference period and end not more than seven days before or more than seven days after the end of that period, as the directors may determine. As regards subsequent accounting reference periods, the period in respect of which the profit and loss account is to be made up must begin with the day after the date to which the last preceding profit and loss account was made up and end not more than seven days before or more than seven days after the end of the accounting reference period.

The directors of every company must prepare a balance sheet as at the date to which any profit and loss account is made up.

---

[5] (1962) Cmnd. 1749, para. 423.   [6] *Ante* p. 43.

In respect of each accounting reference period of a company the directors must lay before the company in general meeting a copy of every document required to be comprised in the accounts of the company, *i.e.*—

(1) the profit and loss account;
(2) the balance sheet;
(3) the auditors' report required to be attached to the balance sheet by section 156 of the 1948 Act *post*[7];
(4) the directors' report required to be so attached by section 157 of the 1948 Act *post*.[7]

Subject as below, in respect of each accounting reference period of a company the directors must deliver a copy of documents (1), (2), (3) and (4) *ante* to the Registrar and, if any such document is in a language other than English, annex to the copy delivered to the Registrar a translation into English certified to be a correct translation.

Section 9 (3) of the European Communities Act 1972, as amended by section 1 of the Companies Act 1976, provides that the Registrar must cause to be published in the *Gazette* notice of the receipt by him of any document delivered by a company in pursuance of section 1.

In the case of an unlimited company, the directors are excepted from the need to deliver a copy of documents (1), (2), (3) and (4) *ante* to the Registrar if—

(a) at no time during the relevant accounting reference period has the company been, to its knowledge, the subsidiary of a company (whether incorporated under the law in force in Great Britain or that in force elsewhere) which was then limited and at no time, to its knowledge, have there been held or been exercisable, by or on behalf of two or more limited companies, shares or powers which, if they had been held or exercisable by one of them, would have made the company its subsidiary;
(b) at no such time has the company been the holding company of a company then a limited company;
(c) at no such time has the company been carrying on business as the promoter of a trading stamp scheme within the meaning of the Trading Stamps Act 1964.

[7] p. 440.

It follows that such an unlimited company can keep its financial position private, *i.e.* such a company is in the same position as partnerships and individual traders who trade with unlimited liability.

Accounting reference period of a company

The accounting reference period of a company ends on March 31 each year unless the company gives notice to the Registrar before section 1 *ante* comes into operation or within six months after the incorporation of the company, whichever last occurs, in which case the accounting reference period ends on the date specified in the notice. Further, if notice is not given, the Registrar may, within two years after section 1 comes into operation, determine with the consent of the company that some date other than March 31 shall be the company's accounting reference date.

The first accounting reference period of a company is the period ending with the company's accounting reference date which—

(1) begins or began on the day after the date to which the profit and loss account last laid before the company in general meeting before section 1 came into operation is or was made up; or

(2) if no profit and loss account is or was so laid, begins or began on the date of incorporation;

and, in either case, is or was a period exceeding six months but not 18 months.

Each successive period of 12 months beginning after the end of the company's first accounting reference period and ending with the company's accounting reference date is an accounting reference period: section 2 of the 1976 Act.

Alteration of accounting reference period

Section 3 of the 1976 Act makes provision for alteration of the accounting reference period. During an accounting reference period the company may give notice in prescribed form to the Registrar specifying a new accounting reference date on which the current accounting reference period and each subsequent accounting reference period of the company is to end or (as the case may require) has ended. After the end of an accounting reference period the company may give notice in prescribed form specifying a new accounting reference date on which the previous accounting reference period and each subsequent accounting reference period is to end or has ended. In the latter case the notice has no effect unless the company is a subsidiary or holding company of another company and the new accounting reference date coincides with that of the other company, and the period allowed for laying and delivering accounts in relation to the previous accounting reference period has not expired.

Any notice must state whether the current or previous accounting reference period is to be treated as shortened or lengthened so as to end on the first or the second occasion that the new accounting reference date occurs, an extension must not exceed 18 months and there are certain other limits to the power to extend an accounting reference period.

The period allowed for laying and delivering accounts

Subject as below, the period allowed for laying and delivering accounts in relation to any accounting reference period is ten months after the end of the accounting reference period in the case of a private company and seven months in the case of a public company: 1976 Act, s. 6.

Where a company carries on business, or has interests, outside the U.K., the Channel Islands or the Isle of Man and, in respect of any accounting reference period, the directors, before the end of the period allowed for laying and delivering accounts, so notify the Registrar, and claim a three months' extension of the period, that period is extended accordingly.

Where the first accounting reference period of a company begins or began on the date of incorporation of the company and is or was a period exceeding 12 months, the period which would otherwise be allowed for laying and delivering accounts is reduced by the number of days by which the accounting reference period is or was longer than 12 months but never to less than three months after the end of the accounting reference period.

In relation to the accounting reference period of a company as respects which notice is given by the company under section 3 *ante* and which is treated as shortened, the period allowed for laying and delivering accounts is the period allowed by section 6, or three months beginning with the date of the notice, whichever last expires.

If for any special reason the Secretary of State thinks fit to do so, he may by written notice to the company extend the period allowed for laying and delivering accounts by the further period specified in the notice.

Penalties for not complying with section 1 of the 1976 Act

Section 4 of the 1976 Act provides that if, in respect of any accounting period, a copy of every document required to be comprised in the accounts of the company is not laid before the company in general meeting or, where appropriate, is not delivered to the Registrar plus, where necessary, a certified translation into English, within the period allowed for laying and delivering accounts, then every person who immediately before the end of such period was a director of the company is guilty of an offence and liable on summary conviction to a fine not exceeding the aggregate of £400 and £40 for each day which falls after the end of such period and before all the requirements of section 1 have been complied with, unless he proves that he took all reasonable steps to see that the requirements would be complied with before the end of such period.

If, in respect of any accounting reference period, a copy of every document required to be delivered to the Registrar is not delivered within the period allowed, the company is liable to a penalty (recoverable in civil proceedings by the Secretary of State) of an amount determined by reference to the length of the time between the end of the period allowed and the date by which all the requirements have been complied with and ranging from £20 where the length of time is not more than one month to £450 where it is more than 12 months.

For the purpose of any proceedings under section 4 it is no defence to prove that a document was not in fact prepared as required by section 1.

Default order

If, in respect of any accounting reference period, a copy of every document required to be delivered to the Registrar is not delivered within the period allowed, and the directors fail to make good the default within 14 days after service of a notice on them requiring them to do so, the court may, on an application by any member or creditor of the company or by the Registrar, make an order directing the directors or any of them to make good the default within such time as may be specified: section 5 of the 1976 Act. The order may provide that the costs of and incidental to the application shall be borne by the directors.

Extracts from the 1975 Reports and Accounts of a company are set out at the end of this Chapter.[8]

Clause 69 of the Companies Bill 1973 would have empowered the Secretary of State to prescribe the matters to be disclosed in accounts, and in directors' and auditors' reports and annual returns.

Profit and loss account

"A profit and loss account is an historical record. It shows as the profit or loss the difference between the revenue for the period covered by the account and the expenditure chargeable in that period."[9]

Every profit and loss account must give a true and fair view of the profit or loss of the company for the financial year. It must also comply with the requirements of the Eighth Schedule to the 1948 Act as amended by the 1967 Act, except so far as such requirements are modified by the Department of Trade on the application of the directors: 1948 Act, s. 149; 1967 Act, s. 9.

The Eighth Schedule as amended[10] requires the profit and loss account to show:

(1) The amount charged to revenue by way of provision for depreciation, renewals or diminution in value of fixed assets.

If, in the case of any assets, an amount is charged by way of provision for depreciation or diminution in value, and an amount is also charged by way of provision for renewal thereof, the latter amount must be shown separately. If the charge by way of provision for depreciation or diminution in value of fixed assets (other than investments) has been determined otherwise than by reference to the amount of such assets for the purpose of making up the balance sheet, that fact must be stated.

(2) The amount of the interest on loans to the company, whether secured by debentures or not, and whether (a) bank loans or overdrafts or (b) loans repayable otherwise than by instalments and due for repayment within five years after the end of the financial year or repayable by instalments the last of which is repayable within such five years.

(3) The charge to revenue for United Kingdom corporation tax and what it would have been but for relief from double taxation, and the charge for United

---

[8] *Post* p. 443 *et seq.*
[9] Jenkins Report, para. 333.
[10] The Eighth Schedule as amended by the 1967 Act is set out in full in Schedule 2 to the 1967 Act. It is further amended by the 1976 Act, Sched. 2.

Kingdom income tax and that for taxation imposed outside the United Kingdom
of profits, income and capital gains.

(4) The amounts provided for redemption of share capital and of loans respectively.

(5) The amount set aside to, or withdrawn from, reserves.

(6) Provisions,[11] other than provisions for depreciation, renewals or diminution in value of assets, or the amount withdrawn from such provisions and not
applied for the purposes thereof.

The Department of Trade, if satisfied that it is not required in the public interest and would prejudice the company, may dispense with this requirement on
condition that any heading stating an amount arrived at after taking into account
these provisions shall indicate the fact.

(7) Income from investments, distinguishing between listed and unlisted
investments.

(8) Rents from land (after deduction of ground-rents, rates and other outgoings[12]) forming part of the company's revenue.

(9) The charge to revenue in respect of the hire of plant and machinery.

(10) The amount (before deduction of income tax) of dividends paid and proposed.

(11) Under a separate heading, if not otherwise included, any charge or
credit arising in consequence of the occurrence of an event in a preceding financial
year.

(12) The remuneration (including expenses) of the auditors.

(13) By way of note, if not otherwise shown:

(a) Other than in the case of a company which is neither a holding company
nor a subsidiary of another company and whose turnover does not exceed
£250,000,[13] the turnover for the financial year and the method by which it
is arrived at, except so far as attributable to banking or discounting
business or to such other business as may be prescribed.

If turnover is omitted as being attributable as aforesaid, the fact that
it is so omitted must be stated: Schedule 8, as amended, paragraph 13A.

In accordance with the recommendation of the Jenkins Committee,
turnover is not defined. However, as the Committee said, it is, generally
speaking, "the total amount receivable by a company in the ordinary
course of its business for goods sold or supplied by it as a principal and
for services provided by it."[14]

(b) If depreciation or replacement of fixed assets is provided for by some
method other than a depreciation charge or provision for renewals, or is
not provided for, the method by which it is provided for or the fact that
it is not provided for.

(c) The basis on which United Kingdom corporation tax and income tax are
computed.

(d) Any special circumstances affecting liability in respect of taxation of
profits, income or capital gains for the financial year or succeeding financial years.

(e) Except in the first profit and loss account, the corresponding amounts for
the immediately preceding financial year for all items shown in the profit
and loss account.

---

[11] *Post* p. 431.
[12] Including, for Scotland, feu-duties and ground annuals: Sched. 8, as amended, Pt.
IV, para. 31.   [13] Companies (Accounts) Regulations 1971 (S.I. 1971 No. 2044).
[14] Cmnd. 1749, para. 394.

(*f*) Any material respects in which any items shown in the profit and loss
account are affected—

    (i) by transactions of a sort not usually undertaken by the company or
otherwise by circumstances of an exceptional or non-recurrent
nature; or

    (ii) by any change in the basis of accounting.

Balance sheet

In the Cohen Report,[15] the function of a balance sheet was said
"to be an endeavour to show the share capital, reserves . . . and
liabilities of a company at the date as at which it is prepared, and the
manner in which the total moneys representing them are distributed
over the several types of assets. A balance sheet is thus an historical
document and does not as a general rule purport to show the net
worth of an undertaking at any particular date or the present realisable value of such items as goodwill, land, buildings, plant and
machinery, nor, except in cases where the realisable value is less
than cost, does it normally show the realisable value of stock-in-trade.
Moreover, if a balance sheet were to attempt to show the net worth
of the undertaking, the fixed assets would require to be revalued at
frequent intervals and the information thus given would be deceptive
since the value of such assets while the company is a going concern
will in most cases have no relation to their value if the undertaking
fails." The "historical cost" basis of accounting was also endorsed
in the Jenkins Report which stated that it reduces to a minimum the
extent to which the accounts can be affected by the personal opinions
of those responsible for them.[16]

Every balance sheet must give a true and fair view of the state of
affairs of the company as at the end of its financial year. It must
also comply with the requirements of the Eighth Schedule to the
Companies Act 1948 as amended by the 1967 Act, except so far as
such requirements are modified by the Department of Trade on the
application of the directors: 1948 Act, s. 149; 1967 Act, s. 9.

The requirements of the Eighth Schedule as amended[17] are:

(1) The balance sheet must summarise the authorised share capital, the issued
share capital, and the liabilities and assets, with such particulars as are necessary
to disclose the general nature of the liabilities and assets, and must specify—

[15] (1945) Cmd. 6659, para. 98.
[16] (1962) Cmnd. 1749, para. 333.
[17] Printed as amended by the 1967 Act in Sched. 2 to that Act. Further amended by
Sched. 2 to the 1976 Act.

(*a*) any part of the issued capital that consists of redeemable preference shares, and the earliest and latest dates on which the company has power to redeem them, whether the company must or may redeem them and whether any (and, if so, what) premium is payable on redemption;

(*b*) so far as it is not given in the profit and loss account, any share capital on which interest has been paid out of capital during the financial year, and the rate of interest;

(*c*) the amount of the share premium account;

(*d*) particulars of any redeemed debentures which the company has power to reissue.

(2) The following must be stated under separate headings, so far as they are not written off—

(*a*) the preliminary expenses;

(*b*) any expenses incurred in issuing shares or debentures;

(*c*) commission paid in respect of shares or debentures;

(*d*) discount allowed in respect of debentures;

(*e*) discount allowed on any issue of shares at a discount.

(3) The reserves, provisions, liabilities and assets must be classified under headings appropriate to the company's business.

Fixed assets, current assets and assets that are neither fixed nor current must be separately identified, and the method of arriving at the amount of the fixed assets under each heading must be stated. The normal method of arriving at the amount of any fixed asset is to take the difference between (*a*) its cost, or, if it is in the company's books at a valuation, the valuation, and (*b*) the aggregate amount provided or written off for depreciation since the date of acquisition or valuation. The balance sheet need show only, for the assets under each heading, the aggregate of the amounts of (*a*) above and the aggregate of the amounts of (*b*) above.

The normal method of arriving at the amount of a fixed asset does not apply to any listed investments.

When there are assets the replacement of which is provided for (i) by making provision for renewals and charging the cost of replacement against that provision, or (ii) by charging the cost of replacement to revenue, there must be stated the means by which their replacement is provided for, and the aggregate amount of the provision made for renewals and not used.

(4) In the case of unlisted investments in equity share capital[18] of other companies (other than any whose values as estimated by the directors are separately shown) there must be stated by way of note or in a statement or report annexed, if not otherwise shown—

(*a*) the amount of the company's income for the financial year ascribable to the investments;

(*b*) the amounts of the company's share before and after taxation of the net aggregate profits of the companies in which the investments are held, being profits for the several periods to which accounts sent by them during the financial year related, after deducting their losses (or vice versa);

(*c*) the amount of the company's share of the net aggregate undistributed profits (or losses) accumulated by such companies since the time when the investments were acquired;

(*d*) the manner in which any losses incurred by such companies have been dealt with in the company's accounts.

[18] *Ante* p. 58.

(5) The aggregate amounts of reserves and provisions (other than provisions for depreciation, renewals or diminution in value of assets) must be stated under separate headings. Where either of these shows an increase over the amount for the preceding year, the source of the increase must be shown and, if there is a decrease, the application of the amount by which it has decreased must be shown.

A provision is a reasonable amount written off or retained by way of providing for depreciation, renewals or diminution in value of assets, or retained by way of providing for any known liability the amount of which cannot be accurately determined, *e.g.* repairs under a lease. The expression "reserve" does not include a provision or any sum set aside to be used to prevent undue fluctuation in charges for taxation: see Schedule 8, as amended, Part IV, paragraph 27 (1) (*b*).

(6) An amount set aside to be used to prevent undue fluctuations in charges for taxation must be stated.

(7) The following must be shown under separate headings—

(*a*) the aggregate amounts of the company's listed and unlisted investments;

(*b*) the amount of the goodwill, patents and trade marks (stated together as a single item), if shown separately in or otherwise ascertainable from the books, so far as not written off;

(*c*) the aggregate amount of outstanding loans to enable shares to be bought for or by employees of the company under section 54;[19]

(*d*) (i) the aggregate amount of bank loans and overdrafts, and

(ii) the aggregate amount of loans to the company repayable otherwise than by instalments and repayable after the expiration of five years after the end of the financial year or repayable by instalments any of which are repayable after such period;

(*e*) the aggregate amount (before deduction of income tax) recommended for distribution as dividend.

A listed investment is an investment listed on a recognised stock exchange, or on a stock exchange of repute outside Great Britain: Schedule 8, as amended, Part IV, paragraph 28.

In relation to loans falling under (*d*) (ii) *ante*, the terms of repayment and the rate of interest payable must be stated.

(8) The nominal amount of any of the company's debentures held by a nominee of or trustee for the company must be stated, together with the amount at which they are stated in the books.

(9) There must be stated by way of note, or in a statement or report annexed, if not otherwise shown—

(*a*) the number, description and amount of any of the company's shares for which any person has an option to subscribe, giving the period during which the option is exercisable and the price to be paid for shares subscribed;

(*b*) the amount of any arrears of fixed cumulative dividends and the period for which they are in arrear;

(*c*) particulars of any charge on the assets of the company to secure the liabilities of any other person, including, where practicable, the amount secured;

(*d*) the general nature of any other contingent liabilities not provided for and, where practicable, the amount;

(*e*) where practicable, the amount of contracts for capital expenditure, so

[19] *Ante* p. 192.

far as not provided for, and the amount of capital expenditure authorised by the directors which has not been contracted for;

(*f*) in the case of fixed assets whose amount is arrived at in accordance with the normal rule stated in (3) *ante* (other than unlisted investments) and is arrived at by reference to a valuation, the years (so far as known to the directors) in which the assets were severally valued and the values and, in the case of assets valued during the financial year, the names of the valuers or their qualifications for doing so and (whichever is stated) the basis of valuation;

(*g*) if fixed assets under any heading (other than investments) include assets acquired during the financial year, or if fixed assets included in the last balance sheet (other than investments) have been disposed of or destroyed, the aggregate amount thereof as determined for the purpose of making up the balance sheet;

(*h*) of the amount of fixed assets consisting of land, how much is ascribable to freeholds and how much to leaseholds [20] and, of the latter, how much to long leases and how much to short leases (a long lease is a lease of which the unexpired residue at the end of the financial year is at least 50 years and the word "lease" includes an agreement for a lease: Schedule 8, as amended Part IV, paragraph 29);

(*i*) if in the opinion of the directors any of the current assets would not realise in the ordinary course of business the value put upon them, that opinion;

(*j*) the aggregate market value of the company's listed investments where it differs from the value stated, and the stock exchange value of any investments when the value shown is higher than their stock exchange value;

(*k*) if a sum set aside to be used to prevent undue fluctuations in charges for taxation has been used during the year for another purpose, the amount thereof and the fact that it has been so used;

(*l*) if the amount carried forward for stock-in-trade or work in hand is material to enable members to appreciate the company's state of affairs or its profit or loss for the year, the manner in which the amount has been computed;

(*m*) where material, the basis on which foreign currencies have been converted into sterling;

(*n*) the basis on which the amount, if any, set aside for United Kingdom corporation tax is computed;

(*o*) except in the case of the first balance sheet, the corresponding amounts at the end of the immediately preceding financial year for almost all items shown in the balance sheet.[21]

Every balance sheet of a company and every copy of such a balance sheet which is laid before the company in general meeting or delivered to the Registrar must be signed by two directors or, if there is only one director (as there might be in the case of a private company), by that director: section 155 of the 1948 Act, as amended by Schedule 2 of the 1976 Act.

[20] In Scotland, how much is ascribable to land owned by and how much to land let to the company: Sched. 8, as amended, Pt. IV, para. 31.
[21] Amended by Companies (Accounts) Regulations 1970 (S.I. 1970 No. 1333).

In *Jones* v. *Bellgrove Properties Ltd.*[22] it was held that a statement in a balance sheet "To sundry creditors £7,638," the balance sheet being signed by the company's agents, a firm of chartered accountants, was an acknowledgment, within the meaning of section 24 (2) of the Limitation Act 1939,[23] of a debt of £1,807 owed to a shareholder and included in the £7,638. Consequently[23] the right of action to recover the debt was by section 23 (4) of the 1939 Act deemed to have accrued on the date of the acknowledgment and the action was not barred by the six-year limitation period fixed by section 2 (1) of the 1939 Act. The *Jones* case was distinguished in *Re Transplanters* (*Holding Co.*) *Ltd.*[24] (where the directors had made the acknowledgment in favour of one of themselves) and considered in *Good* v. *Parry*,[25] but in *Consolidated Agencies Ltd.* v. *Bertram Ltd.*,[26] where a section of the Indian Limitation Act 1908, which was similar to but not identical with section 23 (4) of the 1939 Act, was construed, it was held that the word "acknowledgment" meant acknowledgment of a debt existing at the date of signature and, since the balance sheet was signed many months after the year to which it related, it was not an acknowledgment of such an existing debt but an acknowledgment of a past debt as at the date when the balance sheet was made up. It was said that the *Jones* case was rightly decided on its facts (no question arose there as to the date to which the acknowledgment related although it was taken to be the date of the annual general meeting) and that is questionable whether a signature on a balance sheet, which must of necessity be made some time after the date to which the balance sheet has been made up, can amount to an acknowledgment of an existing debt. However, in *Re Gee & Co.* (*Woolwich*) *Ltd.*,[27] the *Consolidated Agencies* case was distinguished and it was held that a balance sheet, duly signed by the directors, is capable of being an effective acknowledgment of the state of the company's indebtedness as at the date of the balance sheet, so that the cause of action should, in an appropriate case, be deemed to have accrued at that date, being the date to which the signature of the directors relates. On the facts of the *Gee* case, the acknowledg-

[22] [1949] 2 K.B. 700 (C.A.).
[23] Not applicable to Scotland; any similar question arising in Scotland would be governed by the Prescription and Limitation (Scotland) Act 1973.
[24] [1958] 1 W.L.R. 822, *ante* p. 353; *post* p. 458.
[25] [1963] 2 Q.B. 418 (C.A.) (for there to be an acknowledgment the debt must be quantified in figures or it must be liquidated in the sense that it is capable of ascertainment by calculation or by extrinsic evidence without further agreement of the parties).
[26] [1965] A.C. 470 (P.C.).   [27] [1975] Ch.D. 52.

ment was effective even though it was made by the directors in favour
of one of themselves, because it was sanctioned by every member of
the company.

Other requirements as to accounts

There must also be shown in the accounts (either the balance
sheet or the profit and loss account) laid before the company in
general meeting:

(1) Subject to exceptions, the amount of any loans to any officer
of the company during the financial year, or outstanding at
the end of the year, made, guaranteed or secured by the
company or its subsidiary: 1948 Act, s. 197.

(2) The amount of the directors' emoluments as prescribed by
section 196 of the 1948 Act and section 6 of the 1967 Act.[28]

(3) Particulars of directors' emoluments the rights to receive
which have been waived: 1967 Act, s. 7.

(4) Particulars of salaries of employees exceeding £10,000 a year.

Particulars in accounts of salaries of employees receiving more than £10,000 a year

Section 8 of the Companies Act 1967 requires the accounts to show the number
of the company's employees (other than (*a*) directors, and (*b*) employees who
worked mainly outside the United Kingdom) whose several emoluments exceed
£10,000 but not £12,500, and exceed £12,500 but not £15,000 and so on in bands of
£2,500.

For the purposes of the section a person's emoluments include any paid to or
receivable by him from the company, its subsidiaries (as defined below) and any
other person in respect of his services as an employee of the company or a subsidiary thereof or as a director of such a subsidiary (except sums to be accounted
for to the company or a subsidiary).

The expression "emoluments" includes fees and percentages, expenses allowance so far as charged to United Kingdom income tax and the estimated money
value of any other benefits received otherwise than in cash.

The word "subsidiary" in the section means a subsidiary[29] at the time when
the services were rendered and includes a company of which a director was nominated by the accounting company, such director being an employee of the latter
company.

The amounts to be brought into account as respects a financial year are the
sums receivable in respect of that year, whenever paid, or, in the case of sums not
receivable in respect of a period, the sums paid during that year.

If accounts do not comply with section 8 the auditors must, so far as they
reasonably can, include the required particulars in their report.

Obligation to lay group accounts before holding company[29]

By section 150 of the 1948 Act, as amended by section 8 of the
1976 Act, the general rule is that where, at the end of its financial

[28] *Ante* p. 339.   [29] *Ante* p. 57.

year, a company has subsidiaries, the profit and loss account and balance sheet required by section 1 of the 1976 Act to be prepared in respect of the accounting reference period must include group accounts dealing with the state of affairs and profit or loss of the company and the subsidiaries, and such group accounts are included in the documents a copy of which under section 1 the directors lay before the company in general meeting in respect of the accounting reference period.

However, group accounts are not necessary—

(1) if the holding company is itself the wholly owned subsidiary of another company incorporated in Great Britain; or
(2) if the directors are of opinion that—

    (*a*) such accounts are impracticable, or would be of no real value to the members, in view of the insignificant amounts involved, or would involve expense or delay out of proportion to their value to members; or

    (*b*) the result would be misleading, or harmful to the business of the company or its subsidiaries; or

    (*c*) the business of the holding company and that of the subsidiary are so different that they cannot be treated as a single undertaking.

    In case (*c*), and when they are said to be harmful, group accounts can only be dispensed with by approval of the Department of Trade.

For the purposes of section 150 a company is deemed to be the wholly owned subsidiary of another if it has no members except that other and that other's wholly owned subsidiaries and its or their nominees: section 150 (4).

The group accounts usually comprise a consolidated balance sheet and a consolidated profit and loss account for the company and its subsidiaries. They may be wholly or partly incorporated in the holding company's own balance sheet and profit and loss account: section 151. Group accounts must give a true and fair view of the state of affairs and profit or loss of the holding company and the subsidiaries dealt with thereby as a whole, so far as concerns members of the company: section 152. To enable this to be done properly, the directors of the holding company, except where there are good reasons to the contrary, have to secure that the financial year of each subsidiary coincides with that of the holding company: section 153. The group accounts, if prepared as consolidated accounts, must comply with the requirements of the Eighth Schedule as amended, and if not so prepared must give the same or equivalent information. The Department of Trade, on the application of the directors, may modify such requirements to adapt them to the company's circumstances: section 152.

If any group accounts, a copy of which is laid before a company in general meeting or delivered to the Registrar, do not comply with the requirements of section 151 or 152 *ante*, every person who, when the copy was laid or delivered, was a director of the company is guilty of an offence and liable, on conviction on indictment, to a fine, or on summary conviction, to a fine not exceeding £400, unless he can prove that he took all reasonable steps for securing compliance with the requirements.

Special provisions for holding or subsidiary company

The Eighth Schedule as amended, Part II, contains *additional requirements* for holding and subsidiary companies.

In the case of a *holding company*, the balance sheet must set out, separately from the company's other assets, the company's shares in or amounts owing from its subsidiaries, distinguishing shares from indebtedness, and the indebtedness of the holding company to its subsidiaries must be set out separately from its other liabilities. The balance sheet must show, by a note or annexed statement, the number, description and amount of the shares[30] in and debentures of the holding company held by its subsidiaries or their nominees, but excluding any shares or debentures where the subsidiary is concerned as personal representative, or where it is concerned as trustee and neither the company nor any subsidiary is beneficially interested under the trust otherwise than by way of security for the purposes of a transaction entered into in the ordinary course of a business which includes the lending of money.

If group accounts are not submitted, there must be annexed to the balance sheet a statement showing (*a*) the reason why; (*b*) the net aggregate amount, so far as it is not dealt with in the holding company's accounts, of the subsidiaries' profits after deducting losses (or vice versa) for the financial year and also for their previous financial years since they became subsidiaries of the company; (*c*) the net aggregate amount of the same profits (or losses), for the same periods, so far as they are dealt with in the company's accounts—so far as the profits or losses of the subsidiaries in (*b*) and (*c*) above can properly be treated in the holding company's accounts as revenue profits or losses; (*d*) any qualifications in the report of the auditors of the subsidiaries on their accounts for those years. It is unnecessary to show (*b*) and (*c*) *ante* if the directors state that in their opinion the value of the company's investments in its subsidiaries is not less than the amount

---

[30] *i.e.* shares held *before* the commencement of the 1948 Act. See s. 27 (3).

at which they are stated in the balance sheet.[31] Where group accounts are not submitted, and the financial years of any subsidiaries do not end with that of the holding company, there must be annexed to the balance sheet a statement giving the reasons why the directors think that the financial years should not coincide, and the dates when the subsidiaries' years did end.

In the case of a *subsidiary company*, the balance sheet must show its aggregate indebtedness to all its holding companies or fellow subsidiaries and the aggregate amount of the indebtedness of those companies to it, distinguishing between debentures and other indebtedness, and the aggregate amount of assets consisting of shares in fellow subsidiaries. A company is deemed to be a fellow subsidiary of another company if both are subsidiaries of the same holding company but neither subsidiary is a subsidiary of the other.

Consolidated accounts

A consolidated balance sheet and profit and loss account must combine the information contained in the separate balance sheets and profit and loss accounts of the holding company and of the subsidiaries dealt with by the consolidated accounts, with such adjustments as the directors of the holding company think necessary. The emoluments of the directors, including emoluments which have been waived, loans to officers, salaries of employees, and particulars of companies, not subsidiaries, whose shares are held,[32] need not be shown in the consolidated accounts.

Statement in holding company's accounts of identities and places of incorporation of subsidiaries, and particulars of shareholdings therein

The 1967 Act, s. 3, provides that, subject as below, where, at the end of its financial year, a company has subsidiaries, there must be stated in, or in a note on, or statement annexed to, the accounts—

(1) the name of each subsidiary;

(2) if a subsidiary is incorporated outside Great Britain, the country where it is incorporated (and if a subsidiary is incorporated in Great Britain and registered in England but the holding company is registered in Scotland, or vice versa, the country where it is registered); and

(3) the identity and the proportion of each class of the subsidiary's shares held by the holding company, and the extent to which such proportion consists of shares held by, or by a nominee for, (*a*) the company, and (*b*) another of its subsidiaries.

Section 154 (3)[33] of the 1948 Act applies for the purpose of determining whether shares of one company are or are not held by another.

Disclosure of information is not required with respect to a subsidiary which is incorporated outside the United Kingdom, or is incorporated in the United Kingdom but carries on business outside the United Kingdom, if disclosure would, in the opinion of the directors of the holding company, be harmful to the business of it or any of its subsidiaries and the Department of Trade agrees to non-disclosure: section 3 (3).

If in the directors' opinion the number of subsidiaries is such that compliance with the section would result in excessive particulars being given, it is enough to

[31] Companies (Accounts) Regulations 1973 (S.I. 1973 No. 1150).

[32] See 1967 Act, s. 4, *post* p. 438.

[33] *Ante* p. 59.

comply only as regards the subsidiaries whose businesses the directors consider principally affected the profit or loss or the assets of the company and its subsidiaries: subsection (4).

Subsection (5) provides that if a company takes advantage of subsection (4)—

(*a*) the statement required by the section must state that it deals only with the subsidiaries carrying on the businesses referred to; and

(*b*) particulars of *all* the company's subsidiaries must be annexed to the annual return first made after the accounts are laid before the company in general meeting.

Failure to comply with subsection (5) (*b*) renders the company and every officer in default liable to a default fine of £5 a day: 1967 Act, s. 3 (6); 1948 Act, s. 440.

Statement in company's accounts of identities and places of incorporation of companies not subsidiaries whose shares it holds, and particulars of those shares

By section 4 of the 1967 Act, subject as below, if a company holds shares of any class comprised in the equity share capital of another company (not being its subsidiary) exceeding one tenth of the nominal value of the issued shares of that class, its accounts must state—

(1) the name of the other company and,

(*a*) if it is incorporated outside Great Britain, the country where it is incorporated;

(*b*) if it is incorporated in Great Britain and registered in England but the company is registered in Scotland (or vice versa), the country where it is registered;

(2) the identity of the class and the proportion of the shares of that class held; and

(3) if the company also holds shares of other classes (whether or not comprised in its equity share capital), the like particulars as respects each of those other classes.

If the amount of the shares held by a company in another company exceeds one tenth of the amount of its assets, its accounts must state—

(1) above; and

(2) the identity and the proportion of each class of shares held.

Section 154 (3) of the 1948 Act, omitting paragraph (*b*) (ii), applies for the purpose of determining whether shares of one company are or are not held by another.

Section 4 (3), (4), (5) and (6) is similar to section 3 (3), (4), (5) and (6) *ante.*

Statement in subsidiary's accounts of name and place of incorporation of its ultimate holding company

Subject as below, section 5 of the 1967 Act provides that where at the end of its financial year a company is the subsidiary of another, its accounts must state the name of the company regarded by the directors as being the company's ultimate holding company and, if known to them, the country in which it is incorporated.

Disclosure is not required by a company carrying on business outside the United Kingdom if it would, in the directors' opinion, be harmful to the business of the ultimate holding company or the company or any other of the holding company's subsidiaries and the Department of Trade agrees.

Exceptions for special classes of company

Certain banking companies' and insurance and shipping companies' balance sheets and profit and loss accounts must be kept in accordance with the amended Eighth Schedule as modified by Part III of that Schedule.

At the end of 1974, 101 companies satisfied the Department of Trade that they ought to be treated as banking or discount companies. They may, *e.g.*, make undisclosed transfers to and from reserves before arriving at published profits (although they are required to disclose their true profits and reserves to the Bank of England and the Department of Trade). Full disclosure of the fluctuations in the value of their investments and of their periodical losses on lendings might lead to a loss of confidence on the part of depositors and the general public.

Section 12 of the 1967 Act gives the Department of Trade power to revoke the exception from the amended Schedule 8 for banking and discount companies. The Jenkins Report[34] recommended that the Department of Trade should revoke the exception for shipping companies.

Power to alter tables and forms

The Department of Trade, by regulations made by statutory instrument, can alter or add to, *inter alia*, the requirements of the Act as to the matters to be set out in the balance sheet, profit and loss account and group accounts: 1948 Act, s. 454. Section 12 of the 1967 Act, above, extends section 454 to banking and discount companies.

DOCUMENTS TO BE ANNEXED OR ATTACHED TO BALANCE SHEET

The following documents must be annexed or attached to the balance sheet:
  (1) The profit and loss account, approved by the directors before the balance sheet is signed, must be annexed.
  (2) Any group accounts of a holding company, so far as they are not incorporated in the balance sheet or profit and loss account, must be annexed.
  (3) The auditors' report must be attached: section 156[35] of the 1948 Act as amended by Schedule 2 of the 1976 Act.
  (4) The directors' report must be attached: section 157[36] of the 1948 Act as amended by Schedule 2 of the 1976 Act.

[34] Para. 416. [35] *Post* p. 459. [36] *Post.*

RIGHT TO RECEIVE ACCOUNTS

The general rule is that a copy of every balance sheet, including every document required by law to be annexed thereto, of which a copy is to be laid before the company in general meeting, together with a copy of the auditors' report, must be sent to every member, whether or not he is entitled to receive notices of general meetings, and also to every debenture holder, at least 21 days before the date of the meeting. If all the members entitled to attend and vote so agree, a shorter time will suffice. Any member or debenture holder, whether entitled to receive a copy or not, is entitled to a copy on demand without charge: 1948 Act, s. 158, as amended by the 1976 Act, Schedule 2.

Section 24 of the 1967 Act gives a right to receive copies of the directors' report by providing that section 158 above shall have effect as if references to the auditors' report included references to the directors' report.

Where the shares of a member are vested in his personal representatives who have not been entered in the register of members, clause 76 (3) of the Companies Bill 1973 would have entitled the personal representatives to demand without charge a copy of the last balance sheet and of every document required to be annexed or attached to it.

DIRECTORS' REPORT

The directors' report must deal with the company's affairs generally, the amount recommended as dividend and the amount proposed to be carried to reserves: 1948 Act, s. 157 (1).

Sections 16 to 23 of the 1967 Act require certain additional matters to be dealt with in the directors' report. These include the principal activities of the company during the year, the attribution of turnover to businesses of different classes, the average number of employees in each week, certain particulars of political or charitable gifts, and, in the case of certain companies, particulars of exports.

Additional matters of general nature

Section 16 of the 1967 Act provides that the directors' report must state the names of the persons who, at any time during the financial year, were directors, and the principal activities of the company and its subsidiaries in the course of the year and any significant changes in such activities.

Further:

(1) If significant changes in the fixed assets of the company or any of its subsidiaries have occurred during the year, particulars must be given, and if, in the case of interests in land, the market value at the end of the year differs substantially from the amount included in the balance sheet and the directors consider the difference requires the attention of members or debenture holders, the difference must be indicated. This is not necessary in the case of a banking, insurance or shipping company.

(2) If, in the year, the company has issued shares or debentures, the reason therefor, the classes issued and, as respects each class, the number or amount issued and the consideration received, must be stated.

(3) If, at the end of the year, there subsists, or, during the year, there subsisted, a contract with the company (other than a director's contract of service or a contract between the company and another company in which a director is or was interested only as a director of the other company) which the directors consider significant in relation to the company's business and in which a director has or had an interest which the directors consider material, the following must be stated—

(*a*) the fact of the contract's subsisting;
(*b*) the names of the other parties;
(*c*) the name of the director (if not a party);
(*d*) the nature of the contract;
(*e*) the nature of the director's interest in it.

(4) If, during or at the end of the year, there subsist or have subsisted arrangements to which the company is or was a party, being arrangements one object of which is to enable the directors to acquire benefits by the acquisition of shares in or debentures of the company or any other company, the effect of the arrangements and the names of the directors during the year must be stated.

(5) As respects every director at the end of the year there must be stated whether or not he was interested in shares in or debentures of the company or its subsidiary or holding company or co-subsidiary and, if he was, the number and amount of shares in or debentures of each company (specifying it), and whether or not he was interested at the beginning of the year or when he became a director and, if he was, the number and amount of shares in or debentures of each company (specifying it).

(6) If there are any other matters which are material for the members' appreciation of the state of the company's affairs and the disclosure of which will not, in the directors' opinion, harm the business of the company or any of its subsidiaries, particulars must be given.

Turnover[37] and profitability of businesses of different classes

If, during a financial year, a company which is subject to paragraph 13A of Schedule 8 as amended[37] but does not have subsidiaries at the end of the year and does not submit group accounts prepared as consolidated accounts,[38] has carried on business of two or more classes (other than banking or discounting or other prescribed class) that in the directors' opinion differ substantially from each other, the directors' report must state—

(1) the proportions in which the turnover[37] for the year is divided amongst those classes (describing them); and

[37] *Ante* p. 428.   [38] *Ante* p. 435.

(2) the extent (in monetary terms) to which the directors consider each class contributed to or restricted the company's profit or loss.

Similarly, if a company has subsidiaries at the end of the year and submits group accounts prepared as consolidated accounts,[38] and the company and its subsidiaries carried on between them during the year businesses of two or more substantially different classes.

Classes of business which do not differ substantially are treated as one class: 1967 Act, s. 17.

Number of employees and amount of wages[39]

The directors' report must state the average number of employees of the company (or, if the company has subsidiaries, of it and the subsidiaries) in each week of the financial year, and the amount of their gross remuneration, including bonuses, during the year: 1967 Act, s. 18.

Section 18 (3) contains provisions for ascertaining the average number of employees. Persons who worked mainly outside the United Kingdom are ignored: section 18 (6).

The section does not apply if the average number of employees is less than 100 or if the company is a wholly owned subsidiary[40] of a company incorporated in Great Britain.

Political or charitable gifts

If a company (other than a wholly owned subsidiary[40] of a company incorporated in Great Britain) has given more than £50 during the financial year for political or charitable purposes, the directors' report must state, in the case of each purpose, the amount of the gift and, in the case of political purposes, (1) the name of each person to whom more than £50 was given and the amount of the gift and (2) if more than £50 is given by way of donation or subscription to a political party, the identity of the party and the amount of the gift: 1967 Act, s. 19.

"Giving money for political purposes" is defined as giving a donation or subscription to—

(1) a political party in the United Kingdom; or
(2) a person who, to the company's knowledge, is carrying on, or proposing to carry on, activities which can at the time reasonably be regarded as likely to affect public support for such a political party.

Money given for charitable purposes to a person ordinarily resident outside the United Kingdom is ignored. "Charitable purposes" mean exclusively charitable purposes.

Section 19 (2) contains similar provisions with respect to a company with subsidiaries which have given money where the company is not the wholly owned subsidiary of a company incorporated in Great Britain and the gifts by the company and its subsidiaries exceed £50.

Export particulars

Where, at the end of a financial year, a company subject to paragraph 13A of Schedule 8 as amended[37] whose business includes the supplying of goods does

---

[39] The 1974 Labour Party Green Paper, "The Reform of Company Law," p. 26, describes the details required by s.18 as "rather crude."
[40] *Ante* p. 435.

not have subsidiaries,[37] then, unless the turnover[37] for the year does not exceed £50,000, the directors' report must state—

(1) If, in that year, the company has exported goods from the United Kingdom otherwise than as agent of another person, the value of such goods;
(2) if no goods have been so exported, that fact: 1967 Act, s. 20.

If a company has subsidiaries then, unless neither the company's business nor that of any subsidiary includes supplying goods, or the company submits group accounts prepared as consolidated accounts[37] and the turnover[38] does not exceed £50,000, there must be stated—

(1) the aggregate of the values of the goods exported;
(2) as for (2) above.

The section does not apply if the Department of Trade is satisfied that in the national interest the information should not be disclosed.

Items included under authority of section 163 of principal Act

By the proviso to section 163 of the 1948 Act, any information required to be given in accounts, and allowed to be given in a statement annexed, may be given in the directors' report instead, in which case the report must be annexed to the accounts and the auditors must report thereon so far as it gives such information.

If advantage is taken of the proviso to section 163, above, the directors' report must also show the corresponding amount for, or as at the end of, the preceding financial year of the item in question: 1967 Act, s. 22.

Penalisation of failure to comply with above requirements

In respect of any failure, in the case of a company, to comply with the requirements of section 157 (1) of the 1948 Act or sections 15 to 22 of the 1967 Act, every person who is a director immediately before the end of the period allowed by section 6 of the 1976 Act for laying and delivering accounts is guilty of an offence and liable on conviction on indictment to a fine or on summary conviction to a fine not exceeding £400, unless he can prove that he took all reasonable steps for securing compliance with the requirements.

Note paragraphs 10–12 of the 1973 White Paper and clause 69 of the 1973 Bill *ante*.[41]

EXTRACTS FROM REPORTS AND ACCOUNTS
X COMPANY (EXPORT) LIMITED

X COMPANY (EXPORT) LIMITED

DIRECTORS:	AB
	CD
	EF
	GH
	IJ
SECRETARY:	KL
REGISTERED OFFICE:	X House, Chancery Lane, London, WC2A 1PP
AUDITORS:	MN & Co. Chartered Accountants

---

[41] pp. 419 and 427 respectively.

Report of Directors 1975

The Directors of X Company (Export) Limited submit their Report together with the Accounts of the Company for the year ended September 30, 1975 which will be laid before the Members at the Annual General Meeting to be held on March 30, 1976 at X House, Chancery Lane, London WC2A 1PP.

The Balance of Profit for the year ended September 30, 1975 after making the necessary provision for taxation was

£ 48,851

This has been appropriated as follows:
Interim Ordinary Dividend of £48,851 for the year ended September, 30, 1975 on 26,000 shares of £1 each payable on March 1, 1976.

48,851

The Directors recommend that the interim ordinary dividend payable as above be confirmed and that it be termed the "Final Dividend" for the year.

During the year a new branch of the Company was established in Utopia, and technical liaison offices in Oxonia and Cantabria.

The principal activities of the Company during the year continued to be the sale of X and other products in certain overseas countries.

The Company exported goods to the value of £8,369,623 (c.i.f.) during the year.

With the exception of Mr EF who resigned from the Board on June 30, 1975, having served as a Director since his appointment on January 14, 1972, the Directors shown at the head of this Report were Directors of the Company throughout the year 1975.

At the Annual General Meeting Mr GH retires pursuant to Article 98 and being eligible, is recommended for re-election as a Director at the next Annual General Meeting.

The interests of the Directors holding office on September 30, 1975 in the shares, stock and debentures in X Company ("X") (Holding Company) Group are set out below:

DIRECTORS	CLASS OF SHARE/STOCK DEBENTURE	HOLDING AT OCT. 1, 1974	HOLDING AT SEPT. 30, 1975
AB	X Ordinary Stock	£995	£1,213
	X 7¼% Loan Stock	£140	£140
CD	X Ordinary Stock	£2,641	£2,937
GH	X Ordinary Stock	£2,127	£2,349
IJ	X Ordinary Stock	£2,443	£2,426

The Auditors, MN & Co, are willing to continue in office and a resolution authorising the Directors to fix their remuneration will be submitted to the Annual General Meeting.

BY ORDER OF THE BOARD
KL

SECRETARY

X House, Chancery Lane
London WC2A 1PP
March 4, 1975

X COMPANY (EXPORT) LIMITED

AUDITORS' REPORT

We have audited the books and records of X Company (Export) Limited for the year ended September 30, 1975. The attached accounts have been properly prepared in accordance with the provisions of the Companies Acts 1948 and 1967.

The Statement of Standard Accounting Practice No. 1 (accounting for the results of associated companies) has not been complied with for the reasons given in note 8, with which we concur.

In our opinion the accounts give a true and fair view of the state of affairs and profit of the company.

MN & Co.
Chartered Accountants
London
February 13, 1976

X COMPANY (EXPORT) LIMITED

PROFIT AND LOSS ACCOUNT
FOR THE YEAR ENDED SEPTEMBER 30, 1975

	Notes		1974
SALES	2	£9,705,379	£7,625,832
TRADING PROFIT	3	£162,607	£220,737
Provision for amount owing by subsidiary company no longer required		19,883	—
		182,490	220,737
Employees' profit-sharing scheme	4	(218)	(105)
PROFIT BEFORE TAX		182,272	220,632
Taxation on the profit for the year	5	(133,421)	(108,164)
PROFIT AFTER TAX		48,851	112,468
Proposed dividend		£48,851	£112,468

The attached notes form part of the accounts.

X COMPANY (EXPORT) LIMITED

BALANCE SHEET AS AT SEPTEMBER 30, 1975

	Notes		1974
ASSETS EMPLOYED			
FIXED ASSETS	6	£282,581	£224,108
INTEREST IN SUBSIDIARY COMPANY	7	—	—
INTEREST IN ASSOCIATED COMPANY	8	34,389	34,389

CURRENT ASSETS		
Stocks	4,879,394	3,401,887
Amounts due by subsidiaries of X Company Limited	1,229,509	382,054
Debtors	1,637,499	1,147,889
Short term deposits	21,218	49,685
Cash	246,587	115,708
	8,014,207	5,097,223

LESS CURRENT LIABILITIES		
Amounts due to X Company Limited and its subsidiaries	6,694,474	3,723,205
Creditors	456,408	348,516
Current taxation	50,406	71,920
Bank overdrafts	263,722	312,295
Proposed dividend	48,851	112,468
	7,513,861	4,568,404

NET CURRENT ASSETS	500,346	528,819
	817,316	787,316
DEFERRED TAXATION		
Corporation tax due January 1, 1977	(63,000)	(33,000)
	£754,316	£754,316

FINANCED BY			
SHARE CAPITAL	9	£26,000	£26,000
RESERVES		728,316	728,316
		£754,316	£754,316

DIRECTOR AB
DIRECTOR IJ
The attached notes form part of the accounts

> We certify that this is a true copy of the only Balance Sheet laid before the Company in General Meeting during the period to April 13, 1976 to which the Return relates (including every document required by law to be annexed to the Balance Sheet) and a true copy of the report of the Auditors, and of the Report of the Directors accompanying such Balance Sheet.
>
> Signed. . . . . . . AB . . . . . Director
>
> Signed . . . . . . KL . . . . . Secretary

X COMPANY (EXPORT) LIMITED

NOTES TO THE ACCOUNTS SEPTEMBER 30, 1975

1 *Accounting Policies*

The following paragraphs describe the accounting policies of the company.

Depreciation

The book value of each asset is written off over its estimated life.

Stock Valuation

Stocks are stated at the lower of cost and net realisable value.

Foreign currencies

Assets, liabilities and profit and loss accounts in foreign currencies are converted into sterling at rates of exchange ruling at the year end. Differences arising from changes in exchange rates are taken to profit and loss account.

2 *Sales*

Sales represent the amounts charged during the year to:

		1974
External customers	£8,804,928	£7,623,179
Subsidiaries and divisions of X Company Limited	900,451	2,653
	£9,705,379	£7,625,832

3 *Trading Profit*

The following amounts have been charged/(credited) in arriving at trading profit:

		1974
Depreciation	£82,922	£45,377
Profit on sale of fixed assets	(4,632)	(6,053)
Pension fund contributions, pensions and gratuities	134,606	146,659
Audit fees and expenses	13,788	9,865
Interest payable	45,303	35,902
Interest receivable	—	(1,355)
Dividends received from associated company	(10,582)	(12,933)

4 *Employees' Profit-Sharing Scheme*

		1974
Provision for 1974	£150	£75
Underprovision in previous year	68	30
	£218	£105

1974

5 Taxation

U.K. corporation tax at 52% (1974 : 52%)	£94,834	£100,655
Double taxation relief	(31,834)	(67,655)
Overseas taxation	59,303	70,973
	122,303	103,973
Prior years' adjustments	11,118	4,191
	£133,421	£108,164

6 Fixed Assets

	Freehold property	Plant and equipment	Total
Cost			
At beginning of year	£66,780	£349,302	£416,082
Capital expenditure	—	132,566	132,566
Disposals	(1,279)	(55,528)	(56,807)
Exchange adjustments	8,816	24,370	33,186
At end of year	74,317	450,710	525,027
Depreciation			
At beginning of year	47,089	144,885	191,974
Disposals	(1,278)	(43,910)	(45,188)
Depreciation for year	4,288	74,002	78,290
Exchange adjustments	6,222	11,148	17,370
At end of year	56,321	186,125	242,446
Net book value September 30, 1975	£17,996	£264,585	£282,581
Net book value September 30, 1974	£19,691	£204,417	£224,108

7 Interest in subsidiary company

The investment comprises 400,000 shares of 1 dollar each fully paid (100% holding (1974 : 100%)) in X Company (Tomtopia) Limited. The company's interest in X Company (Tomtopia) Limited is as follows:

		1974
Shares at cost	£163,264	£163,264
Amount owing by subsidiary company on current account	211,110	230,993
	374,374	394,257
Less amount provided	374,374	394,257
	£ —	£ —

Consolidated accounts have not been prepared as X Company (Export) Limited is a wholly owned subsidiary of another body corporate. No profits or losses of X Company (Tomtopia) Limited, from its formation to September 30, 1975, have been brought into the accounts of X Company (Export) Limited. At September 30, 1975 the accumulated profits of X Company (Tomtopia) Limited amounted to £380,256 (1974: £200,641).

8 *Interest in associated company*

This investment comprises 98,000 (1974 : 73,500) shares of 10 dollars each fully paid (49% holding (1974 : 49%)) in X Company (Ruritania) Limited, a company incorporated in Ruritania. The shares in this company are quoted on the Ruritanian Stock Exchange and the market value of the company's shareholding at September 30, 1975 amounted to £94,420 (1974 : £70,815).

The policy of X Company Limited for dealing with the results of associated companies is to consolidate the results of its major associated companies only. In the context of the X group the interest in X Company (Ruritania) Limited is not significant and the results of this company therefore will not be consolidated in the group accounts. For this reason also the results have not been consolidated in these accounts.

9 *Share Capital*

	Authorised	Issued and fully paid
10% cumulative preference shares of £1 each	£4,000	£ —
Ordinary shares of £1 each	26,000	26,000
	£30,000	£26,000

10 *Contingent liability*

At September 30, 1975 there were contingent liabilities of £22,979 (1974: £5,227).

11 *Capital commitments*

Capital expenditure, authorsied and contracted but not provided for in these accounts, amounted to £11,279 (1974 : £4,077).

12 *Holding company*

The company's ultimate holding company is X Company Limited which is incorporated in England.

Disclosure of information to Ministers and Trade Unions (Part IV of the Industry Act 1975)

Section 28 of the Industry Act 1975 provides that for the purpose of obtaining information which in the opinion of either the Secretary of State or the Minister of Agriculture, Fisheries and Food, is needed to form or to further national economic policies, or needed for consultations between government, employers or workers on the outlook for a particular sector of manufacturing industry, the minister concerned may serve a preliminary notice on the company or companies if it appears to him that—

(1) a company or group of companies is carrying on in the U.K. an undertaking wholly or mainly engaged in manufacturing industry (defined in section 37);

(2) the undertaking makes a significant contribution to a sector of such industry important to the economy of the U.K.;

(3) it is desirable that the company or companies should provide the government and a representative of each trade union recognised by the company or companies with information relating to the undertaking.

The minister may make an order under the section if it appears to him that the company or companies will not voluntarily furnish the information.

Section 30 provides that a minister who has made an order under section 28 may by notice require a company or companies to furnish him within a specified reasonable time with certain information as to specified matters relating to the business in the U.K. of the undertaking, *e.g.* persons employed, capital expenditure, fixed capital assets, productive capacity and capacity utilisation, output and productivity, sales of products, exports of products, sales of industrial or intellectual property owned or used in connection with the undertaking, expenditure on research or development programmes.

After he has received the information specified in a notice under section 30 above, the minister may require the company or companies to furnish the whole or part of the information to the authorised representative of each relevant trade union within a reasonable period, being at least 28 days. He must not require information to be furnished if he considers that reasons of national policy (*e.g.* it would be undesirable in the national interest) or special reasons (*e.g.* it would cause substantial injury to the undertaking or a substantial number of its employees) apply. (Section 31.)

Information furnished to the minister under section 30 but not furnished to the authorised representatives under section 32 must not be disclosed, without the consent of the person furnishing it, except, for example, to a government department for the purposes of the exercise by them of their functions (section 33).

Section 34 provides for penalties for a person who, *e.g.*, refuses or fails without reasonable cause to furnish information required under Part IV or, in furnishing such information, makes a statement which he knows to be false in a material particular or recklessly makes a statement which is false in a material particular.

CHAPTER 20

AUDITORS

THE position of the auditor has become a very important one. As we shall see,[1] he is given wide powers by section 14 of the Companies Act 1967, and can enforce them by qualifying his report and, in an extreme case, by refusing to certify the accounts.

The most important matters dealt with in this chapter are the way in which auditors are appointed, their qualifications (in effect they must be qualified accountants who are not, *e.g.*, officers or servants of the company), and their powers and duties, including their duty to make a report to the members of the company.

APPOINTMENT OF AUDITORS

1. The first auditors of a company may be appointed by the directors at any time before the first general meeting at which the directors lay before the company a copy of every document required to be comprised in the accounts in respect of the relevant accounting reference period, in which case they hold office until the end of that meeting. If the directors do not appoint the first auditors, the company in general meeting may do so: Companies Act 1976, s. 14 (3), (4).

2. Every company must, at each general meeting at which the directors lay before the company a copy of every document comprised in the accounts, appoint an auditor or auditors to hold office from the end of that meeting until the end of the next such general meeting: 1976 Act, s. 14 (1).

If no auditor is appointed or reappointed at a general meeting, the company must give the Secretary of State notice of the vacancy within one week, whereupon he may appoint an auditor: 1976 Act, s. 14 (2). If the company fails to give due notice, the company and every officer in default is guilty of an offence and liable, on summary conviction, to a default fine: 1976 Act, s. 14 (7).

The Jenkins Report[2] recommended that the appointment of an

---

[1] *Post* p. 461.　　　　　　　　　　[2] Paras. 427, 435.

English firm to be auditors of a company should be deemed to be the appointment of all the duly qualified individuals who are from time to time members of the firm during the period of appointment—at present such an appointment is merely the appointment of the individuals who, at the time of appointment, are members of the firm and qualified for appointment.

3. Any casual vacancy in the office of auditor may be filled by the directors or the company in general meeting, but while the vacancy continues the surviving or continuing auditor or auditors, if any, may act: 1976 Act, s. 14 (5).

Special notice[3] must be given of a resolution—

(a) appointing as auditor a person other than a retiring auditor, or

(b) filling a casual vacancy in the office, or

(c) reappointing a retiring auditor appointed by the directors to fill a casual vacancy, or

(d) removing an auditor before the expiration of his term of office[4]: 1976 Act, s. 15 (1).

On receipt of such notice the company must forthwith send a copy—

(a) to the person to be appointed or removed;

(b) where some other person is to be appointed, to the retiring auditor;

(c) where a casual vacancy was caused by a resignation, to the auditor who resigned: 1976 Act, s. 15 (2).

Where notice is given of a resolution to appoint as auditor someone other than a retiring auditor or to remove an auditor, the retiring auditor or the auditor to be removed may make written representations of a reasonable length whereupon the position is the same as that where a director is being removed under section 184 of the 1948 Act *ante*[5]: 1976 Act, s. 15 (3), (4), (5).

[3] *Ante* p. 295.
[4] Removal of an auditor is dealt with *post*, p. 455.
[5] p. 328.

QUALIFICATIONS OF AUDITORS

No person can be appointed auditor unless—

(1) he is a member of a body of accountants established in the United Kingdom and recognised for the purpose by the Department of Trade; or

(2) he is authorised by the Department of Trade to be appointed because—

(a) he has similar qualifications obtained outside the United Kingdom, or

(b) he has obtained adequate knowledge and experience in the course of his employment by a member of a body of accountants recognised as above (the Secretary of State cannot grant an authorisation under (b) after the expiration of 12 months after section 13 of the 1976 Act came into operation), or

(c) he practised in Great Britain as an accountant before August 6, 1947, and he applied to the Board of Trade to be authorised before January 27, 1968: 1948 Act, s. 161 (1); 1967 Act, ss. 2, 13 (4); 1976 Act, s. 13 (4).

The following bodies are recognised by the Secretary of State for the purposes of (1) *ante*: The Institute of Chartered Accountants in England and Wales; The Institute of Chartered Accountants of Scotland; The Association of Certified Accountants; The Institute of Chartered Accountants in Ireland: 1976 Act, s. 13 (1). The Secretary of State may alter the above list of bodies by the procedure laid down in section 13 (2).

In 1974 the Department of Trade authorised for appointment as auditors 217 persons who were not members of the recognised bodies, making a total since July 1, 1948, of 3,792.

None of the following persons can be appointed auditor:

(1) An officer or servant of the company.

(2) A partner or employee of an officer or servant of the company. This does not prevent a person employed by the auditor from being an officer or servant of the company. "Officer" includes a director, manager or secretary (s. 455).

(3) A body corporate. This prevents a limited company from being an auditor.

(4) A person who, by reason of (1) or (2) *ante*, cannot be appointed auditor of the company's holding company or subsidiary or co-subsidiary: 1948 Act, s. 161 (2), (3); 1967 Act, s. 2.

No person must act as auditor of a company when he knows that he is disqualified for appointment, and if an auditor to his knowledge becomes disqualified during his term of office he must thereupon vacate office and give written notice thereof to the company: 1976 Act, s. 13 (5). Any person who acts as auditor in contravention of subsection (5) *ante*, or fails without reasonable excuse to give notice of vacating his office, is guilty of an offence and liable, on conviction on indictment, to a fine, and on summary conviction, to a fine of up to £40 for every day during which the contravention continues: 1976 Act, s. 13 (6).

Subject to section 161 (2) and (3) above, a person can be appointed auditor of a company if, at the time of his appointment, the following conditions are satisfied, *i.e.* that no shares or debentures of it or of its holding company have been listed on a stock exchange or offered to the public for subscription or purchase, and he is authorised by the Department of Trade as having for the 12 months ending on November 3, 1966, been mainly occupied in practising as an accountant (otherwise than as an employee) and on that date been the duly appointed auditor of a company which was then an exempt private company[6]: 1967 Act, s. 13 (1). The Secretary of State cannot grant an authorisation under section 13 (1) of the 1967 Act after the expiration of 12 months after section 13 of the 1976 Act came into operation: 1976 Act, s. 13 (4).

A Scottish firm may be appointed auditor if, but only if, all the partners are qualified for appointment as auditor of the company in question: 1948 Act, s. 161 (4).

VACATION OF OFFICE BY AUDITORS

Removal of auditors

A company may, by ordinary resolution, remove an auditor before the expiration of his period of office, notwithstanding anything in any agreement between it and him (1976 Act, s. 14 (6)), although nothing in subsection (6) *ante* is to be taken as depriving a removed

[6] *Ante* p. 10.

auditor of compensation or damages payable to him in respect of
the termination of his appointment as auditor or of any appointment
terminating with that as auditor: 1976 Act, s. 14 (10).

Special notice [7] of the resolution is required: 1976 Act, s. 15. This
has been explained already. [8]

A removed auditor is entitled to attend the general meeting at
which his term of office would otherwise have expired, and any
general meeting at which it is proposed to fill the vacancy, to receive
all notices of, and other communications relating to, any such meeting which any member of the company is entitled to receive, and to
be heard at any such meeting which he attends on any part of the
business which concerns him as former auditor of the company:
1976 Act, s. 15 (6).

Within 14 days after a resolution removing an auditor is passed
at a general meeing the company must give notice thereof to the
Registrar (1976 Act, s. 14 (6)), and if the company fails to give notice,
the company and every officer in default is guilty of an offence and
liable, on summary conviction, to a default fine: 1976 Act, s. 14 (7).

Resignation of auditors

An auditor of a company may resign by depositing a notice of
resignation at the company's registered office and his term of office
will end on the date of deposit or any later date specified in the notice,
provided that the notice contains either a statement that there are no
circumstances connected with his resignation which he considers
should be brought to the attention of the members or creditors of the
company or a statement of any such circumstances: 1976 Act, s. 16
(1), (2).

Within 14 days after the deposit of a notice of resignation the
company must send a copy to the Registrar and, if it contains a
statement of circumstances which should be brought to the attention
of the members or creditors, to every member, whether or not he is
entitled to receive notices of general meetings, and to every debenture
holder: 1976 Act, s. 16 (3).

Within 14 days after the receipt of a notice containing a statement
of circumstances which the auditor considers should be brought to
the attention of the members or creditors, the company or any

[7] *Ante* p. 295.
[8] *Ante* p. 453.

aggrieved person may apply to the court for an order that copies need not be sent out and that the auditor pay the whole or part of the company's costs on the application. The court may make such an order if the auditor is using the notice to secure needless publicity for defamatory matter: 1976 Act, s. 16 (4), (5).

Within 14 days of a court order being made the company must send a statement of the effect of the order to the members and creditors. If no order is made, a copy of the statement of circumstances must be sent: 1976 Act, s. 16 (6).

If section 16 (3) or (6) of the 1976 Act is not complied with, the company and every officer in default is guilty of an offence and liable, on conviction on indictment, to a fine, and on summary conviction, to a default fine of £40: 1976 Act, s. 16 (7). Further, section 428 [9] of the 1948 Act applies: 1976 Act, s. 16 (8).

Right of auditor who resigns to requisition meeting of company

When an auditor's notice of resignation contains a statement of circumstances which he considers should be brought to the attention of the members or creditors, he may deposit with it a signed requisition that the directors forthwith duly convene an extraordinary general meeting of the company to receive and consider an explanation of the circumstances connected with his resignation. Further, in such a case he may require the company to circulate to the members a written statement of a reasonable length of such circumstances before the general meeting at which his term of office would otherwise have expired or before the general meeting at which the vacancy is to be filled or convened on his requisition: 1976 Act, s. 17.

The auditor is entitled to attend such meeting, to receive notices of, and other communications relating to, the meeting and to be heard thereat on any part of the business which concerns him as former auditor to the company.

If the directors do not within 21 days of the deposit of the requisition proceed duly to convene a meeting on not more than 28 days' notice, every director who failed to take all reasonable steps to see that it was convened is guilty of an offence and liable, on conviction on indictment, to a fine, and on summary conviction, to a fine not exceeding £400. If the written statement is not sent out as required, the auditor may have it read out at the meeting.

[9] *Ante* p. 71.

The written statement need not be sent out or read out if the court considers that the auditor is abusing his rights to secure needless publicity for defamatory matter.

POSITION OF AUDITORS

The auditor is not a person included in the definition of "officer" in section 455, *ante*. Nor is he an officer for the purposes of section 161 (2) *ante*. However, he is an officer of the company for the purpose of a misfeasance summons under section 333,[10] or for the purpose of offences under sections 328 and 330 of the Companies Act 1948 (which sections also are concerned with offences by officers of companies in liquidation). An auditor is presumably an officer for the purpose of the Theft Act 1968,[11] section 19, *ante*[12] which is concerned with false statements by an officer of a body corporate, but an auditor appointed *ad hoc* for a limited purpose, *e.g.* appointed by the directors for a private audit, is not an officer.[13]

An auditor is an agent of the company for the purposes of section 167, dealing with investigations[14] and may be examined on oath by an inspector. Otherwise the auditor is not (in the absence of special contract) an agent of the company, and his normal certificate as to the correctness of the balance sheet, under what is now section 14 of the Companies Act 1967, cannot constitute an acknowledgment by an agent within the Limitation Act 1939, section 24.[15]

An auditor is treated in the same way as an officer by sections 205 (provisions relieving officers and auditors from liability) and 448 (relief of officers and auditors).[16]

There is no provision in the Companies Acts or in Table A to the effect that an auditor shall cease to hold office on becoming bankrupt or insane. His position in these respects should be compared with that of a director.

[10] *Re Londond and General Bank* [1895] 2 Ch. 166 (C.A.). S. 333 is dealt with *ante* p. 394.
[11] Not applicable to Scotland.
[12] *Ante* p. 156.
[13] *R.* v. *Shacter* [1960] 2 Q.B. 252 (C.C.A.).
[14] *Ante* p. 399.
[15] *Re Transplanters* (*Holding Co.*) *Ltd.* [1958] 1 W.L.R. 822, *ante* p. 433.
[16] *Ante* pp. 354, 355.

REMUNERATION OF AUDITORS

The remuneration of the auditor of a company appointed by the directors or by the Secretary of State, is fixed by the directors or by the Secretary of State, as the case may be. In any other case it is fixed by the company in general meeting or as the company in general meeting may determine. "Remuneration" includes sums paid by the company in respect of his expenses: 1976 Act, s. 14 (8).

The auditor's remuneration (including expenses paid by the company) must be shown under a separate heading in the profit and loss account: Schedule 8, as amended, paragraph 13.

AUDITORS' REPORT

The auditors must report *to the members*[17] on the accounts examined by them, and on every balance sheet, every profit and loss account and all group accounts prepared under section 1 of the Companies Act 1976, of which, in accordance with section 1 (6) of the 1976 Act, a copy is laid before the company in general meeting during their tenure of office: 1967 Act, s. 14 (1), as amended by 1976 Act, Sched. 2.[18] The auditors' report must be read before the company in general meeting and be open to inspection by any member: section 14 (2).

The report must state (except in the case of a company entitled to the benefit of Part III of Schedule 8 as amended[19])—

(*a*) whether in the auditors' opinion the balance sheet and profit and loss account and (in the case of a holding company submitting group accounts) group accounts have been properly prepared in accordance with the provisions of the Companies Acts 1948 to 1976; and

(*b*) whether in their opinion a true and fair view is given—

    (i) in the case of the balance sheet, of the state of the company's affairs at the end of its financial year;

    (ii) in the case of the profit and loss account (if not framed

---

[17] The 1974 Labour Party Green Paper on Reform of Company Law said, at p. 31, "In law, the auditors derive their position and authority from the shareholders to whom they report on [the] company's affairs; in practice, auditors work closely with the company's Directors and senior executives and their relationship with shareholders particularly in non-director-controlled companies is frequently very tenuous indeed."

[18] See also the proviso to s. 163 of the 1948 Act, *ante* p. 443.

[19] *i.e.* a banking, insurance or shipping company, *ante* p. 439.

as a consolidated profit and loss account), of the company's profit or loss for its financial year;

(iii) in the case of group accounts, of the state of affairs and profit or loss of the company and its subsidiaries dealt with thereby, so far as concerns members of the company: section 14 (3).

In the excepted case,[19] the report must state whether in the auditors' opinion the balance sheet and profit and loss account and, if applicable, group accounts, have been properly prepared in accordance with the provisions of the Acts: section 14 (3).

If the auditors think that proper accounting records or returns have not been kept or received, or that the balance sheet and (unless framed as a consolidated profit and loss account) profit and loss account are not in agreement with the accounting records and returns, they must state that fact in the report: 1967 Act, s. 14 (4), as amended by 1976 Act, Sched. 2.

Further, if auditors fail to obtain all the information and explanations which, to the best of their knowledge and belief, are necessary for their audit, they must state that fact in the report: section 14 (6).

If the accounts do not contain particulars of the directors' emoluments, the auditors' report must normally include the required particulars: 1967 Act, ss. 6 and 7.[20]

In preparing their report the auditors must carry out certain investigations, namely those which will enable them to form an opinion as to—

(a) whether proper accounting records have been kept by the company and proper returns adequate for their audit have been received from branches not visited by them;

(b) whether the balance sheet and (unless framed as a consolidated profit and loss account) profit and loss account are in agreement with the records and returns: 1967 Act, s. 14 (4), as amended by 1976 Act, Sched. 2.

If the auditors in their report wilfully make a statement false in a material particular, knowing it to be false, they are liable to four months' imprisonment or a £100 fine or both: section 438 and Schedule 15.

The auditors perform their duty to the members by forwarding

[20] *Ante* p. 339.

their report to the secretary. They are not responsible if the report is not put before the members.[21] However, they must pay due regard to the possibility of fraud and must warn the appropriate level of management promptly and without waiting for the general meeting to report to the shareholders.[22]

The articles cannot preclude the auditors from availing themselves of all the information to which they are entitled as material for their report.[23]

POWERS OF AUDITORS

The auditors have a right of access at all times to the books and accounts and vouchers of the company, and are entitled to require from the officers of the company such information and explanation as they think necessary for the performance of their duties as auditors: 1967 Act, s. 14 (5). This power is necessary to enable them to obtain particulars of the directors' emoluments, including expenses charged to tax and benefits in kind[24] which may not be ascertainable from an examination of the books.

The auditors cannot require the information to be furnished in any particular form or that it should be certified in some way, as by the board of directors. There is no power to require the information to be supplied in writing but auditors can reasonably say that they are not in a position to perform their duties without making further inquiries if they are asked to act on unrecorded oral statements. If proper information is not given, the auditors' remedy is to qualify their report.

If an officer of the company makes a statement to the auditors which purports to convey any information or explanation which they are entitled to require, and it is misleading, false or deceptive in a material particular, he is guilty of an offence and liable, on conviction on indictment, to imprisonment for up to two years or a fine or both, or, on summary conviction, to imprisonment for up to six months or a fine of up to £400 or both: 1976 Act, s. 19.

Auditors also have the right to attend any general meeting of the company and to receive the same notices of general meetings as the

---

[21] *Re Allen, Craig & Co. (London) Ltd.* [1934] Ch. 483.
[22] *Pacific Acceptance Corpn. Ltd.* v. *Forsyth* (1970) 92 W.N. (N.S.W.) 29 (First Australian Supplement to Charlesworth & Cain, p. 229).
[23] *Newton* v. *Birmingham Small Arms Co. Ltd.* [1906] 2 Ch. 378.
[24] *Ante* p. 338.

members, and to be heard at any general meeting on any part of the business which concerns them as auditors: 1967 Act, s. 14 (7).

Powers in relation to subsidiaries

If a subsidiary company is incorporated in Great Britain, the subsidiary and its auditors must give the auditors of the holding company such information and explanation as they may reasonably require for the purposes of their duties. In any other case, the holding company, if required by its auditors to do so, must take such steps as are reasonably open to it to obtain from the subsidiary such information and explanation: 1976 Act, s. 18.

If a subsidiary or holding company fails to comply with section 18, it and every officer in default is guilty of an offence. Similarly with an auditor of a subsidiary who fails to comply.

DUTIES OF AUDITORS

The duties of auditors depend on the terms of the articles as well as on the statutory provisions.

Table A, article 130, provides: Auditors shall be appointed and their duties regulated in accordance with section 161 of the 1948 Act, section 14 of the 1967 Act and sections 13 to 18 of the 1976 Act.[25]

Their duties may be summarised as follows:

(1) They must acquaint themselves with their duties under the articles and the Acts.[26]

(2) They must report to the members on the accounts examined by them, and on every balance sheet, every profit and loss account and all group accounts prepared under section 1 of the 1976 Act, of which, in accordance with section 1 (6) of the 1976 Act, a copy is laid before the company in general meeting during their tenure of office: 1967 Act, s. 14 (1) as amended, *ante*.[27] The report must state the matters specified in sections 6, 7 and 14 (3), (4) and (6) of the 1967 Act, *ante*.[27] In preparing the report they must carry out the investigations specified in section 14 (4), *ante*.[27]

---

[25] Sched. 2 of the 1976 Act.
[26] *Re Republic of Bolivia Exploration Syndicate Ltd.* [1914] 1 Ch. 139.
[27] pp. 459 *et seq.*

They must ascertain and state the true financial position of the company by an examination of the books. This examination must be not merely to ascertain what the books show, but also to ascertain that the books show the true financial position.[28]

"The duty of the auditor" is "not to confine himself merely to the task of verifying the arithmetical accuracy of the balance sheet, but to inquire into its substantial accuracy, and to ascertain that it . . . was properly drawn up, so as to contain a true and correct representation of the state of the company's affairs": *per* Stirling J. in *Leeds Estate Co.* v. *Shepherd* (1887) 36 Ch.D. 787 at p. 802.

An auditor "is not to be written off as a professional 'adder-upper and subtractor'. His vital task is to take care to see that errors are not made, be they errors of computation, or errors of omission or commission, or downright untruths. To perform this task properly he must come to it with an inquiring mind—not suspicious of dishonesty, I agree—but suspecting that someone may have made a mistake somewhere and that a check must be made to ensure that there has been none": *per* Lord Denning in *Fomento (Sterling Area) Ltd.* v. *Selsdon Fountain Pen Co. Ltd.* [1958] 1 W.L.R. 45 (H.L.) at p. 61.

The statutory duty of an auditor, *e.g.* to state whether in his opinion a true and fair view is given by the balance sheet and the profit and loss account, is a personal one, and if he adopts the opinion of the company's accountant, and he is sued by the company for wrongly stating that a true and fair view is given, he has no cause of action against the accountant.[29]

(3) They must act honestly, and with reasonable care and skill.

"An auditor is not bound to be a detective, or . . . to approach his work . . . with a foregone conclusion that there is something wrong. He is a watchdog, but not a bloodhound. He is justified in believing tried servants of the company in whom confidence is placed by the company. He is entitled to assume that they are honest, and to rely on their representations, provided he takes reasonable care. If there is anything calculated to excite suspicion he should probe it to the bottom; but in the absence of anything of that kind he is only bound to be reasonably cautious and careful": *per* Lopes L.J. in *Re Kingston Cotton Mill Co.* (*No. 2*) [1896] 2 Ch. 279 (C.A.) at p. 288.

"It is the duty of an auditor to bring to bear on the work he has to perform that skill, care and caution which a reasonably competent, careful, and cautious auditor would use. What is reasonable skill, care and caution must depend on the particular circumstances of each case. An auditor . . . is not bound to do more than exercise reasonable care and skill in making inquiries . . . He is not an insurer; he does not guarantee that the books do correctly show the true position of the company's affairs; . . . he must be honest—*i.e.*, he must not certify what he does not believe to be true, and he must take reasonable care and skill before he believes that what he certifies is true. . . . Where there is nothing to

28 *Per* Lindley L.J. in *Re London and General Bank* (*No. 2*) [1895] 2 Ch. 673 (C.A.) at p. 682 *et seq.*
29 *Dominion Freeholders Ltd.* v. *Aird* [1966] 2 N.S.W.R. 293 (C.A.) distinguishing *Hedley Byrne & Co. Ltd.* v. *Heller & Partners Ltd.*, [1964] A.C. 465, *ante* p. 147.

excite suspicion very little inquiry will be reasonably sufficient. . . . Where suspicion is aroused more care is obviously necessary; but, still, an auditor is not bound to exercise more than reasonable care and skill, even in a case of suspicion. . . .": *per* Lindley L.J. in *Re London and General Bank (No. 2)* [1895] 2 Ch. 673 (C.A.) at p. 683.

It may be that entries in or omissions from the books ought to make the auditors suspicious. In such a case they must make full investigations into the suspicious circumstances, but they are not liable for "not tracking out ingenious and carefully laid schemes of fraud when there is nothing to arouse their suspicion."[30]

B. was the managing director of the company and the senior partner of E. & Co., stockbrokers. E. & Co. owed £250,000 to the company but on February 27, just before the close of the financial year, E. & Co. bought Treasury Bills for £200,000 and credited the company with them, thus reducing their debt to £50,000. The company's balance sheet accordingly showed an investment in Treasury Bills for £200,000, and a debt from E. & Co. for £50,000. On March 3, after the close of the financial year, E. &. Co. sold the Treasury Bills and became debtors again for £250,000. This was done for three successive years. *Held*, although the transactions, when isolated, should have led the auditors to conclude that fraud had taken place, yet as they formed only one item in a large audit, there was no negligence on the part of the auditors: *Re City Equitable Fire Insurance Co. Ltd.* [1925] Ch. 407 (C.A.).

If payments are made or sums borrowed by the company, the auditors should see that they are authorised and made in accordance with the articles and the Acts.[31]

"When it is shewn that audited balance sheets do not shew the true financial condition of the company and that damage has resulted, the onus is on the auditors to shew that this is not the result of any breach of duty on their part."[32]

They must satisfy themselves that the securities of the company in fact exist and are in safe custody. This duty is discharged by their making a personal inspection of the securities in question. If, however, the securities are in the possession of a person who in the ordinary course of his business keeps securities for his customers, *e.g.* a banker, and that person is regarded as trustworthy, the auditors may safely accept his certificate that the securities are in his custody.

The auditor accepted the certificate of the company's stockbrokers that they held securities on the company's behalf. In fact they did not hold the securities

---

[30] *Per* Lopes L.J. in *Re Kingston Cotton Mill Co. (No. 2)* [1896] 2 Ch. 279 (C.A) at p. 290.
[31] See *Thomas* v. *Devonport Corpn.* [1900] 1 Q.B. 16 (C.A.).
[32] *Per* Astbury J. in *Re Republic of Bolivia Exploration Syndicate Ltd.* [1914] 1 Ch. 139 at p. 171.

and the company suffered heavy loss. *Held*, by Romer J., the auditor was negligent, as he should have inspected the securities and either insisted on their being put in proper custody or reported the matter to the shareholders[33]: *Re City Equitable Fire Insurance Co. Ltd.* [1925] Ch. 407.

They must check the cash in hand and also the balance at the bank, by inspecting the pass book (or bank statement) or obtaining a certificate from the bank.[34]

Auditors are under no duty to take stock.[35] This is part of the wider question of the auditors' duty as to the value of the assets.

The duty of the auditors as to the value to be placed on the fixed assets is discussed in the previous chapter.[36] Apart from complying with the requirements of the Eighth Schedule as amended, if the auditors have formed an opinion that the assets are overvalued, they are bound to report it to the shareholders.

Auditors made a confidential report to the directors, calling their attention to the fact that the security for loans was insufficient, and that there was a difficulty in realisation. They also reported that in their opinion no dividend should be paid for the year. In their report to the shareholders, however, they merely said that the value of the assets was dependent upon realisation. A dividend of seven per cent. was declared out of capital. *Held*, the auditors were guilty of misfeasance and liable to make good the dividend paid: *Re London and General Bank* (*No. 2*) [1895] 2 Ch. 673 (C.A.).

As to current assets, they are entitled to take the values of stocks and work in progress from the manager or other responsible official of the company, unless they have any reason to suppose them inaccurate.

The auditors accepted the certificate of J., the manager, a person of acknowledged competence and high reputation, as to the value of the stock-in-trade. This was grossly exaggerated, as a result of which dividends were paid out of capital. Had the auditors compared the amount of stock at the beginning of the year with the purchases and sales during the year, they would have been put on inquiry, but they did not do so. *Held*, the auditors were not liable, as they were entitled to rely on J.'s certificate in the absence of anything to excite suspicion: *Re Kingston Cotton Mill Co.* (*No. 2*) [1896] 2 Ch. 279 (C.A.).

The facts were similar to those in the *Kingston Cotton Mill* case except that on discovery of the invoices with altered dates (by which the managing director had caused the price payable on purchases of stock made shortly before the end of each period of account to be included in the outgoings of the succeeding period) the auditor accepted the explanation of the managing director, whom he believed to be of the highest integrity, when he should have examined the suppliers' state-

---

[33] The Court of Appeal expressed no concluded opinion on this point. In any event, the articles protected the auditors from liability. See *ante* p. 363.
[34] *Fox & Son* v. *Morrish, Grant & Co.* (1918) 35 T.L.R. 126.
[35] *Re Kingston Cotton Mill Co.* (*No. 2*), *ante*.
[36] *Ante* p. 430.

ments and where necessary have communicated with the suppliers, and having ascertained the precise facts so far as possible he should have informed the board. By not taking these steps he failed in his duty and was liable for, *inter alia*, the amount of the dividends: *Re Thomas Gerrard & Son Ltd.* [1968] Ch. 455.

"The standards of reasonable care and skill are, upon the expert evidence, more exacting today than those which prevailed in 1896": *per* Pennycuick J. at p. 475.

If directors do not allow auditors time to conduct such investigations as are necessary in order to make the statements required to be contained in their report, the auditors must either refuse to make a report or make an appropriately qualified report: they are not justified in making a report containing a statement the truth of which they have not had an opportunity of ascertaining.[37]

Auditors are not concerned with the policy of the company or whether the company is well or ill managed.

"It is no part of an auditor's duty to give advice, either to directors or shareholders, as to what they ought to do. An auditor has nothing to do with the prudence or imprudence of making loans with or without security. It is nothing to him whether the business of a company is being conducted prudently or imprudently, profitably or unprofitably. It is nothing to him whether dividends are properly or improperly declared, provided he discharges his own duty to the shareholders. His business is to ascertain and state the true financial position of the company at the time of the audit": *per* Lindley L.J. in *Re London and General Bank* (*No. 2*) [1895] 2 Ch. 673 (C.A.). at p. 682.

Auditors cannot be relieved from liability for any breach of duty by any provision in the articles or any contract (s. 205), but in certain circumstances they may obtain relief from the court (s. 448).[38]

In England the auditors can plead the Limitation Act after six years.[39]

Apart from the auditor's contractual duty of care to the company he owes a duty of care to third persons with whom he is not in contractual or fiduciary relationship if, as a reasonable man, he knows that he is being trusted or that his skill and judgment are being relied on and he does not make it clear that he accepts no responsibility for information or advice which he gives.[40] For breach of this duty an action for negligence lies if damage results.

---

[37] *Per* Pennycuick J. in *Re Thomas Gerrard, ante,* at p. 477.
[38] *Ante* pp. 354, 355.
[39] *Leeds Estate Co.* v. *Shepherd* (1887) 36 Ch.D. 787.
[40] *Hedley Byrne & Co. Ltd.* v. *Heller & Partners Ltd.* [1964] A.C. 465, disapproving *Candler* v. *Crane, Christmas & Co.* [1951] 2 K.B. 164 (C.A.). And see *Dimond Mfg. Co. Ltd.* v. *Hamilton* [1969] N.Z.L.R. 609 (C.A.) and *M.L.C. Assce. Co. Ltd.* v. *Evatt* [1971] A.C. 793 (P.C.).

". . . to whom do these professional people owe this duty? I will take accountants, but the same reasoning applies to . . . others. They owe the duty, of course, to their employer or client; and also I think to any third person to whom they themselves show the accounts, or to whom they know their employer is going to show the accounts, so as to induce him to invest money or take some other action on them": *per* Denning L.J. in *Candler* v. *Crane, Christmas & Co.* [1951] 2 K.B. 164 (C.A.) at p. 180.

VALUATION OF SHARES

Articles of private companies often provide that a member who wants to sell his shares must first offer them to the existing members at a price to be fixed by the auditors. Similar provisions are often applicable in the case of a member's death.[41] In valuing the shares for this purpose, the auditor is not obliged to explain the basis of his valuation or to give his reasons for it, and he is not liable to an action by a party who is dissatisfied with it unless he is dishonest.[42] If, however, he does give an explanation, the court can inquire into it and, if satisfied that the valuation has been made on the wrong basis, can declare that it is not binding, *i.e.* the valuation can be impeached for[43] fraud, mistake or miscarriage, but on matters of opinion the court will not interfere.[44] In the latest case[45] in this area it was held that for a valuer to establish immunity from suit he must show that a dispute between at least two parties was sent to him to resolve in such a way that he had to exercise a judicial discretion. An auditor of a private company who, on request, values its shares in the knowledge that this valuation will determine the price to be paid under a contract owes a duty of care to both the vendor and the purchaser. Accordingly, on the facts of the case, the plaintiffs' statement of claim disclosed a cause of action.

---

[41] *Ante* p. 249 *et seq.*

[42] *Finnegan* v. *Allen* [1943] K.B. 425 (C.A.), where it was alleged that the valuation was not made in the way contemplated by the instructions.

[43] The Scottish equivalent of "impeached for" is "challenged on the ground of."

[44] *Dean* v. *Prince* [1954] Ch. 409 (C.A.). In this case the articles of a private company provided that a decreased directors' shares should be purchased by the surviving directors at a price to be certified by an auditor as a fair value. The director who held a controlling interest died. The auditor stated that he had not regarded the company as a going concern but had valued on a "break-up" basis because in his opinion the shares had no value on any other basis because of losses made by the company. *Held*, the auditor was right. See further *Jones (M.)* v. *Jones (R. R.)* [1971] 1 W.L.R. 840, where the valuation was not made by the stipulated expert.

[45] *Arenson* v. *Casson Beckman Rutley & Co.* [1975] 3 W.L.R. 815 (H.L.), applying *Sutcliffe* v. *Thackran* [1974] A.C. 727.

CHAPTER 21

DIVIDENDS

A DIVIDEND is the share, received by a shareholder, of the company's profits legally available for dividend and divided among the members. Commercial companies are formed to earn profits for the shareholders out of which dividends can be paid[1], and no express power to pay dividends is required in the memorandum or the articles. It has been held that dividends must only be paid out of profits and articles, *e.g.* Table A, articles 114–122 *post*, usually so provide and also deal with such things as interim dividends, the method of payment of dividends and the creation of reserve funds.

Dividend must be distinguished from interest. Interest is a debt which, like all debts, is payable out of the company's assets generally. A dividend, however, is not a debt until it has been declared by the company, and dividends cannot be declared out of the assets generally; they can be declared only out of the divisible profits.

PROFITS AVAILABLE FOR DIVIDEND

Dividends must only be paid out of profits

We have seen that a fundamental principle of company law is that the issued share capital must be maintained.[2] Paid-up capital must not be paid to the shareholders except by leave of the court. It must be spent only upon the objects defined in the memorandum. Any other expenditure is *ultra vires* and reduces the fund available for the company's creditors in satisfaction of their claims.[3]

W. guaranteed the preference dividends for three years and the company agreed to repay to W. on demand any sums paid by him under the guarantee. *Held*, the company's agreement was *ultra vires* and void, as it might involve capital being reduced otherwise than by expenditure on the company's objects: *Re Walters' Deed of Guarantee* [1933] Ch. 321.

The principle that share capital must be maintained requires that

---

[1] Under s. 19, *ante* p. 66, a company may be prohibited from paying a dividend.
[2] *Ante* p. 232 *et seq.*
[3] See *per* Jessel M.R. in *Flitcroft's Case* (1882) 21 Ch.D. 519 (C.A.) at p. 533.

468

a dividend, in money or kind,[4] declared by a company, must not be paid except out of profits. The terms "dividend" and "profits" are not defined in the Companies Acts and it has been said that although a dividend presupposes profits of some kind, the word "profits" is by no means free from ambiguity.[5] However, the courts have evolved a number of rules for ascertaining the profits available for payment of dividend.

For the purposes of dividends, capital account and revenue account must be kept distinct. When expenses are incurred, whether they should be charged to capital account or revenue account depends on the nature of the expenses in question and what is usual in the particular trade. This is a business question, and if the directors honestly and reasonably form a view that an expense is of the one kind or the other and their view is adopted by the shareholders, the courts will not, subject to what is stated *ante*, interfere with their judgment.

"There is nothing at all in the Acts about how dividends are to be paid, nor how profits are to be reckoned; all that is left, and very judiciously and properly left, to the commercial world. It is not a subject for an Act of Parliament to say how accounts are to be kept; what is to be put into a capital account, what into an income account, is left to men of business": *per* Lindley L.J. in *Lee* v. *Neuchatel Asphalte Co.* (1889) 41 Ch.D. 1 (C.A.) at p. 21.

The rules for ascertaining distributable profits are:

(1) A dividend cannot be paid if it would result in the company's assets being insufficient to pay its debts.[6]

(2) A dividend cannot be paid out of borrowed money unless the company has divisible profits available.[7]

(3) A dividend can usually be paid out of revenue profits without a loss, realised or unrealised, of fixed capital (fixed assets) being made good first,[8] although this might be commercially unwise in the case of a realised loss.[9]

---

[4] *Post* p. 478.

[5] *Per* Lindley L.J. in *Verner* v. *General and Commercial Investment Trust* [1894] 2 Ch. 239 (C.A.) at p. 266.

[6] *Per* Lindley L.J. in *Lee* v. *Neuchatel Asphalte Co.* (1889) 41 Ch.D. 1 (C.A.) at p. 24; *per* Buckley J. in *Dimbula Valley (Ceylon) Tea Co. Ltd.* v. *Laurie* [1961] Ch. 353 at p. 373.

[7] *Re Mercantile Trading Co. (Stringer's Case)* (1869) 4 Ch.App. 475.

[8] *Lee* v. *Neuchatel Asphalte Co. ante*; *Verner* v. *General and Commercial Investment Trust ante*.

[9] For the recommendation of the Jenkins Committee, see *post* p. 474.

Revenue profits are the excess of receipts over expenses as shown in the profit and loss account.

Fixed capital is capital which "is fixed in the sense of being invested in assets intended to be retained by the company more or less permanently and used in producing an income," for example the money invested in the machinery and plant of a manufacturing company, the shares held by a trust company or the business premises of a bank.[10]

The company is not a debtor to capital, and therefore, although the fixed assets are of less value than the nominal capital, the company is not obliged to make them up to the level of its nominal capital.

A company was formed in 1873 to acquire and work a concession from the Neuchatel Government for quarrying bituminous rock and mineral products. The concession was due to expire in 1907. In 1885 there was a profit shown on revenue account and the company proposed to pay a dividend. A shareholder objected on the grounds that (1) a large part of the capital had been lost, (2) the assets were not equal to the share capital, and (3) the concession being a wasting asset, dividing its annual proceeds was dividing the capital assets of the company. *Held*, on none of these grounds could the company be restrained from declaring a dividend: *Lee* v. *Neuchatel Asphalte Co.* (1889) 41 Ch.D. 1 (C.A.).[11]

The case just quoted does not decide that all companies with wasting assets need have no depreciation fund. If the memorandum expressly authorises the acquisition and working of such an asset, no depreciation fund need be provided before profits are ascertained, but in other cases "it is for the court to determine in each case on evidence whether the particular company ought, or ought not, to have such a fund."[12]

"If a company is formed to acquire and work a property of a wasting nature, for example, a mine, a quarry, or a patent, the capital expended in acquiring the property may be regarded as sunk and gone, and if the company retains assets sufficient to pay its debts . . . there is nothing whatever in the Act to prevent any excess of money obtained by working the property over the cost of working it, from being divided amongst the shareholders": *per* Lindley L.J. in *Lee's* case at p. 24.

A company "may or may not have a sinking fund or a deterioration fund, and the articles of association may or may not contain regulations on those matters. If they do, the regulations must be observed": *per* Lindley L.J. in *Lee's* case at p. 25.

---

[10] *Per* Swinfen Eady L.J. in *Ammonia Soda Co. Ltd.* v. *Chamberlain* [1918] 1 Ch. 266 (C.A.) at p. 286.

[11] See also *City Property Investment Trust Corpn. Ltd.* v. *Thorburn* (1897) 25 R. 361 *per* Lord Trayner at p. 367 and Lord Moncreiff at p. 368.

[12] *Per* Farwell J. in *Bond* v. *Barrow Haematite Steel Co.* [1902] 1 Ch. 353 at p. 368; *per* Buckley L.J. in *Re Crabtree* (1912) 106 L.T. 49 (C.A.).

The business of a company was to invest its funds in shares and other securities, its income being derived from the dividends on the shares it held. Owing to a fall in the market values of its investments, the assets of the company were greatly depreciated in value, but the income for the year exceeded the expenses. An action was brought on behalf of the debenture holders to restrain the company from declaring a dividend without first providing for the loss of capital. *Held*, the loss was a loss of fixed capital, and need not be made good before a dividend was declared: *Verner* v. *General and Commercial Investment Trust* [1894] 2 Ch. 239 (C.A.).

"Fixed capital may be sunk and lost, and yet . . . the excess of current receipts over current payments may be divided, but . . . floating or circulating capital must be kept up, as otherwise it will enter into and form part of such excess, in which case to divide such excess without deducting the capital which forms part of it will be contrary to law": *per* Lindley L.J. at p. 266.

(4) A loss of circulating capital (circulating assets) during the year must be made good before revenue profits can be ascertained.

Circulating capital is "a portion of the subscribed capital of the company intended to be used by being temporarily parted with and circulated in business, in the form of money, goods or other assets, and which, or the proceeds of which, are intended to return to the company with an increment, and are intended to be used again and again, and always to return with some accretion," for example capital expended by a trader in buying goods for resale at a profit, by a banker in making loans to customers who are to repay with interest or by a manufacturer in buying raw materials from which goods are to be manufactured and sold at a profit.[13]

The distinction between fixed and circulating capital means no more than that you cannot take the gross receipts of the year without taking into account in finding the profits that part of the capital which has been parted with in order to obtain the profit.[14] For example, when goods are sold the profits are not the gross amount obtained from the sale but only the sum produced by taking the gross amount and deducting the expenses of sale, including the money spent in buying the goods for sale. The result so obtained is exactly the same as if the money spent in buying the goods is regarded as circulating capital which has to be replaced before the true profit can be ascertained.

---

[13] *Per* Swinfen Eady L.J. in *Ammonia Soda Co. Ltd.* v. *Chamberlain* [1918] 1 Ch. 266 (C.A.) at p. 286.
[14] *Per* Scrutton L.J. in *Ammonia Soda Co. Ltd.* v. *Chamberlain, ante,* at p. 297.

The objects of a Scottish company were similar to those in *Verner's* case *ante* but the Scottish company differed from the English company in that it trafficked in securities and treated profits made on sales as income. *Held*, the securities were part of the circulating capital, with the result that preference shareholders received a smaller dividend than they would otherwise have received: *City Property Investment Trust Corpn. Ltd.* v. *Thorburn* (1897) 25 R. 361.

(5) In England, a dividend can be paid out of the revenue profits of any one year without first making good the losses of previous years, *i.e.* "a company, which has operated at a loss and thus accumulated a deficit on revenue account, may distribute revenue profits of subsequent years without either making good any part of the accrued loss or cancelling the loss by reducing its capital."[15]

In 1911 a company had £12,970 to the debit of its profit and loss account. The company's land and buildings then stood in the balance sheet at the value of £63,246. The directors then entered the value of the land and buildings at £83,788, being what they honestly thought they were worth. They also carried £20,542 (the amount of the increased value) to a reserve account to which they charged the debit balance of the profit and loss account. Trading profits were subsequently made and dividends declared. *Held*, (1) the dividends were paid out of profits and not out of capital; (2) the previous losses were losses of capital as there were no profits which could have been lost, and there was no obligation to replace a capital loss before declaring dividends; (3) there was no objection to the revaluation and the treatment of the appreciation in value thereby ascertained: *Ammonia Soda Co. Ltd.* v. *Chamberlain* [1918] 1 Ch. 266 (C.A.).

Scottish authority is to the opposite effect.

A company had "A," or non-cumulative preference, shares and "B," or ordinary, shares. For several years there had been a loss on the revenue account, with the result that at April 30, 1889, there was a debit balance of £7,867. During the year ended April 30, 1890, net profits of £6,909 were earned. *Held*, these profits were properly applied in reducing the debit balance on the revenue account and therefore the "A" shareholders were not entitled to a dividend for that year: *Niddrie etc. Coal Co. Ltd.* v. *Hurll* (1891) 18 R. 805.

"When a loss on the revenue account has been sustained, there is, of course, no profit until the loss has been made good either by set-off of previous undivided profits still in hand, or by profits subsequently earned": *per* Lord Adam at p. 808.

If, instead of retaining goodwill as an asset in the balance sheet and carrying profits to a goodwill depreciation reserve fund, a company has eliminated goodwill by writing it off against the reserve fund, but the profits are not finally capitalised, there is nothing to prevent it from writing back to profit and loss account so much of the depreciation written off goodwill as proves to be in excess of proper requirements.[16]

---

[15] Jenkins Report (Cmnd. 1749), para. 341.
[16] *Stapley* v. *Read Brothers Ltd.* [1924] 2 Ch. 1.

(6) A dividend may be declared out of profits in a reserve fund, *i.e.* undistributed profits from previous years, which profits have not been capitalised.[17]

(7) Unless the articles otherwise provide, a dividend can be declared out of a realised capital profit, *i.e.* a realised profit on the sale of fixed assets, provided that upon a balance of account there has been an accretion to paid-up capital.[18]

The company is forbidden to distribute any part of its capital among its shareholders, but if the capital is intact there is nothing in the Companies Acts to prevent it from distributing any increase as dividend.

A company with a paid-up capital of £500,000 sold part of its undertaking for £875,000. After deducting the capital and certain expenses from this sum, a balance of £205,000 was left which the company proposed to divide as dividend. *Held*, the company could do so: *Lubbock* v. *British Bank of South America* [1892] 2 Ch. 198.

The question of what is profit available for dividend depends upon the result of the whole accounts fairly taken for the year, capital, as well as profit and loss, and although dividends may be paid out of earned profits in proper cases, although there has been a depreciation of capital, a realized accretion to the estimated value of one item of the capital assets cannot be deemed to be profit divisible among the shareholders without reference to the result of the whole accounts fairly taken.[19]

It has been held that a company which has redeemed its debentures at a discount cannot distribute the amount of the discount as profit when there has been an equivalent fall in value of the fixed assets of the company.[20]

The articles frequently restrict the fund from which dividends can be paid. Table A, article 116, provides that no dividend shall be paid otherwise than out of profits. This does not prevent dividends from being paid from an appreciation of the fixed assets of the company. If, however, the articles provide that dividends shall only be paid out of the profits of the business of the company or out of trading profits, an appreciation of fixed assets cannot be divided as dividend.

[17] *Re Hoare & Co. Ltd.* [1904] 2 Ch. 208 (C.A.), *post* p. 479; *Blyth's Trustees* v. *Milne* (1905) 7 F. 799.
[18] *Lubbock* v. *British Bank of South America* [1892] 2 Ch. 198; *Forgie's Trustees* v. *Forgie*, 1941 S.C. 188; *Australasian Oil Exploration Ltd.* v. *Lachberg* (1958) 101 C.L.R. 119 (First Australian Supplement to Charlesworth & Cain, p. 233).
[19] *Foster* v. *New Trinidad Lake Asphalt Co. Ltd.* [1901] 1 Ch. 208.
[20] *Wall* v. *London and Provincial Trust Ltd.* [1920] 1 Ch. 45.

In England, if the articles authorise it, a reserve resulting from the revaluation of capital assets, *i.e.* an unrealised increase in the value of fixed assets, due to a revaluation made in good faith by competent valuers and not likely to fluctuate in the short term, may be distributed by way of dividend.[21]

It is otherwise in Scotland.[22]

Recommendations of the Jenkins Committee

The Jenkins Report[23] made the following recommendations:

(1) A net realised capital profit should not be a distributable profit unless the directors are satisfied that the net aggregate value of the assets remaining after distribution of the profit will be not less than the book value so that the share capital and reserves remaining will be fully represented by the remaining assets.

A capital surplus arising on the revaluation of unrealised fixed assets should not be directly or indirectly available for distribution in dividend.

This would reverse to some extent the law as laid down in *Dimbula Valley (Ceylon) Tea Co. Ltd.* v. *Laurie* and give statutory recognition to the law as laid down in the Scottish case *Westburn Sugar Refineries Ltd.* v. *Inland Revenue, ante.* It is a fundamental principle of accounting practice that profit is normally established when it is realised by transfer of ownership or completion of services rendered.

(2) Past revenue losses should be eliminated before profits of subsequent years are distributable.

This would reverse the law as laid down in *Ammonia Soda Co. Ltd.* v. *Chamberlain* and establish the law as laid down in the Scottish case *Niddrie etc. Coal Co. Ltd.* v. *Hurll, ante.* The revenue account of a company should be regarded as a continuous account.

(3) In general, pre-acquisition profits attributable to shares in another company should not be available for distribution as profits of the acquiring company.

(4) In computing distributable profits provision for depreciation,

---

[21] *Per* Buckley J. in *Dimbula Valley (Ceylon) Tea Co. Ltd.* v. *Laurie* [1961] Ch. 353 at p. 373. In many cases such a course of action might not be a wise commercial practice.

[22] *Westburn Sugar Refineries Ltd.* v. *Inland Revenue*, 1960 S.L.T. 297.

[23] Para. 350.

replacement or diminution of value of wasting assets should normally be obligatory.

At present there are doubts as to (3) and (4).

Clause 72 (1) and (2) of the Companies Bill 1973 would have prohibited the payment of a dividend except out of profits available for dividend and would have defined such profits as the aggregate of a company's revenue profits and realised capital profits so far as not previously utilised (whether by distribution, capitalisation or otherwise) less the aggregate of its revenue losses and realised capital losses so far as not previously written off. Clause 72 (3) would have given effect to the first Jenkins recommendation. Clause 72 (4) would have allowed an unrealised capital profit to be treated as profits available for dividend for the purposes of the articles so far as they provide for applying such profits in paying up bonus shares. Clause 72 (5) would have prevented a company from applying an unrealised capital profit in writing off revenue losses or realised capital losses, or in paying up debentures or partly paid shares.

The Second Draft Directive submitted by the Commission to the Council of the EEC, article 13, provides that dividends may only be taken from the clear profits.

Payment of interest out of capital

Interest can be paid out of capital under section 65. When the shares of a company are issued for the purpose of raising money to defray the expenses of the construction of any works or buildings or the provision of any plant which cannot be made profitable for a lengthened period, interest on so much of that share capital as is paid up may be paid out of capital, provided that:

(1) The payment is authorised by the articles or by a special resolution.
(2) The sanction of the Department of Trade is obtained.
(3) Payment is only made for such period as the Department of Trade determines and the period must not extend beyond the end of the half-year next after the half-year in which the works or buildings are completed or the plant provided.
(4) The rate of interest does not exceed 4 per cent. per annum or that for the time being prescribed by the Treasury: section 65.

Effect of paying dividends out of capital

All directors who are knowingly parties to the payment of dividends out of capital (*e.g.* where debts known to be bad were entered as assets in reports and balance sheets, so that an apparent profit was shown, and the shareholders, relying on these documents, declared dividends) are jointly and severally liable to the company to replace the amount of dividends so paid, with interest, and ratification is impossible so as to bind the company.[24] In such a case they are entitled to be indemnified by each shareholder who received dividends, *knowing them to be paid out of capital*, to the extent of the dividends received.[25] A shareholder who has knowingly received a dividend paid out of capital cannot, individually or on behalf of the company, maintain an action against the directors to replace the dividends so paid, at any rate until he has repaid the money he has received.[26]

PAYMENT OF DIVIDENDS

Dividends are paid in the manner laid down in the articles.

Table A, article 114, provides:

"The company in general meeting may declare dividends, but no dividend shall exceed the amount recommended by the directors." This relates to the final dividend, declared at the annual general meeting. As to an interim dividend, which is a dividend paid on some date between two annual general meetings of the company,[27] article 115 provides: "The directors may from time to time pay to the members such interim dividends as appear to the directors to be justified by the profits of the company."

Before recommending a dividend, directors should have a complete and detailed list of the company's assets and investments prepared for their information, and should not rely for their value merely on the opinion of the chairman or the auditors.[28]

In the absence of anything to the contrary in the articles,[29] a company cannot be compelled to declare a dividend, and no action can be brought for its recovery until it has been declared.[30] In England the declaration of a dividend creates a specialty debt due

---

[24] *Flitcroft's Case* (1882) 21 Ch.D. 519 (C.A.), *ante* p. 234; *Liquidators of City of Glasgow Bank v. Mackinnon* (1881) 9 R. 535.

[25] *Moxham* v. *Grant* [1900] 1 Q.B. 88 (C.A.).

[26] *Towers* v. *African Tug Co.* [1904] 1 Ch. 558 (C.A.); *Liquidators of City of Glasgow Bank* v. *Mackinnon* (1881) 9 R. 535.

[27] *Per* P. O. Lawrence J. in *Re Jowitt* [1922] 2 Ch. 442 at p. 447.

[28] *Per* Romer J. in *Re City Equitable Fire Insce. Co. Ltd.* [1925] Ch. 407 at pp. 471, 474.

[29] For articles which were interpreted as requiring the whole profits to be divided, see *Paterson* v. *R. Paterson & Sons Ltd.*, 1917 S.C. (H.L.) 13; 1916 S.C. 452.

[30] *Bond* v. *Barrow Haematite Steel Co.* [1902] 1 Ch. 353. See, however, what is said on p. 393 *ante* with regard to s. 210.

from the company to the shareholder which will be barred in 12 years from the date of declaration.[31] In Scotland the period of prescription is 20 years.[32]

When preference shares entitle the holders to receive out of the profits of the company for each year a fixed dividend, the "profits of the company" are the profits available for dividend after setting aside such reserves as the directors think fit. If the whole of the profits are transferred to reserve the preference shareholders are not entitled to any dividend.[33]

When the articles, *e.g.* Table A, article 115, above, give the directors power to pay interim dividends, a resolution by the company in general meeting requiring the directors to declare an interim dividend is inoperative.[34]

In English law, unless the articles otherwise provide, dividends are payable to the shareholders in proportion to the nominal amounts of their shares, irrespective of the amounts paid up.[35] Section 59, however, permits a company, if so authorised by its articles, to pay dividend in proportion to the amount paid up on each share where a larger amount is paid up on some shares than on others. Table A, article 118, accordingly provides that "subject to the rights of persons, if any, entitled to shares with special rights as to dividend, all dividends shall be declared and paid according to the amounts paid or credited as paid on the shares."

In Scots law if articles provide that "the directors may . . . declare a dividend to be paid to the members in proportion to their shares" and define "shares" as shares in the nominal capital, dividends fall to be declared according to the nominal amounts of the shares, irrespective of the amounts paid up,[36] where, however, there is no provision in the articles as to how dividends are to be paid, the common law principle applicable is that they are payable in proportion to the amounts paid up on the shares.[37]

The articles usually provide, as does Table A, article 121, that

---

[31] *Re Artisans' Land Corpn.* [1904] 1 Ch. 796; Limitation Act 1939, s. 2 (3).
[32] Prescription and Limitation (Scotland) Act 1973.
[33] *Re Buenos Ayres Great Southern Ry. Co. Ltd.* [1947] Ch. 384; *cf.* the Scottish case *Wemyss Collieries Trust Ltd.* v. *Melville* (1905) 8 F. 143, in which transfer of a sum to reserve was, on an interpretation of the articles, held to be valid, although preference shareholders were thereby deprived of an additional non-cumulative dividend.
[34] *Scott* v. *Scott* [1943] 1 All E.R. 582.
[35] *Birch* v. *Cropper* (1889) 14 App.Cas. 525.
[36] *Oakbank Oil Co. Ltd.* v. *Crum* (1882) 10 R.(H.L.) 11; (1881) 9 R. 198.
[37] *Hoggan* v. *Tharsis Sulphur, etc., Co. Ltd.* (1882) 9 R. 1191.

dividends payable in cash may be paid by cheque or warrant sent through the post to the registered address of the shareholder, or to such person and to such address as the shareholder may in writing direct. In the absence of such a provision in the articles, the company will have to issue a fresh dividend warrant to the shareholder should the warrant first sent be lost in the post.[38]

Unless power is given in the articles, dividends declared must be paid in cash, and a shareholder can restrain the company from paying them in any other way.

A company declared a dividend and passed a resolution to pay it by giving to the shareholders debenture bonds bearing interest and redeemable at par, by an annual drawing, over thirty years. The articles empowered the company to declare a dividend "to be paid" to the shareholders. *Held*, the words "to be paid" meant paid in cash, and a shareholder suing on behalf of himself and the other shareholders could restrain the company from acting on the resolution on the ground that it contravened the articles: *Wood* v. *Odessa Waterworks Co.* (1889) 42 Ch.D. 636.

Accordingly, if it is desired to have the power to pay dividends otherwise than in cash, the articles should give such power, as they usually do.

Table A, article 120, provides: "Any general meeting declaring a dividend or bonus may direct payment of such dividend or bonus wholly or partly by the distribution of specific assets and in particular of paid-up shares, debentures or debenture stock of any other company or in any one or more of such ways."

CREATION OF RESERVE

The articles often contain provisions dealing with the creation of a reserve fund.

Table A, article 117, states: "The directors may, before recommending any dividend, set aside out of the profits of the company such sums as they think proper as a reserve or reserves which shall, at the discretion of the directors, be applicable for any purpose to which the profits of the company may be properly applied, and pending such application may, at the like discretion, either be employed in the business of the company or be invested in such investments (other than shares of the company) as the directors may from time to time think fit. The directors may also without placing the same to reserve carry forward any profits which they may think prudent not to divide."

Even without such a power in the articles a company may create a reserve, as this is a business question for the decision of the company itself.[39] "The general practice of companies certainly is not to

---

[38] See *Thairlwall* v. *Great Northern Ry.* [1910] 2 K.B. 509.
[39] *Burland* v. *Earle* [1902] A.C. 83 (P.C.). Scottish cases decided on the interpretation of articles were *Cadell* v. *Scottish Investment Trust Co. Ltd.* (1901) 9 S.L.T. 299,

divide the total profits, but to carry forward a part to make provision for meeting current liabilities."[40]

A reserve fund may at any time be distributed as dividend or employed in any other way authorised by the articles.[41] The fact that it has been used in the business does not show that it has been capitalised so as not to be available for dividend.[42]

CAPITALISATION OF PROFITS

If the articles so provide, as they usually do, a dividend may be paid by the issue to members of bonus shares credited as fully paid.

Table A, article 128, provides: "The company in general meeting may upon the recommendation of the directors resolve that it is desirable to capitalise any part of the amount for the time being standing to the credit of any of the company's reserve accounts or to the credit of the profit and loss account or otherwise available for distribution, and accordingly that such sum be set free for distribution amongst the members who would have been entitled thereto if distributed by way of dividend and in the same proportions on condition that the same be not paid in cash but be applied either in or towards paying up any amounts for the time being unpaid on any shares held by such members respectively or paying up in full unissued shares or debentures of the company to be allotted and distributed credited as fully paid up to and amongst such members in the proportion aforesaid, or partly in the one way and partly in the other, and the directors shall give effect to such resolution:

Provided that a share premium account and a capital redemption reserve fund may, for the purposes of this regulation, only be applied in the paying up of unissued shares to be issued to members of the company as fully paid bonus shares."

When profits are capitalised, instead of the shareholders getting a dividend in cash, the profits available for dividend are retained by the company and unissued shares or debentures of the company, credited as fully paid up, are allotted to the shareholders, the shares or debentures being called "bonus shares" or "bonus debentures." In such cases there is said to be a "bonus issue" but the term "bonus" is misleading, because if the shareholder had not received, *e.g.*, bonus shares, he might have received a dividend in cash. Consequently, the term "capitalisation issue" is preferable to "bonus issue." Alter-

---

affirming (1901) 8 S.L.T. 480 (O.H.) (power to carry forward profits to the next year instead of paying a larger dividend on deferred shares), and *Wemyss Collieries Trust Ltd.* v. *Melville* (1905) 8 F. 143 (transfer of profits to reserve fund instead of paying additional dividend on preference shares).

[40] *Per* Lord M'Laren in *Cadell* v. *Scottish Investment Trust Co. Ltd.* (1901) 9 S.L.T. 299 at p. 300.

[41] *e.g. Blyth's Trustees* v. *Milne* (1905) 7 F. 799.

[42] *Re Hoare & Co. Ltd.* [1904] 2 Ch. 208 (C.A.).

natively, already issued partly paid shares may be credited with a
further amount paid up. In any event, the appropriate sum will be
transferred from profit and loss account or from reserve account to
share capital account or loan capital account in the balance sheet.

If the articles authorise it, a reserve resulting from the revaluation
of capital assets, *i.e.* an unrealised increase in the value of fixed assets
due to a revaluation, made in good faith by competent valuers and
not likely to fluctuate in the short term, can be capitalised and used
to pay for bonus shares.[43]

Bonus shares

As shown above, bonus shares can be paid for out of profits
available for dividend, if the articles so provide. In addition, by
sections 56[44] and 58,[45] a share premium account and a capital
redemption reserve fund can be used to pay for unissued shares of
the company to be issued to members as fully paid bonus shares.

If bonus shares are to be issued:

(1) There must be authority in the company's articles.[46]
(2) Its nominal share capital must be sufficient.
(3) The members must resolve to capitalise profits, or to apply
the share premium account or the capital redemption reserve
fund, and to issue bonus shares.
(4) The shares must be allotted by the board in the proportions
specified in the articles, usually the same proportions as those
in which the members would have received a cash dividend.[47]
(5) A return of allotments and a contract between the members
and the company (which may be signed on the members'
behalf by the person authorised by the articles) must be
delivered to the Registrar within one month after the allotment.[48] The Jenkins Report[49] recommended that it should be
enough to file a copy of the resolution authorising the issue of
the shares credited as fully paid up.

---

[43] *Dimbula Valley (Ceylon) Tea Co. Ltd.* v. *Laurie* [1961] Ch. 353.
[44] *Ante* p. 176.
[45] *Ante* p. 222.
[46] *Wood's* case, *ante* p. 478.
[47] See Table A, article 128, *ante*.
[48] s. 52, *ante* p. 181.
[49] Para. 495.

CHAPTER 22

DEBENTURES

THIS chapter is concerned with the borrowing of money by a company where the borrowing is on debentures or on debenture stock, and with fixed and floating charges which the company may create over its property in order to secure the principal sum borrowed and interest thereon until repayment. Thus the chapter deals fully with a number of matters touched upon in Chapter 1, including registered debentures and trust deeds.

Ultra vires borrowing is also dealt with and it will be seen that here, the general law has been modified by the European Communities Act 1972, s. 9 (1).

Perhaps the most important part of the chapter is that with regard to charges and the registration of charges, particularly registration with the Registrar of Companies under section 95. It will be seen that the former differences between English law and Scots law (under which it was formerly impossible to create floating charges) have been largely removed by statute, the present statute being the Companies (Floating Charges and Receivers) (Scotland) Act, 1972.

Finally, receivers are dealt with and here it will be seen that the 1972 Act now enables a receiver to be appointed in Scotland.

A COMPANY'S POWER TO BORROW MONEY

As stated earlier,[1] the memorandum of association of a company usually contains an express power to borrow money, although a *trading* company, unless prohibited by its memorandum or articles, has implied power to borrow money for the purposes of its business, and to give security for the loan by creating a mortgage or charge over its property,[2] since such a power is incidental to the objects of a trading company. A non-trading company requires express power to borrow.

A *public* company with a share capital cannot exercise a borrow-

[1] pp. 75, 85.
[2] *General Auction Estate, etc. Co.* v. *Smith* [1891] 3 Ch. 432; *Paterson's Trustees* v. *Caledonian Heritable Security Co. Ltd.* (1885) 13 R. 369.

ing power until the requirements of section 109, *ante*,[3] have been complied with. Sometimes the borrowing powers of a company are restricted by the memorandum and articles to, *e.g.*, two-thirds of the paid-up capital of the company.

If there is nothing to the contrary in the memorandum and articles, a power to borrow by mortgage or otherwise includes the power to charge the uncalled capital of the company.[4] A power given by the memorandum to raise money upon any security of the company etc. authorises a charge on the uncalled capital.[5] In Scots law an assignation of uncalled capital in security confers no preference on the assignee unless the assignation is validly intimated to the shareholders.[6] Capital which can only be called up in the event of winding up cannot be charged as security for a loan.[7]

A company's powers to borrow and issue debentures are usually exercised by the directors, as they are under article 79 of Table A.

Table A, article 79, provides: "The directors may exercise all the powers of the company to borrow money, and to mortgage or charge its undertaking, property and uncalled capital, or any part thereof, and to issue debentures, debenture stock, and other securities whether outright or as security for any debt, liability or obligation of the company or of any third party."

Sometimes a limit is placed upon the power of the directors to borrow on behalf of the company.

Table A, article 79, provides: ". . . the amount for the time being remaining undischarged of moneys borrowed or secured by the directors . . . (apart from temporary loans obtained from the company's bankers in the ordinary course of business) shall not at any time, without the previous sanction of the company in general meeting, exceed the nominal amount of the share capital of the company for the time being issued, but nevertheless no lender or other person dealing with the company shall be concerned to see or inquire whether this limit is observed."

Obtaining an overdraft from the company's bank is borrowing.[8]

---

[3] *Ante* p. 182.
[4] *Re Pyle Works* (1890) 44 Ch.D. 534 (C.A.).
[5] *Newton* v. *Debenture-holders, etc., of Anglo-Australian Investment Co.* [1895] A.C. 244 (P.C.).
[6] *Liquidator of Union Club Ltd.* v. *Edinburgh Life Assce. Co.* (1906) 8 F. 1143; the reading out at a company meeting of a report that an assignation has been made is not a valid intimation, at least to shareholders not attending the meeting.
[7] *Re Mayfair Property Co.* [1898] 2 Ch. 28 (C.A.) (reserve liability), *ante* p. 211; *Robertson* v. *British Linen Co.* (1890) 18 R. 1225 (O.H.) (statutory guarantee fund in company limited by guarantee); contrast *Lloyds Bank Ltd.* v. *Morrison & Son*, 1927 S.C. 571 (assignation of additional independent guarantee fund held valid).
[8] *Brooks & Co.* v. *Blackburn Benefit Socy.* (1884) 9 App.Cas. 857.

Ultra vires borrowing

Under the general law

1. If there is borrowing beyond the powers of the company, *e.g.* for an *ultra vires* purpose, the position under the general law is that the borrowing and any security given for it, is void, and no ratification can render it valid. Such borrowing does not give rise to any indebtedness either at law or in equity [9] on the part of the company.[10] Consequently, no action can be brought on the contract, or in quasi-contract for money had and received. However, it will be seen later [11] that the general law rule has been modified by statute.

Even under the general law the lender has the following remedies:

(*a*) If the money borrowed has been applied in paying off debts incurred by the company *intra vires*, he ranks as a creditor to the extent to which the money has been so applied and can recover from the company.[12]

Whether this is based on the ground that the contract of loan is validated to such extent because the *ultra vires* borrowing does not increase the indebtedness of the company, or on the principle that the *ultra vires* lenders are subrogated to the rights of the legitimate creditors who have been paid off, is doubtful.[12] If the contract is validated one would expect any security given to be validated too.[12]

However, it has been held that the lender is not, in such a case, entitled to any securities or priorities of the creditors who are paid by means of his money.

A company had A, B and C debenture stock, and in issuing this stock had exhausted its borrowing powers. A bank advanced money to pay the interest on these three classes of debentures. A receiver was then appointed, who had funds in hand sufficient to pay the interest to the A stockholders, but not enough to pay the B and C stockholders in full. The bank claimed (i) that before any interest was paid to the stockholders they were entitled to be repaid their advance, (ii) alternatively that they were entitled to be repaid the sum lent by them to pay interest to the A stockholders before any payment was made to the B and C stockholders. *Held*, as the advance was not a valid one, they were not entitled to either of these claims: *Re Wrexham, etc., Rlwy. Co.* [1899] 1 Ch. 440 (C.A.).

---

[9] This distinction has no place in Scots law.
[10] *Baroness Wenlock* v. *River Dee Co.* (1885) 10 App.Cas. 354; *Sinclair* v. *Brougham* [1914] A.C. 398.
[11] p. 485.
[12] *Per* Lord Parker of Waddington in *Sinclair* v. *Brougham* at p. 441.

On the other hand, the lender may retain any securities deposited with him as security for such part of the money lent as has been applied in paying the company's debts.[13]

(b) At law, if the lender can identify his money, or any property purchased with it, he is entitled to what is known as a tracing order,[14] and can recover.[12] If tracing is impossible at law, the lender may be able to obtain an equitable tracing order.[15]

A building society started an *ultra vires* banking business. The contracts of borrowing from depositors were therefore void. In the liquidation of the society the assets were insufficient to pay the shareholders and the depositors in full after outside creditors had been paid. The depositors claimed repayment in quasi-contract on the ground that the deposits were money had and received by the society to their use. This claim failed but it was held that the mixed mass of assets in the liquidator's hands was in part shareholders' money wrongfully employed in the banking business and in part depositors' money. Each class could follow their property into the assets by an equitable tracing order, *i.e.* the assets were divided proportionately between them: *Sinclair* v. *Brougham* [1914] A.C. 398.

"A company or other statutory association cannot by itself or through an agent be party to an *ultra vires* act. If its directors or agents affecting to act on its behalf borrow money which it has no power to borrow, the money borrowed is in their hands the property of the lender. At law, therefore, the lender can recover the money, so long as he can identify it, and even if it has been employed in purchasing property, there may be cases in which, by ratifying the action of those who have so employed it, he may recover the property purchased. Equity, however, treated the matter from a different standpoint. It considered that the relationship between the directors or agents and the lenders was a fiduciary relationship, and that the money in their hands was for all practical purposes trust money. Starting from a personal equity, based on the consideration that it would be unconscionable for anyone who could not plead purchase for value without notice to retain an advantage derived from the misapplication of trust money, it ended . . . in creating what were in effect rights of property, though not recognised as such by the common law": *per* Lord Parker of Waddington in *Sinclair* v. *Brougham, ante*, at p. 441.

(c) The lender may recover damages from the directors, *e.g.* for breach of warranty of authority—unless the fact that the borrowing was *ultra vires* could have been discovered from the company's registered documents.

F. did work for the company. The company, being unable to pay cash, agreed to allot debenture stock to F. At the time, although F. was ignorant of it, all the debenture stock which the company had power to issue had already been

---

[13] *Blackburn Bdg. Socy.* v. *Cunliffe, Brooks & Co.* (1882) 22 Ch.D. 61; 9 App. Cas. 857.

[14] A term of English law.

[15] *Sinclair* v. *Brougham* [1914] A.C. 398; *Re Hallett's Estate* (1880) 13 Ch.D. 696; *Re Diplock* [1948] Ch. 465.

issued. *Held,* the defendant directors were liable on an implied warranty that they had authority to issue valid debenture stock which would be a good security and in the circumstances F. was entitled to recover as damages against the directors the par value of the debenture stock he ought to have received. F. could not know that the company had issued all the debenture stock it was authorised to issue: *Firbank's Exors.* v. *Humphreys* (1886) 18 Q.B.D. 54 (C.A.), applying *Collen* v. *Wright* (1857) 8 El. & Bl. 647; 120 E.R. 241.

A guarantee by directors that the company will repay money borrowed *ultra vires* may be binding on the directors.[16]

2. If borrowing is in excess merely of the directors' powers and not of the powers of the company, it can be ratified and rendered valid by the company in general meeting.[17]

Where such borrowing is not so ratified, if the excess consists of non-compliance with some internal regulation of the company, the lender may be able to rely on the rule in *Royal British Bank* v. *Turquand*[18] and recover the amount of the loan from the company.

Under the European Communities Act 1972, s. 9 (1)

1. We have seen[19] that the *ultra vires* doctrine has been modified by the European Communities Act 1972, s. 9 (1). If a company borrows beyond its powers from a lender who does not actually know that the borrowing is *ultra vires,* he can enforce the contract provided that it is decided upon by the directors or the managing director, although they will be in breach of duty to the company and liable accordingly.

2. As to the case where directors merely exceed their borrowing powers, it will be recalled that section 9 (1) provides, *inter alia,* that in favour of a person dealing with a company in good faith, the powers of the directors to bind the company shall be deemed free of any limitation under the memorandum or the articles, and a party to a transaction decided upon by the directors shall not be bound to inquire as to any such limitation on the powers of the directors, and shall be presumed to have acted in good faith unless the contrary is proved.

[16] *Garrard* v. *James* [1925] Ch. 616; *Heald* v. *O'Connor* [1971] 1 W.L.R. 497, *ante* p. 82.
[17] *Irvine* v. *Union Bank of Australia* (1877) 2 App.Cas. 366 (P.C.).
[18] (1856) 6 El. & Bl. 327; 119 E.R. 886, *ante* p. 411; *Gillies* v. *Craigton Garage Co. Ltd.,* 1935 S.C. 423.
[19] p. 84.

DEBENTURES AND DEBENTURE STOCK

A debenture is a document which creates or acknowledges a debt due from a company. Such document need not be, although it usually is, under seal, it need not give, although it usually does give, a charge on the assets of the company by way of security, and it may or may not be one of a series.[20] Thus debentures may be (1) secured, or (2) unsecured. A debenture is always for a specified sum, *e.g.* £100, which can only be transferred in its entirety. As will be seen, debentures may be collaterally secured by a trust deed.[21] Convertible debentures, *i.e.* debentures which the holder has the right to convert, at stated times, into shares in the company, have already been mentioned.[22]

It may be helpful to mention here that some of the differences between shares and debentures are:

(1) The holder of a debenture is a creditor, not a member, of the company; a shareholder is a member.[23]
(2) Debentures may be issued at a discount; shares may not be.[24]
(3) A company may purchase its own debentures; it must not purchase its own shares.[25]
(4) Interest at the specified rate on debentures may be paid out of capital; dividends on shares must be paid out of profits.[26]

The Companies Act 1948, s. 455, defines "debenture" as including debenture stock, bonds, and any other securities[27] of a company whether constituting a charge on the assets of the company or not. A mortgage of land by a company is a debenture.[28]

Debenture stock is borrowed money consolidated into one mass for the sake of convenience. This is normally done by a trust deed,[21] which may give the trustees a charge on the company's property. Where there is no charge, debenture stock is commonly called unsecured loan stock. The main advantage of debenture stock is that it is transferable in fractional amounts, although the trust deed may

---

[20] See *Lemon* v. *Austin Friars Investment Trust Ltd.* [1926] Ch. 1 (C.A.).
[21] *Post* p. 488.
[22] See *Mosely* v. *Koffyfontein Mines* [1904] 2 Ch. 108, *ante* p. 175.
[23] *Ante* p. 36.
[24] *Ante* p. 174.
[25] *Ante* p. 190; *post* p. 496.
[26] *Ante* p. 468.
[27] "Securities," as used in s. 455, does not include shares.
[28] *Knightsbridge Estates Trust Ltd.* v. *Byrne* [1904] A.C. 613, *post* p. 497.

specify the minimum fractional amount which can be transferred. Again, the debenture stockholders will be given simple debenture stock certificates instead of debentures.

ISSUE OF DEBENTURES

As we saw earlier in this chapter,[29] debentures are issued in accordance with the provisions of the articles, usually by a resolution of the board of directors.

Debentures cannot be issued to persons resident outside the Scheduled Territories without Treasury consent.[30]

Debenture prospectuses and offers for sale were dealt with in Chapter 7.[31]

When debentures have been issued, the prospectus cannot be looked at to ascertain the contract, but if the contract was intended to be contained in the prospectus and the debenture together, or if the prospectus contains a collateral contract the consideration for which was the taking up of the debentures, the prospectus can be looked at.[32]

Debentures or debenture stock certificates must be completed and ready for delivery within two months after allotment or after the lodging of a transfer, unless the conditions of issue otherwise provide: section 80.

There is no objection to the issue of debentures at a discount[33] but when any commission, allowance or discount has been paid or made to any person in consideration of his subscribing or procuring subscriptions for debentures, particulars of the amount or rate of the commission or discount must be sent to the Registrar within 21 days. The omission to do this does not, however, affect the validity of the debentures. The deposit of debentures as security for a debt of the company does not, for this purpose, amount to the issue of debentures at a discount: sections 95 (9) and 106A (8).

A contract to take up debentures may be enforced by specific performance: section 92. This section provides an exception to the

---

[29] p. 482.
[30] Exchange Control Act 1947, Pt. III, *ante* p. 97.
[31] *Ante* p. 130; for an action of damages by a debenture holder against a promoter on the ground that by false and fraudulent representations of the promoter he had been induced to advance money to the company, see *Dunnett* v. *Mitchell* (1885) 12 R. 400.
[32] *Jacobs* v. *Batavia and General Plantations Trust Ltd.* [1924] 2 Ch. 329 (C.A.).
[33] *Ante* p. 175.

rule, laid down in *South African Territories Ltd*. v. *Wallington*,[34] that specific performance will not be granted of a contract to lend money since damages are an adequate remedy for breach of such contract.

Apart from the section, an agreement to issue debentures made in consideration of an actual advance of money has the effect in English law of putting the lender in equity in the same position as if the debentures had actually been issued.

A syndicate agreed to sell goods to a company on the terms that, as part payment, £3,000 debentures charged upon all the company's assets were issued. On this agreement the syndicate allowed the company to remove the goods, which were subsequently taken in execution by F. *Held*, although no debentures were actually issued, the syndicate was in the same position as if they had been and so F. was entitled subject to the charge: *Simultaneous Colour Printing Syndicate* v. *Foweraker* [1901] 1 K.B. 771.

TRUST DEEDS

Debentures and debenture stock are usually secured by a trust deed.[35]

Contents of a trust deed

The main terms of a *debenture trust deed* are:

(1) A covenant by the company for payment to the debenture holders of the principal moneys and interest.

(2) Clauses giving the trustees a legal mortgage by demise of the company's freeholds and leaseholds, which are specified,[36] and a floating charge over the rest of the undertaking and property.

(3) A clause specifying the events in which the security is to become enforceable, *e.g.* default in the payment of interest or principal moneys, order made or resolution passed for winding up, appointment of a receiver, cessation of business, breach of covenant by the company.

(4) A clause giving the trustees power to take possession of the property charged when the security becomes enforceable, to carry on the business and to sell the property charged and to apply the net sale moneys in payment of the principal and interest and to pay the balance to the company.

[34] [1898] A.C. 309.   [35] *Ante* p. 486.
[36] In Scotland security over specified heritable property would be created by the execution of a standard security which would be referred to in the trust deed.

(5) Power for the trustees to concur with the company in dealings with the property charged.

(6) Covenants by the company to keep a register of debenture holders, to insure and to keep in repair the property charged.

(7) Provision for meetings of debenture holders.

(8) Power for the trustees to appoint a receiver when the security becomes enforceable.

(9) Provision for serving notices on the debenture holders by post.

A *debenture stock trust deed*, in addition to containing the foregoing terms, constitutes the stock by acknowledging that the company is indebted to the trustees in a specified sum and provides for the issue of debenture stock certificates.

A trust deed usually contains a clause providing that the rights of the debenture holders against the company or any property charged by the deed may be modified or compromised by extraordinary resolution of the debenture holders.

Clause 37 of the Companies Bill 1973 would have provided that where, in the case of debentures forming part of a series issued by a company and ranking *pari passu* with other debentures of the series, or debenture stock, the debentures or the trust deed provide for meetings of the holders of the debentures or stock then, subject thereto, sections 132 (convening of meeting on requisition), 135 (power of court to order meeting), 136 (proxies), 137 (2) (right to demand a poll) and 138 (voting on a poll) apply.[37]

Advantages of a trust deed

The advantages of a trust deed are:

(1) The trustees will have a legal mortgage[38] over the company's land, so that persons who subsequently lend money to the company cannot gain priority over the debenture holders or debenture stockholders.

(2) Events are specified on the happening of which the principal moneys and interest become payable, *e.g.* non-payment of interest or non-performance of the covenants in the deed; the appointment of trustees, who are usually paid, ensures that there are definite persons whose duty it is to take action on the happening of these events.

---

[37] *Ante* pp. 287, 288, 300, 301.
[38] In Scotland a fixed security.

(3) The company is given a number of powers over the property mortgaged which it can exercise with the consent of the trustees, *e.g.* powers of sale, exchange or leasing. This enables the company to use the property advantageously for the purposes of its business without prejudicing the interests of the debenture holders or debenture stockholders.

(4) Covenants are entered into by the company for insurance, repair and other matters, and can be enforced by the trustees.

(5) Power is given to the trustees to appoint a receiver or to enter into possession of the property and carry on the business of the company in case of urgency.

Liability of trustees

Trustees for debenture holders are in the same position towards their beneficiaries as any other trustees, and cannot purchase the debentures, the subject of the deed, without making full disclosure of all the information relating to them which is in their possession.[39] Any provision in a trust deed, or in a contract with the holders of debentures secured by a trust deed, for exempting the trustees from, or indemnifying them against, liability for breach of trust where they fail to show the degree of care and diligence required of them as trustees, is void, except that the trustees may be released from liability by a release given after the liability has arisen, and a provision in a trust deed for the giving of such a release by a majority of not less than three-fourths in value of the debenture holders present and voting in person or by proxy at a meeting summoned for the purpose is not void: section 88. (Contrast section 205 *ante*[40] as regards officers and auditors.)

Section 448 (power of court to grant relief) *ante*[41] does not apply to the trustees although the Trustee Act 1925, s. 61, and the Trusts (Scotland) Act 1921, s. 32, do, and so in an appropriate case the court may relieve the trustees from liability.

Right to copy of trust deed

A debenture holder is entitled to require a copy of the trust deed on payment of 20p in the case of a printed trust deed or 10p per 100

---

[39] *Re Magadi Soda Co.* (1925) 41 T.L.R. 297.
[40] p. 354.   [41] p. 355.

words or part thereof in other cases: 1948 Act, s. 87 (3); 1967 Act, s. 52 (1).

REGISTERED DEBENTURES

Debentures or debenture stock may be payable to either (1) the registered holder; or (2) the bearer.

Contents of a registered debenture

Where there is a trust deed, the usual form of debenture payable to the registered holder is a document issued under the seal of the company and containing two clauses. The clauses are as follows:

(*a*) The company for valuable consideration received covenants to pay the registered holder the principal sum on a specified day or on such earlier day as it becomes payable under the indorsed conditions, and in the meantime to pay interest by equal half-yearly payments on specified dates at a specified rate.

(*b*) The debenture is said to be issued subject to and with the benefit of the conditions indorsed thereon.

The indorsed conditions usually include the following:

(i) The debenture is said to be one of a series, each for securing a specified sum.

(ii) The registered holders of all the debentures of the issue are said to be entitled *pari passu* to the benefit and subject to the provisions of the trust deed, the date of execution of which and the parties to which are specified, and the charges conferred by the trust deed are recited.

This has the effect of putting all the debentures of the issue on an equal footing; in the absence of such a clause the debentures would rank according to the order in which they were executed.[42]

(iii) The company is empowered, at any time after a specified date, by giving not less than a specified number of months' notice, to pay off the principal moneys secured with interest to the date of payment.

---

[42] *Gartside* v. *Silkstone and Dodworth Coal, etc., Co.* (1882) 21 Ch.D. 762.

(iv) Provision is made for keeping a register of debenture holders at the registered office. We shall see that this will comply with section 86 and that a right of inspection is given by section 87.[43]

(v) The company is not to be bound to recognise anyone as having any title to the debenture except the registered holder, or his personal representative, and is not to be bound to enter notice of any trust in the register.

Section 117 of the Act, which provides that trusts are not to be entered on the register of members, does not apply to the register of debenture holders, and consequently such a clause is necessary. If the company does receive notice of a trust, the clause relieves it from the obligation of entering it on the register, but if it deals with the debentures as a trader, *e.g.* by advancing money on them, after notice of a trust, it will be bound by that trust.[44]

(vi) Transfer of the debenture is provided for. Every transfer must be in writing, as will be explained later.

(vii) Equities or, in Scots law, rights of compensation, between the company and any person other than the registered holder are excluded. This will be explained later.[45]

(viii) The principal moneys and interest are made payable at the company's registered office or at its bankers.

If this clause is not inserted it is the company's duty to follow the usual rule and seek out its creditor and pay him.

F. held 18 £100 debentures repayable in June, 1913, in the M. Corporation. Before the date of redemption F. died, and her executors neglected to present the debentures to the company for payment. In June, 1916, the company was sued for principal and interest. *Held*, as the debentures contained no clause to the effect set out above, it was the company's duty to seek out the debenture holder and pay her; as this had not been done, the company was liable to pay the principal with interest until the date of actual payment: *Fowler* v. *Midland Electric Corpn.* [1917] 1 Ch. 656 (C.A.).

(ix) The company is empowered to purchase any of the debentures of the issue at any time.

(x) Interest is made payable by warrant on the company's bank

---

[43] *Post* p. 494.
[44] *Bradford Banking Co.* v. *Briggs & Co.* (1886) 12 App.Cas. 29; *Mackereth* v. *Wigan Coal Co. Ltd.* [1910] 2 Ch. 293, *ante* pp. 275, 276.
[45] *Post* p. 494.

payable to the order of the registered holder and sent by post to his registered address.

(xi) The principal moneys are made immediately payable if the company defaults in the payment of interest for a specified number of months, or if a winding-up order is made or resolution passed, or if the security constituted by the trust deed becomes enforceable and the trustees enforce it.

The debenture holder is entitled to repayment of his principal on the company's going into liquidation, whether or not the date fixed for repayment has arrived.[46]

Transfer of registered debentures

Registered debentures are transferred in the manner laid down in the indorsed conditions (which usually require a transfer to be in writing under the hand of the registered holder or of his personal representatives) or by a stock transfer under the Stock Transfer Act 1963. As in the case of a transfer of shares[47] it is unlawful for a company to register a transfer of debentures unless a "proper instrument of transfer" has been delivered to the company: section 75.

The company must have the debenture or debenture stock certificate ready for delivery within two months of the lodging of the instrument of transfer unless the conditions of issue otherwise provide: section 80. If registration of a transfer is refused, notice of refusal must be given to the transferee within two months: section 78.

Registered debentures are in England choses in action, and in Scotland incorporeal moveable property to the assignation of which the rule *assignatus utitur jure auctoris* ("the assignee acquires no higher right than his cedent had") applies. They are not negotiable instruments, and consequently a transferee takes them subject to all claims which the company may have against prior holders at the date of the transfer.

After a receiver had been appointed and a winding-up petition had been presented, P., a debenture stockholder, transferred £10,000 debenture stock to X, who was registered as the owner. P. was also a director of the company and a claim was made against him for money had and received by him while a director. *Held*, X was not entitled to payment until the amount due from P. to the company had been ascertained and deducted: *Re Rhodesia Goldfields Ltd.* [1910] 1 Ch. 239.

[46] *Hodson* v. *Tea Co.* (1880) 14 Ch.D. 859.
[47] *Ante* p. 254 *et seq.*

To avoid this result, the indorsed conditions usually provide that the principal and interest shall be paid to the registered holder without regard to any equities or rights of compensation existing between the company and any prior holder of the debenture. Such a clause amounts to a contract by the company that it will not rely on equities or rights of compensation, and its effect is to make the debentures more marketable.

A company was in liquidation. C., who had been a director of the company, transferred debentures to R. as security for a loan. The debentures contained a clause similar to that set out above. It was then discovered that C. had been guilty of misfeasance and he was ordered to pay a sum of money to the liquidator in respect thereof. The liquidator refused to register R.'s transfer. *Held*, the right to transfer and to have the transfer registered was not affected by the winding up, and R. was entitled to payment without regard to C.'s debt to the company: *Re Goy & Co. Ltd.* [1900] 2 Ch. 149.

A transferee cannot claim the benefit of such a clause unless and until he is registered.

B. held debentures containing a clause similar to that set out above. After a resolution for winding up had been passed he transferred them for value to C., who took without notice of any defect in B.'s title. Notice of transfer but no request for registration was given to the liquidator. C. claimed payment but the court found that B. had paid nothing for the debentures and had obtained them by misrepresentation. *Held*, notwithstanding the clause, C. took subject to the company's claim against B. *Re Goy & Co.*, *ante*, was distinguished on the ground that when the transfer in that case was sent for registration the company was not aware of and was not setting up any equities between itself and the transferor: *Re Palmer's Decoration and Furnishing Co.* [1904] 2 Ch. 743.

Section 79 (certification of transfers) *ante*[47a] applies to transfers of debentures as well as to transfers of shares.

Register of debenture holders

A company registered in England must not keep its register of debenture holders in Scotland, and vice versa. The register must be kept at the registered office or at any other office of the company where it is made up or, if it is made up by an agent, it may be kept at the agent's office: section 86. Debenture holders and shareholders in the company may, without fee, inspect the register of debenture holders subject to such reasonable restrictions as the company may in general meeting impose, so that no less than two hours a day is allowed for inspection. Other persons may inspect the register on

[47a] p. 259.

payment of a fee of 5p. The register may be closed for not more than 30 days in any year. A copy may be demanded on payment of 20p for every 100 words or part thereof: 1948 Act, s. 87; 1967 Act, s. 52 (1).

Clause 81 of the Companies Bill 1973 would have allowed a company to use a computer to keep the register of debenture holders.

The Jenkins Report[48] recommended that a company which issues a series of debentures ranking *pari passu* or debenture stock not transferable by delivery should be required to keep a register of the holders. At present a company is not required to keep a register of debenture holders.

Clause 35 of the 1973 Bill would have required a register to be kept in Great Britain.

BEARER DEBENTURES

Debentures payable to bearer are in the same form as registered debentures except that they are expressed to be made payable to bearer and coupons for the interest are attached. The indorsed conditions are also in the same form with the necessary modifications for bearer, instead of registered, instruments.

Bearer debentures are negotiable instruments and consequently a transferee in good faith and for value takes them free from any defects in the title of a prior holder.

The B. Company owned some bearer debentures and kept them in a safe. The secretary fraudulently took them from the safe and deposited them with the bank, who took them in good faith and as security for advances to the secretary. *Held*, the debentures were negotiable instruments transferable by delivery and the bank was entitled to them as against the B. Company: *Bechuanaland Exploration Co.* v. *London Trading Bank* [1898] 2 Q.B. 658.

The courts take judicial notice of the fact that bearer debentures are negotiable instruments.[49]

Bearer debentures are transferable by delivery and no stamp duty is payable on transfer. Interest is payable by means of the coupons which are cut off and presented for payment to the company's bankers when the date of payment arrives.

Treasury consent is necessary for the issue of bearer debentures

---

[48] Para. 306.
[49] *Edelstein* v. *Schuler* [1902] 2 K.B. 144.

and bearer debentures must be deposited with an authorised depositary.[50]

Debentures to bearer issued in Scotland are expressly declared by section 93 of the 1948 Act to be valid and binding notwithstanding anything in the Blank Bonds and Trusts Act 1696 (Scots Act 1696 c. 25).[51]

REDEEMABLE DEBENTURES

Debentures may be (1) redeemable at the option of the company, or (2) irredeemable or perpetual.

Sometimes debentures are issued on the terms that the company is bound to redeem a certain number each year by "drawings" (in which case, in effect, the numbers of the debentures to be redeemed are drawn out of a hat),[52] or that it may purchase, *e.g.* on the Stock Exchange, or that it is bound to set aside a sinking fund for redemption purposes on a specified date. When debentures have been so redeemed, section 90 empowers the company to reissue them or issue other debentures in their place, unless—

(a) the company, in its articles or otherwise, has contracted not to reissue them; or

(b) the company has shown an intention to cancel the debentures by passing a resolution to that effect, or by some other act.

Under the general law, once a debenture was transferred to the company the debt was absolutely gone and the security ceased to exist.[53]

On a reissue of redeemed debentures, the person entitled to them has the same priorities as if the debentures had never been redeemed: section 90. The date of redemption of the reissued debentures cannot be later than that of the original debentures.[54]

Particulars of any redeemed debentures which can be reissued must be included in the balance sheet: Schedule 8 as amended, paragraph 2 (*d*).

Reissued debentures are treated as new debentures for the purpose of stamp duty: section 90.

---

[50] Exchange Control Act 1947, Part III.   [51] *Ante* p. 269.
[52] For difficulties which may arise from the company's inability to trace the holders to whom repayment is due, see *United Collieries Ltd.* v. *Lord Advocate*, 1950 S.C. 458.
[53] *Re George Routledge & Sons Ltd.*, [1904] 2 Ch. 474.
[54] *Re Antofagasta (Chile) and Bolivia Ry. Co.'s Trust Deed* [1939] Ch. 732.

PERPETUAL DEBENTURES

Debentures are not invalid merely because they are made irredeemable, or redeemable on the happening of a contingency, however remote, *e.g.* the winding up of the company, or on the expiration of a period, however long, *e.g.* 100 years after the issue of the debentures, *i.e.* the legal or contractual date for redemption may be postponed, despite any rule of equity to the contrary: section 89.

A company mortgaged 75 houses and other properties to secure £310,000 repayable by instalments over 40 years. There was no right of redemption before the 40 years expired. *Held*, the mortgage was a debenture and valid under what is now section 89: *Knightsbridge Estates Trust Ltd.* v. *Byrne* [1940] A.C. 613.

The issue of perpetual debentures amounts to the granting of a perpetual annuity.[55] If the debentures are secured by a floating charge, the money secured will become payable on the company's going into liquidation and the security will be enforceable on the class of assets charged as it exists at that time.[56]

In English law, subject to section 89 *ante*, the equitable doctrine against clogging the equity of redemption applies to a floating charge securing debentures. The debentures may, however, provide for a collateral advantage for the debenture holder, to endure after the debentures have been paid off, provided it is not (a) unfair and unconscionable; or (b) in the nature of a penalty clogging the equity of redemption; or (c) inconsistent with the contractual or equitable right to redeem.[57]

By an agreement dated August 24, 1910, a firm of woolbrokers agreed to lend a company carrying on the business of meat preservers £10,000 with interest at six per cent. per annum. If interest was punctually paid the loan was not repayable until September 30, 1915, but the company might repay at any time on giving one month's notice. The loan was secured by a floating charge on the undertaking and property of the company. The agreement stipulated that for five years from the date thereof the company should not sell sheepskins to anyone other than the lenders so long as the lenders were willing to buy at the best price offered by anyone else. The loan was repaid in January 1913, whereupon the lenders claimed to exercise their option of pre-emption. *Held*, the stipulation for the option was a collateral advantage entered into as a condition of the company obtaining the loan; it was not a clog on the equity of redemption or repugnant to the right to redeem; and the lenders were entitled to an injunction restraining the company from selling sheepskins to anyone else: *Kreglinger* v. *New Patagonia Meat etc. Co. Ltd.* [1914] A.C. 25.

[55] *Re The Southern Brazilian Rio Grande do Sul Ry. Co. Ltd.* [1905] 2 Ch. 78.
[56] *Hodson* v. *Tea Co.* (1880) 14 Ch.D. 859.
[57] *Kreglinger* v. *New Patagonia Meat, etc., Co. Ltd.* [1914] A.C. 25.

In Scotland, the Conveyancing and Feudal Reform (Scotland) Act 1970, ss. 11 and 18, conferred on the debtor in a standard security the right, which could not be varied by agreement, to redeem the security on giving two months' notice. The Redemption of Standard Securities (Scotland) Act 1971, however, amended the 1970 Act on this point by providing that the condition relating to the debtor's right of redemption might be varied by agreement. The 1971 Act also, for the avoidance of doubt, declared that the provisions of the 1970 Act relating to the standard security do not affect the operation of section 89 of the 1948 Act.

CHARGES SECURING DEBENTURES

A charge on the assets of a company given by a debenture or a trust deed in order to secure money borrowed by the company may be either (1) a specific or fixed charge, or (2) a floating charge. If the debentures are issued in a series and give a specific charge on the company's property, *e.g.* its land, they are always secured by means of a trust deed. The trust deed usually gives a floating charge, *e.g.* on the rest of the company's property, in addition to the fixed charge.

Debentures secured by a fixed charge on the company's assets are often called "mortgage debentures." The Stock Exchange will not list debentures as "Mortgage Debentures" unless they are secured by a specific mortgage or charge.[58]

Fixed charges (English law)

A fixed charge is a mortgage of ascertained and definite property, *e.g.* a legal or an equitable mortgage of a specified factory, and prevents the company from realising that property, *i.e.* disposing of it free from the charge, without the consent of the holders of the charge.

Floating charges (English law)

In *Re Yorkshire Woolcombers Association Ltd.*[59] Romer L.J. said that if a charge has the three characteristics set out below it is a floating charge:

[58] Rules of The Stock Exchange, App. 34, Sched. VII, Pt. B.
[59] [1903] 2 Ch. 284 (C.A.) at p. 295.

(1) it is a charge on a class of assets of a company, present and future;

(2) which class is, in the ordinary course of the company's business, changing from time to time;

(3) it is contemplated by the charge that, until the holders of the charge take steps to enforce it, the company may carry on business in the ordinary way as far as concerns the class of assets charged.

Thus a floating charge is an equitable charge on some or all of the present and future property of a company, *e.g.* the company's undertaking, *i.e.* all its property, present and future.[60] It is effective as to future property only when that property is acquired by the company. The company may, in the ordinary course of business, realise property which is subject to the charge. However, when the security is enforceable, *i.e.* there is default with regard to payment of interest or repayment of the principal sum, and the debenture holders or the trustees enforce it, *e.g.* they appoint a receiver of the property charged,[61] the floating charge is said to crystallise, *i.e.* it becomes a fixed charge on the assets in the class charged at the time of crystallisation or, where the floating charge so provides, assets which come to the company after crystallisation.[62] Crystallisation also occurs on the commencement of the winding up of the company, even if it is a voluntary winding up for the purpose of reconstruction,[63] or when the company ceases business.

The characteristics of a floating charge are therefore:

(1) It is an equitable charge on assets for the time being of the company.[64]

(2) It attaches to the class of assets charged in the varying condition in which they happen to be from time to time,[64] *i.e.* it does not fasten on any definite property but is a charge on property which is constantly changing.

(3) It remains dormant until the undertaking charged ceases to be a going concern, or until the person in whose favour it is created intervenes. His right to intervene may be suspended by agreement but if there is no agreement for suspension he

---

[60] *Re Panama, etc., Royal Mail Co.* (1870) L.R. 5 Ch.App. 318.
[61] *Post* p. 519.
[62] *N. W. Robbie & Co. Ltd.* v. *Whitney Warehouse Co. Ltd.* [1963] 1 W.L.R. 1324 (C.A.); *Ferrier* v. *Bottomer* (1972) 126 C.L.R. 597.
[63] *Re Crompton & Co.* [1914] 1 Ch. 954.
[64] *Per* Lord Macnaghten in *Governments Stock Investment Co. Ltd.* v. *Manilla Ry. Co. Ltd.* [1897] A.C. 81 at p. 86.

may intervene whenever he pleases after default.[63] When this happens the charge is said to crystallise and become fixed.[65]

(4) Although it is an immediate and continuing charge, until it becomes fixed the company can, without consent, deal with the class of assets in the ordinary course of business, *e.g.* it has been held that a company can sell all or any of its business or property for shares or debentures of another company if the memorandum gives it power to do so, and the debenture holders cannot prevent such a sale if the company remains a going concern[66]; similarly, a company with three businesses may sell one of the three.[67]

Where, before crystallisation of a floating charge over all the company's assets and undertaking, the company contracted to sell goods to a buyer to whom it owed money under a previous contract, and the goods were delivered after crystallisation, the company's right to sue for the debt due to it was embraced, when it arose, by the floating charge, but the debenture holder could not be in a better position to assert the rights under the previous contract than the company.[68]

The advantage of a floating charge from the *company's* point of view is that the company can give security for a loan to it by charging property which changes in the course of business and over which it is impracticable to create a fixed charge, *e.g.* the company's stock-in-trade. Further, until crystallisation the company can carry on business in the ordinary way.

A floating charge can be created only by a registered company and not by a partnership or a sole trader. One reason is that such a charge created by a firm over chattels would be a bill of sale within the Bills of Sale Acts 1878 and 1882, and would have to be registered and, as a mortgage bill, would have to be in the statutory form and specify the chattels, which is impossible.[69]

From the *chargee's* point of view, an important advantage is that, upon crystallisation of the floating charge, the chargee obtains

---

[66] *Evans* v. *Rival Granite Quarries Ltd.* [1910] 2 K.B. 979 (C.A.).
[66] *Re Borax Co.* [1901] 1 Cn. 326.
[67] *Re H. H. Vivian & Co. Ltd.* [1900] 2 Ch. 654.
[68] *Rother Iron Works Ltd.* v. *Canterbury Precision Engines Ltd.* [1974] Q.B. 1 (C.A.) applied in *George Barker (Transport) Ltd.* v. *Eynon* [1974] 1 W.L.R. 462 (C.A.).
[69] Gower, *Modern Company Law*, 3rd ed., p. 79. An instrument executed by a registered society whose registered office is in England or Wales and which creates a fixed or floating charge on its assets is not a bill of sale if an appropriate application for recording is made: Industrial and Provident Societies Act 1967.

priority in the payment of debts over unsecured creditors. However, there is a number of disadvantages attached to a floating charge. For example:

(1) As will be seen, a floating charge is postponed to certain other interests.

(2) A floating charge may be invalidated under section 322, *post*.[70]

Priority of charges (English law)

A company which has created a floating charge cannot later create another floating charge over some of the same assets ranking in priority to or *pari passu* with the original charge unless the provisions of the original charge allow this.[71]

On the other hand, since a company which has created a floating charge can, without the consent of the holders of the charge, deal with the class of assets in the ordinary course of business, it follows that the company can, in the ordinary course of business, create a later fixed charge, legal or equitable, over specific assets and with priority over the floating charge,[72] unless the floating charge provides that the company is not to create any mortgage or charge ranking *pari passu* with or in priority to the floating charge, in which case any fixed chargee taking *with notice of this provision* will be postponed to the floating charge. In spite of such a provision the holder of a specific charge will obtain priority over a floating charge on all the company's property if:

(1) taking a legal mortgage, he obtains his mortgage without notice of the provision, even though he has notice of the debentures[73]—the maxim "where the equities are equal the law prevails" will apply; or

(2) taking an equitable mortgage, he obtains the title deeds without notice of the debentures[74]—the maxim "where the equities are otherwise equal the earlier in time has priority" will not apply since the debenture holders left the title deeds

---

[70] *Post* p. 506.
[71] *Re Automatic Bottle Makers Ltd.* [1926] Ch. 412 (C.A.).
[72] *Wheatley* v. *Silkstone, etc., Coal Co.* (1885) 29 Ch.D. 715.
[73] *English and Scottish Mercantile, etc., Co. Ltd.* v. *Brunton* [1892] 2 Q.B. 700 (C.A.).
[74] *Re Castell & Brown Ltd.* [1898] 1 Ch. 315.

with the company so as to enable it to deal with its property as if it was incumbered so that the equities are not equal.

Further, registration of a floating charge under the Companies Acts, *post*,[75] although constructive notice of the charge, is not notice that the charge contains a provision prohibiting the creation of subsequent charges with priority over the floating charge.[76]

The following also have priority over a floating charge:

(1) an execution creditor if the goods are sold by the sheriff,[77] or the company pays out the sheriff to avoid a sale,[78] or the creditor obtains a garnishee order absolute[79] (not a garnishee order nisi)[80], *before* crystallisation of the floating charge;
(2) a landlord's distress for rent levied before crystallisation[81];
(3) the rights of persons such as one who has sold goods to the company under a hire-purchase agreement by which the goods are still the property of such person;[82]
(4) *after* crystallisation, certain *un*secured but preferential debts: sections 94, 319, *post*.[83]

Fixed securities and floating charges (Scots law)

Before 1961 any attempt by a Scottish company to create a floating charge was of no effect, since such a charge violated the principle of the common law expressed in the maxim "*traditionibus, non nudis pactis, dominia rerum transferuntur*," *i.e.* "delivery, and not mere agreement, is required for the transfer of real rights."

"There is no principle more deeply rooted in the law than this, that in order to create a good security over subjects delivery must be given. If possession be retained no effectual security can be granted": *per* Lord Shand in *Clark* v. *West Calder Oil Co. Ltd.* (1882) 9 R. 1017 at p. 1033 (a case in which trustees for debenture holders to whom the company had assigned certain leasehold and moveable property in security were held to have no preference over the ordinary trade creditors of the company since no possession had followed on the assignation).

[75] p. 508 *et seq.*
[76] *Per* Eve J. in *Wilson* v. *Kelland* [1910] 2 Ch. 306 at p. 313; *Dempsey* v. *Traders' Finance Corpn.* [1933] N.Z.L.R. 1258 (C.A.).
[77] *Re Standard Manufacturing Co.* [1891] 1 Ch. 627 (C.A.).
[78] *Heaton and Dugard Ltd.* v. *Cutting Bros. Ltd.* [1925] 1 K.B. 655.
[79] *Evans* v. *Rival Granite Quarries Ltd.* [1910] 2 K.B. 979 (C.A.).
[80] *Norton* v. *Yates* [1906] 1 K.B. 112.
[81] *Re Roundwood Colliery Co.* [1897] 1 Ch. 373 (C.A.).
[82] See *Re Morrison, Jones and Taylor Ltd.* [1914] 1 Ch. 50 (C.A.).
[83] pp. 526, 592.

"The whole method of creating a floating charge . . . is absolutely foreign to our law": *per* Lord President Dunedin in *The Ballachulish Slate Quarries Co. Ltd.* v. *Bruce* (1908) 16 S.L.T. 48 at p. 51 (an attempt to create a floating charge in English form on the uncalled capital and other assets of a company was held to give a debenture holder no valid security).

A company registered in Scotland and having a place of business and assets in England borrowed money under debentures which were in English form and by which the company purported to create a floating charge over its whole undertaking, property and assets. *Held*, that no valid and effectual floating charge had been created even over the company's assets in England: *Carse* v. *Coppen*, 1951 S.C. 233.

"It is clear in principle and amply supported by authority that a floating charge is utterly repugnant to the principles of Scots law and is not recognised by us as creating a security at all. In Scotland the term 'equitable security' is meaningless. Putting aside the rare and exceptional cases of hypothec, we require for the constitution of a security which will confer upon the holder rights over and above those which he enjoys in common with the general body of unsecured creditors of a debtor, (*a*) the transfer to the creditor of a real right in specific subjects by the method appropriate for the constitution of such rights in the particular classes of property in question, or (*b*) the creation of a nexus over specific property by the due use of the appropriate form of diligence. A floating charge, even after appointment of a receiver, satisfies none of these requirements": *er* Lord President Cooper at p. 239.

Floating charges were introduced to Scots law by the Companies (Floating Charges) (Scotland) Act 1961, but there was no power under that Act to appoint receivers. Subsequently, on the recommendation of the Scottish Law Commission,[84] the Companies (Floating Charges and Receivers) (Scotland) Act 1972 was passed with the twofold purpose of:

(1) re-enacting with substantial modification the provisions of the Act of 1961; and

(2) making it competent under Scots law for receivers to be appointed.

Scottish floating charges and receivers have statutory definitions and statutory incidents which distinguish them in some respects from their English common law originals. The term "fixed security" is used in the statutory provisions to denote a security other than a floating charge.[85]

In the two following subdivisions of this chapter the sections referred to are, except where there is a statement to the contrary, those of the Companies (Floating Charges and Receivers) (Scotland) Act 1972.

[84] *Report on the Companies* (*Floating Charges*) (*Scotland*) *Act 1961*, (1970) Cmnd. 4336.
[85] Companies (Floating Charges and Receivers) (Scotland) Act 1972, s. 31.

Floating charges (Scots law)

The main characteristics of the Scottish floating charge are:

(1) It is a charge created by an incorporated company [86] "over all or any part of the property (including uncalled capital) which may from time to time be comprised in its property and undertaking."

(2) It may be created for the purpose of securing any debt or other obligation (including a cautionary obligation) incurred or to be incurred by, or binding upon, the company or any other person. It is therefore possible, for instance, for a subsidiary company to create a floating charge over its own property to secure a debt due by its parent company (another person), or for a subsidiary company to guarantee a debt due by its parent company and create a floating charge over its own property to secure its liability under the guarantee.

(3) On the commencement of the winding up or on the appointment of a receiver it attaches (provided it is not invalid under section 106A [87] or section 322 [88] of the 1948 Act) to the property then comprised in the company's property and undertaking.

The term "crystallisation" is not a statutory term in relation to the Scottish floating charge.

(4) Once attached it has the same effect as if it were a fixed security over the property for the principal of, and any interest due or to become due on, the debt or obligation to which it relates. The security extends to interest stipulated for from the date of attachment until payment. [89]

(5) It is postponed to the rights of certain creditors [90]: section 1.

(6) It can be created by a Scottish company only by the execution, under the seal of the company, of an instrument or bond or other written acknowledgment of debt or obligation which purports to create a floating charge. There is no longer any

[86] Floating charges may also be created by industrial and provident societies registered in Scotland: Industrial and Provident Societies Act 1967, as amended by the Companies (Floating Charges and Receivers) (Scotland) Act 1972, s. 10.
[87] *Post* p. 516.
[88] *Post* p. 506.
[89] *National Commercial Bank of Scotland Ltd.* v. *Liquidators of Telford Grier Mackay & Co. Ltd.*, 1969 S.C. 181, followed in *Royal Bank of Scotland Ltd.* v. *Williamson*, 1972 S.L.T. (Sh.Ct.) 45, and given statutory force by s. 1 (4).
[90] *Post* p. 506.

statutory form as there was under the 1961 Act. An alternative to execution by the company itself is execution by an attorney who has been authorised for that purpose by writing under the company's common seal: section 2.

The document creating a floating charge may contain:

(*a*) provisions prohibiting or restricting the creation of any fixed security or any other floating charge having priority over, or ranking equally with, the floating charge; or

(*b*) provisions regulating the order in which the floating charge is to rank with any other subsisting or future floating charges or fixed security over the property or part of it: section 5.

A floating charge may be altered by an instrument of alteration: section 7.

The advantage of a floating charge from the *company's* point of view is that the company can give security for a loan to it by charging property such as stock-in-trade and other moveables which it would be impracticable to deliver to the lender. Until the floating charge has attached to the property the company can, in the ordinary course of business, realise any of its assets without the consent of the creditor who is entitled to the benefit of the floating charge.

From the *creditor's* point of view, the two disadvantages exemplified on page 501, *ante*, in relation to English law, apply also in Scots law, but for the protection of the creditor it is provided that a Scots company may be wound up by the court "if there is subsisting a floating charge over property comprised in the company's property and undertaking and the court is satisfied that the security of the creditor entitled to the benefit of the floating charge is in jeopardy." The security of the creditor is deemed to be in jeopardy "if the court is satisfied that events have occurred or are about to occur which render it unreasonable in the interests of the creditor that the company should retain power to dispose of the property which is subject to the floating charge": section 4.

Priority of charges (Scots law)

Where all or any part of a company's property is subject both to a fixed security and to a floating charge, the fixed security has as a general rule priority over the floating charge. This is always so if the fixed security is one arising by operation of law (*e.g.* by a statutory provision). If the fixed security is not of that nature (*e.g.* is a standard security over heritable property under the Conveyancing and Feudal Reform (Scotland) Act 1970), the order of ranking may be regulated by provisions in the document which creates the floating charge or in any instrument of alteration.

Where there are two or more floating charges, the charges as a general rule rank with one another according to the time of their registration,[91] and if received by the Registrar by the same postal delivery they rank equally with one another. Here again the order of ranking may be regulated by provisions in the document creating a floating charge or in any instrument of alteration. There is, however, the following statutory restriction on the priority which may be obtained: where the holder of a floating charge which has been registered receives written intimation of the subsequent registration of another floating charge over the same property or part of it, the preference in ranking of the first floating charge is restricted to security for:

(*a*) the holder's present advances;
(*b*) future advances which he may be required to make;
(*c*) interest due or to become due on advances within (*a*) and (*b*), above; and
(*d*) expenses or outlays reasonably incurred by the holder: section 5.

The following have priority over a floating charge:

(1) the rights of any person who has effectually executed diligence on the property or any part of it: section 1;
(2) the rights of persons such as one who has sold goods to the company under a hire-purchase agreement by which the goods are still the property of such person;
(3) certain *un*secured but preferential debts: 1948 Act, s. 319.

Avoidance of floating charges

To prevent insolvent companies from creating floating charges to secure past debts to the prejudice of their general (unsecured) creditors, section 322 provides that where a company is being wound up

[91] *Post* p. 508.

a floating charge on the undertaking or property of the company created within 12 months before the commencement of the winding up is, unless the company was solvent immediately after the charge was created, invalid except to the amount of any cash paid to the company at or after the time when the charge was created and in consideration for the charge, with interest at five per cent. per annum or the rate prescribed by the Treasury.

Whether cash was paid at the time when the charge was created is a question of fact, and "a payment made on account of the consideration for the security, in anticipation of its creation and in reliance on a promise to execute it, although made some days before its execution, is made at the time of its creation within the meaning of the section." [92]

> Moneys were advanced on the security of a floating charge to be created by a company, which was insolvent. The first advance was 54 days, and the last five days, before the charge was created. Five days after the charge was created the company went into liquidation. *Held*, (1) as the delay was not procured or suggested or acquiesced in by the lender, the payments were made at the time of the creation of the charge, and the charge was accordingly valid; (2) as the payments were made at the time of the creation of the charge, the charge could not be a fraudulent preference: *Re F. and E. Stanton Ltd.* [1929] 1 Ch. 180.

The words "in consideration for the charge" in section 322 mean "in consideration of the fact that the charge exists."

> A company created a floating charge to secure its overdrawn current account with its bank. *Held*: (1) Every payment made by the bank to the company after the creation of the charge was "cash paid to the company" and was made in consideration of the charge. Consequently the charge was not invalid against the liquidator, and the bank was a secured creditor as to such payments. (2) The rule in *Clayton's Case* [93] applied. Each payment by the bank after the date of the charge was a provision of "new money" and there was nothing to displace the presumption that payments in by the company after the charge should be set in the first instance against the company's debt to the bank at the date of the charge: *Re Yeovil Glove Co. Ltd.* [1965] Ch. 148 (C.A.).

The effect of section 322 is merely to invalidate the charge, so that the creditor remains an unsecured creditor. If, therefore, the debt secured by a charge rendered void by that section is repaid by the company before the commencement of liquidation, the liquidator cannot recover it. [94]

Cash may have been paid to the company although it was only

---

[92] *Per* Neville J. in *Re Columbian Fireproofing Co. Ltd.* [1910] 1 Ch. 758 at p. 765.
[93] (1816) 1 Mer. 572.
[94] *Re Parkes Garage* [1929] 1 Ch. 139.

paid on condition that it be applied in paying a specified debt of the
company

D. was a director of the company and a partner in the firm of D. & Co. who
supplied goods to the company. The company owed D. & Co. £1,954 and D. &
Co. refused to supply any more goods until this debt was paid. In March D.,
who wished to save the company, agreed to lend the company £3,000 on the
security of a floating charge if the company would, out of this sum, pay £1,954
to D. & Co. This was done. The company was insolvent at the time. In July
the company went into liquidation. *Held*, the floating charge was valid, the
whole £3,000 being cash paid to the company: *Re Matthew Ellis Ltd.* [1933] 1
Ch. 458.

The cash must, however, have been intended to benefit the company and not certain creditors.

An insolvent company granted a floating charge to Z. to secure £900. The
money was provided by D., for whom Z. was a nominee, and the same day as it
was paid to the company the company paid £350 each to B. and S. for directors'
fees and £200 to D., the amount guaranteed by D. in respect of the company's
overdraft. Within 12 months the company went into liquidation. *Held*, the
charge was invalid, as its object was to benefit B., S. and D. and not the company
—in substance, no cash was paid to the company: *Re Destone Fabrics Ltd.* [1941]
Ch. 319 (C.A.).

Fraudulent preferences

Any charge made by a company, within *six* months before the
commencement of winding up, is void if it is a fraudulent preference
of any of the company's creditors: section 320, *post.*[95]

REGISTRATION OF CHARGES

Charges created by a company are required to be registered (1) in the
company's own register, and (2) with the Registrar of Companies.

Registration in company's own register

Section 104, applicable in England, provides that every *limited*
company must keep at its registered office a register of *all* charges
specifically affecting the property of the company and *all* floating
charges on the undertaking or any property of the company. The
register must give—

   (*a*) a short description of the property charged;
   (*b*) the amount of the charge;

[95] p. 570.

(*c*) the names of the persons entitled thereto, except in the case of bearer securities.

There is a corresponding provision for Scotland in section 106I [96] but that section applies to *every* company and is not restricted to *limited* companies.

The omission to comply with section 104 or section 106I merely results in a fine of £50 on every officer who is knowingly a party to the omission. The validity of the charge is *not* affected.

Every company must keep a copy of every instrument creating a charge required to be registered under section 104, section 106I, or under sections 95 and 97 (for Scotland, sections 106A and 106C), *post*, at the registered office of the company. In the case of a series of uniform debentures a copy of one of the series is sufficient: sections 103, 106H.

These copies, and also the company's register of charges, are open to the inspection of any creditor or member of the company without fee for at least two hours each day during business hours. The register of charges *only* is similarly open to the general public on payment of a fee not exceeding five pence: sections 105, 106J.

In Australia, the Company Law Advisory Committee could see no reason why the company should keep a register of charges as provided by the section corresponding to sections 103 to 105 (N.S.W.s. 107)—a searcher cannot rely on such a register in preference to searching the records at the Corporate Affairs Commission (Companies Registration Office). [97]

Registration with Registrar

There are some differences between the registration requirements imposed on English companies by the 1948 Act and those imposed on Scottish companies by the Companies (Floating Charges and Receivers) (Scotland) Act 1972.

---

[96] ss. 106A–106K are set out in the Schedule to the Companies (Floating Charges and Receivers) (Scotland) Act 1972.

[97] Seventh Interim Report (1972), para. 69.

Registration in England

Section 95 provides that prescribed [98] particulars of certain specified charges *created* by companies registered in England, together
with the instrument, if any, creating them, must be delivered to the
Registrar within 21 days after their creation. The object of registration is to protect the grantee of the charge. [99]

The charges to which the section applies are:

(a) A charge to secure an issue of debentures.

(b) A charge on uncalled share capital.

(c) A charge created or evidenced by an instrument which, if
executed by an individual, would require registration as a bill
of sale. [1]

(d) A charge on any land or any interest therein.

The general rule is that a deposit of title deeds by a company to
secure a debt, whether owed by the company or a third party, creates
an equitable charge on the land, despite section 40 of the Law of
Property Act 1925, and not just a naked lien on the documents themselves, which charge is registrable under section 95 since it is contractual in nature even though created as a result of a presumption of
law. [2]

On the true construction of sections 34, 35 and 36 of the Administration of Justice Act 1956, a charging order on specific land of
a company obtained by a judgment creditor does not require registration under section 95. [3] (It must be registered under the Land Charges
Act or the Land Registration Act, as the case may be, *post*.)

(e) A charge on book debts of the company.

If a company which has entered into hire-purchase agreements
for the disposal of its products deposits the agreements as security
for advances, there is a charge on the company's book debts. [4]

---

[98] See the Companies (Forms) Order 1949 (S.I. 1949 No. 382), Form 47; Companies
(Forms) (Amendment No. 4) Order 1972 (S.I. 1972 No. 1636), Form 47 (Scot.).

[99] *Per* Bankes L.J. in *National Provincial Bank* v. *Charnley* [1924] 1 K.B. 431 (C.A.)
at p. 442.

[1] See *Stoneleigh Finance Ltd.* v. *Phillips* [1965] 2 Q.B. 537 (C.A.).

[2] *Re Wallis & Simmonds (Builders) Ltd.* [1974] 1 W.L.R. 391, distinguishing *London
and Cheshire Insce. Co. Ltd.* v. *Laplagrene Property Co. Ltd.* [1971] Ch. 499 (unpaid
vendor's lien created by law not registrable). And see *post* p 516. In *Wallis &
Simmonds* there was no lien on the title deeds having a separate existence and the
charge was void for non-registration.

[3] *Re Overseas Aviation Engineering (G.B.) Ltd.* [1963] Ch. 24 (C.A.), *post* p. 566.

[4] *Independent Automatic Sales Ltd.* v. *Knowles & Foster* [1962] 1 W.L.R. 974.

A charge on future book debts is registrable under section 95.[4] However, where the subject-matter of a charge at the date of its creation is the benefit of a contract which does not then comprehend a book debt, *e.g.* a contract of insurance, the contract cannot be brought within section 95 merely because it might ultimately result in a book debt.[5]

(*f*) A floating charge on the undertaking or property of the company.

(*g*) A charge on calls made but not paid.

(*h*) A charge on a ship (or aircraft[6]).

(*i*) A charge on goodwill, on a patent or a licence under a patent, on a trademark or on a copyright or a licence under a copyright.

A land charge for securing money created by a company on or after January 1, 1970 (other than a floating charge) must also be registered under the Land Charges Act 1925 to the same extent as such a charge created by an individual.[7] In the case of land the title to which is registered, a charge created by a company must also be protected by an entry on the land register under the Land Registration Act 1925.[8]

The Jenkins Report[9] recommended that a charge on shares held by a company in a subsidiary should be registrable under section 95. The Committee found it anomalous that such a charge is not now registrable whereas a charge on the book debts or real property of one of a company's branches is registrable. Clause 83 of, and Schedule 2 to, the Companies Bill 1973 would have given effect to the Jenkins recommendation.

Registration in Scotland

For Scotland section 106A, corresponding to section 95, requires registration of prescribed particulars of certain specified charges created by companies, together with *certified copies* of any instruments creating the charges.

---

[5] *Paul & Frank Ltd.* v. *Discount Bank (Overseas) Ltd.* [1967] Ch. 348.
[6] See Mortgaging of Aircraft Order 1972 (S.I. 1972 No. 1268), art. 16 (2).
[7] Law of Property Act 1969, s. 26.
[8] s. 25.
[9] Para. 306.

The section applies to the following charges:

(a) A charge on land wherever situated or any interest therein. Hence registration with the Registrar in Scotland is required of a charge created by a Scottish company over heritable property in England.[10]

(b) A security over the uncalled share capital.

(c) A security over incorporeal moveable property of any of the following categories—

  (i) the book debts of the company;
  (ii) calls made but not paid;
  (iii) goodwill;
  (iv) a patent or a licence under a patent;
  (v) a trademark;
  (vi) a copyright or a licence under a copyright.

(d) A security over a ship (or aircraft[11]).

(e) A floating charge.

A security over incorporeal moveable property not falling within any of the categories specified (*e.g.* shares in other companies) does not require registration, and if particulars of such a charge have been registered the court will order their deletion from the register.[12]

It is to be observed that a charge to secure an issue of debentures which is the first in the English list is absent from the Scottish list. "For some inscrutable reason no corresponding provision has been made in regard to Scotland."[13]

In the 1961 Act no provision was made for re-registration of any instrument creating a charge,[14] or for registration of an instrument increasing the amount secured.[15] Consequently if at a later date the amount secured by a fixed charge was to be increased, the security had to be re-created from the beginning, a "cumbersome and expensive" practice for which the Scottish Law Commission suggested a remedy.[16] The 1972 Act accordingly provides that where the amount

---

[10] *Amalgamated Securities Ltd., Petitioners*, 1967 S.C. 56.

[11] See Mortgaging of Aircraft Order 1972 (S.I. 1972 No. 1268), art. 16 (2).

[12] *Scottish Homes Investment Co. Ltd., Petitioners*, 1968 S.C. 244.

[13] *Per* Lord President Clyde in the *Scottish Homes* case, above, at p. 248 (shares in other companies assigned to trustees in security for an issue of debenture stock).

[14] *Archibald Campbell, Hope & King Ltd., Petitioners*, 1967 S.C. 21.

[15] *Scottish and Newcastle Breweries Ltd.* v. *Liquidator of Rathburne Hotel Co. Ltd.*, 1970 S.C. 215 (O.H.).

[16] (1970) Cmnd. 4336, paras. 17, 18.

secured by a fixed charge is increased, a further charge is to be held to have been created, and that the registration provisions apply to that further charge.

A fixed charge on land cannot now be created in any form other than a "standard security" under the Conveyancing and Feudal Reform (Scotland) Act 1970. For the creation of a real right the standard security must be recorded in the Register of Sasines: 1970 Act, ss. 9, 11.

Section 106A provides that the date of creation of a floating charge is the date on which the instrument creating the floating charge is executed by the company, and the date of creation of any other charge is the date on which the right of the person entitled to the benefit of the charge becomes a real right, *e.g.* in the case of a standard security, the date of recording in the Register of Sasines.[14]

The registration provisions extend to any instrument of alteration under section 7 of the 1972 Act if the instrument:

(*a*) prohibits or restricts the creation of any fixed security or any other floating charge having priority over, or ranking equally with, the floating charge; or

(*b*) varies, or otherwise regulates the order of, the ranking of the floating charge in relation to fixed securities or to other floating charges; or

(*c*) releases property from the floating charge; or

(*d*) increases the amount secured by the floating charge.

Registration in England and Scotland

In the case of a series of debentures containing, or giving by reference to another instrument, a charge to the benefit of which the debenture holders are entitled *pari passu*, it is sufficient if the following particulars are registered—

(*a*) the total amount secured by the series;

(*b*) the dates of the resolutions authorising the issue of the series and the date of the covering deed, if any, by which the security is created;

(*c*) a general description of the property charged;

(*d*) the names of the trustees, if any, for the debenture holders; and

(*e*) in the case of a Scottish floating charge, a statement of the

restrictions, if any, on the company's power to grant further
securities ranking prior to or equally with the floating charge;

together with the deed (or in Scotland a copy of the deed) creating the
charge or, if there is no deed, one of the debentures (or in Scotland a
copy of one of the debentures) of the series: sections 95, 106A.

Particulars of the amount or rate per cent. of the commission,
allowance or discount on an issue of debentures must be registered:
sections 95, 106A.

The register contains the following particulars—

(*a*) in the case of a series of debentures, the particulars set out
ante;

(*b*) in other cases—

   (i) the date of the creation of the charge;
   (ii) the amount secured by the charge;
   (iii) short particulars of the property charged;
   (iv) the persons entitled to the charge; and
   (v) in the case of a Scottish floating charge, a statement of
   the restrictions, if any, on the company's power to grant
   further securities ranking prior to or equally with the
   floating charge: sections 98 (1), 106D (1).

It is the duty of the company to register the particulars required
by section 95 or section 106A. Registration, however, may be effected
by any person interested in the charge and the registration fees may
be recovered from the company: sections 96, 106B.

On the registration of a charge the Registrar gives a certificate of
registration which is conclusive evidence that the requirements of the
Act as to registration have been complied with: sections 98 (2), 106E.
The particulars delivered to the Registrar may incorrectly state the
property charged, or the amount or date of the charge, but if a certificate is given the grantee of the charge is protected. The certificate is
conclusive evidence that the Registrar has entered the particulars in
the register and that the prescribed, *i.e.* accurate, particulars have
been presented to him.[17]

In the course of its business in 1960 a company bought properties. R., a
shareholder, advanced money for each purchase and the company undertook to
execute formal mortgages on demand. In 1961 the directors and R. agreed that
the company should implement its undertakings, and memoranda of deposit of
title deeds purporting to charge some of the properties with payment to R. of
certain sums on demand were signed but not dated on June 5, 1961. On July 11

---

[17] *Re C. L. Nye Ltd.* [1971] Ch. 442 (C.A.).

the memoranda were registered with the Registrar, the date of execution being given as June 23. On August 4 the company went into voluntary winding up. *Held*, (1) the charges were not void under section 95 (1)—by section 98 (2) the certificate of registration was conclusive that all the requirements of the Act had been complied with within 21 days of execution, although the particulars submitted for registration incorrectly stated the date of the charges; (2) they were fraudulent preferences of R. and so void under section 320 (1)[18]: *Re Eric Holmes* (*Property*) *Ltd.* [1965] Ch. 1052, applied in *Re C. L. Nye Ltd.* [1971] Ch. 442 (C.A.).

"If a charge fraudulently deceives the registrar, a creditor personally damaged by the fraud can take proceedings in personam": *per* Russell L.J. at p. 474. However, on the facts no one gave credit between the date by which registration should have been effected and the date when it was effected.

"It is . . . possible that there is some lacuna in the Act . . . inasmuch as the Act gives, apparently, protection where the certificate is made upon the basis of particulars which are incorrect and might even be fraudulent": *per* Pennycuick J. at p. 1072.

To discover the exact terms of a charge one has to look at the document creating it (which document, or in Scotland a copy of which document, will have been filed) and not at the register.[19]

Cl. 82 of, and Sched. 2 to, the Companies Bill 1973 would have made the Registrar's certificate of registration conclusive evidence only that the statutory particulars have been filed within the requisite time, not that they are correct.

In England, a copy of the certificate of registration must be indorsed on every debenture or debenture stock certificate issued by the company and the payment of which is secured by the charge registered. The penalty for neglect is a fine of £100: section 99. The Jenkins Committee saw no need for this section and recommended its repeal,[20] and clause 82 of, and Schedule 2 to, the 1973 Bill would have given effect to that recommendation. Under the 1972 Act there is no corresponding provision for Scotland.

When the debt for which any registered charge was given is satisfied, in whole or in part, or part of the property charged is released or ceases to form part of the company's property, the Registrar enters a memorandum of satisfaction or release on the register. The company is entitled to a copy of the memorandum: sections 100, 106F (1).

In Scotland the Registrar must not enter any such memorandum on the register unless either:

(*a*) the creditor entitled to the benefit of the floating charge, or a person authorised by the creditor, certifies as correct the particulars submitted to the Registrar with respect to the entry; or

[18] *Post*, p. 570.
[19] *Re Mechanisations* (*Eaglescliffe*) *Ltd.* [1966] Ch. 20, following *National Provincial Bank* v. *Charnley* [1924] 1 K.B. 431 (C.A.). [20] Cmnd. 1749, para. 306.

(*b*) the court, on being satisfied that such certification cannot readily be obtained, directs the Registrar to make the entry: section 106 F(2).

The register is open to public inspection on the prescribed fee, not exceeding five pence, being paid: sections 98 (3), 106D (2).

Effect of non-registration

If a charge which ought to be registered under section 95 or section 106A is not so registered—

(*a*) the company and every officer who is knowingly a party to the default, is liable to a default fine of £50 (ss. 96, 106B, 440);

(*b*) the charge is, so far as any security on the company's property is concerned, void against the liquidator and any creditor of the company, but without prejudice to the contract to repay the money secured, which becomes immediately repayable (ss. 95, 106A). The result is that the holder of the charge is reduced to the level of an *unsecured* creditor.

In March the company gave T. a legal mortgage of specific land to secure £500. The mortgage was not registered. In December the company issued debentures secured by a floating charge on its undertaking and assets to J. to secure another £500. This charge was registered. *Held*, although J., when he took his security, had actual notice of T.'s mortgage, he nevertheless had priority over T.: *Re Monolithic Building Co.* [1915] 1 Ch. 643 (C.A.).

In order to secure repayment of a loan a company gave the lenders sub-charges on properties and deposited deeds and documents (such as legal charges and charge certificates) "to the intent that" they might "be equitably charged." The charges were void for non-registration (as charges on land or on book debts) under section 95. *Held*, the lenders had no common law lien on the documents. The deposit was merely ancillary to the equitable charge and the contractual right to retention of the documents was lost when the charges were avoided. The contract had no independent existence apart from the charge: *Re Molton Finance Ltd.* [1968] Ch. 325 (C.A.), applied in *Re Wallis & Simmonds (Builders) Ltd.* [1974] 1 W.L.R. 391.

Rectification of register

Under section 101 for England and section 106G for Scotland the court may, on application by the company or any person interested, extend the time for registration or rectify the register if—

(*a*) the omission to register a charge within the required time or the omission or mis-statement of a particular with respect to a charge is—

    (i) accidental; or

    (ii) due to inadvertence or some other sufficient cause; or

    (iii) not of a nature to prejudice the creditors or shareholders; or;

(*b*) on other grounds it is just and equitable to grant relief.

Sections 101 and 106G require the court to be satisfied with respect to certain matters before it orders an extension of time and, therefore, if serious issues of fact are involved it should arm itself with the best information and evidence available.[21] The section does not empower the court to grant interim relief.[21]

Relief will usually only be granted "without prejudice to the rights of parties acquired prior to the time when [the charge is] actually registered".[22] This proviso protects rights acquired *against the company's property in the extension of time*,[23] so that a secured creditor whose charge is created and registered in such time will not lose priority.[24]

It is otherwise when the second charge is created and registered within the 21 day period allowed by section 95 for registration of the first charge, *i.e.* the second chargee's rights do not gain priority by reason of the proviso—such rights are acquired at the date of execution of the second charge.

On January 22 a company created two floating charges on its undertaking and property by issuing a first debenture to X to secure £10,000 lent by him to the company and a second debenture to Y to secure £5,000. The second debenture was registered on January 28 but, by mistake, the first was returned to X unregistered. On October 20, X applied under section 101 for an extension of the time allowed for registration and on October 28 the court ordered an extension to November 11 with a proviso that the order was "without prejudice to the rights of any parties acquired prior to the time when the said debenture is to be registered." Also on October 28, Y appointed a receiver under the second debenture. The first debenture was registered on November 5 and a receiver appointed thereunder on November 8. On November 9, the company went into a creditors' voluntary liquidation.

Held, (1) Y's rights under the second debenture were acquired at the date of its execution and not at the expiration of the 21 days allowed by section 95 for registration of the first debenture (February 12), when the first debenture being then unregistered became void, nor in the ensuing period, during which it

---

[21] *Re Heathstar Properties Ltd.* [1966] 1 W.L.R. 993. In *Re Heathstar Properties Ltd. (No. 2)* [1966] 1 W.L.R. 999, it was found that the omission to register was due to inadvertence and the time for registration was extended notwithstanding that an action was proceeding in which the validity of the charge was in issue.

[22] *Re Joplin Brewery Co. Ltd.* [1902] 1 Ch. 79.

[23] *Re Ehrmann Bros. Ltd.* 2 Ch. 697 (C.A.).

[24] *Re Monolithic Building Co.* [1915] 1 Ch. 643 (C.A.), *ante*.

remained void, between the expiration of the 21 days and the date of its actual registration, and accordingly such rights did not gain priority over the first debenture by reason of the proviso to the court order; (2) although the appointment by Y of a receiver crystallised his floating charge, Y did not thereby acquire rights but merely exercised a power acquired when the debenture was executed (*Watson* v. *Duff, Morgan and Vermont* (*Holdings*) *Limited* [1974] 1 W.L.R. 450).

"The effect of an order extending the time for registration under section 101, followed by registration within that extended time, is to constitute the charge valid *ab initio* subject only to such conditions as might be imposed by a judge giving the extended time": *per* Templeman J. at p. 454.

Unsecured creditors with no charge on the company's property do not qualify for the purposes of the proviso. However, if the company has gone into liquidation there will be, as a general rule, no benefit in obtaining an extension of time, as the unsecured creditors will then have acquired rights against the property of the company.[25] A very exceptional case has to be made out to justify the court ordering rectification of the register after the company has gone into liquidation and the rights of unsecured creditors have crystallised.[26] The court has no power under section 101 to delete a whole registration.[27]

A clear case for the exercise of the court's power was held to have been made out where a Scottish company had failed to register a charge created over heritable property in England.[28] In a sheriff court case an extension of time was granted where there had been a misunderstanding as to which party was to effect registration.[29]

Registration of charges existing on property acquired

If a company acquires any property which is already subject to a charge which, if created by the company, would have required registration under section 95 or 106A, *the company* must register particulars of the charge and a copy of the instrument creating or evidencing it within 21 days after the acquisition is completed. Default renders the company and every officer in default liable to a

[25] *Re S. Abrahams & Sons* [1902] 1 Ch. 695.
[26] *Per* Buckley J. in *Re Mechanisations* (*Eaglescliffe*) *Ltd.* [1966] Ch. 20 at p. 36.
[27] *Per* Russell and Megaw L.JJ. in *Re C. L. Nye Ltd.* [1971] Ch. 442 (C.A.) at pp. 474, 476.
[28] *Amalgamated Securities Ltd., Petitioners*, 1967 S.C. 56, *ante* p. 512; contrast *Archibald Campbell, Hope & King Ltd., Petitioners*, 1967 S.C. 21, *ante* p. 512, in which a prayer for extension was held inept under the 1961 Act where the instrument creating the charge had already been registered and the company was seeking to re-register it for the purpose of securing an additional sum; see now s. 106A (9) in the Schedule to the 1972 Act.
[29] *M. Milne Ltd., Petitioners*, (1963) 79 Sh.Ct. Rep. 105.

default fine of £50 (ss. 97, 106C, 440) but the validity of the charge is not affected. This is as it should be since the person entitled to the benefit of the charge will have no opportunity of ensuring that registration is effected.[30]

REMEDIES OF DEBENTURE HOLDERS

1. If a debenture confers no charge, a debenture holder is an ordinary unsecured creditor. Thus, if there is default in the payment of principal or interest he may (*a*) sue for the principal or interest and, after obtaining judgment, levy execution against the company,[31] or (*b*), as will be explained later,[32] petition for the winding up of the company by the court on the ground that the company is unable to pay its debts.

2. When a charge is conferred on the company's assets by way of security, and default is made in the payment of principal or interest, a debenture holder, or the trustees where there is a trust deed, may:

(*a*) sue for the principal or interest; or

(*b*) present a petition for the winding up of the company; or

(*c*) exercise any powers conferred by the debenture or the trust deed, *e.g.* of appointing a receiver of the assets charged, of selling the assets charged or of taking possession of the assets and carrying on the business; or

(*d*) if the debenture or the trust deed does not contain powers in that behalf, apply to the court for:

  (i) the appointment of a receiver or a receiver and manager; or

  (ii) an order for sale or foreclosure.

A debenture or trust deed will normally contain an express power to appoint a receiver of, or to sell, the company's assets charged by way of security. If there is no express power there will be an implied power under the Law of Property Act 1925, s. 101,[32a] if the debenture or trust deed is under seal. Failing an express or an implied power, an application may be made to the court for the appointment of a receiver or an order for sale.

---

[30] Seventh Interim Report of the Australian Company Law Advisory Committee, para. 3.

[31] The Scots equivalent is "do diligence on the decree obtained."

[32] *Post* p. 545.

[32a] not applicable to Scotland; see *post*, pp. 520, 528 *et seq.*

In England, where there are numerous debentures of the same class, a *debenture holders' action* is usually brought. This is brought by one debenture holder on behalf of himself and all other debenture holders of the same class as himself. In it a claim may be made for:

(1) a declaration that the debenture holders are entitled to a (first) charge on the property of the company;
(2) if there is a trust deed, the enforcement of the trusts;
(3) an account of what is due to the debenture holders;
(4) the enforcement of the charge by sale or foreclosure;
(5) the appointment of a receiver and manager.[33]

An order for foreclosure will only be made if all the debenture holders of the same class as the plaintiff are before the court.[34]

If the assets require immediate protection an application for the appointment of a receiver is made.[34]

In Scotland, prior to the Companies (Floating Charges and Receivers) (Scotland) Act 1972, there was no provision for the appointment of receivers, and this constituted a major difference between Scots and English law in the remedies available to the holder of a floating charge and in the procedure for enforcing the security. On the recommendation of the Scottish Law Commission[35] receiverships were introduced to Scotland by the Act of 1972. Though based in general on the English model, the Scottish provisions form a distinct self-contained code comprising Part II of the 1972 Act, and are given separate consideration below.

RECEIVERS (ENGLISH LAW)

A receiver takes possession of the property of the company over which he is appointed and realises it for the benefit of the debenture holder(s). He should not be confused with a liquidator. A liquidator is appointed with the object of winding up the company and terminating its existence whereas a receiver may be paid out whereupon the company will resume business as before.

As shown above, a receiver may be appointed to enforce a charge given by a debenture or a trust deed (1) under a power contained in the debenture or the trust deed; or (2) by an order of the court.

[33] Palmer's *Company Precedents*, 16th ed., Pt. III, p. 498.
[34] *Re Continental Oxygen Co.* [1897] 1 Ch. 511.
[35] *Report on the Companies (Floating Charges) (Scotland) Act 1961*, (1970) Cmnd. 4336, para. 38.

Receiver appointed by the court

The court may appoint a receiver when—

(1) the principal or interest is in arrear[36]; or

(2) the company is being wound up[37]; or

(3) the security is in jeopardy.

A creditor obtained judgment against the company and was in a position to issue execution. There was no default in payment of debenture principal or interest. *Held*, the debenture holders with a floating charge on the undertaking and property of the company were entitled to the appointment of a receiver because the security was in jeopardy: *Re London Pressed Hinge Co. Ltd.* [1905] 1 Ch. 576.

The security is in jeopardy when there is a risk of its being seized and taken to pay claims which are really not prior to the debenture holders' claims. Accordingly a receiver was appointed where the company's works were closed and creditors were threatening actions,[38] where execution was actually levied by a judgment creditor,[39] where a creditor's winding-up petition was pending and compulsory liquidation was imminent,[40] and where the company proposed to distribute its reserve fund, which was its only asset, among its members.[41]

Mere insufficiency of security is not jeopardy where the company is a going concern, is not being pressed by its creditors and there is no risk of its assets being seized by its creditors.[42]

Who cannot be appointed receiver

A body corporate is disqualified for appointment as receiver[43]: section 366. Also, an undischarged bankrupt is disqualified from acting as receiver or manager, unless he is appointed by the court: section 367. Where an application is made to the court to appoint a receiver and the company is being wound up by the court, the Official

[36] *Bissill* v. *Bradford Tramways* [1891] W.N. 51.
[37] *Wallace* v. *Universal Automatic Machines Co.* [1894] 2 Ch. 547 (C.A.).
[38] *McMahon* v. *North Kent Ironworks* [1891] 2 Ch. 148.
[39] *Edwards* v. *Standard Rolling Stock Syndicate* [1893] 1 Ch. 574.
[40] *Re Victoria Steamboats Ltd.* [1897] 1 Ch. 158.
[41] *Re Tilt Cove Copper Co.* [1913] 2 Ch. 588.
[42] *Re New York Taxicab Co.* [1913] 1 Ch. 1.
[43] An attempted appointment of a body corporate is a nullity, and the body corporate does not thereby become an agent for the purposes of the Law of Property Act 1925, s. 109, and the Limitation Act 1939: *Portman Bldg. Socy.* v. *Gallwey* [1955] 1 All E.R. 227.

Receiver may be appointed (s. 368) and, unless there are special circumstances, he or the liquidator will be appointed so as to avoid unnecessary expense and the possibility of conflict.[44]

When a receiver is appointed by the court, he must give security to the satisfaction of the court.

Clause 90 of the Companies Bill 1973 would have added the following to the persons disqualified from acting as receiver—

(1) a person subject to a disqualification order under Clause 38 *ante*, unless leave of the court is obtained;

(2) a person who is, or has at any time during the preceding 12 months been—

    (*a*) a director of the company; or

    (*b*) interested in at least five per cent. of the issued shares of the company; or

    (*c*) interested in debentures of the company.

For the purposes of (2) above, an interest of a member of a person's family was to be treated as an interest of that person.

Appointment of manager

If the debentures give a charge over the company's "business" or "undertaking and property," a manager may be appointed. The same person is usually appointed receiver and manager. A manager is appointed to carry on the business with the object of selling it as a going concern and, therefore, when appointed by the court he is invariably appointed only for a limited time, usually three months. If he acts beyond the limited period, without an order extending the time, his expenditure will be disallowed.[45]

The conduct of a receiver and manager appointed by a debenture holder cannot be examined in misfeasance proceedings under section 333[46] but the company may obtain the appointment of an inspector to investigate his transactions under section 165 (a).[47]

Time of appointment of receiver

A receiver is appointed when the document of appointment is handed to him by a person having authority to appoint and in cir-

[44] *British Linen Co.* v. *South American and Mexican Co.* [1894] 1 Ch. 108 (C.A.).

[45] *Re Wood Green Steam Laundry* [1918] 1 Ch. 423.

[46] *Re B. Johnson & Co. (Builders) Ltd.* [1955] Ch. 634 (C.A.), *ante* p. 395.

[47] *R.* v. *B.o.T., ex p. St. Martins Preserving Co. Ltd.* [1965] 1 Q.B. 603, *ante* p. 397.

cumstances from which it may fairly be said that he is appointing the receiver and the receiver accepts the proffered appointment.[48]

Effect of appointment of receiver

When a receiver is appointed:

(1) Floating charges crystallise and become fixed. This prevents the company from dealing with the assets charged, without the receiver's consent.[49]

(2) When a receiver of the undertaking of the company is appointed, the directors' power of controlling the company is suspended. They cannot claim remuneration from the receiver unless he employs them, but they can still claim from the company any remuneration to which they are entitled.[50]

> ". . . a floating charge purporting to extend . . . to the whole of the assets and undertaking of a company, does not upon appointment of a receiver and manager thereunder, extend to fettering the capacity or power of the directors of the company to cause proceedings to be instituted in the name of the company challenging that debenture": *per* Street J. in *Hawkesbury Development Co. Ltd.* v. *Landmark Finance Pty. Ltd.* (1970) 92 W.N. (N.S.W.) 199 at p. 210.

(3) When the appointment is by the court, the company's servants are automatically dismissed, for which they may be entitled to damages for breach of contract although they may be employed by the receiver.[51]

As to the position where a receiver is appointed by the debenture holders, in *Re Foster Clark Ltd.'s Indenture Trusts*,[52] it was held that the sale by the receiver of the company's business to a subsidiary operated as a dismissal of the company's employees. Plowman J. observed [52a] that there appears to be no good reason in principle why an appointment out of court of a receiver who is the agent of the company should of itself determine contracts of employment made with the company, and this observation was applied in *Re Mack Trucks (Britain) Ltd.*[53] Further, in *Griffiths* v. *Secretary of State for Social*

---

[48] *R. A. Cripps & Son Ltd.* v. *Wickenden* [1973] 1 W.L.R. 944, applying *Windsor Refridgerator Co. Ltd.* v. *Branch Nominees Ltd.* [1961] Ch. 375 (C.A.).
[49] *Ante* p. 499.
[50] *Re South Western of Venezuela, etc., Rlwy.* [1902] 1 Ch. 701.
[51] *Reid* v. *Explosives Co. Ltd.* (1887) 19 Q.B.D. 264 (C.A.), *ante* p. 370.
[52] [1966] 1 W.L.R. 125.   [52a] at p. 132.
[53] [1967] 1 W.L.R. 780.

Services[54] it was held that the mere appointment out of court by debenture holders of a receiver and manager as agent of a company did not automatically terminate an employee's subsisting contract of employment with the company where the continuation of his employment was not inconsistent with the role and functions of the receiver and manager. And see *per* Lawson J. at pp. 845, 6.

(4) Every invoice, order for goods or business letter which is issued by or on behalf of the company or the receiver and on which the company's name appears must contain a statement that a receiver has been appointed: section 370.

(5) A receiver of the whole, or substantially the whole, of the company's property, appointed on behalf of the holders of debentures secured by a floating charge, must forthwith give notice of his appointment to the company: section 372 (1).

(6) Within seven days after the appointment, the person who made or obtained the appointment must give notice of the fact to the Registrar who must enter it in his register of charges: section 102 (1).

(7) Within a period of, usually, 14 days after the receiver gives the company notice of his appointment as required by section 372 (1), above, a statement of the company's affairs must be submitted to him, giving particulars of the assets, debts and liabilities, the names and addresses of the creditors, the securities they hold, the dates when they were given and such other information as may be prescribed. The statement must usually be submitted by, and verified by affidavit of, one of the directors and the secretary or, if the receiver is appointed out of court, verified by statutory declaration of the same persons. In certain circumstances the receiver may require past or present officers, persons who have taken part in the formation of the company or past or present employees, to submit and verify the statement: sections 372 (1), 373.

Clause 92 and Schedule 4 of the Companies Bill 1973 would have amended the law relating to the making of statements of a company's affairs on the appointment of a receiver or manager.

(8) Within two months after the receipt of the statement, the receiver must send to the Registrar, and to the court if he was appointed by the court, a copy of the statement and of his

[54] [1974] Q.B. 468.

comments thereon. He must also send to the Registrar a summary of the statement and of his comments thereon, to the company a copy of his comments or a notice that he does not see fit to make any comments, and to the trustees for debenture holders and to all the debenture holders a copy of the summary: section 372 (1).

(9) When a receiver appointed under a power in an instrument ceases to act, he must give notice to the Registrar: section 102 (2).

Position of receiver

A receiver appointed by the court is an officer of the court, and cannot sue or be sued without leave of the court.[55] By leave of the court an action can be brought against him by a person at whose instance he was appointed.[56] In the case of a receiver appointed under a power in a debenture or a trust deed the debenture usually provides that he is to be the agent of the company. Consequently the debenture holder(s) or the trustees are not liable for his acts. A receiver appointed out of court may apply to the court for directions in any matter concerning the performance of his functions: section 369 (1).

A receiver appointed by order of the court is personally liable on contracts made by him in the course of his receivership. (A liquidator is not personally liable on contracts which he enters into as liquidator.[57])

B. was appointed receiver and manager by the court. He gave a signed order for goods, with the words "receiver and manager" appended to his signature. *Held*, he was personally liable to pay for the goods: *Burt, Boulton and Hayward* v. *Bull* [1895] 1 Q.B. 276 (C.A.).

The receiver is entitled to be indemnified out of the company's assets,[58] so far as they are sufficient.[59]

Contracts made by the company and current at the date of his appointment are not binding on the receiver personally, unless they become binding by a novation.[60] They remain binding, however, on

---

[55] *Viola* v. *Anglo-American Cold Storage Co.* [1912] 2 Ch. 305; *Searle* v. *Choat* (1884) 25 Ch.D. 723 (C.A.).
[56] *L. P. Arthur* (*Insurance*) *Ltd.* v. *Sisson* [1966] 1 W.L.R. 1384.
[57] *Post* p. 578.   [58] *Re Glasdir Mines* [1906] 1 Ch. 365.
[59] *Boehm* v. *Goodall* [1911] 1 Ch. 155.
[60] *Parsons* v. *Sovereign Bank of Canada* [1913] A.C. 160 (P.C.).

the company, so that in the event of a breach the company will be liable for damages. The receiver must carry out the company's current contracts if not to do so would injure the company's good-will,[61] but if the contracts can only be carried out by borrowing money ranking in priority to the debenture holders and are unprofitable, he need not carry them out.[62]

Under section 369 (2) a receiver appointed under a power in any instrument is, to the same extent as if he had been appointed by the court, personally liable on contracts made by him in the performance of his functions except so far as they otherwise provide. He has the same right of indemnity as a receiver appointed by order of the court and he may also, as a condition of accepting the appointment, require an express indemnity from the debenture holders. On the commencement of a winding up of the company the receiver ceases to be the company's agent and his authority to bind the company ceases[63] but his powers with regard to the property charged are unaffected.[64]

The Jenkins Report[65] recommended that the court should be empowered to relieve a receiver appointed, *e.g.*, under an invalid charge, from personal liability. At present, such a person is a trespasser and may incur heavy liabilities.

Borrowing by receiver

To enable the receiver to carry on the business of the company or to preserve the property of the company, the court can authorise the receiver to borrow sums ranking in priority to the debentures.[66]

Preferential payments

Section 94 (1) provides that where, in the case of a company registered in England, either a receiver is appointed on behalf of the holders of debentures secured by a *floating charge*, or possession is taken by or on behalf of those debenture holders of any property subject to the charge, then, if the company is not at the time in the course of being wound up, the preferential debts, *i.e.* certain un-

---

[61] *Re Newdigate Colliery Ltd.* [1912] 1 Ch. 468 (C.A.). And see *Airlines Airspares Ltd.* v. *Handley Page Ltd.* [1970] Ch. 193.
[62] *Re Thames Ironworks Co. Ltd.* (1912) 106 L.T. 674.
[63] *Gosling* v. *Gaskell* [1897] A.C. 575; *Thomas* v. *Todd* [1926] 2 K.B. 511.
[64] *Gough's Garages Ltd.* v. *Pugsley* [1930] 1 K.B. 615.
[65] Para. 306.
[66] *Greenwood* v. *Algesiras Ry. Co.* [1894] 2 Ch. 205 (C.A.).

secured debts,[67] must be paid out of any assets coming to the hands of the receiver or other person taking possession in priority to any claim for principal or interest in respect of the debentures. The receiver is under a positive duty to pay the preferential debts of which he has notice out of any assets coming to his hand in priority to all other creditors.[68]

The receipt of moneys by the debenture holder with notice of a statutory duty under which the moneys should have been applied in settlement of a prior claim makes the debenture holder directly liable to the preferential creditors as a constructive trustee.[68]

At the date of the appointment of a receiver in 1940, a company owed £63 for rates. This was a preferential debt. In the following month a winding-up order was made but the receiver continued to carry on the business of the company. From time to time a demand was made upon him for payment of the £63 but no payment was made. In 1945 the receiver had £91 in hand but by 1948 he had no assets in hand and so informed the rating authority. *Held*, the receiver was liable in damages because section 94 was not merely a negative provision preventing the receiver from paying the debenture holders until after the preferential debts had been paid, but it also imposed a positive duty upon him to pay those debts out of any assets in his hands: *Westminster Corporation* v. *Haste* [1950] Ch. 442.

Any preferential payment made out of the assets secured by the floating charge can be recouped as far as may be out of the assets of the company available for payment of the general creditors: section 94 (5).

Section 94 (1) not only protects preferential creditors where a debenture holder takes possession of assets as mortgagee but also extends to cases where the debenture holder arrogates all the assets to himself with notice of the preferential creditors' claim and is guilty of wrongfully procuring and being a party to a breach of statutory duty.[68]

If the debentures give a fixed charge on specified assets and a floating charge on the company's undertaking and assets, the *fixed charge* is not subject to the payment of the preferential debts.[69]

---

[67] *Post* p. 592 *et seq*. In this case the periods mentioned in s. 319 run from the appointment of the receiver.

[68] *Inland Revenue Commissioners* v. *Goldblatt* [1972] Ch. 498, where, by the direction of and on the receipt of an indemnity from the debenture holder, the receiver transferred the assets of which he had taken possession to the company and he knew or ought to have known that the company would transfer them to the debenture holder without paying off the preferential creditors.

[69] *Re Lewis Merthyr Collieries Ltd.* [1929] 1 Ch. 498 (C.A.).

Remuneration of receiver

A receiver appointed by the court has the amount of his remuneration fixed by the court.

A receiver appointed under a power in the debentures has his remuneration fixed by agreement. The court may, however, on the application of the *liquidator*, fix the receiver's remuneration. Under this power the remuneration may be fixed retrospectively, and any excess paid before the making of the order must be accounted for: section 371.

Delivery of accounts

By the terms of his appointment the receiver may be required to render accounts to the debenture holders. Apart from any such duty, a receiver or manager of the whole or substantially the whole of the company's property, who is appointed on behalf of debenture holders with a floating charge, is obliged by section 372 (2), every year and on his ceasing to act, to send to the Registrar, any trustees for the debenture holders, the company and all the debenture holders, an abstract in the prescribed form of his receipts and payments during the year, and the aggregate amounts of his receipts and payments during the time of his appointment. Section 372 (3) contains a similar provision where a receiver is appointed under the powers contained in any instrument. Penalties are imposed in the event of default. Except where section 372 (2) applies, a receiver appointed under a power in the debentures must, every six months and on his ceasing to act, deliver to the Registrar an abstract in the prescribed form of his receipts and payments. Penalties are imposed in the event of default: section 374.

The court may order the receiver to make any returns or give any notices which he is by law required to make or give: section 375.

RECEIVERS (SCOTS LAW)

The reasons for the introduction of the office of receiver to Scotland by the Companies (Floating Charges and Receivers) (Scotland) Act 1972[70] were:

[70] A petition for the appointment of a judicial factor and interim on the affairs of a limited company is competent at common law: *Fraser, Petitioner*, 1971 S.L.T. 146

(*a*) to enable the fortunes of a company to be revived and thus prevent unnecessary liquidation;

(*b*) to strengthen the rights of a holder of a floating charge by making it possible for him to take possession of and realise the security without liquidation; and

(*c*) to lessen the difficulties which could arise from the difference between Scots and English law where a group of companies included both Scottish and English companies.[71]

In this part of this chapter the sections referred to are, except where there is a statement to the contrary, those of the Companies (Floating Charges and Receivers) (Scotland) Act 1972.

A receiver may be appointed by either the holder of a floating charge or the court on the application of the holder of a floating charge: section 11. The term "holder of the floating charge" is sufficiently widely defined as to include, in the case of a series of debentures, the trustees acting for the debenture holders under a trust deed, or, if there are no such trustees, specified majorities of the debenture holders: section 28 (2).

Appointment by holder of floating charge

A receiver may be appointed by the holder of the floating charge on the occurrence of any event which, by the instrument creating the charge, entitles the holder to make that appointment, and, in so far as the instrument does not provide otherwise, on the occurrence of any of the following:

(*a*) expiry of 21 days after the making of a demand—which is unsatisfied—for payment of the whole or part of the principal sum secured;

(*b*) expiry of two months during which interest has been in arrears;

(*c*) making of an order or passing of a resolution to wind up the company;

(*d*) appointment of a receiver by virtue of any other floating charge created by the company: section 12 (1).

(O.H.) (appointment made in a "position of chaos requiring urgently to be dealt with").

[71] Report on the Companies (Floating Charges) (Scotland) Act 1961, (1970) Cmnd. 4336, paras. 37, 38.

The appointment is made by means of an "instrument of appointment," validly executed by the holder of the charge or by a person having his written authority. A certified copy of the instrument of appointment must be delivered by the person making the appointment to the Registrar within seven days of its execution, and the registrar enters particulars of the appointment in the register of charges. The receiver is regarded as having been appointed on the date of the execution of the instrument of appointment, and as from that date the floating charge, subject to sections 106A and 322 of the 1948 Act, attaches to the property and takes effect as if it were a fixed security. Failure without reasonable excuse duly to register the certified copy of the instrument of appointment attracts a fine of £5 for every day during which the default continues, but does not affect the validity of the appointment: section 13.

Appointment by court

The circumstances in which a receiver may be appointed by the court are the same as those for an appointment by the holder of the floating charge (*ante*, p. 529) except that for paragraph (*d*) there must be substituted:

(*d*) where the court is satisfied that the position of the holder of the charge is likely to be prejudiced if no appointment is made: section 12 (2).

The application to the court for the appointment is by petition, which must be served on the company. A certified copy of the court's interlocutor making the appointment must be delivered by or on behalf of the petitioner to the Registrar within seven days of the date of the interlocutor or such longer period as the court may allow, and the Registrar enters particulars of the appointment in the register of charges. The receiver is regarded as having been appointed on the date of the interlocutor, and as from that date the floating charge attaches to the property and takes effect as if it were a fixed security. Failure without reasonable excuse duly to register the certified copy of the interlocutor attracts a fine of £5 for every day during which the default continues, but does not affect the validity of the appointment: section 14 and R.C. 218A.[72]

[72] See *post*, p. 552; "Section 3A—Receivers," consisting of R.C. 218A, was added to the Rules of Court as from March 31, 1973.

Who can be appointed receiver

The following are disqualified from being appointed as receiver:

(*a*) a body corporate;
(*b*) an undischarged bankrupt; and
(*c*) a Scottish firm: section 11 (3).

It is permissible to have joint receivers: section 11 (5).

Where there are two or more floating charges, the same person may be appointed receiver by virtue of both or all of them: section 16 (7).

Powers of receiver

A receiver has the powers, if any, conferred on him by the instrument creating the floating charge, and in addition he has the extensive powers listed in section 15 in so far as these are not inconsistent with any provision contained in the instrument creating the charge. The statutory powers are such as to place the receiver in a position comparable to that of a receiver and manager in England, and include the following powers:

(a) to take possession and dispose of the company's property;
(b) to borrow money and grant security over the property;
(c) to appoint agents, employees and professional persons such as a solicitor and an accountant;
(d) to apply to the court for directions;
(e) to bring or defend legal proceedings in the name and on behalf of the company, and to refer questions to arbitration;
(f) to insure the company's business and property;
(g) to use the company's seal and execute documents, including bills of exchange and promissory notes, in the name and on behalf of the company;
(h) to carry on the company's business so far as he thinks it desirable to do so;
(i) to grant and take on leases;
(j) to present or defend a petition for the winding up of the company; and
(k) to do all things incidental to the exercise of his other powers: section 15 (1).

The exercise by the receiver of his powers is subject to the rights of persons who have effectually executed diligence[73] before his appointment and to the rights of persons who hold fixed security or floating charges with prior or equal ranking: section 15 (2).

A receiver or manager of an English company which has property in Scotland has the same powers in relation to the Scottish property as he has in relation to the English property in so far as these powers are not inconsistent with Scots law: section 15 (4).[74]

A person transacting with a receiver has no duty to inquire whether any event has happened to authorise the receiver to act: section 15 (3).

Precedence among receivers

Where there are two or more floating charges, a receiver may be appointed by virtue of each charge, but the receiver whose charge has priority of ranking is entitled to exercise the statutory powers to the exclusion of any other receiver. Where two or more floating charges rank equally and two or more receivers have been appointed by virtue of these charges, the receivers are deemed to be joint receivers. The powers of a receiver whose charge has a ranking postponed to that of another charge by virtue of which a receiver has later been appointed are, from the date of the later appointment, suspended so far as is necessary to enable the second-mentioned receiver to exercise his statutory powers, and they revive when the prior floating charge ceases to attach to the property: section 16.

Agency and liability of receiver for contracts

A receiver is deemed to be the agent of the company in relation to the property attached by the floating charge. Subject to that general principle, a receiver is personally liable on any contract entered into by him in the performance of his functions, except in so far as the contract otherwise provides, but he is entitled to be indemnified out of the property in respect of which he was appointed.

Contracts entered into by or on behalf of the company before the receiver's appointment continue in force, subject to the terms of the

---

[73] An arrestment which has not been followed by a decree of furthcoming is not an "effectually executed diligence" for this purpose: *Lord Advocate* v. *Royal Bank of Scotland Ltd.*, 1976 S.L.T. 130 (O.H.).

[74] On interpretation of this provision, see *Gordon Anderson (Plant) Ltd.* v. *Campsie Construction Ltd.* 1977 S.L.T. 7.

contract, after the appointment, but the receiver does not, merely by his appointment, incur personal liability on such contracts. Contracts entered into by a receiver whose powers are later suspended under section 16, *ante*, continue in force, subject to the terms of the contract, after that suspension: section 17.[75]

Remuneration of receiver

The remuneration to be paid to a receiver is fixed by agreement between the receiver and the holder of the floating charge, but where there has been no such agreement or the remuneration fixed is disputed by the receiver, the holder of any floating charge or fixed security, the company or the liquidator, it may be fixed instead by the Auditor of the Court of Session: section 18.

Preferential payments and distribution of monies

The 1972 Act provides that where a company is not at the time of the receiver's appointment in course of being wound up the debts which would be preferential payments in winding up[67] must be paid out of any assets coming into the receiver's hands in priority to claims of the holder of the floating charge. This applies only to debts which have been intimated to the receiver or have become known to him within six months after he has advertised for claims in the *Edinburgh Gazette* and in a local newspaper. Payments made in accordance with these provisions must be recouped as far as may be out of the assets available for ordinary creditors: section 19.

The monies received by the receiver are distributed in the following order:

(*a*) to the holder of any fixed security which ranks prior to or equally with the floating charge, persons who have effectually executed diligence on any part of the property, creditors to whom the receiver has incurred liability, the receiver himself in respect of his liabilities, expenses and remuneration, and preferential creditors entitled to payment under section 19, *ante*;

(*b*) to the holder of the floating charge in or towards satisfaction of the debt secured by the floating charge; and

(*c*) to any other receiver, to the holder of a fixed security over the

[75] See *Macleod* v. *Alexander Sutherland Ltd.* 1977 S.L.T. (Notes) 44 (O.H.) (Decree of implement refused.)

property, and to the company or its liquidator, according to their respective rights and interests.

Where there is doubt as to the person entitled to a payment, or where a receipt or discharge of a security cannot be obtained for a payment, the receiver must consign the amount in a bank of issue in Scotland in name of the Account of Court for behoof of the person entitled to it: section 20.

Cessation of appointment

A receiver appointed by the holder of a floating charge may resign on giving one month's notice to:

(*a*) the holders of floating charges over any part of the company's property;
(*b*) the company or its liquidator; and
(*c*) the holders of any fixed security over the particular property in respect of which the receiver was appointed.

A receiver appointed by the court may resign only with the authority of the court and on such terms and conditions as may be laid down by the court.

The holder of the floating charge by virtue of which a receiver was appointed may apply to the court for the removal of the receiver on cause shown.

On the cessation of his appointment a receiver is entitled to be indemnified out of the property subject to the floating charge for any expenses, charges or other liabilities incurred in the performance of his functions.

Except where the cessation of a receiver's appointment is due to his death or removal by the court, he must give notice of the cessation to the Registrar within seven days. Where the receiver has been removed by the court, the duty to give such notice lies on the holder of the floating charge. The Registrar enters the notice in the register of charges.

If, on the expiry of one month after cessation of a receiver's appointment, no other receiver has been appointed, the charge then ceases to attach to the property and becomes again a floating charge: section 22.

Powers of court

Under the 1972 Act the court may exercise certain powers in relation to receiverships, whether the receiver has been appointed by the holder of the floating charge or by the court:—

(*a*) The court may give directions in connection with the performance by the receiver of his functions. The application to the court may be made either by the receiver or by the holder of the floating charge: sections 15 (1), 23 (1).

(*b*) The court may, on the application of the holder of the floating charge, remove the receiver on cause shown: section 22, *ante*.

(*c*) Where the property which is subject to the floating charge is also subject to another security or burden or is affected by diligence, and the receiver wishes to dispose of the property but is unable to obtain the necessary consent of the other parties, the court may, on the application of the receiver, authorise the disposal of the property free of the security or burden or diligence. A fixed security ranking prior to the floating charge must always be met or provided for in full, but in other respects the court has a discretion both as to whether it will authorise the disposal at all and as to the terms or conditions on which it does so. The right of any creditor to rank for his debt in the winding up of the company is not prejudiced by these provisions: section 21.

(*d*) Where the floating charge is discovered to have been invalid, the court has a discretion to relieve, in whole or in part, a person who has acted as receiver from personal liability for actings which, had his appointment been valid, would have been proper. The court also has a discretion to impose personal liability instead on the person by whom the invalid appointment was made: section 23 (2).

(*e*) If the receiver makes default in delivering the documents or giving the notices which are required of him, *post*, the court may order him to make good the default within a specified time. Application to the court for this purpose may be made by any member or creditor of the company or by the Registrar. Similarly, if the receiver fails, on the liquidator's request, to render proper accounts of receipts and payments and to pay over the proper amount to the liquidator, the court may, on the liquidator's application, order the receiver to make good the default within a specified time: section 27.

Requirements as to notification and information

When a receiver is appointed:—

(*a*) Every invoice, order for goods or business letter which is issued by or on behalf of the company or the receiver or the liquidator and on which the company's name appears must contain a statement that a receiver has been appointed: section 24.

(*b*) The receiver must forthwith send notice of his appointment to the company: section 25 (1).

(*c*) Within a period of, usually, 14 days after the receipt by the company of the last-mentioned notice, a statement of the company's affairs must be submitted to the receiver. The statement must give particulars of the assets, debts and liabilities, the names and addresses of the creditors, the securities held by them, the dates when the securities were given and such other information as may be prescribed. It must usually be submitted by, and verified by the statutory declaration of, one of the directors and the secretary. In certain circumstances the receiver may require past or present officers, persons who have taken part in the formation of the company or past or present employees to submit and verify the statement: sections 25 (1), 26.

(*d*) Within two months after the receipt of the statement, the receiver must send to the Registrar, and to the court if he was appointed by the court, a copy of the statement and of his comments thereon. He must also send to the Registrar a summary of the statement and of his comments thereon, to the company a copy of his comments or a notice that he does not see fit to make any comments, and to the holder of the floating charge, to the trustees for debenture holders and to all the debenture holders a copy of the summary: section 25 (1).

(*e*) On the expiration of each year from the date of his appointment and also on his ceasing to act the receiver must prepare an abstract in the prescribed form showing his receipts and payments during the year or other period and the aggregate amounts of his receipts and payments during all preceding periods, and must send this abstract to the Registrar, the company, the holder of the floating charge, any trustees for the debenture holders, all the debenture holders and also the holders of all other floating charges or fixed securities over property of the company: section 25 (2).

Penalties are imposed for failure to comply with the requirements of sections 24 and 25.

CHAPTER 23

WINDING UP BY THE COURT

THIS chapter and the following three chapters deal with the winding up of a company, which may be—

(1) by the court; or
(2) voluntary; or
(3) subject to the supervision of the court (s. 211),

and with the two kinds of voluntary winding up, namely—

(a) a members' voluntary winding up; and
(b) a creditors' voluntary winding up (s. 283 (4)).

It will be recalled that winding up by the court on the "just and equitable ground" was explained in Chapter 17. Chapter 24 (Contributories and Creditors) and Chapter 25 (Completion of Winding up by the Court), deal with winding up by the court as well as Chapter 23. Chapter 26 is concerned with voluntary winding up and winding up under the supervision of the court. Winding up under supervision is unimportant in practice.

The diagram on page 539 may assist the reader to obtain an overview of winding up.

Section 353, which is explained in Chapter 25,[1] provides a method of dissolving a defunct company by striking it off the register without a winding up, and under section 208, *post*,[2] the court may order dissolution without winding up where there is a compromise or an arrangement to facilitate a reconstruction or an amalgamation.

A company cannot in England be made bankrupt[3] or in Scotland be sequestrated.[4]

---

[1] *Post* p. 601.
[2] p. 640.
[3] Bankruptcy Act 1914, s. 126.
[4] *Standard Property Investment Co. Ltd.* v. *Dunblane Hydropathic Co. Ltd.* (1884) 12 R. 328. A Scottish company could, however, be made notour bankrupt for the purpose of the statutory provisions relating to equalisation of diligences: *Clark* v. *Hinde, Milne & Co.* (1884) 12 R. 347; see now section 327.

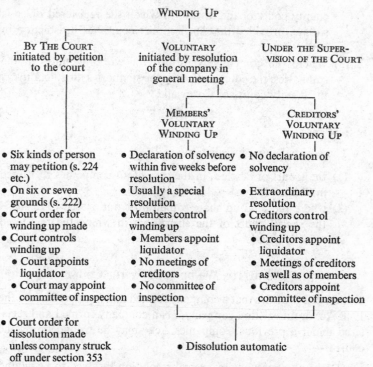

WINDING UP

BY THE COURT
initiated by petition
to the court

VOLUNTARY
initiated by resolution
of the company in
general meeting

**UNDER THE SUPER-
VISION OF THE COURT**

**MEMBERS'
VOLUNTARY
WINDING UP**

**CREDITORS'
VOLUNTARY
WINDING UP**

- Six kinds of person
  may petition (s. 224
  etc.)
- On six or seven
  grounds (s. 222)
- Court order for
  winding up made
- Court controls
  winding up
  - Court appoints
    liquidator
  - Court may appoint
    committee of inspection

- Declaration of solvency
  within five weeks before
  resolution
- Usually a special
  resolution
- Members control
  winding up
  - Members appoint
    liquidator
  - No meetings of
    creditors
  - No committee of
    inspection

- No declaration of
  solvency
- Extraordinary
  resolution
- Creditors control
  winding up
  - Creditors appoint
    liquidator
  - Meetings of creditors
    as well as of members
  - Creditors appoint
    committee of inspection

- Court order for
  dissolution made
  unless company struck
  off under section 353

- Dissolution automatic

In 1974 out of a total of 7,466 liquidations notified in England and Wales, 1,395 were compulsory. Of the 6,071 which were voluntary, 3,746 were members' and 2,325 were creditors'. There were 5 supervision liquidations in the years 1970 to 1974.

In Scotland, out of 419 liquidations notified, 42 were compulsory. Of the 377 which were voluntary, 264 were members' and 113 were creditors'.

JURISDICTION TO WIND UP COMPANIES

In England

To obtain a winding up by the court, a petition must be presented to the court having the necessary jurisdiction. Section 218 provides that the courts having jurisdiction are—

(1) the High Court, *i.e.* the Companies Court,[5] in the case of all companies registered in England;

(2) Where the paid-up share capital does not exceed £120,000, the

---

[5] *Eastern Holdings* v. *Singer & Friedlander Ltd.* [1967] 1 W.L.R. 1017.
[5a] As amended by the Insolvency Act 1976, s. 1 and Sched. 1.

county court of the district in which the registered office is situate, provided that such county court has jurisdiction in bankruptcy.[6]

(3) Where the company is formed for working mines in the stannaries, the court exercising the stannaries jurisdiction, *i.e.* the county courts of Cornwall.[7]

In Scotland

The courts having jurisdiction are—

(1) the Court of Session, in the case of all companies registered in Scotland;

(2) where the paid-up share capital does not exceed £120,000,[5a] the sheriff court of the sheriffdom in which the registered office is situate: section 220.

GROUNDS FOR WINDING UP BY THE COURT

Section 222 provides that a company formed and registered under the 1948 Act or an existing company, *i.e.* a company formed and registered under a previous Companies Act,[8] may be wound up by the court if—

(1) the company has by special resolution resolved to be wound up by the court;[9] or

(2) in the case of a public company, default is made in delivering the statutory report to the Registrar or in holding the statutory meeting;[10] or

(3) the company does not commence business within a year after its incorporation, or suspends business for a whole year;[11] or

(4) the number of members is reduced below seven in the case of a public company or below two in the case of a private company; or

---

[6] See County Courts (Bankruptcy and Companies Winding-up Jurisdiction) Order 1971 (S.I. 1971 No. 656), amended by County Courts (Bankruptcy and Companies Winding-up Jurisdiction) (Amendment) Order 1971 (S.I. 1971 No. 1983).

[7] As a result of the Lord Chancellor's direction under the Stannaries Court Abolition Act 1896.

[8] s. 455.

[9] *Cf.* s. 278, *post* p. 614, under which a company may pass a special resolution to wind up voluntarily.

[10] *Ante* pp. 284, 285.

[11] *Cf.* s. 353, *post* p. 601, under which a defunct company may be struck off the register and so dissolved without being wound up.

(5) the company is unable to pay its debts; or

(6) the court is of opinion that it is just and equitable that the company should be wound up. This part of the section was explained in connection with statutory protection of the minority.[12] It should be added that the power to wind up a company under this part is not confined to cases in which there are grounds analogous to those mentioned earlier in the section;[13] or

(7) in the case of a Scottish company, there is subsisting a floating charge over property comprised in the company's property and undertaking and the court is satisfied that the security of the creditor entitled to the benefit of the floating charge is in jeopardy.[14]

Of the 2,900 petitions presented in England and Wales in 1974, 2,733 were by creditors; 2,504 petitions were to the High Court.

The Jenkins Report[15] recommended that section 222 should be extended to provide that a company may be wound up by the court if the event occurs on the occurrence of which the memorandum or the articles provide that it is to be dissolved, and section 278[16] should be correspondingly amended. Special articles or clauses in the memorandum could provide that on the death of one of two members the survivor should have an opportunity to buy the deceased's shares at a price to be fixed by agreement or, in default of agreement, by arbitration, and to pay the price by instalments over a reasonable period, and that in the event of default in the payment of an instalment dissolution should ensue automatically. This would meet a common grievance of the personal representative left with shares in a private company which is making a surplus sufficient to pay the salaries of the remaining working directors but not a reasonable return on the shares.[17]

Clause 84 (1) of the Companies Bill 1973 would have given effect to the Jenkins recommendation.

The Report[18] also proposed that the court should be empowered, on application by the Registrar, to order a company in persistent

---

[12] *Ante* p. 384.
[13] *Loch* v. *John Blackwood Ltd.* [1924] A.C. 783 (P.C.); *Symington* v. *Symington's Quarries Ltd.* (1905) 8 F. 121; *Baird* v. *Lees*, 1924 S.C. 83.
[14] Companies (Floating Charges and Receivers) (Scotland) Act 1972, s. 4; for the meaning of "in jeopardy" see *ante* p. 505.
[15] Para. 78.
[16] *Post* p. 614.
[17] See *ante* p. 392.
[18] Para. 511.

breach of its statutory duties, or being carried on for an unlawful purpose, to be wound up. This power could be exercised where a company has failed to appoint the statutory minimum of directors.

Clause 85 (2) and (4) would have enabled a company to be wound up by the court on the petition of the Secretary of State in certain cases, *e.g.* where it has been persistently in breach of its obligations under the Companies Acts.

Ground (2): Default in delivery of statutory report, etc.

A winding-up petition on the ground of default in the delivery of the statutory report, or in the holding of the statutory meeting, by a public company, can be presented only by a shareholder, and even he cannot petition until the expiration of 14 days after the last day on which the meeting should have been held: section 224. In such a case the court may, instead of making a winding-up order, direct that the report shall be delivered or that a meeting be held, and that the costs be paid by the persons responsible for the default: section 225.

Ground (3): Company not carrying on business

The period of a year is fixed by section 222 *ante* so as to give the company a reasonable time in which to commence or resume business, as the case may be.

A winding-up order will only be made on this ground if the company has no intention of carrying on business.[19]

A company was formed to build and use assembly rooms. Owing to a depression in trade in the neighbourhood, building was suspended for more than three years although the company intended to continue its operations when trade prospects improved. A shareholder presented a winding-up petition which was opposed by four-fifths of the shareholders. *Held*, the petition should be dismissed. Since the conduct of the majority was not unreasonable or something of which the minority had a right to complain, the wishes of the majority were not to be disregarded. It would have been different if business could not have been carried on or there was an intention to abandon the undertaking: *Re Middlesborough Assembly Rooms Co.* (1880) 14 Ch.D. 104 (C.A.).

If a company is formed to carry on business in England and abroad and has carried on business abroad, it will not be wound up merely on the ground that it has not started its business in England within the year if it intends to do so as soon as possible.[20] There is

[19] *Re Metropolitan Rlwy. Warehousing Co.* (1867) 36 L.J.Ch. 827.
[20] *Re Capital Fire Insurance Association* (1882) 21 Ch.D. 209.

no need to wait a year if it is apparent within the year that the company cannot carry out the objects for which it was formed.[21]

Ground (5): Company unable to pay its debts

This is the ground on which a petition for a compulsory winding up is usually presented.

A company is *deemed* to be unable to pay its debts if—

(a) a creditor by assignment or otherwise, to whom the company is indebted in a sum exceeding £200 [21a] then due has served on the company, by leaving it at the registered office, a demand under his hand requiring the company to pay the sum so due, and the company has for three weeks thereafter neglected to pay the sum due or to secure[22] or compound for it to the creditor's satisfaction; or

(b) in England, execution issued on a judgment in favour of a creditor is returned unsatisfied in whole or in part; or

(c) in Scotland, the induciae of a charge for payment on an extract decree have expired without payment being made; or

(d) it is proved to the satisfaction of the court that *the company's contingent and prospective liabilities, being taken into account,* the company is unable to pay its debts: section 223.

A company has not neglected to pay a debt within (a), *ante,* if it bona fide disputes the debt, and consequently the creditor is not in such a case entitled to a winding-up order.[23] Where there is no doubt that the petitioner is a creditor for a sum which would otherwise entitle him to a winding-up order, a dispute as to the precise sum owed to him is not of itself a sufficient answer to his petition where the company is commercially insolvent in that it does not have assets presently available to meet its current liabilities.[24]

The period of three weeks' neglect required in (a) above is a

---

[21] *Re German Date Coffee Co.* (1882) 20 Ch.D. 169 (C.A.), *ante* p. 80.
[21a] Substituted for £50 by the Insolvency Act 1976, s. 1 and Sched. 1.
[22] The security must be a marketable security covering the amount of the debt: *Commercial Bank of Scotland Ltd.* v. *Lanark Oil Co. Ltd.* (1886) 14 R. 147.
[23] *Re London and Paris Banking Corporation* (1874) L.R. 19 Eq. 444; *Cuninghame* v. *Walkinshaw Oil Co. Ltd.* (1886) 14 R. 87; *W. & J. C. Pollok* v. *Gaeta Pioneer Mining Co. Ltd.,* 1907 S.C. 182. Where it is doubtful whether there is a *bona fide* dispute, the Scots court may sist the petition in order that the petitioners may constitute their debt: *Landauer & Co.* v. *Alexander & Co. Ltd.,* 1919 S.C. 492.
[24] *Re Tweeds Garages Ltd.* [1962] Ch. 406.

period of three clear weeks, excluding the day of service of the demand for payment and the day of presentation of the petition.[25]

It seems that in English practice an order will not usually be made even in cases (*b*) and (*d*), *ante*, unless the petitioner's debt is £200 or more, or the petition is supported by other creditors and the combined debt is £200 or more, since there must be circumstances which justify an inference that the company is insolvent.[26] Where a company refused to pay a debt of £35 on the ground that it was too small to be the foundation of a petition, an order was made.[27] The Scottish practice has been to apply the rule that "any creditor, whatever the amount of his debt, is entitled to a winding-up order, unless special circumstances exist for refusing it."[28]

The Insolvency Act 1976, section 1 empowers the Secretary of State to increase the minimum amount of the debt in section 223 above £200 by statutory instrument.

A company is unable to pay its debts if its acceptances have been dishonoured,[29] or it has informed a judgment creditor that it has no assets on which to levy execution,[30] or the petitioner has demanded payment of the sum due to him without success.[31] A company is not unable to pay its debts just because it is carrying on a losing business, if its assets exceed its liabilities.[32] However, a company may be unable to pay its debts where its assets exceed its liabilities if its assets are not presently available to meet its current liabilities.

Persons who may Petition for Winding Up by the Court

Subject as below, a winding-up petition may be presented on any of the grounds mentioned above, by any of the following parties—

(1) the company;
(2) a creditor;
(3) a contributory;

---

[25] See *Re Lympne Investments Ltd.* [1972] 1 W.L.R. 523.
[26] *Re Industrial Assurance Assocation* [1910] W.N. 245.
[27] *Re World Industrial Bank* [1909] W.N. 148.
[28] *Per* Lord Johnston in *Speirs & Co.* v. *Central Building Co. Ltd.*, 1911 S.C. 330 at p. 333.
[29] *Re Globe, etc., Steel Co.* (1875) L.R. 20 Eq. 337; *Gardy, Petitioner*, 1912 2 S.L.T. 276.
[30] *Re Flagstaff, etc., Co. of Utah* (1875) L.R. 20 Eq. 268; *Re Douglas Griggs Engineering Ltd.* [1963] Ch. 19.
[31] *Stephen, Petitioner* (1884) 21 S.L.R. 764.
[32] *Re Joint Stock Coal Co.* (1869) L.R. 8 Eq. 146.

(4) in England, where, *e.g.*, the company is already being wound up voluntarily, the Official Receiver (Companies Act 1948, s. 224);

(5) the Department of Trade (Companies Act 1967, s. 35[33]; Insurance Companies Act 1974, s. 46; Protection of Depositors Act 1963, s. 16); or

(6) in England, in the case of a charitable company, the Attorney-General (Charities Act 1960, s. 30).

Under section 16 of the 1963 Act as amended by Schedule 2 of the 1976 Companies Act the Department of Trade may petition for the compulsory winding up of a company which advertises for deposits if—

(*a*) it is unable to pay sums due and payable to its depositors, or is able to pay such sums only by obtaining additional deposits or by defaulting in its obligations to its other creditors; or

(*b*) its assets are less than its liabilities taking into account its contingent and prospective liabilities; or

(*c*) it has failed to deliver accounts required by the 1963 Act; or

(*d*) it has failed to comply with the 1976 Act, section 12 (accounting records), or to produce books kept pursuant to that section, and the Department cannot ascertain its financial position.

A creditor

A compulsory liquidation is usually initiated by a creditor's petition. A secured creditor may petition but will normally rely on his security so that the petitioner is almost always an unsecured creditor. Where a petitioning creditor's debt is disputed on a substantial ground the court will restrain the prosecution of the petition as an abuse of the process of the court, even if the company appears to be insolvent.[34]

A creditor whose debt is presently due and who cannot obtain payment normally has a right as between himself and the company *ex debito justitiae* to a winding-up order,[35] even if the company is being wound up voluntarily.[36] This is not displaced merely by show-

---

[33] *Ante* p. 401.   [34] *Mann* v. *Goldstein* [1968] 1 W.L.R. 1091.

[35] See *Re Chapel House Colliery Co.* (1883) 24 Ch.D. 259 (C.A.); *Gardner & Co.* v. *Link* (1894) 21 R. 967.

[36] *Re James Millward & Co. Ltd.* [1940] Ch. 333 (C.A.), *post* p. 627; *Smyth & Co.* v. *The Salem (Oregon) Capitol Flour Mills Co. Ltd.* (1887) 14 R. 441.

ing that the company has appealed against the judgment giving rise
to the debt,[37] or has a disputed claim against the petitioning judgment creditor which is the subject of litigation in other proceedings.[38]
Where there is a cross-claim the matter is one for the discretion of
the judge.[39]

The above rule applies only between the petitioning creditor and
the company. As to all matters relating to winding up the court may
have regard to the wishes of the creditors or contributories of the
company, as proved by sufficient evidence, and may, for the purpose
of ascertaining those wishes, direct meetings to be called, and in the
case of creditors regard must be had to the value of each creditor's
debt: section 346.

Where the company is insolvent the views of the creditors alone,
as the only persons interested, are considered. In other cases the
views of the contributories are considered. Where there are different
classes of creditors the wishes of those particularly interested will be
given most weight and, in particular, where the company's assets are
not entirely charged in favour of debenture holders the wishes of the
unsecured creditors will be primarily considered.[40] Where the assets
are entirely charged in favour of debenture holders, if the petition of
an unsecured creditor is opposed by the debenture holders the petitioner is entitled to a winding-up order unless the opposing creditors
can show that there is no reasonable possibility of the unsecured
creditors obtaining a benefit from a winding up.[41] The court must
not refuse a winding-up order just because the assets of the company
have been mortgaged to an amount in excess of those assets or there
are no assets: section 225 (1).

If the petition of an unsecured creditor is opposed by the majority
in value of the unsecured creditors, although the court has a complete
discretion under section 346, *ante*, to make or refuse an order and the
fact of the majority opposition is not conclusive, if they oppose for
good reason (*e.g.* because the assets exceed the liabilities and there
are prospects of the company being able to continue business) their
wishes will prevail in the absence of special circumstances making
winding up desirable.[42]

[37] *Re Amalgamated Properties of Rhodesia (1913) Ltd.* [1917] 2 Ch. 115 (C.A.).
[38] *Re Douglas Griggs Engineering Ltd.* [1963] Ch. 19.
[39] *Re L. H. F. Wools Ltd.* [1969] 3 All E.R. 882 (C.A.).
[40] Palmer's *Company Precedents*, 17th ed., Pt. II, p. 81.
[41] *Re Crigglestone Coal Co. Ltd.* [1906] 2 Ch. 327 (C.A.); *Gardner's* case, *ante*.
[42] *Re Vuma Ltd.* [1960] 1 W.L.R. 1283 (C.A.); *Re P. & J. Macrae Ltd.* [1961] 1 W.L.R.
229 (C.A.). See also *Re A.B.C. Coupler Co.* [1961] 1 W.L.R. 243.

If a company is being wound up voluntarily a compulsory order will not usually be made if the majority of the creditors want the voluntary liquidation to continue.[43] Where there are special circumstances the court may give effect to the wishes of the minority.[44]

Any assignee of a debt or of a definite part of a debt can petition,[45] unless a petition was presented in respect of the debt before the assignment.[46] A secured creditor can petition, and his security will not be prejudiced; the holder of bearer debentures can also petition.[47] It has been held that the holder of debenture stock secured by a normal trust deed cannot present a petition as he is not a creditor of the company,[48] the trustees being the proper persons to present the petition in such a case. However, it has been said that it is doubtful whether this decision can be supported.[49]

A contingent or prospective creditor can petition, but the court cannot hear his petition until he has given such security for costs as the court thinks reasonable and established a prima facie case to the court's satisfaction: section 224. It is enough if section 224 is satisfied by the time the petition comes on for hearing.[50]

A judgment creditor for more than £20, who has issued a writ of *fi. fa.*, who is informed that the sheriff holds prior executions against the company so that a forced sale of the available effects will not satisfy all the executions and who is unaware that the company has paid the sheriff a sum to discharge the judgment debt, cannot petition for a winding-up order. The payment to the sheriff extinguished the debt, and the creditor is not a "contingent creditor" within section 224 just because in certain events under section 326 (2)[51] his claim against the sheriff is subject to defeasance: *Re William Hockley Ltd.* [1962] 1 W.L.R. 555.

It has been held in England that a garnishor of a debt due from the company cannot petition, because he is not a creditor, a garnishee order only giving him a lien on the debt and not operating as a transfer of the debt,[52] and that a petition cannot be presented by a person

---

[43] *Re Home Remedies Ltd.* [1943] Ch. 1; *Re B. Karsberg Ltd.* [1956] 1 W.L.R. 57 (C.A.); *Re J. D. Swain Ltd.* [1965] 1 W.L.R. 909 (C.A.), *post* p. 627; *cf. Pattisons Ltd.* v. *Kinnear* (1899) 1 F. 551 and *Elsmie & Son* v. *The Tomatin etc., Distillery Ltd.* (1906) 8 F. 434.
[44] *Bell's Trustees* v. *The Holmes Oil Co. Ltd.* (1900) 3 F. 23; *Bouboulis* v. *Mann, Macneal & Co. Ltd.*, 1926 S.C. 637.
[45] See *Re Steel Wing Co.* [1921] 1 Ch. 349.
[46] *Re Paris Skating Rink* (1877) 5 Ch.D. 959.
[47] *Re Olathe Silver Mining Co.* (1884) 27 Ch.D. 278.
[48] *Re Dunderland Iron Ore Co. Ltd.* [1909] 1 Ch. 446.
[49] Palmer's *Company Law*, 21st ed., p. 742.
[50] *Re A Company* [1973] 1 W.L.R. 1566.
[51] *Post* p. 568.
[52] *Re Combined Weighing Machine Co.* (1889) 43 Ch.D. 99 (C.A.).

with a claim against the company for unliquidated damages.[53] However, it has been said that such persons can petition as "contingent or prospective creditors."[54]

A contributory

The term "contributory" means every person liable to contribute to the assets of the company in the event of its being wound up: section 213. As we shall see, it includes the present members and certain past members of the company: section 212.[55] A holder of fully paid-up shares in a limited company is a contributory and entitled to present a winding-up petition.[56]

A contributory cannot present a petition unless—

(1) the number of members is reduced below seven in the case of a public company or below two in the case of a private company; or

(2) his shares, or some of them, were originally allotted to him or have been held by him, and registered in his name, for at least six months[57] during the 18 months before the commencement of the winding up, or have devolved on him through the death of a former holder: section 224.

The object of the latter provision is to prevent a person acquiring shares to qualify himself to present a petition to "wreck the company."[58]

A shareholder whose calls are in arrear can petition, but he must first pay the amount of the call into court.[59]

---

[53] *Re Pen-y-Van Colliery Co.* (1877) 6 Ch.D. 477.
[54] Palmer's *Company Law*, 21st ed., p. 742, and in *Re A Company* [1973] 1 W.L.R. 1566 it was pointed out by Megarry J. at p. 1571 that the *Pen-y-Van* case was decided on section 82 of the 1862 Act which, unlike the present section 224, says nothing about contingent or prospective creditors and it is very doubtful whether it is an authority for the proposition that a claim for unliquidated damages will not support a petition.
[55] *Post* p. 582.
[56] *Re National Savings Bank Association* (1866) L.R. 1 Ch.App. 547; *Walker and ors, Petitioners* (1894) 2 S.L.T. 230 and 397 (O.H.).
[57] See *Re Gattopardo Ltd.* [1969] 1 W.L.R. 619 (C.A.), where an order was made that a name be entered on the register of members but the company was not a party to the proceedings and therefore was not bound to register the individual as a shareholder, and so the six months' period did not commence when the order was made.
[58] Palmer's *Company Law*, 21st ed., p. 744.
[59] *Re Diamond Fuel Co.* (1879) 13 Ch.D. 400 (C.A.).

The court will not, as a rule, make an order on a contributory's petition unless the contributory alleges and proves, at least to the extent of a prima facie case, that there will be assets for distribution among the shareholders,[60] or that the affairs of the company require investigation in respects which are likely to produce a surplus of assets available for such distribution.[61] The reason is that unless there are such assets, the contributory has no interest in a winding up. The rule is not affected by section 225 (1), *ante*,[62] but does not apply where a contributory's petition on the just and equitable ground[63] is based on the company's failure to supply accounts and information about its affairs, so that he cannot tell whether there will be a surplus for contributories.[64] The Jenkins Report[65] recommended that a contributory's petition for winding up should not fail just because there are no assets available for contributories.

On a contributory's petition the court cannot properly determine the beneficial ownership of shares registered in the name of an opposing contributory but to which the petitioner raises an adverse claim. That is an issue which can only be determined in proceedings between the person claiming to have the interest in the shares as plaintiff and the registered owner as defendant.[66]

A petition by a contributory is uncommon. Such a petition which is opposed by the majority of the contributories will not be granted except where the conduct of the majority is something of which the minority have a right to complain.[67]

The right of a contributory to petition cannot be excluded or limited by the articles.

The articles provided that no winding-up petition could be presented without the consent of two directors, or unless a resolution to wind up was passed at a general meeting, or unless the petitioner held one-fifth of the share capital. None of these conditions was fulfilled. *Held*, the restrictions were invalid and a petition could be presented: *Re Peveril Gold Mines Ltd.* [1898] 1 Ch. 122 (C.A.).

[60] *Re Rica Gold Washing Co.* (1879) 11 Ch.D. 36 (C.A.); followed in *Re Expanded Plugs Ltd.* [1966] 1 W.L.R. 514; *ante* p. 312; *Black* v. *United Collieries Ltd.* (1904) 7 F. 18, *per* Lord Trayner at p. 20.
[61] *Re Othery Construction Ltd.* [1966] 1 W.L.R. 69; considering *Re Haycraft Gold etc., Co.* [1900] 2 Ch. 230 and *Re Newman and Howard, post.*
[62] *Re Othery Construction Ltd.* [1966] 1 W.L.R. 69.
[63] *Ante* p. 384.
[64] *Re Newman and Howard Ltd.* [1962] Ch. 257.
[65] Para. 503.
[66] *Re Bambi Restaurants Ltd.* [1965] 1 W.L.R. 750.
[67] *Re Middlesborough Assembly Rooms Co.* (1880) 14 Ch.D. 104 (C.A.), *ante* p. 542; *Galbraith* v. *Merito Shpg. Co. Ltd.*, 1947 S.C. 446; and see *Re Tivoli Freeholds Ltd.* [1972] V.R. 445, *ante* p. 385.

In the case of the holder of a share warrant the shares are not "registered in his name," so that unless, *e.g.*, he is an original allottee, he cannot petition.[68]

The trustee in bankruptcy of a bankrupt shareholder, where the trustee is not on the register of members, is not a contributory and cannot petition.[69] In similar circumstances, it seems that the personal representative of a deceased shareholder is a contributory.[70] The Jenkins Report[71] recommended that section 224 should empower the trustee in bankruptcy or the personal representative of a contributory to petition the court for a winding up.

The Official Receiver

The Official Receiver can petition for a winding up by the court when a company is already in voluntary liquidation or is being wound up under the supervision of the court in England. An order will only be made if the court is satisfied that the existing liquidation cannot be continued with due regard to the interests of the creditors or contributories: section 224 (2). It has been said that a strong case must be made out.[72] However, in the latest case,[73] it was said that to give the court jurisdiction under section 224 it must merely be satisfied on a balance of probabilities that the voluntary winding up cannot be continued with due regard to the interests of creditors or contributories.

[68] *Per* Chitty J. in *Re Wala Wynaad India Gold Mining Co.* (1882) 21 Ch.D. 849 at p. 853.

[69] *Re H. L. Bolton Engineering Co. Ltd.* [1956] Ch. 577. (S. 216 (*a*), by which the trustee represents the bankrupt shareholder, does not come into effect until a winding-up order is made.) In the Scottish case *Ker, Petitioner* (1897) 5 S.L.T. 126 (O.H.), a trustee in bankruptcy was held entitled as a contributory to petition for the removal of a liquidator and for a supervision order.

[70] See *Re Norwich Yarn Co.* (1850) 12 Beav. 366; *Re Cuthbert Cooper & Sons Ltd.* [1937] Ch. 392 at p. 399, where Simonds J. assumed, without deciding, that such a personal representative is a contributory; *per* Wynn-Parry J. in *Re H. L. Bolton Engineering Co. Ltd.* [1956] Ch. 577 at p. 582; and *Re Meyer Douglas Pty. Ltd.* [1965] V.R. 638, *ante* p. 389, where Gowans J. pointed out at p. 655 that in *Re Norwich Yarn Co.* the statutory definition of "contributory" included not only every member, but also every other person liable to contribute, whether as heir, devisee, executor or administrator of a deceased member. See also *Re Bayswater Trading Co. Ltd.* [1970] 1 W.L.R. 343, *post* p. 602, and *Howling's Trustees* v. *Smith* (1905) 7 F. 390.

[71] Para. 503.

[72] *Re 1897 Jubilee Sites Syndicate* [1899] 2 Ch. 204. Such a case was made out in *Re Ryder Installations Ltd.* [1966] 1 W.L.R. 524.

[73] *Re J. Russell Electronics Ltd.* [1968] 1 W.L.R. 1252.

The Department of Trade

Where a petition for compulsory winding up is presented by the Secretary of State for Trade after he has reached the conclusion, as a result of investigations, that it is expedient in the public interest to wind up the company compulsorily,[74] his conclusion, without being decisive, ought to be given appropriate weight by the court; where there are circumstances of suspicion it is highly desirable that the winding up be by the court; and the passing of a resolution for voluntary winding up shortly before the petition is presented ought not to be allowed to put the voluntary winding up in an entrenched position which can only be demolished if the Secretary of State can show that voluntary winding up would be markedly inferior to compulsory winding up.[75]

A report of inspectors appointed by the Department is prima facie evidence on which the court may act in deciding to make a winding up order on a petition by the Secretary of State.[76]

Clause 85 (1) of the Companies Bill 1973 would have enabled the Secretary of State to petition that a company be wound up by the court on the ground that the number of members is reduced below the statutory minimum (which is seven for a public and two for a private company).

PETITION FOR WINDING UP BY THE COURT

In England the winding-up petition must be in the form specified in the Companies (Winding-up) Rules 1949, as amended,[77] and set out —(1) the date of the company's incorporation, (2) the address of the registered office, (3) the capital, (4) the objects, and (5) the grounds on which the petitioner asks for an order to be made: rule 26.

The Companies (Winding-up) Rules 1949, which were made by the Lord Chancellor, with the concurrence of the President of the Board of Trade, under section 365 (1), do not apply to Scotland. Under section 365 (1) the Court of Session may by Act of Sederunt make general rules for carrying into effect the objects of the Act in relation to the winding up of Scottish companies.[78] Rules of Court,

---

[74] See p. 401 *ante.*
[75] *Re Lubin, Rosen and Associates* [1975] 1 W.L.R. 122.
[76] *Re Armvent Ltd.* [1975] 3 All E.R. 441.
[77] By the Companies (Winding-up) (Amendment) Rules 1957, 1962, 1967, 1971, 1972 and 1975.
[78] Acts of Sederunt regulating winding up are A.S. Sheriff Court Liquidations 1948

which were consolidated in 1965,[78] relate to Court of Session practice in general, but Chapter IV, section 3, thereof, comprising Rules 202–218, is almost entirely devoted to winding-up procedure. In this work "R.C." denotes the Rules of Court 1965 as amended, whereas "r." denotes the Companies (Winding-up) Rules 1949 as amended. The contents of a petition for winding up by the Court of Session are prescribed by Rule of Court 202.

In England the petition must be presented to the Registrar of the court[79] who fixes a time and place for the hearing. Seven clear days, excluding Saturdays and Sundays,[80] before the hearing the petition must be advertised in the *London Gazette* and, depending upon the situation of the company's registered office, in a London daily morning newspaper or a local newspaper circulating in the district in which the registered office is situated. An error in the name of the company in the advertisements makes them absolutely void except where the error is a very trifling error in spelling.[81] The advertisement is an invitation to the creditors and contributories of the company to support or oppose the petition. The petition must then be served on the company at its registered office: rules 27–29.

The petition must be verified by affidavit filed within four days after the presentation of the petition: rule 30.[82] Where a contributory's petition is for the winding up of a private company on the ground of deadlock, evidence of his legal rights in the company must be given, *e.g.* the articles should be put in evidence.[83]

In the Court of Session the petition must be presented to the Outer House, where it is dealt with by a liquidation judge appointed by the Lord President: see R.C. 202.

In England it has been held (in a case where the Board of Trade presented the petition on the ground that winding up was expedient by reason of matters referred to in a report of inspectors appointed to investigate the affairs of the company) that when grave charges are levelled against individuals in a petition, the court will not be satisfied with merely prima facie evidence. The petitioner must, if practicable, prove facts by the evidence of witnesses who have first-hand know-

---

(S.I. No. 2293), A.S. The Companies (Winding-up) Forms 1949 (S.I. No. 1065), and A.S. Rules of Court, Consolidation and Amendment 1965 (S.I. No. 321).

[79] "Registrar," in the Companies (Winding-up) Rules, means the Registrar of the court.

[80] *Re Display Multiples Ltd.* [1967] 1 W.L.R. 571.

[81] Which it will normally be if four conditions are satisfied, as to which see *Re Videofusion Ltd.* [1974] 1 W.L.R. 1548.   [82] Altered by S.I. 1967 No. 1341.

[83] *Re Davis Investments (East Ham) Ltd.* [1961] 1 W.L.R. 1396 (C.A.).

ledge of the matters on which they give evidence.[84] However, in a later case it was held that the report of inspectors stands in a wholly different position from ordinary affidavit evidence and represents the conclusions of a statutory fact-finding body, after hearing oral evidence and examination of books. The court is entitled to look at the report and accept it not as hearsay evidence but as material of a different character. At least where the report is not challenged by the company, the court does not have to be satisfied anew by evidence of the ordinary nature as to the facts found in the report.[85]

After the presentation of a petition in England, the petitioner or his solicitor must attend before the Registrar to satisfy the Registrar that the rules have been complied with. Unless this is done, no order will be made (r. 33), *i.e.* no order in favour of the petitioner will be made—an order dismissing the petition with costs against the petitioner may be made.[86]

After the presentation of a petition (which has not been struck out or dismissed[87]) an application may be made to the court for the appointment of a *provisional liquidator*. In England the appointment may be made at any time before the making of a winding-up order, and the person usually appointed is the Official Receiver. In Scotland the appointment may be made at any time before the first appointment of liquidators: section 238. An appointment is made if the assets are in jeopardy,[88] or to avoid possible prejudice.[89] The provisional liquidator takes all the company's property into his custody or under his control (s. 243), and after his appointment no legal proceedings can be commenced or continued against the company without leave of the court: section 231. An interpleader summons to which the company is made respondent is a proceeding against the company.[90] The appointment of a provisional liquidator has the

---

[84] *Re A.B.C. Coupler Co. (No. 2)* [1962] 1 W.L.R. 1236; not followed in *Re Travel & Holiday Clubs Ltd., post.*

[85] *Re Travel & Holiday Clubs Ltd.* [1967] 1 W.L.R. 711, where it was said (at p. 716c) that it is undesirable that inspectors who have conducted an inquiry should have to give evidence of their findings upon which they would be liable to be cross-examined. This case was followed in *Re S.B.A. Properties Ltd.* [1967] 1 W.L.R. 799. And see *Re Allied Produce* [1967] 1 W.L.R. 1469.

[86] *Re Royal Mutual Benefit Bldg. Socy.* [1960] 1 W.L.R. 1143.

[87] *Re A Company* [1973] 1 W.L.R. 1566.

[88] *e.g. Levy* v. *Napier*, 1962 S.C. 468, in which a deferred shareholder whose petition was opposed by the controlling ordinary shareholder averred that he was apprehensive that the proceeds of the sale of the company's business and assets were being depleted to his prejudice.

[89] *e.g. McCabe* v. *Andrew Middleton (Enterprises) Ltd.*, 1969 S.L.T. (Sh.Ct) 29.

[90] *Eastern Holdings* v. *Singer & Friedlander Ltd.* [1967] 1 W.L.R. 1017.

same result as the making of a winding-up order in that the board of directors of the company becomes *functus officio* and its powers are assumed by the liquidator,[91] but notwithstanding the appointment the board has some residuary powers, *e.g.* it can instruct solicitors and counsel to oppose the petition and, if a winding-up order is made, to appeal against it.[92] The board can also act in interlocutory proceedings, including a motion to discharge the provisional liquidator.

The court may also, after the presentation of a petition (which is still subsisting[87]) and before a winding-up order has been made, on the application of the company or of any creditor or contributory, stay or restrain any pending legal proceedings against the company: section 226. Section 226 is an exception to the rule[93] that proceedings pending in the Supreme Court cannot be restrained by injunction. The object of provisions such as sections 226 and 231 is "to put all unsecured creditors upon an equality, and to pay them *pari passu*."[94]

A petition cannot be withdrawn by a petitioner or be struck out by the court prior to the hearing merely because the petitioner's debt has been paid, or the parties have reached a compromise, but where it is an abuse of the process of the court and therefore bad in its inception, the court has jurisdiction to strike it out before the hearing.[95]

Hearing of petition

The company and any creditor or contributory may attend the hearing of the petition. For this purpose a person is a creditor if he is a creditor for a present debt, a prospective debt or a contingent debt. Whether a person is a contingent creditor depends on circumstances existing at the date of the hearing.[96]

In England any creditor or contributory wishing to appear must give notice to the petitioner of his intention to appear, and state whether he intends to support or oppose the petition: rule 34 as amended.[97] Any affidavit in opposition to the petition must be filed within seven days after the date on which the affidavit verifying the petition was filed. The petitioner can then file affidavits in reply within three days: rule 36. A summons can be taken out for the cross-

[91] *Post* p. 560.
[92] *Re Union Accident Insce. Co. Ltd.* [1972] 1 W.L.R. 640.
[93] In the Supreme Court of Judicature (Consolidation) Act 1925, s. 41.
[94] *Per* Lindley L.J. in *Re Oak Pits Colliery Co.* (1882) Ch.D. 322 (C.A.) at p. 329.
[95] *Re CDPD* (No. 001889 of 1975), June 16, 1975 (Templeman J.).
[96] *Re S.B.A. Properties Ltd.* [1967] 1 W.L.R. 799.
[97] By S.I. 1972 No. 1404.

examination of the deponents on their affidavits. If the company is in default in filing annual returns or other requisite documents, and it is sought to delay or avert the making of a winding-up order, by adjournment or otherwise, there ought usually to be before the court a sufficient indication that steps have been or will be taken for the prompt making good of the default.[98]

In Scotland persons intending to oppose, or otherwise appear in, the petition lodge answers. The induciae within which any answers must be lodged will have been stated in the advertisement of the petition: R.C. 202.

On the hearing of a petition the court may dismiss it, or adjourn the hearing conditionally or unconditionally, or make any interim order, or any other order that it thinks fit: section 225 (1).[99]

The court may have regard to the wishes of the creditors or contributories: section 346.[1]

A petitioner can consent to his petition being dismissed, but he cannot withdraw it without leave of the court.

When a judgment creditor[2] is deprived of the right *ex debito justitiae* to a winding-up order because his petition is opposed by the majority of the creditors, the fair practice is to make no order as to costs.[3] The same is true where the petitioning creditor is not a judgment creditor but his debt is undisputed.[4] *Aliter* if the petitioning creditor acted unreasonably in presenting or prosecuting his petition,[5] or the company is being wound up voluntarily and no evidence is filed on behalf of the petitioner beyond an affidavit verifying the petition.[6]

If a judgment creditor[2] who petitions for the compulsory liquidation of a company which is in voluntary liquidation does more than allege the existence of the voluntary winding up he does so at his own risk as to costs.[7]

When a winding-up order is made, it is usual to order the costs of (1) the petitioner, (2) the company, and (3) one set of creditors and one set of contributories, to be paid out of the assets.

[98] Practice Note (Companies Court) [1974] 1 W.L.R. 1459.
[99] *Ante* p. 546.
[1] *Ante* p. 546. See also *Re Middlesborough Assembly Rooms Co.* (1880) 14 Ch.D. 104 (C.A.), and *Galbraith* v. *Merito Shpg. Co. Ltd.*, 1947 S.C. 446, *ante* p. 549.
[2] Scots equivalent, a creditor who has obtained a decree.
[3] *Re R. W. Sharman Ltd.* [1957] 1 W.L.R. 774; *Re A.B.C. Coupler Co.* [1961] 1 W.L.R. 243.   [4] *Re Sklan Ltd.* [1961] 1 W.L.R. 1013.
[5] *Re A. E. Hayter & Sons (Porchester) Ltd.* [1961] 1 W.L.R. 1008.
[6] *Re Riviera Pearls Ltd.* [1962] 1 W.L.R. 722.
[7] *Re A. & N. Thermo Products Ltd.* [1963] 1 W.L.R. 1341.

In England, three copies of the order must be sent by the court to the Official Receiver. Of these, one must be served on the company at its registered office. Notice of the order is given by the Official Receiver to the Department of Trade, which causes it to be gazetted, and to a local newspaper (r. 42).[8]

A copy of the order must be sent by the company to the Registrar of Companies: section 230.

Section 9 (3) of the European Communities Act 1972 provides that the Registrar must cause notice of the receipt by him of the copy of the order to be published in the *Gazette*. The notice must state the company's name, a description of the document received and the date of receipt.

Clause 88 of the Companies Bill 1973 would have clarified the effect of section 9 (4)[9] of the 1972 Act by providing that section 9 (4) is not to be construed as affecting the operation of section 227, 228, 282, 325 or 327 of the 1948 Act *post*.

The court has power to stay a winding-up order either altogether or for a limited time, on such terms and conditions as it thinks fit, if an application is made to it by the liquidator or (in England) the Official Receiver or any creditor or contributory. In England the court may require the Official Receiver to furnish a report on matters relevant to the application. A copy of any order made by the court under this provision must be sent to the Registrar: section 256. Such an order is not usually made unless all the creditors are paid or satisfied, but the court will have regard to commercial morality and not just to the interests of the creditors.[10] As a matter of practice a stay is never granted, and there are good reasons for the practice.[11]

An appeal from the making of a winding-up order in England may be brought within 21 days: R.S.C., Order 59, rule 4. An order made by a Lord Ordinary in Scotland may be reviewed by the Inner House if a reclaiming motion is enrolled within 14 days: section 277.[12]

Where an order winding up a solvent company was made on a contributory's petition opposed by the company and another contributory, and the company appealed against the order, the company had to provide security for the costs

[8] For Scotland, see R.C. 205.

[9] *Ante* p. 98.

[10] *Re Telescriptor Syndicate Ltd.* [1903] 2 Ch. 174. See also *Re Denistone Real Estate Pty. Ltd.* [1970] 3 N.S.W.R. 327 and *Re Data Homes Pty. Ltd.* [1972] 2 N.S.W.L.R. 22 (C.A.).

[11] See *per* Plowman J. in *Re A. & B.C. Chewing Gum Ltd.* [1975] 1 W.L.R. 579 at p. 592.

[12] *e.g. Levy, Petitioner*, 1963 S.C. 46.

of the appeal otherwise than from the company's assets. It would have been wrong, if the appeal failed, for the petitioner to be liable to bear any proportion of the costs of the appeal or of a liquidation. An order was made that security be provided by the directors or shareholders promoting the appeal: *Re E. K. Wilson & Sons Ltd.* [1972] 1 W.L.R. 791 (C.A.).

CONSEQUENCES OF A WINDING-UP ORDER

The consequences of the making of a winding-up order date back to an earlier date than that on which the order was actually made. This date is called the *commencement of the winding up* and is:

(1) the time of the presentation of the petition;
(2) where, before the presentation of the petition, the company was in voluntary liquidation, the time of the passing of the resolution for voluntary winding up (s. 229).

The consequences of a winding-up order are:

(1) Any disposition of the property of the company, and any transfer of shares or alteration in the status of the members, after the commencement of the winding up, is void unless the court otherwise orders: section 227.

The effect of a winding-up order is to divest the company of beneficial ownership of its assets despite its continuance as legal owner.[13]

The object of section 227 is to prevent, during the period which must elapse before a petition can be heard, the improper alienation and dissipation of the property of a company *in extremis*. However, where a company is trading, the court can, however, sanction transactions in the ordinary course of business—otherwise the presentation of a petition, whether well- or ill-founded, would paralyse the company's trade.[14]

Between the date of the presentation of the petition and the making of a winding-up order X advanced £1,200 to the company to enable it to pay wages due to the staff and took a debenture as security. X knew, at the time of the issue of the debenture, of the presentation of the petition. *Held*, the debenture was valid: *Re Park, Ward & Co. Ltd.* [1926] Ch. 828.

The court may order that a debenture taken after the commencement of the winding up is not void if the money is advanced, not for

---

[13] *Ayerst* v. *C. & K. (Construction) Ltd.* [1976] A.C. 167.
[14] *Per* Lord Cairns in *Re Wiltshire Iron Co.* (1868) L.R. 3 Ch.App. 443 at p. 447; see also *United Dominions Trust Ltd., Notes* 1977 S.L.T. (Notes) 56 (O.H.) (Warrant to all suitable subjects valid).

the payment of wages, but for the company's benefit to enable it to carry out its contracts and the lender has acted in good faith and with the honest intention of benefiting the company.[15]

After the presentation of a petition, property may safely be transferred or payment made *to* the company,[16] but payments made *by* the company in respect of debts previously incurred must be refunded by the recipient.[17]

The word "disposition" in section 227 includes dispositions of a company's property whether made by the company or by a third party, or whether made directly or indirectly.[18]

The court may, under the section, authorise a disposition of a company's property after presentation of the petition notwithstanding that a winding-up order has not yet been made and will do so if the disposition will benefit creditors of the company if an order is made.[19]

Section 227 contains no express provision as to who can apply for the validation of dispositions. However, an applicant must have some discernible interest in the matter. The company can apply under the section. A shareholder has a sufficient *locus standi* to apply. A director may have a sufficient *locus standi*.[20]

The rule which makes transfers of shares and alterations in the status of members void operates for the benefit of the company and its creditors, not for the benefit of third parties, and so an assignation of shares, if duly intimated to the company, cuts out a subsequent arrestment of the shares.[21]

(2) As regards English companies and such property of Scottish companies as is situated in England, any attachment, sequestration, distress or execution put in force against the estate or effects of the company after the commencement of the winding up is void: section 228. As regards Scottish companies

---

[15] *Re Steane's (Bournemouth) Ltd.* [1950] 1 All E.R. 21, applied in *Re Clifton Place Garage Ltd.* [1970] 1 All E.R. 352 (C.A.).

[16] *Mersey Steel Co.* v. *Naylor, Benzon & Co.* (1882) 9 Q.B.D. 648 (C.A.); (1884) 9 App.Cas. 434; *Millar* v. *The National Bank of Scotland Ltd.* (1891) 28 S.L.R. 884 (O.H.).

[17] *Re Civil Service and General Store Ltd.* (1888) 57 L.J.Ch. 119; *M'Lintock* v. *Lithauer*, 1924 S.L.T. 775 (O.H.).

[18] *Re Leslie Engineers Co. Ltd.* [1976] 1 W.L.R. 292. But see *Re Mal Bower's Macquarie Electrical Centre Pty. Ltd. (in Liqdn) etc.* [1974] 1 N.S.W.L.R. 254 to the effect that the s. does not affect agencies such as a bank interposing between a company, as disponor, and the recipient of the property, as disponee.

[19] *Re A. I. Levy (Holdings) Ltd.* [1964] Ch. 19.

[20] *Re Argentum Reductions (U.K.) Ltd.* [1975] 1 W.L.R. 186.

[21] *Jackson* v. *Elphick* (1902) 10 S.L.T. 146 (O.H.).

and such property of English companies as is situated in Scotland, any winding up is, as at the date of its commencement, equivalent to an arrestment in execution and decree of furthcoming, and to an executed or completed poinding, and also to a decree of adjudication of the heritable property of the company for payment of the whole of its debts: section 327.

In spite of its plain words, section 228 is subject to the provisions of section 226, *ante*,[22] and section 231, *post.* Thus an order under section 231 validates, *inter alia*, sequestrations and executions which would otherwise be void under section 228.[23]

The effect of section 327 is to equalise diligence by depriving any creditor who does diligence after the commencement of winding up (or within 60 days before that date) of the benefit which his diligence would otherwise have given him.[24] The section is not restricted by the provisions of section 231, *post.* Accordingly the court could not under section 231 sanction diligence contrary to section 327.[24] Section 327[25] has been held not to render ineffectual an arrestment executed within 60 days before the commencement of winding up but superseded, owing to payment of the debt, before that date.[26]

(3) After a winding-up order has been made or a provisional liquidator has been appointed, no action can be proceeded with or commenced against the company except by leave of the court: section 231.

The purpose of section 231 is to ensure that when a company goes into liquidation the assets are administered for the benefit of all the creditors.[27]

Notwithstanding the section, if a company in liquidation brings an action the defendant may, without leave of the court, set up a cross-demand for liquidated or unliquidated damages, but only as a set-off to reduce or extinguish the plaintiff's claim.[28]

---

[22] p. 554.
[23] *Re Lancashire Cotton Spinning Co.* (1887) 35 Ch.D. 656 (C.A.); *The Constellation* [1966] 1 W.L.R. 272.
[24] For an application of s. 327 (1) (*b*) (decree of adjudication), see *Turnbull* v. *Liquidator of Scottish County Investment Co. Ltd.*, 1939 S.C. 5.
[25] *Allan* v. *Cowan* (1892) 20 R. 36; see also opinion of Lord Trayner in *Radford & Bright Ltd.* v. *D. M. Stevenson & Co.* (1904) 6 F. 429 at p. 431.
[26] *Johnston* v. *Cluny Trustees*, 1957 S.C. 184, *post* p. 569.
[27] *Per* Widgery L.J. in *Langley Constructions (Brixham) Ltd.* v. *Wells* [1969] 1 W.L.R. 503 (C.A.) at p. 508.
[28] *Langley Constructions (Brixham) Ltd.* v. *Wells* [1969] 1 W.L.R. 503 (C.A.).

Since "the court" is defined as "the court having jurisdiction to wind up the company" (s. 455), an action brought in a Scottish court against a company registered in England requires to be sisted until leave of the English court has been obtained.[29]

(4) On a winding-up order being made in England, the Official Receiver by virtue of his office becomes provisional liquidator, and he continues to act until he or another person becomes liquidator: section 239.

(5) On a winding-up order being made, most of the powers of the directors cease,[30] and are assumed by the liquidator. Those which do not have been dealt with already.[31] Some of the duties of the directors cease, too, *e.g.* as to the mode of keeping the company's accounting records under what is now section 12 of the Companies Act.[32] One of the duties which remains after the making of a winding-up order is the duty not to disclose confidential information.[33]

(6) On a winding-up order being made, the servants of the company are *ipso facto* dismissed,[34] and may be able to sue for damages for breach of contract, but a servant who continues to discharge the same duties and receive the same wages as before may be held to have entered by tacit relocation into a contract of service with the liquidator.[35]

Every invoice, order for goods or business letter issued by or on behalf of the company or the liquidator, on which the company's name appears, must contain a statement that the company is being wound up: section 338.

Appointment of special manager in England

When the Official Receiver becomes the liquidator, whether provisionally or otherwise, he may apply to the court for the appointment of a special manager of the company's business other than

---

[29] *Martin* v. *Port of Manchester Insce. Co. Ltd.*, 1934 S.C. 143. And see *Coclas* v. *Bruce Peebles & Co. Ltd.* (1908) 16 S.L.T. 7 (O.H.).
[30] *Fowler* v. *Broad's Patent Night Light Co.* [1893] 1 Ch. 724.
[31] *Ante* p. 554.
[32] *Ante* p. 42.
[33] *Re Country Traders Distributors Ltd.* etc. [1974] 2 N.S.W.L.R. 135.
[34] *Chapman's Case* (1866) L.R. 1 Eq. 346, *ante* p. 371; *Laing* v. *Gowans* (1902) 10 S.L.T. 461 (O.H.), *ante* p. 371.
[35] *Day* v. *Tait* (1900) 8 S.L.T. 40 (O.H.).

himself if the nature of the company's business or the interests of the creditors or contributories require it. The court can appoint the special manager with such powers, including any of the powers of a receiver or manager, as it thinks fit: section 263.

A special manager is appointed in almost all cases where the business of the company is to be carried on pending the appointment of a liquidator.

The special manager must give security to the satisfaction of the Department of Trade. His remuneration is fixed by the court.

PROCEEDINGS AFTER A WINDING-UP ORDER

1. Statement of company's affairs to be submitted to Official Receiver in England

Within 14 days after the appointment of a provisional liquidator or after the winding-up order, a statement of the affairs of the company must be delivered to the Official Receiver unless the court orders otherwise. This statement must be in the prescribed form, verified by affidavit, and must show particulars of the assets, debts and liabilities of the company, the names, residences and occupations of its creditors, the securities held by them and the dates when they were given, and such other information as may be required.

The statement is made by one or more of the directors and by the secretary, or, if the Official Receiver so requires, by other persons, *e.g.* present or past officers of the company. The costs incurred in making the statement are allowed to the makers: section 235.[36]

The statement is open to the inspection of anyone stating himself in writing to be a creditor or contributory.

Clause 91 of the Companies Bill 1973 would have empowered the Official Receiver to require the furnishing of information and the production of books and papers relating to the company.

2. Report by Official Receiver in England

Where a winding-up order is made the Official Receiver must, as soon as practicable after he has received the statement of affairs, submit a preliminary report to the court—

(*a*) as to the amount of capital issued, subscribed and paid up, and the estimated amount of assets and liabilities;

[36] See the 1967 Act, s. 50, *ante* p. 400.

(*b*) if the company has failed, as to the cause of the failure; and

(*c*) whether further inquiry is desirable as to any matter relating to the promotion, formation or failure of the company or the conduct of its business: section 236.

If he thinks fraud has been committed in or since the promotion or formation of the company, the Official Receiver may make a further report to the court and a public examination may be ordered under section 270, *post*.[37]

3. First meetings of creditors and contributories

The Official Receiver must summon separate meetings of the creditors and contributors of the company: section 239.

Unless the court otherwise directs, these first meetings of creditors and contributors must be held within one month, or, if a Special Manager has been appointed, within six weeks, after the winding-up order: r. 121.

The meetings are summoned by at least seven days' notice in the *London Gazette* and in a local paper; and at least seven days before the meeting notice must be sent by post to every creditor and contributory: r. 129.

The Official Receiver must send to the creditors and contributories a summary of the company's statement of affairs, including the causes of its failure, and any observations thereon he may think fit to make. The meetings are not invalidated by reason of any summary or notice not having been sent or received beforehand. The Official Receiver may also summon any director or other officer of the company to attend the meetings. The Official Receiver or his nominee is chairman at the meetings, and the procedure is regulated by the Companies (Winding-up) Rules 1949, rules 121–156. Any other meetings of creditors and contributories are summoned in the same way and regulated by the same procedure.

The object of these meetings is to decide whether to make application to the court to appoint a liquidator in the place of the Official Receiver and, if so, whether to apply for the appointment of a committee of inspection to act with him. If the meetings cannot agree, the court decides: sections 239, 252.

Section 239 and the 1949 Rules do not apply to Scotland, but by section 252 when a winding-up order has been made by the court in

[37] p. 573.

Scotland, the liquidator must summon separate meetings of the creditors and contributories[38] of the company to decide whether or not an application is to be made to the court for the appointment of a committee of inspection to act with the liquidator, and if the meetings do not agree, the court decides.[39]

4. Appointment of liquidator

In England a liquidator may be appointed by the court, on application being made after the meetings of the creditors and contributories have been held. If the two meetings do not agree on the person to be appointed, the court will decide the difference and make such order as it thinks fit. If a liquidator is not appointed by the court, the Official Receiver is the liquidator: sections 237, 239. In Scotland a liquidator is appointed by the court, and is described by the style of "the official liquidator" of the particular company: sections 237, 241. The question of who is to be appointed liquidator is primarily a discretionary matter to be decided by the court which makes the order for winding up, and the exercise of that discretion is not lightly interfered with.[40]

Because liquidation is specialised work carrying heavy responsibilities and a liquidator in a compulsory liquidation is an officer of the court to whom various powers and duties imposed on the court itself are delegated, there has been a rule of practice for thirty years not to appoint an accountant of less than five years' standing. Although the rule is a good working rule, the overall discretion of the court remains.[41]

In England a person other than the Official Receiver who is appointed liquidator cannot act until he has given notice of his appointment to the Registrar of Companies and given security in the prescribed manner to the Department of Trade: section 240. In Scotland all official liquidators must on their appointment find caution of such nature and amount as the court may direct: section 241 and R.C. 206.

In England, the appointment of a liquidator must be gazetted by

---

[38] If the order has been made on the ground that the company is unable to pay its debts, a meeting of contributories need not be summoned: s. 252 (2) proviso.

[39] For Scotland, see R.C. 208, 210.

[40] *Steel Scaffolding Co. Ltd.* v. *Buckleys Ltd.*, 1935 S.C. 617.

[41] *Re Icknield Development Ltd.* [1973] 1 W.L.R. 537 (where exception was made).

the Department of Trade and advertised by the liquidator in such manner as the court directs, after security has been given: r. 58.[42]

Accounts of the liquidator's powers and duties will be found later in this chapter and in Chapter 25.[43]

5. Committee of inspection

The committee of inspection is appointed by the court after the meetings of the creditors and contributories have been held: section 252. It consists of creditors and contributories or persons holding general powers of attorney from creditors or contributories in such proportions as may be agreed on by the meetings or as, in the case of difference, is determined by the court, except that in Scotland if the winding-up order has been made on the ground that the company is unable to pay its debts, the committee consists only of creditors or persons holding general powers of attorney from creditors. It will be shown[44] that the function of the committee is to assist and supervise the acts of the liquidator.

The committee meets at least once a month or oftener if required. The liquidator or any member of the committee may summon a meeting when he thinks necessary. The committee acts by a majority of the members present and a majority of the committee constitutes a quorum.

A person ceases to be a member of the committee if—

(a) he sends his resignation in writing to the liquidator; or

(b) he becomes bankrupt or compounds or arranges with his creditors; or

(c) he is absent from five consecutive meetings without leave of his fellow creditor or contributory representatives; or

(d) he is removed by ordinary resolution of the creditors, if he represents creditors, or of the contributories, if he represents contributories: section 253.

In a winding up in Scotland, the committee has, in addition to the powers and duties conferred and imposed on it by the Act, such of the powers and duties of commissioners on a bankrupt estate as may be conferred and imposed on committees of inspection by general rules:

[42] For Scotland, see R.C. 205.
[43] *Post* pp. 578, 603.
[44] *Post* p. 578.

section 255. The committee has, *e.g.*, a right of access to the liquidator's books and accounts: R.C. 209.[45]

A member of the committee of inspection is in a fiduciary position and cannot, *e.g.*, buy any of the company's assets from the liquidator except by leave of the court: r. 161 *et seq.*[46]

THE PROPERTY OF THE COMPANY IN A WINDING UP BY THE COURT

Custody of company's property. Vesting in liquidator

When a winding-up order has been made, or a provisional liquidator appointed, the liquidator must take into his custody or under his control all the property to which the company is or appears to be entitled. In Scotland, if and so long as there is no liquidator, all the company's property is deemed to be in the custody of the court: section 243.

Winding up does not, as does bankruptcy or sequestration, operate as a *cessio bonorum* or transfer of property: the company's property remains vested in it as before.[47] The liquidator has therefore to get the property into his possession. Under section 244 the court may make an order vesting any of the company's property in him in his official name. Section 258 and, as regards England, section 273 and the Companies (Winding-up) Rules 1949, rule 79, also contain wide powers to enable the liquidator to get the company's property into his custody.

The property to which the company is entitled and which the liquidator can accordingly take into his custody is:

(1) Property belonging to the company at the commencement of the winding up.[48]

---

[45] On R.C. 209 (a) and (b) see *Liquidator of Upper Clyde Shipbuilders Ltd.*, 1975 S.L.T. 39 (O.H.).

[46] For Scotland, see *Liquidators of North British Locomotive Co. Ltd.* v. *Lord Advocate*, 1963 S.C. 272 (O.H.), and *Brewis, Petitioner* (1899) 37 S.L.R. 669 (O.H.), approved in *Liquidators of Pattisons Ltd., Petitioners* (1902) 4 F. 1010.

[47] *Per* Warrington L.J. in *Re H. J. Webb & Co. (Smithfield, London) Ltd.* [1922] 2 Ch. 369 (C.A.) at p. 388; *per* Lord President Inglis in *Queensland Mercantile etc. Co. Ltd.* v. *Australasian Investment Co. Ltd.* (1888) 15 R. 935 at p. 939; *per* Lord Hailsham in *Alexander Ward & Co. Ltd.* v. *Samyang Navigation Co. Ltd.*, 1975 S.L.T. 126 at p. 129.

[48] In Scotland this has been held to include heritable property which the company has come under a personal obligation to convey to a purchaser who has paid the purchase price to the company: *Gibson* v. *Hunter Home Designs Ltd.*, 1976 S.L.T. 94.

(2) Subject as below, property against which execution has been issued by, or which has been attached by the diligence of, a creditor.

Restriction of rights of creditor as to execution or attachment where company being wound up in England

In the case of a company being wound up in England, section 325 (1) provides that where a creditor has issued execution against the goods or lands of a company or has attached any debt due to it, and the company is subsequently wound up, he is not entitled to retain the benefit of the execution or attachment against the liquidator unless he completed the execution or attachment before the commencement of the winding up [49] or, if he had notice of a meeting at which a resolution for voluntary winding up was to be proposed, before such notice. A purchaser in good faith, under a sale by the sheriff, of goods on which execution has been levied acquires a good title to them against the liquidator.

An execution against goods is taken to be completed by seizure and sale, and an attachment of a debt by receipt of the debt, and an execution against land by seizure or the appointment of a receiver: section 325 (2) as amended by the Administration of Justice Act 1956, s. 36 (4).

A judgment creditor who obtains a charging order on specific land of a company under the Administration of Justice Act 1956, section 35 (1), thereby issues "execution" against the land.[50]

Where a judgment creditor issued a writ of *fi. fa.* in respect of the judgment and the sheriff seized the company's goods and, after a petition for a compulsory winding up had been presented (although this was unknown to the sheriff), sold them, when an order for winding up was made the sheriff had to hand over the proceeds to the liquidator.[51]

The phrase "the benefit of the execution" does not refer to "the fruits of the execution" but to the charge conferred on the creditor by the issue of execution.[52]

---

[49] *Ante* p. 557.
[50] *Re Overseas Aviation Engineering (G.B.) Ltd.* [1963] Ch. 24 (C.A.). The Law Commission's tentative view is that charging orders under s. 35 of the Administration of Justice Act 1956 should be placed on the same footing as ordinary charges by amending s. 40 (2) of the Bankruptcy Act 1914 and s. 325 (2) of the Companies Act 1948 so that "execution" would be "completed" by the making of the charging order (Working Paper No. 46: Charging Orders on Land).
[51] *Bluston & Bramley Ltd.* v. *Leigh* [1950] 2 K.B. 548.
[52] *Re Walkden Sheet Metal Co. Ltd.* [1960] Ch. 170.

Where a creditor has issued a writ of *fi. fa.* against a company, money paid to the sheriff or his officers in order to avoid a sale and which remains in their hands at the commencement of the winding up is outside "the benefit of the execution" so that the liquidator is not entitled to such money as against the creditor.[52]

"The benefit of the attachment" means the right to take the necessary steps to complete it.

If a judgment creditor who has obtained a garnishee order obtains payment after receipt by him of notice of a meeting called for the winding up of the company, he must, subject to the court's discretion under section 325 (1), proviso (c), *post*, account to the liquidator for the money.[53]

By section 325 (1), proviso (c), the rights conferred by section 325 (1), *ante*, on the liquidator may be set aside by the court in favour of the creditor. The basic scheme of the Companies Acts is that in a winding up unsecured creditors rank *pari passu* and an execution creditor who has not completed his execution at the commencement of the winding up is for this purpose in the same position as any other unsecured creditor. Section 325 (1), proviso (c), gives the court a free hand to do what is right and fair according to the circumstances of the case,[54] but weighty reasons are necessary to justify the court in exercising its discretion under the proviso.[55]

Where a judgment creditor of a company refrained from levying immediate execution because of a promise of payment by a director, there being no dishonesty by the director, and the execution was not completed before the commencement of the winding up, the court refused to set the liquidator's rights aside. To allow the creditor to retain the benefit of the execution would have been contrary to the basic scheme of the Acts and unfair to the other creditors. During the year before the winding up the company was keeping its general body of trade creditors at bay and there was no reason why one execution creditor who had not completed execution should be preferred to the other creditors whether or not they had obtained judgment or commenced execution.[54]

On the other hand, where before the action the company stalled the creditors' claims by promises and defended the action by disputing a debt already admitted, the liquidator's rights were set aside.[56]

Duties of sheriff as to goods taken in execution

Section 326 (1) provides that, subject to subsection (3), *post*, where any goods of a company are taken in execution and, before the

---

[53] *Re Caribbean Products (Yam Importers) Ltd.* [1966] Ch. 331 (C.A.); overruling *Re Rainbow Tours Ltd.* [1964] Ch. 66.
[54] *Re Redman (Builders) Ltd.* [1964] 1 W.L.R. 541.
[55] *Re Caribbean Products (Yam Importers) Ltd., ante.*
[56] *Re Suidair International Airways Ltd.* [1951] Ch. 165.

sale thereof or the completion of the execution by the receipt or recovery of the amount of the levy, notice is served on the sheriff that
a provisional liquidator has been appointed or a winding-up order
made or that a resolution for voluntary winding up has been passed,
the sheriff must, if so required, deliver the goods and any money
seized or received in part satisfaction of the execution to the liquidator, but the costs of the execution are a first charge on the goods or
such money and the liquidator may sell the goods or part of them for
the purpose of satisfying the charge.

Money paid to the sheriff to avoid a sale is not money received in
carrying out the execution, *i.e.* not money received in part satisfaction
of the execution.[52]

Subject to subsection (3), where under an execution in respect of
a judgment for a sum exceeding £20 the goods of a company are sold
or money is paid to avoid sale, the sheriff must deduct the costs of the
execution from the proceeds of sale or the money paid and retain the
balance for 14 days, and if within that time notice is served on him of
the presentation of a petition for winding up the company or of a
meeting at which a resolution for voluntary winding up is to be proposed, and an order is made or a resolution is passed, as the case may
be, he must pay the balance to the liquidator who is entitled to retain
it as against the execution creditor: section 326 (2).

Where execution is issued against a company and money is paid to the
bailiff to avoid a sale, the payment to the bailiff is payment to the sheriff and if
the 14-day period expires before he receives notice of a winding up the liquidator
is not entitled to the money.[52]

If, after he has sold the company's goods but before he has handed over
the proceeds of sale to the creditor, the sheriff receives notice of a meeting at
which a resolution for *voluntary* winding up is to be proposed and at the meeting
a resolution for *compulsory* winding up is passed, the sheriff is not bound to hand
the proceeds to the liquidator.[51] If the sheriff receives notice, pursuant to section
293, of a meeting of creditors to appoint a liquidator, etc., he is taken to know
that notices of a meeting of members have been sent out too, and the subsection
is satisfied.[57]

Notice of a meeting for the proposal of a resolution for voluntary winding up
was received by the sheriff's officer after he had taken possession of the company's
goods and money was paid to him to avoid their sale. *Held*, there was no evidence
that the sheriff had deputed to him the duty of receiving the notice and no
reason to suppose it implicit in the duties of a sheriff's officer to inform the
sheriff of the receipt of such notice, and it had not been served on the sheriff.
The money was therefore properly paid to the execution creditor: *Hellyer* v.
Sheriff of Yorkshire [1975] Ch.D. 16 (C.A.).

[57] *Engineering Industry Training Board* v. *Samuel Talbot* (*Engineers*) *Ltd.* [1969] 2 Q.B.
270 (C.A.).

Section 326 (3) provides that the rights conferred by the section on the liquidator may be set aside by the court in favour of the creditor.

In the section, the term "sheriff" includes any officer charged with the execution of a writ or other process (subsection (4)). This subsection is intended to cover persons who are in the equivalent situation, so far as execution is concerned, of the sheriff in respect of courts other than the High Court.[58]

Scottish companies, and property of English companies in Scotland

As regards Scottish companies and such property of English companies as is situated in Scotland, section 327 provides as follows:

(*a*) The winding up is, as at the date of its commencement,[49] equivalent to an arrestment in execution and decree of forthcoming, and to an executed or completed poinding, and no arrestment or poinding of the funds or effects of the company executed on or after the sixtieth day before that date is effectual as against the liquidator except to the limited extent that an arrester or poinder who is thus deprived of the benefit of his diligence is entitled to a preference for the expense bona fide incurred by him in his diligence.

C. brought an action of payment against a company and arrested the sum sued for in the hands of S., a debtor of the company. On the instructions of the company, S. paid the sum arrested to C. with the result that the arrestment was superseded. Later, but less than 60 days after the execution of the arrestment, an order was made for the winding up of the company, and the liquidator brought an action to recover the amount paid to C. *Held*, the only arrestments made ineffectual by section 327 were those which, but for it, would have been effectual at the commencement of winding up, and therefore the section did not apply to arrestments which had been withdrawn or superseded by payment of the debt before that date: *Johnston* v. *Cluny Trustees*, 1957 S.C. 184.

(*b*) The winding up is, as at the date of its commencement, also equivalent to a decree of adjudication of the heritable estates of the company for payment of the whole debts of the company, subject to any preferable heritable rights and securities which are valid and unchallengeable and subject to the limited right to poind the ground provided for in (*c*).[59]

[58] Per Russell L.J. in *Hellyer* v. *Sheriff of Yorkshire* [1975] Ch.D. 16 (C.A.) at p. 20.
[59] For an instance of the application of provision (*b*), see *Turnbull* v. *Liquidator of Scottish County Investment Co. Ltd.*, 1939 S.C. 5; on the inter relation of this provision and the Conveyancing and Feudal Reform (Scotland) Act 1970, s. 24 (application to court for warrant to sell), see *United Dominions Trust Ltd.* Notes, 1977 S.L.T. (Note) 56 (O.H.).

(c) A poinding of the ground which has not been carried into execution by sale of the effects 60 days before the commencement of winding up is of no effect in a question with the liquidator unless the poinder holds a heritable security which is preferable to the right of the liquidator, in which case the poinding is available for the interest for the current half-year and for the arrears of interest for the preceding year, but for no more.

(3) Property used by the company to give a fraudulent preference to any of its creditors.

Fraudulent preference

Any conveyance, mortgage, delivery of goods, payment, execution or other act relating to property, made or done by or against a company within six months before the commencement of its winding up, is void if it is a fraudulent preference of any of the company's creditors: section 320. "In this respect the company in liquidation is exactly in the same position as an individual debtor under the Bankruptcy Acts."[60]

In England a payment will be a fraudulent preference if it is—

(a) made with the dominant intention of giving the creditor a preference over the other creditors;[61] and

(b) the voluntary act of the company. A payment made under pressure is not a fraudulent preference.[62]

K. and his wife were the sole directors and shareholders of a company. The company's overdraft was guaranteed by K. On May 12 the directors were advised that the company was insolvent. Between May 12 and 21, payments were made into the bank extinguishing the overdraft, and on May 23 a winding-up resolution was passed. No trade creditors were paid between May 10 and 23. *Held*, a fraudulent preference: *Re M. Kushler Ltd.* [1943] Ch. 248 (C.A.).

Where a creditor making an advance takes from the debtor a promise to execute a charge on request the court will, in the absence of other circumstances, infer that the purpose of the parties is to give the creditor the right to be preferred on request. Such an arrangement, although for value, is fraudulent and unenforceable, and when

---

[60] *Per* Lord Kinnear in *Bank of Scotland* v. *Liquidators of Hutchison, Main & Co. Ltd.*, 1914 S.C. (H.L.) 1 at p. 3.
[61] *Peat* v. *Gresham Trust Ltd.* [1934] A.C. 252.
[62] *Sharp* v. *Jackson* [1899] A.C. 419. And see *Re F.L.E. Holdings* [1967] 1 W.L.R. 1409.

the debtor creates the charge the court, in the absence of other circumstances, will infer that the debtor's intention is to prefer the creditor. Where the creation of the charge is part of a wider arrangement, the debtor's intention must be determined in relation to the arrangement as a whole.[63]

If there is a fraudulent preference of a person interested in property charged to secure the company's debt, that person has the same rights and liabilities as if he were a surety for the debt to the extent of the charge on the property or the value of his interest, whichever is less: section 321. Thus, if a director has secured the company's overdraft, *e.g.* by deposit of the title deeds to his own property, but without undertaking personal liability, and the overdraft is discharged so as to amount to a fraudulent preference of him, and the bank has to repay the liquidator, the bank can sue the director, who can prove against the company.[64]

The bankruptcy rule as to reputed ownership does not apply to companies.[65]

In Scotland fraudulent preferences may be reduced either at common law on the ground of insolvency or under the Bankruptcy Act 1696 (Scots Act 1696, c. 5), as amended by the Companies Act 1947, s. 115 (3), on the ground of notour bankruptcy.

At common law the challenger must prove that—

(*a*) the debtor was insolvent at the date of the transaction and continuously thereafter down to the date of the challenge;

(*b*) the debtor was aware at the date of the transaction that he was insolvent;

(*c*) the transaction was voluntary and in satisfaction or further security of a prior debt; and

(*d*) the transaction was to the prejudice of the debtor's other creditors.

The 1696 Act facilitated challenge of fraudulent preferences. Under that Act, as amended, the challenger must prove that—

(*a*) the debtor is notour bankrupt;

(*b*) the transaction took place at, after, or within six months[66] before, notour bankruptcy;

---

[63] *Re Eric Holmes (Property) Ltd.* [1965] Ch. 1052, *ante* p. 515.
[64] See Gower, *Modern Company Law*, 3rd ed., pp. 661–2.
[65] *Gorringe* v. *Irwell India Rubber Works Ltd.* (1886) 34 Ch.D. 128 (C.A.).
[66] Substituted for 60 days by the Companies Act 1947, s. 115 (3).

(c) the transaction was voluntary and in satisfaction or further security of a prior debt; and

(d) the challenge is made by or on behalf of prior creditors or by a trustee in a sequestration.

Both at common law and under the statute the following are recognised as exceptions and are not reducible unless there is proof of fraudulent contrivance between debtor and creditor—(i) cash payments of debts actually due, (ii) transactions in the ordinary course of trade and (iii) *nova debita*, namely, new debts arising out of new transactions.

A transaction is not "voluntary" if the debtor is doing "the very thing which he is bound to do,"[67] such as implementing a prior obligation to grant a specific security provided that obligation is part of the original contract.[68]

The preference is equally challengeable whether conferred directly (*e.g.* where security is given to a creditor previously unsecured) or indirectly.[69]

An isolated and unprecedented assignation by an insolvent company cannot claim the protection afforded to transactions "in the ordinary course of trade," and is therefore reducible.[70]

The liquidator can sell or otherwise realise the property of the company (s. 245).[71] In England it is his duty to collect the assets of the company and apply them in discharge of its liabilities: sections 257, 273; r. 78. In Scotland it is for the court to cause the assets to be collected and applied in discharge of the company's liabilities, there being no provision for delegation to the liquidator: section 257.

Private examination

After the making of a winding-up order or the appointment of a provisional liquidator, the court may examine on oath any officer of the company or person known or suspected to have in his possession any property of the company or supposed to be indebted to the

---

[67] *Taylor* v. *Farrie* (1855) 17 D. 639 at p. 649 (joint opinion).
[68] *T.* v. *L.*, 1970 S.L.T. 243 (O.H.).
[69] *Walkraft Paint Co. Ltd.* v. *Lovelock*, 1964 S.L.T. 103 (O.H.) (mandates given by the company to certain of its debtors to pay the favoured creditor); *Walkraft Paint Co. Ltd.* v. *James H. Kinsey Ltd.*, 1964 S.L.T. 104 (O.H.) (cheque from company's debtor endorsed by company to the favoured creditor).
[70] *Walkraft Paint Co. Ltd.* v. *James H. Kinsey Ltd.*, *ante.*
[71] *Post* p. 579.

company, or any person whom the court deems capable of giving any information as to the promotion, formation, trade, dealings, affairs or property of the company. The court may reduce his answers to writing and require him to sign them. He may be required to produce books and papers relating to the company. If a person summoned for examination does not appear, he may be apprehended and brought before the court for examination: section 268.

An order for an examination is usually made on the application of the liquidator,[72] but may be made on the application of a contributory. The examination is in private.

It has been said that the section is an extraordinary one giving an extraordinary power of an inquisitorial nature, enabling the court to direct the examination of a person who is not a party to any litigation, and that the process under the section is needed because of the difficulty in which the liquidator in an insolvent company is necessarily placed in that there are almost certain to be many transactions which are difficult to discover or to understand merely from the books and papers of the company.[73]

While it is not a conclusive objection to an order for a private examination under section 268 that proceedings have been commenced against the person concerned, the court ought to act with very great care before ordering an examination of a person who is or who is about to be defendant to an action by the company in liquidation, so that the private examination may be said to be assisting the company to get a favourable judgment.[74]

Public examination in England

In bankruptcy, the bankrupt must always undergo a public examination. When a company goes into liquidation, however, a public examination only takes place if an order for examination has been made. Where the Official Receiver has made a further report[75] to the court stating that in his opinion a *fraud* has been committed by any person in the promotion or formation of the company or by any officer of the company in relation to the company since its formation, the court may make an order for the public examination of such person: section 270.

---

[72] *e.g. M'Lintock* v. *Lithauer*, 1924 S.L.T. 775 (O.H.).
[73] *Per* Megarry J. in *Rolls Razor Ltd.* (*No.* 2) [1970] Ch. 576 at pp. 586 and 591–2.
[74] *Re Bletchley Boat Co. Ltd.* [1974] 1 W.L.R. 630, and see *per* Brightman J. at p. 637.
[75] Under s. 236, *ante* p. 562.

The report must make out a prima facie case of fraud, *i.e.* it must not be flimsy or sketchy. The charge need not be such as would support civil or criminal proceedings. It need not attribute particular pieces of alleged fraud to particular individuals.[76]

The Official Receiver must take part in the examination, and the liquidator, or any creditor or contributory, may take part. Evidence is given on oath. At his own cost, the person ordered to be examined is furnished with a copy of the Official Receiver's report and he may employ a solicitor with or without counsel. Notes of the examination are taken down in writing and signed by the person examined, and may be used in evidence against him: section 270.

The Jenkins Report[77] recommended that section 270 should empower the court to order public examination of directors of an insolvent company where there is some prima facie case of culpability. The Act does not at present provide a sufficient deterrent to dissuade directors from continuing the business of a company which they know to be hopelessly insolvent.

Attendance of officers at meetings in Scotland

While the public examination required in sequestration[78] has no place in the liquidation of a company, the court in the compulsory winding up of a Scottish company has power to require any officer of the company to attend any meeting of creditors or of contributories or of a committee of inspection for the purpose of giving information as to the trade, dealings, affairs or property of the company: section 269.

Fraudulent trading

Section 332 provides that if in the winding up of a company it appears that business has been carried on with intent to defraud creditors or for any fraudulent purpose, the court, on the application of the Official Receiver, the liquidator or any creditor or contributory, may declare that any persons who were knowingly parties to the fraudulent trading shall be personally responsible, without limitation of liability, for all or any of the company's debts or other liabilities

[76] *Tejani* v. *Official Receiver* [1963] 1 W.L.R. 59 (P.C.).
[77] Para. 503.
[78] Bankruptcy (Scotland) Act 1913, s. 83.

as the court may direct, *i.e.* shall lose the privilege of limited liability. Such persons are also liable to two years' imprisonment or a fine of £500 or both: section 332 (3). A company must be in liquidation before a prosecution can be initiated under subsection (3).[79]

In general it may be properly inferred that there is an intent to defraud creditors if a company carries on business and incurs debts when, to the knowledge of the directors, there is no reasonable prospect of the company being able to pay them.[80] The expression "parties to" in section 332 indicates no more than "take part in" or "concur in" and involves some positive steps. Mere omission by the secretary to give certain advice (that the company is insolvent and should cease to trade) is not being a party to carrying on the business in a fraudulent manner.[81]

The court may charge the liability of any such person on any debt due to him from the company, or on any charge on any assets of the company held by him, or any company or person on his behalf, or certain assignees from him or such a company or person: section 332.

It has been held that a claim by a creditor under section 332 is made on his own account and not under a trust for the other creditors or anyone else.[82] Nevertheless it is thought that the section can only result in an accretion to the assets of the company for distribution in due course of winding up.[83]

It is thought that the section does not involve lifting the veil of incorporation.[84]

The Jenkins Report[77] recommended that section 332 be extended to make directors and others who have carried on the business in a reckless manner, personally liable for the company's debts, and to make it clear that section 332 (3) provides a penalty for fraudulent trading if the facts are discovered otherwise than in a winding up, *e.g.* as a result of an investigation by an inspector appointed by the Department of Trade.

---

[79] *R.* v. *Schildkamp* [1971] A.C. 1.
[80] *Re William C. Leitch Bros. Ltd.* [1932] 2 Ch. 71. However, in *Hardie* v. *Hanson* (1960) 105 C.L.R. 451 the High Court of Australia doubted the decision of Maugham J. in *Leitch Bros.* and it was held that the fact that a company continues to trade and to obtain goods on credit and to incur other liabilities without any reasonable prospect of being able to pay therefor does not of itself show that the directors have carried on the business with intent to defraud creditors. The intent to defraud must be express or actual or real; nothing constructive, imputed or implied will do.
[81] *Re Maidstone Buildings Provisions Ltd.* [1971] 1 W.L.R. 1085.
[82] *Re Cyona Distributors Ltd.* [1967] Ch. 889 (C.A.).
[83] See *per* Russell L.J. in the *Cyona* case at p. 908.
[84] *Ante* p. 33.

Clause 107 of the Companies Bill 1973 would have given effect to the latter recommendation.

Misfeasance proceedings

These were explained in connection with statutory protection of the minority.[85]

Disclaimer in case of company wound up in England

When any part of the property of a company which is being wound up consists of—(1) land burdened with onerous covenants;[86] or (2) shares or stock in companies; or (3) unprofitable contracts; or (4) property that is unsaleable, or not readily saleable, because it binds the possessor to the performance of an onerous act or to the payment of money; the liquidator may, with the leave of the court, disclaim the property. The disclaimer must be made, in writing signed by the liquidator, within 12 months after the commencement of the winding up[87] or such extension of time as the court may grant or, if the liquidator was not aware of the property within one month after the commencement of the winding up, within 12 months after his becoming aware of it or such extended period as the court may allow: section 323.

A disclaimer operates to determine the rights and liabilities of the company in respect of the property disclaimed but does not, except for the purpose of releasing the company from liability, affect the rights or liabilities of any other person: section 323 (2). The court will not allow a disclaimer which would cause substantial injury to other parties, *e.g.* a landlord entitled to sue another party on a guarantee of the rent due from the company.[88]

The liquidator cannot disclaim any property if notice in writing is served on him, by a person interested in the property, requiring him to decide whether he will disclaim or not, and he does not, within 28 days or the further period allowed by the court, give notice that he intends to apply for leave to disclaim. In the case of a contract, if the liquidator does not disclaim within such time, the company is deemed to have adopted it.

---

[85] *Ante* p. 394.
[86] In *Re The Nottingham General Cemetery Co.* [1955] Ch. 683, the land disclaimed could not be used except in accordance with contracts between the company and the holders of grave certificates.
[87] *Ante* p. 557.   [88] *Re Katherine et Cie Ltd.* [1932] 1 Ch. 70.

Any person who is, as against the liquidator, entitled to the benefit or subject to the burden of a contract with the company may apply to the court for an order rescinding the contract. The court may grant rescission on such terms as it thinks fit, including the payment of damages for breach of contract. Any damages payable to such person under the order may be proved for in the liquidation.

The court may, on the application of any person interested in disclaimed property, make an order for the vesting of the property in or the delivery of the property to any person entitled thereto, on such terms as the court thinks just.

Where the property is leasehold, a vesting order cannot be made in favour of any person claiming under the company, as underlessee or mortgagee, except—

    (*a*) subject to the same liabilities and obligations as those to which the company was subject under the lease in respect of the property at the commencement of the winding up; or

    (*b*) if the court thinks fit, subject only to the same liabilities and obligations as if the lease had been assigned to that person at that date.

Any person injured by a disclaimer is deemed a creditor of the company to the amount of the injury and may prove for the amount as a debt in the winding up: section 323.

Repudiation in case of company wound up in Scotland

By the common law of Scotland the liquidator may either adopt or repudiate current contracts, and if he repudiates them the company is liable in damages for breach of contract. If the liquidator does not within a reasonable time declare his intention to adopt a contract, he will be held to have abandoned it and to be liable in damages.[89]

Where the company is bound under two separate contracts with the same party, the liquidator is entitled to adopt one and repudiate with the other, and the other party to the contracts is not entitled to retain a sum due to the company under the contract adopted, either in security for the proper fulfilment of that contract by the company

---

[89] *Crown Estate Commissioners* v. *Liquidators of Highland Engineering Ltd.*, 1975 S.L.T. 58 (O.H.).

or in security for a claim for damages in respect of the contract repudiated.[90]

A Working Party of the Scottish Law Commission recommended
that the statutory disclaimer provisions applicable in English liquidations should not be introduced to Scotland.[91]

POWERS OF THE LIQUIDATOR IN A WINDING UP BY THE COURT [92]

Section 245 provides that:

(1) The liquidator (including a provisional liquidator [93]) in a
winding up by the court has power, *with the sanction of the court or
of the committee of inspection*:

(a) To bring or defend actions and legal proceedings in the name
and on behalf of the company.

It is a matter for his discretion whether he should litigate or not
and so the court will not give guidance as to whether he should
appeal to a higher court.[94]

(b) To carry on the business of the company so far as may be
necessary for beneficial winding up.

When a liquidator carries on the business of the company he does
so as the company's agent and is not personally liable on contracts
which he enters into as liquidator.

S. had a contract with the company to deliver cotton in monthly instalments
from November, 1929, to August, 1930. The company went into liquidation
and C. was appointed liquidator by the court in May, 1930. C. did not disclaim
the contract, and arranged with S. that payment should be made after and not
before delivery. The goods were delivered but not accepted by C. *Held*, C. was
not personally liable for damages for non-acceptance: *Stead, Hazel & Co*. v.
Cooper [1933] 1 K.B. 840.

In *Liquidator of Burntisland Oil Co. Ltd.* v. *Dawson* (1892) 20 R. 180, the
court refused the liquidator's application to carry on the business for an indefinite
period on the ground that the company's property could not then be sold except
on ruinous terms but granted power to carry on for six weeks while the property
was advertised for sale. However, in *M'Intyre, Petitioner*, (1893) 30 S.L.R. 386

---

[90] *Asphaltic Limestone Concrete Co. Ltd.* v. *Glasgow Corpn.*, 1907 S.C. 463; see also
Gray's Trustees v. *Benhar Coal Co. Ltd.* (1881) 9 R. 225.
[91] See Scottish Law Commission, Memorandum No. 16: *Insolvency, Bankruptcy and
Liquidation in Scotland*, para. 105 and App.D.
[92] See further *post* p. 610.
[93] *Wilsons (Glasgow and Trinidad) Ltd., Petitioners*, 1912, 2 S.L.T. 330.
[94] *Note for Liquidator in Liquidation of S.S. "Camelot" Ltd.* (1893) 1 S.L.T. 358 (O.H.).

(O.H.) power was granted to carry on business until the time of the year when the company's property, which consisted of a hall let for public entertainments, could be sold to best advantage.

(c) To appoint a solicitor to assist him in his duties.

It is, however, the duty of the liquidator "to perform the business of the liquidation himself, and only to employ the law-agent in such matters as bring him into contact with the Court, in such matters as involve conveyancing, and in such other matters as justify him in obtaining legal advice for his guidance." [95]

(d) To pay any classes of creditors in full.
(e) To make any compromise or arrangement with creditors.
(f) To compromise all calls and liabilities to calls and other debts and liabilities.

In England, if there is no committee of inspection, the Department of Trade may, on the liquidator's application, give any authorisation required to be given by the committee: section 254. In Scotland, if there is no committee of inspection, the court may provide that the liquidator may exercise powers (a) and (b) above without the sanction of the court: section 245 (4).

(2) On his own responsibility and *without obtaining any sanction*, the liquidator can:

(a) Sell the property of the company.
(b) Do all acts and execute, in the name and on behalf of the company, all deeds and documents, and use the company's seal therefor.
(c) Prove, rank and claim in the bankruptcy, insolvency or sequestration of any contributory.
(d) Draw, accept, make and indorse any bill of exchange or promissory note in the name and on behalf of the company.
(e) Raise money on the security of the company's assets.
(f) Take out letters of administration to any deceased contributory and do any other act necessary for obtaining payment of money due from a contributory or his estate.
(g) Appoint an agent to do business which he cannot do himself.
(h) Do all such other things as are necessary for winding up the affairs of the company and distributing its assets.

[95] *Per* Lord Johnston in *Reekie* v. *Liquidator of Leith etc. Shipping Co. Ltd.*, 1911 S.C. 808 at p. 815.

In Scotland the liquidator has, subject to any general rules made by Act of Sederunt under section 365, the same powers as a trustee on a bankrupt estate under the provisions of the Bankruptcy (Scotland) Act 1913, including power to apply to the court for directions in connection with the exercise of his powers: [96] s. 245 (5).

The liquidator has power to vest in trustees for sale property which the company and he are competent to dispose of, if the trusts are framed so as to accord with his statutory duties as liquidator. Table A, article 135, contemplates such an arrangement.[97]

Winding Up of Unregistered Companies

Section 399 provides that an unregistered company may be wound up by the court if—

   (i) it is dissolved, or has ceased business, or is carrying on business only for the purpose of winding up its affairs; or

   (ii) it is unable to pay its debts; or

   (iii) the court is of opinion that it is just and equitable that the company should be wound up.

The expression "unregistered company" includes any partnership, association or company with the exception of, *e.g.*—

   (i) a company registered under the Companies Acts; or

   (ii) an association or company with less than eight members which is not a foreign partnership, association or company; or

   (iii) a limited partnership registered in England or Northern Ireland: section 398.

For the purpose of determining the court having jurisdiction in the winding-up, an unregistered company is deemed to be registered in England or Scotland according to whether its principal place of business is situated in England or Scotland: section 399 (3).

An unregistered company is deemed unable to pay its debts if—

   (i) a creditor, by assignment or otherwise, for at least £50 has served on the company a written demand for payment and the company has neglected to pay the same or to secure or compound it for three weeks;

[96] *Liquidator for Upper Clyde Shipbuilders Ltd.,* 1975 S.L.T. 39 (O.H.).
[97] *Re Salisbury Railway & Market House Co. Ltd.* [1969] 1 Ch. 349.

   (ii) an action has been instituted against a member for any debt due from the company, or from him in his character of member, and written notice of the institution of the action has been served on the company and the company has not within ten days paid, secured or compounded for the debt, or procured the action to be stayed, or indemnified the defendant against the action and against all costs, damages and expenses to be incurred by him by reason of the same;

  (iii) in England, execution issued on a judgment in favour of a creditor against the company or any member thereof is returned unsatisfied;

  (iv) in Scotland, the induciae of a charge for payment of an extract decree, registered bond or registered protest have expired without payment being made;

  (v) it is otherwise proved to the satisfaction of the court that the company is unable to pay its debts: section 399 (6).

Section 402 extends section 226 [98] (stay of proceedings against company) to proceedings against a contributory where the application to stay is by a creditor, and section 403 provides that where an order has been made for winding up an unregistered company, no action or proceeding shall be proceeded with or commenced against any contributory of the company in respect of any debt of the company, except by leave of the court.

The provisions of Part X of the Act (sections 398 to 405) with respect to unregistered companies are in addition to and not in restriction of the provisions with respect to the winding-up of companies by the court, and the court or liquidator has the same powers in the case of unregistered companies as in the case of the winding up of companies formed and registered under the Act: section 404.

[98] *Ante* p. 554.

Chapter 24

CONTRIBUTORIES AND CREDITORS

As soon as may be after a winding-up order is made, it is the duty of the liquidator in England to—

(1) settle a list of contributories;

(2) collect the company's assets and apply them in discharge of its liabilities: sections 257, 273; rules 78, 80.

In Scotland it is for the court to settle a list of contributories and to cause the assets of the company to be collected and applied in discharge of the company's liabilities: section 257. Section 273, which provides for delegation of the court's power to the liquidator, and the Companies (Winding-up) Rules 1949 do not apply to Scotland.

CONTRIBUTORIES

A contributory is a person liable to contribute to the assets of a company in the event of its being wound up: section 213. Section 212 provides that on a winding up every present and past member is liable to contribute to the assets of the company to an amount sufficient for payment of its debts and liabilities, and the costs, charges and expenses of the winding up, and for the adjustment of the rights of the contributories among themselves. This is subject to certain qualifications, *post*, *e.g.* a past member is not liable to contribute if he ceased to be a member one year or more before the commencement of the winding up[1]: section 212 (1) (*a*). This qualification does not apply in the winding up of an unlimited company which has re-registered as limited under the Companies Act 1967, s. 44.[2]

A fully paid shareholder in a limited company is a contributory so that where all debts have been paid in a voluntary liquidation the liquidator is justified in making calls on partly paid-up shareholders for the purpose of adjusting rights between them and the fully paid-up shareholders.[3]

---

[1] *Ante* p. 557.   [2] *Ante* p. 46.

[3] *Re Anglesea Colliery Co.* (1866) L.R. 1 Ch.App. 555, followed, *e.g.*, in *Paterson* v. *M'Farlane* (1875) 2 R. 490.

The list of contributories

The list of contributories is in two parts, the A list and the B list. The A list consists of the members of the company at the commencement of the winding up, *i.e.* present members. The B list consists of persons who were members within a year before the commencement of the winding up. The B list is often not settled at all, and is never settled unless it appears that the A contributories are unable to satisfy their contributions.[4] The list must distinguish between contributories who are liable in their own right and those liable as representatives of others: section 257.

Procedure on settling the list in England (rr. 80–85)[5]: The list contains (1) the address of each contributory, (2) the number of his shares, (3) the amount called up and (4) the amount paid up.

The liquidator appoints a time and place for the settlement of the list, and gives notice in writing to every person whom he proposes to put on it. At the time appointed, the liquidator settles the list after hearing any objectors. He then gives notice to every person whom he has finally placed on the list. The notice must inform that person that any application to remove his name must be made to the court within 21 days. After the expiration of 21 days no application to vary the list can be made, unless the court extends the time. The liquidator can, from time to time, vary or add to the list. This does not entitle him to reopen any question finally settled.[6]

The court may dispense with the settlement of a list of contributories where it appears that it will not be necessary to make calls on or adjust the rights of contributories: section 257. The distribution of surplus assets among the contributories does not of itself involve an adjustment of the rights of the contributories among themselves.[7] The court should not exercise its discretion to dispense with a list of contributories if the company has a large number of shares held by a large number of shareholders.[8]

Liability of contributories

The liability of a contributory on the A list is limited to the amount unpaid on his shares: section 212 (1) (*d*).

The liability of a contributory on the B list is further limited:

(1) No contribution is required from him exceeding the amount

---

[4] See Palmer's *Company Precedents*, 17th ed., Pt. II, p. 400.
[5] For Scotland, see R.C. 211.
[6] *Re Westways Garage Co. Ltd.* [1942] Ch. 356.
[7] *Re Phoenix Oil, etc., Co.* [1958] Ch. 560.
[8] *Re Paragon Holdings Ltd.* [1961] Ch. 346.

unpaid on the shares in respect of which he is liable as a past member: section 212 (1) (*d*).

Example: C and D are the holders of £1 shares, 37½p paid. C transfers his shares to X and D transfers to Y. Within a year the company is wound up, and is insolvent. X pays up his shares in full, but Y pays nothing. No contribution will be required from C. A contribution will be required from D.

If there have been several transfers of the same shares within a year before the winding up, and the A list is exhausted, all the transferors will be placed on the B list at the same time. In such a case the primary liability is that of the latest transferor.[9]

(2) A B contributory is not liable to contribute in respect of any debt or liability of the company contracted *after* he ceased to be a member: section 212 (1) (*b*).

The assets of the company, including the amount received from A contributories, are first applied *pari passu* in payment of the debts of the company, irrespective of the time when they were contracted.[10] The liability of the B contributors is therefore further restricted, because they are liable only for such of the company's debts contracted before they ceased to be members as have not been satisfied by the distribution of the company's other assets among the creditors generally. The B contributories may therefore not be fully called upon although the creditors are not paid in full.

The liquidator made calls on the B contributories of 1s. a share in 1925, and 1s. 6d. a share in 1927. The amount so realised exceeded by about £10,000 the debts of the company contracted while the B contributories were members but the total of all the calls did not suffice to pay the creditors in full. The liquidator asked to retain the full amount of the calls on the B contributories as assets available for the creditors. *Held*, he could not retain the full amount, but must return the £10,000 to the B contributories: *Re City of London Insce. Co. Ltd.* [1932] 1 Ch. 226.

B contributions are part of the general assets of the company, and are not to be applied, preferentially or exclusively, to the payment of debts incurred before the B shareholders ceased to be members.[11]

(3) A B contributory is not liable to contribute unless it appears to the court that the existing members are unable to satisfy their contributions: section 212 (1) (*c*).

---

[9] *Humby's Case* (1872) 26 L.T. 936.
[10] *Morris' Case* (1871) L.R. 7 Ch.App. 200.
[11] *Webb* v. *Whiffin* (1872) L.R. 5 H.L. 711.

It is uncertain whether the liability of a B contributory is fixed at the date of a call on him or at a later date.[12] Thus it is uncertain whether such liability would be reduced by the purchase, after a call has been made on him, of debts incurred by the company before he ceased to be a member.

A member cannot claim any dividend in competition with any other creditor not a member of the company: section 212 (1) (*g*). For the purposes of section 212 (1) (*g*) the word "member" includes a past member.[13] This provision has been held not to apply to dividends which have been carried to an account current between the company and a member.[14]

The liability of a contributory creates a debt (in England of the nature of a specialty) accruing at the time when his liability commenced, but payable when a call is made: section 214.

If a contributory dies either before or after he has been placed on the list of contributories, his personal representatives are liable. They are not personally liable; they are liable in their representative character. In England, if they make a default in payment, proceedings may be taken for administering the estate of the deceased: section 215.

If a contributory becomes bankrupt, his trustee in bankruptcy represents him for all the purposes of the winding up and is a contributory accordingly.[15] Calls already made and the estimated value of the bankrupt's liability to future calls may be proved against the estate: section 216.

There are special provisions as to the liability of B contributories where a company has re-registered under section 43 or 44 of the Companies Act 1967.[16]

Calls on contributories

In England calls on contributories are made by the liquidator with the leave of the court or the sanction of the committee of inspection: sections 260 and 273, and rule 86. In Scotland calls are made by the court: section 260.

Procedure on making calls in England (rr. 86–90)[17]: The liquidator summons a meeting of the committee of inspection by at least seven days' notice stating

---

[12] See *Re Apex Film Distributors Ltd.* [1960] Ch. 378 (C.A.).
[13] *Re Consolidated Goldfields of New Zealand Ltd.* [1953] Ch. 689.
[14] *Liquidator of Wilsons (Glasgow and Trinidad) Ltd.* v. *Wilson's Trustees*, 1915 1 S.L.T. 424 (O.H.).
[15] On the interpretation of this provision, see *ante* p. 550, no. 69.
[16] *Ante* pp. 46, 48. [17] For Scotland, see R.C. 212 and s. 275.

the proposed amount of the call and the purpose for which it is intended. If the winding up is in the High Court, notice of the intended call and meeting is advertised in a London newspaper; in other cases, in a local newspaper. The advertisement must state that any contributory may attend the meeting and be heard, or make a communication in writing, with reference to the call. At the meeting any representations made by a contributory, either personally or in writing, must be heard. The sanction of the committee is given by resolution passed by a majority of the members present.

If there is no committee of inspection, the liquidator must obtain the leave of the court. Even if the committee has refused its sanction, the court may grant leave.[18] The application for leave is made by summons served at least four days before the day appointed for making the call on every contributory proposed to be included in the call, but, if the court directs, notice may instead be given by advertisement.

When the liquidator is authorised to make a call, he must file with the Registrar the document making the call. He must also serve on each contributory included in the call a copy of the resolution or order with a notice of the amount due from him.

Payment of the call may be enforced by order of the court, made in chambers on summons by the liquidator.

Calls may be made either before or after the insufficiency of the assets has been ascertained. They are made for an amount necessary to satisfy the debts and liabilities of the company, and the costs of winding up, and for adjustment of the rights of the contributories among themselves. In fixing the amount regard is had to the probability that some contributors may fail to pay the call: section 260.

A debt due from the company to a contributory cannot be set off against calls, whether made before or after the winding up,[19] except—

(1) where all the creditors have been paid in full (s. 259); or
(2) in the case of an unlimited company, where the debt is due to him on an independent dealing with the company and not due to him as a member in respect of dividend or profit (s. 259); or
(3) where the contributory is bankrupt.[20]

A contributory on the list may be ordered by the court, at any time after the making of a winding-up order, to pay any money due from him to the company: section 259.[21] The court can also order the arrest of, and seizure of the movable personal property of, a con-

---

[18] *Re North Eastern Insurance Co.* (1915) 85 L.J.Ch. 751.
[19] *Grissell's Case* (1866) L.R. 1 Ch.App. 528; *Cowan* v. *Gowans* (1878) 5 R. 581; this has been held to be so where a shareholder deposited money with the company against calls: *Millar* v. *Aikman* (1891) 28 S.L.R. 955 (O.H.).
[20] *Re Duckworth* (1867) L.R. 2 Ch.App. 578.
[21] The effect of s. 259 dies with the company when it is dissolved: *Butler* v. *Broadhead* [1975] Ch.D. 97.

tributory believed to be about to abscond or to remove his property with the object of evading payment of calls: section 271.

CREDITORS

In the winding up of an *insolvent* English company the English bankruptcy rules apply with regard to (1) the respective rights of secured and unsecured creditors, (2) debts provable, and (3) the valuation of annuities and future and contingent liabilities: section 317.

It has been held that the bankruptcy provisions as to priority are applicable, including the provision as to limitation of interest to five per cent. in the Bankruptcy Act 1914, s. 66 (1).[22]

Section 317 has no application once the liquidation throws up a surplus, whatever may have been the position at the commencement of the winding up.[23]

In the winding up of an *insolvent*[24] Scottish company certain provisions of the Bankruptcy (Scotland) Act 1913, namely, sections 45 to 62 (which relate to voting and ranking for payment of dividends), section 96 (as to reckoning of majorities), and section 105 (as to interruption of prescription) apply, so far as is consistent with the 1948 Act: s. 318.

Secured creditors (England)

A secured creditor is one who holds some security for a debt due to him from the company, such as a mortgage, charge or lien. He must give credit for the realised or estimated value of his security unless he surrenders it. Thus he may—

    (1) realise his security and prove, as an unsecured creditor, for any balance due to him after deducting the amount realised; or

---

[22] *Re Theo Garvin Ltd.* [1969] 1 Ch. 624.
[23] *Re Rolls-Royce Co. Ltd.* [1974] 1 W.L.R. 1584, in which Pennycuick V.-C. said at p. 1591: "I reach this conclusion with some regret . . . because . . . it seems fair that a creditor should be compensated for being kept out of his money during the period of administration . . . and, again, because the difference in this respect between the winding up provisions and the bankruptcy provisions appears to be without logical foundation."
[23a] A new section 45 was substituted by the Insolvency Act 1976, s. 5(3).
[24] The word "insolvent" is implied from the general nature of the statutory provision: see *Collins' Trustees* v. *Borland & Co. Ltd.*, 1907 S.C. 1287.

(2) value his security and prove, as an unsecured creditor, for any balance due after deducting the value of the security; or

(3) surrender his security and prove, as an unsecured creditor, for the whole debt; or

(4) where he is fully secured, rely on his security and not prove at all.

A secured creditor who has realised his security for less than the total amount of his debt, part of which is preferential,[25] can appropriate the proceeds of sale to that part of his debt which is not preferential, so that he can prove for the preferential part.[26]

If a secured creditor has valued his security, the liquidator may (*a*) redeem the security at that value, or (*b*) require the security to be sold. The creditor may, on the other hand, serve notice in writing on the liquidator requiring him to elect whether or not he will exercise either of these powers, and if the liquidator does not within six months thereafter signify his intention to elect, he loses his right to exercise the powers: Bankruptcy Act 1914, Sched. 2.

The liquidator may also, within 28 days after a proof, require the creditor to give up the security on payment of the estimated value with an addition of 20 per cent.: Companies (Winding-up) Rules 1949, r. 142.

If the creditor has made a mistake in the valuation of his security, he may amend it by application to the court. If he subsequently realises his security, the amount realised must be substituted for the amount in the proof: Bankruptcy Act 1914, Sched. 2.

If, at a meeting of creditors, a secured creditor votes in respect of his whole debt, he will be deemed to have surrendered his security, unless the court is satisfied that the omission to value it was due to inadvertence: rule 141.

Secured creditors (Scotland)

The rules of the Bankruptcy (Scotland) Act 1913, relating to secured creditors, are to the same general effect as the rules applicable in England.

For the purpose of *voting*, a secured creditor must value his security, deduct that value from his debt and specify the balance. If

---

[25] *Post* p. 592 *et seq.*
[26] *Re William Hall (Contractors) Ltd.* [1967] 1 W.L.R. 948.

the estate over which the security extends has been sold, he must specify his free proceeds, deduct them and specify the balance. In either case he is entitled to vote in respect of the balance and no more, except that in questions as to the disposal or management of the estate which is subject to his security he is entitled to vote as a creditor for the full amount of his debt· 1913 Act, s. 55.

The liquidator within two months after the exercise of a secured creditor's vote, or the majority in value of the other creditors at a creditors' meeting, may require the creditor to convey the security to the liquidator on payment of the specified value with an addition of 20 per cent. The creditor may correct his valuation provided at least 21 days have elapsed since the claim was voted on and he has not been required to convey the security to the liquidator: 1913 Act, ss. 58, 96.

For the purpose of *ranking for dividends*, a secured creditor must value his security, deduct that value from his debt and specify the balance, and the liquidator is entitled to a conveyance of the security on payment of the specified value, or to reserve to the creditor the full benefit of the security. In either case the creditor is ranked for and receives a dividend on the balance and no more: 1913 Act, s. 61.

Proof of debts

If the company is *solvent*, all debts payable on a contingency, and all claims against the company, present or future, certain or contingent, ascertained or sounding only in damages, can be proved: section 316.

In other respects the law and procedure applicable depend on whether the company is registered in England or Scotland.

English companies

The debts which can be proved in a liquidation when the company is insolvent are all debts and liabilities, present or future, certain or contingent, owing at the date of the commencement of the liquidation, except demands in the nature of unliquidated damages arising otherwise than by reason of a contract, promise or breach of trust: section 317; Bankruptcy Act 1914, s. 30.

If the company is solvent, a claim for unliquidated damages for tort may be proved; this is not so if the company is insolvent. Statute-barred debts cannot be proved.[27]

Where there have been mutual credits, mutual debts or other mutual dealings between the company and one of its creditors, an account is taken of what is due from one to the other, and the balance of that account and no more can be claimed or paid: Bankruptcy Act 1914, s. 31.

A Co. borrowed money from B Co. on the security of bills of sale charging some machinery and providing for its insurance against fire. The policies were in the name of B, and A paid the premiums. The machinery was destroyed by fire and the insurance amounting to £1,600 paid to B. A then went into liquidation. £744 was owing to B on the bills of sale at the date of the fire, so that B had £856 in hand, but A owed B £2,099 unsecured book debts. *Held*, B could set off the £856 against the £2,099: *Re H. E. Thorne & Son Ltd.* [1914] 2 Ch. 438.

The holder of a life policy in an assurance company mortgaged the policy to the issuing company. On the company's going into liquidation the policy holder claimed to set off the value of the policy against his mortgage debt. *Held*, he was entitled to do so: *Re City Life Assurance Co. Ltd.* [1926] Ch. 191.

This statutory set-off cannot be excluded by agreement between the parties.[28]

A person is not entitled to set off against the property of a debtor where he had, when he gave credit to the debtor, notice of an available act of bankruptcy by the debtor: Bankruptcy Act 1914, s. 31. The publication of notice of a meeting of creditors of a company under section 293[29] is analogous to the filing of a declaration of inability to pay debts under the bankruptcy legislation.[30]

How debts are proved (rr. 91–118): The liquidator must fix a time within which creditors must prove their claims or be excluded from the benefit of any distribution made before those debts are proved.[31] The time fixed must be not less than 14 days from the date of the notice. The time must be advertised in a newspaper and notice given to every creditor whose claim has not been admitted, and to every preferential creditor whose preferential claim has not been admitted.

Proof is made by delivering or posting to the liquidator an affidavit verifying the debt and (1) giving particulars of the debt and any vouchers by which it can be substantiated, and (2) stating whether the creditor is or is not a secured creditor. The liquidator must then examine the proof and within 28 days must in writing admit or reject it or require further evidence in support of it. If he

---

[27] *Re Art Reproduction Co. Ltd.* [1952] Ch. 89.

[28] *Rolls Razor Ltd.* v. *Cox* [1967] 1 Q.B. 552 (C.A.).

[29] *Post* p. 618.

[30] *Re Eros Films Ltd.* [1963] Ch. 565. So is notice of any act or omission of the company which would found a petition to wind up that company on the ground that it was unable to pay its debts: *Law* v. *James* [1972] 2 N.S.W.L.R. 573 (C.A.).

[31] Ss. 264, 273. "Distribution" in r. 106 includes a distribution to contributories: *Butler* v. *Broadhead* [1975] Ch.D. 97.

rejects it, he must state in writing the grounds of his rejection, and the creditor may then, within 21 days, appeal to the court. On an application to reverse a decision of the liquidator in rejecting a proof, the court must approach the question *de novo*, and decide the claimant's rights in the light of the evidence before it, *i.e.* the court is not bound merely to express a view as to whether the liquidator was right or wrong.[32]

If a proof has been improperly admitted, the court may, on the application of the liquidator, a creditor or a contributory, and after notice to the creditor, expunge the proof or reduce its amount.

The liquidator must, on the first day of every month, file with the Registrar a list of all proofs he has received in the preceding month, distinguishing between those admitted, those rejected, and those standing over. Proofs admitted or rejected must be filed with the Registrar.

If, where the liquidator has advertised for claims, a creditor, whether it is his fault or not, does not put in a claim, then he is barred under section 264 and rule 106 *ante*. There is no room for the application of the principle in *Ministry of Health* v. *Simpson* [1951] A.C. 251.[33]

Scottish companies

Certain provisions of the Bankruptcy (Scotland) Act 1913, *ante*,[34] apply when the company is insolvent.

A creditor, if he is to be entitled to vote or draw a dividend, must produce at the meeting or to the liquidator an oath as to the verity of the debt claimed by him, and stating what other persons, if any, are besides the company, liable for the debt, and also specifying any security which he holds. He must also produce the account and vouchers necessary to prove the debt: 1913 Act, s. 45.[34a]

When the creditor's claim depends on a contingency which is unascertained at the date when the claim is lodged, the creditor may require the liquidator to put a value on the claim, and the creditor is then entitled to vote and draw dividends in respect of that value; otherwise such a creditor is not entitled to vote or draw a dividend: 1913 Act, s. 49.

The court may fix a time within which creditors must prove their claims or be excluded from the benefit of any distribution made before those debts are proved: 1948 Act, s. 264. They may, however, participate in later distributions.[35]

If a creditor's oath or claim is in some respect defective, the court

---

[32] *Re Kentwood Constructions Ltd.* [1960] 1 W.L.R. 646.
[33] *Butler* v. *Broadhead* [1975] Ch.D. 97.
[34] p. 587.
[34a] By the Insolvency Act 1976, s. 5, a notice of claim is made an alternative to an oath.
[35] *Dickey* v. *Ballentine* 1939 S.C. 783 (O.H.).

or the liquidator must call upon the person concerned to rectify it, and if it is not rectified it must be disallowed. Where, however, the defect is due to some improper or fraudulent purpose or where other creditors would suffer loss as a result, an opportunity for rectification need not be given: 1913 Act, s. 47.

Appeals against any deliverance by a liquidator on claims to vote and rank are made by note of appeal and must normally be presented to the appropriate court within seven days of the liquidator's deliverance: R.C. 214.

Order of application of assets

The effect of section 319 is that in a winding up the assets of the company are applicable in the following order:

(1) Costs, charges and expenses properly incurred in the winding up, including the remuneration of the liquidator.

(2) The preferential creditors.

(3) The other (ordinary) unsecured creditors.

Subject to what is said later about debts secured by floating charges being postponed to the winding-up costs and preferential unsecured debts, secured creditors may pay themselves out of their security and, as to any balance remaining unpaid, rank as ordinary or preferential unsecured creditors.[36]

In the event of the assets being insufficient to satisfy the liabilities, the court may make an order for payment of the costs, charges and expenses in such order of priority as it thinks just: section 267.

In England priority is regulated by the Companies (Winding-up) Rules 1949, rule 195.

Unless the court orders otherwise, the order of priority is:

(a) Fees and expenses properly incurred in preserving, realising or getting in the assets.

(b) Costs of the *petition*[37] including costs of those appearing on the petition whose costs are allowed by the court.[38]

(c) Remuneration of the special manager (if any).

---

[36] *Ante* p. 587.

[37] See *Re Bostels* [1968] Ch. 346.

[38] In *Re Bathampton Properties Ltd.* [1976] 1 W.L.R. 168 the company's costs were increased by its unsuccessful and unjustifiable opposition to the petition, and only its costs down to and including the first hearing, when it could have consented, were paid out of the assets.

(*d*) Costs and expenses of any person who makes the company's statement of affairs.

(*e*) Charges of a shorthand writer appointed to take an examination.

(*f*) Disbursements of the liquidator.

(*g*) Costs of any person properly employed by the liquidator.

(*h*) Remuneration of the liquidator.

(*i*) Expenses of the committee of inspection, if approved by the Department of Trade.

Where the company is a lessee rent accrued due after the winding-up order is an expense of the liquidation if the liquidator retained the lease solely for the benefit of the liquidation, and not for the joint benefit of himself and the lessors.[39]

The winding-up costs have priority over the preferential debts and the claims of debenture holders under a floating charge and if necessary are paid out of property subject to the charge.[40]

In Scotland there are no fixed rules corresponding to rule 195 above, it being left to the court, in the exercise of its discretion under section 267, to give such priority as it "thinks just" in the circumstances of each case.[41]

The *preferential debts* rank equally among themselves and must be paid in full, in priority to the other unsecured debts, unless the assets are insufficient to meet them, in which case the preferential debts abate in equal proportions: section 319 (5) (*a*).

Clause 93 (1) of the Companies Bill 1973 would have given the preferential debts in class (*c*) *post* priority over the preferential debts in the other classes but would have limited the sum given precedence to £50 per claimant.

By section 319 (1) the preferential debts include:

(*a*) Rates and value added tax[42] which became payable by the company within 12 months next before the relevant date.

The expression "the relevant date" means, when the company is being wound up compulsorily, the date of the appointment of a provisional liquidator or, if no such appointment was made, the date of the winding-up order; if the company is or was being wound up

---

[39] *Re A.B.C. Coupler & Engineering Co. Ltd. (No. 3)* [1970] 1 W.L.R. 702; and see *Re Downer Enterprises Ltd.* [1974] 1 W.L.R. 1460, where an intermediate lessee paid the arrears of rent and was held entitled to the lessor's rights by way of subrogation.

[40] *Re Barleycorn Enterprises Ltd.* [1970] Ch. 465 (C.A).

[41] See *The Northern Distilleries Ltd.* (1901) 9 S.L.T. 213 (O.H.); *Edinburgh Pavilion Ltd.* (1906) 14 S.L.T. 61 (O.H.); *Robertson* v. *Drummond* (1908) 15 S.L.T. 1067 (O.H.).

[42] Finance Act 1972, s. 41 and Finance Act 1976, s. 22.

voluntarily it means the date of the passing of the resolution for winding up: section 319 (8).

(b) *Any* one year's assessment of assessed tax, *e.g.* corporation tax, assessed up to April 5 next before the relevant date.

Apart from these provisions as to taxes, Crown debts have no priority.[43] The Crown's priority is not limited to tax assessed in the year immediately before the winding up; the Crown may claim priority for any one year before that date.[44]

The Crown can choose different years for different preferential debts.

A company in a creditors' voluntary liquidation owed income tax and profits tax, so that any one year's arrears of each was a preferential debt. *Held*, the Inland Revenue Commissioners could choose one year's arrears in the case of the income tax and a different year's arrears in the case of the profits tax: *Lord Advocate* v. *Liquidators of Purvis Industries Ltd.*, 1958 S.C. 338 (O.H.).

(c) Wages or salary (whether or not earned wholly or partly by way of commission) of a clerk or servant in respect of services rendered to the company within four months next before the relevant date, not exceeding £800[44a] per claimant (subs. (2)).

In England a full-time secretary is a "clerk or servant,"[45] but in Scotland a secretary, *semble* even if full-time, is not.[46] A managing director[47] is not a "clerk or servant," nor is a director as such. However, a director may, under power in the articles, be employed in a salaried position with the company and so be a clerk or servant. Thus, where a director could be, and was, employed as editor of a periodical, he was a preferential creditor.[48]

A chemist engaged two days a week at a salary to work on formulae for perfumiers is a "clerk or servant."[49] A contributor, even a regular contributor, to a newspaper, even though paid by a fixed salary, is not.[48]

---

[43] *Food Controller* v. *Cork* [1923] A.C. 647.
[44] *Re Pratt* [1951] Ch. 225.
[44a] Substituted for £200 by the Insolvency Act 1976, s. 1 and Sched. 1.
[45] *Cairney* v. *Back* [1906] 2 K.B. 746.
[46] *Scottish Poultry Journal Co.* (1896) 4 S.L.T. 167 (O.H.) (secretary and manager); *Clyde Football, etc., Co. Ltd.* (1900) 8 S.L.T. 328 (O.H.); *Laing* v. *Gowans* (1902) 10 S.L.T. 461 (O.H.).
[47] *Re Newspaper Proprietary Syndicate Ltd.* [1900] 2 Ch. 349, although see Wallace & Young, *Australian Company Law & Practice*, pp. 798, 799.
[48] *Re Beeton & Co. Ltd.* [1913] 2 Ch. 279.
[49] *Re G. H. Morison & Co. Ltd.* (1912) 106 L.T. 731.

(d) Wages of a workman or labourer for services rendered within four months next before the relevant date, not exceeding £800[44a] per claimant (subs. (2)).

(e) Accrued holiday remuneration payable to a clerk, servant, workman or labourer on the termination of his employment before or by the effect of the winding-up order or resolution.

(f) All the debts specified in section 93 (2) of the Social Security Act 1973 or section 153 (2) of the Social Security Act 1975, *e.g.* national insurance contributions payable by the company as an employer within 12 months next before the relevant date, unless the winding up is a voluntary winding up for the purposes of reconstruction or amalgamation.

Advances made by a third person to pay the wages or salary of any clerk, servant, workman or labourer employed by the company have the same priority as the persons whose wages are paid out of the money advanced: section 319 (4). It is not necessary to prove that the advance of money was made in pursuance of any agreement if it was in fact made for the purpose of paying wages.[50]

A bank met cheques drawn by the company on its overdrawn wages account. *Held*, (1) the bank was advancing money for the purpose of paying wages and the resulting indebtedness was preferential under section 319 (4), and cheques drawn on current account in favour of wages account transferred part of such indebtedness to current account; (2) the rule in *Clayton's* case applied to sums credited to current account so as to discharge the earliest of the debits on such account: *Re James R. Rutherford & Sons Ltd.* [1964] 1 W.L.R. 1211.

A "labour only" contract between a company and a sub-contractor is not a contract of employment for the purposes of section 319 (4) and so advances by a third person to enable the company to pay the sub-contractor are not entitled to priority.[51]

So far as the assets of the company available for payment of general creditors are insufficient to meet them, the preferential debts have priority over the claims of debenture holders under a floating charge[52] created by the company and are paid out of any property subject to the charge: section 319 (5) (b); Companies (Floating Charges) (Scotland) Act 1961, s. 7.

---

[50] *Re Primrose (Builders) Ltd.* [1950] Ch. 561, where an advance by the bank for paying wages was made on current account on the bank's being satisfied that an amount equal to the advance would shortly be paid in. *Held*, the advance was preferential. See also *Re Rampgill Mill Ltd.* [1967] Ch. 1138, where the bank did not make it a condition of an advance that it should be so satisfied.

[51] *Re C. W. & A. L. Hughes Ltd.* [1966] 1 W.L.R. 1369.

[52] *Ante* pp. 502, 506.

In England if a landlord or other person has distrained on the company's goods within three months next before a winding-up order, the preferential debts are a first charge on the goods or the proceeds of the distress. The landlord or other person, however, has the same priority as the persons paid out of the proceeds: section 319 (7).

If the court is to interfere with the rights of a person seeking to complete distress, there must be some inequitable conduct on the part of such person, and where a collector of taxes, relying on his right of distress under the Taxes Management Act 1970, distrained on the goods of a company for unpaid national insurance contributions, had taken possession prior to the date of winding up he was entitled to complete distress by sale and the fact that he obtained priority over other preferential creditors was not sufficient to justify the court's interference.[53]

The ordinary debts rank and abate equally *inter se.*[54]

It may be mentioned here that a sum of money paid into a company's bank account for behoof of the company's employees and which is at the date of the liquidation "clearly distinguishable and capable of being disentangled from the company's own funds," does not form part of the company's assets but must be paid to the employees.[55]

---

[53] *Re Herbert Berry Associates Ltd.* [1976] 1 W.L.R. 783, where the winding up was a creditors' voluntary winding up.
[54] *Per* Lord Selbourne in *Black & Co.'s Case* (1872) L.R. 8 Ch. 254 at p. 262.
[55] *Smith* v. *Liquidator of James Birrell Ltd.*, 1968 S.L.T. 174 (O.H.).

CHAPTER 25

COMPLETION OF WINDING UP BY THE COURT

WHEN the liquidator has collected the assets and received the proofs of the creditors, he proceeds to divide the assets among the creditors.

Procedure on declaring dividends (*England*): Not more than two months before declaring a dividend the liquidator must give notice to (1) the Department of Trade so that it can be gazetted, and (2) such of the creditors mentioned in the statement of affairs as have not proved. The notice must state the latest date up to which proofs must be lodged, which must be not less than 14 days from the date of the notice. A creditor wishing to appeal against the rejection of a proof must do so within seven days from the date of the notice. Immediately after the time for appealing has expired, the liquidator declares a dividend and gives notice to the Department of Trade, so that they can gazette it, and to each creditor whose proof has been admitted. If it becomes necessary to postpone the declaration of a dividend beyond the limit of two months, the liquidator must give a fresh notice of his intention to declare a dividend to the Department of Trade but need not give notice to the creditors.

When a dividend is declared the liquidator must transmit a list of the proofs filed with the Registrar to the Department of Trade.

Dividends may at the request and risk of the person to whom they are payable be transmitted to him by post: rule 119.

Procedure on declaring dividends (*Scotland*): For the provisions of the Bankruptcy (Scotland) Act 1913 which apply, see *ante* p. 587. See also R.C. 214.

If there is any surplus after the costs of the liquidation and the company's debts have been paid, the court must adjust the rights of the contributories among themselves and distribute any surplus among the persons entitled thereto: section 265. The section requires a court order before the liquidator can distribute surplus assets, whether or not an adjustment has to be made among the contributories.[1] It will be remembered that under normal articles preference shareholders are entitled to priority over ordinary shareholders in the return of capital.[2]

In England the order by which the liquidator is authorised to return capital to contributories contains a list of the names and addresses of the persons to whom the return is to be made, the amount payable to each, and particulars of any variation in the list of contributories which has arisen since the list of contributories was settled: rule 120.

---

[1] *Re Phoenix Oil, etc., Co. Ltd.* (*No. 2*) [1958] Ch. 565, where a list of contributories was dispensed with and the register of members was seven years out of date.

[2] *Ante* p. 215.

For tax purposes a distribution on a winding up does not count as income of the shareholder who receives it, whether it consists of a return of capital or a share in surplus assets.[3]

If the liquidation is not completed within a year after its commencement, the liquidator must send to the Registrar of Companies, at such intervals as may be prescribed, a statement in the prescribed form and giving prescribed particulars as to the position of the liquidation: section 342. This statement can be inspected and sealed copies or extracts obtained: section 426 of the 1948 Act as amended by Sched. 2 and 3 of the 1976 Act.

In the case of a company being wound up in England, if the liquidator has in his hands or under his control for six months money representing unclaimed or undistributed assets of the company, he must pay it into the Insolvency Services Account at the Bank of England. Any person entitled to the money may then apply to the Department of Trade, and the Department may, if the liquidator certifies accordingly, make an order for payment: section 343.

Clause 95 of the Companies Bill 1973 would have replaced the Companies Liquidation Account and the Bankruptcy Estates Account by a single account, the "Insolvency Services Account." See new Insolvency Act 1976, s. 3 and Sched. 2.

In the case of a Scottish company, when the company has been wound up and is about to be dissolved, the liquidator must lodge in a joint stock bank of issue in Scotland in the name of the Accountant of Court all unclaimed dividends or unapplied or undistributable balances, and the deposit receipts for these sums must be sent to the Accountant. Within seven years the Accountant, if satisfied of a claimant's right, must grant him a warrant upon which the bank pays the amount due including any interest which has accrued. On the expiry of seven years from the deposit, the Accountant must hand over the receipt to the Queen's and Lord Treasurer's Remembrancer who then obtains from the bank payment of the whole remaining amount on behalf of the Crown: 1948 Act, s. 344; Bankruptcy (Scotland) Act 1913, s. 153.

Dissolution of company

When the affairs of the company have been completely wound up, the court, if the liquidator makes an application in that behalf,

---

[3] *Post* p. 662.
[3a] Substituted for the Companies Liquidation Account by the Insolvency Act 1976, s. 3 and Sched. 2.

must make an order that the company be dissolved. The liquidator must, within 14 days, send a copy of the order to the Registrar of Companies who must make a minute of the dissolution in his books (s. 274) and cause notice of the receipt by him of the order to be published in the Gazette (European Communities Act 1974, s. 9 (3)). However, because of the expense involved in an application to the court, the modern practice is for the liquidator not to apply for a dissolution order under section 274, but to apply to the Registrar to dissolve the company by striking its name off the register under section 353, *post*. After the liquidator is released under section 251 (which does not apply to Scotland), the Registrar waits two years before striking the company off. The idea is to minimise the possibility of striking off being prejudicial.

In 1974, 1,395 compulsory liquidations were begun in England and Wales. Four companies were dissolved by order of the court, whereas 15,807 companies were struck off under section 353. The corresponding figures for Scotland are 42, nil and 595.

The Jenkins Report[4] recommended that a simple and inexpensive means of formally dissolving companies wound up by the court—on the lines of sections 290 and 300, *post*[5]—should be provided.

Subject to any order which may at any time be made by the court under section 352 or section 353, any property vested in or held on trust for a company immediately before its dissolution (excluding property held by the company on trust for any other person) vests in the Crown as *bona vacantia*: section 354. The Crown may disclaim such property by a notice signed in the case of property in England by the Treasury Solicitor (and in the case of property in Scotland by the Queen's Remembrancer). The effect of such disclaimer is much the same as if the property had been disclaimed under section 323, *ante*.[6] The notice of disclaimer must be executed within 12 months after the vesting of the property came to the notice of the Treasury Solicitor or the Queen's Remembrancer or, where any person interested in the property applies in writing to the Treasury Solicitor or the Queen's Remembrancer requiring him to decide whether he will disclaim, usually within three months after the application. The notice of disclaimer must be delivered to the Registrar of Companies and registered by him, and copies must be published in the *Gazette*

---

[4] Para. 503.   [5] *Post* pp. 617, 620.
[6] p. 576; s. 323 is not applicable to Scotland but, for the purposes of s. 355, is deemed to be so.

and sent to persons who have given the Treasury Solicitor or the Queen's Remembrancer notice of their interest in the property: section 355.

Where a company has been dissolved the court may, within two years, make an order declaring the dissolution void. Such an order may be made on the application of the liquidator or of any other person who appears to the court to be interested: section 352. An order may be made after two years if the application is made within two years.[7] A solicitor acting on behalf of a client with a claim against the dissolved company, and having neither a financial nor a proprietary interest, is not a "person . . . interested" within section 352.[8] A liquidator de son tort, *i.e.* a person who has never been a duly appointed liquidator of the company but who has, without lawful authority, been carrying on the liquidation of the company, is.[9] The Inland Revenue may apply where an assessment for taxes has been made but the assessments were under appeal when the company was struck off the register under section 353, *post*.[10]

When a dissolution is declared void, any property of the company which purported to vest in the Crown never so vested, so that no order is necessary to revest it in the company.[11] An office copy of the order declaring the dissolution void must be delivered to the Registrar of Companies within seven days: section 352. Such an order does not validate proceedings taken on behalf of the company between the dissolution and its avoidance.[12] Thus it does not revive a misfeasance summons issued, but not served, before dissolution.[13]

It is incompetent for the court to declare the dissolution void for a limited purpose only.[14]

Grounds for declaring a dissolution void are that there are unsatisfied claims by creditors,[15] or the discovery of undistributed assets such as a sum wrongly paid to the Inland Revenue,[16] or to enable the

---

[7] *Re Scad Ltd.* [1941] Ch. 386, approved of *obiter* in *Dowling, Petitioner*, 1960 S.L.T. (Notes) 76 (O.H.).

[8] *Re Roehampton Swimming Pool Ltd.* [1968] 1 W.L.R. 1693.

[9] *Re Wood and Martin (Bricklaying Contractors) Ltd.* [1971] 1 W.L.R. 293.

[10] *Re Belmont & Co. Ltd.* [1952] Ch. 10; followed in *Re Test Holdings (Clifton) Ltd.* [1970] Ch. 285. The Inland Revenue can also apply under s. 353 (6), *post*: *Re Avondale Hotel Southport Ltd.* (1951) (unreported).

[11] *Re C. W. Dixon Ltd.* [1947] Ch. 251.

[12] *Morris* v. *Harris* [1927] A.C. 252.

[13] *Re Lewis & Smart Ltd.* [1954] 1 W.L.R. 755.

[14] *Champdany Jute Co. Ltd., Petitioners*, 1924 S.C. 209 (for the purpose of receiving a repayment from the Inland Revenue).

[15] *Re Spottiswoode, Dixon and Hunting Ltd.* [1912] 1 Ch. 410.

[16] *Champdany* case, *ante*.

liquidator to grant a title to property of the company sold since the dissolution.[17]

A testatrix by her will gave a share of her residuary estate to a company but the company was dissolved before she died. An order under section 352 was refused because the share of residue did not belong to the company before dissolution. The next of kin therefore took the lapsed share as on a partial intestacy: *Re Servers of the Blind League* [1960] 1 W.L.R. 564.

In very special circumstances the Court of Session in the exercise of its *nobile officium* may declare a dissolution void, although the application has not been made within the two years.[18]

DEFUNCT COMPANIES

By section 353, if the Registrar of Companies has reasonable cause to believe that a company is not carrying on business or is not in operation, he may, after carrying out a specified procedure, strike the company's name off the register, after which it is dissolved and sections 354 and 355, *ante*, apply.

The procedure under section 353 is:

(1) The Registrar sends to the company by post a letter asking whether the company is carrying on business.

(2) If no answer is received within one month, he sends within the next 14 days a registered letter, stating that if no reply is received within one month a notice will be published in the *Gazette* with a view to striking the company's name off the register.

(3) If no satisfactory reply is received, he sends to the company by post and publishes in the *Gazette* a notice, stating that unless cause is shown to the contrary the company will be struck off after three months.

(4) If cause is not shown to the contrary, he strikes the company off and publishes notice thereof in the *Gazette*, whereupon the company is dissolved.

Striking the company's name off the register does not affect the liability of any director or member of the company, and the company may still be wound up by the court. If the company is to be wound up, it should first be restored to the register under section 353 (6).[19]

Section 353 (6) provides that if the company, or any member or creditor thereof, feels aggrieved by the striking off the register, it or he may, within 20 years, apply[20] to the court which, if satisfied that

[17] *M'Call & Stephen Ltd., Petitioners* (1920) 57 S.L.R. 480.
[18] *Collins Brothers & Co. Ltd., Petitioners*, 1916 S.C. 620.
[19] *Re Cambridge Coffee Room Association Ltd.* [1952] 1 All E.R. 112. *Alliance Heritable Security Co. Ltd., Petitioners* (1886) 14 R. 34.
[20] By petition: R.S.C., O. 102, r. 5; R.C. 190.

it is just that the company be revived, may order that the name of the company be restored to the register. A petition for restoration under section 353 (6) should contain an outline explanation of why the company was struck off.[21] Upon an office copy of the order being delivered to the Registrar the company is deemed to have continued in existence as if its name had not been struck off. The court may, by the order, give directions for placing the company and all other persons in the same position as nearly as may be as if the company had not been struck off. This provision should be compared with section 352, *ante*, as to the persons who may apply for a court order and as to what the court may do by an order. The word "creditor" in subsection (6) extends to a plaintiff claiming damages under the Fatal Accidents Acts 1846 to 1959, and having therefore an unqualified claim against the company.[22] The subsection does not authorise the insertion of such a clause as would put a creditor in the same position as if the company had been struck off.[23]

To qualify as a "member or creditor" within section 353 (6) an applicant for restoration must have been a member or creditor of the company at the date when it was dissolved.[24] However, the personal representative of a deceased shareholder has been held entitled to apply for restoration of a company's name to the register, and then for its winding up, even though he is not registered as a shareholder.[25]

On an application for restoration to the register, the court may only restore or refuse to restore and cannot, *e.g.*, impose a penalty (beyond costs) as a condition of restoration.[26] It may, however, make the restoration conditional on the company's filing such statutory returns to the Registrar as are necessary to bring the company's file up to date.[27]

Clause 89 (5) of the Companies Bill 1973 would have given the court power to direct the company to make a payment to the Registrar in respect of the cost of the exercise of his functions.

The restoration of the company to the register under section 353 (6) validates retrospectively all acts done on behalf of the company

[21] Practice Note (Companies Court) [1974] 1 W.L.R. 1459.
[22] *Re Harvest Lane Motor Bodies Ltd.* [1969] 1 Ch. 457.
[23] *Re Lindsay Bowman Ltd.* [1969] 1 W.L.R. 1443, not following *Re Rugby Auto Electric Services* (No. 00973 of 1959 (Dec. 14, 1959) unreported).
[24] *Re New Timbiqui Gold Mines Ltd.* [1961] Ch. 319.
[25] *Re Bayswater Trading Co. Ltd.* [1970] 1 W.L.R. 343.
[26] *Re Brown Bayley's Steel Works Ltd.* (1905) 21 T.L.R. 374; *Re Moses and Cohen Ltd.* [1957] 1 W.L.R. 1007.
[27] *Healy, Petitioner* (1903), 5 F. 644.

between its dissolution and its restoration.[28] This should be compared with the effect of an order under section 352, *ante*. In one English case, where the petition was that of a contributory and there were assets available for the shareholders or creditors, as the case might be, the court directed that, as regards creditors whose debts were not statute-barred at the date of dissolution, the period between dissolution and restoration to the register was not to be counted for the purposes of any Statute of Limitations.[29] Where, *e.g.*, a creditor petitions and there is no indication that other creditors might be unfairly affected by an order not containing a special provision as to the limitation of actions, no such provision will be inserted in the order.[30]

Where the company is in breach of its statutory obligations and at least one applicant is guilty of some default, the normal order for taxation of costs under R.S.C. Order 62, rule 28, should be on a common fund basis (instead of the usual order on a party and party basis).[31]

The Jenkins Report[32] recommended that the court be empowered, on application by the Registrar, to order a company to be struck off the register and dissolved where winding up would not be appropriate. It appears that in one case a company had no assets and its managing director was in receipt of National Assistance but section 353 was not applicable.

Clause 89 of the 1973 Bill would have given effect to the Jenkins recommendation.

The Liquidator in a Winding Up by the Court

The liquidator in a winding up by the court is an officer of the court.[33]

---

[28] *Tymans Ltd.* v. *Craven* [1952] 2 Q.B. 100 (C.A.), applied in *Re Boxco Ltd.* [1970] Ch. 442 (Legal charge created by company after being struck off. Order for restoration made. Company put in same position retrospectively as if charge duly created and registered).

[29] *Re Donald Kenyon Ltd.* [1956] 1 W.L.R. 1397. *Aliter* where the company is already in liquidation: *Re Vickers & Bott Ltd.* [1968] 2 All E.R. 264n.

[30] *Re Huntingdon Poultry Ltd.* [1969] 1 W.L.R. 204, distinguishing *Re Donald Kenyon*, *ante*, and *Re Rugby Auto Electric Services Ltd.*, *ante*.

[31] *Re Court Lodge Development Co. Ltd.* [1973] 1 W.L.R. 1097.

[32] Para. 511.

[33] *Per* Megarry J. in *Re Rolls Razor Ltd.* (*No. 2*) [1970] Ch. 576 at p. 586.

Appointment

The liquidator is appointed in the manner set out in Chapter 23.[34]

Apart from the necessity for giving security, there is no statutory requirement as to his qualifications. A body corporate cannot be appointed liquidator: section 335. Subject to section 335, a liquidator's acts are valid notwithstanding any defects which may afterwards be discovered in his appointment or qualification: section 242.

The court may appoint as liquidator a person resident beyond the jurisdiction of the court but such an appointment is made only where there is adequate reason.[35]

It is no objection to the appointment of a person as liquidator that he has been a director,[36] the secretary[37] or the auditor[38] of the company, but where there are to be joint liquidators it is not desirable, at least where creditors object, that both should be connected with the company.[38]

Clause 90 of the Companies Bill 1973 would have disqualified the following from acting as liquidator—

(1) an undischarged bankrupt, unless leave of the court is obtained;
(2) a person subject to a disqualification order under clause 38 *ante*, unless leave of the court is obtained;
(3) except in a members' voluntary winding up, a person who is, or who at any time during the preceding year has been—

    (*a*) a director of the company; or
    (*b*) interested in at least five per cent. of the issued shares of the company; or
    (*c*) interested in debentures of the company.

For the purposes of (3) above, an interest of a member of a person's family would have been treated as an interest of that person.

Any person who gives, or agrees or offers to give, any member or creditor of the company any valuable consideration with a view to securing his own appointment or nomination, or to securing or preventing the appointment etc. of someone else, as the liquidator, is liable to a fine of up to £100: section 336.

---

[34] p. 563.
[35] *Brightwen & Co.* v. *City of Glasgow Bank* (1878) 6 R. 244 (appointment as joint liquidator of accountant resident in London refused); see also *Liquidators of Bruce Peebles & Co. Ltd.* v. *Shiells*, 1908 S.C. 692, and contrast *Barberton Development etc., Ltd., Petitioners* (1898) 25 R. 654.
[36] *Liquidators of Bruce Peebles* case, *ante*.
[37] *Gilmour's Trustees* v. *Kilmarnock, etc., Investment Co. Ltd.* (1883) 10 R. 1221.
[38] *Argylls Ltd.* v. *Ritchie & Whiteman*, 1914 S.C. 915.

Resignation

A liquidator may resign before the completion of the liquidation: section 242.

In England resignation is effected by summoning meetings of the creditors and contributories to receive the resignation. If both meetings, by ordinary resolutions, agree to accept the resignation, the liquidator files a memorandum with the Registrar and gives notice to the Official Receiver, and his resignation thereupon becomes effective. If either of the meetings does not accept the resignation, the liquidator reports to the court the result of the meetings and sends a report to the Official Receiver, and the court, on application by the liquidator or the Official Receiver, decides whether or not the resignation shall be accepted: rule 167.

In Scotland leave to resign was granted to an official liquidator where it was stated that there was nothing to recover from the estate, and the liquidator's application was concurred in by substantially all the creditors and was unopposed.[39]

Removal

A liquidator may, on cause shown, be removed by the court: section 242. Grounds on which a liquidator may be removed include personal unfitness (due to, *e.g.*, his character, his residence,[40] or his personal interest or involvement[41]), insanity,[42] prosecuting a claim against the wishes of a majority of the creditors where the company is insolvent,[43] or unwillingness to prosecute a claim, which should have been prosecuted, against directors with whom he was intimate.

"The words 'on cause shown' have not quite the effect of 'if the Court shall think fit.' Jessel M.R. said in *In re Sir John Moore Gold Mining Co.*,[44] 'they point to some unfitness of the person—it may be from personal character, or from his connection with other parties, or from circumstances in which he is mixed up—some unfitness in a wide sense of the term.' But, as pointed out by the Court of Appeal in *In re Adam Eyton, Ld.*[45] this definition was not intended to be exhaustive, and if the Court is satisfied on the evidence that it is desirable in the interests of all those interested in the assets that a particular person shall not manage the assets, the Court has power to remove him, without there being shown any personal misconduct or unfitness."[46]

[39] *Jamieson, Petitioner* (1877) 14 S.L.R. 667.
[40] *Skinner, Petitioner* (1899) 6 S.L.T. 388 (O.H.) (residence in England of sole liquidator).
[41] *Lysons* v. *Liquidator of the Miraflores Gold Syndicate Ltd.* (1895) 22 R. 605.
[42] *Re The North Molton Mining Co. Ltd.* (1886) 54 L.T. 602.
[43] *Re Tavistock Ironworks Co.* (1871) 24 L.T. 605.
[44] (1879) 12 Ch.D. 325 (C.A.) at p. 331.   [45] (1887) 36 Ch.D. 299 (C.A.).
[46] Per Astbury J. in *Re Rubber, etc., Investment Trust* [1915] 1 Ch. 382 at p. 387; *Lyson's* case and *Skinner's* case *ante*.

Cause must be shown: the court will not remove a liquidator merely because he is a shareholder and former director,[47] or because the majority of the creditors or of the contributories desire it.[48]

A vacancy in the office of liquidator appointed by the court is filled by the court: section 242.

Remuneration

A person other than the Official Receiver who is appointed liquidator is remunerated as the court directs: section 242.

If there is a committee of inspection in England the remuneration is fixed by the committee and is in the nature of a commission or percentage, of which one part is payable on the amount realised and the other on the amount distributed in dividend. If the Department of Trade is of opinion that the remuneration so fixed is too high, it may apply to the court, which will then fix the remuneration. If there is no committee of inspection, the remuneration will be on the scale of remuneration payable to the Official Receiver as liquidator, unless the court otherwise orders: rule 159.

A liquidator must not receive any gift, remuneration or consideration of benefit whatever, beyond the remuneration he is entitled to receive under the Act or the Rules: rule 160. He must not, whilst acting, purchase any assets of the company except by leave of the court: rule 161. He must not, without the court's sanction, purchase goods for carrying on the business if he would obtain part of the profit arising from the transaction: rule 162.

Where there are joint liquidators, their remuneration is distributed among them in such proportions as the court directs: section 242. The presumption is in favour of equality, but is displaced by evidence that the liquidators have not shared the responsibility and work equally.[49]

A liquidator is not entitled to renumeration out of the funds of a related Company.[49a]

Duties

A liquidator must:

(1) Take all the property of the company into his custody as soon as possible: section 243.

(2) In England, as soon as may be, settle a list of contributories,[50] collect the company's assets, apply them in discharge of its liabilities and distribute any surplus among the members

---

[47] *M'Knight & Co. Ltd.* v. *Montgomerie* (1892) 19 R. 501.
[48] *Ker, Petitioner* (1897) 5 S.L.T. 126 (O.H.).
[49] *City of Glasgow Bank Liquidators, Petitioners* (1880) 7 R. 1196.
[49a] *Taylor, Petitioner*, 1976 S.L.T. (Sh. Ct.) 82.
[50] But see *ante* p. 583.

according to their rights and interests in the company: sections 257, 265, 273; rule 78.

In Scotland, he must perform such duties as will enable the court to exercise the functions mentioned: sections 257, 265; R.C. 211.

The word "liabilities" excludes claims which are not legally enforceable. Thus it does not include arrears of tax claimed by a foreign state, even one which adheres to the Commonwealth.[51]

If the liquidator distributes the assets without making provision for the liabilities he is liable to pay damages to the unpaid creditors.

The company had a lease of premises expiring in 1938 at a yearly rent of £1,217 10s. The lease was assigned to M., and in 1933 the company went into voluntary liquidation. M. was insolvent and unable to pay the rent. The liquidator distributed the assets without making any provision for the company's liabilities under the lease. *Held*, the liquidator had committed a breach of his duty and was liable in damages to the lessor: *James Smith & Sons* (*Norwood*) *Ltd.* v. *Goodman* [1936] Ch. 216 (C.A.).

(3) In England, have regard to any directions given by resolution of the creditors or contributories at a meeting or by the committee of inspection. Directions of the creditors or contributories override those of the committee of inspection: section 246.

In Scotland it is the duty of the committee of inspection to act with the liquidator and advise him in the management of the company's affairs and the conduct of the liquidation: R.C. 209.

(4) In England, summon meetings of the creditors or contributories when directed by resolution of the creditors or contributories or requested in writing by one-tenth in value of the creditors or contributories: section 246. He may summon meetings on his own initiative whenever he wants to ascertain the wishes of the creditors or contributories: section 246.

In Scotland the committee or any member of it may apply to the court for an order on the liquidator to summon a meeting of creditors or contributories or both: R.C. 209. The liquidator may call a meeting of creditors on his own initiative: section 245 and Bankruptcy (Scotland) Act 1913, s. 93.

For the court's power to have meetings of creditors or contributories summoned, see section 346, *ante*.[52]

[51] *Government of India* v. *Taylor* [1955] A.C. 491.
[52] p. 546.

(5) In England, keep, in manner prescribed, proper books. Any
    creditor or contributory may, subject to the control of the
    court, inspect such books: section 247.

The books to be kept are (*a*) the record book, and (*b*) the cash book.

The record book contains a record of all minutes, all proceedings had and
resolutions passed at meetings of the creditors or contributories, or of the
committee of inspection, and all matters necessary to give a correct view of the
liquidator's administration of the company's affairs, excluding documents of a
confidential nature such as opinions of counsel affecting the interest of the
creditors or contributories: rule 171.

The cash book contains entries made from day to day of the receipts and
payments made by the liquidator: rule 172.

Where the liquidator carries on the business of the company, he must keep a
distinct account of the trading and must incorporate in the cash book the total
weekly amounts of the receipts and payments on that trading account: rule 176.

In Scotland the committee of inspection have a right of access to
the liquidator's books and accounts: R.C. 209.

In both countries, after a winding-up order has been made, the
court may order inspection of the company's books and papers by
creditors and contributories and the books and papers are then not
open to any further or other inspection: section 266.

Sections 246 and 247, *ante*, and sections 248 to 250, *post*, do not
apply to Scotland.

(6) In England, pay all money received by him into the Insolvency
    Services Account[52a] at the Bank of England. If the commit-
    tee of inspection satisfy the Department of Trade that it is
    for the advantage of the creditors or contributories for the
    liquidator to bank with another bank, the Department must
    direct payments to be made into such other bank: section 248.

If a liquidator retains more than £200[52b] for more than 10 days, then,
unless he explains the retention to the satisfaction of the Department
of Trade, he is liable to pay interest on the excess at the rate of 20 per
cent. per annum, to disallowance of his remuneration, to be removed
from his office and to pay any expense occasioned by his default:
section 248.

No money must be paid into the liquidator's private banking
account: section 248.

All payments out of the Companies Liquidation Account are made in the
manner prescribed[53] by the Department of Trade: rule 169.

[52a] Substituted for the Companies Liquidation account by the Insolvency Act 1976,
s. 3 and Sched. 2.

[52b] Substituted for £50 by the Insolvency Act 1976, s. 1 and Sched. 1.

[53] See Regulations issued by the Board of Trade, July 2, 1958.

Payments out of a special bank account are made by cheque payable to order, with the company's name on the face of it, signed by the liquidator, and countersigned by a member of the committee of inspection and such other person as the committee appoint: rule 170.

(7) In England, send his accounts to the Department of Trade for audit twice a year: section 249.

The cash book is audited by the committee of inspection every three months and the trading account is examined and certified by the committee once a month: rules 174, 176.

Six months from the date of the winding-up order, and thereafter every six months, until his release, the liquidator must send to the Department of Trade a copy of the cash book in duplicate, with vouchers and copies of the certificates of audit of the committee of inspection. With the first accounts he must send a summary of the statement of affairs, showing the amounts realised and the cause of the non-realisation of the unrealised assets. Every six months he must send a report upon the position of the liquidation. When the assets have been fully realised and distributed, the liquidator must send in his accounts immediately. The accounts are verified by affidavit: rule 175.

When the accounts have been audited by the Department, one copy is filed with the court. Each copy is open to the inspection of any person: rule 177.

A summary of the accounts must be prepared and a printed copy sent by post to every creditor and contributory: rule 178.

A liquidator is under the control of the Department of Trade and if he does not perform his duties properly the Department must inquire into the matter and take such action as they may think expedient. They may also (*a*) require him to answer any inquiries in relation to the liquidation, (*b*) apply to the court to examine him on oath, (*c*) direct a local investigation to be made of his books and vouchers: section 250.

(8) A court winding up involves more than a mere realisation of the assets and distribution of proceeds. The liquidator is an officer of the court, and as such he has public responsibilities to investigate past activities connected with the company and, in appropriate cases, to initiate such further proceedings, civil and criminal, connected therewith as the circumstances may dictate. It is his duty to discover not only breaches of the Companies Act but also conduct falling short of the requisite standards of commercial morality.[54]

There is no objection to a liquidator accepting funds or indemnities from creditors to enable a winding up to proceed, and indeed such practice is to be encouraged. However, a liquidator must decide

---

[54] *Re Allebart Pty. Ltd.* [1971] 1 N.S.W. L.R. 24.

himself what steps should be taken in the winding up and, where he draws upon the financial assistance of the creditor, it is incumbent upon him to ensure that he does not place in jeopardy his independence in the discharge of his duties. A liquidator should not permit a situation to develop in which it might appear that he has yielded up to any degree whatever his exclusive independent control in the decision-making processes and administration of a winding up.[54]

Powers

The liquidator's powers are set out in Chapter 23.[55]

The exercise of his powers is subject to the control of the court, and any creditor or contributory may apply to the court with respect to such exercise: section 245 (3). If, in England, any person is aggrieved by any act or decision of the liquidator, that person may apply to the court, which may make such order as it thinks just: section 246 (5). The court has been held entitled, on an application under either section, to interfere in circumstances analogous to those in which it would interfere under the Bankruptcy Act 1914, s. 80, *e.g.* where there is fraud, or the liquidator has not exercised a discretion bona fide, or he has acted unreasonably.[56]

In England the liquidator may apply to the court for directions in relation to any particular matter arising under the winding up: section 246. In Scotland the liquidator has the same right by virtue of section 245 (5), since a trustee on a bankrupt estate may apply to the court for directions in connection with the exercise of his powers.[57] The right should be exercised in every case of serious doubt or difficulty in relation to the performance by the liquidator of his statutory duties. The omission to exercise it may lead the liquidator into serious liabilities.[58]

Liability

A liquidator is not strictly speaking a trustee for the individual creditors or contributories, his position being that of agent of the company.

---

[55] p. 578.
[56] *Leon* v. *York-o-Matic Ltd.* [1966] 1 W.L.R. 1450; *Re Mineral Securities Australia Ltd.* (*in Liquidation*), *etc.* [1973] 2 N.S.W. L.R. 207.
[57] *Liquidator of Upper Clyde Shipbuilders Ltd.*, 1975 S.L.T. 39 (O.H.).
[58] See *Re Windsor Steam Coal Co.* (*1901*) *Ltd.* [1929] 1 Ch. 151, and *Re Home and Colonial Insurance Co. Ltd.* [1930] 1 Ch. 102, *post.*

During a liquidation a claim was made by a contributory for damages for delay in handing over to the contributory his proportion of the surplus assets of the company. *Held*, in the absence of fraud, bad faith or personal misconduct, an action for damages would not lie against the liquidator at the suit of a creditor or contributory, the proper remedy being an application to the court to control the liquidator in the exercise of his powers: *Knowles* v. *Scott* [1891] 1 Ch. 717.[59]

On the other hand, for breach of any of his statutory duties the liquidator will be liable in damages to a creditor or contributory for injury caused to them.

A liquidator distributed the assets of the company without paying X, a creditor, who had no notice of the liquidation. The books of the company showed X to be a creditor but the liquidator made no attempt to communicate with X beyond issuing an insufficient advertisement for creditors. The company was dissolved. *Held*, the liquidator was liable in damages to X. The duty of the liquidator was not merely to advertise for creditors but to write to those of whom he knew and who did not send in claims: *Pulsford* v. *Devenish* [1903] 2 Ch. 625.

A liquidator should make provision for contingent claims of which he has notice, *e.g.* where the company, having assigned a lease, is under a contingent liability for the rent,[60] or where he knows of possible claims by workmen for injuries not covered by insurance.[61]

If a liquidator applies the company's assets in paying a doubtful claim, which turns out to be unfounded, without taking proper legal advice or applying to the court for directions, he will be liable to refund the amount paid on a misfeasance summons taken out by a creditor or contributory.[62]

In such a case, although the liquidator may be a trustee for the purposes of sections 30 and 61 of the Trustee Act 1925,[63] he is not entitled to relief, because he has paid away money in his hands to the wrong person.

The Trustee Act 1925 does not apply to Scotland but there are corresponding provisions in the Trusts (Scotland) Act 1921, ss. 3 and 32.

A liquidator, however, is not liable for admitting a proof of debt which is ill-founded, provided he exercises all due care beforehand. But "a high standard of care and diligence is required from a liquidator in a . . . winding up. He is of course paid for his services; he is able to obtain wherever it is expedient the assistance of solicitors and

---

[59] *Cf. Upper Clyde* case, *ante*, *per* Lord Grieve (Ordinary) at p. 40.
[60] *James Smith & Sons (Norwood) Ltd.* v. *Goodman* [1936] Ch. 216 (C.A.), *ante* p. 607; *cf.* Lord Elphinstone v. *Monkland Iron, etc., Co. Ltd.* (1886) 13 R. (H.L.) 98.
[61] *Re Armstrong Whitworth Securities Co. Ltd.* [1947] Ch. 673.
[62] *Re Windsor Steam Coal Co. (1901) Ltd.* [1929] 1 Ch. 151 (C.A.).
[63] The point was left open in *Re Windsor Steam Coal Co. (1901) Ltd., ante.*

counsel; and, which is a most important consideration, he is entitled, in every serious case of doubt or difficulty . . . to submit the matter to the Court and to obtain its guidance." [64]

H. Co. made a reinsurance agreement with L. Co. which was invalid. On H. going into liquidation, L. tendered a proof which the liquidator ultimately accepted for £89,100, on which £38,000 was paid to L. in dividends. On learning that he should have disallowed the claim, the liquidator sued L. but the claim was dismissed, as no mistake of fact on the part of the liquidator was made. A creditor took out a misfeasance summons. *Held*, the liquidator was negligent in admitting so large a proof without taking legal advice or applying for directions, and was liable to pay compensation to the company: *Re Home and Colonial Insurance Co. Ltd.* [1930] 1 Ch. 102, *ante*.[65]

Where a liquidator has paid money to shareholders under an error in law, caused, *e.g.*, by an underestimation of tax liability he is not entitled to recover it under the *condictio indebiti*, his position being in this respect analogous to that of a testamentary trustee who is not entitled to recover an overpayment made under an error in construing documents.[66]

Release (England)

When the liquidator has realised as much of the property of the company as he can, and has distributed the final dividend, if any, to the creditors, and made a final return, if any, to the contributories, or has resigned or been removed, he may apply to the Department of Trade for a report on his accounts to be prepared. After considering the report and any objections of the creditors or contributories, the Department may grant or withhold his release, subject to an appeal to the High Court: section 251.

Before applying for his release, the liquidator must give notice of his intention to the creditors and contributories, and must send with the notice a summary of his receipts and payments. This release, when granted, is gazetted: rule 205.

The release, when granted, discharges the liquidator from all liability in respect of his conduct of the liquidation. It may, however, be revoked on proof that it was obtained by fraud, or by suppression or concealment of any material fact: section 251.

---

[64] *Per* Maugham J. in *Re Home and Colonial Insurance Co. Ltd.* [1930] 1 Ch. 102 at p. 125.
[65] p. 396.
[66] *Taylor* v. *Wilson's Trustees*, 1974 S.L.T. 298 (O.H.).

Discharge (Scotland)

A liquidator may be discharged by the court on his presenting a petition for that purpose. Failure of the liquidator to carry out statutory procedure (*e.g.* to call meetings of creditors and contributories as required by section 252 and Rule of Court 208. and to make up a list of contributories for settlement by the court under Rule of Court 211) is a ground for the dismissal of the petition.[67]

Section 251 does not apply to Scotland.

Summary of Procedure on Compulsory Liquidation

1. Petition presented.
    Provisional liquidator may be appointed.
    Court may stay legal proceedings.
    No transfer of property or shares, or alteration in status of members, unless court otherwise orders.
    No attachment, sequestration, distress or execution.
2. Winding-up order made.
    Official Receiver becomes provisional liquidator in England.
    No actions except with leave of court.
    Powers of directors cease.
    Servants dismissed.
3. Statement of affairs within fourteen days of order in England.
4. As soon as practicable Official Receiver reports to court in England.
5. First meetings of creditors and contributories[68] within one month of order.
6. In England liquidator and committee of inspection, in Scotland committee of inspection, may be appointed.
7. List of contributories may be settled.
8. Assets collected.
9. Proofs of debts received.
10. Dividends paid to creditors.
11. Capital may be returned to contributories.
12. Company struck off register and dissolved.

[67] *Lovat Mantle Manufacturers Ltd., Petitioners*, 1960 S.L.T. (Sh.Ct.) 52.
[68] Meeting of contributories may not be required in Scotland; see *ante* p. 562.

CHAPTER 26

VOLUNTARY WINDING UP

FROM the point of view of the company itself, a voluntary winding up has many advantages over a compulsory winding up, the chief being that there are not so many formalities to be complied with. In consequence the great majority of liquidations are voluntary liquidations.[1]

Initiation of voluntary winding up

Section 278 provides that a company may be wound up voluntarily:

(1) When the period, if any, fixed for its duration by the articles expires, or the event, if any, occurs, on the occurrence of which the articles provide that it is to be dissolved, and the company in general meeting passes a resolution (*i.e.* an *ordinary resolution*) to be wound up voluntarily.

(2) If it resolves by *special resolution* to be wound up voluntarily.

A company can be wound up by special resolution without any reason being assigned.

(3) If the company resolves by *extraordinary resolution* that it cannot by reason of its liabilities continue its business and that it is advisable to wind up.

An extraordinary resolution is allowed here because time is of the essence since the company is insolvent and a special resolution would normally require a longer period of notice.[2]

A resolution for voluntary winding up must be advertised in the *Gazette* within 14 days after it is passed: section 279. In Scotland, where failure to make timeous advertisement was due to inadvertence and no prejudice had been suffered as a result of the failure, the Court of Session, in the exercise of its *nobile officium*, authorised the liquidator to make a belated advertisement, the expenses of the proceedings to be borne by the liquidator personally.[3]

---

[1] *Ante* p. 539.   [2] *Ante* pp. 305, 306.
[3] *Liquidator of Nairn Public Hall Co. Ltd., Petitioner*, 1946 S.C. 395.

Clause 84 (2) of the Companies Bill 1973 would have allowed voluntary winding up on the occurrence of the event in which the articles or the memorandum provide for dissolution, and clause 86 would have fixed a minimum period of seven days' notice of a special resolution for voluntary winding up.

Kinds of voluntary winding up

A voluntary winding up may be either (1) a members' voluntary winding up; or (2) a creditors' voluntary winding up: section 283. About 60 per cent. of voluntary liquidations are members' voluntary liquidations.[1]

MEMBERS' VOLUNTARY WINDING UP

A members' voluntary winding up takes place only when the company is solvent. It is entirely managed by the members, and the liquidator is appointed by them. No meeting of creditors is held and no committee of inspection is appointed. To obtain the benefit of this form of winding up, a declaration of solvency must be filed: section 283. The resolution for voluntary winding up will usually be a special resolution.

Declaration of solvency

This is a statutory declaration made by the directors or, if there are more than two of them, by the majority, at a board meeting, that they have made a full inquiry into the company's affairs and, having done so, they have formed the opinion that the company will be able to pay its debts in full within a specified period not exceeding 12 months from the commencement of the winding up.[4] The declaration has no effect unless it is made within the five weeks immediately preceding the date of the passing of the winding-up resolution and filed with the Registrar before such date. It must be made, at the latest, the day preceding that on which the resolution is passed. Further, the declaration has no effect unless it embodies a statement of the company's assets and liabilities as at the latest practicable date before it is made: section 283. If there is something which can reasonably be described as "a statement of the company's assets and liabilities," then, even if it subsequently appears that there were

[4] *Ante* p. 557.

errors and omissions, these will not prevent the statement from being a statement within section 283.[5]

A director making a declaration of solvency without reasonable grounds is liable to imprisonment for six months, or a fine of £500, or both. If the debts are not paid or provided for within the period stated. he is presumed not to have had reasonable grounds: section 283 (3).

If a declaration is made in accordance with the section the winding up is a members' voluntary winding up: section 283 (4).

The liquidator

Unlike the liquidator in a winding up by the court, a liquidator in a voluntary winding up is not an officer of the court.[6] He is appointed, and his remuneration may be fixed, by the company in general meeting (s. 285), and within 14 days he must give notice of his appointment to the Registrar of Companies and publish it in the *Gazette*: section 305.[7] He may be appointed at the meeting at which the resolution for voluntary winding up is passed. If there is no liquidator acting, the court may appoint one. The court may also, on cause shown, remove a liquidator and appoint another: section 304.[8] Where a person had been appointed liquidator without his knowledge and he declined to act, it was held that the appointment was invalid and there was therefore no need to remove him.[9]

If a vacancy occurs in the office of liquidator, whether by death, resignation or otherwise, the company at a general meeting, summoned by any contributory or by a continuing liquidator, may fill it: section 286.

Conduct of liquidation

Subject to section 291,[10] within three months after the end of the first and every succeeding year of the liquidation, the liquidator must summon a general meeting of the company and lay before it an account of his acts and dealings and of the conduct of the winding up during the preceding year: section 289.

---

[5] *De Courcy* v. *Clement* [1971] Ch. 693.
[6] *Per* Megarry J. in *Re Rolls Razor Ltd.* (*No. 2*) [1970] Ch. 576 at p. 586.
[7] *Cf.* s. 240, *ante* p. 563.　　　　　　[8] *Cf.* s. 242, *ante* p. 605.
[9] *Liquidator of Highland, etc., Dairy Farms Ltd.*, Petitioners, 1964 S.C. 1.
[10] *Post* p. 617.

Subject to section 291,[10] as soon as the affairs of the company are fully wound up the liquidator must call a general meeting of the company. This is done by advertisement in the *Gazette* at least one month before the meeting. At the meeting the liquidator must present an account of the winding up, showing how the winding up has been conducted and how the company's property has been disposed of. A copy of this account, together with a return of the holding of the meeting, must be sent to the Registrar within a week after the meeting: section 290. It is not necessary for the affairs of the company to be fully wound up before the liquidator can validly make his return, only that they should be fully wound up so far as the liquidator is aware.[11]

If a quorum is not present at the final meeting, the liquidator must make a return that the meeting was summoned but no quorum was present, and this has the same effect as a return of the holding of the meeting.

The Registrar must publish in the *Gazette* notice of the receipt of the return (European Communities Act 1972, s. 9 (3)).

If the liquidator of a company which is in a members' voluntary winding up forms the opinion that the company will not be able to pay its debts in full within the period stated in the declaration of solvency, he must forthwith summon a meeting of the creditors, and lay before it a statement of the company's assets and liabilities: section 288. The winding up then proceeds as if it were a *creditors'* voluntary winding up, and sections 299 and 300, *post*, apply to the exclusion of sections 289 and 290: section 291.

Dissolution

The company is automatically dissolved three months after the Registrar registers the return of the final meeting, unless the court makes an order deferring the date of dissolution: section 290.

Any undistributed property passes to the Crown (s. 354), unless the Crown disclaims (s. 355). Within two years after the dissolution, the court may declare the dissolution void: section 352.[12]

---

[11] *Re Cornish Manures Ltd.* [1976] 1 W.L.R. 807.
[12] *Ante* p. 600.

CREDITORS' VOLUNTARY WINDING UP

If no declaration of solvency is filed with the Registrar, a voluntary winding up is a creditors' voluntary winding up: section 283 (4). In such a case the company must summon a meeting of its creditors for the day, or the day next following the day, on which the resolution for voluntary winding up is to be proposed. Notices of the meeting of creditors must be sent by post to the creditors at the same time as notices of the meeting of the company are sent to the members: section 293.

Thus the management of a creditors' voluntary winding up is shared by the members and the creditors but the creditors have control—in effect they appoint the liquidator and decide the composition of any committee of inspection, as will be seen.

Notice of the meeting of creditors must be advertised in the *Gazette* and in two local newspapers circulating in the district in which the company's registered office or principal place of business is situate: section 293.

Meeting of creditors

The meeting of creditors is presided over by one of the directors nominated for that purpose by the directors: section 293. The business of the meeting is:

(1) To receive a full statement by the directors of the position of the company's affairs, together with a list of the creditors and the estimated amount of their claims: section 293.
(2) To appoint a liquidator: section 294, *post.*
(3) To appoint a committee of inspection: section 295.

The liquidator

The creditors and the company at their respective meetings may nominate a liquidator and, if different persons are nominated, the person nominated by the creditors is the liquidator, subject to any order made by the court. If different persons are nominated, any director, member or creditor of the company may, within seven days after the creditors' nomination, apply to the court for an order that the company's nominee be liquidator instead of or jointly with the creditors' nominee, or that some other person be liquidator: section 294.

If the members nominate or appoint a liquidator and no meeting of creditors is held, although a creditors' voluntary winding up is contemplated, until something is done about it at the instance of the creditors the person nominated or appointed is the liquidator of the company.[13]

In England, Rule 134 of the Companies (Winding-Up) Rules 1949 applies to the creditors' meeting so that the creditors' resolution appointing a liquidator must be passed by a majority in number and value of the creditors present and voting in person or by proxy.[14]

Sections 304 and 305, *ante*,[15] apply as regards the appointment of the liquidator.

Any vacancy, by reason of death, resignation or otherwise, in the office of a liquidator, other than a liquidator appointed by the court may be filled by the creditors: section 297.

The liquidator's remuneration is fixed by the committee of inspection or, if there is no committee, by the creditors: section 296.

Committee of inspection

The creditors, at their first or any subsequent meeting, may appoint a committee of inspection of not more than five persons to act with the liquidator.[16] If they do so, the company in general meeting may appoint not more than five persons to act as members of the committee, but the creditors may resolve that these persons ought not to be members of the committee, and thereupon, unless the court otherwise directs, they cannot act on the committee: section 295. It will be recalled that there is no statutory maximum number of members of the committee of inspection in a compulsory liquidation.[17]

Subject as above, section 253, *ante*,[17] and in Scotland, also section 255,[17] apply to a committee of inspection appointed under section 295.

A member of the committee is in a fiduciary position.[17]

[13] *Re Centrebind Ltd.* [1967] 1 W.L.R. 377.
[14] *Re Caston Cushioning Ltd.* [1955] 1 W.L.R. 163.
[15] p. 616.
[16] *Post* p. 624.
[17] *Ante* p. 564.

Conduct of liquidation. Dissolution

Within three months after the end of the first and every succeeding year of the liquidation the liquidator must summon a general meeting of the company and a meeting of creditors, and lay before the meetings an account of his acts and dealings and of the conduct of the winding up during the preceding year: section 299.

When the liquidation is complete, the liquidator must, by at least one month's notice in the *Gazette*, call final meetings of the company and the creditors, and present his account. Within a week after these meetings, a copy of the account and a return of the holding of the meetings or a return that no quorum was present thereat must be filed with the Registrar (s. 300), who must publish it in the *Gazette* (European Communities Act 1972, s. 9 (3)). The company is thereupon dissolved automatically three months after the registration of the account and the return: section 300. Sections 352, 354 and 355, *ante*,[18] apply as in the case of a members' voluntary winding up.

*Summary of Differences Between Members' Voluntary Winding Up
and Creditors' Voluntary Winding Up*

Members' Voluntary Winding Up	Creditors' Voluntary Winding Up
(1) Declaration of solvency.	No declaration of solvency.
(2) Usually initiated by special resolution.	Initiated by extraordinary resolution.
(3) No meetings of creditors.	Meeting of creditors required whenever meeting of contributories held.
(4) Liquidator appointed and his remuneration fixed by company in general meeting.	Liquidator, in effect, appointed by creditors and his remuneration fixed by committee of inspection or, if there is no committee, by creditors.
(5) No committee of inspection.	May be committee of inspection, appointed, in effect, by creditors.

CONSEQUENCES OF ANY VOLUNTARY WINDING UP

The commencement of a voluntary winding up is the date of the passing of the resolution for voluntary winding up: section 280. Even if the company is subsequently wound up by the court, the commencement of the winding up is the date of the passing of the resolution: section 229.

[18] p. 617.

The consequences of a voluntary winding up are:

(1) As from the commencement of the winding up the company must cease to carry on business except so far as is required for its beneficial winding up, although the corporate state and powers continue until the company is dissolved: section 281. Notification that the company is in liquidation must be given on the company's documents on which its name appears: section 338.[19]

(2) No transfer of shares can be made without the sanction of the liquidator and any alteration in the status of the members is void: section 282 (*cf.* s. 227, *ante*).[20] A transfer of debentures can, however, be made.[21]

(3) On the appointment of a liquidator the powers of the directors cease except so far as the company in general meeting or the liquidator (in a members' voluntary winding up), or the committee of inspection or, if there is no such committee, the creditors (in a creditors' voluntary winding up), sanction their continuance: sections 285, 296.

A voluntary winding up does not necessarily operate as a discharge of the company's servants; but if it takes place because the company is insolvent, it will operate as a discharge.

By a written agreement F. was appointed managing director of a company for five years certain. Before the expiration of the five years the company passed a resolution for voluntary winding up as it could not by reason of its liabilities continue its business. F. voted for this resolution. *Held,* the voluntary winding up operated as a wrongful dismissal of F. and a term could not be implied that if the company went into voluntary liquidation with the assent of F. he should lose his right to damages: *Fowler* v. *Commercial Timber Co. Ltd.* [1930] 2 K.B. 1 (C.A.).[22]

"An order for the compulsory winding up of a company puts an end to the employment of the managing director . . . and in my judgment the same result must necessarily follow where there is a resolution for the voluntary winding up of the company which depends upon the company being unable to meet its obligations": *per* Greer L.J. at p. 6.

When the terms of the contract of employment are to be found in the articles, no damages are recoverable.[23]

[19] *Ante* p. 560.
[20] p. 557.
[21] *Re Goy & Co. Ltd.* [1900] 2 Ch. 149, *ante* p. 494.
[22] And see *Reigate* v. *Union Manufacturing Co. (Ramsbottom) Ltd.* [1918] 1 K.B. 592 (C.A.).
[23] *Re T. N. Farrer Ltd.* [1937] Ch. 352, *ante* p. 313.

If the winding up is purely for the purpose of amalgamation it will not operate as a discharge.[24]

After the commencement of the winding up the liquidator may continue the employment of the company's servants to wind up the company.[25]

In England there is no statutory provision for the stay of actions and other proceedings against the company in the case of a voluntary winding up (*cf.* ss. 226, 228, 231, *ante*),[26] but on an application under section 307, *post*,[27] the court has a discretion to stay proceedings.[28] Executions will usually be stayed when it is necessary to ensure the distribution of assets among the creditors *pari passu*,[29] but actions will not be stayed when there is a dispute as to liability, or when no advantage will be gained, *e.g.* no expense will be saved, by a stay.[30] Section 307 extends section 256 (power to stay a winding up), *ante*,[31] to a voluntary winding up.[32] Normally, a stay should not be granted unless each member consents or is bound not to object, *e.g.* because there is a scheme under section 206, or there is secured to him the right to receive what he would have received had the winding proceeded to its conclusion.[32]

In Scotland, the provision now in section 307, *post*,[27] has been interpreted as not giving the court power to stay proceedings against the company,[33] and section 308 provides that, on the application of the liquidator of a Scottish company, the court may direct that no action or proceeding shall be proceeded with against the company except by leave of the court. Section 327 (relating to diligence in Scotland)[34] applies to voluntary, as well as to compulsory, winding up.

DISTRIBUTION OF THE PROPERTY OF THE COMPANY IN A VOLUNTARY WINDING UP

The costs, charges and expenses properly incurred in a voluntary winding up, including the remuneration of the liquidator, are payable

[24] *Midland Counties District Bank Ltd.* v. *Attwood* [1905] 1 Ch. 357.
[25] *Cf. Day* v. *Tait* (1900) 8 S.L.T. 40 (O.H.), *ante* p. 560.
[26] pp. 554, 558, 559.   [27] p. 626.
[28] *Currie* v. *Consolidated Kent Collieries Corpn. Ltd.* [1906] 1 K.B. 134 (C.A.).
[29] *Anglo-Baltic Bank* v. *Barber & Co.* [1924] 2 K.B. 410 (C.A.).
[30] *Cook* v. *"X" Chair Patents Co. Ltd.* [1960] 1 W.L.R. 60.
[31] p. 556.
[32] *Re Calgary and Edmonton Land Co. Ltd.* [1975] 1 W.L.R. 355.
[33] *Sdeuard* v. *Gardner* (1876) 3 R. 577.   [34] *Ante* p. 559.

in priority to all other claims: section 309. Subject thereto the liquidator must apply the property[35] of the company first in paying the preferential debts[36] and then in discharging the liabilities of the company *pari passu*: section 302. Under this section the liquidator has a duty to inquire into all claims against the company.[37] Even where the company is solvent statute-barred debts cannot be paid unless the contributories consent.[38] If the company is insolvent the bankruptcy rules apply as well to a voluntary as to a compulsory winding up: sections 317, 318.[39] Subject as above the property of the company must be distributed among the members according to their rights and interests: section 302.

A contracting out of the provisions of section 302 is contrary to public policy.[40]

In the result, the order of application of assets is the same as that in a compulsory liquidation.[41]

POWERS AND DUTIES OF THE LIQUIDATOR IN A VOLUNTARY WINDING UP

In every voluntary winding up it is the duty of the liquidator to pay the debts of the company and adjust the rights of the contributories among themselves: section 303.

To enable him to do this the section provides that he may *without sanction*:

(1) settle a list of contributories;
(2) make calls;

---

[35] Ss. 325*, 326*, 320, 321*, 332, 333 and 323*, *ante* p. 566 *et seq.*, apply as in a compulsory winding up. And s. 322, *ante* p. 506, may apply in either a compulsory or a voluntary liquidation. Ss. marked * do not apply to Scotland; s. 327 applies to Scotland only.

[36] See s. 319, *ante* p. 593.

[37] *Austin Securities Ltd.* v. *Northgate and English Stores Ltd.* [1969] 1 W.L.R. 529 (C.A.) applying *Pulsford* v. *Devenish* and *Re Armstrong Whitworth Securities Co. Ltd.*, *ante* p. 611.

[38] *Re Art Reproduction Co. Ltd.* [1952] Ch. 89. The Scottish equivalent of "statute-barred" is "prescribed."

[39] *Ante* p. 587.

[40] *British Eagle International Air Lines Ltd.* v. *Compagnie Nationale Air France* [1975] 1 W.L.R. 758 (H.L.), where the rules of the general liquidation prevailed over the International Air Transport Association clearing house arrangements and, despite such arrangements, the plaintiff company was entitled to recover the sums payable to it by other airlines for services rendered by it and not cleared through the I.A.T.A. system, and vice versa.

[41] *Ante* p. 592.

(3) summon general meetings of the company for any purpose he may think fit;

(4) exercise all the powers of a liquidator in a compulsory winding up under section 245, *ante*,[42] except those mentioned below.

He may carry on the business of the company, if he reasonably thinks it is necessary for the beneficial winding up of the company. If he does so, those to whom he incurs obligations are entitled to be paid in priority to the creditors at the commencement of the winding up: *Re Great Eastern Electric Co. Ltd.* [1941] Ch. 241.[43]

In a members' voluntary winding up, *with the sanction* of an extraordinary resolution of the company, and in a creditors' voluntary winding up, *with the sanction* of the court or the committee of inspection or (if there is no such committee) a meeting of the creditors, the liquidator may:

(1) pay any classes of creditors in full;

(2) make any compromise or arrangement with creditors;

(3) compromise all calls and liabilities to calls and other debts and liabilities: section 303.

List of contributories

The rules relating to the settling of the list of contributories in a compulsory winding up, *ante*,[44] are not required to be observed by the liquidator in a voluntary winding up, although as a general rule he should follow them. It is no defence, therefore, to an action for calls that notice has not been given to the contributory.[45]

Proof of debts

The liquidator in a voluntary winding up need not require the creditors to prove their debts. The debts may be proved in the same way as in a compulsory winding up, *i.e.* in England by delivering or posting to the liquidator an affidavit verifying the debt.[46] The liquidator may fix a date before which debts must be proved. In England there is no limit to the time within which a dissatisfied

[42] p. 578.
[43] *Cf. Day* v. *Tait* (1900) 8 S.L.T. 40 (O.H.), *ante* p. 622.
[44] p. 582.
[45] *Brighton Arcade Co.* v. *Dowling* (1868) L.R. 3 C.P. 175.
[46] *Ante* p. 590.

creditor may appeal to the court. In Scotland any application to the court under section 307[47] to have a liquidator's deliverance reversed or varied must normally be presented within seven days of the deliverance: R.C. 214.[47a]

Dividends

Dividends are declared by the liquidator; in England the rules as to dividends in a compulsory winding up[48] have no application to a voluntary winding up. In Scotland section 318 makes certain provisions of the Bankruptcy (Scotland) Act 1913 applicable to *any* winding up of an *insolvent* company.[49]

Meetings

In an English voluntary winding up the Companies (Winding-up) Rules 1949, rules 121–156, *ante*,[50] apply only to meetings of creditors in a creditors' voluntary winding up. In a Scottish voluntary winding up, Rule 208 of the Rules of Court 1965 applies, with some modifications, to all general meetings of creditors or contributories in *any* winding up: R.C. 210.

Remuneration

The rules[51] limiting the liquidator's remuneration and restricting his dealing with the assets and purchasing goods apply in a voluntary winding up.

Books of account

In an English creditors' voluntary winding up, the liquidator must keep such books as the committee of inspection or, if there is no such committee, the creditors direct. The books must be submitted to the committee of inspection or, if there is no committee, to the creditors as and when the committee or the creditors direct: rule 172. In Scotland the committee of inspection have right of access to the liquidator's books and accounts: R.C. 209.

---

[47] *Post*, p. 626.
[47a] See *Knoll Spinning Co. Ltd.* v. *Brown,* 1977 S.L.T. (Notes) (O.H.) (note of appeal dismissed).
[48] *Ante* p. 597.
[49] *Ante* pp. 587, 597.
[50] p. 562.
[51] Rr. 160–162 (not applicable to Scotland), *ante* p. 606.

Neither the English nor the Scottish rules contain provisions relating to the books of account in a members' voluntary winding up, but proper books should be kept. The Jenkins Report[52] recommended that in a voluntary winding up the liquidator's accounts should normally be required to be audited.

Unclaimed assets, dividends, etc.

The provisions of section 343 relating to unclaimed assets in England and of section 344 relating to unclaimed dividends, etc., in Scotland apply as in a compulsory winding up.[53]

Information as to pending liquidations

Section 342, *ante*,[54] applies where a voluntary winding up is not concluded within one year.

Power to apply to court

In a voluntary winding up the liquidator, or any contributory or creditor, may apply to the court to determine any question arising in the winding up or to exercise any of the powers which the court could exercise if the company were being wound up by the court: section 307.[55] This gives the liquidator in a voluntary winding up the same right to the guidance of the court as in a compulsory liquidation. For example, in England, if he is of opinion that fraud has been committed in the formation or promotion of the company or in relation to the company since its formation, he can obtain an order of the court for the public examination[56] of any promoter, director or other officer of the company concerned. Again, he can apply for an order for private examination.[57]

[52] Para. 503. [53] *Ante* p. 598.
[54] *Ante* p. 598.
[55] For examples of applications under s. 307, see *Liquidators of North British Locomotive Co. Ltd.* v. *Lord Advocate*, 1963 S.C. 272 (O.H.), *ante* p. 565, *Smith and another, Petitioners*, 1969 S.L.T. (Notes) 94 (O.H.) (as to exercise of directors' discretionary powers under a pension scheme) and *Booth* v. *Thomson*, 1972 S.L.T. 141 (O.H.) (as to provisional liquidator's right to retain funds to pay his remuneration and expenses). See note 479 *ante*.
[56] *Re Campbell Coverings Ltd.* (*No.* 2) [1954] Ch. 225. As to public examination in a compulsory winding up in England, see s. 270, *ante* p. 573. For Scotland, see s. 269, *ante* p. 574.
[57] As in *Re Rolls Razor Ltd.* (*No.* 2) [1970] Ch. 576. As to private examination in a compulsory winding up, see s. 268, *ante* p. 573.

Duty to report criminal offences

If the liquidator thinks that any past or present officer, or any member, of the company has committed a criminal offence in relation to the company, he must report the matter, in an English winding up, to the Director of Public Prosecutions, and in a Scottish winding up, to the Lord Advocate. The matter may then be referred to the Department of Trade, who may apply to the court for an order conferring upon them the same powers of investigating the company's affairs as there are in the case of a winding up by the court: section 334.

Section 334 lacks the force of section 236[58] in a compulsory winding up—in such a winding up section 236 imposes on the Official Receiver a duty to submit a preliminary report to the court as to the cause of the failure of the company and as to whether further inquiry is desirable into the cause of failure or the conduct of the business; and there is also provision for further reports as to frauds.[59] The English court has been held not entitled, under section 334, to order either a public examination under section 270 or a private examination under section 268.[60]

COMPULSORY LIQUIDATION AFTER COMMENCEMENT OF VOLUNTARY LIQUIDATION

A voluntary liquidation does not bar the right of any creditor or contributory to have the company wound up by the court: section 310. A creditor of a company in voluntary liquidation is entitled *ex debito justitiae* as between himself and the company to a compulsory winding-up order.[61] However, the court is bound to have regard to the wishes of all the creditors,[62] and if the majority favour the continuance of the voluntary liquidation an order will not be made unless the petitioner can show special circumstances.[63] A contribu-

---

[58] *Ante* p. 562.
[59] Per Megarry J. in *Re Lubin, Rosen and Associates Ltd.* [1975] 1 W.L.R. 122 at p. 128.
[60] *Re Campbell Coverings Ltd.* [1953] Ch. 488 (C.A.); however, see *Re Campbell Coverings Ltd. (No. 2)* [1954] Ch. 225, *ante.*
[61] *Re James Millward & Co. Ltd.* [1940] Ch. 333 (C.A.); *Gardner & Co.* v. *Link* (1894) 21 R. 967.
[62] *Re Home Remedies Ltd.* [1943] Ch. 1; *cf. Pattisons Ltd.* v. *Kinnear* (1899) 1 F. 551 and *Elsmie & Son* v. *The Tomatin, etc., Distillery Ltd.* (1906) 8 F. 434.
[63] *Re B. Karsberg Ltd.* [1956] 1 W.L.R. 57 (C.A.); *Re J. D. Swain Ltd.* [1965] 1 W.L.R. 909 (C.A.); for special circumstances, see *Bouboulis* v. *Mann, Macneal & Co. Ltd.*, 1926 S.C. 637.

tory must satisfy the court that the rights of the contributories will be prejudiced by a voluntary winding up: section 310. What the Secretary of State must show when he is the petitioner has been dealt with already.[64]

When a voluntary winding up is superseded by a compulsory winding up, all proceedings in the voluntary winding up are deemed to have been validly taken unless the court, on proof of fraud or mistake, thinks fit to direct otherwise: section 229, *ante*.[65]

ARRANGEMENTS WITH CREDITORS IN A VOLUNTARY WINDING UP

Under section 306[66] a company which is about to be, or is being, wound up voluntarily, may make a binding arrangement with its creditors if the arrangement is—

(1) sanctioned by an *extraordinary* resolution of the company;
(2) acceded to by three-fourths in number and value of the creditors, *i.e.* all the creditors, not just those voting.

Any creditor or contributory may, within three weeks from the completion of the arrangement, appeal to the court against it, and the court may confirm or vary the arrangement as it thinks just. A composition by the company with its creditors with the intention of making the company solvent and preventing a winding up is not an "arrangement" within the meaning of the section.[67]

Summary of Procedure

Members' Voluntary Winding Up

1. Notice of meeting to pass special resolution for voluntary winding up sent out.
2. Declaration of solvency made (may be after notice of meeting is sent out).
3. Declaration of solvency filed with Registrar.
4. Resolution (usually special) passed and liquidator appointed.
    Company ceases to carry on business except for winding up.
    Corporate existence continues.
    No transfer of shares without liquidator's consent.
    Powers of directors cease.
5. Resolution filed with Registrar.
    Gazetted within 14 days.
    Notice of liquidator's appointment gazetted and registered within 14 days.

---

[64] p. 551.   [65] p. 620.
[66] *Cf.* s. 206 (*post* p. 635), s. 245 (*ante* p. 579) and s. 303 (*ante* p. 624).
[67] *Re Contal Radio Ltd.* [1932] 2 Ch. 66; for a Scottish instance of a s. 306 arrangement, see *Gillies* v. *Dawson* (1893) 20 R. 1119 (O.H.).

6–10. As for 7–11 in a compulsory winding up, *ante*.[68]
11. At end of each year, meeting of company summoned and liquidator's account submitted.
12. Final meeting advertised by at least one month's notice in the *Gazette*.
13. Final meeting held and liquidator's account presented.
14. Return of holding of meeting and copy account filed with Registrar.
15. Company automatically dissolved three months after return registered.

Creditors' Voluntary Winding Up

1. Notice of meeting to pass extraordinary resolution for voluntary winding up sent out.
   Notice of meeting of creditors sent out and advertised.
2. Extraordinary resolution passed. Consequences, as in 4 above. Servants dismissed.
3. Liquidator and committee of inspection appointed by creditors.
4. Resolution filed with Registrar.

Other proceedings as in members' voluntary winding up but meetings of creditors are summoned in addition to meetings of the company.

WINDING UP SUBJECT TO SUPERVISION OF COURT

When a company has passed a resolution for voluntary winding up, the court may order that the winding up shall continue subject to such supervision of the court, and with such liberty for creditors, contributories, or others to apply to the court, and generally on such terms and conditions, as the court thinks just: section 311. However, as has been shown,[69] supervision orders are rarely made now because under section 307, *ante*,[70] in a voluntary winding up creditors can apply to the court to determine questions and exercise any power which the court could exercise in a compulsory winding up.

In England, a winding up under supervision resembles a voluntary winding up in that the Official Receiver is never liquidator. It differs from a voluntary winding up in that the order invariably directs the liquidator to file with the Registrar every three months a report of the position of, and the progress made with, the winding up of the company, and also orders the costs to be taxed.[71] In Scotland, in any winding up (including a voluntary winding up) which lasts for more than one year the liquidator must send half-yearly statements to the Registrar.[72]

Although the court will have regard to the wishes of the creditors

---

[68] p. 613.
[69] *Ante* p. 539.
[70] p. 626.
[71] See Companies (Winding-Up) Rules 1949, Appendix, Form 18.
[72] R.C. 213 and Form 35.

or contributories (s. 346),[73] it has an absolute discretion as to the granting of a supervision order and a creditor is not entitled to such an order as of right, but must show some special cause, *e.g.* that there is danger of preference being created or that there is some impropriety, actual or threatened, in the conduct of the liquidation.[74]

A petition for the continuance of a voluntary winding up subject to supervision is, for the purpose of giving the court jurisdiction over actions, deemed to be a petition for winding up by the court: section 312. Consequently the court has the section 226[75] power to stay proceedings against the company, and under section 231[76] actions are stayed when the supervision order is made. For the purposes of sections 227 and 228[77] winding up subject to supervision is deemed to be a winding up by the court: section 313.

One advantage of a supervision order is that where such an order is made, the court may appoint an additional liquidator or remove an existing liquidator and appoint another in his place. A liquidator so appointed is in the same position as if he had been appointed in a voluntary winding up: section 314.

In England a supervision order must be advertised by the petitioner in the *London Gazette* within 12 days, and served on such persons and in such manner as the court directs: rule 42. In Scotland an order must be advertised once in the *Edinburgh Gazette* within 14 days: R.C. 205.

The effect of a supervision order is to allow the liquidator to wind up the company as in a voluntary winding up, subject only to any restrictions imposed by the order. The liquidator can exercise all the powers of a liquidator in a voluntary winding up, but in those cases in which he requires sanction in a voluntary winding up[78] he requires the sanction of the court (instead of the sanction of an extraordinary resolution of the company), or where before the order the winding up was a creditors' voluntary winding up, the sanction of the court or the committee of inspection or, if there is no committee, a meeting of the creditors: section 315.

---

[73] *Ante* p. 546; *e.g. Wilson* v. *Hadley* (1879) 7 R. 178.
[74] *Crawford* v. *A. R. Cowper Ltd.* (1902) 4 F. 849; *cf. Macquisten* v. *Adam, etc., Co. Ltd.* (1896) 23 R. 910 (order granted to a creditor whose claim amounted to four-fifths of the company's debts).
[75] *Ante* p. 554.
[76] *Ante* p. 559.
[77] *Ante* pp. 557, 558; s. 228 does not apply to Scotland; s. 327 relating to diligence in Scotland applies to any winding up.
[78] *Ante* p. 624.

The section also provides that various sections applicable to a compulsory liquidation, which are set out in the Eleventh Schedule, are not to apply to a winding up under supervision, but subject to those exceptions a supervision order is for almost all purposes deemed to be an order for winding up by the court.

The commencement of a winding up subject to the supervision of the court is the date of the resolution for voluntary winding up: section 229.[79]

The Jenkins Report[80] stated that the provisions of the Act relating to winding up under supervision serve no useful purpose and should be repealed. Clause 87 of the Companies Bill 1973 would have done that.

[79] *Ante* p. 557.
[80] Para. 503.

CHAPTER 27

RECONSTRUCTION AND AMALGAMATION

NEITHER of the words "reconstruction" and "amalgamation" has any definite legal meaning. A reconstruction is where a company transfers its assets to a new company with substantially the same shareholders. An amalgamation is the merger of two or more companies into one. This occurs, *e.g.*, where a company acquires the assets of or the shares in two or more companies whose shareholders are issued with the appropriate number of shares in the new company. Again, there is an amalgamation where one company acquires the shares in another in return for shares in the first company. Where one company acquires the assets of another, the other is wound up. Where one company acquires the shares of another, the other will remain in existence as a subsidiary of the first.[1]

Both a reconstruction and an amalgamation may be effected (1) under section 287 or section 298, or (2) under sections 206 to 208. Where an amalgamation[2] is effected by one company acquiring the shares in another section 209 may operate to enable the acquiring company to compel dissentient shareholders to transfer their shares.

The Third Draft Directive submitted by the Commission to the Council of the EEC is concerned with mergers.

RECONSTRUCTION OR AMALGAMATION UNDER SECTION 287

Under section 287 a company (1) which is in a members' voluntary winding up; (2) may transfer or sell the whole or part of its business or property to another company, whether a company within the meaning of the Act or not; and (3) may pass a special resolution authorising the liquidator to receive as consideration cash or shares, policies or other like interests in the transferee company for distribution among the members of the transferor company according to

---

[1] *Per* Buckley J. in *Re South African Supply, etc., Co.* [1904] 2 Ch. 268 at p. 281.

[2] For examples of amalgamation see *Head (Henry) & Co. Ltd.* v. *Ropner Holdings Ltd.* [1952] Ch. 124, *ante* p. 177, *Governments Stock, etc., Investment Co. Ltd.* v. *Christopher* [1956] 1 W.L.R. 237, *ante* p. 132, *Rights and Issues Investment Trust Ltd.* v. *Stylo Shoes Ltd.* [1965] Ch. 250, *ante* p. 112, and *Clydesdale Bank Ltd., Petitioners,* 1950 S.C. 30.

their rights and interests in that company. The sanction of the court is unnecessary.

The sale may be to a foreign company.[3] However, it must be to a company and not to a speculator who hopes to form a company to take over the assets.[4]

The following procedure might be adopted under section 287. A meeting of the transferor company is summoned in order to pass resolutions for reconstruction or amalgamation. At the meeting, resolutions are passed for the voluntary winding up of the company, the appointment of a liquidator, and giving authority to the liquidator to enter into an agreement with the transferee company on the terms of a draft submitted to the meeting. The agreement provides that the transferee company shall purchase the assets of the transferor company, except a sum retained by the liquidator to discharge its liabilities, that the consideration shall be the allotment by the transferee company to the liquidator or his nominees of shares, fully or partly paid up, in the transferee company, that the liquidator shall give notice to the shareholders of the transferor company of the number of shares to which they are entitled, and the time within which they must apply, and that failure to apply for shares within that time shall preclude their rights to any shares.

A reconstruction scheme provided that shareholders in the old company should apply for shares in the new company within ten days after being given notice requiring them to apply, and that the liquidator should dispose of all shares not applied for. On June 12 the liquidator sent out notices requiring application for shares in the new company to be made before June 25. P., a shareholder in the old company, applied on August 24. *Held*, P. was not entitled to an allotment of shares in the new company, or to any other relief: *Postlethwaite* v. *Port Philip, etc., Gold Mining Co.* (1889) 43 Ch.D. 452.

Instead of the liquidator being authorised to dispose of all shares not applied for by the members of the transferor company, an underwriting agreement may be made in respect of such shares.[5] If the agreement is silent as to the disposal of the proceeds of sale of the shares not applied for, the proceeds must be distributed among the members of the transferor company who have not applied for shares in the transferee company.[6]

Shares may be given directly to the members of the transferor company instead of being applied for in the manner explained above.

---

[3] *Re Irrigation Co. of France* (1871) L.R. 6 Ch.App. 176.
[4] *Bird* v. *Bird's Patent, etc., Sewage Co.* (1874) L.R. 9 Ch.App. 358.
[5] *Barrow* v. *Paringa Mines (1909) Ltd.* (1909) 2 Ch. 658.
[6] *Re Lake View Extended Gold Mine Co.* [1900] W.N. 44.

Protection of dissentient members

A sale or arrangement under section 287 is binding on all members of the transferor company, whether they agree to it or not: section 287 (2). However, a member who (1) did not vote in favour of the special resolution, and (2) expressed his dissent from it in writing addressed to the liquidator and left at the registered office within seven days after the passing of the resolution, may require the liquidator either to abstain from carrying the resolution into effect or to purchase his interest at a price to be determined by agreement or arbitration: section 287 (3). Subsection (4) below shows that the election is that of the liquidator. The Jenkins Report[7] recommended that members who vote in favour of the resolution should be able to express dissent.

A transferee of shares whose transfer was not registered when the special resolution was passed may be entitled to have the register of members rectified and to dissent from it.[8]

If the liquidator elects to purchase the member's interest, the purchase money must be paid before the transferor company is dissolved, and be raised by the liquidator as is determined by special resolution: section 287 (4). The agreement usually provides for the retention by the liquidator out of the assets of the transferor company of a sum to cover the interests of the dissentient shareholders.

The articles cannot deprive a member of his statutory right to the value of his shareholding if he dissents.[9]

Protection of dissentient creditors

The liquidator must pay the creditors of the transferor company in the usual way in a winding up. If, however, the creditors conceive that they will be prejudiced by the transfer of all the company's assets to the transferee company, they may petition for a compulsory winding up or a supervision order. Section 287 (5) provides that the special resolution for reconstruction shall not be valid if, within a year, an order is made for winding up the company by or subject to the supervision of the court, unless the court sanctions the resolution.

[7] Para. 503.
[8] *Re Sussex Brick Co.* [1904] 1 Ch. 598 (C.A.), *ante* p. 199.
[9] *Payne* v. *The Cork Co. Ltd.* [1900] 1 Ch. 308.

Application of section to other forms of winding up

Section 287 is limited by its terms to a members' voluntary winding up. It also applies, however, to a creditors' voluntary winding up, except that in this case, in addition to the special resolution of the company, the scheme must be sanctioned by the court or the committee of inspection: section 298.

In the case of a compulsory liquidation the court can, under section 245,[10] sanction a scheme which could be carried out by a liquidator under section 287, and no special resolution will be required.[11]

Sale under power in memorandum

The memorandum of association may give power to a company to sell its undertaking for shares in another company. If, however, the whole of the undertaking is to be sold and the proceeds are to be distributed among the shareholders, the procedure laid down in section 287, including the provisions for the protection of dissentient shareholders and creditors, cannot be excluded.[12]

SCHEME OF ARRANGEMENT UNDER SECTION 206

Where there is no reconstruction or amalgamation

A company cannot validly make any conveyance or assignment of all its property to trustees for the benefit of its creditors: section 320 (2). Under section 306[13] an arrangement with its creditors can be made by a company when it is about to be or is in course of being wound up voluntarily, and in a winding up by the court the liquidator can make arrangements with the company's creditors under section 245,[14] but in both these cases liquidation is either in progress or in contemplation. Under section 206 a company can enter into a compromise or arrangement with its creditors, or its members, or any class thereof, without going into liquidation.

The proper way to distribute the assets of a company otherwise

---

[10] *Ante* p. 578.
[11] See *Re Agra and Masterman's Bank* (1866) L.R. 12 Eq. 509n.
[12] *Bisgood* v. *Henderson's Transvaal Estates Ltd.* [1908] 1 Ch. 743 (C.A.); *cf. Waverley Hydropathic Co. Ltd., Petitioners*, 1948 S.C. 59.
[13] *Ante* p. 628.   [14] *Ante* p. 579.

than strictly in accordance with creditors' rights is by a scheme of arrangement under section 206 which binds all creditors, and not by an agreement of compromise under section 245[14] which would deprive non-assenting creditors of the court's protection and prevent them from expressing their views.[15]

Section 206 provides that a compromise or arrangement will be binding on the company and the creditors or class of creditors or the members or class of members, as the case may be if:

(1) The court, on the application in a summary way of the company or of any creditor or member of the company (or, if the company is being wound up, of the liquidator), orders a meeting of the creditors or class of creditors, or of the members or class of members, to be summoned.

The application for the meeting or meetings in England is by originating summons (R.S.C., O. 102, r. 2) and in Scotland by petition to the Inner House (R.C. 190).

(2) The compromise or arrangement is agreed to by a majority in number representing three-fourths in value of those present and voting either in person or by proxy at the meeting.

(3) It is sanctioned by the court.

The application for sanction is by petition: R.S.C., order 102, rule 5; R.C. 190.

The word "company" in sections 206 and 207[16] means any company liable to be wound up under the Act: section 206 (6). Thus it includes a company formed and registered under the 1948 Act, an existing company (in effect, a company formed and registered under a previous Companies Act), or an unregistered company.[17]

The word "arrangement" has a very wide meaning, and is wider than the word "compromise."[18] An arrangement may involve debenture holders giving an extension of time for payment, accepting a cash payment less than the face value of their debentures,[19] giving up their security in whole or in part, exchanging their debentures for shares in the company[20] or in a new company,[21] or having the rights

---

[15] *Re Trix Ltd.* [1970] 1 W.L.R. 1421.
[16] *Post.*
[17] s. 398, *ante* p. 580.
[18] *Re Guardian Assce. Co.* [1917] 1 Ch. 431 (C.A.).
[19] *e.g., The Philadelphia Securities Co.* v. *The Realisation, etc., Corpn. of Scotland Ltd.* (1903) 11 S.L.T. 217 (O.H.).
[20] *e.g., Gillies* v. *Dawson* (1893) 20 R. 1119 (O.H.).
[21] *Re Empire Mining Co.* (1890) 44 Ch.D. 402.

attached to their debentures varied in some other respect,[22] creditors may take cash in part payment of their claims and the balance in shares or debentures in the company; preference shareholders may give up their rights to arrears of dividends,[23] agree to accept a reduced rate of dividend in the future, or have their class rights otherwise varied[24] (the use of section 206 to vary class rights has already been dealt with[25]). Or the members of a company in liquidation may agree with the company to seek or not to oppose a stay of the winding up, whereunder the members will give up their existing right to have all the proceeds of the company's assets distributed among them and instead be remitted to their contractual rights under the articles.[26] Section 206 itself provides that the expression "arrangement" includes a reorganisation of the share capital of the company by the consolidation of shares of different classes or by the division of shares into shares of different classes. The word "compromise" implies some element of accommodation on each side. It is not apt to describe a total surrender. Similarly, the word "arrangement" implies some element of give and take.[27]

Where an arrangement under section 206 is essentially a scheme for the purchase by an outsider of all the issued shares of a company it is not necessarily treated as a section 209 case which, it will be seen,[28] requires a 90 per cent. majority.[29] However, the count will not allow section 209 to be circumvented by the use of section 206 where the necessary resolution under section 206 can only be passed with the assistance of votes of the wholly-owned subsidiary of the taking-over company.[30] Further, a shareholder which is a wholly-owned subsidiary of a company which is the proposed purchaser of shares pursuant to a scheme of arrangement is in a different class from other shareholders for the purposes of a class meeting.[30]

The meaning of the term "class" has been considered already.[31] The interests of a wholly-owned subsidiary of a company which is

---

[22] *e.g., Wright & Greig Ltd., Petitioners,* 1911 1 S.L.T. 353.
[23] *e.g. Balmenach-Glenlivet Distillery Ltd., Petitioners,* 1916 S.C. 639.
[24] *City, etc., Trust Corporation Ltd., Petitioners,* 1951 S.C. 570.
[25] *Ante* p. 218.
[26] Per Megarry J. in *Re Calgary and Edmonton Land Co. Ltd.* [1975] 1 W.L.R. 355 at p. 363.
[27] *Re N.F.U. Development Trust Ltd.* [1972] 1 W.L.R. 1548.
[28] *Post* p. 642.
[29] *Re National Bank Ltd.* [1966] 1 W.L.R. 819; *The Singer Manufacturing Co. Ltd.* v. *Robinow,* 1971 S.C. 11 (scheme to enable parent company to acquire remaining 7.3 per cent. shareholding in subsidiary held competent).
[30] *Re Hellenic & General Trust Ltd.* [1976] 1 W.L.R. 123.
[31] p. 217.

taking shares in another under a scheme of arrangement, when the subsidiary holds shares in the other, are different from those of the other ordinary shareholders in the other company and therefore the subsidiary is in a different class from the other ordinary shareholders and separate meetings must be held to approve the scheme.[30]   Separate class meetings are required whenever the parties are not all on an equal footing, *e.g.* where some creditors are secured and others unsecured.[32]

It is the responsibility of the petitioners to see that the class meetings are properly constituted, and if they fail the court has no jurisdiction to sanction the arrangement.[30]

As to (1) *ante*, where a meeting of creditors or members is summoned under section 206, with every notice of the meeting there must be sent a statement explaining the effect of the compromise or arrangement and, in particular, stating any material interests of the directors in any capacity and the effect thereon of the compromise or arrangement in so far as it is different from the effect on the like interests of other persons. If the meeting is summoned by advertisement, a similar statement, or a notification of the place where such a statement may be obtained, must be included. Where the compromise or arrangement affects the rights of debenture holders the statement must give the like explanation as respects the trustees of a deed for securing the issue of debentures as it is required to give as respects the directors: section 207.

Section 207 must be faithfully complied with: the court "has no discretionary power to dispense with the procedural requirements of section 207."[33] Thus a scheme will not be sanctioned if the explanatory statement, while stating that the company's assets have been revalued, does not give the amount of the revaluation,[34] or if a copy of the petition[35] or a copy of the scheme[36] has been sent without any further explanation. Material interests of directors must always be stated, even although those interests are in no way differently affected by the scheme from the interests of other persons.[37]

As to (2) *ante*, "three-fourths in value of the members or class of

[32] *La Lainière de Roubaix* v. *Glen Glove, etc., Co. Ltd.,* 1926 S.C. 91.
[33] *Per* Lord Guthrie in *The Scottish Eastern, etc., Trust Ltd., Petitioners,* 1966 S.L.T. 285 at p. 288.
[34] *Re Dorman, Long & Co. Ltd.* [1934] Ch. 635.
[35] *Rankin & Blackmore Ltd., Petitioners,* 1950 S.C. 218.
[36] *Peter Scott & Co. Ltd., Petitioners,* 1950 S.C. 507.
[37] *Coltness Iron Co. Ltd., Petitioners,* 1951 S.C. 476; contrast *Second Scottish Investment Trust, etc., Petitioners,* 1962 S.L.T. 392.

members" in section 206 refers to the size of the stake which each member has in the company. "The purpose is to prevent a numerical majority with a small stake outvoting a minority with a large stake, *e.g.* to prevent 51 members with one share each outvoting 49 members with 10 shares each."[38]

Any proper form of proxy may be used and it is not necessary to its validity that it should be sent to the company's offices before the meeting.[39] Directors who, pursuant to the court's order, receive proxies must use them whether they are for or against the scheme.[38]

As to (3) *ante*, before giving its sanction to a scheme of arrangement the court will see "First, that the provisions of the statute have been complied with. Secondly, that the class was fairly represented by those who attended the meeting and that the statutory majority are acting bona fide and are not coercing the minority in order to promote interests adverse to those of the class whom they purport to represent; and, thirdly, that the arrangement is such as a man of business would reasonably approve."[40]

The court cannot sanction any arrangement involving transactions *ultra vires* the company.[41] Nor can the court approve under section 206 something for which a procedure is provided elsewhere by the Act, *e.g.* a reduction of capital.[42]

An order sanctioning a compromise or arrangement under section 206 has no effect until an office copy has been delivered to the Registrar of Companies. A copy of the order must also be annexed to every copy of the memorandum issued after the making of the order: section 206 (3).

Where there is a reconstruction or an amalgamation

Section 206 *ante* can be used not only to effect arrangements with creditors and members, but also to carry out a scheme of reconstruction or amalgamation. One advantage of using section 206 to carry out such a scheme is that dissentient creditors are bound if the

[38] *Per* Brightman J. in *Re N.F.U. Development Trust Ltd.* [1972] 1 W.L.R. 1548 at p. 1553.
[39] *Re Dorman, Long & Co. Ltd.* [1934] Ch. 635.
[40] *Per* Astbury J. in *Re Anglo-Continental Supply Co. Ltd.* [1922] 2 Ch. 723 at p. 736. See to the same effect *per* Lindley L.J. in *Re Alabama, etc., Rlwy. Co.* [1891] 1 Ch. 213 (C.A.) at p. 238. For adoption in Scotland, see *per* Lord President Dunedin in *Shandon Hydropathic Co. Ltd., Petitioners,* 1911 S.C. 1153 at p. 1155.
[41] *Re Oceanic Steam Navigation Co. Ltd.* [1939] Ch. 41.
[42] *Re St. James' Court Estate Ltd.* [1944] Ch. 6.

scheme is approved by the requisite majority. When the section is so used there is no statutory provision for the protection of dissentient members, and such members are bound by the arrangement if it is approved by the requisite majority. However, the court may, and usually will, as a condition of sanctioning the scheme, if it thinks it reasonable to do so, require dissentient members to be given the same rights as they would have had under section 287 *ante*.

In order to facilitate schemes of reconstruction and amalgamation, section 208 provides that when an application is made to the court under section 206 for the sanctioning of a compromise or arrangement, where the compromise or arrangement is for the purposes of a scheme for the reconstruction of a company or the amalgamation of two or more companies and the scheme involves the transfer of the whole or part of the undertaking or property of a company (called "a transferor company") to another company (called "the transferee company"), the court may make an order providing for the following matters:

(1) The transfer to the transferee company of the whole or part of the undertaking and of the property or liabilities of a transferor company. An order so made cannot operate to transfer to the transferee company the benefit of a personal contract such as a contract of service between a transferor company and a person employed by it.[43] Further, a scheme under section 206, or an order under section 208 for giving effect to such a scheme, cannot transfer the office of executor from one bank to another; such an office of personal trust is incapable of assignment.[44]

(2) The allotting by the transferee company of any shares, debentures, policies or other similar interests in such company to the appropriate persons.

(3) The continuation by or against the transferee company of any legal proceedings pending by or against a transferor company.

(4) The dissolution, without winding up, of a transferor company.

(5) The provision to be made for persons who dissent from the scheme.

This has been dealt with already.

---

[43] *Nokes* v. *Doncaster Amalgamated Collieries Ltd.* [1940] A.C. 1014.
[44] *In the Estate of Skinner (decd.)* [1958] 1 W.L.R. 1043.

(6) Any incidental matters.

An office copy of an order made under section 208 must be registered with the Registrar of Companies within seven days.

The word "company" in section 208 means a company within the meaning of the Act. Thus it means a company formed and registered under the Act or an existing company, in effect a company formed and registered under a previous Companies Act: section 455.

AMALGAMATION BY PURCHASE OF SHARES

Sometimes a company obtains the business of another company not by acquiring the property of the other under section 287, or under sections 206 and 208, *ante*, but by acquiring the shares in the other and keeping it in existence. Whereas there may be a reconstruction or an amalgamation under section 287 or 206, when one company acquires the shares in another there is an amalgamation. In such a case it is usual for the acquiring company (the transferee company) to make an offer (called a "take-over bid") to the shareholders in the other company (the transferor company) to purchase their shares at a stated price, and to fix a time within which the offer is to be accepted, with a condition that if a named percentage of the shareholders do not accept the offer, the offer is to be void. The offer is to buy the transferor company's shares at a higher price (in cash or shares in the transferee company) than their market price, because the transferee company believes that a profit can be made from the transferor company's assets, either in the way of a capital sum or in increased earnings. If the required majority of the transferor company's shareholders accept, the transferee company will then purchase their shares and, under section 209, to prevent a dissentient minority from hampering the scheme, the transferee company is entitled, subject to certain conditions, to acquire the shares of the minority, and the matter may never come before the court. The section provides safeguards for minority shareholders where there is a take-over bid and in a proper case provides machinery for a small minority to be obliged to accept the offer against their wishes.[45]

[45] *Per* Templeman J. in *Re Hellenic & General Trust Ltd.* [1976] 1 W.L.R. 123 at p. 127.

Power to acquire shares of shareholders dissenting from scheme approved by majority

Section 209 provides that where—

(1) there is a scheme or contract involving the transfer of shares or any class of shares in a transferor company to a transferee company, whether a company within the Act or not;

(2) and within four months after it is made, the offer by the transferee company is approved by the holders of not less than nine-tenths in value of the shares whose transfer is involved (other than shares already held at the date of the offer by, or by a nominee for, the transferee company or its subsidiary);

(3) the transferee company may, within two months after the expiration of the four months, give notice in the prescribed form to any dissenting shareholder in the transferor company of its desire to acquire his shares;

(4) whereupon the transferee company is entitled and bound to acquire those shares on the terms approved by the approving shareholders unless, on application by the dissenting shareholder within one month from the date of the notice, the court orders otherwise.

The words "a scheme or contract involving the transfer of shares" include a scheme or contract involving the transfer of an absolute right to shares in a case in which by the terms of a trust deed securing convertible loan stock the effect of an offer to acquire the shares in a company is to entitle the holders of the stock to an allotment of shares, and approval "by the holders of not less than nine-tenths in value of the shares whose transfer is involved" includes approval by persons who have an absolute right to an allotment.[46]

The period of four months after the offer is a maximum period and the transferee company may prescribe a shorter period within which it must be approved.[47] If it does so, however, it usually reserves the right to extend the period up to the statutory maximum of four months.[48] Extension of the closing date for acceptance of an

[46] *Re Simo Securities Trust Ltd.* [1971] 1 W.L.R. 1455.
[47] *Re Western Manufacturing (Reading) Ltd.* [1956] Ch. 436.
[48] *e.g. Musson* v. *Howard Glasgow Associates Ltd.*, 1960 S.C. 371; the right to extend the closing date need not be exercised within the original time limit: *per* Lord Sorn at p. 376.

offer does not amount to a new offer and so the transferee company's right must be exercised within six months of the original offer.[49]

Section 209 (5) provides that the expression "dissenting shareholder" includes a shareholder who has not assented to the scheme or contract and a shareholder who has failed or refused to transfer his shares in accordance with the scheme or contract. If the offer of the transferee company of a share for share exchange is accompanied by a cash offer from a third party and the transferee company wishes to exercise its rights of compulsory acquisition under section 209 (1), a dissenting shareholder has an option to require the transferee to pay him the amount of cash he would have received had he accepted the offer of the third party.[50]

It has been held that the word "court" in the section means the court with jurisdiction to wind up the transferor company.[52] The court will order otherwise and prevent the transferee company from acquiring the shares of dissentient shareholders only if it is satisfied that the scheme is unfair to the general body of shareholders in the transferor company. There is normally a heavy burden of proof on the dissentients[53]—since the scheme has been approved by nine-tenths of the shareholders, prima facie it must be taken to be a fair one.[54] The test is one of fairness to the body of shareholders as a whole and not to individual shareholders, and it is not enough merely to prove that the scheme is open to criticism or capable of improvement.[55] It is not enough that the materials put before the shareholders were inadequate to enable them to form a just conclusion as to the acceptance or refusal of the offer.[56] Where there is a Stock Exchange quotation for the shares, prima facie that can be taken as the value of the shares.[57] The element of control of the transferor company, which would accrue to the transferee company from the acquisition of all the shares in the transferor company, is not to be taken into account in determining the value of the shares of a minority shareholder.[55] The dissentient shareholders, who are not satisfied

---

[49] *Musson's* case, *ante.*
[50] *Re Carlton Holdings Ltd.* [1971] 1 W.L.R. 918.
[51] *Re Samuel Heap & Son Ltd.* [1965] 1 W.L.R. 1458 (C.A.).
[52] See ss. 218, 220, *ante* pp. 539, 540.
[53] *Re Sussex Brick Co. Ltd.* [1961] Ch. 289n; *Nidditch* v. *The Calico Printers' Assocn. Ltd.,* 1961 S.L.T. 282.
[54] The onus is the other way round under s. 206, *ante: per* Templeman J. in *Re Hellenic & General Trust Ltd.* [1976] 1 W.L.R. 123 at pp. 130, 131.
[55] *Re Grierson, Oldham & Adams Ltd.* [1968] Ch. 17.
[56] *Re Evertite Locknuts Ltd.* [1945] Ch. 220.
[57] See *Re Press Caps Ltd.* [1949] Ch. 434 (C.A.).

with the price offered, cannot obtain an order for discovery so as to enable them to carry out an investigation into the value of the shares, unless there are special circumstances.[58]

However, if the dissentient shareholders show that in substance the transferee company is the same as the majority holding in the transferor company the onus is on the majority to satisfy the court that the scheme is one which the minority ought reasonably to be compelled to fall in with.

A and B were the two shareholders, each holding 50 shares, in the transferee company which offered to purchase the shares in the transferor company in which there were three shareholders, A and B, who each held 4,500 shares and who accepted the offer, and C, who held 1,000 shares and who dissented. *Held*, that C, by showing that the transferee company was, for practical purposes, equivalent to the holders of nine-tenths of the shares in the transferor company who accepted the offer, had, prima facie, shown that the case was one in which the circumstances were special and that the court ought to "order otherwise" within the meaning of section 209, and the majority had not shown that there was some good reason in the interests of the company (*e.g.* that the minority shareholder was acting in a manner highly damaging to the interests of the company) for allowing the section to be invoked for the purpose of enabling the majority to expropriate the minority: *Re Bugle Press Ltd.* [1961] Ch. 270 (C.A.).

The directors of an offeree company (*i.e.* a transferor company) have a duty towards their shareholders to be honest and not to mislead them. A shareholder in such a company may be prejudiced if his co-shareholders are misled into accepting the offer. A minority can therefore complain if it is being wrongfully subjected to the power of compulsory purchase as a result of a breach of duty by such directors.[59]

Where, after notice has been given to a dissentient shareholder, no application is made to the court or, if made, it is unsuccessful, the transferee company must send a copy of the notice to the transferor company together with an instrument of transfer executed on behalf of the transferee company and, on behalf of the shareholder, by a person appointed by the transferee company. The transferee company must also pay or transfer the money or other consideration to the transferor company, and is then entitled to be registered as the holder of the shares. The transferor company must pay any money received into a separate bank account, and must hold any money or other consideration received upon trust for the persons entitled to the shares in respect of which it was received: section 209 (3), (4).

[58] *Re Press Caps Ltd.* [1948] 2 All E.R. 638.
[59] *Gething* v. *Kilner* [1972] 1 W.L.R. 337, particularly at pp. 341, 342.

Section 209 does not apply, *e.g.*, where one company acquires shares in another by purchase on the Stock Exchange, or where a "first come, first served" invitation to treat is made by one company to shareholders in another who then offer to sell their shares to the first company, or where an offer to purchase shares is made by an individual. It has been held that the Australian equivalent of section 209[60] does not apply where a "take-over" offer to purchase shares is made by a consortium of two or more companies jointly, or an offer is made to shareholders in two or more companies.[61] Of course, a group of companies can form a joint subsidiary which can make a take-over offer for shares in another company.

One-tenth of shares already held by transferee

Where, at the date of the offer, more than one-tenth in value of the shares or class of shares whose transfer is involved are held by, or by a nominee for, the transferee company or its subsidiary, section 209 does not apply unless:

(1) the transferee company offers the same terms to all the holders of the shares or each class of shares whose transfer is involved; and

(2) the holders who approve the scheme or contract, besides holding at least nine-tenths in value of the shares whose transfer is involved, are also not less than three-fourths in number of the holders of such shares: section 209 (1) proviso.

The date at which a count has to be made to ascertain whether approving shareholders amount in number to three-fourths of the total holders is the most practical date and therefore the fraction must normally be calculated by reference to the total number of shareholders on the register at the offer date.[62]

Transferee acquires nine-tenths of shares

If the shares transferred under the scheme or contract, together with the shares held by, or by a nominee for, the transferee company or its subsidiary at the date of the transfer, amount to nine-tenths in

---

[60] Section 185 of the Companies Act 1961 as amended (N.S.W.).
[61] *Blue Metal Industries Ltd.* v. *Dilley* [1970] A.C. 827 (P.C.).
[62] *Re Simo Securities Trust Ltd.* [1971] 1 W.L.R. 1455.

value of the shares in the transferor company or of any class of such shares, the transferee company must, within a month after the transfer, give notice of that fact to the holders of the remaining shares, or of the remaining shares of the class, who have not assented to the scheme. Thereupon any such holder may, within three months after the notice, *require* the transferee company to acquire the shares in question on the terms on which, under the scheme, the shares of the approving shareholders were transferred, or on such terms as may be agreed, or fixed by the court on the application of either the transferee company or the shareholder: section 209 (2).

Recommendations of the Jenkins Committee

The Jenkins Report[63] made the following recommendations:—

(1) The Department of Trade should have power to make rules (on the lines of the Rules for Licensed Dealers, below) applicable to every take-over offer and to every circular containing or recommending acceptance of such an offer.

Such circulars should no longer be required to be sent through authorised channels or approved by the Department but should be required to be registered with the Registrar before circulation.

Such circulars and circulars recommending rejection of a take-over offer should be subject to a provision on the lines of the Prevention of Fraud (Investments) Act 1958, s. 13,[64] extended so as to give a civil remedy for an untrue statement.

These changes would mean that take-over offers would be regulated broadly in the same way as prospectuses.

(2) An offeror who subsequently varies his offer by increasing the price should be required to pay the higher price for shares accepted on the initial offer. This is already common practice in most take-over offers.

When an offer is declared unconditional the offeror should be required to disclose the number and proportion of shares of each class which he then has or controls. This would enable non-accepting shareholders to re-assess their position.

(3) Every take-over circular offering cash for securities should state what steps the offeror has taken to ensure that the necessary cash will be available. The Licensed Dealers (Conduct of Business)

[63] Para. 294.
[64] *Ante* p. 158.

Rules 1960, below, do not go far enough. The Committee saw no justification for imposing upon all offers to acquire companies or controlling interests therein a requirement that part of the consideration should be in cash. Many mergers or take-overs have gone through on a share exchange basis.

(4) Section 209 should be amended, *e.g.*:

(*a*) To make it clear that it applies only to offers, for all outstanding shares of the company or of a class, made on the same terms to all the shareholders concerned.

(*b*) To provide that subsection (1) operates only where the offer has been approved by the holders of at least nine-tenths of the shares whose transfer is involved other than shares held by, or by a nominee for, the transferee company or any company in the same group as it.

(*c*) To require that all shares held by any member of the same group as the offeror shall be taken into account in deciding whether for the purpose of subsection (2) the right to be bought out has arisen. At present, the rights of an offeree under section 209 (2) can be defeated by procuring the offer to be made by a subsidiary of a company which already has a substantial holding in the transferor company.

Clauses 26 and 27 of the Companies Bill 1973 would have given effect to the recommendations in (4) above.

Other Provisions to be Borne in Mind When a Take-Over Bid is to be Made

When a take-over bid is to be made, apart from the provisions of the Companies Act, the following should also be borne in mind:

(1) The Prevention of Fraud (Investments) Act 1958, section 14,[65] which restricts the channels through which circulars containing offers to sell or purchase shares (not being prospectuses within the meaning of the Companies Act) may be distributed and so controls, *inter alia*, the distribution of take-over circulars.

(2) The Licensed Dealers (Conduct of Business) Rules 1960,[66] which were made by the former Board of Trade under section 7 of the Prevention of Fraud (Investments) Act 1958, and have statutory force only as regards licensed dealers, although they are observed generally.[67] These, *inter alia*, lay down certain requirements for the conduct of take-over offers and

[65] *Ante* p. 158.
[66] S.I. 1960 No. 1216.
[67] Jenkins Report, paras. 268, 269.

the contents of take-over circulars. For example, if an offer is conditional, the latest date on which the offeror may declare it unconditional must be specified, and if the offer relates to less than the total amount in issue of any class of securities it must be open to acceptance by all holders of the class and if too many acceptances are received they must be scaled down *pro rata*. Again, the bidder must be identified, and the extent of the offeror's interest in the securities of the offeree company must be given.

(3) The City Code on Take-overs and Mergers[68] which was prepared at the suggestion of the Stock Exchange, London, and the Governor of the Bank of England, by the Executive Committee of the Issuing Houses Association in co-operation with other organisations including the Committee of London Clearing Bankers. The Code has no statutory force but constitutes a generally accepted code of behaviour on take-over bids. It provides, *e.g.*, that an offer should be made in the first instance to the board of directors of the offeree company or its advisers, that the identity of the offeror company should be disclosed and that an assurance should be given that it has the necessary resources. The operation of the Code is supervised by the Panel on Take-overs and Mergers.

Fair Trading Act 1973

The Fair Trading Act 1973, which *inter alia* repealed, and re-enacted with amendments, the Monopolies and Mergers Act 1965, should be borne in mind because it enables the Secretary of State in certain circumstances to refer a merger to the Monopolies & Mergers Commission.

Sections 64 and 75 of the 1973 Act provide that where it appears to the Secretary of State that—

(1) two or more enterprises, at least one of which was or is carried on in the United Kingdom or by or under the control of a company incorporated here, have ceased to be distinct enterprises within the past six months or without notice to the Secretary of State or the Director General of Fair Trading, or are about to cease to be distinct enterprises; and

(2) either (*a*) as a result at least one-quarter of certain goods or services are or will be supplied in the U.K. by or to any one person, or by or to the persons by whom the enterprises are carried on; or

(*b*) the value of the assets taken, or to be taken, over exceeds £5m.;

the Secretary of State may refer the matter to the Commission for investigation and report within, usually, six months (s. 70).

If conditions (1) and (2) are fulfilled the Commission must decide whether the merger is against the public interest (s. 69) and, if so, what action should be taken. If, according to the report as laid before Parliament, facts found operate against the public interest, the Secretary of State has the powers specified in Schedule 8 (s. 73), *e.g.* he may prohibit bodies corporate from becoming interconnected bodies corporate, or provide for the division of any business by the sale of any part of the undertaking or assets or otherwise, or for the division of any group of inter connected bodies corporate. For this purpose the Secretary of State may order, *inter alia*, the winding up of a company or the amendment of its memorandum and articles.

It is the duty of the Director General of Fair Trading to keep himself in-

[68] Revised edition February, 1973, amended June, 1974.

formed about actual or prospective mergers and to make recommendations to the Secretary of State as to action which it would be expedient for the Secretary of State to take (s. 76).

"Enterprise" is defined in section 63 as the activities or any part of the activities of a business. Two enterprises are treated as ceasing to be distinct enterprises if they are brought under common ownership or control or either enterprise ceases to be carried on at all. The following enterprises are treated as being under common control—

(1) those of interconnected bodies corporate;
(2) those carried on by any two or more bodies corporate controlled by the same person or persons;
(3) that carried on by a body corporate and that carried on by the person or persons controlling the body corporate (s. 65).

For the purposes of section 65 a person or group of persons able to control or materially to influence the policy of a body corporate or that of a person carrying on an enterprise, without having a controlling interest, may be treated as having control.

Associated persons, and any bodies corporate which any of them control, are treated as one person for the purposes of, *e.g.* section 65. Certain persons are deemed to be associated, *e.g.* an individual and that individual's spouse, and any relative, or spouse of a relative, of either (s. 77).

By section 58 a transfer of a newspaper or of newspaper assets to a newspaper proprietor whose newspapers have an average circulation per day, with that of the newspaper concerned, of 500,000 or more copies is unlawful and void unless made with the written consent of the Secretary of State.

Industry Act 1975, Part II

The Industry Act 1975, Part II (sections 11–20), gives the Secretary of State power to prohibit the transfer or to acquire the undertaking if there is a serious and immediate possibility that control over a important manufacturing undertaking (as defined in section 11 (2)) will pass to a person resident outside the United Kingdom and the transfer would be contrary to the national interest.

Section 11 provides that the powers conferred by Part II extend to changes of control of important manufacturing undertakings. Section 12 provides that there is such a change of control only in certain specified events, *e.g.* when a person not resident in the U.K. becomes able to exercise or control the exercise of 30 per cent. or 40 per cent. or 50 per cent. of the votes that may be cast at a general meeting of a body corporate carrying on the whole or part of the undertaking.

Section 13 provides that if it appears to the Secretary of State that there is a serious and immediate possibility of a change of control of an important manufacturing undertaking and that would be contrary to the interests of the U.K. or a substantial part thereof, he may make a prohibition order. In certain circumstances he may make a vesting order vesting the share capital and loan capital of any relevant body corporate or any assets employed in the undertaking in the National Enterprise Board or himself or nominees. A vesting order can be made only if the Secretary of State is satisfied that the order is necessary in the national interest and that it is impossible to protect that interest in any other way.

CHAPTER 28

FOREIGN COMPANIES

Oversea companies

Section 406 provides that sections 407 to 414 apply to oversea companies and that an oversea company is a company incorporated outside Great Britain which establishes a place of business within Great Britain. The expression "Great Britain" includes England and Wales and Scotland but not the Isle of Man,[1] or the Channel Islands. The expression "place of business" includes a share transfer or share registration office: section 415; but a company which only employs agents within Great Britain, and has no office, has not established a place of business.[2]

Documents to be delivered to Registrar by oversea companies

Within one month of the establishment of the place of business an oversea company must deliver certain documents to the Registrar of Companies in England or Scotland as the case may be: sections 407, 413.

At the end of 1974, 4,260 oversea companies had registered documents under section 407.

The documents which must be registered under section 407 of the 1948 Act as amended by Schedule 1 of the 1976 Act are—

   (1) a certified copy of the charter, statutes or memorandum and articles of the company or other instrument defining the constitution of the company and, if the instrument is not written in the English language, a certified translation of it;
   (2) a list of the directors and secretary, with similar particulars to those required by section 200[3] in the case of an English or a Scottish company;
   (3) A list of the names and addresses of one or more persons resident in Great Britain authorised to accept, on behalf of the company, service of process and notices;
   (4) a list of the above-mentioned documents.

[1] *Per* Megarry J. in *Curragh Investments Ltd.* v. *Cook* [1974] 1 W.L.R. 1559.
[2] *Lord Advocate* v. *Huron and Erie Loan Co.*, 1911 S.C. 612.
[3] *Ante* p. 318.

650

If any alteration is made as regards (1), (2) or (3) above, or the corporate name, the company must, within the prescribed time, deliver particulars to the Registrar: section 409 of the 1948 Act as amended by Schedule 2 of the 1976 Act.

Section 31 of the Companies Act 1976 empowers the Secretary of State, if he considers it undesirable for an oversea company to carry on business in Great Britain under its corporate name, to cause the Registrar to serve notice to that effect on the company within six months after it complies with section 407 *ante* or it registers a return that its name has changed, whereupon the company must cease carrying on business in Britain under its corporate name within two months, and there are penalties for default. However, the oversea company then has the right to register a statement specifying another name, approved by the Secretary of State, under which it will carry on business in Britain and this name is for all purposes of the law applying in Britain (including the Registration of Business Names Act 1916) deemed to be the company's corporate name.

Other obligations of oversea companies

(1) In respect of each of its accounting reference periods[4] prepare a balance sheet and profit and loss account (and, if it is a holding company, group accounts) with the appropriate documents annexed or attached, as if it were an English or a Scottish Company[5] and deliver copies to the Registrar: 1976 Act, s. 9.

In general, the period allowed for delivering accounts is thirteen months after the end of the accounting reference period and there are penalties for non-compliance: 1976 Act, s. 11.

If any of the above mentioned documents is not written in English, a certified translation must be annexed. The one exception to section 9 *ante* is where the company would come within section 1 (8) of the 1976 Act if it were an English or a Scottish company.

(2) An oversea company must, in any prospectus inviting subscriptions for its shares or debentures in Great Britain, state the country in which it is incorporated.

---

[4] As regards the accounting reference period of an oversea company, ss. 2 and 3 of the 1976 Act apply subject to the modification specified in s. 10 of that Act.
[5] *Ante* p. 422.

(3) An oversea company must conspicuously exhibit on every place where it carries on business in Great Britain, its name and the country in which it is incorporated.

(4) An oversea company must cause its name and the country in which it is incorporated to be stated in legible characters in all bill-heads and letter paper, and in all its notices and other official publications.

(5) If the liability of its members is limited, an oversea company must cause notice of that fact to be stated in legible characters in every prospectus, and in all bill-heads, letter paper, notices and other official publications of the company in Great Britain, and to be affixed on every place where it carries on its business: section 411.

Compliance with sections 406 to 413 is enforced by a penalty of £50 or, in the case of a continuing offence, £5 a day during the continuance of the default, imposed on the company and every officer or agent of the company who authorises or permits the default: section 414.

(6) An oversea company must register charges on property in England under sections 95, 97 and 104, and on property in Scotland under sections 106A, 106C and 106I[6]: sections 106 and 106K.

An oversea company incorporated in the Channel Islands or the Isle of Man is subject to all the provisions of the Act requiring documents to be delivered to the Registrar as if the company was a company registered in England or in Scotland, depending upon where it has established a place of business: section 416 of the 1948 Act as amended by Schedule 3 of the 1976 Act.

As companies incorporated abroad have, at common law, no restriction upon their trading or issuing shares or debentures in Great Britain, the above provisions are aimed at preventing companies from evading the stringent provisions of the Companies Acts by becoming incorporated abroad.

We saw earlier [7] that an oversea company which carries on business in Britain under a business name must register such name under the Registration of Business Names Act 1916.

If any alteration is made in any of the above documents etc., the

[6] *Ante* p. 509 *et seq.*
[7] *Ante* p. 70.

company must, within the prescribed time, deliver particulars of those alterations to the Registrar: section 409.

Service of process or notices on oversea companies

Section 412 provides that any process or notice may be served on an oversea company by addressing it to, and leaving it with or sending it by post to, the person whose name has been delivered to the Registrar under section 407. Further, that if such a name has not been delivered, or the persons whose names have been delivered are dead or have ceased to reside at the addresses given, or refuse to accept service, or cannot be served, a document may be served on the company by leaving it at or sending it by post to any place of business established by the company in Great Britain. It has been held that the words "any place of business established . . . in Great Britain" mean a place of business established at the time of service. They do not include a former place of business which is no longer such at the material time.[8]

The Jenkins Report[9] recommended that section 412 should be extended to provide that, where an oversea company has ceased to have an established place of business in Great Britain and there is no representative willing to accept service of process, service may be effected at any place at which the company has had an established place of business within the last three years. Further, that an oversea company which has ceased to have an established place of business here should, at the end of three years from cessation, be entitled to have the name of a representative nominated by it for the purposes of section 407 removed from the register. At present, if the representative is prepared to accept service on its behalf, such a company may be made amenable to the jurisdiction of our courts for an indefinite period.

Clause 100 of the 1973 Bill would have given effect to the above recommendations.

Winding up of oversea companies

An oversea company which has ceased to carry on business in Great Britain may be wound up here as an unregistered company[10] even if it has been dissolved under the laws of the country under which it was incorporated: section 400.

[8] *Deverall* v. *Grant Advertising Inc.* [1955] Ch. 111 (C.A.).
[9] Para. 525.　　　　[10] *Post.*

Prospectuses of foreign companies

Prospectuses of oversea companies and other companies incorporated outside Great Britain are subject to much the same rules as those of English or Scottish companies. It is unlawful to issue or circulate in Great Britain a prospectus offering for subscription shares in or debentures of a company incorporated outside Great Britain unless a copy, certified by the chairman and two other directors as having been approved by the managing body, is first registered with the appropriate Registrar of Companies: section 420.[11]

The prospectus must be dated, must state the matters, and set out the reports, required in the case of a prospectus of a British company, and must contain particulars with respect to the following matters—

(1) the instrument defining the company's constitution;

(2) the enactments under which the company is incorporated;

(3) the address in Great Britain where the instrument and enactments, and a certified translation of them, can be inspected;

(4) the date on which, and the country in which, the company was incorporated;

(5) whether the company has established a place of business in Great Britain and, if so, the address of its principal office in Great Britain: section 417.[12]

If the prospectus is issued more than two years after the date on which the company is entitled to commence business, then (1)–(3), *ante*, need not be set out: section 417.[12]

There are provisions as to an expert's consent and material contracts (ss. 419, 420), and a certificate of exemption (s. 418), as there are in the case of British companies.[13] Section 422 extends section 43 (civil liability for mis-statements) to a prospectus of a foreign company and section 423 applies most of section 45 to an offer for sale of shares in or debentures of a foreign company.

These provisions prevent a company, which it is really intended shall carry on business in Great Britain, from evading the Companies Acts by being incorporated abroad.

---

[11] Which corresponds to s. 41, *ante* p. 142, in the case of an English or a Scottish company.

[12] s. 417 corresponds to ss. 37 and 38.

[13] Under ss. 39, 40 and 41.

Winding up of foreign companies as unregistered companies

Any company incorporated outside Great Britain, whether an oversea company or not, is an unregistered company within section 398 *ante*, and may be wound up by the court under section 399.

In normal circumstances, in order to establish jurisdiction under section 399 (*i.e.* to wind up a foreign company as an unregistered company)—

(1) there is no need to establish that the foreign company ever had a place of business or carried on business in the U.K. unless, perhaps, the petition is based on the company carrying on business;

(2) there must be sufficient evidence that the company has some asset(s) within the jurisdiction *and* that there are one or more persons concerned in the proper distribution of the assets;

(3) it suffices if the assets within the jurisdiction are of any nature —they need not be "commercial" assets, or assets which indicate that the company formerly carried on business in the U.K.;

(4) the assets need not be assets distributable to creditors by the liquidator in a winding up—it suffices if, by the making of a winding up order, they would be of benefit to a creditor(s) in some other way;

(5) if there is no reasonable possibility of benefit accruing to creditors from the making of a winding up order, jurisdiction is excluded.[14]

[14] *Re Compania Merabello San Nicholas S.A.* [1973] Ch. 75, applying *Banque des Marchands de Moscou (Koupetschesky)* v. *Kindersley* [1951] Ch. 112 (C.A.); and see *Inland Revenue* v. *Highland Light Engineering Ltd.*, 1975 S.L.T. 203 (O.H.).

CHAPTER 29

TAXATION

INTRODUCTION

PROFITS as defined for tax purposes are liable to be taxed in some way. Individuals pay income tax on their income, capital gains tax on their capital gains. Companies (and also unincorporated associations other than partnerships) pay corporation tax on both their income and capital profits. Both companies and individuals may be liable to pay development land tax if they start projects of material development or dispose of land with development potential.

Losses which are gratuitous, *i.e.* gifts, may be subject to capital transfer tax. This is charged on (1) individuals and (2) settlements. It is not charged on gifts by companies other than close companies (see *post*, p. 668).

Transactions may be taxed. Value added tax is a tax on the supply of goods or services in the course of a business. Stamp duty is charged on certain transactions; capital duty is charged, in effect, on the issue of shares by companies.

The reader who has not appreciated this before will have rapidly realised from the above that the topic—and burden—of taxation is enormous. This short chapter can do no more than introduce the reader to the main features of the taxation of companies; it also attempts to introduce the reader to some of the factors which may influence a person for tax reasons to carry on business through the medium of a company rather than a partnership (there are, of course, many critical non tax factors: see *ante*, p. 37). For further reading, Pinson's *Revenue Law* is recommended; references to Pinson in this chapter are to paragraphs in that invaluable basic work. References to rates of income tax are references to the rates for income tax year 1976–77; for corporation tax, the references are to the rates for Financial Year 1975.

TAX ON BUSINESS PROFITS

Income tax and the unincorporated trader

The individual (or partnership) carrying on a trade pays income tax on his trading profits, as computed for income tax purposes, for each tax year (April 6–April 5 following). He does not normally pay tax on his actual profits for each tax year: his profits will usually be assessed on the "preceding year basis." For the details, see Pinson, paragraphs 2–79 to 2–84. Suffice it to say that the overall result will usually be that the unincorporated trader will find that the date for payment of tax is long after the end of the accounting period which produced the profits—if the right period is selected, one half the tax may not become due until almost 21 months after the end of the period, and the other half a further six months after that.[1] If profits are growing, or there is rapid inflation, a delay of this magnitude in paying tax is clearly beneficial to the trader: effectively, he will be paying tax on an income smaller, or much smaller, than he is actually enjoying. Further, there are special rules for the opening and closing years of a business; when a business is closed down, the unincorporated trader will normally find that the profits for a whole accounting period (or more) have dropped out of the tax net altogether.[2]

Against the undoubted advantages of the preceding year basis, it must be pointed out that the unincorporated trader has to pay income tax on all his profits, whether he withdraws them or not. The amount of tax he pays will depend on the amount of the profits; income tax charged on individuals is graduated. The first part of income is exempted tax by personal reliefs (*e.g.* for 1976/77 a married man is exempted tax on the first £1,085). For tax year 1976/77, the remainder of an individual's income is taxed as follows: next £5,000 at the basic rate of 35 per cent., next £500 at 40 per cent., next £1,000 at 45 per cent., next £1,000 at 50 per cent., next £1,000 at 55 per cent. and so on up to 83 per cent. where total taxable income exceeds £20,000. Thus a person whose trading profits are £7,500 more than his personal reliefs will find that if he earns any more profits he will need to pay tax at 55 per cent. on them.

---

[1] *i.e.* if the accounting period runs from April 7–April 6 following.
[2] See, in particular, illustration in Pinson, para. 2–84.

Capital gains tax and the unincorporated trader

An individual pays capital gains tax on his capital gains, *e.g.* on the disposal of his fixed capital; the rate is 30 per cent., but the small trader may find that he is paying less under "the alternative rate."[3]

Corporation tax and the company

A company pays corporation tax on the profits which actually arise during its accounting period (broadly speaking, the period not exceeding 12 months for which it makes up its accounts).[4] The rate of tax is the rate fixed for the financial year (April 1 to March 31 following) during which the profits arise. There are two rates of corporation tax: there is a small companies rate[5] and a normal rate. Rates are always fixed in arrears; Finance Act 1976 provides for the rates for financial year 1975 (*i.e.* the period from April 1, 1975 to March 31, 1976). The small companies rate is 42 per cent.;[6] it applies to companies whose profits do not exceed £30,000. If profits exceed £50,000, corporation tax at the rate of 52 per cent. is charged;[7] there is a sliding scale of rates between 42 per cent. and 52 per cent. for companies whose profits are between £30,000 and £50,000.[8]

If an accounting period straddles two financial years for which different rates have been fixed, the profits must be apportioned on a time basis.

Corporation tax is normally payable nine months after the end of the accounting period.[9]

If the rates of income tax and corporation tax are compared, it will be seen that companies pay more tax on their profits if those profits are very small, *e.g.* less than £5,000–6,000. On the other hand, if the profits are large, the company pays much less tax. A company pays tax at only 42 per cent. on profits of £30,000; the effective overall rate of tax for an individual earning such profits would be in the region of 60 per cent.; further, the individual would be paying tax at 83 per cent, on, say, the top £8,000 of his profits (the

[3] Finance Act 1965, s. 21 (1); Pinson, para. 16–01.
[4] Income and Corporation Taxes Act 1970, s. 247.
[5] Finance Act 1972, s. 95.
[6] Finance Act 1976, s. 27 (2).
[7] *Ibid.*, s. 25.
[8] *Ibid.*, s. 27 (3) and Finance Act 1972, s. 95.
[9] Income and Corporation Taxes Act, s. 243 (4). There are special rules for companies trading before 1965: *ibid.*, s. 244.

precise amount would depend on the value of the reliefs available to him), making those profits very hard earned indeed.

To that extent, then, corporation tax is favourable. An unfavourable feature, however, is the fact that tax is payable much earlier in the case of a company than it is in the case of an individual—as has been seen, an individual trader will not have to pay any part of his tax on trading profits for up to 21 months after the end of his accounting period, if he has chosen the best possible accounting period, whereas companies generally have to pay their corporation tax nine months after the end of the period.

Further, where a company is concerned, corporation tax may only be part of the story—ultimately, those who have put money or effort into a company will want to see a return coming to them personally—this is considered further, below.

Capital gains and companies

Companies pay corporation tax on their capital gains; however, the rules are such that the effective rate of corporation tax is only 30 per cent.[10] To that extent, it may be thought that the position of a company making a capital gain is little different from the position of an individual. However, a capital gain made by a company (subject to corporation tax at an effective rate of 30 per cent.) will enhance the value of the shareholders' shares, so that they may in turn have to pay capital gains tax when they sell their shares.

For example, a company makes a capital gain of £1,000. Corporation tax on this will amount to £300. Thus, after tax, the company's net gain will be £700. If the shares of the shareholders are valued on an assets basis, they will go up in value by £700. If this gain is realised, there may be further capital gains tax at 30 per cent. to be paid by the shareholders, *i.e.* a further £210 to pay. Thus, the overall rate of tax on capital gains enjoyed through the medium of a company can be as high as 51 per cent. (or higher, when the gain of a subsidiary is enjoyed by a shareholder in the holding company).

TAX ON THE ENJOYMENT OF COMPANY PROFITS

The entrepreneur who is carrying on business through a company may enjoy the company's profits personally in one of four ways—

    (1) he may withdraw them as directors fees; or

    (2) they may be paid to him as interest on a loan; or

[10] Finance Act 1972, s. 93 (2); Finance Act 1974, s. 10 (1).

(3) he may take them as a dividend on his shares; or

(4) he may enjoy them as a capital gain by selling his shares, the value of which has been enhanced by profits retained by the company.

Directors' fees

Directors' emoluments are a deductible business expense for tax purposes; thus a company which pays away all its "profits" to its directors as remuneration will, in fact, have no profits for tax purposes.[11] Instead, the money paid to the directors as remuneration will be taxed as income in their hands.[12] This means that a person who runs a business through the medium of a company, and pays the entire "profits" to himself as director's fees, will be in exactly the same position, as far as rates of tax are concerned, as if he had carried on the business on his own account without incorporating. However, he will be in a worse position as far as payment of the tax is concerned. As a director, he will be an employee for tax purposes and thus have tax deducted from each payment to him at the time when it is made,[13] whereas if he had carried on the business on his own account he would have been able to take advantage of the considerable deferment of tax which can arise under the preceding year basis, as explained above.

Dividends and distributions

Whenever a company pays a dividend to a shareholder, it is liable to pay "advance corporation tax" to the Revenue, *i.e.* the company must pay, in advance, part of the corporation tax which it will be liable to pay on the profits of the accounting period during which the dividend is paid.[14] The rate of advance corporation tax is governed by the basic rate of income tax; the rate for financial year 1976 (the period from April 1, 1976 to March 31, 1977) is 35/65,[15] *e.g.* if a company pays a dividend of £65, it must send £35 to the Revenue, the £35 being a payment in advance of the corporation tax for which

---

[11] So long as the remuneration is not extravagant: see *Copeman* v. *Flood* [1941] 1 K.B. 202.

[12] Under Schedule E. See Pinson, Chapter 3.

[13] The "pay as you earn" system; Income and Corporation Taxes Act 1970, s. 204.

[14] Finance Act 1972, ss. 84–85. See, generally, Pinson, paras. 14–40 and 14–75.

[15] Finance Act 1976, s. 26.

the company will be liable on the profits of the accounting period during which the dividend is paid.

At first sight it would appear that the above means that a company can always distribute 65 per cent. of its profits by way of dividend. However, this is not so. Say, for example, a company makes a profit of £10,000 and distributes £6,500 to shareholders by way of dividend. On paying such a dividend, the company will have to find £3,500 to pay to the Revenue by way of advance corporation tax—in such a case, the dividend plus A.C.T. will equal the full profits of the company. However, on £10,000 profits the company will be liable to pay corporation tax (at the small companies rate) of £4,200, *i.e.* the company will have to find another £700 to pay in tax on top of the £3,500 A.C.T. it has already paid. Thus the company will have had to pay in dividends and taxes £700 more than its total profits. In fact, the maximum proportion of total profits which can be paid out by way of dividend (assuming that reserves are not being used for the purpose) is 58 per cent. in the case of a company charged to tax at the small companies rate of 42 per cent. and 48 per cent. in the case of a company charged to tax at the full companies rate of 52 per cent.

A dividend paid by a company is taxable income in the hands of a shareholder.[16] For income tax purposes, the shareholder is treated as receiving not just the dividend paid to him, but also the A.C.T. paid in respect of it;[17] thus if a company pays a dividend of £65, on which it must pay £35 in A.C.T., the shareholder will be treated as receiving taxable income of £100. However, the A.C.T. paid by the company is credited against his income tax liability;[18] if the shareholder is not liable to tax, he may recover the A.C.T., and if he is liable to tax at the basic rate only, he will not have any further tax to pay. The shareholder will have further tax to pay if he is liable to tax at higher rates than the basic rate (*i.e.* where his income, after deducting reliefs, exceeds £5,000) or if he is liable to the investment income surcharge (below). In other words, as far as the shareholder is concerned he is effectively treated as if he had received his dividend after deduction of income tax at the basic rate.

[16] Income and Corporation Taxes Act 1970, s. 232; Finance Act 1972, s. 87.
[17] Finance Act 1972, ss. 86–87.
[18] *Ibid.*

Qualifying distributions

The above rules apply whenever a "qualifying distribution" is made by a company.[19] To prevent tax avoidance, the term distribution is very widely defined. It includes not only any dividend, but can also include (1) certain issues of bonus shares which are irredeemable, (2) certain reductions of capital, and (3) certain payments of interest.

Subject to the point about stock dividend options (*below*) a bonus issue of irredeemable shares is only a distribution to the extent that the company has repaid capital on shares, other than preference shares, since April 6, 1965.[20]

A reduction of capital is a distribution if (*a*) it exceeds the amount paid up on the shares[21] or (*b*) the company has issued bonus shares of the same class since April 6, 1965.[22] However, a repayment of capital in a winding-up is not a distribution,[23] although it may give rise to a capital gains tax liability in the hands of the shareholder (*e.g.* if he gets back more for his shares than he paid for them).

The rules relating to the circumstances in which "linked" bonus issues and reductions of capital can give rise to a distribution must be borne in mind by any company considering either reducing capital or making a bonus issue. If, *e.g.*, a bonus issue is contemplated, it may be a distribution—and therefore attract tax which would not otherwise have been attracted—if the company has reduced capital since 1965. If the company has not reduced capital since 1965, the bonus issue may not be a distribution; however, it may hinder freedom to manoeuvre in the future because it may cause a subsequent reduction in capital to be a distribution, which it might not otherwise have been.

In the case of (broadly) quoted companies, the rules are tempered to some extent, in that bonus issues and reductions of capital can only be "linked" if they come within ten years of each other.[24]

As mentioned above, certain payments of interest, *e.g.* interest on bonus debentures issued since April 6, 1965, interest which depends on the results of the company's business, and interest in excess of a reasonable commercial rate, are distributions.[25] It should be stressed

---

[19] *Ibid.*, s. 84 (4).
[20] Income and Corporation Taxes Act 1970. s. 234 (1).
[21] *Ibid.*, s. 233 (2) (16). [22] *Ibid.*, s. 235.
[23] *Ibid.*, s. 233 (1).
[24] Finance Act 1972, sched. 22, paras. 5, 6.
[25] Income and Corporation Taxes Act 1970, s. 233 (2) (d).

that this is not the general rule—the general rule is that a payment of interest is a charge on income and not a distribution:[26] thus it is deductible from profits for corporation tax purposes.

Non-qualifying distributions

Bonus redeemable preference shares and bonus debentures are non-qualifying distributions.[27] On making such an issue, the company is not liable to account for advance corporation tax. The recipient, although not liable to basic rate tax, may have to account for "excess liability" (*i.e.* the difference between tax at the basic rate (35 per cent.) and his top rate of higher rate tax.)[28]

Stock dividend options

Where a person is given the choice of accepting bonus shares in lieu of a cash dividend, and he opts for such bonus shares, the issue will not be a distribution (even if it would otherwise be one under the above rules) and the company is not liable to account for A.C.T.; however, the shareholder liable to higher rate tax will, in effect, be charged such tax as if the value of the bonus shares received were a net sum from which income tax at the basic rate had been deducted at source.[29]

Declaration of dividends; preference dividends

It was mentioned earlier that, as far as a shareholder is concerned, a dividend received by a shareholder is, in effect, received by him net of income tax at the basic rate—thus a dividend of 6·5 per cent. (net) is (at the rate of A.C.T. for Financial Year 1976) equivalent to a dividend of 10 per cent. before income tax.

If a company wished to pay a dividend of equivalent effect before April 6, 1973, it would declare a dividend of 10 per cent and deduct income tax from it (the net result would have been different, because the rate of income tax was different, but the cost to the company would have been the same).

However, under the imputation system (as the present system of

[26] *Ibid.*, s. 248.
[27] Finance Act 1972, s. 84 (4).
[28] *Ibid.*, s. 87 (5).
[29] Finance (No. 2) Act 1975, s. 34.

paying dividends is called), introduced on April 6, 1973,[30] the company must now declare a dividend of 6·5 per cent. to get the same result if the dividend, with the addition of A.C.T., is to cost it no more than it intends.

What about paid dividends on preference shares where the rate was fixed before April 6, 1973? These will have been fixed on the basis of a gross dividend, from which income tax would be deducted, rather than as net dividends to which A.C.T. would have to be added. Finance Act 1972[31] provides, therefore, that the fixed dividend becomes a fixed net dividend of such a sum, as with the addition of A.C.T. at the rate in force for Financial Year 1973[32] ($\frac{3}{7}$) equals the fixed gross dividend previously provided for. Thus what was a 10 per cent. (gross) preferential dividend before 1973 becomes now a seven per cent. (net) preferential dividend, with the curious result that holders of preference shares issued before April 6, 1973, are now getting a larger gross dividend than ever before, because the rate of A.C.T. is now, at $\frac{35}{65}$, higher than it was for financial year 1973.[33]

Director's fees, interest payments, dividends and capital gains contrasted

Undoubtedly the most tax efficient income which a company can give to a working proprietor is in the form of director's fees. As explained above, these should normally be a deductible expense in computing its profits for tax purposes, *i.e.* the only tax to which the director's fees will be subject will be income tax in the hands of the director.

Next in line comes interest on money lent to a company. Once again, the payment of interest will normally come out of pre-tax profits, so that the only tax to be attracted will be income tax on the recipient (or corporation tax, if the recipient is a company). However, in the case of an individual recipient, the interest received will be investment income and so might attract the investment income surcharge if his investment income is large enough.[34] No surcharge is payable on the first £1,000 of investment income; a surcharge of

[30] Finance Act 1972, s. 84 (1).
[31] *Ibid.*, sched. 23, para. 18.
[32] Finance Act 1976, s. 46, nullifying the decision in *Sime Darby London Ltd.* v. *Sime Darby Holdings Ltd.* [1976] 1 W.L.R. 59.
[33] See articles by Ralph Inshore on "The Preference Dividend Muddle" (1975) 125 N.L.J. 928 and (1976) 126 N.L.J. 608.
[34] Finance Act 1971, s. 34; Finance Act 1976, s. 24 (b).

10 per cent. (on top of income tax) is payable if investment income exceeds £1,000; the surcharge is 15 per cent. on investment incomes in excess of £2,000.

The least tax efficient payment is a dividend (or payment of interest which ranks as a distribution). This will be taxed as investment income in the hands of the individual recipient. Further, there is an element of double taxation—although part of the corporation tax (*i.e.* the amount of A.C.T.) for which a company is liable may be set off against the income tax for which an individual recipient is liable on a dividend, it is only a partial relief. In other words, unlike payments of interest and directors fees, dividends have to come out of income which is partly taxable in the company's hands.

If the shareholder is prepared to wait before he realises a company's profits, the profits may be retained, subject to payment of corporation tax (but see close companies, *below*) and the benefit of the retained profits taken indirectly by the shareholder on a sale of his shares. In this case, he will be liable normally to capital gains tax of 30 per cent.; however, there are some extremely complex provisions designed to prevent a person taking in a capital form what are essentially a company's reserves of income, and these can operate where a person makes a capital gain on a sale of shares.[35] Broadly, where the provisions operate, the capital gain can be treated as if it were income.

Distributions received by a company

The way in which a company's profits are to some extent double taxed before they reach the shareholder when paid to him as a dividend has been mentioned above. There are complex rules to ensure that there is no multiple taxation when dividends pass through the hands of corporate shareholders before reaching an individual shareholder. Broadly speaking, this is achieved by not charging companies to corporation tax on dividends received by them and (in effect) by allowing recipient companies to pass on such dividends to their shareholders without paying A.C.T.[36]

[35] Income and Corporation Taxes Act 1970, s. 460; see, *e.g.*, *I.R.C.* v. *Cleary* [1968] A.C. 766.
[36] Finance Act 1972, ss. 88–89.

CLOSE COMPANIES

There are extremely involved rules to ensure that small companies are not used as a vehicle for tax avoidance. These rules affect "close companies." A close company is one which is under the control of either (1) five or fewer participators or (2) participators who are directors even if more than five.[37]

The term "participators" is widely defined to include not only shareholders but also (*inter alia*) persons with options to take shares and loan creditors (other than banks lending money in the ordinary course of business). The word "control" is also widely defined and is not limited to voting control. In deciding whether a participator has control, the powers of control of his associates (certain relatives, partners and companies of which he has control) must be attributed to him.[38]

Certain companies which would otherwise fall within the definition are expressly excluded, *e.g.* companies not resident in the U.K., subsidiaries of non-close companies and companies whose ordinary shares carrying not less than 35 per cent. of the voting power are held by the public and quoted on a recognised stock exchange.[39]

Principally, the special rules relating to close companies (1) prevent the company from getting full tax relief for certain payments made to participators and (2) prevent the participators from avoiding income tax on the company's profits by not distributing them.

(1) above is achieved by providing that certain payments made to participators are qualifying distributions and taxable as such. In particular, a payment of interest in excess of the "prescribed limit" to a director–participator or an associate of his is a qualifying distribution. The prescribed limit is an amount equal to 12 per cent. on the lesser of (*a*) the loan made by the director–participator etc. or (*b*) the nominal amount of the company's issued capital plus share premium account plus capital redemption reserve fund.[40] In other words, a person may get very little tax advantage by forming a company and transferring assets to the company in return for debentures instead of shares—under this provision, the interest (or much of it) may be taxed as if it were a dividend on shares.

(2) above is achieved by providing that in so far as a close com-

---

[37] Income and Corporation Taxes Act 1970, s. 282.
[38] *Ibid.*, ss. 302–303.
[39] *Ibid.*, ss. 282–283; Finance Act 1971, s. 25.
[40] Income and Corporation Taxes Act, 1970 s. 285; Finance Act 1974, s. 35.

pany fails to distribute its "relevant income," the company is liable
to account for A.C.T. on the amount undistributed, and this amount
is apportioned among the participators who are liable to income tax
on the amount apportioned as if it had actually been paid to them by
way of dividend.[41] There are complex rules for calculating what is
"relevant income" (*i.e.* the amount of the profits which ought to be
distributed). In the case of a trading company whose profits are
derived wholly from trade, the effect of the rules is, broadly, that
relevant income can never exceed 50 per cent. of profits after tax, *i.e.*
a trading company and its shareholders can never be taxed as if a
distribution had been made if it retains no more than 50 per cent. of
its trading profits. Further, "relevant income" can be reduced (to nil
in appropriate cases) to the extent that the company can show that it
could not have distributed 50 per cent. of its trading profits con-
sistently with the requirements of its business. There are also special
rules for companies with small profits—broadly, the effect is that a
close trading company and its shareholders can never be charged to
tax under these provisions if the company's pre-tax trading profits
do not exceed £10,919.

There can also be a charge to tax on a company when it makes a
loan or gives credit (otherwise than in the ordinary course of business)
to a participator.[42]

Were it not for the above rules, it would be too easy to save tax by
carrying on business through the medium of a company. The
proprietors, as directors, would withdraw fees enough to enable them
to live on; their "savings" they would leave in the company to be
taxed at only the corporation tax rate which might be appreciably
less than the rate of tax they would have to pay if all the company's
profits were distributed to them. Nevertheless, even though the rules
are designed to prevent higher rate income tax being avoided by the
retention of profits, a limited tax saving can still be achieved.

CAPITAL TRANSFER TAX

Capital transfer tax is payable on the open market value of a person's
estate on his death;[43] it is also payable by any person who makes a
disposition which reduces the value of his estate, unless the disposition is on arms length terms without gratuitous intent.[44]

[41] Finance Act 1972, s. 94 and sched. 16.
[42] Income and Corporation Taxes Act 1970, s. 286.
[43] Finance Act 1975, s. 22.   [44] *Ibid.*, s. 20.

As a general rule, dispositions by companies are not subject to capital transfer tax. However, where a close company makes a gift, capital transfer tax is charged as if the gift were made by the participators according to their respective rights and interests in the company immediately before the gift.[45] In relation to companies, the following further capital transfer tax provisions may be noted.

1. If there is an alteration in the unquoted share or loan capital of a close company, the alteration is treated as if it were a disposition made by the participators—in other words, it is not possible to avoid capital transfer tax by an alteration of class rights which effectively passes value out of some shares into other shares.[46]

2. A controlling interest in shares or securities of a company (which is not an investment company nor a company principally engaged in dealing in securities or land) may be valued for capital transfer tax purposes at a 30 per cent. discount on the open market value.[47]

3. There are provisions whereby capital transfer tax on a controlling holding of unquoted securities, and also certain other unquoted securities, may be paid by eight yearly or 16 half-yearly instalments.[48] This, together with the previous point, goes a long way towards getting round one of the principal difficulties affecting controlling shareholdings—the problem of finding the cash to pay capital transfer tax, a problem which sometimes forces those inheriting a controlling interest either to sell their shares to an outsider or to put the company into liquidation. Even now, those inheriting a controlling shareholding in the company may be tempted to bleed the company to pay the instalments of capital transfer tax, and this should be borne in mind by minority shareholders.

STAMP DUTY AND CAPITAL DUTY

1. Capital duty is charged (*inter alia*) whenever a company issues shares other than bonus shares; the charge is on the actual value of the net assets contributed for the shares or the nominal value of the shares, whichever is the greater.[49] The duty is paid by way of stamp, normally on the return of allotments which must be delivered to the Registrar of Companies under section 52 of the Companies Act 1948 (see *ante* p. 181).

[45] *Ibid.*, s. 39 (1) (see also Finance Act 1976, s. 118).
[46] Finance Act 1975, s. 39 (5).   [47] Finance Act 1976, s. 73 and sched. 410.
[48] Finance Act 1975, sched. 4, paras. 13–16.
[49] Finance Act 1973, s. 47; see Pinson, Chapter 32.

2. A transfer of shares attracts stamp duty at the rate of £2 per cent. of the consideration for the shares (market value, in the case of a gift or sale at under value).[50] It will already have been noted that a company may not register a transfer which is insufficiently stamped (see *ante* p. 254).

3. Share warrants bear stamp duty at the rate of £6 per cent.[51] Share warrants are, of course, transferable simply by delivery without the need for a transfer which must be stamped—the heavy rate of duty payable on the issue of bearer shares is a rough and ready attempt to make up for the fact that the Revenue will not get stamp duty when such shares are transferred.

4. No capital duty or stamp duty is payable on the issue[52] or (generally) transfer[53] of loan capital.

TURNING A BUSINESS INTO A COMPANY

Companies are very often formed to take over an established business. The small trader may well start business with the minimum formalities, even though he may be as much (or more) in need of limited liability than the person who is carrying on business in a more substantial way. Later, he may come to consider whether it is desirable to incorporate his business. The non-tax factors which will influence his decision have already been mentioned, *ante* p. 37—limited liability is probably the most important of these. The main tax factors he will have to take into account in deciding whether he will be better off trading as an individual or company have been outlined above—it is largely a question of balancing the advantage of only paying corporation tax on retained profits (subject to the special rules for close companies mentioned above) against the loss of the considerable deferment of tax which the individual trader can enjoy under the preceding year basis of assessment to income tax.

If the trader considers that turning his business into a company will give him an advantage, he will need to consider the cost that may be involved—this can make the exercise not worth while.

1. For tax purposes, the transfer of an unincorporated business to a company involves the discontinuance of that business. This can involve a substantial additional tax bill—in effect, the Revenue will,

---

[50] As a conveyance or transfer on sale or voluntary disposition. The current rate of duty was fixed by Finance Act 1974, s. 49.
[51] Finance Act 1963, s. 59.
[52] Finance Act 1973, s. 49.
[53] Finance Act 1976, s. 126.

to some extent, be able to catch up the deferment of tax which the trader has been enjoying under the preceding year basis.

2. The actual transfer of the business to the newly incorporated company will be a disposal for capital gains tax purposes. However, so long as the whole of the business is transferred in consideration of the issue of shares in the company, the capital gains tax can be postponed until the shares are disposed of.[54] If the consideration only partly consists of shares, there will be a partial deferment. Further, if the business assets include land with development potential, development land tax may be payable, although payment of the tax can be deferred for up to eight years.[55]

3. Capital duty at the rate of £1 per cent. will be payable on the actual value of the assets transferred to the company in return for shares.

4. Stamp duty at the rate of £2 per cent. will be payable on the transfer of many of the business assets to the company—this is a complex topic; for details see Pinson, Chapter 29.

[54] Finance Act 1969, sched. 19, para. 15.
[55] Development Land Tax Act 1976, sched. 8, para. 52.

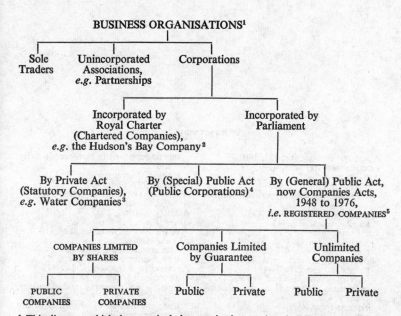

BUSINESS ORGANISATIONS[1]

- Sole Traders
- Unincorporated Associations, *e.g.* Partnerships
- Corporations
  - Incorporated by Royal Charter (Chartered Companies), *e.g.* the Hudson's Bay Company[2]
  - Incorporated by Parliament
    - By Private Act (Statutory Companies), *e.g.* Water Companies[3]
    - By (Special) Public Act (Public Corporations)[4]
    - By (General) Public Act, now Companies Acts, 1948 to 1976, *i.e.* REGISTERED COMPANIES[5]
      - COMPANIES LIMITED BY SHARES
        - PUBLIC COMPANIES
        - PRIVATE COMPANIES
      - Companies Limited by Guarantee
        - Public
        - Private
      - Unlimited Companies
        - Public
        - Private

[1] This diagram, which does not include organisations such as building societies, was inspired by the more complete one in Palmer's *Company Law*, 21st ed., p. 2.

[2] There are not many chartered companies but some of them are important. A chartered company differs from a company incorporated by Act of Parliament in a number of respects. The objects of such a company are to be found in its charter and with one or two obvious exceptions it has the same powers as a natural person. The objects of a statutory company are set out in the Private Act and those of a registered company are set out in its memorandum of association, and each only has power to carry out the specified objects and to do things incidental thereto. Neither a chartered company nor a statutory company is within the definition of "company" in section 455 of the Companies Act, 1948.

[3] Railway, canal and other companies formed for the purpose of public undertakings were incorporated by private or local or special Acts of Parliament because they required powers, *e.g.* to acquire land compulsorily, and privileges which they could not obtain under the Companies Acts. However, many such companies were nationalised in the years 1946 to 1948 and their undertakings were taken over by public corporations, such as the National Coal Board, and today most of the few remaining statutory companies are water companies. In England a statutory company is governed by the Companies Clauses Acts 1845–89 so far as not modified or excluded by the special Act.

[4] A public corporation, which is set up by special public Act of Parliament, *e.g.* the National Coal Board under the Coal Industry Nationalisation Act 1946, should not be confused with a public company. There are no shareholders and its capital is raised by Government loan. Any profits must be "ploughed back." It is run by members appointed by the appropriate Minister: see *per* Denning L.J. in *Tamlin* v. *Hannaford* [1950] 1 K.B. 18 (C.A.) at p. 23. The Atomic Energy Authority and the Independent Television Authority are public corporations. (The British Broadcasting Corporation is formed by Royal Charter limited in duration to, usually, ten years.)

[5] At December 31, 1974, the number of companies on the registers in Great Britain was 657,859, of which 59,480 were in liquidation or course of removal. Of the 657,859, 16,658 were public companies and 641,201 were private companies. (Department of Trade Annual Report for the year ended December 31, 1974 H.M.S.O.)

INDEX

672